A Day-By-Day Review of World Events

TODAY
in HISTORY

A TEHABI BOOK

TEHABI BOOKS

LONDON, NEW YORK, MELBOURNE,
MUNICH, and DELHI

Tehabi Books developed, designed, and produced *Today in History* and has conceived and produced many award-winning books that are recognized for their strong literary and visual content. Tehabi works with national and international publishers, corporations, institutions, and nonprofit groups to identify, develop, and implement comprehensive publishing programs. Tehabi Books is located in San Diego, California. www.tehabi.com

President and Publisher: Chris Capen
Vice President of Operations: Sam Lewis
Director, Corporate Publishing: Chris Brimble

Senior Art Director: John Baxter
Art Director: Curt Boyer
Production Artists: Helga Benz, Mark Santos
Picture Researcher: Mary Beth Farlow
Materials Manager: Cindy Anderson

Editors: Terry Spohn & Nancy Cash
Editorial Assistant: Katie Franco
Copy Editor: Lisa Wolff
Proofreader: Jacqueline Garrett
Researchers: Jeremy Schmidt, Thomas Schmidt, Letitia Burns O'Connor, Phil Harrison, Joseph E. Brown, Ian Harrison, Richard Crowest, Christine Huynh

Tehabi Books offers special discounts for bulk purchases for sales promotions and use as premiums. Specific, large-quantity needs can be met with special editions, custom covers, and by repurposing existing materials. For more information, contact Andrew Arias, Corporate Sales Manager, at Tehabi Books, 4920 Carroll Canyon Road, Suite 200, San Diego, California 92121-3735; or, by telephone, at 800-243-7259.

Editor: Anja Schmidt
Production Manager: Chris Avgherinos
Art Director: Dirk Kaufman
Project Director: Sharon Lucas
Creative Director: Tina Vaughan
Publisher: Chuck Lang

Library of Congress Cataloging-in-Publication Data

Today in history : a day-by-day review of world events.-- 1st ed.
  p. cm.
  "Editors of DK."
  Based on the television series This Week In History.
  ISBN 0-7894-9698-4
  1. World history. 2. Civilization, Ancient. 3. Civilization, Medieval. 4. Civilization, Modern. I. History Channel (Television network) II. This Week In History (Television program)

D20.T65 2003
909--dc22

2003055438

Printed by Toppan Printing Co. in Hong Kong
10 9 8 7 6 5 4 3 2

> ## *"History is the record of an encounter between character and circumstance."*
>
> —*Donald Creighton*

EVERYONE LOOKS AT HISTORY DIFFERENTLY. Some see trends or relationships between events over the centuries; some look for their own personal roots in the distant past; others may find brilliant gems of genius among the mundane, the violent, or the absurd. Each of us interprets it differently, and, at its heart, history itself is made up of individual experiences. Winston Churchill once said, "History will be kind to me for I intend to write it," but in fact, history is neither kind nor unkind. It simply is what it is, and each generation, each culture, judges it differently.

We've tried to do the impossible with this book: to list the most consequential and interesting events that have occurred on each day of the year. Along the way we encountered the enthralling mix of courage and folly and creativity and humor that constitutes human history. Any accounting of history in this form is met with challenges: to be inclusive; to be pertinent; and to be accurate. Limited by what is recorded and by what may prove interesting to our readers, we have tried to impart a sense of the variety of events that have occurred on each day.

To report as accurately as possible, we consulted a variety of sources, defaulting to the *Encyclopaedia Britannica* online for the final word. The multitude of calendars in use throughout the world often added to the challenge by sprinkling a particular event across a number of possible dates. Another challenge was the gradual changeover from the old Roman Julian calendar to the corrected Gregorian calendar used today in the Western world. To make this change, it was necessary that the day following October 4, 1582 become October 15, 1582. This was done by papal decree and the new calendar, with its one-time loss of 10 days, was adopted separately by the nations of Europe over a period of nearly two centuries. (For more specific information on this changeover, see page 738.) The listing of the event dates in this book is based upon our best determination of the local date at the time and place the event occurred.

We have accompanied many events with a current flag denoting the present-day nation to whose history the event is most closely connected. Events with an accompanying image are indicated by the color red differentiating the year. All events without a national flag have been assigned a descriptive icon to indicate one of five categories:

- 🪖 Military/Wars
- 🎭 Arts/Entertainment
- 🔬 Science/Technology/Medicine
- ⚖️ Justice/Crime
- 🏆 Sports

It has not been our intention to definitively assign categories to events, as many could easily have fallen into another category as well. Our goal has been to entertain as much as to educate. We hope we have succeeded.

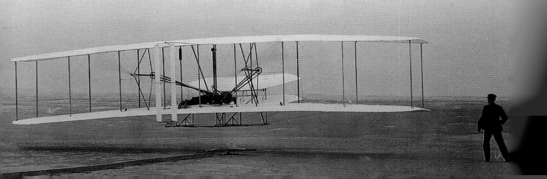

45 B.C. New Year's Day is celebrated in Italy at the beginning of January for the first time in history, with the adoption of the Julian calendar.

1501 Portuguese explorer stops at Cochin, India, to trade for spices. Cabral would also bear another, more significant item back to his king and sponsor, Manuel I of Portugal. On his way to the southern tip of Africa from Portugal, Cabral had taken a wide swing westward and had seen the coast of what is now Brazil. He landed, staying ten days, and claimed the land for Portugal, calling it "Island of the True Cross."

1764 Eight-year-old Austrian music prodigy Wolfgang Amadeus Mozart performs for the French Royal Family at the palace in Versailles.

1788 The *Times,* now London's oldest continuously published newspaper, prints its first edition under this title. It was first published on January 1, 1785, as the *Daily Universal Register.*

1801 Ceres, the first known asteroid, is observed by Giuseppe Piazzi, of Palermo, Italy.

1803 Haiti declares independence from France following defeat of Napoleon Bonaparte's colonial forces.

1814 The first Welsh-language newspaper, *Seren Gomer,* is published in Swansea.

1850 The first iron-piling lighthouse, Minot's Ledge near Boston, Massachusetts, is lighted. It was destroyed by a storm 16 months later.

BORN ON THIS DAY

1449
LORENZO DE' MEDICI (THE MAGNIFICENT)
Arts patron, humanist, and unofficial ruler of Florence (1469–92), father of Pope Leo X

1735
PAUL REVERE
Patriot in the American Revolution who rode his horse to warn of the arrival of British troops

1752
BETSY ROSS
Seamstress traditionally credited with sewing the first American flag

1819
AH CLOUGH
English poet ("Thou shalt not kill; but needst not strive/ Officiously to keep alive," often used as a manifesto for euthanasia.)

1863
PIERRE DE COUBERTIN
French Baron who instigated the modern Olympics.

1879
E. M. FORSTER
English novelist (*A Room with a View; Howard's End; A Passage to India*)

1895
J. EDGAR HOOVER
American director of the FBI from 1924 until his death in 1972

1900
XAVIER CUGAT
Spanish-born "King of Rumbas," who brought Latin music into North American households

1909
BARRY GOLDWATER
U.S. senator who lost the presidential race in 1964

1919
J. D. SALINGER
American author (*The Catcher in the Rye; Franny and Zooey*)

1933
JOE ORTON
English playwright (*Entertaining Mr. Sloane; Loot*)

"The best thing about the future is that it comes one day at a time."
—*Abraham Lincoln*

1863 U.S. president Abraham Lincoln issues the Emancipation Proclamation, the calling for liberation of black slaves in rebellious southern states.

1876 In honor of the American centennial, the first area-wide New Year's Day Mummers' Parade is held in Philadelphia, Pennsylvania.

1877 Britain's Queen Victoria is pronounced Empress of India.

1892 Ellis Island Immigrant Station opens in New York. More than 20 million immigrants would eventually pass through its doors on their way to new lives in America.

1896 German physicist Wilhelm Roentgen announces the discovery of x-rays.

1898 Brooklyn, Manhattan, Queens, Staten Island, and the Bronx are combined into one great city, New York City.

1901 The six British colonies of Australia are joined to become a modern nation, the Commonwealth of Australia. Edmund Barton is the first prime minister.

1902 The first public radio broadcast is made by U.S. inventor Nathan Stubblefield in Murray, Kentucky.

1902 The first Tournament of Roses (the Rose Bowl) football game is played in Pasadena, California, between Michigan and Stanford. Michigan won, 49–0.

1905 The Trans-Siberian Railway officially opens. The journey from Paris to Vladivostok could then be completed in 21 days.

1919 Edsel Ford takes over as president of Ford Motor Company, succeeding his father and the company's founder Henry, and announces a 20 percent increase in Ford's minimum wage from an already generous $5 per day to $6.

1922 Drivers in British Columbia, Canada, switch from the British system and begin driving on the right side of the road.

1937 An American classic gets its title. Spam is named at a party at the Hormel (meatpacking company) Mansion in Minnesota.

Immigrants landing at Ellis Island

1946 In the aftermath of World War II, twenty Japanese soldiers surrender to a lone American serviceman on the island of Corregidor in the Philippines. Having remained in an underground bunker, the Japanese learned of their country's defeat four months earlier from a discarded newspaper picked up on a food-foraging excursion.

1958 The European Economic Community, or Common Market, is launched.

1959 Cuban dictator Fulgencio Batista flees to the Dominican Republic, forced out by the popular revolution of Fidel Castro.

1993 After the fall of communism in eastern Europe, Czechoslovakia separates peacefully into the Czech Republic and Slovakia.

1999 Exchange rates for the European Economic Community's new single currency, the Euro, are set.

President Franklin D. Roosevelt and British prime minister Winston Churchill

1492 The kingdom of Granada falls to the Christian forces of King Ferdinand V and Queen Isabella I, and the Moors lose their last foothold in Spain.

1839 Louis Daguerre, French pioneer of photography, makes the first photograph of the moon.

1842 Traffic rattles across the world's first cable suspension bridge in Fairmount, Pennsylvania.

1870 Construction begins on the Brooklyn Bridge in New York City.

1882 John D. Rockefeller forms the Standard Oil Trust, the first sanctioned monopoly in America.

1897 American writer Stephen Crane survives the sinking of the *Commodore* off the coast of Florida. He will turn the adventure into his short story, "The Open Boat."

1900 The Open Door Policy is announced by U.S. secretary of state John Hay, encouraging European powers and Japan to respect the rights of all nations to trade freely with China. The policy probably helped keep China undivided and independent.

1903 U.S. president Theodore Roosevelt closes a

> *"Never let your sense of morals get in the way of doing what's right."*
>
> —Isaac Asimov

BORN ON THIS DAY

1647
NATHANIEL BACON
Leader of Bacon's Rebellion in the American colonies

1727
JAMES WOLFE
English general, hero of the Battle of Quebec

1732
FRANZ XAVIER BRIXI
Czech composer

1830
HENRY KINGSLEY
English-born Australian author

1861
HELEN HERRON TAFT
First lady to President Robert Taft

1866
GILBERT MURRAY
Australian-born scholar, chairman of the League of Nations (1923–28)

1904
SALLY RAND
American dancer, famous for the use of fans in her act

1920
ISAAC ASIMOV
American author (*Foundation; I, Robot*)

Isaac Asimov

1936
ROGER MILLER
American country music star ("King of the Road"; "Dang Me")

1942
DENNIS HASTERT
Speaker of the U.S. House of Representatives (1999–present)

1961
GABRIELLE CARTERIS
American actress (*Beverly Hills 90210; Malpractice; Full Circle*)

1968
CUBA GOODING, JR.
American actor (*Jerry Maguire*)

post office in Missouri for refusing to employ an African-American postmistress.

1905 During the Russo-Japanese War, Port Arthur, the Russian naval base in China, surrenders to Japanese naval forces under Admiral Heihachirō Tōgō.

1906 Willis Havilland Carrier is granted a patent for an "apparatus for treating air": the first practical air conditioning unit.

1914 Trehawke Davies becomes the first woman to loop the loop, at Hendon airfield in England.

1919 The New York Stock Exchange installs a separate ticker to track bond trading.

1932 Having invaded China's Manchuria region in 1931, Japan creates a puppet state called Manchukuo, to be ruled by Pu Yi, last emperor of the Manchu dynasty.

1935 Bruno Hauptmann, kidnapper and murderer of Charles and Anne Lindbergh's infant son, goes on trial in Flemington, New Jersey. He later was convicted and executed.

1936 In St. Louis, Missouri, television pioneers Vladimir Kosma Zworykin and George Arthur Morton demonstrate an electron tube that is sensitive to ultraviolet and infrared rays. The device represented an important step in the development of television.

1941 The Andrews Sisters record "Boogie Woogie Bugle

Bruno Hauptmann

Boy" for Decca Records. The song became a classic World War II hit.

1942 During World War II, Japanese forces capture Manila, capital of the Philippines, and the U.S. naval base at Cavite.

1954 Pope Pius XII warns that television is a potential threat to family life, but five months later he launches a new Eurovision TV network with the words: "let the nations learn to know each other better."

1959 The Soviet Union launches *Luna I*, the first space vehicle to escape Earth's gravitational field. It passed near the moon and entered a solar orbit.

1967 A U.S. Air Force F-4 Phantom shoots down seven communist MiG-21s over North Vietnam.

1967 Ronald W. Reagan is sworn in as governor of California.

1968 French-Polish film director, screenwriter, and actor Roman Polanski marries American actress Sharon Tate, who is later murdered while pregnant with their baby. Polanski's films include *Knife in the Water, Rosemary's Baby, Chinatown, Macbeth, Frantic, Bitter Moon,* and *The Pianist.*

1974 U.S. president Richard M. Nixon signs the federal law forcing states to set maximum speed limits of 55 miles per hour.

1995 Astronomers using Hawaii's Keck telescope discover 8C 1435+6, a galaxy estimated to be 15 billion light years away—the most distant yet identified.

The Andrews Sisters

1322 Charles IV succeeds to the throne of France upon the death of his brother, Philip V. Among Charles's accomplishments is increasing the royal wealth by devaluation of the coinage.

1521 Pope Leo X issues the papal bull *Decet Romanum Pontificem*, which excommunicates Martin Luther from the Catholic Church.

1777 In the American Revolution, colonial forces under George Washington defeat the army of General Lord Charles Cornwallis at the Battle of Princeton.

1833 Great Britain retakes control of the Falkland Islands following diplomatic and military conflicts with Spain and other claimants.

1841 American writer Herman Melville sails for the South Seas on the whaler *Acushnet*. In 1851, Harper & Brothers published his novel, *Moby-Dick*. The book flopped and was not recognized as a classic for many years.

The Battle of Princeton

MILESTONE

Man of the Year

On this day in 1983, *Time Magazine* names the personal computer *Man of the Year*, predicting that the home computer will dramatically change both office and home. At the time, the most powerful processor on the market was an Intel 286 chip. The Apple II, the first truly mass-market home computer, had come out just six years before. The Macintosh had not yet been invented, and Apple still led the market. In the same year, Microsoft introduced the Microsoft mouse for $200. Xerox and Apple had already released computers with graphical user interfaces, and Microsoft hoped to supply the necessary hardware. However, the mouse took several years to catch on.

"For laws are silent in time of war."

—*Cicero*

1868 Heralding the birth of modern Japan, patriotic samurai from Japan's outlying domains join with antishogunate nobles in restoring the emperor to power after 700 years. Young Emperor Meiji moved the royal court to Tokyo, dismantled feudalism, and enacted widespread reforms along Western models.

1888 Marvin Stone patents the waxed-paper drinking straw, which would soon replace natural straws made of ryegrass stems.

1899 An editorial in the *New York Times* makes reference to an "automobile." It is the first known use of the word.

1903 Bulgaria breaks with Austria-Hungary by renouncing the Treaty of Commerce.

1911 Three anarchists are trapped in a burning house after injuring ten people and killing three policemen in the "Sidney Street siege" in the East End of London.

1924 Two years after British archaeologist Howard Carter discovered the tomb of the pharaoh Tutankhamen near Luxor, Egypt, he finds its greatest treasure—a stone sarcophagus containing a solid gold coffin that holds the mummy of Tutankhamen.

1945 During World War II, in preparation for assaults

against Iwo Jima, Okinawa, and mainland Japan, General Douglas MacArthur takes command of all U.S. ground forces.

⚖️ **1946** German propagandist William Joyce, called "Lord Haw Haw," is hanged in London for treason. Son of an English father and Irish-American mother, the Nazi convert fled from England to Germany as World War II began and made weekly broadcasts from 1939 to 1945.

🔬 **1957** After 10 years of development, the Hamilton Watch Company announces production of the world's first electric watch.

🇺🇸 **1959** Alaska is granted statehood as the 49th state, and first new state to be added since Arizona in 1912.

General Douglas MacArthur

Jack Ruby shoots Lee Harvey Oswald

🇺🇸 **1967** Jack Ruby, the Dallas nightclub owner who killed Lee Harvey Oswald, the alleged assassin of U.S. president John F. Kennedy, dies of cancer in a Dallas hospital.

⚖️ **1973** American political analyst Daniel Ellsberg goes to trial, indicted for giving the Pentagon Papers to the press. Charges were dropped when it became known that President Richard M. Nixon had ordered burglars to search Ellsberg's psychiatrist's office for material that would discredit him.

⚖️ **1990** Panamanian general Manuel Noriega, having taken refuge for 10 days in the Vatican embassy, surrenders to a U.S. invasion force to face charges of drug trafficking.

BORN ON THIS DAY

106 B.C.
MARCUS CICERO
Roman statesman and author

1621
WILLIAM TUCKER
Believed to be the first African American born in the New World

1777
M. A. ELISA BONAPARTE
Corsican monarch of Lucca/Piombino

1793
LUCRETIA COFFIN MOTT
American women's rights advocate and founder of the first Women's Rights Convention

1892
J. R. R. TOLKIEN
English author of the Ring Trilogy

1901
NGO DINH DIEM
South Vietnamese president who was assassinated by his own generals in 1963

1905
RAY MILLAND
Academy Award-winning American actor (*The Lost Weekend*)

1909
VICTOR BORGE
Humorist, entertainer, and pianist known as the "Great Dane"

1939
BOBBY HULL
Canadian Hall of Fame hockey player

1945
STEPHEN STILLS
American musician (Crosby, Stills and Nash)

1950
VICTORIA PRINCIPAL
American actress (*Dallas*)

1956
MEL GIBSON
American actor (*Gallipoli; Lethal Weapon; Hamlet*)

1960
JOAN CHEN
American actress (*Twin Peaks; On Deadly Ground; Judge Dredd*)

1969
MICHAEL SCHUMACHER
German race-car driver

1642 Isaac Newton is born. In addition to theorizing about planetary orbits and gravity, the English scientist was the first to examine the possibility of satellites. He hypothesized that a cannonball shot at high velocity would eventually orbit the Earth.

1757 King Louis XV of France survives an assassination attempt by Robert Frangois Damiens, a soldier who tried to stab the king as he entered his carriage. Damiens was tortured to death.

1847 Samuel Colt rescues the future of his faltering gun company by winning a contract to provide the U.S. government with 1,000 of his .44-caliber revolvers.

1863 New Yorker James Plimpton patents the four-wheeled roller skate, which became popular because it could turn easily.

1877 Fiercely competitive and fabulously wealthy, Cornelius Vanderbilt, one of America's archetypal businessmen, dies. Having built an estate of some $100 million, he was the richest man in America at the time.

1902 In Malta there are protests at the change of the official language from Italian to English. The island had been annexed to Great Britain by the 1814 Treaty of Paris at the end of the Peninsular War and later served nobly as a vital naval base during two world wars. Malta achieved self-government in 1947 and independence in 1964.

BORN ON THIS DAY

1334
AMADEUS VI
"The Green Earl," Earl of Savoye

1710
GIOVANNI BATTISTA PERGOLESI
Italian composer
(*Il Prigioniero Superbo*)

1785
JACOB LUDWIG GRIMM
German philosopher who wrote *Grimm's Fairy Tales* with his brother, Wilhelm

1809
LOUIS BRAILLE
French developer of a reading system for the blind

1838
CHARLES "TOM THUMB" STRATTON
American circus performer

1874
JOSEF SUK
Czech composer, son-in-law of Antonín Dvořák

1905
STERLING HOLLOWAY
American actor, voice of numerous cartoon characters

1914
JANE WYMAN
American actress
(*Johnny Belinda; The Lost Weekend; Magnificent Obsession*)

1935
FLOYD PATTERSON
American heavyweight champion boxer

1917 During World War I, Great Britain and Germany agree to an exchange of all internees over the age of 45.

1920 The first African-American baseball league, the Negro National League, is formed.

1944 U.S. aircraft begin dropping supplies to guerrilla forces throughout western Europe. Virtually every country that experienced Axis invasion raised a guerrilla force; they were especially effective and numerous in Italy, France, China, Greece, the Philippines, Yugoslavia, and the Soviet Union.

1948 Burma gains independence from Great Britain.

1950 *The God That Failed*, a collection of essays by six writers and intellectuals who sympathized with the communist cause before renouncing the ideology, is published by Harper's. The book provided insight into why communism appealed to, and then disappointed, so many adherents.

1958 The Russian satellite *Sputnik I*—the first man-made object in space—falls back to earth after 92 days in orbit.

Sputnik I

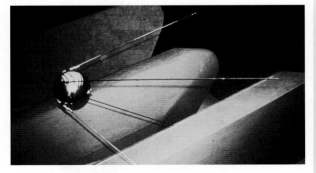

Euro currency

1960 French author and existentialist philosopher Albert Camus is killed in a car crash. Camus' writings include *The Outsider, The Myth of Sisyphus, The Rebel, The Plague,* and *The Fall.* He won the 1957 Nobel Prize in literature.

1962 Beneath the streets of New York City, the first unmanned automatic subway train begins service.

1964 Albert DeSalvo, the Boston Strangler, claims his last murder victim—Mary Sullivan, raped and strangled in her Boston apartment. DeSalvo was stabbed to death by an unidentified inmate at Walpole State Prison in 1973.

1965 In his State of the Union message, President Lyndon B. Johnson reaffirms U.S. commitment to support South Vietnam in fighting communist aggression. He says, "Our own security is tied to the peace of Asia."

"You miss a hundred percent of the shots you never take."

—*Wayne Gretzky*

1974 South Vietnam reports that 55 soldiers have been killed in clashes with communist forces. President Nguyen Van Thieu orders a counteroffensive, ending the fragile cease-fire of the Paris Peace Accords.

1974 U.S. president Richard M. Nixon refuses to turn over documents and tape recordings subpoenaed by the Senate Watergate Committee.

1984 Canadian hockey star Wayne Gretzky, playing for the Edmonton Oilers, scores eight points (four goals and four assists) against the Minnesota North Stars.

1987 Spanish guitar great Andrés Segovia arrives in the United States for his final American tour. Hailed for bringing the Spanish guitar from relative obscurity to classical status, he died four months later in Madrid at the age of 94.

1996 General Motors announces that it will release an electric car, the EV-1, in the fall. The car met with modest success.

1999 Europe's new unified currency, the Euro, takes effect in eleven European Union nations. Its symbol is €.

JANUARY 5

1477 Charles the Bold, Duke of Burgundy and unskilled military commander, loses his life and grand ambitions to Swiss forces at the Battle of Nancy.

1589 Catherine de' Medici, regent queen of France during the bloody Huguenot-Catholic struggles, dies at age 70.

1643 In the first divorce in the American colonies, Anne Clarke of the Massachusetts Bay Colony is granted a divorce from her absent and adulterous husband, Denis Clarke.

1825 Twenty-three-year-old French writer Alexandre Dumas fights his first duel. He sustains no serious injury, although his pants fall down in the fight.

1846 Boldly reversing its longstanding policy of "free and open" occupation in the disputed Oregon Territory, the U.S. House of Representatives calls for an end to British-American sharing of the region.

1861 To reinforce Fort Sumter against possible rebel attack, the unarmed merchant ship *Star of the West* leaves New York harbor with 250 soldiers.

Star of the West

"It's amazing what you can accomplish if you do not care who gets the credit."
—Harry S. Truman

1885 The Long Island Railroad, foreshadowing modern piggy-back carriers, begins transport of farm wagons on railroad flatcars in New York.

1895 French officer Alfred Dreyfus, condemned for passing military secrets to the Germans, is stripped of his rank and later sentenced to life in notorious Devil's Island Prison. In 1898, Major Hubert Henry admitted that he had forged much of the evidence. In 1906 the Dreyfus conviction was overturned.

1900 Physicist Henry Augustus Rowland of Johns Hopkins University in Baltimore, Maryland, discovers the cause of Earth's magnetism.

1919 Anton Drexter founds the German Workers' Party. Adolf Hitler is member number seven.

1922 Irish explorer Sir Ernest Shackleton dies of a heart attack in South Georgia during his fourth expedition to the Antarctic.

1924 American manufacturer Walter Chrysler, a former General Motors executive who had pioneered the introduction of all-steel bodies in automobiles (instead of wood), introduces his first motorcar.

1933 Construction begins on the Golden Gate Bridge spanning the entrance to San Francisco Bay. With its tall towers and famous red paint job, the bridge quickly became an American landmark and a symbol of San Francisco, California.

1934 The National and American baseball leagues agree to use baseballs of the same size.

1940 FM radio is demonstrated for the first time to the U.S. Federal Communications Commission.

1945 On the eve of a major offensive into Poland, the Soviet Union decides to recognize the pro-Soviet Lublin Committee as the Provisional Government of Poland, a move that turned the exhausted and battered Poland into a nondemocratic satellite country, which it remained until 1989.

1947 Coal mines are nationalized in Great Britain.

1949 Newly elected U.S. president Harry S. Truman, in his State of the Union Address, names his administration the "Fair Deal," a play on his predecessor's "New Deal."

1951 The Chinese Army drives United Nations forces from Inchon, South Korea.

1952 British prime minister Winston Churchill arrives in Washington, D.C., to discuss world problems with President Harry S. Truman.

1976 Khmer Rouge leader Pol Pot announces a new constitution changing the name of Cambodia to Kampuchea, and legalizing its Communist government. During the next three years, Pol Pot's regime would murder more than a million Cambodian people in the infamous "killing fields."

1981 Peter Sutcliffe is arrested in London. Believed to be the Yorkshire Ripper, he was accused of killing 13 women.

Killing Fields memorial

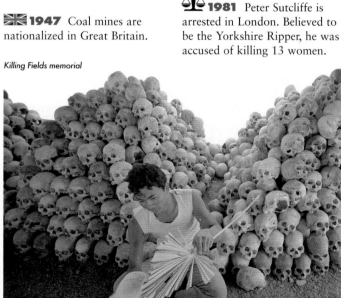

First Space Shuttle, STS-1

1066 Harold II is crowned king of England. The last Anglo-Saxon king's reign ended in October when William the Conqueror, Duke of Normandy, invaded from France. Harold was killed in battle, William was crowned the first Norman king of England, and English language and culture were changed forever.

1540 England's King Henry VIII takes Anne of Cleves (Cleves was a small German state) to be his fourth wife in a marriage that would last only six months before annulment.

1759 George Washington marries the wealthy widow Martha Dandridge Custis, who later became the first woman to be depicted on U.S. currency when she appeared on the $1 bill in 1886. She was also the first woman to be depicted on a U.S. postage stamp, which was issued in 1902, a century after her death.

1839 A powerful storm hits Ireland, destroying homes, smashing windows, sinking ships, killing livestock, and destroying crops. The storm killed more than 200 and left thousands homeless.

George and Martha Washington's wedding

BORN ON THIS DAY

367
RICHARD II
King of England, son of Edward the Black Prince

1412
JOAN OF ARC
French saint and national heroine

1799
JEDEDIAH SMITH
Explorer, first American to reach California by land

1811
CHARLES SUMNER
American antislavery senator from Massachusetts

1832
GUSTAVE DORÉ
French painter and illustrator

1838
MAX BRUNCH
German composer

1878
CARL SANDBURG
American journalist, poet, and biographer

1880
TOM MIX
American actor in silent movies who starred in over 300 westerns

1882
SAM RAYBURN
U.S. congressman from Texas and speaker of the house

1883
KAHLIL GIBRAN
Lebanese artist, philosopher, and author (*The Prophet; The Beloved*)

1913
LORETTA YOUNG
American actress (*Naughty But Nice; The Loretta Young Show*)

1913
EDWARD GIEREK
Polish politician who became leader of the Polish United Workers' Party in 1970 and was forced to resign in 1980

1914
NICHOLAS DE STAEL
French painter

1920
SUN MYUNG MOON
Controversial Korean founder and head of the Unification Church, whose followers are commonly known as "Moonies"

"Nine-tenths of wisdom is being wise in time."

—*Theodore Roosevelt*

1898 American inventor Simon Lake, submerged in a homemade submarine at the bottom of Maryland's Patapsco River, telephones the mayor of Baltimore. Despite his success, regular ship-to-shore telephone service was not instituted until 1929.

1910 The German Society of Geography honors Irish explorer Ernest Shackleton for his pioneering exploration of the Antarctic. In 1909, Shackleton had come within 97 miles of the South Pole, the closest approach to that date.

1919 Theodore Roosevelt, the 26th president of the United States, dies at Sagamore Hill, his estate overlooking New York's Long Island Sound. He was 60 years old.

1921 To help promote nonmilitary aviation, the U.S. Navy orders the sale of "flying boat" aircraft to commercial airlines. Pan Am flew "China Clippers" across the Pacific.

1925 Finnish long-distance runner and Olympic champion Paavo Nurmi sets two world records in New York's Madison Square Garden.

1928 The River Thames bursts its banks, drowning 14 Londoners, flooding the vaults of the Houses of Parliament, and filling the usually dry moat of the Tower of London. At the Tate Gallery, twelve paintings

We Can Do It!

Female factory worker Rosie the Riveter

by Landseer were damaged by the flood but the gallery's Turner collection was unharmed.

1942 During World War II, President Franklin D. Roosevelt announces the largest armaments production in U.S. history: 45,000 aircraft, 45,000 tanks, 20,000 antiaircraft guns, and 8 million tons in new ships in the first year of production, saying, "These figures will give the Japanese and Nazis a little idea of just what they accomplished." Such large-scale production was possible due to the number of women who had entered the factories to replace men who had gone to war.

1942 Arriving in New York, Pan Am's Pacific Clipper completes the first round-the-world trip by a commercial aircraft.

1958 The Soviet Union announces plans to cut its standing army by 300,000 troops in the coming year. The reduction was part of Nikita Khrushchev's policy of "peaceful coexistence" with the West and an indication that Cold War relations were undergoing a slight thaw in the mid- to late 1950s.

1971 During the Vietnam War, the U.S. Army drops charges in the My Lai massacre against four officers, leaving only Lieutenant William Calley, Captain Ernest Medina, and Captain Eugene Kotouc to face trial. Calley was found guilty of murdering at least 22 South Vietnamese civilians and sentenced to life in prison. Kotouc and Medina were acquitted.

1973 A Mercedes-Benz 770K sedan, supposedly Adolf Hitler's parade car, was sold at auction for $153,000, the most money ever paid for a car at auction at that time.

1991 Appearing on television, Iraqi president Saddam Hussein predicts a long war against what he calls tyranny in the form of the United States.

1993 Rudolf Nureyev, the famous Russian ballet dancer and defector from the Soviet Union, dies in Paris at age 54.

1994 American Olympic hopeful Nancy Kerrigan is attacked at a Detroit ice rink two days before the American National Figure Skating Championships.

Nancy Kerrigan

🇬🇧 **1327** King Edward II of England, the inept son of Edward I, is deposed, and later murdered.

🇫🇷 **1558** The French recapture Calais, the last English holding in continental France.

🔬 **1610** Italian astronomer Galileo Galilei sees three of Jupiter's moons through his telescope. He thought they were stars, but in subsequent observations noted that they moved with the planet.

The moons of Jupiter

🔬 **1714** English inventor Henry Mill patents the typewriter "for the impressing or transcribing of letters singly or progressively one after another, as in writing."

🇺🇸 **1782** The Bank of North America throws open its doors in Philadelphia, Pennsylvania, making it the first commercial bank in the United States.

🇫🇷 **1785** Frenchman Jean-Pierre Blanchard and American John Jeffries become the first to cross the English Channel in a gas balloon. To do it, they had to jettison nonessentials such as anchors, a nonfunctional hand-operated propeller, silk-covered oars with which they hoped to row their way through

---

BORN ON THIS DAY

1718
ISRAEL PUTNAM
American Revolutionary War hero

1745
ETIENNE MONTGOLFIER
French inventor who, with his brother, launched the first successful hot air balloon

1800
MILLARD FILLMORE
13th president of the United States

Millard Fillmore

1834
PHILIPP REIS
German schoolteacher and inventor who demonstrated the first telephone in 1860, sixteen years before Bell patented his telephone

1845
LOUIS III
Last king of Bavaria

1899
FRANCIS POULENC
French composer

1912
CHARLES ADDAMS
American cartoonist (*The Addams Family*)

1922
VINCENT GARDENIA
Emmy and Tony Award-winning Italian actor

1922
JEAN-PIERRE RAMPAL
French jazz and classical flutist

1925
GERALD DURRELL
English writer and zoologist, younger brother of Lawrence Durrell

1928
WILLIAM PETER BLATTY
American author (*The Exorcist*)

1948
KENNY LOGGINS
American singer (Loggins and Messina)

---

the air, and even Blanchard's trousers.

🇺🇸 **1789** The United States' first presidential election is held to choose state electors; voters included only white men with property.

🇺🇸 **1872** American financier James Fisk, one of Wall Street's more colorful and unscrupulous characters, dies from a gunshot wound involving a squabble with his lover, Josie Mansfield, a.k.a. the "Broadway Beauty."

🏆 **1887** Thomas Stevens finishes the first round-the-world bicycle trip. Leaving San Francisco, California, in 1884, he pedaled a Columbia high-wheeler to Boston, Massachusetts. He sailed to London and rode across Europe, the Middle East, and Asia.

🔬 **1894** A patent for motion picture film is granted to W. K. Dickson.

🇺🇸 **1901** A new single-day record is set for trading on the New York Stock Exchange: two million shares.

🔬 **1904** The Marconi Company proposes an international distress call. The C.Q.D. signal meant "Stop sending and listen," although the popular interpretation of the letters was "Come quick! Danger!" The code went into effect on the

> *"All truths are easy to understand once they are discovered; the point is to discover them."*
>
> —*Galileo Galilei*

next month, and was used until 1908, when it was replaced by the S.O.S. signal.

1927 Commercial phone service across the Atlantic is inaugurated in a call from Walter Sherman Gifford, president of AT&T in New York, to Sir George Evelyn Pemberton Murray, secretary of the British General Post Office, in London. A three-minute call cost $25.

1931 U.S. president Herbert Hoover's Committee for Unemployment Relief releases its report detailing depression woes: some 4 to 5 million Americans unemployed. However, the Great Depression continued to worsen; by 1932, some 13 million Americans were without jobs.

1932 Germany announces that it will not continue World War I reparations payments.

1939 U.S. gangster Al Capone is moved from Alcatraz to San Pedro's "Terminal Island" prison.

1942 During World War II, Japanese forces launch the siege of Bataan.

1953 President Harry S. Truman announces that the United States has built a hydrogen, or thermonuclear, bomb. Based on fusion, as compared to the fission-based atomic bomb, it had been tested in 1952 at Eniwetok atoll.

1954 The Allen B. Du Mont Laboratories demonstrate the Duoscopic, a forerunner of today's picture-in-picture television set, in New York City and Chicago. Viewers wore Polaroid glasses to separate the two signals displayed on the screen. Earphones allowed each ear to hear a different program.

1959 Six days after President Fulgencio Batista fled Cuba, the United States recognizes the new provisional government, despite fears that Fidel Castro might have communist leanings.

1971 U.S. defense secretary Melvin Laird arrives in South Vietnam to check on the progress of "Vietnamization"—President Richard M. Nixon's effort to increase the strength of South Vietnamese forces so U.S. troops could withdraw. Laird warned Nixon and his cabinet of "some tough days ahead."

1979 Vietnamese troops seize the Cambodian capital of Phnom Penh, toppling the brutal regime of Pol Pot and his Khmer Rouge.

1989 Showa Tenno Hirohito, the 124th Japanese monarch in an imperial line dating back to 660 B.C., dies after serving six decades as the emperor of Japan. After U.S. atomic bombs destroyed Hiroshima and Nagasaki during World War II, he argued for his country's surrender, explaining to the Japanese people that the "unendurable must be endured." He was succeeded by his only son, Akihito.

1999 The impeachment trial of President Bill Clinton, charged with lying under oath and obstructing justice, begins in the U.S. Senate. Congress had attempted to remove a president on only one other occasion: the 1868 impeachment trial of President Andrew Johnson.

MILESTONE

First Practical Camera

The Daguerreotype, named for its inventor Louis Daguerre, and the first practical means of making a photograph, is announced in France on this day in 1839. The Daguerreotype plate was difficult and time consuming to make. A sheet of copper was plated with a thin coat of silver. This was then polished until the surface was mirror-like. The picture usually had a brass mat placed directly on the plate, and then glass was placed over this, without touching the photographic plate. Since the photograph is silver on copper, it will not attract a magnet. The Daguerreotype is considered by many to be the most beautiful, artistic form of photography ever developed. The method was able to capture very fine, rich detail—superb even by today's standards.

Louis Daguerre

1598 Genoa, Italy, orders the expulsion of Jews.

1656 The world's oldest present-day newspaper, the *Haarlems Dagblad*, begins publication in Holland.

1790 U.S. president George Washington delivers the first State of the Union Address, at Federal Hall in New York, and welcomes North Carolina into the Union.

1798 Congress ratifies the 11th Amendment to the U.S. Constitution, which stops lawsuits against a state by residents of other states or foreign countries.

1800 The Wild Boy of Aveyron, later named Victor, walks into San Sernin, France, looking for shelter.

1806 Members of the Lewis and Clark expedition find a beached blue whale on the Oregon coast.

1811 In Louisiana, 500 slaves led by a man named Charles, and inspired by the successful revolt of slaves in Haiti, attempt their own uprising. The revolt lasted two days.

1815 Two weeks after the War of 1812 officially ended with the signing of the Treaty of Ghent, U.S. General Andrew Jackson achieves the greatest American victory of the war at the Battle of New Orleans.

1838 Alfred Vail of Morristown, New Jersey, demonstrates a telegraph code he devised using dots and dashes as letters, a predecessor to Samuel Morse's code. Vail

---

MILESTONE

Voting Rights for African-American Men

On this day in 1867, Congress overrides President Andrew Johnson's veto of a bill granting adult male citizens of the District of Columbia—without regard to race—the right to vote. It was the first law in American history that granted voting rights to African-American men. The Thirteenth and Fourteenth Amendments, in conjunction with congressional reconstruction, set the stage for extending suffrage to African-American males. It would take the Fifteenth Amendment to actually guarantee their voting rights.

The Battle of New Orleans

> *"It is far better to be alone than to be in bad company."*
>
> —*George Washington*

transmitted the message "a patient waiter is no loser."

1877 Outnumbered, low on ammunition, and forced to use outdated weapons to defend themselves, Sioux Indian chief Crazy Horse and his warriors fight their final losing battle against the U.S. Cavalry in Montana.

1889 Dr. Herman Hollerith receives a U.S. patent for his electric tabulating machine, which tallies numbers from punch cards. The Tabulating Machine Company later grew into the International Business Machines Corporation (IBM).

1916 During World War I, Allies retreat from the Gallipoli Peninsula in Turkey, ending a disastrous invasion of the Ottoman Empire that resulted in 250,000 Allied casualties and greatly discredited the Allied military command.

1918 U.S. president Woodrow Wilson outlines to Congress the aims of the United States in World War I and describes his "14 Points" for achieving a lasting peace in Europe.

1926 Abdul-Aziz ibn Sa'ud becomes the king of Hejaz. In 1932, he combined it with Nejd and called the country Saudi Arabia.

1940 Benito Mussolini sends a message to Adolf Hitler warning against war with Britain. Mussolini asked if it was truly necessary, but he had his own imperial ambitions. Italy was not prepared to join the effort, and Il Duce did not want to be outshined by the upstart Hitler.

1946 In the aftermath of World War II, the trial of Hermann Goering and Joachim von Ribbentrop begins in Nuremburg. Both were condemned to death, but Goering committed suicide by poison shortly before he was due to be executed.

1951 Breeding pairs of cahow, a species of petrel once believed extinct, are found in Bermuda.

1959 Charles de Gaulle takes the oath of office as president of France.

1962 In his first professional appearance, 21-year-old American golfer Jack Nicklaus finishes 50th.

1972 Russian composer Dimitri Shostakovitch's 15th Symphony is performed in Moscow for the first time.

1973 U.S. national security advisor Henry Kissinger and Hanoi's Le Duc Tho resume peace negotiations in Paris. A month earlier, the North Vietnam delegation had walked out. Nixon's intense bombing of Hanoi contributed to their return.

1976 Zhou Enlai, premier of the People's Republic of China since 1949, and second to Mao Zedong, dies of cancer at age 77.

1976 *Ragtime* by American author E. L. Doctorow is awarded the National Book Critics Circle Award.

1987 In the New York Exchange, the Dow Jones Industrial Average closing bell rings above 2,000 for the first time.

1988 The stock market crash of 1987 is blamed on automated computer trading. In February, the New York Stock Exchange announced trading curbs to prevent a repeat.

1998 Ramzi Yousef, convicted of the bombing the World Trade Center in 1993 is sentenced to life in prison.

Premier Benito Mussolini

1317 Phillip V assumes the French crown, succeeding his brother who left only a daughter as heir and establishing in France the exclusion of females in royal succession.

1349 Aroused by rumors that Jews were intentionally spreading bubonic plague, mobs in Basel, Switzerland, burn hundreds alive.

1493 Thinking he has found mermaids in the New World, Italian explorer Christopher Columbus describes manatees as being "not half as beautiful as they are painted."

1570 Russian czar Ivan the Terrible slaughters more than 3,000 people in Novgorod to teach them loyalty.

1643 Italian astronomer Giovanni Riccioli reports a faint glow on the dark side of Venus —the mysterious "Ashen Light."

1718 France declares war on Spain in the two-year War of the Quadruple Alliance.

1768 In London, England, Philip Astley stages

Ivan the Terrible, czar of Russia

BORN ON THIS DAY

1554
GREGORY XV
Roman Catholic pope

1728
THOMAS WARTON
Poet laureate of England

1890
KAREL CAPEK
Czech writer and playwright whose play "R.U.R." contained the first use of the word "robot"

1898
DAME GRACIE FIELDS
English singer

1904
GEORGE BALANCHINE
Russian-born ballet choreographer

1908
SIMONE DE BEAUVOIR
French socialist, feminist, and writer (*The Second Sex, The Mandarins*)

1913
RICHARD M. NIXON
37th president of the United States and first president to resign from office

1928
JUDITH KRANTZ
American author (*Heartburn*)

1934
BART STARR
American football Hall of Fame quarterback

1935
BOB DENVER
American actor (*Dobie Gillis; Gilligan's Island*)

1941
JOAN BAEZ
American folk singer and activist

1941
SUSANNAH YORK
English actress (*The Killing of Sister George; Tom Jones*)

1944
JIMMY PAGE
English musician (Led Zeppelin)

1951
CRYSTAL GAYLE
American singer ("Don't It Make My Brown Eyes Blue")

---

the first modern circus. Trick riders, acrobats, clowns, trained animals, and other such acts weren't new, but had never before been organized in the form of a circus.

1816 The Davy safety lamp, designed to prevent the light's flame from igniting flammable gases in the surrounding air, is first used in a coal mine.

1861 The merchant ship *Star of the West*, carrying reinforcements from New York, is driven back by South Carolina forces in the first hostile action of the American Civil War.

1879 In a desperate escape attempt, Chief Dull Knife and 150 Cheyenne captives break out of Fort Robinson, Nebraska. All were killed by guards.

1887 In Montana, Wyoming, and the Dakotas, a summer of drought is followed by deep snow, intense cold, and a layer of hard ice. Montana ranchers alone lost an estimated 362,000 head of cattle, more than half the territory's herd.

1909 Irish explorer Ernest Shackleton reaches 88°22' south latitude, the closest approach to the South Pole yet achieved.

1944 During World War II, Maungdaw, Burma, is recaptured by British and Indian forces.

1952 In his State of the Union Address, President Harry S. Truman warns Americans that they are "moving through a perilous time" and calls for vigorous action to meet the communist threat.

1958 The Toyota and Datsun (later Nissan) brand names make their first appearances in the United States at the Imported Motor Car Show in Los Angeles, California.

1959 The western television series *Rawhide* premieres, starring Clint Eastwood as a cattle-driving cowboy. The show was one of 30 westerns aired in the 1959–60 television season.

1960 Construction begins on the controversial Aswan High Dam on the Nile River in southern Egypt. Built with Soviet aid, the dam was opened in 1971.

1967 Construction of the Volga Automobile Works begins in Togliatti in the Soviet Union. By April of 1970, Zhiguli automobiles (later known as "Lada" autos) were rolling off the assembly lines. The Volga works became and remains the

> *"The easiest kind of relationship is with ten thousand people; the hardest is with one."*
>
> —*Joan Baez*

largest producer of small European automobiles.

1972 In Hong Kong harbor, a fire breaks out aboard RMS *Queen Elizabeth*, which is being refitted as a seagoing university. By the next morning the famous luxury liner lay in a wreck on the harbor floor.

1984 Angelo Buono, one of the Hillside Stranglers, is sentenced to life in prison for his role in the rape, torture, and murder of 10 young women in Los Angeles, California. Buono's cousin and partner in crime, Kenneth Bianchi, testified against Buono to escape the death penalty.

U.S. troops unload supplies on Lingayen Gulf, Luzon Island (milestone)

Thomas Paine

1613 French explorer Samuel de Champlain publishes *Voyages*, recounting his explorations and adventures along the New England coast.

1645 William Laud, the dictatorial archbishop of Canterbury, is beheaded. Among the charges is that he set himself above all national laws.

1724 King Philip V, grandson of France's Louis XIV and Spain's first Bourbon king, abdicates the throne to his son Louis. He came out of retirement the same year, when Louis died of smallpox.

1776 American colonist Thomas Paine publishes his influential pamphlet *Common Sense*. He argues against the concept of monarchy, and for separation from Great Britain. Although little used today, pamphlets were an important medium for the spread of ideas in the 16th through 19th centuries.

1811 U.S. federal troops end the Louisiana Slave Revolt with bullets. Fifty-six African Americans die on the spot, or later by execution. The heads of many were displayed on poles as a warning to others.

BORN ON THIS DAY

1738
ETHAN ALLEN
American Revolutionary War fighter

1834
LORD ACTON (JOHN E. E. DALBERG)
English historian, editor of *The Rambler*

1864
GEORGE WASHINGTON CARVER
American chemist and agronomist, who helped change the agricultural economy of the South

1880
CHJARLES ADRIEN WETTACH
Swiss clown, famous around the world as "Grock"

1903
BARBARA HEPWORTH
English sculptor (*Contrapuntal Forms; The Unknown Political Prisoner; Three Monoliths*) who was made a Dame of the British Empire in 1965 and died in 1975 after a fire in her studio

1904
RAY BOLGER
American dancer and actor (*The Wizard of Oz*)

1910
GALINA ULANOVA
Russian ballerina

1912
GUSTÁV HUSÁK
Former president of Czechoslovakia (1975–87) who was imprisoned for his politics in 1951, rehabilitated in 1960, and became deputy premier in 1968

1917
JERRY WEXLER
American record producer

1921
RODGER WARD
American race-car driver and two-time Indianapolis 500 winner

1927
JOHNNIE RAY
American singer ("Cry"; "Walkin' My Baby Back Home"; "Just Walking in the Rain")

"Society is produced by our wants, and government by our wickedness."

—*Thomas Paine*

1811 Canadian explorer David Thompson crosses the Continental Divide at Athabasca Pass. After wintering on the west slope, he explored the Columbia River from its source to the Pacific.

1839 Tea from India first arrives in the United Kingdom.

1878 California senator A. A. Sargent introduces a constitutional amendment granting women the right to vote. It took 42 years to become law.

1878 The British House of Lords approves the Representation of the People Bill, giving the vote to married women over the age of 30.

1902 German chancellor Bernhard Ernst von Bulow leads an attack on British activity in South Africa.

1903 Argentina, concerned about sanitation issues, bans import of American beef.

1917 Colonel William Frederick Cody, better known as Buffalo Bill, dies. William Cody earned his nickname by killing nearly 5,000 buffalo in order to fulfill a contract to supply meat to the workers building the Kansas Pacific Railway.

1920 In the aftermath of World War I, the Treaty of Versailles takes effect.

1920 The League of Nations is formally established according to a covenant ratified by 42 nations in 1919. The League turned over its assets to the newly formed United Nations in 1946.

1922 Arthur Griffith, the founder of Sinn Féin and one of the architects of the 1921 peace treaty with Britain, is elected president of the newly established Irish Free State.

1923 Four years after the end of World War I, President Warren G. Harding orders U.S. occupation troops stationed in Germany to return home.

1929 The cartoon character Tintin makes his first appearance. Drawn by the Belgian cartoonist Hergé, Tintin first appeared in the paper *Vingtième Siècle* ("Twentieth Century").

1941 President Franklin D. Roosevelt's Lend-Lease program is brought before the U.S. Congress for consideration. By the end of World War II, more than $50 billion in funds, weapons, aircraft, and ships were distributed to 44 countries through the program. After the war, the Lend-Lease program grew into the Marshall Plan.

1942 The Ford Motor Company signs on to make Jeeps, the new general-purpose military vehicles desperately needed by American forces in World War II.

1946 The first General Assembly of the United Nations, comprising 51 nations, convenes at Westminster Central Hall in London, England.

1957 Harold Macmillan becomes prime minister of Great Britain.

1967 President Lyndon B. Johnson, in his State of the Union message to the U.S. Congress, asks for a 6 percent surcharge on personal and corporate income taxes to help support the Vietnam War. Congress eventually passed the surcharge.

1967 Massachusetts Republican Edward Brooks takes office as the first African American in the U.S. Senate.

1968 U.S. satellite *Surveyor 7* lands safely on the moon and starts sending back photos of the surface.

1989 Cuban troops begin their withdrawal from Angola, but the terrible civil war rages on for more than a decade.

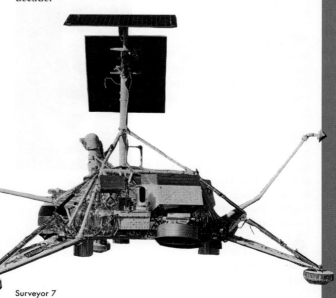

Surveyor 7

1753 Irish-born British physician and naturalist Sir Hans Sloane dies at the age of 92. Sloane founded the Chelsea Physic Garden and his collection of artifacts, books, and manuscripts formed the basis of the British Museum. London's Sloane Square is named after him.

1775 Francis Salvador, the first Jew elected to public office in the Americas, takes his seat on the South Carolina Provincial Congress. In June 1776, Salvador, a patriot, became known as the "Southern Paul Revere" when he warned Charleston, South Carolina, of the approaching British naval fleet.

1787 British astronomer William Herschel, who discovered Uranus in 1781, today discovers its first moon, Titania.

1813 Pineapples are planted in Hawaii for the first time.

1902 American magazine *Popular Mechanics* publishes its first issue.

1904 British troops soundly defeat the fighting dervishes of Mohammed bin Abdullah Hassan, whom they called the "Mad Mullah," at Jidballi, Somaliland.

1908 Declaring that "the ages had been at work on it, and man can only mar it," U.S. president Theodore Roosevelt designates the mighty Grand Canyon a national monument.

1913 The world's first closed hard-topped production car is introduced: Hudson Motor Car Company's Model 54 sedan.

MILESTONE

Stalin Banishes Trotsky

On this day in 1928, Leon Trotsky, a leader of the Bolshevik revolution and early architect of the Soviet state, is deported by Soviet leader Joseph Stalin to Alma-Ata in remote Soviet Central Asia. A year later he was banished from the U.S.S.R. forever. He was received by the government of Turkey and settled on the island of Prinkipo. After four years in Turkey, Trotsky lived in France and then Norway and in 1936 was granted asylum in Mexico. He was found guilty of treason in absentia during Stalin's purges of his political foes. Trotsky survived a machine-gun attack on his home but on August 20, 1940, fell prey to a Spanish communist, Ramón Mercader, who wounded him with an ice ax. He died of his wounds the next day.

Leon Trotsky

Amelia Earhart

1922 At Toronto General Hospital, 14-year-old Canadian Leonard Thompson becomes the first person to receive an experimental insulin injection as treatment for diabetes.

1935 Amelia Earhart departs Wheeler Field in Honolulu on the first solo flight from Hawaii to North America.

The Grand Canyon

> *"Courage is the price that life asks for granting peace."*
>
> —Amelia Earhart

She landed in Oakland 18 hours later.

1939 Marguerite Perey, of the Curie Institute in Paris, discovers the element francium.

1940 Benjamin Davis becomes the first African-American general in the U.S. Army.

1942 During World War II, Japanese forces invade Borneo, Dutch East Indies.

1945 Fighting in the Greek Civil War stops with a political truce between the British-backed Democratic National Army and the communist rebel National Liberation Front.

1949 On Connecticut Avenue in Washington, D.C., the cornerstone is laid at the first mosque of note in the United States.

1963 The Los Angeles nightclub Whiskey-A-Go-Go opens for business on Sunset Boulevard.

1963 The Beatles release new hits: "Please Please Me" and "Tell Me Why."

1964 For the first time, the U. S. Surgeon General gives an official warning that smoking cigarettes can be fatal.

1816 By French decree, the Bonaparte family is excluded from France forever.

1820 Britain's Royal Astronomical Society is founded.

1836 English naturalist Charles Darwin, aboard the *Beagle*, arrives in Australia.

1838 Joseph Smith abandons Ohio to avoid arrest following failure of his Mormon bank in the Panic of 1837 and heads for Missouri to rebuild his religious community.

1879 The British-Zulu War begins as British troops under Lieutenant General Frederic Augustus invade Zululand from the southern African republic of Natal.

1900 The Detroit Automobile Company finishes its first commercial vehicle, a delivery wagon designed by a young engineer named Henry Ford. Ford soon quit to start his own company.

1904 American race-car driver Barney Oldfield sets a new speed record—91.37 miles per hour—on the frozen surface of Lake St. Clair in a stripped-down Ford automobile.

1906 In New York, the Dow Industrials close over 100 for the first time.

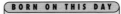

BORN ON THIS DAY

1483
HENDRIK VAN NASSAU DILLENBURG EN DIETZ
Governor and viceroy of Holland

1588
JOHN WINTHROP
First governor of Massachusetts Bay Colony

1665
PIERRE DE FERMAT
French lawyer and mathematician

1729
EDUMUND BURKE
Irish statesman and philosopher

1737
JOHN HANCOCK
First signer of the Declaration of Independence

1822
JEAN JOSEPH ÉTIENNE LENOIR
French inventor of the first practical internal combustion engine

1876
JACK LONDON
American writer (*The Call of the Wild*)

Jack London

1893
HERMANN GOERING
Nazi leader, commander of the Luftwaffe

1904
MISSISSIPPI FRED MCDOWELL
American jazz artist

1922 The British government announces an amnesty for all Irish political prisoners.

1926 In Paris, the Pasteur Institute announces the discovery of an antitetanus serum.

1932 Ophelia Wyatt Caraway, a Democrat from Arkansas, becomes the first woman elected to the U.S. Senate. The first female senator was Rebecca Felton, appointed in 1922 to fill a vacancy but never elected.

1937 Chester Lawton of Ridgewood, New Jersey, and Captain Melville Bloomer of Halifax, Nova Scotia, patent the first submarine cable plow, which allows submarines to dig trenches and lay cable simultaneously for telegraph or telephone systems.

1943 During World War II, Soviet troops create a breach in the German siege of Leningrad, which has lasted for a year and a half. In 1942, 650,000 Leningrad citizens died from starvation, disease, exposure, and injuries suffered from the continual German bombardment. The siege ended in 1944 after 872 days.

1944 Alfred Hitchcock's *Lifeboat* premieres at the Astor Theater in New York. *Lifeboat* demonstrated Hitchcock's mastery of suspense by confining all action to the space of one small boat.

1945 The Japanese lose 41 ships in the Battle of the South China Sea.

1954 U.S. secretary of state John Foster Dulles

Barney Oldfield and Henry Ford

Demonstrators burn the flag of the Romanian Communist Party

announces that the United States will protect its allies through the "deterrent of massive retaliatory power." The policy was a signal that the Eisenhower administration would rely on the nation's nuclear arsenal for defense against communist aggression.

1962 During the Vietnam War, the U.S. Air Force launches Operation Ranch Hand, a "modern technological area-denial technique"—defoliation by the herbicide Agent Orange. It killed vegetation, but did not stop the Vietcong.

1970 On its first transatlantic proving flight, a Boeing 747 lands in London, England.

1970 The would-be Republic of Biafra, its people dying of starvation, gives up its war of secession against Nigeria.

1976 English mystery writer Dame Agatha Christie dies at age 85.

1984 Construction workers restoring the Great Pyramids in Egypt stop using wet concrete, which causes

limestone blocks to split. Instead, they adopted a system of interlocking blocks—the system used by the original builders.

1986 Dr. Franklin Chang-Diaz, first Hispanic American in space, takes off in the space shuttle Columbia.

1990 The Communist Party is outlawed in Romania, still smarting from 24 years under corrupt dictator Nicolae Ceauçescu.

1991 The U.S. Congress gives the green light to military action against Iraq in the Persian Gulf crisis.

1996 Troops from Russia and the United States arrive in Bosnia to help with peacekeeping in the two countries' first joint military action since World War II.

> *"A bone to the dog is not charity. Charity is the bone shared with the dog, when you are just as hungry as the dog."*
>
> —*Jack London*

1404 The Act of Multipliers, which prohibits alchemy, the making of gold from base materials, is passed by the English Parliament—this despite no one ever having succeeded.

1610 Italian astronomer Galileo discovers the fourth moon of Jupiter, Callisto.

1842 A British army doctor reaches the British sentry post at Jalalabad, Afghanistan, the lone survivor of a 16,000-strong Anglo-Indian expeditionary force that was massacred in its retreat from Kabul.

1846 On the brink of war with Mexico, U.S. general Zachary Taylor and 4,000 troops march to the Texas border.

1861 In the charity ward of New York's Bellevue Hospital, Stephen Foster, America's first professional songwriter ("Oh! Susannah," "The Old Folks at Home") dies of a protracted fever at the age of 64.

General Zachary Taylor

MILESTONE

"The Twist" in Number 1 Spot Twice

On this day in 1962, Chubby Checker's hit "The Twist" becomes the first song to reach the No. 1 spot in American music charts twice in two years. "The Twist" had already hit the top of the charts in September 1960.

"One forges one's style on the terrible anvil of daily deadlines."

—Émile Zola

1893 The British Independent Labour Party is founded. Its main objective: "to secure the collective ownership of the means of production, distribution and exchange."

1898 French writer Émile Zola's inflammatory editorial entitled "J'Accuse" is printed. The letter exposes a military cover-up of evidence that French army Captain Alfred Dreyfus—convicted by secret tribunal and sentenced to life in a penal colony—was innocent.

1906 *Scientific American* runs an advertisement for a radio receiver and transmitter, the Telimco. Priced at $8.50, it included a spark coil and a four-cell dry battery and was guaranteed to receive signals from as far as a mile away.

1910 New York's Metropolitan Opera takes part in the first live radio broadcast of opera, transmitting strains of *Pagliacci* and *Cavalleria Rusticana*. The broadcast could be heard only by a few amateur hobbyists who had built their own radio receivers.

1919 California casts its vote in favor of national prohibition of alcoholic beverages.

1928 Tiny television sets are installed in three homes in Schenectady, New York.

James Joyce self-portrait

RCA and General Electric installed the sets, which displayed a 1.5-inch-square picture. The first successful public broadcast of TV also happened on this day.

1929 Nearly 50 years after the famous gunfight at the O.K. Corral, American lawman Wyatt Earp dies quietly in Los Angeles at the age of 80.

1933 Olympic champion Babe Didrikson Zaharias (winner of the javelin and 80m sprint at the 1932 Los Angeles Olympics) scores nine points in her professional basketball debut with the Brooklyn Yankees. Her motto: "Loose your girdle and let'er fly!" Zaharias went on to become a golfer, winning the U.S. National Women's Amateur Championship in 1946, the British Ladies' Amateur Championship in 1947, and the U.S. Women's Open in 1948, 1950, and 1954.

1935 In a referendum dictated by the Treaty of Versailles, voters in the Saar coal-mining region on the border of Germany and France vote overwhelmingly to join Adolf Hitler's Reich.

1937 It becomes illegal for an American to serve in the Spanish Civil War.

1941 James Joyce, widely regarded as Ireland's greatest author, dies in Zürich, Switzerland, at the age of 58. Joyce's masterpiece *Ulysses* is ranked among the greatest works in the English language.

1942 Representatives of nine German-occupied countries meet in London to declare that all those found guilty of war crimes would be punished after World War II ended.

1957 The first Pluto Platters, or Frisbees, start spinning off the production line of the Wham-O company.

1972 President Richard M. Nixon announces that 70,000 U.S. troops will leave South Vietnam over the next three months, reducing U.S. troop strength there by May 1 to 69,000.

1990 Douglas Wilder becomes the governor of Virginia and the first African-American governor in U.S. history.

President Richard M. Nixon

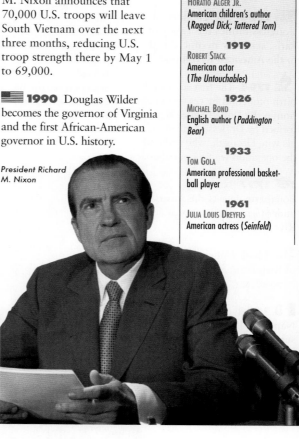

1526 By signing the Treaty of Madrid, King Francis I of France gains his freedom (after a year as a prisoner of Spanish King Charles V) but gives up claims in Italy and France.

1601 In Rome, officials of the Catholic Church hold a burning of Hebrew books.

1639 In Hartford, Connecticut, the first constitution in the American colonies, the "Fundamental Orders," is adopted by representatives of the three major Puritan settlements.

1690 Johann Christoph Denner invents the clarinet in Nuremburg, Germany.

1784 The Continental Congress ratifies the Treaty of Paris, and puts an official end to the American Revolution.

1794 The first successful birth of a child by cesarean section in the United States is performed by Dr. Jesse Bennett on his wife Elizabeth, who endured the operation without anesthesia.

1797 Napoleon Bonaparte defeats the Austrians under General Alvinczy at Rivoli, Italy.

1814 Under the Treaty of Kiel, Denmark cedes Norway to Sweden.

1858 France's Emperor Napoleon III and his Empress survive an assassination attempt by Italian Felice Orsini. Orsini hurled a bomb that exploded under their carriage but left the ruler and his wife unhurt.

MILESTONE

First Moving Assembly Line

On this day in 1914, Ford introduces the moving assembly line, in which car bodies are pulled slowly past production teams. The old system involved teams—and parts—moving down a line of stationary autos. To improve the flow of the work, it needed to be arranged so that as one task was finished, another began, with minimum time spent in set-up. Ford was inspired by the meat-packing houses of Chicago and a grain mill conveyor belt he had seen—if he brought the work to the workers, they'd spend less time moving about. Then he divided the labor by breaking the assembly of the Model T into 84 distinct steps. Each worker was trained to do just one of these steps. Production time was cut from 17 hours per car to 90 minutes.

Sherman's march to the sea

1864 In the American Civil War, General William T. Sherman begins his scorched-earth march through the South.

1868 A convention to write a new state constitution meets in South Carolina with a majority of African-American delegates.

1878 Great Britain's first private telephone call is placed by Queen Victoria at Osborne House to Thomas Biddulph at Osborne Cottage, both on the Isle of Wight.

1894 British novelist Joseph Conrad returns to London to begin writing after a long career at sea. In 1889 he had commanded a Congo River steamboat, which set

> *"As soon as man does not take his existence for granted, but beholds it as something unfathomably mysterious, thought begins."*
>
> —*Albert Schweitzer*

Governor George Wallace, right

the stage for his classic *Heart of Darkness*.

1896 Carlo Ponzi immigrates to America from Italy. He ran a pyramid scam—a type of crime now named for him, the "Ponzi scheme." Caught and deported in 1934, Ponzi was given a high position in Italy's financial sector. He embezzled money from the treasury, escaped to Brazil, and died in 1949.

1917 Poland establishes a provisional parliament. On January 22, U.S. president Woodrow Wilson acknowledged "the emergence of Poland united, independent, and sovereign."

1918 Russia and Finland adopt the modern Gregorian calendar.

1919 In the aftermath of World War I, Germany releases all Allied prisoners of war.

1920 In Paris, the British Liberal prime minister, Welshman David Lloyd George, is awarded the Grand Cross of the Legion of Honour. Hitler later described Lloyd George as "the man who won the (first world) war."

1943 British prime minister Winston Churchill and U.S. president Franklin D. Roosevelt meet in Casablanca, Morocco, to discuss strategy and study the next phase of World War II. They announced that the Allies would accept only unconditional surrender from the Axis powers.

1963 George Wallace is inaugurated as the governor of Alabama, promising his followers, "Segregation now, segregation tomorrow, segregation forever!"

1980 In a crushing diplomatic rebuke to the Soviet Union, the U.N. General Assembly votes 104 to 18 to "deplore" the Russian intervention in Afghanistan.

1559 Two months after the death of her half-sister, Queen Mary I of England, Elizabeth Tudor, the 25-year-old daughter of Henry VIII and Anne Boleyn, is crowned Queen Elizabeth I at Westminster Abbey.

1782 In a report to the U.S. Congress, Superintendent of Finance Robert Morris recommends establishment of a national mint and outlines plans for decimal coinage.

1831 French author Victor Hugo finishes writing *Notre Dame de Paris*, also known as *The Hunchback of Notre Dame*.

1865 During the American Civil War, Fort Fisher in North Carolina falls to Union forces, resulting in the closure of Wilmington, the Confederacy's most important blockade-running port.

1870 The first recorded use of a donkey to represent the U. S. Democratic Party appears in a *Harper's Weekly* cartoon by Thomas Nast. Four years later in another cartoon, Nast originates the use of an elephant to symbolize the Republican Party.

The Battle of Fort Fisher

BORN ON THIS DAY

1432
AFONSO V "THE AFRICAN"
King of Portugal (1438–81)

1622
MOLIÉRE (JEAN BAPTISTE POQUELIN)
French comic dramatist
(*La Tartuffe*)

1823
MATHEW BRADY
American Civil War photographer

1845
ELLA FLAGG YOUNG
First woman president of an American organization (National Educational Association)

1870
PIERRE S. DUPONT
American industrialist, chairman of the board of the DuPont Company

1893
IVOR NOVELLO
Welsh composer and actor

1902
SAUD IBN ABD AL-AZIZ
King of Saudi Arabia who became prime minister in 1953, three months before succeeding his father as king

1908
EDWARD TELLER
Hungarian-born U.S. physicist known as the "Father of the H-bomb"

1918
GAMAL ABDEL NASSER
Egyptian statesman who became president of the newly formed United Arab Republic in 1958

1929
MARTIN LUTHER KING, JR.
American civil rights leader and winner of the Nobel Peace Prize

---

"Coming together is a beginning, staying together is progress, and working together is success."
—Henry Ford

1907 American inventor Dr. Lee De Forest, widely regarded as the "father of radio and the grandfather of television," patents the Audion radio tube, which made wireless broadcasting feasible.

1909 A motorized hearse is used for the first time ever in a Chicago funeral procession by funeral director H. D. Ludlow, in a break with the ancient tradition of stately horse-drawn hearses.

1918 English-born comedian Stan Laurel first starts work with the Hal Roach movie studio. In late 1926, director Leo McCarey suggested that the skinny Laurel team up with rotund comic Oliver Hardy, and a classic team was born.

1933 After nearly a century of cooperative living, the utopian Amana colonists of Iowa begin using U.S. currency for the first time.

1936 American auto baron Henry Ford establishes the Ford Foundation, a philanthropic organization.

1942 The first "blackout" Cadillacs are completed. As part of the war effort, these cars had painted trim rather than chrome. They also lacked spare tires and other luxuries.

1951 Ilse Koch, wife of the commandant of the

U.S. combat advisers with the South Vietnamese

Buchenwald concentration camp, is sentenced to life imprisonment in a court in West Germany. She was nicknamed the "Witch of Buchenwald" for her extraordinary sadism during World War II.

1962 Asked at a news conference if U.S. troops are fighting in Vietnam, President John F. Kennedy says "No." He was technically correct, but U.S. soldiers were serving as combat advisers with the South Vietnamese Army.

1962 The British Meteorological Office adopts the Celsius scale of temperature, 220 years after it was devised by Swedish scientist Anders Celsius.

1970 Muammar al-Qaddafi, the young Libyan Army captain who deposed King Idris in September 1969, is proclaimed premier of Libya by the General People's Congress. Son of a Bedouin farmer and an ardent Arab nationalist, Qaddafi and a group of fellow officers overthrew the Libyan monarchy on September 1, 1969.

1973 Citing "progress" in the Paris peace negotiations between U.S. secretary of state Henry Kissinger and Le Duc Tho of North Vietnam, President Richard M. Nixon halts the most concentrated bombing of the Vietnam War.

1973 American singer Carly Simon tops the charts with "You're So Vain."

1975 "I've got bad news and I don't expect any applause," warns U.S. president Gerald Ford before delivering his first State of the Union Address. He was referring to the economy, not the aftermath of Richard M. Nixon's scandal-wracked administration.

1981 *Hill Street Blues*, television's landmark cops-and-robbers drama, debuts on NBC. Steven Bochco's first show invigorated American television, paving the way for more realistic and gritty fare.

1992 Tim Berners-Lee, inventor of the World Wide Web, releases the first web browser on the Internet.

Tim Berners-Lee

John C. Fremont

1847 A leader in the successful fight to grab California from Mexico, explorer and map-maker John C. Fremont briefly becomes governor of the newly won American territory.

1861 The Crittenden Compromise, the last chance to keep the North and South together, dies in the U.S. House of Representatives. It would have protected slavery in the District of Columbia, forbade federal interference with the interstate slave trade, and compensated owners whose slaves escaped to the free states.

1919 Prohibition, in the form of the 18th Amendment to the U.S. Constitution, prohibiting the "manufacture, sale, or transportation of intoxicating liquors for beverage purposes," becomes the law of the land.

MILESTONE

Castro Forces Take Over Cuban Government

Fidel Castro's Cuban revolutionaries formally overtake and supplant the government of Fulgencio Batista in 1959. Manuel Urrutia was placed as provisional president, while Castro was named head of the Cuban military. As news of the revolution reached the people, there was celebration and some violence in the streets. Within days, the U.S. government had formally recognized the new regime. It did not seem to matter much whether, as the non-existent former government claimed, 3,000 rebel casualties filled the streets of Santa Clara as the body of Castro forces retreated to the east, or whether the government forces had been cut in three and all government buildings were occupied by Castro's men. In two years Castro had converted 40 audacious guerrillas into a conquering army capable of disrupting the life and economy of Cuba and dictating the character of the next government.

1936 Albert Fish is executed at Sing Sing Prison in New York. The "Moon Maniac" was one of America's most notorious and disturbed killers. He went to the electric chair telling guards, "It will be the supreme thrill, the only one I haven't tried."

1945 Adolf Hitler, having decided to remain in Berlin for the last great siege of World War II, takes to his underground bunker, where he would remain for 105 days before committing suicide.

1969 In Paris, representatives of the United States, South Vietnam, North Vietnam, and the National Liberation Front sit at a circular table without name-plates, flags, or markings. Seemingly trivial, agreement on the shape of the furniture allowed peace talks during the Vietnam War to proceed.

U.S. government agents pouring liquor into the sewer

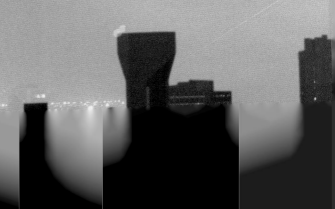

Anti-Shah demonstration outside the U.S. Embassy in Iran

1972 Don McLean's "American Pie" tops the American music charts.

1979 Faced with an army mutiny and violent demonstrations against his rule, Mohammad Reza Shah Pahlavi, leader of Iran since 1941, is forced to flee the country. Fourteen days later, the Ayatollah Ruhollah Khomeini, spiritual leader of the Islamic revolution, returned after 15 years of exile and took control of the country.

1981 John Lennon tops the American music charts with "Starting Over."

1990 In the wake of vicious fighting between Armenian and Azerbaijani forces in Azerbaijan, the Soviet government sends in 11,000 troops to quell the conflict.

1991 The United Nations deadline for the Iraqi withdrawal from Kuwait expires at midnight. Within hours, fighter aircraft launched bombing missions from Saudi Arabia and from aircraft carriers in the Persian Gulf.

"What luck for the rulers that men do not think."

—*Adolf Hitler*

35

1893 On the Hawaiian Islands, a group of American sugar planters under Sanford Ballard Dole overthrow Queen Liliuokalani, the Hawaiian monarch, and establish a new provincial government with Dole as president.

1899 French driver Camille Jenatzy captures the land-speed record in an electric car of his own design: 41.425 miles per hour at Acheres Park, France. On the same day, previous record-holder Gaston Chasseloup-Laubat raises the record again, posting 43.690 miles per hour in an electric Jeantaud automobile.

1900 Mormon Brigham Roberts is refused a seat in the U.S. House of Representatives because he is a polygamist.

1904 In Moscow, Anton Chekhov's *The Cherry Orchard* is performed for the first time.

1905 Fifty-nine people die in Bergen, Norway, when a rock-fall causes a 20-foot wave in the fjord.

1923 At Getafe, Spain, the first successful flight of designer Juan de la Cierva's

Cierva's Autogiro

BORN ON THIS DAY

1504
PIUS V
Italian pope (1566–72)

1706
BENJAMIN FRANKLIN
American statesman, diplomat, scientist, and inventor who helped draft the Declaration of Independence and wrote *Poor Richard's Almanac*

Benjamin Franklin

1820
ANNE BRONTË
English poet and novelist, the youngest of the Brontë sisters

1863
DAVID LLOYD GEORGE
British prime minister during World War I

1883
COMPTON MACKENZIE
English author

1899
NEVILLE SHUTE
English novelist (*A Town Like Alice; On the Beach*)

1899
AL CAPONE
American mobster known as "Scarface Al"

1913
VIDO MUSSO
Italian-born musician who played with Benny Goodman

1942
MUHAMMAD ALI (CASSIUS CLAY)
American boxer, the only three-time heavyweight champion

1962
JIM CARREY
American actor and comedian (*Dumb and Dumber; The Truman Show; Ace Ventura: Pet Detective*)

"The definition of insanity is doing the same thing over and over and expecting different results."
—*Benjamin Franklin*

Autogiro proves the feasibility of helicopters.

1938 American bandleader Benny Goodman and his orchestra perform the first jazz concert at Carnegie Hall in New York.

1942 American actress Carole Lombard, one of Hollywood's most glamorous stars, dies in a plane crash at age 34.

1945 During World War II, Soviet troops cross the Vistula River, liberate the city of Warsaw, and grab it for the U.S.S.R. Since the German invasion in 1939,

Aftermath of Northridge, California, earthquake on Route 14 near Sylmar (milestone)

Warsaw's population of approximately 1.3 million had shrunk to 153,000.

1949 The first Volkswagen Beetle arrives in the United States from Germany. The little Volkswagen ("people's car") was designed by Ferdinand Porsche at the request of Adolf Hitler to be a workhorse car for the common German.

1950 A team of 11 thieves, in a precisely planned strike, steals more than $2 million from the Brinks Armored Car depot in Boston, Massachusetts. It was an almost perfect crime: The thieves were caught only days before the statute of limitations for the theft expired.

1961 In his farewell address to the nation, U.S. president Dwight D. Eisenhower warns the American people to keep a careful eye on what he calls the "military-industrial complex" and calls for diplomacy, restraint, and compassion in dealing with the Soviet Union.

1966 A United States Air Force B-52 bomber collides with a jet tanker over Spain's Mediterranean coast, dropping three 70-kiloton hydrogen bombs near the town of Palomares and one in the sea. The bombs were not armed, but radioactive plutonium was scattered over the fields of Palomares, requiring decontamination.

1977 Gary Gilmore, convicted in the double murder of an elderly couple, is executed by firing squad in Utah—the first execution in the United States since reinstatement of the death penalty in 1976.

1535 Spanish conquistador Francisco Pizarro founds Lima, Peru.

1562 After 10 years in recess, the Council of Trent reconvenes to help the Catholic Church deal with the challenges of the Reformation.

1733 The first polar bear shown in the United States, a nine-month-old cub captured in Greenland, goes on exhibit in Boston.

1778 English explorer Captain James Cook becomes the first European to sight the Hawaiian Islands when he sails past Oahu.

1788 The first Australian penal colony is established with the arrival of 736 convicts banished from Great Britain to Botany Bay. Over the next 60 years, approximately 50,000 criminals would be transported from Great Britain to the "land down under."

1803 In a confidential message to the U.S. Congress, President Thomas Jefferson requests $2,500 to finance Lewis and Clark's exploration of the West. A week earlier, Congress approved $9,375,000 for the purchase of land near French-held New Orleans—a move that led to the Louisiana Purchase.

1817 Argentine revolutionary Jose de San Martín begins an epic crossing of the Andes to Chile with an army—a feat that ranks him with Hannibal and Napoleon.

1854 In La Paz, Mexico, William Walker, a self-styled

American "conquistador," proclaims the independent Republic of Sonora. The Mexicans weren't interested, and drove him out. Later, he made himself president of Nicaragua.

1871 William, king of Prussia, becomes German emperor at Versailles.

1910 In Japan, 25 people are condemned to death for plotting to kill the Mikado (former title of the emperor of Japan).

1911 Lieutenant Eugene Ely lands his Curtiss biplane on a special platform mounted on the deck of a ship in San Francisco Harbor, thereby demonstrating the feasibility of aircraft carriers.

1912 After a two-month ordeal, English explorer Robert Falcon Scott arrives at the South Pole only to find that Roald Amundsen, a Norwegian explorer, has preceded him by just over a month. Disappointed, his exhausted expedition began the long journey back to their base camp, but died en route.

Robert F. Scott expedition of 1912

> *"One of the advantages of being disorderly is that one is constantly making exciting discoveries."*
>
> —A. A. Milne

1915 The U.S. Revenue Marine Corps changes its name to the U.S. Coast Guard.

1918 Vladimir Lenin proclaims the existence of the Union of Soviet Socialist Republics.

1919 Bentley Motors is established in England. The manufacturer of sports cars and luxury automobiles was later acquired by Rolls-Royce. Over time, the two makes became nearly indistinguishable from one another.

1943 During World War II, the Soviet Army announces that the siege of Leningrad has been broken.

1943 The United States institutes a wartime ban on the sale of presliced bread, to reduce metal demand by bakeries.

1943 During World War II, after a four-month hiatus, Germany resumes the deportations of Jews from the Warsaw ghetto to Treblinka death camp. This time Jewish rebels fought back, forcing SS troops to withdraw temporarily. There was no happy ending. Before this new incursion was over, 6,000 more Jews had been transported.

1964 Architect Minoru Yamasaki reveals his plan for the World Trade Center in New York.

Senator George McGovern with one of his campaign workers, future president Bill Clinton

1970 An attempt is made to destroy the grave of Karl Marx in Highgate Cemetery in London.

1971 Senator George S. McGovern of South Dakota begins his antiwar campaign for the 1972 Democratic presidential nomination by vowing to bring home all U.S. soldiers from Vietnam.

1978 The U.S. Centers for Disease Control isolate the cause of Legionnaire's disease: stagnant water.

1980 English designer and photographer Cecil Beaton dies. Beaton was a photographer for *Vanity Fair* and *Vogue* magazines, and later designed sets for ballet, opera, theater, and film, including *My Fair Lady* and *Gigi*.

1983 American rock musician Frank Zappa defines the music-news process: "Most rock journalism is by people who can't write, interviewing people who can't talk, for people who can't read."

MILESTONE

World War I Peace Conference Begins

The Paris Peace Conference opens in France on this day in 1919. The conference sought to produce treaties that would officially mark the end of World War I. In attendance were 70 delegates from 27 countries. Germany was excluded from the conference until the treaty terms were ironed out and then submitted to the German government. Notable attendees of the conference were Georges Clemenceau of France, David Lloyd George of Great Britain, Woodrow Wilson of the United States, and Vittorio Emanuele Orlando of Italy—a group that became known as the "Big Four." Results of the Paris Peace Conference include the Covenant of the League of Nations and the Treaty of Versailles. President Wilson was successful in insisting on a League of Nations, predecessor to the United Nations, whose purpose is to promote international peace and security.

49 B.C. With the words *Lacta alea est* (The die is cast), Julius Caesar leads his army across the Rubicon River to civil war in Italy.

1840 Captain Charles Wilkes sights the coast of eastern Antarctica and claims it for the United States. Wilkes' group explored a 1,500-mile stretch of the eastern Antarctic coast that later became known as Wilkes Land.

1847 Angered by the abusive behavior of American soldiers occupying the city, Mexicans in Taos, New Mexico, strike back by murdering the American-born governor, Charles Bent.

1903 King Edward VII and President Theodore Roosevelt exchange coded greetings in the first transatlantic radio broadcast between heads of state.

1904 Thomas A. Edison patents an electric automobile.

1907 In Tehran, Mohammed Ali Mirza is formally crowned Shah of Persia.

1915 Parisian George Claude wins a U.S. patent for the neon advertising sign.

1915 During World War I, Great Britain suffers its first casualties from an air attack when two German zeppelins drop bombs on the eastern coast of England.

1936 English poet and Nobel laureate Rudyard Kipling dies at the age of 70. Kipling's best-known works were the two *Jungle Books, Stalky and Co,*

Kim, and the *Just So Stories*. He wrote the poem "Recessional (Lest We Forget)" for Queen Victoria's diamond jubilee in 1897.

1937 English ballet dancer Margot Fonteyn makes her debut in *Giselle* at Sadler's Wells Theatre in London.

1937 Howard Hughes flies a plane from Los Angeles, California, to New York in seven hours, 22 minutes.

1940 The Three Stooges film *You Natzy Spy* is released. Anticipating Charlie Chaplin's *The Great Dictator* by nine months, Moe (Moses Howard) played a Hitler-like dictator of a fictional country, Moronica.

1941 During World War II, British forces in East Africa, acting on months of intercepted intelligence communiqués, invade Italian-occupied Eritrea—a solid step toward victory in Africa.

President Theodore Roosevelt and King Edward VII

Howard Hughes

570
MOHAMMED
Islamic prophet (*The Koran*)

1736
JAMES WATT
Scottish inventor who improved steam engines, adapted the telescope for use in measuring distance, and coined the term "horsepower"

1807
ROBERT E. LEE
Confederate general during the American Civil War

1809
EDGAR ALLAN POE
American author and poet ("The Raven")

1839
PAUL CÉZANNE
French post-Impressionist painter

1869
ALFRED R. ZIMMERMAN
Rotterdam mayor 1906–22, director of the League of Nations

1905
ANNE SCHUMACHER HUMMERT
American radio pioneer who, with her husband Frank, wrote and produced radio soap operas during the golden age of radio (*Just Plain Bill*)

1919
JOHN H. JOHNSON
American editor and publisher (*Ebony; Jet*)

1920
JAVIER PÉREZ DE CUÉLLAR
Peruvian diplomat, secretary-general of the U.N. (1982–92)

1922
GUY MADISON
American actor (*Wild Bill Hickok*)

1923
JEAN STAPLETON
American actress (*All in the Family*)

1943
JANIS JOPLIN
American singer ("Me and Bobby McGee"; "Mercedes Benz"; "Piece of My Heart")

1955
SIMON RATTLE
English conductor

1950 American singer Merv Griffin has a top hit: "I've Got a Lovely Bunch of Coconuts."

1955 U.S. president Dwight D. Eisenhower holds the first presidential press conference filmed for TV and newsreels. NBC did the filming and then shared it with other networks.

1961 Dr. Michael Ramsey succeeds Geoffrey Fisher as archbishop of Canterbury. Ramsey made a historic visit to the pope in the Vatican in 1966.

1966 Following the death of Indian prime minister Lal Bahadur Shastri, Indira Gandhi becomes head of the Congress Party and thus prime minister of India. The daughter of independent India's first prime minister, Jawaharlal Nehru, Gandhi was India's first female head of government.

1969 American musician Marvin Gaye tops the charts with "I Heard It Through the Grapevine."

Indira Gandhi

> *"I have great faith in fools; my friends call it self-confidence."*
> —Edgar Allan Poe

1327 Edward II, king of England, is forced from power by his wife, Eleanor of Castille, and her lover, Roger Mortimer, in the name of the younger Edward. However, after Edward III was crowned, he had Mortimer executed and his mother imprisoned.

1616 Samuel de Champlain, French explorer and founder of Quebec City, arrives for the winter in a Huron Indian village after being wounded in a battle with Iroquois in New France.

Samuel de Champlain

1649 Following the English Civil War, King Charles I is tried for treason.

1783 France and Spain, allies of America during the American Revolutionary War, sign a peace agreement with Great Britain.

1841 During the First Opium War, China cedes the island of Hong Kong and surrounding territory to the British with the signing of the Chuenpi Convention.

1870 Victoria Woodhull and her sister Tennessee Claflin open the doors of Woodhull, Claflin & Co., America's first brokerage firm run solely by women.

1885 L. A. Thompson patents the roller coaster. His first model, at Coney Island in Brooklyn, New York, was 450 feet from start to finish with a maximum 30-foot drop.

1887 The U.S. Senate approved the leasing of Pearl Harbor for construction of a naval base.

1892 Students of the YMCA Training School in Springfield, Massachusetts, play the world's first official basketball game.

1908 The Sullivan Ordinance forbids smoking by women in American public places.

1930 American aviator Charles Lindbergh touches down in New York, having set a new record for flying across the country: 14.75 hours.

1936 King George V of Great Britain and Ireland, the 71-year-old grandson of Queen Victoria, dies after 26 years on the throne. In 1917, during World War I, he renamed his line the House of Windsor to break the family association with its German relations. He was succeeded by Edward VIII.

1937 Franklin D. Roosevelt, in keeping with the 20th Amendment to the Constitution, is the first U.S. president inaugurated on this day. Ratified during his first term in 1933, the amendment set January 20 as the official date henceforth.

1942 During World War II, Nazi officials, including Adolf Eichmann and Reinhard

> ## "You exist only in what you do."
> —Federico Fellini

Heydrich, meet at Wannsea, a suburb of Berlin, to discuss details of the "Final Solution" to the "Jewish question." Minutes of this conference later provided key evidence during the Nuremberg war crimes trials.

1953 AT&T links its lines to the Bell Telephone Company of Canada and transmits Canada's first television show over a 66-mile microwave link between Buffalo, New York, and Toronto.

1954 In Korea, more than 22,000 anticommunist prisoners are released to U.N. forces in the aftermath of the Korean War.

1958 American singer Elvis Presley receives orders from the Memphis, Tennessee, draft board to report for duty.

1961 Eighty-seven-year-old Robert Frost recites his poem "The Gift Outright" at U.S. president John F. Kennedy's inauguration. Although Frost had written a new poem for the occasion, titled "Dedication," faint ink in his typewriter made the words difficult to read, so he recited "The Gift Outright" from memory.

1977 Newly inaugurated U.S. president Jimmy Carter turns down the traditional limousine and walks from the Capitol to the White House.

1981 Minutes after Ronald W. Reagan's inauguration as the 40th president of the United States, the 52 American captives held at the U.S. embassy in Tehran, Iran, are released, ending the 444-day Iran Hostage Crisis.

1986 The federal holiday to commemorate slain American civil rights leader Martin Luther King, Jr. is observed for the first time.

1986 Great Britain and France announce a joint effort to build a tunnel beneath the English Channel.

1996 Yāsir Arafāt is elected president of the Palestinian National Council with 88.1 percent of the popular vote, becoming the first democratically elected leader of the Palestinian people.

Elvis Presley

1472 A comet passes within 10.5 million km of Earth. It was bright enough to be seen in daylight.

1793 One day after being convicted of conspiracy with foreign powers and sentenced to death by the French National Convention, deposed King Louis XVI is executed by guillotine in the Place de la Revolution in Paris.

1899 The five Opel brothers begin production of the Opel-Lutzmann automobile in Russelheim, Germany. In 1902 Opel introduced its first original car, a two-cylinder runabout.

1914 The Victoria Memorial is completed. The Memorial, designed by Sir Aston Webb and incorporating a statue by Thomas Brock, stands outside the east front of Buckingham Palace facing the Mall.

1916 The American National Board of Review, a volunteer group of film fans representing movie studios founded in 1909 as the National Board of Censorship, agrees it will not accept nudity in films.

1919 The first meeting of the unofficial Irish parliament,

King Louis XVI being led to the guillotine

1821
JOHN BRECKINRIDGE
Fourteenth U.S. vice president

1824
THOMAS "STONEWALL" JACKSON
Confederate American Civil War general

Thomas "Stonewall" Jackson

1855
JOHN (MOSES) BROWNING
American gun designer

1905
CHRISTIAN DIOR
French fashion designer

1905
PAUL SCOFIELD
English actor best known for his role as Sir Thomas More in *A Man For All Seasons*

1925
BENNY HILL
British comedian

1927
TELLY (ARISTOTLE) SAVALAS
Emmy Award-winning American actor (*Kojak*)

1933
WILLIAM WRIGLEY III
American chewing gum manufacturer and longtime owner of the Chicago Cubs baseball team

1934
PLACIDO DOMINGO
Spanish opera singer

1939
WOLFMAN JACK (BOB SMITH)
American radio disc jockey who pioneered in promoting rock-and-roll music

the Dail Eirann, is held in Dublin by 25 Sinn Fein MPs who refuse to attend the House of Commons in Westminster.

1924 Vladimir Lenin, the architect of the Bolshevik Revolution and the first leader of the Soviet Union, dies of a brain hemorrhage at the age of 54. His body was embalmed and placed in a mausoleum near the Kremlin, and Petrograd was renamed Leningrad in his honor.

1950 In one of the most spectacular trials in U.S. history, former State Department official Alger Hiss is convicted of perjury regarding his alleged involvement in a Soviet spy ring before and during World War II. Hiss served nearly four years in jail, but steadfastly protested his innocence.

1950 English author Eric Arthur Blair, better known as George Orwell, dies of tuberculosis. Orwell's work included *Down and Out in Paris and London, Homage to Catalonia, Keep the Aspidistra Flying, Coming Up for Air, Animal Farm,* and *Nineteen Eighty-Four.*

1950 Scientists in Berkeley, California, announce the discovery of the 93rd element of the Periodic Table, which they name berkelium.

1958 Buddy Holly's "Peggy Sue" tops the American music charts.

> *"A lie told often enough becomes the truth."*
> —*Vladimir Lenin*

1959 American director, producer, and screenwriter Cecil B. De Mille dies at age 78. His 70 films included *Cleopatra*, *The Crusades*, and *The Ten Commandments*.

1968 The Battle for Khe Sanh begins. One of the most publicized and controversial battles of the Vietnam War, it was an attempt by North Vietnam to overrun an old French outpost reactivated by U.S. Marines. The siege lasted 66 days and ended with no clear victory for either side.

1976 On simultaneous flights from London and Paris, the first Concordes with commercial passengers take flight, headed for Bahrain and Rio de Janeiro, Brazil. The supersonic Concordes flew at 1,350 miles per hour, cutting air travel time by more than half.

1977 One day after taking office, U.S. president Jimmy Carter grants pardon to hundreds of thousands of Americans who avoided the draft during the Vietnam War. The pardon allowed draft-dodgers to come back to the United States without fear of prosecution.

1980 The U.S. price of gold hits $850 per ounce, up from $381 in less than three months.

1985 "Like a Virgin" by Madonna tops the American music charts.

1985 Don DeLillo wins the American Book Award for his breakthrough novel *White Noise*.

Message written on the back of a U.S. Marine in Khe Sanh

1840 The first British colonists in New Zealand arrive at Port Nicholson on Auckland Island. Originally part of the Australian colony of New South Wales, New Zealand became a separate colony in 1841 and was made self-governing in 1852.

1879 In trying to defend a ford across the Buffalo River during the Zulu War in South Africa, 139 British troops repel the attacks of between 3,000 and 4,000 Zulus at the famous Battle of Rorke's Drift.

1901 Queen Victoria dies, ending a 63-year reign, the longest in British history. She saw the growth of an empire on which the sun never set, restored dignity to the English monarchy, and ensured its survival as a ceremonial political institution.

1903 Colombia sells America the right to build the Panama Canal, and assigns U.S.

Queen Victoria

control in perpetuity of a narrow strip of land known as the Canal Zone.

1905 The first Russian revolution begins on "Bloody Sunday," when czarist troops open fire on a peaceful group of workers marching to the Winter Palace in St. Petersburg to present their grievances to Czar Nicholas II. Some 500 protestors were massacred. Months of disorder followed throughout Russia.

1927 The second-to-last surviving Confederate general of the American Civil War, John A. McCausland, dies in Mason, West Virginia, an unreconstructed Rebel to the end. He died 13 months before Felix Robertson, the last surviving Confederate general.

MILESTONE

Roe v. Wade

On this day in 1973, the U.S. Supreme Court rules in *Roe v. Wade* that women can terminate a pregnancy during the first two trimesters. The Court held that a woman's right to an abortion falls within the right to privacy protected by the 14th Amendment. The decision also defined different levels of state interest for regulating abortion in the second and third trimesters. As a result, the laws of 46 states were affected by the Court's ruling. Although defended by the Court on several occasions, the legalization of abortion became a divisive and intensely emotional public issue. The debate intensified during the 1980s, and both pro-choice and pro-life organizations strengthened their membership and political influence.

A British officer helps an Italian prisoner near Tobruk, Libya

1939 Scientists split a uranium atom for the first time in the cyclotron at New York City's Columbia University. Their work led to the Manhattan Project and the atom bomb.

1941 During World War II, British and Commonwealth forces take the coastal fortress of Tobruk, Libya, and capture 30,000 Italian prisoners, 236 guns, and 87 tanks. The battle marked the beginning of the end for Italy's occupation of North Africa.

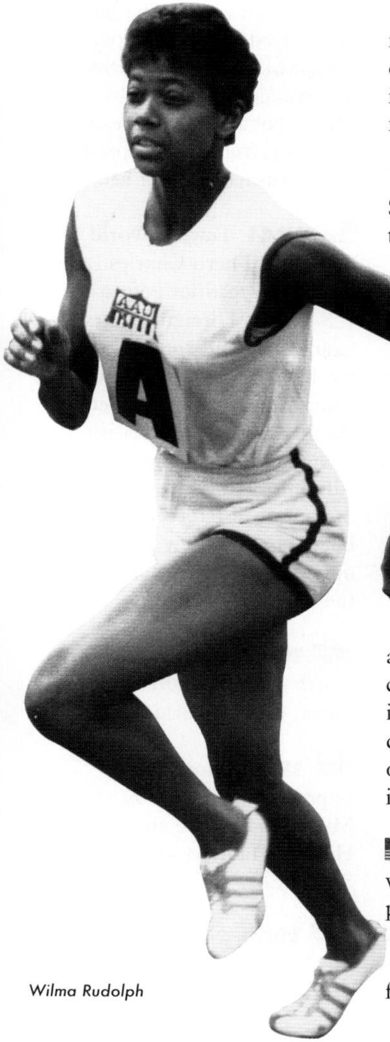

Wilma Rudolph

> ***"Be thou the rainbow in the storms of life. The evening beam that smiles the clouds away, and tints tomorrow with prophetic ray."***
>
> *—Lord George Byron*

1960 Paul Pender beats Sugar Ray Robinson for the American middleweight boxing championship.

1961 Olympic gold-medal winner Wilma Rudolph of the United States sets a world indoor record—6.9 seconds—for the women's 60-yard dash.

1966 "The Sound of Silence" by Simon and Garfunkel tops the American music charts.

1968 *Rowan and Martin's Laugh-In* premieres on American television. It was an instant smash that ran for five years on NBC.

1980 Andrei Dmitriyevich Sakharov, the Soviet physicist who helped build the U.S.S.R.'s first hydrogen bomb, is arrested in Moscow after criticizing Soviet military intervention in Afghanistan. He was subsequently stripped of his numerous scientific honors and banished to remote Gorky.

1997 Lottie Williams, walking in a Tulsa, Oklahoma, park, becomes the first human hit by man-made space junk—a six-inch metal piece from a falling Delta II rocket.

BORN ON THIS DAY

1440
Ivan III (the Great)
Grand prince of Russia (1462–1505)

1561
Sir Francis Bacon
English philosopher, statesman, and essayist (*The Advancement of Learning*)

1775
André Marie Ampère
French mathematician and physicist who gave his name to the SI unit of electrical current (ampère or amp)

1788
Lord George Byron
English romantic poet ("Lara"; "Don Juan")

1849
August Strindberg
Swedish dramatist, novelist, and painter

1875
D. W. (David Wark) Griffith
American film director (*Birth of a Nation; Intolerance*)

1890
Fred Vinson
Thirteenth chief justice of the U.S. Supreme Court

1906
Willa Brown Chappell
Pioneer aviator who was the first African-American female officer in the Civil Air Patrol and the first black woman to hold a commercial pilot's license in the United States

1909
U Thant
Burmese statesman and secretary-general of the United Nations (1962–71), who played a major diplomatic role in the Cuban Missile Crisis

1911
Bruno Kreisky
Austrian statesman and prime minister

1937
Joseph Wambaugh
American author (*Choirboys; The Onion Field*)

1957
Mike Bossy
NHL All-Star player, led the New York Islanders to 4 Stanley Cups

1579 The Union of Utrecht is signed, leading to formation of the Dutch Republic.

1870 Declaring that he doesn't care if they are the rebellious band of renegades he has been searching for, Colonel Eugene Baker orders his men to attack a sleeping camp of peaceful Blackfeet in northern Montana.

1896 In Wurzburg, Germany, Wilhelm Roentgen gives the first public exhibition of his x-ray device.

1901 Edward VII, king of Great Britain and Ireland, makes his accession speech following the death of his mother, Queen Victoria, the previous day.

1907 Charles Curtis of Kansas begins his term as the first Native American elected to the U.S. Senate.

1911 The all-male membership of the French Academy of Science rejects admission of Nobel Prize-winner Marie Curie.

1912 The Aermore Manufacturing Company, a Chicago concern, receives a

---

BORN ON THIS DAY

1574
LUCAS I. FRANCHOYS
Belgian painter

1752
MUZIO CLEMENTI
Italian composer considered the father of modern piano playing

1832
ÉDOUARD MANET
French Impressionist painter (*Luncheon in the Grass*)

1898
SERGEI MIKHAILOVICH EISENSTEIN
Russian film director (*The Battleship Potemkin; Ten Days That Shook the World; Ivan the Terrible*)

1899
HUMPHREY BOGART
American actor (*Treasure of the Sierra Madre; Key Largo; Casablanca*)

1910
DJANGO REINHARDT
Belgian jazz guitarist

1914
NAPOLEON L. BONAPARTE
French pretender to the throne

1919
ERNIE KOVACS
Comedian and television personality

1928
JEANNE MOREAU
French actress (*Jules et Jim; La Femme Nikita*)

1933
CHITA RIVERA
American actress (*Sweet Charity*)

"Things are never so bad they can't be made worse."

—*Humphrey Bogart*

patent for a multiple-pipe auto horn that plays a chord like a church organ. It never caught on.

1930 The planet Pluto is photographed for the first time by American astronomer Clyde Tombaugh.

1931 Russian ballerina Anna Pavlova dies at her home in Hampstead Heath, London, at the age of 49. The Dying Swan solo was created for her by Michel Fokine, and the dessert of meringue, fruit, and whipped cream was named after her.

1941 During World War II, national hero Charles Lindbergh testifies before the U.S. House Foreign Affairs Committee and suggests that the United States negotiate a neutrality pact with Hitler. He denounced "the British, the Jewish, and the Roosevelt Administration" as instigators of American intervention, but eventually flew combat missions over the Pacific for the Allies.

1943 British forces in North Africa capture Tripoli, Libya, during World War II.

1944 Norwegian Expressionist painter Edvard Munch dies at the age of 80. His most famous work was *The Scream*.

1956 Nelson Riddle tops the American music charts with "Lisbon Antigua."

Senator Charles Curtis, right, riding with President and Mrs. Coolidge

The USS Pueblo

1956 Sir Alexander Korda, the Hungarian-born film producer credited with saving the British film industry, dies at the age of 67. Korda directed in Vienna, Berlin, and Hollywood (for First National) before moving to Great Britain, where he founded London Film Productions and Denham Studios. His films include *The Scarlet Pimpernel*, *The Fallen Idol*, *The Third Man*, and *Richard III*.

1957 Princess Grace of Monaco gives birth to her first child, Caroline.

1960 Jacques Piccard and Lieutenant Don Walsh set an ocean depth record in the bathyscaphe *Trieste*, descending 35,810 feet into the Challenger Deep.

1961 The U.S. Supreme Court upholds a Chicago law that forbids the showing of any motion picture without approval of city censors.

1968 During the Vietnam War, North Korean patrol boats open fire on and capture the USS *Pueblo*, a Navy intelligence vessel engaged in surveillance. One sailor was killed and several were wounded. Negotiations to free the 82 survivors dragged on for 11 months, causing a crisis of confidence in American foreign policy.

1971 Prospect Creek Camp, Alaska, records the record low temperature for the United States: minus 80° F.

1973 George Foreman beats Joe Frazier for the world heavyweight boxing title.

1977 The miniseries *Roots* debuts on ABC. The show traced four generations of an African-American family based on author Alex Haley's account of his own family and became the single most-watched program in American history.

1978 In Paris, gunmen kidnap Belgian industrialist Baron Edouard Empain. Four days later the kidnappers send part of Empain's finger to his family in the mail. On March 26, he was released by his captors.

1985 O. J. Simpson is elected to the American Football Hall of Fame.

1544 Dutch astromomer Reinerus Gemma-Frisius uses a camera obscura to view a solar eclipse and later publishes the first illustration of the method.

1848 A millwright named James Marshall discovers gold along the banks of Sutter's Creek in northern California. Nine days later Mexico ceded California to the United States, and the gold rush was on.

1860 French inventor Etienne Lenoir is issued a patent for the first successful internal-combustion engine—a converted steam engine that burned a mixture of coal gas and air.

1907 Engineer Glenn Curtiss sets an unofficial land-speed record on a self-built V-8 motorcycle: 136.29 miles per hour. Also in 1907, Curtiss established one of the first airplane manufacturing companies in the United States.

1908 The Boy Scouts movement begins in England with the publication of the first installment of Robert Baden-Powell's handbook *Scouting for Boys.*

Glenn Curtiss

1670
WILLIAM CONGREVE
English dramatist and poet

1679
CHRISTIAN VON WOLFF
German philosopher

1712
FREDERICK II (THE GREAT)
King of Prussia (1740–86)

Frederick II

1732
PIERRE DE BEAUMARCHAIS
French dramatist (*The Barber of Seville; The Marriage of Figaro*)

1862
EDITH WHARTON
American novelist (*Ethan Frome; The Age of Innocence*)

1880
ELISABETH ACHELIS
American creator and promoter of the World Calendar

1888
ERNST HEINKEL
German aircraft engineer

1913
MARK GOODSON
American TV game show producer (*What's My Line?; I've Got a Secret; The Price Is Right*)

1925
MARIA TALLCHIEF
American ballerina

1928
DESMOND MORRIS
English anthropologist and writer (*The Naked Ape; Manwatching; The Human Animal*)

1949
JOHN BELUSHI
American comedian and actor (*Saturday Night Live; The Blues Brothers; Animal House*)

1915 During World War I, British warships sink the *Blucher* on Dogger Bank in the North Sea. The *Blucher* was the pride of the German fleet and had been described as "the most powerful battle cruiser in the world."

1922 Christian Nelson of Onawa, Iowa, patents the Eskimo Pie.

1927 Young director Alfred Hitchcock's first film, *The Pleasure Garden,* is released in England.

1935 The world's first canned beer—Krueger—goes on sale in Richmond, Virginia.

1935 Mussolini dismisses every member of the Italian cabinet.

1936 American clarinenist and bandleader Benny Goodman records the hit "Stompin' at the Savoy."

1943 During World War II, German general Friedrich von Paulus, commander of the German 6th Army at Stalingrad, urgently requests permission from Adolf Hitler to surrender his position there, but Hitler refuses. Paulus surrendered a week later, having lost more than half of his 280,000 men.

1946 The U.S. Army bounces a radar signal off the moon back to Earth.

"If only we'd stop trying to be happy we'd have a pretty good time."
—*Edith Wharton*

U.S. Army radar receiver

earnings record: over $30 million, with more to come.

 1965 Sir Winston Leonard Spencer Churchill, the British leader who guided Great Britain and the Allies through the crisis of World War II, dies in London at the age of 90.

● **1972** Farmers in Guam discover Shoichi Yokoi, a Japanese sergeant who spent 28 years in hiding, unaware that World War II had ended. He got a big welcome in Japan, married, and returned to Guam for his honeymoon.

1955 The first atomic clock is developed at Columbia University in New York.

1964 In the world's first heart transplant operation, 58-year-old Boyd Rush gets a chimpanzee heart and survives three hours.

1964 American jockey Willie Shoemaker sets a career

1984 The first Macintosh computers go on sale. Price: $2,495.

1986 The *Voyager II* space probe flies past Uranus at close range, discovering new moons and sending back pictures to the United States.

The first Apple Macintosh computer

1533 King Henry VIII marries Anne Bolyn despite Pope Clement's refusal to annul his first marriage. Later, Henry disavowed the pope's authority and declared himself the head of the Church of England.

1554 In England, Sir Thomas Wyatt raises an army in rebellion against Queen Mary I.

1839 At the Royal Institution, English scientist Michael Faraday announces the development of photography.

1858 Vickie, the oldest daughter of Queen Victoria of Great Britain and Ireland, chooses Mendelssohn's "Wedding March" for her wedding to Frederick William of Prussia and sets a tradition followed today.

1863 During the American Civil War, President Abraham Lincoln removes General Ambrose Burnside from command of the Army of the Potomac. Burnside served only two months, saw only failure, and was replaced by General Joe Hooker.

1890 Coal miners band together to form the United Mine Workers of America, one of the United States' most potent, and at times most troubled, labor organizations.

1890 News reporter Elizabeth Cameron, a.k.a.

Construction of locks on the Panama Canal

BORN ON THIS DAY

1477
ANNA DE BRETAGNE
Wife of Maximilian of Austria and Louis XII

1540
EDMUND CAMPION
English saint and Jesuit martyr

1627
ROBERT BOYLE
Irish physicist and chemist

1759
ROBERT BURNS
Scottish poet ("Auld Lang Syne"; "Comin' Thru the Rye")

1874
SOMERSET MAUGHAM
British author (*The Moon and Sixpence; Cakes and Ale; East of Suez; The Razor's Edge*)

1882
VIRGINIA WOOLF
English author (*Mrs. Dalloway; Orlando*)

Virginia Woolf

1899
PAUL HENRI SPAAK
Belgian prime minister and first president of the U.N. General Assembly

1933
CORAZON AQUINO
President of the Philippines who defeated Ferdinand Marcos after government agents had assassinated her husband in 1983

"What's done we partly may compute, but know not what's resisted."

—*Robert Burns*

Nellie Bly, makes it around the world in 72 days, 6 hours, 11 minutes, and 14 seconds, beating the fictional journey of Jules Verne's story *Around the World in 80 Days.*

1905 Arthur MacDonald of Great Britain set a new land speed record of 104.65 miles per hour at Daytona Beach, Florida.

1906 The spectacular 12-mile Simplon Tunnel is opened to rail traffic between Switzerland and Italy.

1909 In Dresden, Germany, Richard Strauss's opera *Elektra* is performed for the first time.

1920 Italian painter and sculptor Amedeo Modigliani dies in Paris at the age of 35. The following night his model and mistress Jeanne Hebuterne, who was nine months pregnant, killed herself by jumping out of a fifth-floor window.

1924 The first Winter Olympics is held at Chamonix in the French Alps. Competition featured ski jumping, bobsled, and 12 other events.

1947 Chicago gangster Al Capone dies in Miami from syphilis at age 48.

1949 The National Academy of Television Arts and Sciences presents its first industry award—the Emmy—at the Hollywood Athletic Club in Los Angeles. The most popular program: *Pantomime Quiz Time*.

1951 President Harry S. Truman gives the first tape-recorded presidential press conference at the White House. The U.S. Army Signal Corps recorded the conference for the White House archives.

1955 The United States and Panama sign the Panama Canal Treaty.

1959 American Airlines flies a Boeing 707 from California to New York—the first scheduled flight across the United States.

1964 The Beatles get their first number one hit: "I Want to Hold Your Hand."

1971 In Los Angeles, California, cult leader Charles Manson is convicted, along with followers Susan Atkins, Leslie Van Houten, and Patricia Krenwinkle, of the brutal 1969 murders of actress Sharon Tate and six others.

1971 Idi Amin Dada Oumée takes over Uganda in a military coup.

1974 South African surgeon Dr. Christian Barnard conducts the first human heart transplant.

1980 A U.S. Navy hovercraft hits the top speed attained by a warship: 103 miles per hour.

1981 Jiang Qing, the widow of Chinese leader Mao Zedong, is sentenced to death for her "counter-revolutionary crimes" during the Cultural Revolution. Two years later, the Chinese government commuted her sentence to life, which ended in 1991 when she died in prison of an apparent suicide.

1983 Nazi war criminal Klaus Barbie is arrested in Bolivia.

1995 Russia comes close to launching nuclear missiles when early-warning radar detects a missile launched near Norway, apparently headed for Moscow. Norway had notified Russia of the planned scientific launch, but the Russian Defense Ministry failed to pass the information to radar personnel. The missile landed outside Russia.

2002 The American daytime soap opera *The Guiding Light* becomes the longest-running daily program in broadcast history, having run for 65 consecutive years. The serial began in 1937 as a 15-minute radio show.

1500 Spanish explorer Vicente Yáñez Pinzón, who had commanded the Niña during Christopher Columbus's first expedition to the New World, makes the first recorded sighting by a European of the Brazilian coast.

1699 The Treaty of Carlowitz ends hostilities between the Holy League and the Ottoman Empire.

1784 In a letter to his daughter, Benjamin Franklin writes that the turkey would be a more fitting national symbol for the United States than the bald eagle.

1838 The first Prohibition law in the history of the United States is passed in Tennessee, making it a misdemeanor to sell alcoholic beverages in taverns and stores.

1875 Pinkerton detectives shoot up the James family home in Missouri, thinking they have outlaws Frank and Jesse James cornered. They managed only to maim the outlaws' mother and kill their nine-year-old half brother.

1875 George Green patents the electric-powered dental drill.

1885 Mahdist fighters kill British general George "Chinese" Gordon on the palace steps in Khartoum, Sudan.

1905 The world's largest diamond is found at the Premier mine in Pretoria, South Africa—a 3,106-carat monster named the "Cullinan." It was later cut into 106 polished diamonds including

---

BORN ON THIS DAY

1715
CLAUDE HELVÉTIUS
French philosopher

1826
JULIA DENT GRANT
Wife of U.S. president Ulysses S. Grant

Julia Dent Grant

1880
DOUGLAS MACARTHUR
20th-century American general

1892
BESSIE COLEMAN
American pioneer aviator

1908
STÉPHANE GRAPELLI
French jazz violinist

1918
NICOLAE CEAUSESCU
Leader of the Romanian Communist Party (1965–89), deposed and shot in the bloody Christmas Revolution of 1989

1925
PAUL NEWMAN
American actor (*Hud*, *Cool Hand Luke*)

1928
EARTHA KITT
American singer

1945
JACQUELINE DU PRÉ
English cellist

General George Gordon

"We are not retreating— we are advancing in another direction."
—Douglas MacArthur

the 530-carat "Star of Africa I," the largest cut fine-quality colorless diamond in the world.

1905 American Fred Marriot, driving a Stanley Steamer, sets a land-speed record of 121.57 miles per hour at Daytona Beach, Florida.

1906 Fred Marriot sets the final land-speed record for a steam-powered vehicle: 127.66 miles per hour.

1910 In Paris, the River Seine floods to more than three times its normal level, endangering the sculpture gallery of the Louvre, which houses the *Venus de Milo*.

1911 Glenn Curtiss, the father of naval aviation, makes the first successful take-off from water.

1920 The Lincoln Motor Car Company is founded in the United States. It was acquired by the Ford Motor Company just two years later, but the brand survived.

1924 St. Petersburg (Petrograd), Russia, is renamed Leningrad.

1932 American inventor Ernest Orlando Lawrence applies for a patent on the cyclotron, the first atom-smasher.

1934 American producer Samuel Goldwyn buys the film

Refugees fleeing Spain after the fall of Barcelona

rights to *The Wonderful Wizard of Oz*, by L. Frank Baum. Released in 1939, the film made 17-year-old Judy Garland an international star.

1934 New York's Apollo Theater opens in Harlem under new management, starting its long history as an African-American musical mecca.

1939 During the Spanish Civil War, Barcelona, the Republican capital of Spain, falls to the Nationalist forces of Generalissimo Francisco Franco.

1940 Twenty-nine-year-old actor Ronald Reagan marries actress Jane Wyman. Their marriage lasted until 1948. Four years later, he married former actress Nancy Davis.

1945 American lieutenant Audie Murphy, the most decorated soldier of World War II, is wounded in France. Winner of 37 medals and decorations, he was wounded three times, fought in nine major campaigns, and was credited with killing 241 Germans. He played himself in the monumentally successful film *To Hell and Back*—and admitted publicly that he suffered from post-traumatic stress syndrome. He died in a plane crash in 1971.

1950 The Republic of India is born. In August 1947, Great Britain granted independence to this part of its former empire, which was partitioned into Pakistan and India. An Indian constitution was adoped in late 1949, and the Republic was established on this date.

1970 U.S. Navy lieutenant Everett Alvarez Jr. spends his 2,000th day in captivity in Southeast Asia during the Vietnam War. Shot down on August 5, 1964, and released in 1973, he was the longest-held POW in U.S. history.

1972 Renowned American gospel singer Mahalia Jackson dies at the age of 61.

1980 The U.S. Olympic Committee votes to cancel or move the upcoming Moscow Olympics in response to the Soviet invasion of Afghanistan. The games were held as scheduled, but many countries stayed away.

1988 Aborigines in Australia begin the "year of mourning," a protest of the nation's founding. This day marks the bicentennial celebration of Australia Day.

Audie Murphy postage stamp

1302 Italian poet and politician Dante Alighieri is exiled from Florence, where he served as one of six priors governing the city. He wrote his masterpiece, *The Divine Comedy*, as a virtual wanderer, seeking protection for his family in town after town.

1649 Charles I, king of England, Scotland, and Ireland, is sentenced to death for being a traitor, murderer, public enemy, and tyrant.

1825 Indian Territory is approved by Congress, thus beginning the "Trail of Tears" and the forced westward relocation of Native Americans from eastern U.S. states.

1880 American inventor Thomas Edison patents an incandescent electric light.

1887 St. Jean Marie Muzeyi, one of the 22 Martyrs of Uganda, is beheaded by Mwanga, ruler of what was then Buganda.

1888 The National Geographic Society is founded in Washington, D.C.

1899 Frenchman Camille Jenatzy captures the land-speed record (49.932 miles per hour) in a battery-powered CGA Dogcart automobile.

1901 Italian composer Giuseppe Verdi (*Aida; La Traviata*) dies in Milan at age 87.

1901 Edward VII, king of Great Britain and Ireland, makes his nephew, the German Kaiser, a field marshal in the British army.

BORN ON THIS DAY

1756
WOLFGANG AMADEUS MOZART
Austrian composer

Wolfgang Amadeus Mozart

1808
DAVID F. STRAUSS
German theologian (*Jesus' Life*)

1832
LEWIS CARROLL (CHARLES DODGSON)
English mathematician and writer (*Alice's Adventures in Wonderland*)

1834
DMITRI MENDELEYEV
Russian chemist who created the periodic table of the elements

1850
SAMUEL GOMPERS
First president of the American Federation of Labor

1851
RAFAEL OBLIGADO
Argentinian author (*Santos Vega*)

1859
KAISER WILHELM II
German emperor during World War I who was forced to abdicate in 1918

1900
HYMAN RICKOVER
American admiral, considered the "Father of the Atomic Submarine"

1919
DAVID SEVILLE (ROSS BAGDASARIAN)
American cartoonist (*Alvin and the Chipmunks*)

1936
TROY DONAHUE
American actor (*A Summer Place; Surfside Six*)

1948
MIKHAIL BARYSHNIKOV
Russian ballet star

1964
BRIDGET FONDA
American actress (*Scandal; Point of No Return; Single White Female*), daughter of Peter Fonda, grand

---

Nevada nuclear test

1904 American racer William K. Vanderbilt sets a new land-speed record of 92.308 miles per hour in a gasoline-powered Mercedes at Daytona Beach, Florida.

1913 Jim Thorpe, the American athlete dubbed "the greatest athlete in the world" after winning gold medals in the pentathlon and decathlon at the 1912 Stockholm Olympics, is stripped of his medals and his titles after admitting to being paid to play minor-league baseball during 1909 and 1910. The payments made Thorpe a professional and therefore ineligible for the Olympics.

1918 *Tarzan of the Apes* is released. The silent movie, based on Edgar Rice Burroughs's novel, was the first in a long line of Tarzan productions.

William K. Vanderbilt

1923 In Munich, Germany's National Socialist (Nazi) Party holds its first rally.

1924 The body of Soviet leader Vladimir Lenin is laid to rest in a mausoleum on Red Square near the Kremlin.

1931 In the United States, Francis Davis of the truck division of the Pierce Arrow Motor Car Company is granted the first patent for a power steering system.

1944 Two weeks after puncturing German lines, World War II Soviet forces break the siege of Leningrad, an 872-day battle that cost hundreds of thousands of Russian lives.

1945 At the close of World War II, Soviet troops enter Auschwitz, Poland, freeing the survivors of the network of concentration camps and finally revealing to the world the depth of the horrors perpetrated there.

1951 France recognizes the People's Republic of China.

1951 The first of a series of nuclear detonations inaugurates the new Nevada test site.

1959 Candidates for the first U.S. space flight are selected by NASA. Among the 110 chosen is John Glenn, who became the first American to orbit the Earth.

1967 A launch-pad fire during Apollo program tests at Cape Canaveral, Florida, kills astronauts Virgil "Gus" Grissom, Edward H. White II, and Roger B. Chafee.

1968 A week after he died in a plane crash, American singer Otis Redding's "Sitting on the Dock of the Bay" is released.

1973 The Paris Peace Accords are signed by the United States and North Vietnam, bringing an official end to America's participation in its most unpopular foreign war. The accords, however, did not end the Vietnam conflict.

> *"The labor of a human being is not a commodity or article of commerce. You can't weigh the soul of a man with a bar of pig-iron."*
>
> —*Samuel Gompers*

M I L E S T O N E

Americans Bomb Germans for the First Time

On this day in 1943, 8th Air Force bombers, dispatched from their bases in England, fly the first World War II American bombing raid against the Germans, targeting the Wilhelmshaven port. Of the 64 planes participating in the raid, 53 reached their target and managed to shoot down 22 German planes— and lost only three planes in return. The 8th Air Force was activated in February 1942 as a heavy bomber force based in England. Its B-17 Flying Fortresses, capable of sustaining heavy damage while continuing to fly, and its B-24 Liberators, long-range bombers, became famous for precision bombing raids, the premier example being the raid on Wilhelmshaven. Commanded at the time by Brigadier General Newton Longfellow, the 8th Air Force was amazingly effective and accurate in bombing warehouses and factories in this first air attack against the Axis power.

1077 Holy Roman Emperor Henry IV receives absolution at Canossa, Italy, thus acknowledging secular submission to the Church.

1547 English king Henry VIII dies in London at age 55.

1573 The Compact of Warsaw guarantees religious freedom in Poland.

1596 Sir Francis Drake, English admiral and explorer known to the Spanish as "the master-thief of the unknown world," dies at sea near Panama.

1613 Italian astronomer Galileo records a star that might have been the planet Neptune, but cloudy weather prevents him from further observations, and Neptune went unconfirmed until 1846.

Neptune

1787 The Free Africa Society is founded by former slaves Absalom Jones and Richard Allen in Philadelphia, Pennsylvania.

1807 Gaslights illuminate a street for the first time: London's Pall Mall.

1855 The Panama Railway, which carried thou-

BORN ON THIS DAY

1457
HENRY VII
First Tudor king of England
(1485–1509)

1611
JOHANNES HEVELIUS
Polish astronomer

1693
ANNA "IVANOVNA"
Czarina of Russia (1730–40)

1706
JOHN BASKERVILLE
English inventor of the "hot-pressing" method of printing

1841
SIR HENRY MORTON STANLEY
Welsh-born American explorer who led the African expedition to find missing missionary David Livingstone

Sir Henry Morton Stanley

1853
JOSÉ MARTIY PEREZ
Cuban poet, essayist, and politician who struggled for Cuban independence

1884
AUGUSTE PICCARD
Swiss scientist, explorer, and balloonist who, in 1935, ascended to 55,000 feet in a balloon

1912
JACKSON POLLOCK
Abstract Expressionist whose style of dripping paint onto canvases made him one of the most influential American artists of the 20th century

1933
SUSAN SONTAG
American author (*The Style of Radical Will*; *Illness as a Metaphor*)

---

sands of unruly miners to California via the dense jungles of Central America, dispatches its first train across the Isthmus of Panama. It ran until the Panama Canal opened in 1914.

1871 In the events leading to the establishment of the Third Republic, France signs an armistice with victorious Prussian invaders.

1878 America's first college daily, *The Yale News*, publishes its first edition.

1878 New Haven, Connecticut, opens the first commercial phone exchange, providing eight lines for twenty-one telephones.

1885 British gunboats arrive in Khartoum, Sudan, two days too late to save General George "Chinese" Gordon and his beseiged garrison.

1916 President Woodrow Wilson nominates Louis Brandeis to the U.S. Supreme Court. The appointment was confirmed despite bitter opposition, and Brandeis became the first Jew on the high court.

1917 American forces are recalled from Mexico after nearly 11 months of fruitless searching for Mexican revolutionary Pancho Villa.

1921 German physicist Albert Einstein theorizes that the universe can be measured.

1921 In Paris, the Allies set Germany's war reparation payments at £10 billion over 42 years. The payments were

---

> *"I was not looking for my dreams to interpret my life, but rather for my life to interpret my dreams."*
>
> —*Susan Sontag*

reduced by two-thirds the following January.

1925 American film star Gloria Swanson marries the Marquis de la Falais de la Coudraie, one of six marriages.

1934 In Vermont, Robert Royce starts up America's first ski lift—a rope tow powered by a Model T engine.

1937 The prototype of the Rolls-Royce Silver Wraith makes its first test run. It became the British company's principal luxury sedan in the decades following World War II.

1938 Rudolf Caracciola hits 268.496 miles per hour on the German autobahn, the highest speed ever achieved on a public road. Later the same day, Bernd Rosemeyer crashed and died on the autobahn trying to surpass Caracciola's record.

1945 Toward the end of World War II, the 717-mile "Burma Road" is reopened by the Allies, allowing supplies to flow from British-held northern Burma to Kunming, China.

1958 American Charles Starkweather kills the family of his girlfriend, 14-year-old Caril Ann Fugate. The two take off on a cross-country killing spree dramatized in the 1973 film *Badlands*.

1986 The space shuttle *Challenger* lifts off from Cape Canaveral, Florida; 73 seconds later it explodes, killing the crew, which included high-school teacher Christa McAuliffe.

The Challenger *explodes*

M I L E S T O N E

Carnegie Institution Established

Rather than retire and play with his riches, Andrew Carnegie follows his belief that a "man who dies rich dies disgraced" and donates his fortune to various philanthropic causes. Carnegie donated $350 million, $10 million of which he hands over on this day in 1902 to establish the Carnegie Institution in Washington, D.C. According to Carnegie, it was designed "to encourage, in the broadest and most liberal manner, investigation, research, discovery, and the application of knowledge to the improvement of mankind." Carnegie's mission translated into an organization dedicated to research and education in biology, astronomy, and the earth sciences.

King George III

🏴󠁧󠁢󠁥󠁮󠁧󠁿 **1820** Ten years after mental illness forced him to retire from public life, King George III, the British king who lost the American colonies, dies at the age of 82.

🇺🇸 **1834** Workers building the Chesapeake and Ohio Canal riot over labor conditions. President Andrew Jackson calls in the military—the first time federal troops were deployed to settle an American labor dispute.

🎭 **1845** American writer Edgar Allan Poe's famous poem "The Raven," beginning "Once upon a midnight dreary," is published in the *New York Evening Mirror*.

🇺🇸 **1861** Kansas enters the Union as the 34th state. In the midst of the secessions of eight states over the previous six weeks, it entered as a free state despite armed conflict between pro-slavery and antislavery foces.

🔬 **1886** German manufacturer Karl Benz earns a patent for his three-wheeled "Motorwagen," the first practical internal-combustion vehicle ever constructed.

First Inductees to the Hall of Fame

On this day in 1936, the U.S. Baseball Hall of Fame received its first members in Cooperstown, New York. The original inductees were Ty Cobb, Babe Ruth, Honus Wagner, Christy Mathewson, and Walter Johnson. There are currently 254 members in the National Baseball Hall of Fame. Included are 189 former major-league players, 23 executives or pioneers, 18 Negro leaguers, 16 managers, and 8 umpires. The Hall of Fame currently has 58 living members. Inducted into the Hall of Fame in 2003 were Gary Carter and Eddie Murray.

> *"One must be a god to be able to tell successes from failures without making a mistake."*
>
> —*Anton Chekhov*

🔱 **1891** Following the death of her brother, King Kalakaua, Liliuokalani becomes the last monarch of the Hawaiian Islands. Two years later, with the help of U.S. Marines, Sanford B. Dole and his "Committee of Safety" removed her from the throne.

🇪🇸 **1930** Spanish dictator General Primo de Rivera resigns. His son José Antonio later founded the Spanish Fascist Party and was executed by the Republicans.

🇮🇷 **1942** Iran signs a Treaty of Alliance with Great Britain and the U.S.S.R., assuring a wartime supply route from the

Edgar Allan Poe

President Johnson visits troops at Cam Rahn Bay in South Vietnam

West to Russia during World War II.

🎬 **1958** Creating one of the most enduring of Hollywood marriages, American movie stars Paul Newman and Joanne Woodward wed.

🎬 **1958** The American group The Silhouettes have a top hit with "Get a Job."

🎬 **1964** American director Stanley Kubrick's black comic masterpiece, *Dr. Strangelove or: How I Learned to Stop Worrying and Love the Bomb,* opens in theaters. The movie focused on the actions of a rogue U.S. officer who orders U.S. bombers to launch atomic attacks against the Soviet Union.

🎬 **1967** The Mamas and The Papas top the American music charts with "Words of Love."

🇺🇸 **1968** In his annual budget message, U.S. president Lyndon B. Johnson asks for $26.3 billion to continue the war

in Vietnam and announces an increase in taxes to pay for it.

🇺🇸 **1979** Brenda Spencer, 16, kills two men and wounds nine children as they enter the Cleveland Elementary School in San Diego, California. Asked for an explanation, she said, "I just don't like Mondays. I did this because it's a way to cheer up the day."

🇨🇳 **1979** Chinese Communist leader Deng Xiaoping meets U.S. president Jimmy Carter to sign new accords reversing decades of hostility between the two countries.

🎬 **1980** American comedian Jimmy Durante, nicknamed Schnozzola for his notable nose, dies in Santa Monica, California, at the age of 97.

🇺🇸 **1989** Global Motors, the American company that imported the Yugo, files for bankruptcy. The Yugo was a Yugoslavian-made economy car—inexpensive and worth even less.

1349 Günther, count of Schwarzburg-Blankenburg, is elected king of Germany, a crown he would lose in May to the other elected king, Charles IV.

1648 The Peace of Westphalia is signed by the Dutch and Spanish, bringing an end to the Eighty Years' War.

1649 In London, King Charles I is beheaded for treason. His opponents abolished the monarchy and Oliver Cromwell assumed control of the new English Commonwealth. When Cromwell died, the monarchy was restored and Cromwell was convicted of treason. For good measure, his body was disinterred and hanged.

1782 José Antonio Galán, peasant leader of the Comunero (Commoner's) Rebellion in Colombia, is hanged.

1790 English builder Henry Greathead tests the first lifeboat designed for shore-based rescue of shipwrecked sailors. Oar-powered, super buoyant, and self-righting, it served for 40 years on the coast of England.

1820 English explorer Edward Bransfield, in HMS *Williams*, becomes the first man to sight the Antarctic mainland. From near Deception Island, he charted "high mountains, covered with snow."

1835 President Andrew Jackson survives the first attempt against the life of a U.S. president when a deranged man fires two pistols at him in the House chamber of the U.S. Capitol.

BORN ON THIS DAY

1882
FRANKLIN D. ROOSEVELT
32nd U.S. president (1933–45) who led the nation out of the Great Depression and through World War II

Franklin D. Roosevelt

1885
JOHN HENRY TOWERS
American naval aviation pioneer who during World War II led the air arm of the largest fleet ever assembled in recorded history

1899
MAX THEILER
American microbiologist who won the Nobel Prize in 1951 for his work in combating yellow fever

1911
(DAVID) ROY "LITTLE JAZZ" ELDRIDGE
American trumpeter

1912
BARBARA TUCHMAN
American historian (*The Guns of August*)

1915
JOHN PROFUMO
English Conservative politician who was forced to resign in 1963 after a scandal involving his relationship with Christine Keeler, who was also involved with Russian diplomat Yevgeny Ivanov

1927
OLOF PALME
Swedish politician who was elected prime minister in 1969, 1982, and 1985

1937
VANESSA REDGRAVE
Academy Award-winning British actress (*Morgan; Isadora; Mary, Queen of Scots*)

1847 Yerba Buena, a California settlement of 200 shacks, gets a new name: San Francisco.

1875 After the fall of Napoleon III, France adopts the Third Republic.

1889 Rudolf, Archduke and Crown Prince of Austria, kills himself and his 17-year-old lover in a suicide pact.

1901 Humphrey Haines discovers Waimangu Geyser, the world's tallest, near Rotorua, New Zealand. On a cycle of about 36 hours, it erupted 600 feet in the air, with occasional bursts to 1,600 feet. After four years, it stopped.

1917 The first jazz recording is made in New York City, featuring five jazz innovators calling themselves the Original Dixieland Jazz Band.

1920 The Toyo Kogyo Company, Ltd., future maker of Mazda vehicles, is founded in Hiroshima, Japan.

1933 Adolf Hitler, leader of the National Socialist Nazi Party, becomes chancellor of Germany.

1933 With the stirring notes of the *William Tell Overture* and a shout of "Hi-yo, Silver! Away!" *The Lone Ranger* debuts on Detroit's WXYZ radio station in Michigan.

1942 The last automobiles to be produced by Chevrolet and DeSoto before America joins World War II roll off the assembly lines. Chrysler, Plymouth, and Studebaker plants followed suit

Original Dixieland Jazz Band

the next day. World War II restrictions shut down the commercial automobile industry, and auto manufacturers retooled for production of military gear.

1964 The United States launches an unmanned spacecraft called *Ranger 6*. The craft, carrying television cameras, crash-landed on the moon.

1968 In coordinated attacks all across South Vietnam, communist forces launch the Tet Offensive. Dozens of cities, towns, and military bases—including the U.S. embassy in Saigon—were attacked. The attack's size and intensity shook the confidence of Americans who believed the Vietnam War would soon be over.

1972 In Derry (also known as Londonderry), Northern Ireland, 13 unarmed civil rights demonstrators are shot dead by British Army paratroopers in an event that becomes known as "Bloody Sunday."

1975 Hungarian professor of interior design Erno Rubik files a patent for the Rubik's Cube®, published as patent number HU 170062.

1979 With the shah gone, Iran's new civilian government announces that Ayatollah Ruhollah Khomeini is free to return from exile in France.

1995 On the most propitious day of India's Kumbh Mela festival, millions of Hindu pilgrims bathe in the Ganges at Allahabad.

1996 The U.S. Centers for Disease Control and Prevention reports that AIDS is the leading cause of death for Americans aged 25 to 44.

> *"Almost anything you do will be insignificant, but it is very important that you do it."*
> —*Mohandas Karamchand Gandhi*

1606 In London, Guy Fawkes, a chief conspirator in the "Gunpowder Plot," a Catholic plan to blow up the British Parliament building and annihilate the entire Protestant government, jumps to his death moments before his execution for treason.

1863 The first African-American infantry regiment is mustered into the U.S. Army at Beaufort, South Carolina.

1897 The first auto hill climb is held on the final stage of a race from Marseilles to Nice. The uphill dash was won by M. Pary in a steam-powered DeDion-Bouton.

1900 Scottish peer Sir John Sholto Douglas, 8th Marquis of Queensberry, dies at the age of 56. Queensberry supervised the formulation by John Graham Chambers of the rules of boxing, which became known as the Queensberry Rules. In 1895 Irish writer Oscar Wilde had unsuccessfully sued the Marquis for libel following allegations of a homosexual relationship with Queensberry's son Lord Alfred Douglas, allegations which ultimately led to Wilde's imprisonment in Reading Gaol.

1901 In Moscow, Anton Chekhov's play *Three Sisters* is performed for the first time.

1902 A French soccer team plays in England for the first time: Paris loses, 4-0, to Marlow FC.

1906 The coast of Ecuador is shaken by the century's fifth-largest earthquake,

---

Jackie Robinson

World War I gas masks

measuring 8.8 on the Richter scale.

1913 The British House of Lords rejects a bill tabled by the Liberal government and passed by the House of Commons on January 16 proposing home rule for Ireland. One peer said that home rule would make the Irish "a men-

> *"I sit here all day trying to persuade people to do the things they ought to have sense enough to do without my persuading them."*
>
> —*Harry S. Truman*

development of the hydrogen bomb, based on nuclear fusion. It was far more powerful than fission, or atom bombs.

1966 The Soviet Union launches *Luna 9*, the first spacecraft to land softly on the moon.

ace in war and a disturbing influence in peace."

1915 On the Russian Front, Germany uses poison gas for the first time.

1917 During World War I, Germany announces renewal of unlimited submarine warfare in the Atlantic, warning that submarines will attack all ships, including civilian passenger carriers, in war-zone waters.

1930 For the first time, a U.S. Navy glider is released from a dirigible, but the idea of an aerial aircraft carrier never caught on.

1943 German troops surrender at Stalingrad in the first major defeat of Germany's armies during World War II.

1944 U.S. forces invade the Japanese-held Marshall Islands during World War II.

1950 U.S. president Harry S. Truman orders the

1968 As part of the Tet Offensive during the Vietnam War, 19 Vietcong soldiers on a suicide mission seize the U.S. embassy in Saigon and hold it for six hours until American paratroopers land by helicopter on the roof and rout them.

1971 *Apollo 14*, piloted by astronauts Alan B. Shepard Jr., Edgar D. Mitchell, and Stuart A. Roosa, is launched from Cape Canaveral, Florida. In 1961, Shepard was the first American in space. He became the fifth man to walk on the moon and celebrated by hitting golf balls from the lunar surface.

1990 The Soviet Union's first McDonald's fast-food restaurant opens in Moscow. Throngs of people line up to pay the equivalent of several days' wages for burgers.

Hundreds of Muscovites line up for McDonald's opening day

FEBRUARY 1

682 To pressure Jews to convert to Christianity or emigrate, King Erwig, Visigoth king of Spain, prohibits the practice of any Jewish rites and urges the "utter extirpation of the pest of the Jews."

1587 Queen Elizabeth I of England signs the warrant of execution for Mary, Queen of Scots.

Mary, Queen of Scots

1789 Vietnamese forces drive Chinese troops from the Vietnamese capital of Thang Long.

1790 The Supreme Court of the United States convenes in New York City for its first session, Chief Justice John Jay presiding.

1814 English Romantic poet Lord Byron publishes "The Corsair," a gloomy work that sells roughly 10,000 copies on its first day in print.

1814 Twelve hundred people die when the volcano Mayon erupts on the Philippine island of Luzon.

1861 Texas becomes the seventh state to secede from the

Union over the issue of slavery, doing so despite the objections of its governor, Sam Houston, who predicts an "ignoble defeat" for the South.

1862 American writer Julia Ward Howe's patriotic song "Battle Hymn of the Republic" is published in the *Atlantic Monthly*.

1884 The first volume of the *Oxford English Dictionary*, spanning entries from "a" to "ant," is published. It took another 43 years for the editors to finish the Z entries.

1887 Real-estate developer Harvey Wilcox subdivides 120 acres in southern California and calls the development Hollywood.

1902 Chinese empress Tzu-hsi outlaws the binding of women's feet.

1908 Portuguese king Carlos I and his heir, Luis Filipe, are assassinated while riding in an open carriage through Portugal's capital city, Lisbon.

1917 During World War I, Germany resumes the unrestricted use of submarine warfare against Allied shipping.

1919 At the Paris peace conference in Versailles, agreement is reached between the United States, United Kingdom, Italy, and France on the founding principles of the League of Nations.

1928 The tomb of Tutankhamen yields its final secrets as jars containing the king's vital organs are found.

> *"I believe that unarmed truth and unconditional love will have the final word in reality. This is why right, temporarily defeated, is stronger than evil triumphant."*
>
> —*Martin Luther King, Jr.*

1935 The BBC announces that it will launch the world's first public television service later in the year. A German service was the first to air on March 22.

1937 Thirteen men, accused of colluding with the exiled Leon Trotsky to overthrow Stalin, are executed in Moscow. Trotsky denied having links with the men and accused Stalin of staging the trials in order to cling to power.

1938 The ninth-largest earthquake of the century, measuring 8.5 on the Richter scale, occurs on the ocean floor of Indonesia's Banda Sea.

1943 During World War II, Japanese forces begin evacuating the island of Guadalcanal after seven months of intense, often hand-to-hand jungle fighting that killed more than 25,000 Japanese and 1,600 Americans.

1954 The U.S.S.R. calls for Emperor Hirohito of Japan to be tried for war crimes.

1957 Friedrich von Paulus, the World War II German field marshal who surrendered at Stalingrad against Hitler's orders to fight to the death, dies at 66.

1960 The USA conducts the first test firing of the Minuteman intercontinental ballistic missile.

1965 Police arrest Martin Luther King, Jr. and 700 U.S. civil rights demonstrators in Selma, Alabama.

1979 Shiite Muslim cleric Ayatollah Ruhollah Khomeini returns to Iran in triumph after 15 years in exile and is greeted by revolutionaries eager to establish a fundamentalist Islamic state.

2003 The U.S. space shuttle *Columbia* disintegrates 200,000 feet above Texas while reentering the atmosphere near the end of its mission, killing seven astronauts and scattering debris over east Texas and western Louisiana. The 22-year-old *Columbia*, the oldest in NASA's fleet of reusable space vehicles, was traveling approximately 12,500 miles per hour when the disaster occurred.

M I L E S T O N E

North Carolina Lunch Counter Sit-in

On this day in 1960, four African-American students, refused service at a Woolworth's lunch counter in Greensboro, North Carolina, stage a sit-in. Similar protests in other southern cities during the next few days led to the arrests of more than 1,600 people. The four black youths were attacking the social order of the time. The unwritten rules of society required black people to stay out of white-owned restaurants, to use only designated drinking fountains and restrooms, to sit in the rear of Greensboro city buses, in a separate balcony at the Center Theatre, and in segregated bleachers during sports events at War Memorial Stadium. All four would emerge unscathed and eventually be recognized as heroes of the civil rights movement.

Space shuttle Columbia: Commander Rick Husband, center waving; front row from left, Kalpana Chawla, William McCool; second row from left, Ilan Ramon, Laurel Clark; third row from left, Michael Anderson, David Brown

FEBRUARY 2

962 German king Otto I invades Italy at the request of Pope John XII and is crowned Holy Roman Emperor.

1046 The first known observation of the beginning of the Little Ice Age (a 200-year period of exceptional cold) appears in the *Anglo-Saxon Chronicle*: "no man alive . . . could remember so severe a winter."

1494 Italian explorer Christopher Columbus begins using Native Americans as slaves.

Christopher Columbus, center

1536 The city of Buenos Aires, Argentina, is founded by the Spaniard Pedro de Mendoza.

1556 More than 800,000 people die in an earthquake in the Chinese provinces of Shanxi and Henan.

1585 English playwright William Shakespeare's twins, Hamnet and Judith, are baptized. Hamnet died eleven years later.

1624 Dutch settlers establish New Amsterdam at the southern end of Manhattan Island. The British later renamed the community New York.

1626 Charles I inherits the English throne. His subsequent power struggle with

BORN ON THIS DAY

1650
NELL GWYNNE
Actress and mistress of King Charles II of England

1875
FRITZ KREISLER
Austrian-born American violinist and composer

1882
JAMES JOYCE
Irish novelist (*Dubliners; Portrait of the Artist as a Young Man; Ulysses*)

1895
GEORGE S. HALAS ("PAPA BEAR")
American cofounder of the National Football League, coach and founder of the Chicago Bears

1905
AYN RAND
American author (*The Fountainhead; Atlas Shrugged*)

1923
JAMES DICKEY
American poet (*Buckdancer's Choice; The Zodiac; Falling*), novelist (*Deliverance*), and critic

1925
ELAINE STRITCH
American actress and singer in musicals, movies, and television

1937
TOM SMOTHERS
Comedian, singer who teamed with brother Dickie Smothers as The Smothers Brothers

1942
GRAHAM NASH
Musician in Crosby, Stills, Nash and Young, ("Southern Cross")

Fort Ross

Parliament leads to the English Civil War and, finally, to his execution.

1709 Marooned British sailor Alexander Selkirk, upon whom Daniel Defoe modeled his fictional character Robinson Crusoe, is rescued from the Juan Fernandez islands.

1812 Russians establish Fort Ross on the Pacific coast north of San Francisco as a base for exploiting the sea otter trade.

1848 The Treaty of Guadalupe Hidalgo is signed by the United States and Mexico, ending the Mexican-American War and giving the Southwest to the United States in exchange for $15 million.

1852 Great Britain's first public restroom opens, for men, in London's Fleet Street.

1863 American author Samuel Clemens uses the pseudonym "Mark Twain" for the first time, in a piece for the *Virginia City Enterprise*.

1876 American baseball's National League forms with teams from eight cities: Boston, Chicago, Cincinnati, New York, Philadelphia, St. Louis, Louisville, and Hartford.

> *"The trouble with the world is that the stupid are cocksure and the intelligent are full of doubt."*
>
> —*Bertrand Russell*

1887 The first Groundhog Day is celebrated, in Punxsutawney, Pennsylvania.

1892 The longest boxing match under modern rules goes 77 rounds, between Harry Sharpe and Frank Crosby.

1893 The first motion-picture close-up is filmed in New Jersey, using Thomas Edison's Kinetoscope. The subject was a comedian sneezing.

1913 New York City's Grand Central Station opens.

1931 Austrians make the first use of a rocket to deliver mail.

1933 Adolf Hitler, Germany's elected chancellor for just two days, dissolves parliament.

1935 A lie detector machine is used for the first time, in Portage, Wisconsin, by its inventor, Leonard Keeler.

1942 Nazi collaborator Vidkun Quisling is installed as leader of a puppet government in Norway. His surname has since entered the language as a name for one who aids the enemy.

1947 The first instant camera is demonstrated to the Optical Society of America by its inventor Edwin H. Land. The first Polaroid camera went on sale the following year.

1949 An American B-50 bomber completes the first non-stop flight around the world, refueling four times in mid-air during its 94-hour flight of 23,452 miles.

1970 English philosopher, antinuclear campaigner, and winner of a Nobel Prize in literature Bertrand Russell dies at 97.

1985 O. J. Simpson and Nicole Brown are married. The marriage ended in divorce in 1992, and Nicole was found brutally murdered two years later. Simpson was eventually acquitted of the crime after the most publicized trial in legal history.

1989 South Africa's last apartheid president, P. W. Botha, resigns.

1990 South African President F. W. de Klerk legalizes the African National Congress and pledges to free its imprisoned leader, Nelson Mandela.

Bertrand Russell, British philosopher

MILESTONE

Battle of Stalingrad
The tide of World War II begins to turn as the five-month Battle of Stalingrad comes to an end with the surrender of the last pockets of German resistance on this day in 1941. The battle was effectively over two days earlier when Field Marshal von Paulus surrendered to the Red Army. The German troops had survived by eating the horses of the Romanian cavalry division, and von Paulus had twice rejected surrender terms. As he was at last about to give in, Hitler ordered him to keep fighting, promoting him to field marshal as no German officer of that rank had yet surrendered, but he could obey orders no longer. About 90,000 surviving German troops surrendered to the Red Army between January 31 and February 2. Of those, just 5,000 would survive the Soviet prisoner-of-war camps.

✈ **1160** Frederick Barbarossa, Holy Roman Emperor and German king, flings prisoners, including children, at the besieged Italian city of Crema, forcing it to surrender.

1238 The Mongols seize control of the Russian trading city of Vladimir.

1458 Johann Gutenberg of Germany, inventor of printing with moveable type, dies.

1690 The Massachusetts Bay Colony issues the first paper money in America, in order to pay its soldiers in the war against Quebec.

1749 Sicily, to restore flagging trade, invites Jews to return after having banned them for nearly 300 years.

1783 Spain formally recognizes the independence of the United States.

1815 The world's first commercial cheese factory is established in Switzerland.

1865 Informal peace talks at Hampton Roads, Virginia, between U.S. president Abraham Lincoln and representatives of the Confederacy, fail. Lincoln had insisted on reunion

Johann Gutenberg

BORN ON THIS DAY

1817
SAMUEL RYAN CURTIS
U.S. Army Civil War major general (Union Volunteers)

1820
ELISHA KENT KANE
American arctic explorer

1821
ELIZABETH BLACKWELL
First British woman to qualify as a doctor, graduating from the University of Geneva, New York State, USA, in 1849

Elizabeth Blackwell

1830
ROBERT CECIL, 3RD MARQUESS OF SALISBURY
Three-time British prime minister between 1885 and 1902

1859
HUGO JUNKERS
German aircraft engineer, designer of the first all-metal airplane

1874
GERTRUDE STEIN
American writer who coined the phrase "the lost generation" about the survivors of the fighting in World War I

1894
NORMAN ROCKWELL
American artist whose portrayals of idealized American life were featured on *Saturday Evening Post* covers

1904
CHARLIE "PRETTY BOY" FLOYD
American Depression-era criminal

---

of the nation and emancipation of slaves, the southerners wanted independence.

⚖ **1889** American outlaw Belle Starr, 40, called the "Bandit Queen," is killed by an unknown assailant who shoots her twice in the back.

1913 The 16th Amendment to the U.S. Constitution, authorizing a federal income tax, is ratified.

✈ **1917** A German sub torpedoes and sinks the American liner *Housatonic* off the Sicilian coast. The United States then cut diplomatic ties with Germany.

1923 The century's eighth-largest earthquake rattles Russia's far eastern Kamchatka Peninsula. It measured 8.5 on the Richter scale.

🔬 **1925** Australian anthropologist Raymond Dart announces his discovery in South Africa of the first "missing link" fossil, a skull of *Australopithecus africanus*.

1935 Hugo Junkers, the German aircraft designer who built the first successful all-metal airplane in 1915, dies. During World War II, his company built trimotor troop transports, "Stuka" dive bombers,

> *"From birth, man carries the weight of gravity on his shoulders. He is bolted to earth. But man has only to sink beneath the surface and he is free."*
>
> —*Jacques-Yves Cousteau*

Junkers trimotor planes with German troops, 1936

and other planes for the *Luftwaffe*.

1944 American troops invade and take control of the Marshall Islands from Japan, which had used them as a base for military operations throughout World War II.

1948 Cadillac produces the first car with tailfins, signaling the dawn of a new era in automotive aesthetic design.

1953 French oceanographer Jacques-Yves Cousteau publishes *The Silent World,* his most famous and lasting book.

1959 American rock stars Buddy Holly, Ritchie Valens, and J. P. "The Big Bopper" Richardson die when their chartered plane crashes in Iowa. Holly and his band, the Crickets, had just scored a No. 1 hit with "That'll Be the Day."

1960 British prime minister Harold Macmillan, on a tour of Africa, gives a speech to the South African parliament describing "a wind of change" blowing through the continent. His remarks, urging the government there to embrace racial equality, are not well received.

1966 The Soviet Union achieves the first controlled lunar landing when the unmanned *Luna 9* touches down on the Ocean of Storms.

1994 U.S. president Bill Clinton lifts the 19-year-old trade embargo against Vietnam.

1998 A U.S. Marine jet smashes into a Mt. Cermis cable car in the Dolomite mountains near Calavese, in northern Italy.

Mount Cermis cable-car tragedy

211 B.C. Roman emperor Septimius Severus dies at York in England while on campaign.

1194 English king Richard I (Richard the Lion-Heart) is released from captivity in Austria by Holy Roman Emperor Henry VI after paying an enormous ransom and surrendering his kingdom.

1789 George Washington, commander of American forces during the Revolutionary War and a pivotal figure in the adoption of the U.S. Constitution, is elected as the first U.S. president.

1795 France abolishes slavery and confers citizenship upon those formerly enslaved.

1818 At his home in Hempstead, Leigh Hunt challenges his fellow English poets Percy Bysshe Shelley and John Keats to a sonnet-writing contest and declares himself the winner.

1826 American novelist James Fenimore Cooper publishes *The Last of the Mohicans*, perhaps the most famous of his Leatherstocking Tales.

1847 The first telegraph company opens, in Maryland.

President George Washington

The Magnetic Telegraph Company soon linked New York with Washington, D.C., charging a nickel a word to send messages.

1861 Representatives of six Southern states meet in Montgomery, Alabama, to form the Confederate States of America, a new independent government with Mississippian Jefferson Davis at its head.

1868 English naturalist Charles Darwin, 69, begins writing *The Descent of Man and Selection in Relation to Sex*.

1873 Prolific American inventor Thomas Edison receives the first of three patents issued on this date, for an "Improvement to Circuits for Chemical Telegraphs." The other patents were for a quadruplex telegraph in 1890 and a reversible galvanic battery in 1902.

1889 Horse thief Harry Longabaugh is released from jail in Sundance, Wyoming, and later makes a name for himself, "The Sundance Kid," after teaming up with Butch Cassidy to rob banks and trains.

1899 Fighting breaks out around Manila between American and Philippine forces, beginning two years of bloody guerrilla warfare that would end in 1901 with the capture of Philippine leader Emilio Aguinaldo.

> *"If I had to choose, I would rather have birds than airplanes."*
>
> —*Charles Lindbergh*

Emilio Aguinaldo

1906 Police in New York City begin using fingerprints for identification.

1913 American Louis Henry Perlman patents the first demountable tire-carrying rim, thus relieving the motorist of the need to replace the entire wheel when a tire wears out.

1915 Dr. Joseph Goldberger begins experimenting on prison volunteers in Jackson, Mississippi, in order to find the cause of the disease pellagra, which was killing thousands annually in the United States. His groundbreaking study not only showed that pellagra is caused by poor diet but launched the "biological age" of nutrition research, which linked diseases with a lack of essential vitamins.

1923 French and Belgian troops occupy the German industrial region of the Ruhr in accordance with the treaty that ended World War I.

1941 Roy Plunkett patents "Tetrafluoroethylene Polymers," or Teflon, a substance used to fabricate nonstick cookware.

1945 Allied leaders convene in the Soviet Union for the Yalta Conference, which anticipated the end of World War II and foreshadowed the Cold War. During the week-long talks, Franklin D. Roosevelt, Winston Churchill, and Josef Stalin decided that Germany would be divided after its defeat, that part of Poland would be controlled by the Soviet Union, and that the Soviets would declare war on Japan.

1951 The longest operation in medical history—four days—commences in Chicago to remove Gertrude Levandowski's 308-pound ovarian cyst.

1965 The sixth-largest earthquake of the century strikes the Rat Islands, part of Alaska's Aleutian chain. The quake measured 8.7 on the Richter scale.

1994 Russian cosmonauts aboard the *Mir* space station unfurl a plastic mirror 65 feet in diameter, prompting talk of placing huge mirrors in orbit to illuminate cities and extend growing seasons.

Patty Hearst (milestone)

🔫 **45 B.C.** Roman statesman Cato the Younger, a militant opponent of Julius Caesar, dies by his own hand after Caesar's army crushes Scipio's at Thapsus in Africa.

1265 French cardinal Gui Folques is elected to the papacy. As Pope Clement IV, he enlisted the military help of Charles of Anjou and nearly wiped out the powerful Hohenstaufen family of German rulers.

1631 Roger Williams, founder of Rhode Island and an important American religious leader, arrives in the Massachusetts Bay Colony. His later dissent against Puritan leadership and his objections to the confiscation of Native American land led him to resettle in present-day Rhode Island.

🔫 **1762** French forces surrender Martinique, a major military base in the Lesser Antilles of the West Indies, to the British.

1778 South Carolina becomes the first state to ratify the Articles of Confederation, which formed the government of the United States before the present Constitution of 1789.

1783 Sweden recognizes the independence of the United States.

> *"Man is a strange animal. He generally cannot read the handwriting on the wall until his back is up against it."*
>
> —Adlai Stevenson

Dwight Lyman Moody

George, Prince of Wales

🇬🇧 **1811** George, Prince of Wales, becomes prince regent in order to rule in the place of his father, George III, who had suffered from periods of insanity for more than 20 years.

🎭 **1816** Rossini's opera *The Barber of Seville* is performed for the first time, in Rome.

1846 The first newspaper on the Pacific coast of the United States, the *Oregon Spectator*, is published.

🔬 **1850** Du Bois Parmelee of New Paltz, New York, patents the first depressible-key adding machine, which he called a calculator. The impractical design proved unpopular.

🎭 **1897** French novelist Marcel Proust meets critic Jean Lorrain in a pistol duel. Both fire two shots and miss.

1901 Ed Prescot patents the loop-the-loop centrifugal railroad, better known in amusement parks the world over as the roller coaster.

🏆 **1905** Pilot T. S. Baldwin pits his dirigible against an automobile in a 10-mile race and wins by a margin of three minutes.

1917 After seven years of revolution, Mexican president Venushortio Carranza proclaims the modern Mexican constitution, which promised land reform and separation of church and state.

1917 The U.S. Congress overrides President Woodrow Wilson's veto and passes the Immigration Act, which required literacy tests for immigrants and barred most Asiatic laborers.

1924 A British broadcasting institution is established when the BBC transmits the first Greenwich time signal at 9:30 P.M. Created automatically by chronometers at the Royal Observatory, the "pips" counted down the last five seconds of each quarter hour, but they are now generally broadcast only on the hour.

1937 President Franklin D. Roosevelt announces his plan to expand the U.S. Supreme Court to as many as 15 justices and is criticized by opponents for trying to "pack" the court with his own appointees.

1943 American middle-weight boxer Jake La Motta beats Sugar Ray Robinson in the second of their six famous bouts. It was Robinson's first defeat and the only time "The Bronx Bull" would prevail over Robinson.

1945 During World War II, American troops commanded by General Douglas MacArthur enter Manila.

1952 New York City erects the first "Don't Walk" sign as a response to pedestrian fatalities in crowded Manhattan streets.

1988 The United States indicts Panamanian military strongman and former CIA informant Manuel Noriega on drug smuggling and money laundering charges.

1994 The lengthiest murder case in U.S. history ends with the conviction of Byron de la Beckwith in the shooting death 31 years earlier of civil rights leader Medgar Evers.

1994 The U.S. Coast Guard icebreaker *Polar Sea* sails within 690.1 miles of the South Pole, thus establishing a new, southernmost point on Earth accessible by surface ship.

The Soviet Army on the Afghan-Soviet border (milestone)

43 The Trung sisters, heroines of Vietnam's first independence movement, drown themselves after the Chinese rout their armies near present-day Hanoi and Son Tay.

1643 Dutch navigator and explorer Abel Janszoon Tasman discovers the Fiji Islands.

1659 The earliest recorded check is written, on a British bank.

1685 British king Charles II, the first on the throne after the restoration of the monarchy following the English Civil War, dies.

1788 Massachusetts becomes the sixth state to ratify the U.S. Constitution.

1820 The first organized immigration of freed slaves to Africa from the United States sails from New York harbor on a voyage to Freetown, Sierra Leone, in West Africa.

1836 English naturalist Charles Darwin, aboard the HMS *Beagle*, arrives in Tasmania.

1840 Great Britain signs the Treaty of Waitangi with the Maori tribes of New Zealand. The pact protected tribal land interests in exchange for recognition of British sovereignty and marks the national birthday of New Zealand.

1862 The Union wins its first major victory of the American Civil War when naval forces under Commodore Andrew Hull Foote capture the Confederate stronghold

BORN ON THIS DAY

1564
CHRISTOPHER MARLOWE
English poet ("Hero and Leander"; "The Passionate Shepherd to His Love") and dramatist (*The Jew of Malta; Edward the Second*)

1665
QUEEN ANNE
The last of the Stuart monarchs of England and Scotland

1756
AARON BURR
Third U.S. vice president, who killed Alexander Hamilton in a duel

1838
SIR HENRY IRVING
English actor-manager, the first actor to be knighted

1895
GEORGE HERMAN "BABE" RUTH
American Hall of Fame baseball player

1903
CLAUDIO ARRAU
Chilean concert pianist

1911
RONALD W. REAGAN
American actor and 40th president of the United States (1981–89)

1913
MARY LEAKEY
American archeologist and anthropologist

1950
NATALIE COLE
American singer ("Unforgettable"; "Pink Cadillac"), daughter of Nat "King" Cole

> *"Who ever loved, that loved not at first sight?"*
>
> —*Christopher Marlowe*

of Fort Henry on the Tennessee River.

1868 Uncle Sam—the stern, bewhiskered symbol of American patriotism—makes his first appearance, as a character in a Thomas Nast illustration for *Harper's Weekly*.

1891 The Dalton Gang bungles its first train robbery, near Alila, California, when a guard in the Southern Pacific express car fires on them and forces them to flee.

1904 Japan severs diplomatic ties with Russia as war looms between the two countries.

1911 English manufacturer Rolls-Royce adorns its automobiles with the "Spirit of Ecstasy" mascot, a silver-winged hood ornament that becomes the company's symbol.

1917 British women over the age of 30 are granted the right to vote.

Bombardment and capture of Fort Henry

The Union Jack being hoisted over Benghazi

1919 Germany adopts a democratic federal constitution and becomes known as the Weimar Republic. The republic weathered the economic recovery of postwar Germany, but succumbed to Adolf Hitler during the worldwide depression of the early 1930s.

1936 In Munich, Germany, Adolf Hitler opens the fourth Winter Olympic Games.

1937 American author John Steinbeck publishes *Of Mice and Men*, a novella about the bond between two Depression-era migrant workers.

1941 During World War II, British forces occupy Benghazi, Libya, after a bold flanking maneuver by the 7th Armoured Division cuts off an Italian retreat along the North African coast. The British, with just 29 tanks and 3,000 men, captured 20,000 prisoners, 120 tanks, and 216 artillery pieces. On the same day, Adolf Hitler gives Erwin Rommel command of Germany's Afrika Korps.

1943 Italian dictator Benito Mussolini fires his son-in-law, Count Ciano, from his post as foreign minister because of Ciano's growing antiwar sentiments during World War II.

1944 U.S. Army troops take Kwajalein Island in the Central Pacific during World War II.

1952 Princess Elizabeth, 26, elder daughter of English king George VI, becomes queen of the United Kingdom upon the death of her father. He was 54.

1958 An airplane carrying the Manchester United soccer team home from a European Cup tie crashes on the runway at Munich, killing eight of the team and fifteen other passengers and crew.

1959 The United States successfully test-launches a Titan intercontinental missile, capable of carrying a 4.5-megaton warhead.

1966 President Lyndon B. Johnson meets South Vietnamese premier Nguyen Cao Ky in Honolulu and pledges U.S. support to establish democracy in South Vietnam.

King George VI, Queen Elizabeth, and princesses Elizabeth and Margaret Rose

FEBRUARY 7

1569 The Spanish Inquisition establishes a branch office in South America.

1668 England, Sweden, and the Netherlands form the Triple Alliance to counter French King Louis XIV after his invasion of the Spanish Netherlands during the War of Devolution.

1783 Spanish and French forces lift their 41-month siege of the British colony at Gibraltar.

1788 A flotilla of British ships bearing 730 transported convicts and 250 free persons establishes a settlement along the southeast coast of Australia in Sydney Cove. The settlement would grow into the city of Sydney.

1807 The Battle of Eylau breaks out in eastern Prussia between Napoleon's army and a coalition of Russian and Prussian forces. The two-day stalemate cost each side between 18,000 and 25,000 men and was the first deadlock suffered by Napoleon.

1882 American boxing great John L. Sullivan becomes the last bare-knuckle world heavyweight champ with a victory over Patty Ryan in Mississippi.

1896 Doctors in Liverpool, England, use x-rays to locate a bullet in a boy's head just weeks

John L. Sullivan

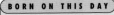

> *"A day without laughter is a day wasted."*
> —Charlie Chaplin

after the new technology was unveiled.

1898 French writer Émile Zola is tried for libel for writing a newspaper editorial that attacked the French Army for wrongly convicting Captain Alfred Dreyfus of espionage. Though the army was indeed guilty of suppressing Dreyfus's innocence, Zola was convicted of libel, sentenced to a year in prison, and fined 3,000 francs.

1904 The Great Baltimore Fire begins when a small fire in the Maryland city's business district is whipped by wind into an uncontrollable blaze that soon engulfs a large portion of the city.

1914 English actor Charlie Chaplin debuts his "Little Tramp" character in *Kid Races* in Venice, Italy. The meek, baggy-panted fellow with the mustache, bowler hat, and cane would become Chaplin's trademark.

1917 During World War I, a German submarine sinks the British steamer *California* off the coast of Ireland.

1920 Pilot Sadi-Joseph Lecointe sets a new air-speed flying record, 171.4 miles per hour, in a Nieuport 29V.

1920 Bolsheviks execute Admiral Alexandr Kolchak, a principal leader of White Russian forces during the Russian Civil War.

1942 During World War II, the U.S. government officially orders all automakers to stop making passenger cars and start manufacturing military hardware, such as tanks. Automakers were guaranteed profits regardless of production costs throughout the war.

1943 During World War II, Polish Jews in the Warsaw ghetto launch an armed uprising against the German Nazis.

1944 Germany starts its second attack against Allied forces at the Anzio beachhead in Italy during World War II.

1965 U.S. Navy jets from aircraft carriers *Coral Sea* and *Hancock* raid a guerrilla training camp in North Vietnam to retaliate for communist attacks on Camp Holloway and the Pleiku airfield the previous day.

1979 Dr. Josef Mengele, the infamous German Nazi doctor who performed sadistic medical experiments on children at Auschwitz during World War II, dies of a stroke while swimming in Brazil.

1984 American astronaut Bruce McCandless becomes the first human satellite when he exits the space shuttle *Challenger* and flies untethered, using a jet-powered backpack of his own design.

1986 The people of Haiti take to the streets after Jean-Claude "Baby Doc" Duvalier flees the country. Their celebrations turn to violence as people take revenge on Duvalier's hated Tontons Macoutes secret police.

1990 Signaling the impending collapse of the Soviet system, the Communist Party's Central Committee gives up its monopoly on power and allows political challenges to its dominance.

1991 Jean-Bertrand Aristide, a Catholic priest and champion of the poor, is sworn in as Haiti's first freely elected president.

1992 Western European nations establish the European Union by signing the Maastricht Treaty, which called for greater economic integration and laid the groundwork for a single European currency, the Euro.

1996 A faulty speedometer leads to the crash of a Boeing 757 jetliner off the coast of the Dominican Republic; 189 people die in shark-infested waters.

Astronaut Bruce McCandless

"If you think it's hard to meet new people, try picking up the wrong golf ball."

—*Jack Lemmon*

1692 Hysteria over witches in Salem, Massachusetts, starts when a doctor declares that the teenage niece and daughter of a local pastor are under the influence of "an evil hand." Before long, Salem's jails filled with alleged witches. Nineteen were executed and 100 imprisoned.

1693 In order to educate clergy and civil servants for the colony of Virginia, King William III and Queen Mary II of England grant a charter to William and Mary College, making it the second-oldest institute of higher education in the United States.

1725 Peter the Great, emperor of Russia, dies at the age of 53 and is succeeded by his wife, Catherine. His sweeping reforms of the military, economy, culture, and politics of the country built Russia into a major European power.

1862 In the American Civil War, Union forces capture Roanoke Island in North Carolina. This major victory gave the North control of the mouth of Albemarle Sound and allowed it to threaten the Confederate capital of Richmond.

1874 Russian composer Modest Mussorgsky's opera *Boris Gudunov*, based on

---

BORN ON THIS DAY

1819
JOHN RUSKIN
English art critic and social commentator who brought the Pre-Raphaelites to public notice and campaigned for the preservation of historic buildings

1820
WILLIAM TECUMSEH SHERMAN
Major general of the Union Army during the American Civil War

1828
JULES VERNE
French author (*From the Earth to the Moon; Twenty Thousand Leagues Under the Sea*)

1888
DAME EDITH EVANS
English actress on the stage and in movies (*The Importance of Being Earnest; Look Back in Anger*)

1894
BILLY BISHOP
Canadian World War I flying ace

1906
CHESTER F CARLSON
Inventor of xerography (photocopy machines)

1920
OSCAR BRAND
American folk singer, author, and humorist

1925
JACK LEMMON
American actor (*Mister Roberts; Some Like It Hot; JFK; Short Cuts*)

1931
JAMES DEAN
American actor (*Rebel Without a Cause; Giant*)

Aleksandr Pushkin's drama, premieres in St. Petersburg.

1887 U.S. president Grover S. Cleveland signs the Dawes Severalty Act, which divided communal Indian lands into individual, privately owned plots and opened much of the land to white settlement.

1898 John Sherman of Worcester, Massachusetts, patents the first machine to fold and gum envelopes. His invention cut the cost of producing a thousand envelopes from sixty cents to eight.

1904 Japan starts the Russo-Japanese War by launching a devastating surprise attack that destroys the Russian fleet at its Port Arthur base in China.

1908 American inventors Orville and Wilbur Wright close the first sale of a military aircraft by contracting to sell a Model A flyer to the U.S. Army for $25,000. The Army agrees to pay a $5,000 bonus if the plane can fly faster than 40 miles per hour.

1915 American producer D. W. Griffith's film *Birth of a Nation* premieres in Los Angeles. The three-hour epic

The capture of Roanoke Island

South Vietnamese soldiers enter Laos

about the Civil War was a box-office smash, but is now considered one of the most offensive films ever made because of its explicit racism.

1928 The first transatlantic television image, a picture of Mrs. Mia Howe, is transmitted from Purley, England, to Hartsdale, New York, by John Logie Baird.

1943 The Soviet Union's Red Army retakes Kursk 15 months after Germany captured the key industrial city during World War II. On the same day, Britain's 77th Indian Infantry Brigade, also called the Chindits, begins launching guerrilla raids behind Japanese lines in Burma.

1949 The highest-ranking Catholic official in Hungary, Joseph Cardinal Mindszenty, is convicted of treason by the Communist People's Court and sentenced to life in prison.

1952 Queen Elizabeth II arrives back in Great Britain from Kenya, where she had learned of the death of her father, King George VI. She is greeted at the airport by Prime Minister Winston Churchill, and is proclaimed Queen the same day.

1964 The Iraqi National Oil Company is incorporated in Baghdad. In years to come, oil wealth would help the nation play an important part in Middle East politics.

1967 Topping the American music charts: "Georgy Girl," by the Seekers and "The Beat Goes On," by Sonny and Cher.

1969 A shower of meteorites falls on Pueblito de Allende, Chihuahua, Mexico. The meteorites came from the explosion of a single meteor weighing several tons which created a large fireball as it fell through the atmosphere. More than two tons of fragments have been recovered in Chihuahua, Mexico.

1971 During the Vietnam War, South Vietnam invades southern Laos to disrupt a communist supply and infiltration network adjacent to the two northern provinces of South Vietnam.

1993 An Iranian jetliner bearing pilgrims to Meshed collides with a military aircraft during takeoff, explodes, and crashes into the ground. All 132 people aboard were killed.

Queen Elizabeth I

474 Zeno, the father of Rome's five-year-old emperor Leo II, is made co-emperor. Leo II lived for just a few months more, leaving the throne to Zeno.

1119 Calixtus II ascends to the papal throne. During his 25-year reign he condemned lay investiture, excommunicated the Holy Roman emperor, and provided a considerable amount of protection for Roman Jews.

1567 Lord Darnley, the second husband of Mary, Queen of Scots, and father of King James VI of Scotland and I of England, is strangled to death and his house blown up in Edinburgh, Scotland.

1674 British and Dutch representatives sign the Treaty of Westminster, ending the Third Anglo-Dutch War.

1825 The U.S. House of Representatives votes to elect John Quincy Adams president despite his clear loss to Andrew Jackson in both the popular and electoral-college voting.

1861 Jefferson Davis is formally elected president of the Confederate States of America in Montgomery, Alabama.

President John Quincy Adams

BORN ON THIS DAY

1773
WILLIAM HENRY HARRISON
Ninth U.S. president, who caught a cold on inauguration day and died 30 days later, the shortest term of any U.S. president

William Henry Harrison

1808
SIR FRANCIS PETIT SMITH
English inventor who developed the first ships with screw propellers

1863
SIR ANTHONY HOPE
English novelist (*The Prisoner of Zenda*)

1865
MRS. PATRICK CAMPBELL
British actress (*Pygmalion*) and lover of George Bernard Shaw

1866
GEORGE ADE
American journalist and playwright (*Fables in Slang; The Sultan of Sulu; The College Widow*)

1874
AMY LOWELL
Pulitzer Prize-winning American poet (*A Dome of Many-Coloured Glass; Men, Women and Ghosts*)

1891
RONALD COLEMAN
British-born American actor (*A Tale of Two Cities; The Prisoner of Zenda*)

1914
ERNEST TUBB
American singer ("Walkin' the Floor Over You"; "Have You Ever Been Lonely?")

1923
BRENDAN BEHAN
Irish playwright (*The Hostage; The Quare Fellow*)

1942
CAROLE KING
American singer ("I Feel the Earth Move"; "It's Too Late") and songwriter ("Take Good Care of My Baby"; "The Locomotion")

1875 A Boston and Maine Railroad train becomes the first to pass through the 4.75-mile Hoosac Tunnel, which bores through the Berkshire Mountains. It had taken 20 years and had cost 200 lives to complete the tunnel.

1895 The first American college basketball game is played, with the Minnesota State School of Agriculture beating the Hamline College Porkers, 9–3.

1900 Tennis's Davis Cup, an elegant silver trophy bowl, is first put up for competition when college tennis champ Dwight Filley Davis challenges British players to cross the Atlantic and play his Harvard team.

1909 American Carl G. Fisher incorporates the Indianapolis Motor Speedway Corporation, thus founding "The Brickyard," site of the Indy 500, which would become the world's largest single-day sporting event.

1916 Conscription begins in Great Britain for men ages 18 to 41. During the course of World War I, 4.5 million Britons would serve.

1918 The Ukrainian Republic signs a peace treaty with the Central Powers at Brest-Litovsk, thus ending its armed participation in World War I.

1933 Actors Mae West and Cary Grant open in *She*

> *"You only live once, but if you do it right, once is enough."*
>
> —Mae West

Done Him Wrong, a risqué American film that features West as "one of the finest women who ever walked the streets."

1934 In response to charges of corrupt practices among airmail delivery companies, U.S. president Franklin D. Roosevelt cancels all domestic airmail contracts and orders the U.S. Army to fly the mail.

1950 Wisconsin Republican senator Joseph McCarthy waves his infamous sheet of paper in Wheeling, West Virginia, and claims it is a list of more than 200 "known communists" working in the U.S. State Department.

1964 The English rock group The Beatles appear live on America's *The Ed Sullivan Show* before an audience of 728 screaming fans and play five songs, including "All My Lovin'" and "She Loves You."

1965 The United States commits its first combat troops to South Vietnam, initiating American involvement in the Vietnam War.

1969 The world's largest passenger airplane, the Boeing

Senator Joseph McCarthy, left, with his attorney, Roy Cohn

747, makes its first flight, lasting 76 minutes. The aircraft is the second prototype of the "Jumbo jet," and is powered by four Pratt & Whitney engines.

1971 A 6.5-magnitude earthquake strikes California's San Fernando Valley, claiming 58 lives and causing more than a half billion dollars in damage.

1971 American baseball pitching legend Satchel Paige is inducted into the sport's Hall of Fame, the first Negro League star to be selected.

1991 Japan suffers its worst nuclear accident when a steam generator pipe bursts and 55 tons of radioactive coolant water leak into a secondary generating unit.

French luxury liner Normandie lying capsized in New York Harbor (milestone)

1258 Baghdad falls to Mongol armies led by Hulegu, grandson of Genghis Khan. The conquest led to a long period of cultural, political, and economic decline in Iraq.

1616 English playwright William Shakespeare's second daughter, Judith, marries Thomas Quiney, a disreputable vintner who was soon prosecuted by the ecclesiastical courts for fathering a child with another woman.

1667 The Royal Society, London, publishes Nicolaus Steno's classic paleontology paper, "Head of a shark dissected," the first scientific paper to recognize that fossils are the petrified remains of organisms.

1675 American settler Mary Rowlandson and her three children are captured by Native Americans in Lancaster, Massachusetts. She later wrote America's first "captivity narrative."

1720 Sir Edmund Halley is appointed as Great Britain's second Astronomer Royal. He had identified the comet that bears his name in 1682.

1763 The Seven Years' War, a global struggle known in America as the French and Indian War, ends in victory for Great Britain. In the Treaty of Paris, France relinquished all claims to Canada and gave Louisiana to Spain; Great Britain got Spanish Florida and Upper Canada.

1778 Exiled French writer Voltaire makes a triumphant return to Paris after 28 years abroad to direct his play *Irene*. The following day,

BORN ON THIS DAY

1775
CHARLES LAMB ("ELIA")
English essayist

1824
SAMUEL PLIMSOLL
English politician and social reformer whose name was applied to the load line he introduced for shipping

1880
JESSE G. VINCENT
Engineer who designed the first V-12 engine

1890
BORIS PASTERNAK
Russian author (*Doctor Zhivago*)

1893
WILLIAM TATEM TILDEN
American tennis champion

1893
JIMMY DURANTE
American actor and comedian

1894
HAROLD MACMILLAN, EARL OF STOCKTON
British prime minister (1957–1963), known as "Super Mac"

1898
BERTOLT BRECHT
German playwright (*Mother Courage and Her Children; The Measures Taken*)

> *"Because things are the way they are, things will not stay the way they are."*
> —*Bertolt Brecht*

he was welcomed by hundreds of intellectuals and other well-wishers.

1814 French general Napoleon Bonaparte attacks enemy columns advancing on Paris, beating the Russians at Champqubert.

1837 Aleksandr Pushkin, the great Russian poet and novelist, dies from wounds he received defending his wife's honor in a duel forced on him by influential enemies two days earlier. His opponent was his brother-in-law, Baron Hecheren d'Anthes, who had turned and fired after only four paces.

1840 Queen Victoria of England, dressed completely in items of British manufacture, marries Prince Albert, a man

A battle during the French and Indian War

1943 During World War II, Nazi Germany and fascist Spain sign a secret protocol in which Germany promises to supply modern military equipment in exchange for Spain's pledge to fight any Allied invasion of the Iberian Peninsula or of Spanish territories elsewhere, including Africa, the Mediterranean, and the Atlantic.

1962 American spy pilot Francis Gary Powers is released in Berlin by the Soviets in exchange for Rudolf Abel, a senior KGB spy captured in the United States five years earlier. Powers's U-2 spy plane had been shot down in 1960.

1996 In Japan, a 50,000-ton rock falls on a highway tunnel and crushes 20 people to death.

1996 World chess champion Gary Kasparov loses the first game of a six-game match against Big Blue, an IBM computer capable of evaluating 200 million moves per second. Kasparov won the match with three wins, two ties.

U-2 spy plane pilot Francis Gary Powers

she had described months earlier as "quite charming, and so extremely handsome." Victoria detested babies, pregnancy, and childbirth, but produced nine children.

1846 Mormon leader Brigham Young and 1,600 followers abandon Nauvoo, Illinois, and cross the frozen Mississippi on the first leg of their long westward journey to the Great Salt Lake in Utah.

1861 On the verge of the American Civil War, Jefferson Davis learns by telegram that he has been selected as president of the Confederate States of America.

1863 Tom Thumb (Charles Stratton) marries Lavinia Warren. The diminutive pair starred in American showman P. T. Barnum's circus.

1878 A ten-year Cuban revolt against Spain ends with the signing of the Peace of Zanjon, which was arranged by Spanish general Arsenio Martinez Campos.

Gary Kasparov

1349 Jews of Uberlingen, Switzerland, are massacred.

1573 English explorer Francis Drake, on a privateering voyage to the West Indies, climbs a ridge on the Isthmus of Panama and sees the Pacific Ocean for the first time. Five years later, he sailed into the Pacific during his circumnavigation of the globe.

1650 French philosopher and scientist René Descartes, who coined the phrase "I think, therefore I am," dies in Sweden.

1673 England's Charles II exempts Jews from prosecution under the Conventicle Act of 1664, which defined as seditious any prayer meeting of more than five persons not conducted in accord with the Book of Common Prayer.

1752 The first American hospital, the Pennsylvania Hospital, opens in Philadelphia thanks in large part to Benjamin Franklin, who helped raise funds.

1805 Sacajawea, the Shoshone Indian woman who served as an interpreter and occasional guide for the Lewis and Clark Expedition across western North America, gives birth to a son, Jean-Baptiste Charbonneau. Meriwether Lewis assisted at the birth. William Clark nicknamed the boy "Pomp."

> *"There is nothing like returning to a place that remains unchanged to find the ways in which you yourself have altered."*
>
> —*Nelson Mandela*

BORN ON THIS DAY

1657
BERNARD LE BOVIER DE FONTENELLE
French author

1800
WILLIAM HENRY FOX TALBOT
English photographic pioneer

1812
ALEXANDER HAMILTON STEPHENS
Vice president of the Confederate States of America

Alexander Stephens

1847
THOMAS ALVA EDISON
American inventor of the kinetoscope, which led to motion pictures, the incandescent light bulb, the phonograph, and over 1,000 other devices

1908
SIR VIVIAN FUCHS
British explorer and geologist, leader of the first expedition to cross the Antarctic (1958)

1917
SIDNEY SHELDON
American screenwriter (*Annie Get Your Gun; Easter Parade*), television scriptwriter (*I Dream of Jeannie; Hart to Hart*), and novelist (*Bloodlines; Windmill of the Gods*)

1920
KING FAROUK I
Last king of Egypt (1936–52)

1936
BURT REYNOLDS
American actor (*Smokey and the Bandit; Deliverance; Semi-Tough*)

1941
SERGIO MENDES
Brazilian bandleader

1809 American inventor Robert Fulton patents the steamboat, two years after his first successful steamboat journey between New York City and Albany, New York.

1809 Jesse Fell of Wilkes-Barre, Pennsylvania, devises a method for burning anthracite coal in his fireplace, thus opening a vast home-heating market for the cheap, clean-burning fuel.

1828 Edinburgh "body-snatchers" Burke and Hare commit their first premeditated murder. They sold corpses to anatomy schools for dissection by students.

1852 London, England, establishes its first public rest room for women, on Bedford Street.

1858 A 14-year-old French peasant girl, Marie-Bernarde Soubirous, claims to have seen the Virgin Mary at a grotto near Lourdes in southern France. Years later she was canonized as St. Bernadette.

1861 With the American Civil War in the offing, President-elect Abraham Lincoln departs for Washington, D.C., telling a crowd in Springfield, Illinois, that he faces "a task . . . greater than that which rested upon Washington."

1928 The La-Z-Boy reclining chair is designed by American Ed Shoemaker and his cousin Edward Knabusch, using a sheet of plywood and a yardstick.

1929 The Vatican State in Rome comes into existence at midday with the signing of the

The "Big Three" at the Yalta Conference

Lateran Treaty by Italian leader Benito Mussolini and the Pope's secretary of state Cardinal Gaspari.

1937 American auto workers win a major victory when General Motors signs the first union contract in U.S. auto history. The agreement came after a 44-day sit-down strike at the Fisher Body plant in Flint, Michigan.

1939 Swedish-Austrian physicist Lise Meitner and her nephew Otto Fritsch publish a paper on nuclear fission in the journal *Nature*. Her work contributed to the development of the atomic bomb.

1942 During World War II, German battleships *Gneisenau* and *Scharnhorst*, along with the heavy cruiser *Prinz Eugen* start their famous "Channel Dash" from Brest to the safety of German waters.

1945 The "Big Three" Allied leaders—Roosevelt, Churchill, and Stalin—wrap up the Yalta Conference, which divided postwar Germany and Poland between East and West.

1956 Two former members of the British Foreign Office, Donald Maclean and Guy Burgess, surface in Moscow after having disappeared from England in 1951. The pair denied having spied for the Soviet Union.

1970 Japan becomes the world's fourth space power by launching its *Ohsumi* satellite into orbit.

1975 Margaret Thatcher becomes the first woman to lead a British political party when she is elected leader of the Conservatives, beating four male rivals. She went on to become Great Britain's first woman prime minister in 1979.

1990 South African anti-apartheid leader Nelson Mandela is released from prison after spending 27 years behind bars.

Nelson Mandela and wife, Winnie, upon his release from prison

FEBRUARY 12

1049 Leo IX is enthroned as pope. His 5 years in Peter's chair led up to the East-West Schism of 1054.

1541 Spanish conquistador Pedro de Valdivia founds the city of Santiago, Chile, after marching across the coastal desert of northern Chile and defeating a large force of Indians in the Valley of Chile.

1554 Lady Jane Grey, who reluctantly wore the English crown for nine days in 1553, is beheaded at the age of 16 in the Tower of London on orders from Mary Tudor. Her husband was executed the same day; her father, 11 days later.

1793 The U.S. Congress passes America's first fugitive slave law, which required all states, including those that forbade slavery, to return escaped slaves to their original owners.

1804 German philosopher Immanuel Kant, one of the Enlightenment's foremost thinkers, dies in Konigsberg.

1808 For the first time, a lifeline fired by an explosive mortar is used to save lives during a shipwreck off Gorleston on the east coast of England.

Immanuel Kant

> *"No man is good enough to govern another man without that other's consent."*
> —*Abraham Lincoln*

The device was the invention of George William Manby, who had attended school with naval hero Lord Nelson.

1817 Shortly after leading his army across the Andes, Argentine revolutionary José de San Martín launches a surprise attack against Spanish loyalists and captures Santiago, Chile.

1839 British bare-knuckle heavyweight champ James Burke loses his title to William "Bendigo" Thompson in 10 rounds.

1851 Australian prospector Edward Hargraves touches off the Australian gold rush when he announces finding the precious metal at Summerhill Creek in New South Wales.

1865 Reverend Dr. Henry Highland Garnet, a former slave, becomes the first African American to address the U.S. House of Representatives. His sermon commemorated Union victories in the American Civil War and the deliverance of the country from slavery.

1877 The *Boston Globe* receives the first telephone news dispatch, using equipment provided by American inventor Alexander Graham Bell.

1912 China's last emperor, six-year-old Hsuan-

An American POW talking through a barred door port to fellow a prisoner in Hanoi

T'ung, abdicates following Sun Yat-sen's republican revolution. The move ended 2,000 years of imperial rule.

1924 American composer George Gershwin, 26, debuts his revolutionary work, *Rhapsody in Blue*, which was written in such haste that he had to improvise much of the piano solo at its premiere in New York City.

1941 During World War II, German general Erwin Rommel and his Afrika Korps arrive in Libya to reinforce the beleaguered Italian army.

1953 Willys-Overland, the American Jeep manufacturer, celebrates its 50th anniversary. The company produced 600,000 Jeeps for the U.S. Army during World War II.

1972 During the Vietnam War, about 6,000 Cambodian soldiers attempt to drive 4,000 North Vietnamese from Angkor Wat, a Buddhist temple complex seized in 1970.

1973 North Vietnam begins the release of 591 American prisoners captured during the Vietnam War.

1983 American jazz great Eubie Blake, who helped launch the ragtime piano genre, dies five days after his 100th birthday. "If I knew I was going to live so long," he once said, "I'd have taken better care of myself."

1986 After spending eight years in Soviet prisons and labor camps for championing the cause of Russian Jews to practice Judaism, Anatoly Scharansky is released and allowed to emigrate to Israel.

1996 More than 2,000 people carrying paper doves hold a vigil outside the city hall in Belfast, the main city of Northern Ireland. They were indicating their desire for continued peace following the I.R.A. bomb two days earlier that ended a 17-month cease-fire.

1999 After a five-week impeachment trial, the U.S. Senate acquits President William Jefferson Clinton on charges of perjury and obstruction of justice related to his extramarital affair.

President Bill Clinton

Joan of Arc

1429 Joan of Arc, disguised as a man, begins her journey through English-occupied France in order to reach the dauphin, Charles, and ask his permission to raise an army against English king Henry VI.

1542 Catherine Howard, fifth wife of English king Henry VIII, is beheaded in the Tower of London for having had affairs prior to her marriage to the king.

1588 Borrowing from both Ptolemy and Copernicus, Danish astronomer Tycho Brahe outlines his own idea for how the solar system works: the sun and moon revolve around Earth (Ptolemy); and the remaining planets orbit the sun (Copernicus).

1633 Italian astronomer Galileo Galilei arrives in Rome for his trial before the Inquisition on heresy charges for stating his belief that Earth revolves around the Sun.

1689 William and Mary are proclaimed joint sovereigns of Great Britain following Britain's Glorious Revolution,

which drove James II from the throne and established a new bill of rights that curtailed the power of the crown.

1692 In Glencoe, Scotland, soldiers under the command of Archibald Campbell treacherously slaughter thirty-three men, two women, and two children of the MacDonald clan. The incident becomes known as the Massacre of Glencoe.

1822 American fur-trade entrepreneur William Ashley places his famous newspaper ad seeking 100 "enterprising young men" to engage in what became the Rocky Mountain fur trade.

1858 British explorers Richard Burton and John Speke become the first Europeans to set eyes on Lake Tanganyika in Tanzania.

1866 Jesse James, a Confederate veteran of the American Civil War and one of the best-known outlaws of the American West, robs his first bank, in Liberty, Missouri.

1867 Johann Strauss premieres his "Blue Danube Waltz" at a public concert in Vienna.

1875 American Edna Kanouse gives birth to five sons in the first well-documented U.S. birth of quintuplets.

1907 Marcel-Alexandre Bertrand, the French geologist

> *"Man is the only animal that blushes. Or needs to."*
>
> —Mark Twain

who theorized that certain mountain ranges were created by the folding of Earth's crust, dies at age 59.

1929 Scottish bacteriologist Alexander Fleming presents a paper to the Medical Research Club describing his discovery of a mold that had begun to kill some bacterial cultures while he was on vacation. Fleming's discovery led to the development of the first antibiotic, penicillin, for which he shared the Nobel Prize in medicine in 1945.

1935 Bruno Hauptmann is found guilty of kidnapping and murdering the baby of American aviation great Charles Lindbergh. He was later executed, maintaining his innocence to the end.

1942 During World War II, Japanese paratroopers invade Palembang, in Sumatra.

1945 Soviet troops capture Budapest, Hungary, during World War II.

1958 In the United States, Ford introduces the first four-seater Thunderbird, which sported a 352-cubic-inch, 300-horsepower engine.

1959 The first Barbie doll, an impossibly proportioned blonde in a black-and-white bathing suit, makes its debut at the American Toy Fair in New York City.

1960 France detonates its first nuclear bomb, from a 330-foot tower in a remote portion of the Sahara Desert.

1965 U.S. president Lyndon B. Johnson approves the sustained bombing of North Vietnam. During the three-year campaign, dubbed Operation Rolling Thunder, 643,000 tons of bombs were dropped and 900 U.S. aircraft lost.

1984 Konstantin Chernenko, the last of Russia's communist hard-liners to rule the Soviet Union, succeeds Yuri Andropov as general secretary of the Soviet Communist Party.

1991 Sotheby's announces the discovery of a long-lost Mark Twain manuscript: the first half of his original version of *Huckleberry Finn*, which had languished in a librarian's trunk for more than a century.

2000 The last original *Peanuts* comic strip appears as a signed farewell from its originator, American cartoonist Charles M. Schulz, who had died the previous day of colon cancer.

Charles M. Schulz

CA. 380 Western pilgrim Etheria attends a festival in Jerusalem commemorating the presentation of Jesus at the temple. The custom soon spread to other cities and eventually developed into the festival of Candlemas, now celebrated on February 2.

1014 Henry II is crowned Holy Roman emperor. The German king's reign, marked by cooperation between church and state, would last 10 years. He was canonized in 1146.

1349 Two thousand Jews are burned to death in Strasbourg, Germany.

1400 Deposed English king Richard II dies at Pontefract castle in Yorkshire where he has been imprisoned by Henry Bolingbroke, Duke of Lancaster and later King Henry IV. Richard was either murdered or allowed to starve to death.

1493 On the return from Christopher Columbus's first voyage across the Atlantic, a dreadful storm separates the mariner's two ships, the Niña and the Pinta.

1556 Thomas Cranmer, first Protestant archbishop of Canterbury and adviser to Henry VIII and Edward VI of England,

Thomas Cranmer

MILESTONE

No Love Lost

On this day in 1929 in what would became known as the St. Valentine's Day Massacre, three men dressed as police officers enter the headquarters of Chicago gangster Bugs Moran, line up seven of his men, and shoot them to death. The killings marked the climax of a gang war between Moran and his archrival, Al Capone. The St. Valentine's Day Massacre stirred a media storm centered on Capone and his illegal Prohibition-era activities and motivated federal authorities to redouble their efforts to take him off the streets, finally convicting him of tax evasion. At Alcatraz, the syphilis Capone had contracted in his youth entered a late stage, and he spent his last year in prison in the hospital ward. In 1939, he was released after only six and a half years in jail as the result of good behavior and work credits.

On the same day, in 1943, Germany's Afrika Korps attacks the American position at Kasserine Pass in Tunisia. Though initially repulsed, Field Marshal Erwin Rommel's troops eventually broke through, killing more than 1,000 Americans and handing the United States its first major battlefield defeat in the European theater during World War II.

---

is declared a heretic and handed over to be burned at the stake.

1779 English explorer and navigator Captain James Cook is killed by Hawaiians during his third visit to the Pacific island group.

1797 The British fleet defeats the Spanish in the Battle of St. Vincent, off the coast of Portugal. During the battle, Captain Horatio Nelson distinguishes himself by dividing the Spanish fleet and capturing two ships.

1842 Well-heeled American fans of English novelist Charles Dickens throw an elite party in New York for the writer, who was on a five-month tour of the United States. The "Boz Ball," named after Dickens's early pseudonym, sold out despite the then-outrageous ticket price of $10 a head.

1876 In the United States, rival inventors Alexander Graham Bell and Elisha Gray both apply for telephone patents.

1886 California orange growers ship their first trainload of fruit from Los Angeles.

"Where justice is denied, where poverty is enforced, where ignorance prevails, and where one class is made to feel that society is an organized conspiracy to oppress, rob, and degrade them, neither persons nor property will be safe."

—*Frederick Douglass*

Premier Nikita Khrushchev

1895 *The Importance of Being Earnest,* probably Irish playwright Oscar Wilde's most famous work, premieres at St. James's Theatre in London. The Marquis of Queensberry, outraged at Wilde's homosexual relationship with his son, is denied admission to the theatre when he arrives to present Wilde with a bouquet of root vegetables.

1896 Edward, Prince of Wales, later King Edward VII, becomes the first member of the British royal family to ride in an automobile.

1927 English director Alfred Hitchcock premieres his first suspense film, *The Lodger.*

1938 Hollywood socialite Hedda Hopper publishes her first gossip column in the *Los Angeles Times.*

1956 At the Soviet Communist Party's 20th congress, Nikita Krushchev announces a new, softer line in Soviet foreign policy: coexistence with states of different social systems.

1962 First Lady Jacqueline Kennedy hosts the first televised tour of the White House. On the same day,

President John F. Kennedy authorizes American troops in Vietnam to return fire.

1978 Texas Instruments patents the first microchip.

1989 Anglo-Indian novelist Salman Rushdie is forced into hiding when Iranian ayatollah Ruhollah Khomeini condemns his book *The Satanic Verses* and offers a reward to anyone who would kill him.

1989 At a meeting of five Central American presidents, a cease-fire is arranged between the leftist Sandinista government of Nicaragua and American-backed anti-Sandanista rebels based in Honduras.

1990 The American space probe *Voyager I* snaps a photo of the entire solar system.

1993 Fifteen ice fishermen die near Perm, Russia, when a hydroelectric plant releases hot water into the river and the frozen surface breaks apart.

2000 An unmanned American spacecraft arrives at 433 Eros, the largest near-Earth asteroid, and begins a yearlong survey of the object.

The asteroid Eros

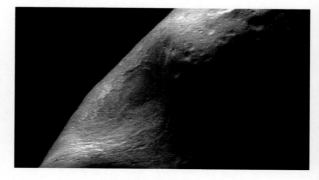

339 B.C. Greek philosopher Socrates is sentenced to death.

1113 Pope Paschal II formally recognizes the Knights Hospitaller. Still in existence, the order originated in the 11th century to care for pilgrims in Jerusalem.

1145 Eugenius III, a Cistercian abbot and disciple of St. Bernard of Clairvaux, is elected pope. Later exiled to France, he helped organize the Second Crusade.

1758 Mustard makes its debut in America, manufactured in a German section of Philadelphia, Pennsylvania.

1764 The American city of St. Louis, Missouri, is founded as a French trading post at the confluence of the Missouri and Mississippi rivers. It was to become the hub of a vast fur-trading empire and a key site in the exploration of the American West.

1804 New Jersey becomes the last northern state to abolish slavery.

1861 Mary Miller Chestnut begins writing *A Diary from Dixie*, her famous, first-hand account of southern society during the American Civil War. She accompanied

---

1564
GALILEO GALILEI
Italian physicist and astronomer persecuted by the Catholic Church

1748
JEREMY BENTHAM
English social reformer who brought in the registration of births, marriages, and deaths

1803
JOHN SUTTER
Early California settler at whose mill gold was discovered in 1848

1809
CYRUS HALL McCORMICK
American inventor of the mechanical reaper

1820
SUSAN B. ANTHONY
American suffragist

Susan B. Anthony

1874
ERNEST H. SHACKLETON
British Antarctic explorer

1905
HAROLD ARLEN
Pen name of Hyam Arluck, American songwriter ("It's Only a Paper Moon"; "Somewhere Over the Rainbow")

1929
GRAHAM HILL
English race-car driver, member of the International Motor Sports Hall of Fame

---

"The unexamined life is not worth living."

—Socrates

her husband, a Confederate staff officer, on his military missions.

1879 The U.S. Congress allows women lawyers to argue cases before the Supreme Court.

1903 The first teddy bear goes on sale at a toy store in Brooklyn, New York. The bear was made by the store's owner, Russian immigrant Rose Michtom, and named "Teddy's Bear" for President Teddy Roosevelt.

1922 The Permanent International Court of Justice holds its first session in the Hague, Netherlands. Today this court is the principal justice organ of the United Nations, notably the seat of war crimes tribunals.

1933 President-elect Franklin D. Roosevelt survives an assassination attempt in Miami, Florida. The assassin's bullets instead struck Chicago mayor Anton Cernak, who later died from his wounds.

1939 Early in World War II, Germany launches the battleship *Bismarck*.

1944 During World War II, Allied bombers destroy the 1,400-year-old Benedictine monastery at Monte Cassino in the mistaken belief that the Germans had occupied and fortified it. The Germans evacuated the monks, then returned to occupy and fortify the ruins.

1950 The Soviet Union and communist China sign a mutual defense and assistance treaty, creating a force that one prominent Chinese official declared would be "impossible to defeat."

1951 The first atomic reactor used for medical therapy is placed in service by the U.S. Atomic Energy Commission.

1954 French oceanographers Georges Houot and Pierre Willm set a new ocean exploration depth record of 13,287 feet when their submersible touches the floor of the Atlantic Ocean off Dakar, Senegal.

1965 Nat "King" Cole, American swing-era jazz pianist and singer, dies in Santa Monica, California.

1965 Canada first flies its new national flag, adorned with a prominent red maple leaf.

1971 England bids farewell to the shilling,

Abdullah Ocalan

adopting instead a decimal system of coinage.

1988 Richard Feynman, Nobel Prize-winning American nuclear physicist who worked on the Manhattan project that developed the first atomic bomb, dies at the age of 69.

1994 After a twelve-month standoff, North Korea agrees to allow officials of the International Atomic Energy Agency to inspect seven key nuclear installations.

1994 Forty people die in Hengyang, China, when train passengers stampede in a crowded railway station following the Chinese New Year.

1999 Turkish security forces seize Kurdish rebel leader Abdullah Ocalan from the Greek embassy in Nairobi, Kenya.

FEBRUARY 16

1086 A solar eclipse visible in Sicily and southern Italy prompts local citizens to break out lamps and torches during normal daylight hours.

1852 American brothers Henry and Clement Studebaker found a blacksmith and wagon-building business that eventually develops into one of the nation's largest independent automakers.

1862 Fort Donelson, an important American Civil War stronghold on the Cumberland River in Tennessee, falls to Union troops under General Ulysses S. Grant. The victory captured 15,000 Southern soldiers and forced a general Confederate withdrawal from central Tennessee.

1894 Gunslinger John Wesley Hardin is pardoned after serving fifteen years in a Texas prison for murder. Hardin probably killed more than 40 people—one man, it was said, just for snoring.

1909 America's first subway car with side doors is placed in service in New York City.

> *"Ideas are far more powerful than guns. We don't allow our enemies to have guns, why should we allow them to have ideas?"*
>
> —*Joseph Stalin*

1923 The sepulchral chamber of King Tutankhamen's tomb in Thebes, Egypt, is unsealed by English archaeologist Howard Carter.

1937 A DuPont chemist, Wallace Carothers, patents nylon as well as the process for making the now-ubiquitous material.

1940 During World War II, the HMS *Cossack* rescues 300 British prisoners of war from the German prison ship *Altmark* in a Norwegian fjord. The British government protested that officials from neutral Norway had failed to find the prisoners when the ship had earlier been searched at the Norwegian port of Bergen.

1943 During World War II, the White Rose student group posts a sign in Munich reading "Out with Hitler! Long live freedom!" The perpetrator was soon caught and beheaded.

1945 Three years after the infamous Bataan Death March during World War II, U.S. Army troops under General Douglas MacArthur recapture the Bataan Peninsula in the Philippines.

1946 The first commercial helicopter, a four-seat single-rotor Sikorsky S51, makes its

Battle at Fort Donelson

Fidel Castro becomes prime minister

1987 The trial of Ivan Demjanjuk opens in Jerusalem. A Ukrainian Secret Service volunteer during World War II, Demjanjuk was accused of being "Ivan the Terrible," a notoriously cruel guard who oversaw the gas chambers in Treblinka.

1992 An Israeli helicopter strike kills the secretary-general of Hezbollah, Abbas al-Musawi, who Western officials held responsible for many terrorist attacks, including the 1983 Beirut bombings that killed 300 U.S. and French soldiers.

1993 More than 1,200 die when a triple-decker ferry carrying between 1,500 and 2,000 people capsizes and sinks off the coast of Haiti.

2000 In an address before the Israeli Knesset, German president Johannes Rau asks forgiveness for Germany's murderous treatment of Europe's Jews during World War II.

German president Johannes Rau at the Yad Vashem Holocaust memorial in Jerusalem

maiden flight. The chopper had a range of 250 miles at a speed of 100 miles per hour.

1951 Reacting to the war in Korea, Soviet premier Joseph Stalin launches a scathing verbal assault on the United Nations, warning that "warmongers" in the West could trigger a world war.

1959 Cuban revolutionary Fidel Castro is sworn in as prime minister of Cuba, after leading a guerrilla war that forced right-wing dictator Fulgencio Batista from the country.

1968 During the Vietnam War, U.S. officials report that the Tet Offensive in South Vietnam has created 350,000 new refugees since January 30, boosting the total number of refugees in South Vietnam to 1.1 million.

1979 Disco music continues to dominate the American pop scene as The Bee Gees win a Grammy for their album *Saturday Night Fever*.

MILESTONE

To the Shores of Tripoli

On this day in 1804, during the First Barbary War, American Lieutenant Stephen Decatur leads a military mission that famed British Admiral Horatio Nelson calls the "most daring act of the age."

In October 1803, the U.S. frigate *Philadelphia* ran aground near Tripoli and was captured by Tripolitan gunboats. The Americans feared that the well-constructed warship would be both a formidable addition to the Tripolitan navy and a model for building future Tripolitan frigates. Hoping to prevent the Barbary pirates from gaining this military advantage, Lieutenant Stephen Decatur led a daring expedition into Tripoli harbor to destroy the captured American vessel.

After disguising himself and his men as Maltese sailors, Decatur's force of 74 men, which included nine U.S. Marines, sailed into Tripoli harbor on a small, two-masted ship. The Americans approached the USS *Philadelphia* without drawing fire from the Tripoli shore guns, boarded the ship, and attacked its Tripolitan crew, capturing or killing all but two. After setting fire to the frigate, Decatur and his men escaped without the loss of a single American. The *Philadelphia* subsequently exploded when its gunpowder reserve was lit by the spreading fire.

1454 During a gargantuan banquet featuring performances by trained exotic beasts, the flamboyant Philip the Good of Burgundy, France, swears the "oath of the pheasant," thereby pledging to go on the Third Crusade.

1461 In England's long-running War of the Roses, the houses of York and Lancaster battle for the second time at St. Alban's. The Lancastrians gain the upper hand on the battlefield, but the Yorkists soon take London and the crown for Edward IV.

1600 Italian philosopher, astronomer, and mathematician Giordano Bruno is burned at the stake in Rome for heresy after refusing to recant his theories of an infinite universe, which went beyond the accepted Copernican view of a finite universe centered around the sun.

1621 Puritan pilgrim Miles Standish is appointed as the first commander of the Plymouth colony in Massachusetts.

1673 French dramatist Molière collapses on a Paris stage during the fourth performance of his last play, *The Imaginary Invalid,* and is carried home to die.

Miles Standish

BORN ON THIS DAY

1766
THOMAS MALTHUS
British economist and demographer who developed the Malthusian theory

1781
RENÉ LAËNNEC
French physician and inventor of the stethoscope

1844
MONTGOMERY WARD
American merchant and department store mogul

1864
ANDREW BARTON PATERSON
Australian poet and journalist famous for the words of "Waltzing Matilda"

1877
ANDRÉ MAGINOT
French minister of war, creator of the fortified "Maginot Line" to defend France from German attack

1889
H. L. (HAROLDSON LAFAYETTE) HUNT
American industrialist and oil magnate (Hunt Oil) who was also one of the founders of the American Football League

1902
MARION ANDERSON
African-American classical singer with a "voice that comes once in a hundred years"

1930
RUTH RENDELL
English crime writer

1934
ALAN BATES
English actor (*Far from the Madding Crowd; Women in Love; Gosford Park*)

1936
JIM BROWN
American Hall of Fame football player and actor (*The Dirty Dozen; Ice Station Zebra; He Got Game*)

1954
RENE RUSSO
American actress (*The Thomas Crown Affair; Major League*)

1963
MICHAEL JORDAN
American professional basketball player

"The fortune of our lives . . . depends on employing well the short period of our youth."

—*Thomas Jefferson*

1772 Prussia, Austria, and Russia carve up Poland for the first of three times, virtually extinguishing it as a nation until its restoration after World War I with the Versailles Treaty.

1776 English scholar Edward Gibbon publishes the first volume of his classic history *The Decline and Fall of the Roman Empire.*

1801 Thomas Jefferson is elected third president of the United States after tying Aaron Burr in the electoral college and finally winning the necessary tie-breaking votes in the House of Representatives.

1817 A street in Boston, Massachusetts, becomes the first in the United States illuminated with gas streetlights.

1818 German baron Karl von Drais de Sauerbrun patents a forerunner of the bicycle called the "draisine."

1864 During the American Civil War, the Confederate hand-cranked submersible *H. L. Hunley* becomes the world's first submarine to sink an enemy ship, the Union sloop *Housatonic*, with a spar torpedo, in the harbor of Charleston, South Carolina. Both vessels were destroyed, however, with the loss of all hands on the submarine.

Karl von Drais de Sauerbrun's draisine, forerunner of the bicycle

1911 In the United States, Cadillac introduces the first automobile with a self-starting engine, an attractive alternative to Ford's hand-cranked starter, which caused its share of broken jaws and ribs.

1933 Blondie Boopadoop marries Dagwood Bumstead in American cartoonist Chic Young's popular comic strip *Blondie.*

1944 American troops storm Eniwetok, a strategic atoll along Japan's inner defensive perimeter in the Marshall Islands. On the same day, the U.S. fleet launches the first of many World War II attacks against the Japanese base at Truk, in the Caroline Islands.

1945 German rocket scientist Wernher von Braun, later a key figure in the American missile and space programs, flees Adolf Hitler's V2 rocket site in Peenemunde, East Germany, as Soviet troops advance.

1947 The Voice of America beams its first radio broadcast into the Soviet Union as part of the U.S. propaganda campaign during the Cold War.

1952 Prime Minister Winston Churchill announces that England is developing an atomic bomb, the third nation to do so, after the United States and the Soviet Union.

1968 The weekly U.S. casualty rate in Vietnam hits an all-time high as officials report that 543 Americans were killed in action and 2,547 wounded during the previous seven days of the Vietnam War.

1972 The Volkswagen Beetle surpasses the Ford Model T's production record and becomes the most heavily produced car in history as the 15,007,034th Beetle rolls off the assembly line in Wolfsburg, Germany.

1979 Chinese forces invade Vietnam in response to the Vietnamese invasion of Cambodia in January. Nine days of bitter fighting ensued, and the Chinese were forced to withdraw.

U.S. Marines carry their wounded atop a tank in Vietnam

1478 George, Duke of Clarence, is murdered in the Tower of London after opposing his brother, King Edward IV. Several accounts said he was drowned in a barrel of malmsey wine.

1546 Martin Luther, German leader of the Protestant Reformation and a pivotal figure in Western civilization, dies in Eisleben after mediating a quarrel between two princes.

1564 Italian artist Michelangelo Buonarroti, one of the greatest artists of all time, dies in Rome. Michelangelo considered himself primarily a sculptor, but some of his works in painting and architecture also rank among the most famous in existence.

1678 English author John Bunyan publishes *Pilgrim's Progress*, which is now said to be the most frequently reprinted book in English after the Bible.

1688 At a meeting in Germantown, Pennsylvania, Quakers and Mennonites compose the "Germantown Protest," which lodged the first formal complaint against slavery and the slave trade by a white group in America.

1837 "Spring-Heeled Jack," a seemingly demonic masked attacker, strikes for the

MILESTONE

Cortés Conquers Mexico
On this day in 1519, Spanish conquistador Hernán Cortés sets sail for Mexico with 508 soldiers, 100 sailors, and 16 horses. During the next two years, Cortés would overthrow the Aztec empire. He was greeted by messengers of the Aztec ruler Montezuma. Wanting to show the Aztec his power, Cortés had the ships' cannons fired. The Aztec were stunned. Montezuma welcomed the Spanish into Tenochtitlan, but soon learned he had made a terrible mistake. Six months later, one of Cortés' leaders massacred thousands of Aztec people, causing a massive Aztec rebellion. Cortés lost most of his army in his retreat. Finally, on August 13, 1521, with most of their warriors dead from disease, starvation, or war wounds, the Aztec gave up. Within two years' time the Spanish had destroyed the Aztec Empire.

> *"No man should escape our universities without knowing how little he knows."*
> —*Robert Oppenheimer*

first time in central London, having already spread terror to the south of the river Thames. The assailant, who wore a cloak, horned helmet, and long metal claws, was named for the huge strides he took escaping from the scenes of his crimes. He was never caught.

1865 In the American Civil War, Confederate troops evacuate Charleston, South Carolina, site of Fort Sumter and focus of a 19-month Union siege that ended with the approach of General William T. Sherman's troops.

1873 The U.S. House of Representatives censures Massachusetts congressman Oakes Ames after finding him guilty of bilking the federal government out of millions of dollars in the Credit Mobilier scandal.

1876 Great Britain and New Zealand establish a direct telegraphic link.

1878 A New Mexico posse murders English rancher John Tunstall, igniting the range war in Lincoln County between cattlemen and merchants that made gunslinger Billy the Kid famous.

1885 Mark Twain publishes *The Adventures of Huckleberry Finn*, a book that novelist Ernest Hemingway

Fort Sumter

Lusitania, sunk by a German U-Boat in 1915

later said marked the beginning of American literature.

1915 During World War I, Germany begins treating the waters around the British Isles as a war zone in which any ship, enemy or not, could be sunk by its submarines. Few ships were destroyed, but the threat brought long-term hostility from neutral countries.

1918 American novelist F. Scott Fitzgerald is discharged from the U.S. Army after spending his entire enlistment in the United States.

1930 Pluto, the ninth planet from the sun, is discovered after years of searching by American astronomer Clyde W. Tombaugh using a new observational technique that employed photographic plates and a blink microscope.

1946 Clemens August Galen, the Roman Catholic bishop of Münster, Germany, and a powerful public opponent of the Nazis during World War II, is named a cardinal.

1948 Eamon de Valera, the most dominant Irish political figure of the 20th century, resigns as Irish prime minister after leading independent Ireland for 16 years. Born in

New York, de Valera participated in the 1916 Easter Rising against the British in Dublin and remained active in Irish politics into his 90s.

1967 Robert Oppenheimer, the American physicist who headed the quest for the atomic bomb, dies in Princeton, New Jersey, at 62. During World War II, Oppenheimer led the "Manhattan Project," which developed the bombs that were dropped on Nagasaki and Hiroshima, Japan.

1977 In the United States, NASA flight-tests the first space shuttle, the *Enterprise*, by flying it atop a 747 jumbo jet. Four more captive flights would pass before the orbiter was released to land on its own.

1984 Italy and the Vatican agree to drop Roman Catholicism as the official state religion of Italy.

1997 A massive Peruvian mudslide buries two villages in the Andes, killing as many as 300 people.

2001 American stock-car racing legend Dale Earnhardt dies in a crash on the last lap of the Daytona 500.

Dale Earnhardt

▌▌ **197** Albinus, a powerful Roman general, proclaimed emperor by his troops, is defeated and killed by his rival emperor, Severus, during a battle near present-day Lyon, France.

607 Boniface III is elected pope just four years after obtaining an edict from the Byzantine emperor recognizing the see of Rome as the head of all the churches.

1090 Henry IV, Holy Roman emperor and German king, makes a hollow pledge to guarantee Jews protection and freedom of trade within his empire.

1408 The third and final rebellion by Henry Percy, Earl of Northumberland, against King Henry IV of England ends with the Earl's death at the Battle of Bramham Moor.

1601 In England, Henry Wriothesley, earl of Southampton and patron of William Shakespeare, is tried for treason for reviving *Richard II*, a play that tells the story of overthrowing a monarch.

1674 New York City is transferred from the Netherlands

> *"Let me assert my belief that the only thing that we have to fear is fear itself— nameless, unreasoning, unjustified terror that paralyzes needed efforts to convert retreat into advance."*
>
> —*Franklin D. Roosevelt*

MILESTONE

Bloody Fighting in Asia
On this day in 1905, the final land battle of the Russo–Japanese War commences near the Manchurian city of Mukden with 270,000 Japanese troops attacking a Russian force of 330,000. The Russians would withdraw two days later, having suffered 89,000 casualties to 71,000 Japanese.

On this same day in 1945, U.S. Marines invade Iwo Jima, a Pacific island of strategic importance because it lay close enough for American planes to launch bombing raids against Japan. Heavily fortified and occupied by 21,000 Japanese troops dug into a network of caves, Iwo Jima presented the Marines with some of the most difficult fighting of the second world war. By nightfall, more than 550 Americans had been killed and 1,800 wounded. When the American flag was finally raised on Iwo Jima, the memorable image was captured in a famous photograph that later won the Pulitzer Prize.

The Russo-Japanese War in Manchuria

Earl of Southampton

to England through the Peace of Westminster.

⚖ **1807** Former U.S. vice president Aaron Burr is arrested in Alabama for treason. Burr had led a group of well-armed colonists toward New Orleans, Louisiana, allegedly for the purpose of establishing an independent republic west of the Mississippi.

🔬 **1831** In Pennsylvania, the first coal-burning locomotive in the United States makes its trial run.

1847 The first rescuers reach the Donner Party, a group of California-bound emigrants who had resorted to cannibalism after they were stranded by heavy snow the previous autumn in the Sierra Nevada Mountains.

▌▌ **1855** The first weather map is presented at the French Academy of Sciences.

1861 Russian czar Alexander II abolishes serfdom.

🔬 **1878** Prolific American inventor Thomas A. Edison patents the phonograph.

1906 Michigan cereal makers W. K. Kellogg and

Charles Bolin incorporate the Battle Creek Toasted Corn Flake Company.

1915 In an attempt to remove Turkey as a force in World War I, Allied forces begin a campaign to push through the straits of the Dardanelles between the Aegean and the Sea of Marmara. The Gallipoli campaign is little short of a disaster, ending with an evacuation in January 1916 and costing 252,000 Allied and 251,000 Turkish lives.

1942 U.S. president Franklin D. Roosevelt signs Executive Order 9066, which was used to relocate more than 110,000 Japanese Americans from their homes on the West Coast to remote internment camps around the country.

1942 The New York Yankees announce that the baseball team will offer free seats to 5,000 uniformed servicemen at each home game during the coming season.

1965 Dissident South Vietnamese officers launch an abortive coup in Saigon against the leader of the country, General Nguyen Khanh, during the Vietnam War.

1970 The Chicago Seven, a group of American Vietnam War protesters, are convicted of inciting riots at the 1968 Democratic National Convention. The judge also found them guilty of 175 counts of contempt of court during their turbulent trial. Their convictions were overturned on appeal.

1977 Off the Galápagos Islands, deep-sea research scientists discover a thriving ecosystem of worms, clams, and crabs centered around geothermal hot water vents on the floor of the ocean, far beyond the reach of sunlight. The ecosystem was later found to depend on the oxidation of hydrogen sulfide spewing from the vents.

1997 Detroit's 19-month newspaper strike ends with a settlement between six unions and the *Detroit News* and *Detroit Free Press*.

The Chicago Seven, from left to right: Lee Weiner, John Froines, Abbie Hoffman, Rennie Davis, Jerry Rubin, Tom Hayden, and David Dellinger

1408 Henry Percy, first earl of Northumberland and a key figure in the abdication of English king Richard II, is killed in the Battle of Bramham Moor as he fights to unseat King Henry IV, the man he had helped to crown in Richard II's place.

1422 Pope Martin V issues a bull (withdrawn the following year) that reminds the faithful that Christianity derived from Judaism and warns church officials to refrain from inciting the public against Jews.

1437 King James I of Scotland is killed by a group of nobles angered at his liberal reforms. The king took refuge in a water closet and killed two of the attackers, but was fatally stabbed with a sword.

1725 A posse of New Hampshire volunteers scalp 10 Native Americans and collect a bounty of 100 pounds per scalp. It was the first recorded instance of this grim practice

"There is nothing worse than a brilliant image of a fuzzy concept."
—*Ansel Adams*

being used by Europeans in the American colonies.

1809 During the Napoleonic Wars, the Spanish city of Saragossa falls to the French after a protracted and bloody siege, which was later described in Lord Byron's poem "Childe Harold."

1864 In the American Civil War's battle of Olustee, a Confederate force beats back a Union attack west of Jacksonville, Florida, thus preserving Southern control of Florida's interior for the remainder of the war.

1872 Massachusetts inventor Luther Childs Crowell patents a machine for making square-bottomed paper bags.

Battle of Olustee

1907 Dmitri Mandeleyev, the Russian chemist who developed the periodic table of the elements, dies in St. Petersburg. He left gaps in his table, correctly predicting that they would be filled later by elements not then known.

1921 Reza Khan Pahlavi, an Iranian army officer, leads a bloodless coup and takes control of the country's military. He would later become shah.

1942 Navy fighter pilot Edward O'Hare becomes the first American flying ace of World War II, downing five Japanese bombers in just four minutes as the enemy planes approached the U.S. aircraft carrier *Lexington* off the Solomon Islands. He was later awarded the Medal of Honor.

1943 Paricutin, a new cinder cone volcano, erupts from a Mexican farm field, burying two neighboring towns in lava and ash. Within a year, the cone stood 1,475 feet high.

1962 John Glenn makes the first American orbital space flight, riding the *Friendship 7* Mercury capsule around Earth three times before splashing down near the Bahamas.

1968 In direct response to the Tet Offensive in Vietnam, the U.S. Senate Foreign Relations Committee begins its investigation of American policy in Vietnam.

1974 The editor of the *Atlanta Constitution*, Reg Murphy, is kidnapped and held for a $700,000 ransom. The money was paid two days later and the kidnapper, who claimed to represent a right-wing American militia group, was arrested.

1976 The Southeast Asia Treaty Organizaion, one of the anchors of American Cold War policies in Asia and a primary player in the Vietnam War, quietly disbands.

1985 Ireland, predominantly Catholic, approves the sale of contraceptives after decades of controversy.

1986 The Soviet Union launches the core module of the *Mir* space station, a stepped cylinder about 43 feet long and 14 feet in diameter at its widest point.

1994 A mild earthquake shakes up the 18th Winter Olympic Games in Nagano, Japan.

1997 A boat full of Tamil refugees capsizes off the northern coast of Sri Lanka, drowning 165 people.

Mir space station

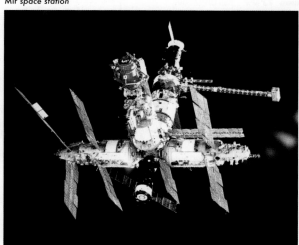

1173 Pope Alexander III canonizes Thomas Becket, martyred archbishop of Canterbury who was killed on orders of English king Henry II.

1431 French national heroine Joan of Arc, captured and imprisoned by enemies of Charles VII, faces her interrogators for the first time before her trial on charges of heresy.

1543 Ethiopian emperor Galawdewos uses European arms and tactics to defeat a Muslim army near Lake Tama, thus securing north-central Ethiopia for Christian forces.

1595 English poet Robert Southwell is hanged, then drawn and quartered at Tyburn in London, having been imprisoned and tortured for his Jesuit beliefs. He became a Catholic saint and martyr.

1677 Dutch-Jewish philosopher Benedict de Spinoza, the most important exponent of 17th-century rationalism, dies in The Hague.

1707 Aurungzebe, Mogul emperor of Hindustan, dies after a 49-year reign.

1804 Richard Trevithick, Cornish inventor of the high-pressure steam engine, wins a bet when his recently constructed railway locomotive successfully

> *"Some books are undeservedly forgotten; none are undeservedly remembered."*
>
> —*W. H. Auden*

BORN ON THIS DAY

1855
ALICE (ELVIRA FREEMAN) PALMER
American educator and administrator, president of Wellesley College

1875
JEANNE LOUISE CALMENT
Frenchwoman who was the world's oldest woman when she died at age 122, one year after she released a rap CD

1893
ANDRÉS SEGOVIA
Spanish classical guitarist

1903
ANAÏS NIN
French author (*Cities of the Interior; Seduction of the Minotaur; Delta of Venus: Erotica*)

1907
W. H. AUDEN
Pulitzer Prize-winning British/American poet (*City Without Walls; For the Time Being*)

1922
MURRAY "THE K" KAUFMAN
American disc jockey known as the "Fifth Beatle"

1931
LARRY HAGMAN
American actor (*Dallas*)

1934
RUE McCLANAHAN
American actress (*They Might Be Giants; The Dreamer of Oz; Starship Troopers*)

1943
DAVID GEFFEN
American movie and television producer (*Beetlejuice; The West Wing*)

hauls 10 tons of iron and 70 men for 10 miles along a Welsh tramway.

1828 The Cherokee Nation in New Echota, Georgia, receives its first printing press, designed to print a Cherokee-language newspaper in the newly invented Cherokee alphabet.

1848 John Quincy Adams, sixth U.S. president and congressman from Massachusetts, collapses from a stroke on the floor of the House of Representatives while speaking against the recently concluded Mexican-American War.

1848 Karl Marx, with help from Friedrich Engels, publishes *The Communist Manifesto*, perhaps the most influential political pamphlet in history. In it, Marx predicted imminent revolution. Within days, a revolt in France forced King Louis-Philippe to abdicate.

1849 British forces in India defeat the Sikhs at Gujarat to win the Second Sikh War.

John Quincy Adams after his stroke

Karl Marx

1862 In the American Civil War's first major battle of the far West (the Battle of Val Verde), a Confederate army under General Henry Sibley attacks Union troops near Fort Craig in New Mexico Territory but is repulsed after a day of indecisive fighting.

1885 The Washington Monument, a 555-foot-high marble obelisk built in honor of America's Revolutionary War hero and first president, is dedicated in Washington, D.C.

1919 Kurt Eisner, the German socialist and statesman who led a 1918 revolt that overthrew the monarchy in Bavaria, is assassinated by a reactionary zealot.

1925 The renowned American literary magazine *The New Yorker* publishes its first issue.

1926 Swedish-born actress Greta Garbo, later a superstar of both silent and talking films, makes her U.S. film debut in *The Torrent*.

1937 A California aeronautics company test-flies the first successful automobile-airplane combination, the Arrowbile, which claimed a top speed of 120 miles per hour in the air, 70 on land.

1944 Japanese war leader Hideki Tōjō adds another position to his portfolio by taking over as army chief of staff, thus giving himself direct control of the Japanese military during World War II. The virtual dictator was already prime minister, army minister, war minister, and minister of commerce and industry.

1965 African-American nationalist and religious leader Malcolm X is assassinated by rival Black Muslims while giving a speech at a New York City ballroom.

1970 During the Vietnam War, American national security advisor Henry Kissinger opens secret peace talks with North Vietnamese representative Le Duc Tho, in a villa outside Paris, France.

Malcolm X

MILESTONE

Germans Launch Battle of Verdun

On this day in 1916, German forces open one of the most cataclysmic engagements of World War I, the Battle of Verdun, with a devastating bombardment of French positions along the Meuse River. The five-month battle would kill hundreds of thousands on both sides. The Battle of Verdun is considered the greatest and longest in world history. Never before or since has there been such a lengthy battle, involving so many men, situated on such a tiny piece of land. The battle, which lasted until December 19, 1916, caused over 700,000 casualties. The battlefield was not even ten kilometers square. The battle had degenerated into a matter of prestige for two nations who continued fighting literally for the sake of fighting.

EDITÉ PAR LA COMPAGNIE DES CHEMINS DE FER DE L'EST

Verdun

899 Arnulf of Carinthia is crowned Holy Roman emperor by Pope Formosus in Rome, but his rival Lambert of Spoleto keeps the imperial throne anyway.

1281 Simon De Brion is elected pope and takes the name Martin IV.

1371 David II, bumbling king of Scots, dies in Edinburgh at age 46.

1475 The first known Hebrew book—a copy of the Bible—is printed in southern Italy.

1495 Charles VIII, king of France, enters Naples in triumph to claim his hereditary rights. It was a pointless, costly expedition by an inept king; Italian armies gave him a quick boot back to France.

1797 General William Tate, an American mercenary, leads a force of French troops and convicts in an attack on Great Britain. The invasion was short-lived, partly because the soldiers landed at the Welsh village of Fishguard instead of

---

MILESTONE

Ancient Holiday

Every morning since its construction in the 13th century B.C., the first rays of sunlight would on this day (and again on October 22) illuminate the innermost shrine of the temple to sun god Amon-Re at Abu Simbel, Egypt. In 1257 B.C., Pharaoh Ramses II had two temples carved out of solid rock at a site on the west bank of the Nile south of Aswan in the land of Nubia and known today as Abu Simbel. Long before Ramses II, the site had been sacred to Hathor of Absek. The temple built by Ramses, however, was dedicated to the sun gods Amon-Re and Re-Horakhte. Because of their remote location near the Sudanese border in southern Egypt, the temples were unknown until their rediscovery in 1813. They were first explored in 1817 by the Egyptologist Giovanni Battista Belzoni.

---

their intended target, the English city of Bristol.

1799 The new emperor of China forces corrupt courtier Ho-shen to commit suicide. Ho-shen had advanced himself from the Imperial guard to a high ministerial position which he used to enrich himself at great cost to the nation.

1819 Spain and the United States sign the Florida Purchase Treaty, in which Spain agrees to cede the remainder of its old province of Florida to the United States.

1828 Michael, younger son of King John VI of Portugal, assumes the regency, and later the throne, of an empire that included Brazil.

1847 During the Mexican-American War, forces under Mexican general Santa Anna and U.S. general Zachary Taylor fight the Battle of Buena Vista.

1848 The French royal government forbids a planned banquet of left-wing reformers, who start a riot that brings down the monarchy two days later. It is the start of the Second Republic.

1864 In the American Civil War's Battle of West Point, Mississippi, Confederate general Nathan Bedford Forrest routs a far larger Union force and helps end Union general William T. Sherman's expedition into Alabama.

1879 Frank Winfield Woolworth kicks off a retail revolution by opening the Great 5 Cents Store in Utica, New

U.S. general Zachary Taylor leading the charge at the Battle of Buena Vista

> *"Frankly, I don't mind not being president. I just mind that someone else is."*
>
> —Edward M. Kennedy

York, pledging to sell nothing that cost more than a nickel.

🏆 **1888** In New York, Scot John Reid and his friend John Upham play the first round of golf in America using clubs and balls imported from Scotland. The course: an improvised three holes.

🇨🇦 **1913** Francisco Madero, revolutionary and president of Mexico, is arrested during a military coup and assassinated by the soldiers taking him to prison. His death made him a martyr in the struggle against military dictatorship.

🇺🇸 **1918** Swept along by hysterical fears of treacherous German spies and domestic labor violence, the Montana legislature in the USA passes a Sedition Law that severely restricts freedom of speech and assembly. Three months later, Congress adopted a federal Sedition Act modeled on the Montana law.

1942 During World War II, U.S. president Franklin D. Roosevelt orders General Douglas MacArthur out of the Philippines, as the American defense of the islands collapses.

1965 During the Vietnam War, General William Westmoreland, commander of Military Assistance Command, requests two battalions of U.S. Marines to protect the U.S. air base at Da Nang. By 1969 over 540,000 American troops were in South Vietnam.

1967 Indonesian president Achmed Sukarno surrenders all executive authority to military dictator General Raden Suharto, remaining president in title only.

🇬🇧 **1972** An I.R.A. bomb kills six civilians and a Catholic priest at the headquarters of the 16th Parachute Brigade in Aldershot, England

🏆 **1980** In one of the most dramatic upsets in Olympic history, the underdog U.S. hockey team, made up of collegians and second-rate professional players, defeats the defending champion Soviet team at the XIII Olympic Winter Games in Lake Placid, New York.

🇺🇸 **1994** American CIA operative Aldrich Ames is arrested for selling secrets to the Soviet Union.

U.S. vs Soviet 1980 Olympic hockey game

303 Roman emperor Diocletian begins the "Great Persecution" against Christians to force universal adherence to the imperial religion.

1138 In Rome, Pietro Pierleoni and Gregorio Papareschi, elected by rival groups of Catholic cardinals, are consecrated as rival popes.

1540 Spanish conquistador Francisco Vásquez de Coronado sets off to find the fabled and nonexistent Seven Golden Cities of Cibolo.

1768 By signing the Treaty of Masulipatam, the nizam (ruler) of Hyderabad, India, submits to British control.

1786 British general Charles Cornwallis, best known for his defeat in the American Revolution, accepts a new job: governor-general of India.

1813 In Waltham, Massachusetts, the world's first company to mill cotton from raw material to finished fabric using powered machines is incorporated.

1821 English poet John Keats, whose work includes "The Eve of St. Agnes," dies of tuberculosis in Rome at age 25.

1835 Mexican general Anonio López de Santa Anna lays siege to the Alamo in Texas.

1848 Revolution erupts in Paris, France.

1874 Lawn tennis is created when Major Walter Clopton Wingfield of London patents the first recognizable

version of the game under the name "Sphairistike."

1885 In Exeter, England, 19-year-old John Lee is sent to the gallows, which mysteriously and repeatedly malfunctions until authorities ascribe it to an act of God. Lee's death sentence was commuted, and he spent the next 22 years in prison.

1886 U.S. chemist Charles Hall develops a process for separating aluminum from its ore. His process led to the first practical commercial production of the metal.

1893 Rudolf Diesel receives a German patent for the diesel engine.

1896 Leo Hirshfield introduces the Tootsie Roll.

1910 The United Wireless Telegraph Company in Philadelphia, Pennsylvania, sponsors the first-ever Morse code radio contest. Contestants were judged on speed and accuracy.

1920 The world's first wireless telegraph broadcasting service is transmitted in Chelmsford, England.

1927 The Federal Radio Commission, later called the Federal Communications Commission (FCC), starts work governing the American airwaves.

1936 A Russian unmanned gas balloon sets a new altitude record: 25 miles.

1938 In an action more symbolic than effective, 12 Chinese planes drop bombs on Japan.

> *"If poetry comes not as naturally as leaves to a tree it had better not come at all."*
>
> —John Keats

1942 During World War II, a submarine lobs shells at a California oil refinery in the first Japanese attack on the U.S. mainland.

1945 U.S. Marines raise the American flag atop Mount Suribachi, the highest point on Iwo Jima, during World War II.

1946 In the aftermath of World War II in Manila, the Philippines, Japanese general Yamashita is hanged for war crimes.

1954 Children in Pittsburgh, Pennsylvania, receive the first mass inoculation of the Salk polio vaccine.

U.S. Marines raise the American flag atop Mt. Suribachi, Iwo Jima

1958 Argentine auto-racing champion Juan Manuel Fangio is kidnapped by communist guerrillas in Cuba one day before the second Havana Grand Prix. The kidnappers wanted publicity for their cause and might have saved Fangio's life: he missed a major accident during the race.

1960 Demolition begins at Ebbets Field, former home of New York's Brooklyn Dodgers.

1965 English comedian Stan Laurel dies at age 74, eight years after the death of his long-time comedy partner, Oliver Hardy.

1966 During the Vietnam War, U.S. military headquarters in Saigon announce that 14 percent of South Vietnamese army soldiers deserted in 1965, a much higher rate of desertion than among the Vietcong.

19 B.C. In Jerusalem, King Herod dedicates the renewed temple but offends Jews by trying to put a Roman imperial eagle above the entrance.

616 Ethelbert, Anglo-Saxon king of Kent, dies. Canonized as St. Æthelberht, his kingdom included most of southern England.

1147 In Wurzburg, Germany, rioters kill 22 Jews on rumors that a corpse found in the river could perform miracles, viewed as a sign that Jews murdered the person.

1208 Francis of Assisi hears a sermon describing Christ's instructions to his apostles to renounce all possessions and become wandering preachers. Inspired, Francis did just that.

1479 Isabella I, queen of Castile, secures her throne after four years of civil war. She married Ferdinand II of Aragon the same year; together they unified Spain.

1642 Marco da Gagliano, a pioneer of Italian opera, dies in Naples.

1658 At the Battle of Bahadurpur in India, Sulayman

Isabella I

Shikoh defeats his uncle Shah Shuja' in a war of succession among sons of Mughal emperor Shah Jahan. Shikoh loses the throne, and his head, to Aurangzeb.

1669 Poet and scholar Sor Juana Inés de la Cruz enters a Mexican convent to avoid marriage and to have the freedom to spend her life in intellectual pursuit—something not done by women of her time.

1739 Iranian adventurer Nadir Shah defeats the Mughal emperor of India at the Battle of Karnal, massacres residents of Delhi, and makes off with plunder including the Peacock Throne of Shah Jahan.

1821 Mexican independence leader Agustin de Iturbide issues the Iguala Plan, calling for a European prince, if one could be found, to rule an independent Mexico. Iturbide himself became emperor.

1825 Thomas Bowdler dies in Wales. By stripping Shakespeare's plays of language he thought inappropriate, and publishing acceptable versions in *The Family Shakespeare*, he made his name a verb: to bowdlerize is to expurgate.

1826 King Bagyidaw of Burma signs the Treaty of Yandabo, surrendering a large territory plus indemnity payments to Great Britain.

"Where there is charity and wisdom, there is neither fear nor ignorance."
—*St. Francis of Assisi*

Royal carriages being burned during the French Revolution

1836 Texan colonel William Travis sends a desperate plea for help for the besieged defenders of the Alamo, ending the message with the famous last words, "Victory or Death." He got death, but also immortality in the slogan "Remember the Alamo," which quickly became the rallying cry for the Texas revolution.

1836 Samuel Colt receives a patent for an invention that became a central symbol of the American West: the Colt revolver.

1848 French king Louis Philippe, the "Citizen King," is overthrown by revolutionary citizens.

1852 Russian writer Nikolai Gogol, influenced by the fanatic Father Konstantinovsky, burns the manuscript of the second volume of his seminal novel *Dead Souls*. He died 10 days later.

1868 The U.S. House of Representatives votes to impeach President Andrew Johnson, citing Johnson's removal of Secretary of War Edwin M. Stanton as a violation of the Tenure of Office Act. The first American president to be impeached, Johnson was not convicted.

1917 Great Britain releases the "Zimmermann Note," a coded message from Germany to its ambassador in Mexico suggesting an alliance if the U.S. entered World War II. As a reward, Mexico would get Texas, New Mexico, and Arizona. The note helped turn U.S. public opinion firmly against Germany.

1942 The *Sturma*, an immigrant ship carrying Jews to Palestine, is torpedoed in the Black Sea after being turned away from Istanbul. All but one of the 769 passengers perish.

1946 Juan Domingo Perón, the controversial former vice president of Argentina, is elected president. Ousted in a 1955 military coup, he was again elected in 1973 after 18 years in exile.

1949 At White Sands Proving Grounds in New Mexico, a two-stage rocket becomes the first to reach outer space.

1968 The discovery of pulsars, pulsating radio sources in space, is announced.

1975 Birendra Bir Bikram Shah Dev is crowned king of Nepal, three years after acceding to the throne.

U.S. Marines in a stone fortress of Hué during the Tet Offensive (milestone)

FEBRUARY 25

161 B.C. Jewish rebels under Judas Maccabaeus defeat Seleucid general Nicanor, who boasted that he would destroy the Temple in Jerusalem and mount Judas's head near the city gates.

1451 To prevent Christians from converting to Judaism, Pope Nicholas V bans all social contact between members of the two religions. In many Catholic countries, the penalty for conversion was death.

1570 Pope Pius V excommunicates Queen Elizabeth I of England in response to her having beheaded Mary, Queen of Scots, and offers advance pardons to the person or persons who might assassinate her.

1601 The Earl of Essex, Robert Devereux, is executed in the Tower of London for high treason. He was a former favorite of Queen Elizabeth I.

1723 Sir Christopher Wren, architect of St. Paul's Cathedral in London, dies at age 90.

1730 In Russia, Anna Ivanovna, having agreed to conditions imposed by the Supreme Privy Council that would create a limited monarchy, changes her mind and reinstates imperial dictatorship with herself in the empress chair.

"The nicest thing is to open the newspapers and not to find yourself in them."
—George Harrison

Domingo Ortega

Hiram Rhoades Revels

1831 During the "November Insurrection," Polish patriots attempting to overthrow Russian rule fight the Russian Army to a standstill at Grochów. They lost their war three months later.

1837 American inventor Thomas Davenport, applying magnetism and electro magnetism, patents the first workable electric motor.

1856 The Congress of Paris convenes to develop a final settlement of the Crimean War. The Treaty of Paris was signed at the end of March.

1862 The U.S. Congress passes the Legal Tender Act, authorizing the use of paper notes to pay the government's bills. By replacing gold or silver, paper money allowed the government to finance the costly war long after its precious metal reserves were depleted.

1870 Hiram Rhoades Revels, a Republican from Natchez, Mississippi, is sworn in to the U.S. Senate, the first African American to sit in Congress. He was elected to fill the Senate seat once held by Jefferson Davis, former president of the Confederacy.

1875 Kuang-hsü, ninth Ching Dynasty emperor of China, ascends to the throne at age four. As an adult, he sought to reform the decaying imperial system, but was stymied by his dominating aunt, the empress dowager. He died under questionable circumstances the day before she did.

1902 English inventor and bridge engineer Hubert Booth issues the prospectus for the company operating the world's first power vacuum cleaner. The size of a refrigerator and mounted on a horse-drawn cart, it had an 800-foot hose and took two people to operate. Later in the year, Booth's invention was used to clean the enormous blue carpet in Westminster Abbey for Edward VII's coronation.

1909 American movie studios including Biograph, Vitagraph, the Edison Studio, and others, begin submitting films to the New York-based Board of Censorship for review. The board was set up by movie studios as a self-policing body to avoid threatened government censorship.

1913 The 16th Amendment to the U.S. Constitution, which paved the path for the United States' adoption of an income tax, is ratified, although its roots can be traced back to 1895.

1919 Oregon becomes the first U.S. state to impose a tax on gasoline. The funds collected from the one-percent tax were used for road construction and maintenance.

1928 The Federal Radio Commission (later the FCC) issues the first television license for a broadcast station, in Washington, D.C.

1938 Miami's first drive-in movie theater opens. The drive-in craze would reach its peak in 1963, when 3,502 theaters were in operation across the United States.

1949 American actor Robert Mitchum, star of classics such as *Cape Fear* and *Night of the Hunter*, is released after serving two months in a Los Angeles County prison for marijuana possession. Police meant the arrest as a deterrent to other would-be pot smokers.

1952 Windscale, Great Britain's plutonium plant, begins operation at Sellafield one week after announcement of plans to build a British atomic bomb.

1955 Great Britain completes construction of HMS *Ark Royal*, its largest-ever aircraft carrier.

Cassius Clay defeats Sonny Liston (milestone)

1147 Crusaders eager to liberate the Holy Land massacre Jews in Wurzburg, Germany.

1266 Manfred, de facto king of Sicily, dies in battle against Charles of Anjou, who was offered the crown by Pope Urban IV on the condition that he take it from Manfred.

1403 Widow Joan of Navarre, remarried to King Henry IV of England, is crowned at Westminster in London. Her former subjects in Brittany are unimpressed, and remain hostile to England.

1548 Lorenzino de' Medici, Italian writer and assassin, is murdered in Venice.

1577 Erik XIV, king of Sweden, dies in prison after being deposed by his half brothers, one of whom he had locked up years earlier.

1658 By signing the Treaty of Roskilde, Denmark cedes fertile agricultural provinces and parts of Norway to Sweden. Together with the Treaty of Copenhagen, signed later, it effectively determined the modern boundaries of the three countries.

1815 French general Napoleon Bonaparte returns to France from exile in Elba.

1839 The first Grand National Steeplechase, one of the most famous horse races in England, is run at Aintree near Liverpool.

1870 Inventor Alfred Beach demonstrates a 300-foot pneumatic subway beneath Broadway in New York City. A

1802
VICTOR HUGO
French author (*The Hunchback of Notre Dame; Les Misérables*)

Victor Hugo

1832
JOHN GEORGE NICOLAY
American author who was Abraham Lincoln's biographer

1846
WILLIAM "BUFFALO BILL" CODY
American frontiersman and showman

1852
JOHN HARVEY KELLOGG
American surgeon who also developed the process of flaking grains that inspired the flaked cereal industry

1876
PAULINE MUSTERS
Dutchwoman who was the shortest known adult (1' 11.2")

1903
ORDE WINGATE
British General who led the jungle force called the Chindits in Burma during World War II

1916
JACKIE GLEASON
American comedian and actor (*The Honeymooners*)

1921
BETTY HUTTON
American actress (*Annie Get Your Gun; The Perils of Pauline*)

1931
ROBERT NOVAK
American political columnist and author (*Lyndon B. Johnson: The Exercise of Power; Nixon in the White House; The Reagan Revolution* (all co-authored with Rowland Evans Jr.))

1932
JOHNNY CASH
American country singer ("I Walk the Line,"; "Ring of Fire")

"Science says the first word on everything and the last word on nothing."
—Victor Hugo

huge fan pushed the car one way and then pulled it back. His pneumatic technique eventually lost out to electric power.

1878 French lexicographer Paul-Émile Littré coins the term "microbe."

1896 Shortly after discovering that phosphorescent crystals exposed to light can create images on tightly wrapped photographic plates, French physicist Arbine Henri Becquerel learns that uranium salts can do the same even if kept in the dark.

1903 In Florida, Alexander Winton, driving his Winton Bullet, sets the first Daytona Beach speed record: over 65 miles per hour for a full mile. The engine was a massive water-cooled four-cylinder unit with a displacement of 792 cubic inches.

1935 The first radar (radio detection and ranging) system is demonstrated in England, tracking a Royal Air Force bomber. The invention proved crucial to Great Britain's defense in World War II.

1935 The Pontiac "Indian Maiden" mascot is patented. Before General Motors adopted his name, Pontiac was a famous war chief of the Ottawa tribe during the French and Indian Wars. For some obscure reason the

Buffalo Creek, West Virginia, after the flood

"Indian Maiden" became Pontiac's hood ornament.

1935 In violation of the Versailles Treaty, which prohibited military aviation in Germany, Adolf Hitler signs a secret decree establishing the Reich *Luftwaffe*, or air force, with World War I air hero and high-ranking Nazi Hermann Goering at its head.

1936 In Japan, ambitious young army officers attempt a coup, assassinating Prime Minister Saito Makoto and several cabinet members.

1938 Radar is installed on the American passenger ship *New York*. The following year, the first battleship equipped with radar was put into service.

1946 The *Lucky Lady II*, a B-50 Superfortress, leaves Texas on the first nonstop round-the-world flight. Refueled in the air four times, the plane took 94 hours to fly 23,452 miles.

1968 During the Vietnam War, Allied troops who had recaptured the imperial capital of Hué from the North Vietnamese during the Tet Offensive discover the first mass graves in Hué. The victims were thousands of civilians killed for being sympathizers with the Saigon government.

1972 At Buffalo Creek, West Virginia, floodwaters break through badly constructed strip-mine dams. The toll: 25 dead, 4,000 homeless.

World Trade Center (milestone)

425 Theodosius II, scholarly Eastern Roman emperor, helps establish the University of Constantinople.

1531 German Protestants form the Schmalkaldic League to protect Lutheran churches from attacks by Holy Roman Emperor Charles V, a Catholic.

1670 Jews are expelled from Austria.

1700 The island of New Britain, in Papua New Guinea, is discovered by English buccaneer and explorer William Dampier.

1706 John Evelyn, English author and diarist, dies in 1706. Evelyn was one of the founders of the Royal Society, and a friend of Samuel Pepys. His diaries were not published until 1818.

1782 The British House of Commons votes to end the war with the United States.

1788 Massachusetts declares the American slave trade illegal after a group of free blacks were kidnapped and taken to the island of Martinique as slaves.

1827 New Orleans, Louisiana, kicks off its first Mardis Gras.

1831 The first commercially successful steam carriage

> *"Some of my best leading men have been horses and dogs."*
>
> —Elizabeth Taylor

BORN ON THIS DAY

289
CONSTANTINE THE GREAT
Roman emperor (306–37) who adopted Christianity

1807
HENRY WADSWORTH LONGFELLOW
American poet (*Endymion; The Wreck of the Hesperus; The Village Blacksmith*)

Henry Longfellow

1847
DAME ELLEN TERRY
English stage actress

1848
SIR HUBERT PARRY
English composer (*Jerusalem*)

1869
ALICE HAMILTON
American physician and writer who promoted worker's compensation laws

1873
ENRICO CARUSO
Italian tenor, considered by many to be the greatest opera tenor of all time

1902
JOHN STEINBECK
Nobel Prize-winning American author (*The Grapes of Wrath; Of Mice and Men; East of Eden*)

1912
LAWRENCE DURRELL
English novelist (*The Alexandria Quartet*)

1932
ELIZABETH TAYLOR
English-born American Academy Award-winning actress (*National Velvet; Butterfly 8; Cat on a Hot Tin Roof; Cleopatra*)

1934
RALPH NADER
American consumer advocate and author (*Unsafe at Any Speed*)

Execution of Henry Wirz

—noisy, smoky, dangerous, and destructive of roadways—begins passenger service on the nine-mile run between the English cities of Gloucester and Cheltenham.

1862 In the American Civil War, Union prisoners start arriving at Andersonville prison in southern Georgia, an infamous site where nearly a quarter of the inmates would die in wretched, overcrowded conditions. Camp commander Henry Wirz became the only Confederate official executed in the aftermath of the war.

1879 Constantine Fahlberg discovers the artificial sweetener saccharine, at Johns Hopkins University in Baltimore, Maryland.

1906 American engineer Samuel Pierpont Langley, builder of the first heavier-than-air flying machine to achieve sustained flight, dies in Aiken, South Carolina. His flying machine weighed 26 pounds, had two sets of 14-foot wings, and was powered by a small steam engine.

1932 In England, Cambridge University physicist James Chadwick discovers the neutron. He later won a Nobel Prize.

1933 An arson fire guts Germany's historic parliamentary building, the Reichstag, an incident the Nazis conveniently blamed on the communists, thus paving the way for Adolf Hitler to seize dictatorial powers.

1936 Nobel laureate Ivan Pavlov, the Russian physiologist who developed the concept of conditioned reflex by teaching a hungry dog to salivate at the sound of a bell, dies in Leningrad.

1939 Borley rectory, "the most haunted house in England," burns to the ground.

1942 In the heroically defiant World War II Battle of the Java Sea, a vastly outgunned Allied fleet attacks the Japanese invasion fleet, damaging just one Japanese destroyer at the cost of five Allied warships.

1962 Two South Vietnamese air force pilots bomb and strafe the presidential palace in Saigon in an attempt to assassinate President Ngo Dinh Diem. The attack confirmed Diem's view that his principle enemies were domestic and fueled his

brother Nhu's brutal campaign to crush political dissent.

1964 Italy announces that it is looking for advice on how to save the Leaning Tower of Pisa from collapse. The 180-foot 12th-century tower had already leaned 17 feet off center, and the tilt was increasing year by year. Italy's appeal produced no good answers until 1999, when successful restoration began.

1973 Motivated by a long history of violated treaties, mistreatment, and discrimination, 200 members of the American Indian Movement occupy the small South Dakota town of Wounded Knee, site of an infamous 1890 massacre of Sioux Indians by the U.S. Army.

1991 With all objectives met in the Gulf War against Iraq, U.S. president George H. Bush announces a cease-fire would take effect just 100 hours after the ground war began.

1994 Astronomer Alexander Wolszcan of Pennsylvania State University confirms the existence of two planets orbiting a star 1,300 light-years from Earth.

Members of the National Woman's Party

Wounded Knee protestors

54 B.C. Julius Caesar's term as a Roman consul ends in the midst of his triumphant conquest of Gaul.

1638 Scots sign the National Covenant, which denounces attempts by King Charles I to force English liturgical practices upon the Scottish church.

Charles I, wife Henrietta, and their children

1646 Massachusetts Puritans put Roger Scott on trial for falling asleep in church.

1749 British novelist Henry Fielding publishes his rollicking and monumental tale *The History of Tom Jones, a Foundling.*

1803 The U.S. Congress approves President Thomas Jefferson's plan for an overland expedition to the Pacific and appropriates $2,500 to cover expenses for what became known as the Lewis and Clark Expedition.

1844 During a Potomac River cruise aboard the U.S. Navy's new steamship *Princeton,* Secretary of State Abel Upshur and several others are killed when the ship's 12-inch cannon explodes during a firing demonstration. President John Tyler was also on board, but escaped injury.

MILESTONE

Common Currency
On this day in 2002, the Euro becomes the sole currency for 12 members of the European Union: Germany, France, Italy, Spain, Portugal, Belgium, Luxembourg, the Netherlands, Austria, Finland, Greece, and Ireland. Their national currencies, among them the French franc, the Deutschmark, and the Greek drachma, cease to exist. Three E.U. countries have yet to adopt the Euro—the United Kingdom, which opted out of the process when it first became E.U. policy in 1991; Denmark, whose voters rejected joining in a 2000 referendum; and Sweden, whose economy has not met the conditions for entry. The Euro came into existence in electronic form on January 1, 1999, and notes and coins were first issued three years later.

1847 During the Mexican-American War, U.S. troops under Colonel Alexander Doniphan win the Battle of Sacramento and occupy Chihuahua.

1859 The Arkansas legislature votes to exile free blacks from the state.

1861 The U.S. Congress creates the Colorado Territory, which during the previous three years had become a major producer of gold and silver.

1864 In the American Civil War, the Union launches a major cavalry raid, sending 3,500 men through Virginia to free federal prisoners and spread the word about President Abraham Lincoln's offer of amnesty to any Confederate who would give up the fight. The raid was repulsed and 335 Union troops were killed.

1893 American inventor Edward G. Acheson patents silicon carbide, a highly effective synthetic abrasive with a hardness approaching that of diamonds.

1900 During the Boer War, British general Sir Redvers Buller breaks the 119-day siege of Ladysmith, South Africa.

1928 The Soviet government sets up a 14,200-square-mile Jewish district in Eastern

> *"If people don't like Marxism, they should blame the British Museum."*
>
> —Mikhail Gorbachev

Siberia to be used as a buffer against China. Most of the area was uninhabitable.

1932 Ford Motor Company produces the last Model A, ending a five-year production run that put about five million Model As on America's highways. With a 40-horsepower engine and a self-starter, the cars had a base price of $460.

1940 The American epic film *Gone with the Wind* nearly sweeps the Oscars, winning awards for best picture, director, actress, and supporting actress.

1942 Japanese troops invade Java during World War II, landing at three points and rapidly expanding their beachheads.

1944 During World War II, Hannah Reitsch, ardent Nazi and the world's first female test pilot, suggests to Adolf Hitler that Germany establish a squad of suicide bombers who would guide specially designed versions of the V-1 rocket onto their targets.

1982 After years of legal wrangling, the J. Paul Getty Museum in Malibu, California, receives a $1.2 billion bequest from its late founder, making it the most richly endowed museum in the world.

1987 Soviet leader Mikhail Gorbachev indicates that his nation is ready to sign a treaty that would eliminate all U.S. and Soviet medium-range nuclear missiles from Europe.

1993 Ten people die in a Waco, Texas, gun battle as agents of the U.S. Treasury Department's Bureau of Alcohol, Tobacco, and Firearms (ATF) raid the compound of the Branch Davidians, a Christian cult. Six Davidians and four ATF agents were killed. David Koresh, the cult's founder, is among the wounded.

1994 In the first combat engagement of NATO's 45-year history, NATO jets shoot down four Serbian warplanes in the no-fly zone over Bosnia.

1997 A 6.1-magnitude earthquake kills 965 people in the border region of Armenia, Azerbaijan, and Iran.

1998 The U.S. military test-flies the Global Hawk unmanned reconnaissance aircraft, which could fly 13,500 nautical miles and remain aloft for 40 hours.

Iranian President Ali Akbar Hashemi Rafsanjani visits earthquake damage

Christopher Columbus

992 Saint Oswald, archbishop of York, a leading force in monastic reform and founder of several Benedictine monasteries, dies in Worcester, England.

1212 Honen, a Buddhist priest and founder of Japan's Pure Land sect, dies in Kyoto.

1288 A Scottish law takes effect allowing women to propose marriage to men on February 29 and requiring men to pay fines if they refuse.

1504 Italian explorer Christopher Columbus, marooned in Jamaica with a mutinous crew during his fourth voyage to the New World, uses a lunar eclipse to frighten the natives into providing food. Columbus, who knew that European astronomers had predicted an eclipse that night, told them the moon would lose its light because they had refused to share food.

1528 Scottish Protestant Patrick Hamilton is burned at the stake for heresy, making him the first martyr of the Scottish Reformation. The 24-year-old Hamilton had spent time with Martin Luther and William Tyndale and had begun promoting the Reformation in Scotland.

MILESTONE

U.S. Civil Rights

On this day in 1968, the Kerner Commission, a government board set up to investigate civil disorder in the U.S., blames 1960s riots on white racism and warns of further racial polarization and violence unless drastic and costly remedies are undertaken. The report, which declared that "our nation is moving toward two societies, one black, one white—separate and unequal," called for expanded aid to African-American communities in order to prevent further racial violence and polarization. Unless drastic and costly remedies were undertaken at once, the report said, there would be "continuing polarization of the American community and, ultimately, the destruction of basic democratic values."

White racism

1704 In the bloodiest American event of Queen Anne's War, a combined force of French and Native Americans raid Deerfield, Massachusetts, killing 56 men, women, and children, capturing 109, and burning half the town.

1864 In the American Civil War, Union naval lieutenant William B. Cushing leads a landing party into Smithville, North Carolina, to capture Confederate brigadier general Louis Hebert. Finding the general absent for the night, Cushing left a note: "I deeply regret that you were not here when I called."

1880 After eight years of underground work, crews complete the nine-mile St. Gotthard Tunnel through the Alps, linking Milan, Italy, with Lucerne, Switzerland.

1908 Dutch scientists produce helium in solid form.

1920 Czechoslovakia's National Assembly passes a constitution establishing a democratic republic.

1920 Hungary, a newly independent nation since the break-up of the Austro-Hungarian empire, becomes a monarchy again as Miklos Horthy overthrows the communist government and establishes himself as regent. The following month he dissolved parliament, ruling as a dictator until 1944.

> *"Poetry makes things happen, but rarely what the poet wants."*
>
> —Howard Nemerov

Jungle fighting in the southwest Pacific

gering a tidal wave and touching off fires.

1960 The world's first Playboy Club, featuring shapely young women in revealing bunny costumes, opens its doors in Chicago, Illinois. About 40 other such clubs would be established throughout the world.

1972 As the Vietnam War winds down, South Korea pulls 11,000 of its roughly 48,000 combat troops out of South Vietnam.

1988 Black South African archbishop Desmond Tutu is arrested for demonstrating against the apartheid regime outside the parliament building.

1988 A Nazi document is discovered that implicates Kurt Waldheim, Austrian president and former U.N. secretary general, in World War II deportations of Jews.

1996 A jetliner crashes into a mountain near Arequipa, Peru, killing all 123 passengers.

1936 German physicist Niels Bohr publishes his "bowl of balls" explanation to describe the behavior of particles bombarding a nucleus, in the British journal *Nature*.

1936 The Japanese government puts down a three-day army revolt in Tokyo that had led to the assassinations of several leading statesmen and an attempt on the life of the prime minister, Okada Keisuke.

1940 Nobel Prize winner Ernest O. Lawrence, an American physicist, skips the Stockholm festivities and gives his acceptance speech in Berkeley, California, so he can keep raising funds for his cyclotron research.

1944 As part of the Allied "island-hopping" campaign in the Pacific during World War II, American troops invade Los Negros in the Admiralty Islands northeast of Papua New Guinea.

1956 U.S. president Dwight D. Eisenhower announces that he will run for re-election.

1960 More than 12,000 people die when an earthquake strikes in Agadir, Morocco, trig-

Peruvian rescue workers searching for the crashed jetliner's "black box"

293 Roman emperor Diocletian forms a tetrarchy with Maximian, Constantius, and Galerius to rule the eastern and western divisions of the empire.

492 Pope Felix III, whose excommunication of the patriarch of Constantinople had triggered the 35-year Acacian Schism, dies in Rome.

1349 Riots break out in Worms, Germany, leading to the deaths of 420 Jews, the exile of many more, and the seizure of Jewish property.

1360 The young English author Geoffrey Chaucer, who later wrote *The Canterbury Tales*, is ransomed during the Hundred Years' War by King Edward III, who paid 16 pounds for his release.

1469 William Caxton, the first English printer, begins his laborious translation of *The Recuyell of the Historyes of Troye*, which would become the first book printed in English.

1510 Francisco de Almeida, explorer and the first viceroy of Portuguese India, is killed by natives in a skirmish at present-day Cape Town, South Africa, where his ship had stopped to take on fresh water.

1546 Protestant reformer George Wishart is burned at the stake on orders of David Beaton, the Roman Catholic archbishop of St. Andrews, England.

1633 George Herbert, the English religious poet, breathes his last in Wiltshire, England.

BORN ON THIS DAY

772
PO TJIU-I
Chinese poet and governor of Hang-tsjow

1810
FRÉDÉRIC CHOPIN
Polish pianist and composer (the *Barcarolle*, opus 60; the *Fantasia*, opus 49; the *Berceuse*, opus 57)

1864
REBECCA LEE
First African-American woman to get a medical degree

1904
GLENN MILLER
American musician and composer ("Moonlight Serenade")

1914
RALPH ELLISON
First African-American author to win the National Book Award (*The Invisible Man*)

1917
ROBERT LOWELL
American poet ("For the Union Dead"; "Near the Ocean"; "Notebook 1967–68")

1924
DEKE (DONALD) SLAYTON
American astronaut, one of the original seven Project Mercury crewmembers

1926
PETE ROZELLE
American commissioner of the National Football League (1960–89)

1930
BENNY POWELL
American jazz musician, trombonist with the Count Basie Orchestra and the *Merv Griffin Show* band

1944
ROGER DALTREY
English rock singer (The Who)

1954
RON HOWARD
American actor (*American Graffiti; Happy Days*) and director (*Cocoon; Apollo 13*)

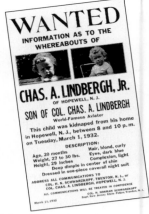

Lindbergh kidnapping poster

1815 After escaping from exile on the island of Elba, French general Napoleon Bonaparte lands in Cannes with 1,500 men and begins his march on Paris.

1864 French inventor Louis Ducos du Hauron patents (but does not build) a machine for making and projecting motion pictures.

1864 In the American Civil War, Ulysses S. Grant is given supreme command of all Union forces and promoted to lieutenant general, a rank previously attained only by George Washington.

1872 The world's first national park, Yellowstone, is established in the American West on account of its geysers, hot pools, and other geothermal curiosities.

1875 The U.S. Congress passes the last of the Force Acts, post–Civil War laws that protected the constitutional rights guaranteed African Americans through the 14th and 15th Amendments to the Constitution.

> *"All novels are about certain minorities: the individual is a minority."*
>
> —Ralph Ellison

1877 Jack McCall, the murderer of Old West legend Wild Bill Hickok, is hanged in Deadwood, South Dakota.

1896 At the Battle of Adwa, the Ethiopian army routs an Italian force of 14,500 and forces it into a disorderly retreat, thus checking Italy's colonial ambitions in Africa.

1917 The American press publishes the Zimmerman Telegram, a secret message from the German foreign minister that offered Mexico territory in the United States if Mexico sided with Germany in World War I. The telegram helped push the United States into the war.

1918 During World War I, Germany launches a massive offensive against Russia in order to force the Bolshevik government to agree on peace terms.

1932 The newborn son of American aviation hero Charles Lindbergh is abducted from the Lindbergh mansion in Hopewell, New Jersey, and a ransom note for $50,000 is left behind.

1937 American steelworkers represented by the Congress of Industrial Organizations sign their first union contract with U.S. Steel, winning a 40-hour work week, overtime pay, and a raise to $5 a day.

1941 Bulgaria signs the Tripartite Pact, which aligns that Balkan nation with Nazi Germany and the other Axis powers during World War II.

1954 Four Puerto Rican nationalists open fire from a visitors' gallery in the U.S. House of Representatives and wound five congressmen.

1966 The Soviet space probe *Venera 3* inadvertently collides with Venus, thus becoming the first spacecraft to reach the surface of another planet. The probe had been launched to analyze the Venusian atmosphere.

1971 A bomb explodes in a U.S. Senate bathroom, causing $300,000 in damage but injuring no one. A leftist radical group protesting the Vietnam War later claimed responsibility.

1975 The Japanese-made Honda Civic is introduced in the United States as an economical, gas-efficient alternative to large American cars.

1999 The *Breitling Orbiter 3* lifts off from Chateau d'Oex in Switzerland at the start of the world's first nonstop circumnavigation by balloon. The pilots were Brian Jones and Bertrand Piccard, grandson of August Piccard who set ballooning altitude records in the 1930s.

Peace Corps stamp

1975 Honda Civic

426 A total lunar eclipse is seen from Europe, prompting one chronicler to note that the moon had "turned into blood."

1127 Charles the Good, count of Flanders, who declined the crown of Jerusalem and refused to be nominated as Holy Roman emperor, is murdered at prayer in the church of St. Donat at Bruges.

1476 The Swiss Confederation routs Charles the Bold of Burgundy at the Battle of Grandson.

1498 Portuguese explorer Vasco da Gama reaches the island of Mozambique during his first voyage to India and learns that Arab merchant ships trade along the east coast of Africa.

MILESTONE

Congress Abolishes the African Slave Trade

On this day in 1807, the U.S. Congress passes an act to "prohibit the importation of slaves into any port or place within the jurisdiction of the United States . . . from any foreign kingdom, place, or country." As slave labor was not a crucial element of the northern economy, most northern states soon passed legislation to abolish slavery. However, in the South, the invention of the cotton gin made cotton a major industry and increased the demand for slaves. Some southern congressmen joined with the North in voting to abolish the slave trade, an act that became effective January 1, 1808.

"You can get help from teachers, but you are going to have to learn a lot by yourself, sitting alone in a room."

—Theodor Geisel (Dr. Seuss)

1714 German Baroque composer and organ master Johann Sebastian Bach becomes concertmaster at Weimar, a post requiring the 28-year-old to compose a new cantata every month.

1809 French emperor Napoleon Bonaparte officially adds the Italian region of Tuscany to his empire.

1861 In the American Civil War, controversial Union general John C. Fremont is relieved of command after declar-

Slave trade (milestone)

ing martial law and proclaiming freedom for all slaves in Missouri.

1877 Rutherford Birchard Hayes is declared the 19th president of the U.S. by an electoral commission. The electoral results of four states were disputed, and it is likely that both Republican and Democrat partisans had attempted to defraud the ballot. This is the only occasion on which a commission has been used to decide the result of a U.S. presidential election.

1896 In the first recognition of what would later be called radioactivity, French scientist Henri Becquerel reports his discovery of penetrating rays from a uranium compound.

1919 The Comintern, an association of national communist parties devoted to the promotion of world revolution, is founded in Russia. The body helped exert Soviet control over the international communist movement.

1927 American baseball legend Babe Ruth signs a three-year contract with the New York Yankees worth $210,000, making him the highest-paid player to that point in history.

1946 Ho Chi Minh is elected president of the Democratic Republic of Vietnam.

1949 A U.S. Air Force crew completes the first non-stop flight around the world, in an American B-50 Superfortress, which was refueled in flight several times.

1958 A 12-man British expedition, led by Dr. Vivian

Nicholas Leeson

Fuchs, completes the first land journey across Antarctica, traveling 2,500 miles in 99 days from the Filchner Ice Shelf to McMurdo Sound.

1960 Penguin Books, the publisher of an unexpurgated version of English author D. H. Lawrence's novel *Lady Chatterley's Lover*, is acquitted of obscenity charges.

1962 Basketball great Wilt "The Stilt" Chamberlain scores 100 points in the game between the Philadelphia Warriors and the New York Knicks.

1962 Burmese general Ne Win led a military coup replacing the elected government of premier U Nu. Ne dominated the government even after he yielded the presidency in 1982, until he relinquished his party chairmanship in 1988.

1995 German police arrest Nicholas Leeson, a financial trader whose concealed losses on the futures market of more than $1 billion led to the collapse of Barings PLC, Great Britain's oldest merchant bank.

1575 Indian Mughal emperor Akbar wins the decisive Battle of Tukaroi by scattering the army of the Afghan sultan of Bengal, Da'ud Khan.

1776 American naval forces make their first amphibious landing in history, on New Providence Island in the Bahamas, in order to capture ordnance and gunpowder for the Revolutionary War.

1803 German composer Ludwig van Beethoven publishes "Moonlight Sonata."

1820 The U.S. Congress averts civil war, for the time being, by passing the Missouri Compromise, which admits Missouri as a state without restrictions on slavery in exchange for bringing in Maine as a free state.

1859 At the largest recorded slave auction in American history, 400 men, women, and children are sold to pay off the gambling debts of their owner, Pierce M. Butler.

1861 Russian emperor Alexander II, convinced that radical social reform is needed for his country to compete with the West, frees the serfs of the Russian Empire.

1863 During the American Civil War, Congress passes a conscription act that produces America's first wartime draft. It covered all males between the ages of 20 and 45, but draftees could buy exemptions for $300 or find substitutes.

1865 The United States establishes the Freedmen's

BORN ON THIS DAY

1831
GEORGE M. PULLMAN
American inventor of the railway sleeping car

1838
GEORGE W. HILL
American astronomer

1845
GEORG CANTOR
German mathematician

1847
ALEXANDER GRAHAM BELL
American inventor of the telephone

1867
GUSTAV STRUBE
German composer, one of the first conductors of the Boston Pops

1911
JEAN HARLOW
American actress (Goldie; Hell's Angels; Dinner at Eight)

1920
JAMES DOOHAN
Canadian actor (Star Trek)

1953
ALEKSANDR VIKTOROVICH BORODIN
Russian cosmonaut

1962
JACKIE JOYNER-KERSEE
American track and field athlete, Olympic gold medalist

Bureau to help freed blacks make the transition from slavery to freedom by providing them with relief, medical care, education, and land.

1873 The Comstock Law takes effect in the United States, making it illegal to send any "obscene, lewd, or lascivious" material through the mail.

1887 American tutor Anne Sullivan begins teaching six-year-old Helen Keller, who had lost her sight and hearing after a severe illness at the age of 19 months.

1903 In a shift in U.S. immigration policy, the Congress passes a bill aimed at reducing the number of people settling in the country. The bill introduced a two dollar head tax on aliens arriving in U.S. ports, and sought to exclude certain classes of people, including "anarchists, or persons who believe in, or advocate, the overthrow by force or violence of the government of the United States."

1913 As thousands of woman suffrage supporters march past a huge crowd in

Helen Keller and Anne Sullivan

Washington, D.C., onlookers attack the marchers, injuring 200.

1918 With German troops advancing on St. Petersburg during World War II, the Bolshevik government of Russia signs the Treaty of Brest-Litovsk, thus ending hostilities with the Central Powers. The treaty removed Finland, Poland, the Ukraine, and Baltic states from Russian control.

1924 The Turkish Republic exiles the Ottoman sultan Abdulmecid and abolishes the title of caliph, in use by Muslim leaders since Muhammad's death in 632.

1931 Francis Scott Key's patriotic hymn "The Star-Spangled Banner" becomes the official national anthem of the United States.

1932 Italian automotive legend Alfieri Maserati dies at age 44 from complications from injuries he received during a 1927 auto-racing crash.

1934 Notorious American bank robber John Dillinger escapes from prison in Indiana by threatening guards with a fake pistol. As he left, he sang, "I'm heading for the last roundup."

1952 The U.S. Supreme Court allows the state of New York to prohibit communists from teaching in its public schools.

1971 The U.S. Fifth Special Forces Group, the Green Berets, withdraw from South Vietnam after years of training guerrillas and overseeing counterinsurgency operations during the Vietnam War.

1991 A bystander videotapes an all-white squad of Los Angeles police officers beating Rodney King, an African American the police had chased down for a traffic offense. Riots followed when the tape was broadcast.

1993 American microbiologist Albert Bruce Sabin, developer of the first oral vaccine for polio, dies in Washington, D.C. His live vaccine was easier to administer and provided longer protection than Jonas Salk's killed, injected vaccine.

1998 Flash floods in Baluchistan, Pakistan, kill as many as 1,800 people and leave 25,000 homeless.

Pakistan flash flood survivors

581 Having ousted the Chous from the Chinese throne, Wen-ti holds his first imperial audience and founds the Sui dynasty.

1386 Wladyslaw II is crowned king of Poland. He soon built his country into the leading power of eastern Europe.

1461 The first stage of England's Wars of the Roses comes to an end as Edward, earl of March, enters London and is hailed as the rightful king. The son of Richard, duke of York, he was the first of the Yorkist kings and brother of the notorious Richard III.

1675 English religious thinker and writer John Bunyan is imprisoned for preaching without a license. While in prison, he wrote *Pilgrim's Progress*, one of the spiritual classics of the age.

1681 King Charles II of England grants William Penn the American province of Pennsylvania as a place where Penn's fellow Quakers would be free to worship.

MILESTONE

FDR Inaugurated

On this day in 1933, at the height of the Great Depression, Franklin Delano Roosevelt is inaugurated as the 32nd president of the United States. In his famous inaugural address, delivered outside of the U.S. Capitol, Roosevelt outlined his New Deal—an expansion of the federal government as an instrument of employment opportunity and welfare—and told Americans, "the only thing we have to fear is fear itself." He delivered a speech that radiated optimism and competence. A broad majority of Americans united behind Roosevelt and his radical economic proposals to lead the nation out of the Great Depression.

Franklin Delano Roosevelt

1776 During the American Revolutionary War, American general George Washington seizes and places cannons upon strategic Dorchester Heights in British-occupied Boston, Massachusetts. The move soon forced the British to evacuate the city and its harbor.

1789 The first session of the U.S. Congress opens in New York City, as the nation's new Constitution takes effect. Only 22 of the 81 senators and representatives attend.

1793 During the French Revolution, riots break out in Cholet in the west of France and touch off a counterrevolutionary insurrection that sweeps the Vendée region.

1840 The world's first commercial photography studio opens in New York City, offering to make Daguerreotype portraits.

1861 On the brink of the American Civil War, Abraham Lincoln is inaugurated as the 16th U.S. president. "In your hand, my fellow countrymen," he said, "and not in mine, is the momentous issue of civil war."

1887 German automotive pioneer Gottlieb Daimler tests his first four-wheel motor vehicle, which has a one-cylinder engine and a top speed of 10 miles per hour.

William Penn (holding paper) standing and facing King Charles II

> *"Repetition does not transform a lie into a truth."*
>
> —*Franklin D. Roosevelt*

1890 A Scottish landmark is born as the Forth Railway Bridge, crossing the Firth of Forth to the north of Edinburgh, opened by the Prince of Wales. The 1.5-mile cantilever bridge was designed by engineers Sir John Fowler and Benjamin Baker.

1902 The American Automobile Association is founded to address the problems that commonly plague motorists.

1941 During World War II, British navy commandos raid a German outpost in the Lofoten Islands off the coast of Norway and damage an armed German trawler. Operation Claymore boosted British public morale but failed in its principal objective: the capture of an Enigma decoding machine.

1944 American gangster Louis "Lepke" Buchalter, head of Murder, Inc., and the leader of America's largest crime syndicate during the 1930s, is executed at Sing Sing Prison in New York.

1944 During World War II, U.S. Air Force bombers attempt the first American night bombing raid of the German capital of Berlin. Though few planes were lost to German defenses, all but one dropped their loads elsewhere.

1952 American novelist Ernest Hemingway completes *The Old Man and the Sea* and describes it as the best writing he has ever done.

1954 U.S. secretary of state John Foster Dulles pressures the leftist government of Guatemala by warning that "international communism" has made inroads in the Western Hemisphere and asking Latin American nations to condemn the danger.

1960 American operatic baritone Leonard Warren dies onstage during a performance of Verdi's *La Forza del Destino* (*The Power of Destiny*).

1962 The American Atomic Energy Commission announces that the U.S. Navy is operating Antarctica's first atomic power plant, built in just three months from prefabricated parts.

1968 U.S. president Lyndon B. Johnson's Ad Hoc Task Force on the Vietnam War backs off from another major esclation of the Vietnam War by advising against the Pentagon's request for more than 200,000 additional troops.

1980 Robert Mugabe, leader of the Zimbabwe African National Union Patriotic Front (Zanu PF), is elected first prime minister of the new state of Zimbabwe.

1997 Explosions in three interconnected Chinese coal mines kill 86 miners and injure 12.

Ernest Hemingway

1179 Pope Alexander III convenes the Third Lateran Council, which gave the college of cardinals the exclusive right to elect future popes.

1328 In Navarre, France, a Catholic friar incites anti-Jewish riots in which virtually all of the city's 6,000 Jews are murdered and their homes pillaged and destroyed.

1496 English king Henry VII authorizes the Italian sailor John Cabot (Giovanni Caboto) to explore the New World on behalf of England. Cabot sailed to Newfoundland in 1497.

1590 Danish astronomer Tycho Brahe discovers a comet in the Pisces constellation.

1616 A Roman Catholic decree declares the Copernican theory "false and erroneous" and prohibits anyone from teaching or believing that the Earth orbits the sun.

1750 A Shakespearean play, *Richard III,* is staged for the first time in America, in New York City.

1770 British troops guarding the Customs House in Boston, Massachusetts, open fire on a mob of protesters, killing five in what became known as the Boston Massacre. On the same day, Great Britain repealed most of the hated Townshend Acts and ordered the removal of troops from Boston.

1798 French forces under Napoleon invade Switzerland and occupy Bern, thus smashing the ancient Swiss Confederation of the Thirteen Cantons.

BORN ON THIS DAY

1574
WILLIAM OUGHTRED
English mathematician and inventor of the slide rule

1637
JOHN VAN DER HEYDEN
Dutch painter and inventor of the fire extinguisher

1824
JAMES MERRITT IVES
American lithographer (Currier & Ives)

1897
SOONG MEI-LING
Wife of Chinese leader Chiang Kai-shek

Soong Mei-ling

1908
REX HARRISON
English actor (*Blythe Spirit; My Fair Lady*)

1935
PHILIP K. CHAPMAN
Australian astronaut

1939
SAMANTHA EGGAR
English actress (*The Collector; Walk, Don't Run; The Molly Maguires*)

1958
ANDY GIBB
English rock musician

1966
MICHAEL IRVIN
American professional football player

1972
BRIAN GRANT
American professional basketball player

Boston Massacre

1811 The French army begins an evacuation of Portugal, harried continuously by English and Portuguese attacks.

1827 Alessandro Volta, Italian inventor of the first electric battery, dies in Como, Italy.

1830 Limelight is demonstrated in a scientific trial at the Tower of London in England. The innovation, which used jets of oxygen to heat lime to incandescence, was used in lighthouses and theaters.

1839 English author Charlotte Brontë, 23, turns down a marriage proposal from the Reverend Henry Nussey, telling him that she is too "romantic and eccentric" to be a clergyman's wife. Eight years later she wrote her classic Victorian novel *Jane Eyre.*

1864 In the American Civil War, Confederate general John C. Breckinridge takes command of southern forces in the Appalachian Mountains of western Virginia.

1868 C. H. Gould, of Birmingham, England, patents the stapler.

> *"Courage is the first of human qualities because it is the quality which guarantees all others."*
>
> —*Winston Churchill*

1872 American inventor George Westinghouse patents the railroad air brake.

1875 The state of Wisconsin officially begins a search for a motorized wagon by offering a $10,000 reward to anyone who can supply "a cheap and practical substitute" for the horse and wagon.

1915 During World War I, British warships bombard the Turkish port of Smyrna.

1922 American sharpshooter Annie Oakley breaks all existing records in women's trap shooting by blasting 98 of 100 clay targets, at the Pinehurst Gun Club in North Carolina.

1929 Colonel Victor Barker, apparently a decorated World War I soldier, is arrested in Great Britain for bankruptcy. On being strip-searched at Brixton prison, he is found to be a woman, Valerie Lilias Arkell-Smith.

1933 The Nazi Party polls just 43.9 percent of the vote in German legislative elections despite a decree suspending all guarantees of freedom and a violent campaign against Nazi opponents.

1933 On his first full day in office, U.S. president Franklin D. Roosevelt declares a four-day "bank holiday," which closed the nation's banks, thus halting a frantic run on the banks and giving FDR time to push the Emergency Banking Act through Congress.

1936 Great Britain flight-tests its new fighter plane, the *Spitfire*, for the first time, at Eastleigh aerodrome, in Southampton.

1946 Former British prime minister Winston Churchill makes his famous "Iron Curtain" speech, which condemned the Soviet Union's policies in Europe and is considered one of the opening volleys of the Cold War.

1970 The Nuclear Nonproliferation Treaty, signed by 45 nations including the major nuclear powers, comes into force.

1971 The United States withdraws the Eleventh Armored Cavalry Regiment from Vietnam, where it had fought during the Vietnam War since 1966.

British Spitfire fighter planes

1239 James I of Aragon issues an edict that validates the privileges of the Jews of Aragon, and also forbids all harassment of Jews except for proven financial debt.

1447 Saint Colette, who reformed the order of the Poor Clares, dies in Ghent, Belgium.

1665 Britain's Royal Society publishes the first issue of *Philosophical Transactions of the Royal Society*, which would become the world's oldest continuing periodical.

1835 English philosopher John Stuart Mill gives his friend, the historian Thomas Carlyle, some bad news: Mill's maid had burned Carlyle's manuscript of *The French Revolution*, which Mill had borrowed to read. Carlyle had already disposed of his notes.

1836 In the Texas war for independence, Mexican troops overrun the Alamo in San Antonio after besieging the fiercely defended outpost for 13 days. Nearly all of the 184 Texan defenders were killed, but they inflicted heavy casualties on the Mexicans and

Alamo under attack

M I L E S T O N E

Aspirin Is Patented in Germany

What will become one of the most common drugs in household medicine cabinets is patented on this day in 1899. Aspirin was originally the trade name given by German pharmaceutical company Bayer to acetylsalicylic acid. The success of the drug, together with a ruling after World War I that forced Bayer to give up the trademark, led to aspirin becoming the universal name. The drug is derived from a chemical found in the bark of willow trees, which had been known for its pain relieving properties for centuries. A purified form of the active ingredient, salicylic acid, had been known since the 1830s, but it was very unpleasant to take and damaging to the stomach. French chemist Charles Frederic Gerhardt had created what was probably aspirin in 1853, but did not market or patent it. In 1897, Bayer employee Felix Hoffman found a way to create a stable form of the drug, which he gave to his father to ease his arthritis. Aspirin is still used to treat mild arthritic inflammation today.

"Let no one till his death be called unhappy. Measure not the work until the day's out and the labor done."

—*Elizabeth Barrett Browning*

bought time for Sam Houston to defend the rest of Texas.

1857 At the end of an eleven-year legal battle, Dred Scott, a slave from Missouri in the United States, is told that he must remain a slave. He and his wife had filed a suit for their freedom, but the U.S. Supreme Court issued a clear victory for slave-holding southern states by ruling that Congress and territorial governments were powerless to exclude slavery from American territories. The case added significantly to the tension that led to the American Civil War four years later.

1886 Some 9,000 members of the Knights of Labor strike Jay Gould's Southwestern Railroad system, halting service along 5,000 miles of American track and impeding the nation's transcoastal trade.

1896 Charles Brady King drives the first automobile to appear on the streets of Detroit, Michigan, later known as Motor City. When King's car broke down, a passerby told him to get a horse.

1898 Italian left-wing journalist and political leader Felice Cavallotti, sometimes called Italy's "Poet of the Democracy," dies in a duel fought against a Venice newspaper editor.

Biosphere 2 sits in the desert near Oracle, Arizona

1913 Danish physicist Niels Bohr writes the first of his three historic papers describing his ideas on atomic structure.

1913 The word "jazz" appears in print for the first time in a sports report in the *San Francisco Bulletin,* describing the energy of a baseball player.

1915 Dario Resta of Italy, driving a Peugeot, wins the tenth Vanderbilt Cup Race at the Pan-Pacific International Speedway in San Francisco, California.

1930 The first individually packaged frozen foods go on sale in Springfield, Massachusetts.

1933 Anton Cermak, the mayor of Chicago, Illinois, dies from wounds he sustained several days earlier in an assassination attempt on President-elect Franklin D. Roosevelt.

1945 During World War II, Dutch resistance fighters in Apeldoorn, Holland, hijack a truck filled with food for the German army and unwittingly shoot Lieutenant General Hanns Rauter, an SS officer. Rauter lived, and the special police force executed 263 Dutchmen in retaliation for the attack.

1946 Vietnamese president Ho Chi Minh signs an agreement with France recognizing Vietnam as a "free state with its own government, army, and finances," but integrated into a French Union.

1951 The espionage trial of Americans Julius and Ethel Rosenberg, accused of selling atomic secrets to the Soviet Union, opens in New York.

1964 American heavyweight boxing champion Cassius Clay changes his name to Muhammad Ali.

1965 At the reluctant invitation of the South Vietnamese government, the United States sends 3,500 Marine combat troops to Vietnam in order to secure the air base at Da Nang during the Vietnam War.

1994 A group of seven people from five countries enter *Biosphere 2,* a glass-enclosed ecosystem in Arizona, to begin a study in self-contained living.

161 Roman emperor Antoninus Pius, fourth of the "five good emperors," dies after a 23-year reign of peace and prosperity.

1080 During the Investiture Controversy, a protracted struggle for supremacy between the papacy and the Holy Roman emperors, Pope Gregory VII excommunicates and deposes the Holy Roman emperor, Henry IV, for the second time.

1274 Italian thinker Thomas Aquinas, later canonized and regarded as the Roman Catholic Church's foremost Western philosopher and theologian, dies in Fossanova.

1778 English explorer Captain James Cook sights the coast of Oregon, at Yaquina Bay.

1808 The Portuguese royal family, forced into exile by Napoleon's 1807 invasion, arrives in Rio de Janeiro, Brazil, under the protection of the British fleet.

1820 British astronomers and mathematicians found the Royal Astronomical Society in London in order to promote celestial research.

1862 During the American Civil War, the Battle of Pea Ridge (Elkhorn Tavern) opens in Arkansas and ends the following day in a decisive Union victory that would help secure the Mississippi Valley. The Union lost 1,384 men; the Confederates, 2,000.

1876 American inventor Alexander Graham Bell receives his patent for the telephone,

---

The Battle of Pea Ridge

---

which describes not only the instrument, but also the idea of a telephone system.

1897 Dr. John Kellogg serves the world's first cornflakes to mental patients in Battle Creek, Michigan.

1903 English auto buff (and later manufacturer) C.S. Rolls sets a new speed record, 84.84 miles per hour, while driving downhill with a tailwind.

1911 American inventor Willis Farnsworth patents the first coin-operated locker.

1916 Two German manufacturers merge their companies to form the Bayerische Motoren-Werke, or BMW, to make aircraft engines. The company built its first motorcycle in 1923 and its first car in 1929.

1918 During World War I, German air raids on the English counties of Kent, Essex, Hertfordshire, Bedfordshire, and London kill 23 and injure 39.

1926 The first successful transatlantic wireless telephone conversation takes place, between New York and London.

Chancellor Adolf Hitler, left, reviews troops at Cologne, Germany, in the Rhineland

1932 Four labor protesters are shot to death by private security forces outside Ford Motor Company's River Rouge plant in Detroit.

1933 The board game "Monopoly" is trademarked by American businessman Charles Darrow, of Atlantic City, New Jersey.

1936 In the most important turning point of the interwar years, Adolf Hitler sends 22,000 troops into the Rhineland. Hitler was prepared to beat a hasty retreat, but France, Britain, and Italy did nothing.

1939 In the Spanish Civil War, fighting breaks out in Madrid between communist and anticommunist factions while the Republican Army continues to melt away.

1941 During World War II, British and Australian troops from North Africa land in Greece to occupy the Olympus-

Vermion line and to support the Greek Army in its repulse of Benito Mussolini's short-lived invasion of the country.

1945 American armored troops under General George Patton capture Cologne, cross the Rhine River, and establish the first World War II Allied bridgehead on the east bank of the river, at Remagen.

1960 An American aircraft carrier in the Pacific rescues four Russian soldiers who had been drifting for 49 days in a 50-foot landing craft.

1972 During the Vietnam War, U.S. jets fight five North Vietnamese MiGs and shoot one down during the largest air battle in the region in three years.

1973 Bangladesh, having survived a brutal war with Pakistan that killed a million of its people, elects its first democratic leader, Sheikh Mujib Rahman, in a landslide.

1982 At the top of the American music charts: "Who Can it Be Now?" by Men at Work; "Up Where We Belong" by Joe Cocker and Jennifer Warnes; and "Somebody's Baby," by Jackson Browne.

> *"The nation that secures control of the air will ultimately control the world."*
>
> —*Alexander Graham Bell*

🔬 **1618** German astronomer Johannes Kepler works out his famous third, or harmonic, law of planetary motion.

🏴 **1702** English king William III dies following a fall caused by his horse stumbling on a molehill.

🔬 **1775** English chemist Joseph Priestley, the discoverer of oxygen, begins suffocating mice at his home laboratory to determine whether the gas is necessary to support life.

🇺🇸 **1796** For the first time, the U.S. Supreme Court issues a ruling on whether congressional legislation is constitutional. It declares, in *Hylton v. United States*, that the carriage tax is constitutional.

💥 **1801** During the Napoleonic Wars, combined British and Ottoman forces capture the strategic naval port of Abukir, in French-occupied Egypt. Great Britain lost 1,100 men in the amphibious operation.

🎭 **1839** French tenor Adolphe Nourrit, despondent over illnesses that ruined his voice, jumps to his death from a hotel room in Naples, Italy.

🏴 **1844** Oscar I ascends to the throne of Sweden and Norway as a progressive social reformer.

🇺🇸 **1857** Female garment workers in New York City protest for better pay and working conditions. Police halt the demonstration.

💥 **1862** In the American Civil War, the Confederate iron-

MILESTONE

Russian Revolution

This day in 1917 sees food riots and strikes erupt in Petrograd, triggering Russia's February Revolution (known as such because the country was still using the Julian calendar, under which the date was February 23). Unrest had been growing for some time, owing to the shortage and high price of food during World War I. Events had been brought to a head the day before, when workers at the Putilov ironworks were locked out after demanding higher wages. Czar Nicholas II attempted to force the Russian parliament, the Duma, to disband, but without success. A week later he abdicated, bringing to an end three centuries of rule by the Romanov family, and setting the stage for the Bolshevik Revolution later in the year.

"We should be eternally vigilant against attempts to check the expression of opinions that we loathe."

—*Oliver Wendell Holmes Jr.*

clad *Virginia* (better known as the *Merrimac*) attacks a Union fleet off Newport News, Virginia, sinking a wooden 50-gun frigate, running another aground, and destroying a wooden sloop.

⚖️ **1893** American outlaw Emmet Dalton, sole survivor of the Dalton Gang's disastrous attempt to rob two Kansas banks, begins serving a life sentence in the Kansas State Penitentiary.

🏴 **1912** In a telegram from Tasmania, Norwegian polar explorer Roald Amundsen announces to the world that he reached the South Pole on December 14, 1911.

💥 **1916** During World War I, a British attack on Dujaila Redoubt, a Turk-held fortress in Iraq, fails after the Turks inflict 3,500 casualties.

The sinking of the frigate Cumberland *by the ironclad* Merrimac

An Egyptian coast guardsman watches as a ship passes through the Suez Canal

1921 Spanish prime minister Eduardo Dato is assassinated in Madrid by an anarchist.

1931 Spaniard Domingo Ortega makes his first appearance as a matador. He would become one of Spain's most admired bullfighters.

1933 The American musical film *42nd Street* makes its premiere, with elaborate dance numbers choreographed by Busby Berkeley. Berkeley went on to choreograph more than two dozen films and direct more than 20.

1942 During World War II, Dutch forces surrender Java to the Japanese, ending nearly 400 years of Dutch colonial control over the East Indies. More than 100,000 Allied troops were made prisoners of war; many died in captivity.

1951 The state of New York executes Martha Beck and Raymond Fernandez, the "Lonely Hearts Killers," who had used newspaper personal ads to seduce, rob, and murder at least four women.

1957 Egypt reopens the Suez Canal following the Suez Crisis, which had led to an invasion and occupation of the canal region by British, French, and Israeli troops.

1965 During the Vietnam War, the United States lands 3,500 Marines on a beach near Da Nang, South Vietnam, in order to secure the city's airbase.

1969 Panamanian boxer Roberto Duran wins the first professional bout of his illustrious career. Duran would go on to claim the world lightweight, welterweight, junior middleweight, and middleweight crowns.

1973 During The Troubles that followed the Bloody Sunday shootings in Northern Ireland, the Irish Republican Army (IRA) begins its campaign of terrorist bombing against civilians in mainland Great Britain. Two car bombs explode in central London, killing one man and injuring 180 others. Another two bombs were safely defused after 10 members of the IRA team were arrested at Heathrow airport.

1976 A stony meteorite weighing 1,774 kilograms falls to Earth in Jilin, China, during a meteor shower that dropped more than 4,000 kilograms of space debris.

886 Albumazar, leading astrologer of the Muslim world, dies in Iraq. He predicted that the world would end when the seven known planets came into conjunction in the last degree of Pisces.

1074 Pope Gregory VII excommunicates all married priests.

1497 Polish astronomer Nicolaus Copernicus watches the moon eclipse Alpha Centauri, "the brightest star in the eye of the Bull," and later uses the observation to measure the moon's diameter.

1566 David Riccio, secretary and trusted advisor to Mary, Queen of Scots, is dragged from the queen's presence and stabbed to death, apparently with the connivance of the queen's deranged husband, Lord Darnley.

1698 Czar Peter the Great, one of Russia's greatest reformers, departs Moscow incognito on his Grand Embassy to western Europe. The trip was intended to strengthen anti-Turk alliances and to learn about the economic and cultural life of the West.

1796 French General Napoleon Bonaparte marries

MILESTONE

The Firebombing of Tokyo

On this day in 1945, U.S. warplanes launch a new bombing offensive against Japan, dropping 2,000 tons of incendiary bombs on Tokyo. Almost 16 square miles in and around the Japanese capital were incinerated and between 80,000 and 130,000 Japanese civilians were killed in the worst single firestorm in recorded history. Shitamachi was a neighborhood composed of roughly 750,000 people living in cramped quarters in wooden-frame buildings. Setting ablaze this paper city was a kind of experiment in the effects of firebombing; it would also destroy the light industries, called shadow factories, that produced prefabricated war materials destined for Japanese aircraft factories.

> *"I could have gone on flying through space forever."*
>
> —*Yuri Gagarin*

Josephine de Beauharnais in a civil ceremony at a hotel in Paris.

1822 Charles Graham of New York patents false teeth.

1831 French king Louis Philippe founds the French Foreign Legion, in part to rid France of foreigners.

1841 The U.S. Supreme Court frees the African slaves who had seized the slave ship *Amistad*, on the grounds that they had been illegally forced into slavery. The United States had abolished the African slave trade in 1807.

1847 In the Mexican-American War, some 10,000 U.S. soldiers make an amphibious landing near the fortified city of Vera Cruz without a single casualty.

USS Monitor, foreground, and CSS Merrimac (Virginia)

1862 The world's first battle between ironclad naval vessels ends in a draw after the Confederate steam frigate *Virginia* and the Union *Monitor* pound one another with cannon fire for four hours at Hampton Roads, Virginia, during the American Civil War.

1915 The British destroyer *Ariel* rams and sinks the German submarine *U12* in a World War I battle.

1916 During World War I, Germany declares war on Portugal. On the same day, the Italian army launches its fifth offensive along the Isonzo River, in an attempt to take pressure off the French at Verdun.

1917 Reacting to German U-boat attacks during World War I, U.S. president Woodrow Wilson orders the arming of merchant ships.

1917 Several hundred Mexican guerrillas under Pancho Villa raid the small border town of Columbus, New Mexico, and kill 17 Americans. U.S. cavalry pursued the raiders into Mexico, killing several dozen before turning back.

1918 French and British troops land at Murmansk, along Russia's Arctic shore, in order to support anti-Bolshevik "White" forces in the Russian Civil War.

1932 Henry Pu Yi, exiled emperor of China, becomes regent of the Japanese puppet state of Manchukuo, comprising Manchuria and the Chinese province of Rehe.

1938 American comedian Bob Hope makes his film debut, singing "Thanks for the Memories" in *The Big Broadcast of 1938*.

1942 Some 20,000 Allied troops in Java surrender to the Japanese during World War II.

1955 American teen idol James Dean makes his first appearance in a major film role in *East of Eden*.

1974 Japanese soldier Hiroo Onada, 51, finally gives up the fight after hiding out in the Philippines for 29 years after the end of World War II. He did not know the war was over.

Dante Alighieri

241 B.C. In the First Punic War, Roman naval forces defeat the Carthaginian fleet near the Aegusae Islands, leading to Carthage's cession of Sicily and other possessions.

1302 In Florence, Italy, poet Dante Alighieri is condemned in absentia to death by burning for crimes he did not commit. He survived, and the experience largely shaped his masterwork, *The Divine Comedy*.

1496 Italian-born Spanish explorer Christopher Columbus sets sail for Spain declaring that Cuba was in fact Cathay, hoping to gain support for a third voyage of conquest.

1762 French Huguenot Jean Calas, wrongly convicted of murdering his son, is tortured to death. The event inspired the philosopher Voltaire to lead a campaign for religious tolerance and legal reform.

1864 In Virginia City, Montana, local hell-raiser Jack Slade is hanged in one of the more troubling incidents of frontier vigilantism. Slade was guilty of nothing worse than drunken rowdiness. The vigilantes, who had hanged a series of genuine murderers, apparently

---

BORN ON THIS DAY

1452
FERDINAND II THE CATHOLIC
King of Aragon and Sicily

1787
WILLIAM ETTY
English painter (*Pandora Crowned by the Seasons; Youth on the Prow and Pleasure at the Helm*)

1845
ALEXANDER III
Russian Romanov czar
(1881–94)

Alexander III

1903
BIX BEIDERBECKE
American jazz musician ("In a Mist"; "Candlelight"; "Flashes"; "In the Dark")

1916
JAMES HERRIOT
English author (*All Creatures Great and Small*)

1940
CHUCK NORRIS
American actor and martial artist (*A Force of One; Firewalker; Sidekicks*)

1940
WAYNE DYER
American psychologist and author (*Your Erroneous Zones; You'll See It When You Believe It*)

1947
KIM CAMPBELL
First female prime minister of Canada

1958
SHARON STONE
American actress (*Basic Instinct; Casino; Last Dance*)

1977
SHANNON MILLER
American gymnast, Olympic gold medalist

---

let illegitimate power go to their heads.

1876 Discernible speech is transmitted for the first time over a telephone system when American inventor Alexander Graham Bell summons his assistant in another room by saying, "Mr. Watson, come here; I want you." Bell had received a comprehensive telephone patent just three days before.

1902 In the case of *Edison v. American Mutoscope Company*, a U.S. Court of Appeals rules that despite his claims, Thomas Edison did not invent the movie camera.

1908 The first Mother's Day is celebrated in the United States when Anna Jarvis of Grafton, West Virginia, holds a service of commemoration for her mother. The celebration is not related to the old religious festival of Mothering Sunday, held on the fourth Sunday in Lent.

1918 Warner Bros. releases its first film, *Four Years in Germany*. The American company failed to become a major player in the cinema world until 1927, when it released *The Jazz Singer*, the first feature with sound.

1922 Hindu religious leader Mohandas Karamchand Gandhi is arrested in India. Tried for sedition, and sentenced to six years in prison, he was

> *"Men are like steel. When they lose their temper, they lose their worth."*
>
> —*Chuck Norris*

released after two years. He later became known as Mahatma, meaning "Great Soul."

1923 Soviet premier Vladimir Ilich Lenin suffers a stroke, loses the ability to speak, and ceases political activity. He died after other strokes on January 21, 1924.

1926 In the United States, the first Book-of-the-Month Club selection is published by Viking Press: *Lolly Willowes, or The Loving Huntsman*, by English novelist, poet, and short-story writer Sylvia Townsend Warner.

1938 For the first time since the American Academy Awards (Oscars) began in 1927, the winners' names are kept secret until their announcement at the gala ceremony.

1938 The American film *Jezebel* opens, and marks a breakthrough for Bette Davis, whose portrayal of a hot-tempered southern belle would win her an Oscar for Best Actress.

1945 U.S. troops land at Zamboanga on Mindanao Island, in the Allied campaign to retake the Philippines during World War II.

1952 General Fulgencio Batista overthrows the Cuban government. Within a year, Fidel Castro began organizing the revolution that would end in Batista's ouster in 1959.

1956 At Royal Naval Air Station Ford, near Chichester in England, pilot Peter Twiss shatters the previous air-speed flying record, pushing the limit by 310 miles per hour to 1132.13 mph in a Fairey Delta Two Turbojet. Fewer than 50 years earlier, the first air-speed record was set at 25.65 mph.

1964 The first Ford Mustang is produced, although the sporty little American car wouldn't be released to the public until April 16. An enormous success, it brought in over a billion dollars in its first two years.

The Dalai Lama (aboard white horse) in the Himalayas, pursued by Red Chinese troops (milestone)

105 In China, paper is invented by Tsai Lun, an official of the Han dynasty. He developed a process for converting vegetable fibers to sheets of paper.

1669 Italy's Mount Etna begins its most violent recorded eruption, throwing out nearly a million cubic yards of ash and lava over a four-month period.

1702 Britain's first regular daily newspaper, *The Daily Courant* is published in London by Mr. E. Mallet. The paper runs to just a single side of a single sheet. Its offices were in the Fleet Street area of London, which remained the heart of the British newspaper industry until the 1980s.

1744 In London, England, Samuel Baker holds his first auction of books from a private library, thus establishing the Sotheby's auction business.

1811 In England, laborers displaced by new textile machinery attack the devices they blame for their misery. Taking its name from Ned Ludd, a young man from Leicester who is thought to have smashed machinery that was replacing workers in 1799, the Luddite movement was sparked by unemployment, hard times, and failing hope. The term Luddite has since

> *"Humans are not proud of their ancestors, and rarely invite them round to dinner."*
>
> —Douglas Adams

1811
URBAIN JEAN JOSEPH LE VERRIER
French astronomer who co-discovered Neptune

1846
ANTÓNIO C. G. CRESPO
Brazilian poet

1885
MALCOLM CAMPBELL
English auto racer who was the first to travel five miles per minute

Malcolm Campbell

1903
LAWRENCE WELK
American bandleader and television producer (*The Lawrence Welk Show*)

1926
RALPH ABERNATHY
American minister and civil rights leader

1931
RUPERT MURDOCH
Australian-born British media mogul

1934
SAM DONALDSON
American television news journalist

1950
BOBBY McFERRIN
American singer ("Don't Worry Be Happy")

1952
DOUGLAS ADAMS
English author (*The Hitchhiker's Guide to the Galaxy*)

1969
DAN LACROIX
Canadian professional hockey player

Confederate states five cent stamp

come to refer to anyone who dislikes or resists new technology.

1818 *Frankenstein; or, The Modern Prometheus,* by 21-year-old English author Mary Wollstonecraft Shelley, is published. The book, in which a scientist animates a creature constructed from dismembered corpses, is often called the world's first science-fiction novel.

1861 In Montgomery, Alabama, delegates from South Carolina, Mississippi, Florida, Alabama, Georgia, Louisiana, and Texas adopt the Permanent Constitution of the Confederate States of America. Closely modeled on the U.S. Constitution, it guaranteed the continuation of slavery, and effectively established the Confederate states as a separate nation with their own federal government and president. The first battle of the American Civil War followed a month and a day later.

1917 During World War I, British forces occupy Baghdad, then part of the Ottoman Empire. Baghdad would become the capital of Iraq when the nation was created in 1920. British rule continued until 1932.

1917 In Petrograd (St. Petersburg), Russia, disorder erupts in the midst of a general

American and Filipino soldiers surrender to the Japanese on Corregidor island

strike, and the czar's government loses control. Four days later, the czar abdicated.

1918 Spanish flu hits the United States. Unusually dangerous, the virus would kill more than 600,000 Americans, and some 40 million people worldwide.

1927 The Flatheads Gang stages the first armored truck holdup in U.S. history, near Pittsburgh, Pennsylvania. The armored truck, carrying $104,250 of payroll money for the Pittsburgh Terminal Coal Company, blew up when it hit a land mine planted by the bandits. Five guards were badly injured.

1942 Under orders from President Franklin D. Roosevelt, U.S. general Douglas MacArthur abandons the island fortress of Corregidor during World War II. Left behind at Corregidor and on the Bataan Peninsula were 90,000 American and Filipino troops, who, lacking food, supplies, and support, would soon succumb to the Japanese offensive.

1960 *Pioneer V* is launched from Cape Canaveral,

Florida. The first of its kind, the beachball-sized space probe orbited the sun and relayed scientific data for about three months.

1970 Iraq's Baath government proclaims the Manifesto of March 11, which promises self-rule to the country's Kurdish minority.

1971 Papua New Guinea adopts its national flag in preparation for independence from Australia, which would come on September 16, 1975.

1981 Guatemala, British Honduras, and Great Britain reach a preliminary agreement leading to independence for Belize, which would come in September.

1990 Lithuania proclaims its independence from the U.S.S.R. The Soviet government responded by imposing an oil embargo and economic blockade against the Baltic republic, and later sent in troops. On September 6, 1991, the crumbling Soviet Union agreed to grant independence to Lithuania and the other Baltic republics of Estonia and Latvia.

Mikhail Gorbachev

Pope Gregory I

1479
GIULIANO DE' MEDICI
Monarch of Florence

1835
SIMON NEWCOMB
Canadian-born American mathematician, astronomer, and economist

1862
JANE DELANO
American nurse and teacher who founded the Red Cross

1922
JACK KEROUAC
American Beat poet and novelist (*On the Road; The Subterranean; The Dharma Bums*)

1928
EDWARD ALBEE
American playwright (*Who's Afraid of Virginia Woolf?; The Sandbox; A Delicate Balance; Three Tall Women*)

Edward Albee

1932
ANDREW YOUNG
U.S. ambassador to the United Nations and mayor of Atlanta, Georgia

1940
AL JARREAU
American jazz musician ("Mornin'"; "We're in This Love Together"; "Ain't No Sunshine")

1946
LIZA MINNELLI
American actress and singer (*Cabaret; New York, New York; Arthur*), daughter of Judy Garland

1948
JAMES TAYLOR
American musician ("Carolina on My Mind"; "Fire and Rain"; "How Sweet It Is (To Be Loved by You)")

"All of life is a foreign country."

—Jack Kerouac

604 Pope Gregory I, architect of the medieval papacy and staunch supporter of monasticism, dies in Rome after 14 years in Peter's chair. Gregory the Great's reform of the mass gave rise to the Gregorian chant.

641 Tibetan king Songzan Gambo marries Chinese princess Wen Cheng. The marriage would later form the basis of China's claim to sovereignty over the region.

1088 French cardinal Odo of Lagery is elected as Pope Urban II. During his 11-year reign, Urban would launch the First Crusade.

1171 During an ongoing struggle for Venetian independence from the Byzantine Empire, the Byzantine emperor orders the arrest of all Venetians and the seizure of their ships and goods. His act triggered a war that was disastrous for Venice.

1609 The Bermuda Islands become an English colony.

1622 Pope Gregory XV canonizes four saints: Ignatius Loyola, founder of the Jesuit order; Teresa of Avila, a Spanish mystic; Philip Neri; and Francis Xavier.

1689 James II, the Roman Catholic king of Britain who was deposed during the Glorious Revolution that brought William and Mary to the throne, lands in Ireland.

1755 The first reported use of a steam engine in the United States takes place at a copper mine in New Jersey. Imported from England, it was used to power a water pump.

1841 English inventor Orlando Jones patents a process for producing starch from rice.

1864 In the American Civil War, the Union launches its disastrous Red River Campaign, which would send 27,000 infantry and 20 gunboats up Louisiana's Red River toward Texas. The infantry was routed and the gunboats ran aground.

1888 A devastating blizzard dumps 40 inches of snow on New York City, stranding the metropolis for several weeks, killing hundreds of people, and causing millions of dollars in property damage.

1894 The first bottles of Coca-Cola go on sale in the United States.

1901 American industrialist Andrew Carnegie gives away $5.2 million to build 65 branch libraries in New York City.

1923 The first movie with sound recorded on film is unveiled in Los Angeles, California. It shows a couple dancing to music played by four musicians, but there is no dialogue.

1930 Indian independence leader Mohandas Gandhi and 78 followers begin a defiant 241-mile march to the sea in order to protest the British monopoly on salt by making their own from seawater.

1933 U.S. president Franklin D. Roosevelt delivers the first of his national radio addresses, which came to be known as "fireside chats."

1938 During World War II, German troops accompanied by Adolf Hitler march into Austria to proclaim an *Anschluss*, or annexation of the German-speaking country. Ecstatic crowds of Austrians hail them as they pass.

1940 The Russo-Finnish War ends in a Soviet victory after a heroic two-month defense by the heavily outgunned and outnumbered Finns.

1947 U.S. president Harry S. Truman asks Congress for $400 million to help the governments of Greece and Turkey stave off communist domination. His speech outlined the broad parameters of U.S. foreign policy for the Cold War and became known as the Truman Doctrine.

1952 German automaker Mercedes-Benz introduces the sleek 300 SL race car, with a detachable steering wheel and gull-wing doors that opened vertically.

1968 U.S. senator Eugene McCarthy surprises President Lyndon B. Johnson in the New Hampshire Democratic presidential primary, polling 42 percent against Johnson's 48 percent.

1969 Police in London, England, raid the home of George Harrison and arrest the Beatles' bass guitarist for possession of hashish. On the same day, fellow Beatle Paul McCartney marries photographer (and later campaigner for vegetarianism and animal rights) Linda Eastman.

1972 During the Vietnam War, Australia withdraws the last of its troops from Vietnam.

1994 In ceremonies at Bristol Cathedral, the Church of England ordains 32 women as priests, thus breaking with 460 years of tradition.

Mercedes-Benz 300 SL

483 Felix III becomes pope and soon excommunicates Acacius, the patriarch of Constantinople, thus triggering the 35-year Acacian Schism.

1107 An unusually heavy snowstorm in Ireland kills many cattle.

1352 Ashikaga Tadayoshi, the Japanese military and administrative genius who was instrumental in the founding of Japan's Ashikaga shogunate, dies in Kamakura.

1519 Spanish conquistador Hernán Cortés lands on the coast of Yucatan, befriends the local Indians, and makes plans to conquer the Aztec Empire.

1569 During the French Wars of Religion, Catholic forces defeat the Huguenots in the Battle of Jarnac.

1809 Gustav IV, the absolutist king of Sweden, is driven from power in a coup.

1813 English inventor William Hedley patents a design for the first commercially useful adhesion-type steam locomotive (one that depends on friction between wheels and rails).

BORN ON THIS DAY

1615
ANTONIO PIGNATELLI
Italian pope Innocent XII (1691–1700)

1696
ARMAND DU PLESSIS, DUKE DE RICHELIEU
French marshal

1770
DANIEL LAMBERT
English giant who weighed 739 pounds at his death

1855
PERCIVAL LOWELL
American astronomer

1883
ENRICO TOSELLI
Italian composer ("Serenade")

1911
L. RON HUBBARD
American founder of Scientology and author (*Scientology; Dianetics; Clear Body, Clear Mind*)

1913
WILLIAM CASEY
Director of the U.S. Central Intelligence Agency

1936
CLARENCE NASH
Voice of animation character Donald Duck

1939
NEIL SEDAKA
American singer/songwriter ("Breaking Up Is Hard To Do"; "Love in the Shadows"; "Should've Never Let You Go")

1972
BRIAN SAXTON
American professional football player

1815 With Napoleon gathering strength as he advances on Paris, French king Louis XVIII flees to Ghent.

1836 In Texas's war for independence from Mexico, American general Sam Houston begins a series of strategic retreats in order to buy time to train his poorly prepared army.

1839 Danish crown prince Frederick VI, a social reformer, ascends the throne upon the death of his mentally incompetent father, Christian VII.

1842 English general Henry Shrapnel, inventor of the shrapnel artillery shell, which was filled with small projectiles, dies.

1865 With the tide of the American Civil War running strongly against the South, the Confederacy reluctantly decides to enlist black slaves as soldiers.

1868 For the first time in U.S. history, the impeachment trial of an American president, Andrew Johnson, begins in the Senate. Johnson, reviled for his post-Civil War Reconstruction policies, was charged with violating the Tenure of Office Act.

1877 Maine teenager Chester Greenwood patents earmuffs.

Andrew Johnson's impeachment

"There is a condition worse than blindness, and that is, seeing something that isn't there."

—L. Ron Hubbard

1881 Czar Alexander II, a reformer who freed Russia's serfs and did much to modernize his country, dies from wounds inflicted by an assassin's bomb.

1882 English inventor Eadweard Muybridge demonstrates his zoopraxiscope at the Royal Institution to an audience including the Prince of Wales and Alfred, Lord Tennyson. The device was a forerunner of the movie projector, and his pioneering film clearly showed that a galloping horse lifted all four hooves off the ground at the same time.

1891 Norwegian playwright Henrik Ibsen's drama *Ghosts*, which deals with the subject of syphilis, premieres on the London stage.

1917 Shortly after Baghdad falls to the British during World War I, Great Britain opens the costly Samarrah Offensive north of the city to seize a strategic railway from the Turks.

1920 In turbulent interwar Germany, a band of radical nationalists briefly seize control of the government in the so-called Kapp Putsch, named for the monarchist who planned it, Wolfgang Kapp.

1938 CBS launches *European Roundup,* an American radio news program that covered events leading up to World War II.

1940 The first of seven successful American "road" film comedies, *The Road to Singapore,* premieres, with Bob Hope, Bing Crosby, and Dorothy Lamour in lead roles.

1942 During World War II, German Nazis open a second extermination camp at Belzec in Poland, and gas the first 6,000 deportees.

1954 The siege of Dien Bien Phu begins in Vietnam as 40,000 Vietminh soldiers surround 15,000 French troops and launch a massive artillery barrage.

1961 In an attempt to patch up relations with Latin America, U.S. president John F. Kennedy proposes a multibillion-dollar aid program called the Alliance for Progress.

1975 Toward the end of the Vietnam War, North Vietnamese troops capture the strategic provincial capital of Ban Me Thuot in the Central Highlands of South Vietnam.

1979 Socialists in Grenada stage a bloodless coup and take control of the Caribbean nation.

1996 In the 13th-century Scottish village of Dunblane, a former Boy Scout leader bursts into a school gymnasium and shoots to death 16 kindergarten students and their teacher before shooting himself.

Queen Elizabeth lays a floral bouquet at Dunblane Primary School

190 B.C. Roman historian Livy describes a solar eclipse as having occurred in early July. However, astronomers calculate that the eclipse happened on March 14, showing that the Roman calendar was inaccurate by more than three months.

1471 Sir Thomas Malory, of Warwickshire, England, thought by many to be the author of *Le Morte d'Arthur*, the history of King Arthur, dies.

1629 Charles I of England grants a royal charter to the Massachusetts Bay Company for their colony in New England.

1647 In the Thirty Years' War, Maximilian I, elector of Bavaria, signs the Treaty of Ulm, concluding a separate peace with France, Sweden, and Cologne, and ending his alliance with Holy Roman Emperor Ferdinand III.

1794 American inventor Eli Whitney patents the cotton gin and changes the face of the textile industry. Cotton becomes a dominant commercial crop in the southern United States, greatly increasing the demand for slaves to work the fields.

1812 The U.S. Congress approves issue of America's first war bond, worth some 11 million dollars, to help finance the War of 1812 against Great Britain.

> *"If A equals success, then the formula is A equals X plus Y plus Z. X is work. Y is play. Z is keep your mouth shut."*
>
> —Albert Einstein

BORN ON THIS DAY

1681
GEORG PHILIPP TELEMANN
German baroque composer

1804
JOHANN STRAUSS THE ELDER
Austrian violinist and composer
("Loreley-Rhein-Klänge";
"Radetzky-Marsch")

1835
GIOVANNI V. SCHIAPARELLI
Italian astronomer who first detected "channels" on the surface of Mars

Giovanni V. Schiaparelli

1861
GEORGE FREDERIC HANDEL
German-born composer of baroque operas and cantatas
(*Messiah; The Triumph of Time and Truth*)

1912
LES BROWN
American musician and big band leader (Les Brown and His Band of Renown)

1920
HANK KETCHAM
American cartoonist (*Dennis the Menace*)

1928
FRANK BORMAN
American astronaut, commander of the 1968 *Apollo 8* mission

1933
QUINCY JONES
American musician and composer ("Just Once"; "Baby, Come to Me"; "You Put a Move on My Heart")

1933
MICHAEL CAINE
Academy Award-winning English actor (*Alfie; A Bridge Too Far; The Quiet American*)

1947
BILLY CRYSTAL
American comedian and actor (*When Harry Met Sally; City Slickers; Monsters, Inc.*)

1836 English naturalist Charles Darwin leaves Australia aboard HMS *Beagle* on the last leg of his five-year voyage.

1864 English explorer Samuel Baker discovers one source of the Nile River, Lake Albert Nyanza, on the border of modern Uganda and Congo.

1885 *The Mikado*, an operetta by English composers Gilbert and Sullivan, debuts at London's Savoy Theatre.

1903 By executive order, President Theodore Roosevelt establishes the United States' first national bird sanctuary—Pelican Island in Florida.

1913 American industrialist John D. Rockefeller establishes the Rockefeller Foundation with a $100 million endowment.

1915 During World War I, British ships sink the German light cruiser *Dresden* off the coast of Chile, virtually ending German raids by conventional ships. Germany turned with lethal effect to submarines.

1917 The Petrograd Soviet, fearing counterrevolution,

Charles Darwin

Polish Jews deported by Nazis

issues "Order No. 1," which calls on soldiers to disarm their officers. The result is chaos in an already demoralized military still trying to fight World War I.

1918 In California, the first American ship made of concrete is launched.

1935 Six-year-old actress Shirley Temple leaves her handprints in cement outside Grauman's Chinese Theater in Los Angeles. Since first winning attention with a song and dance in the 1934 movie *Get Up and Cheer,* Temple became America's biggest box-office draw.

1943 During World War II, German troops reenter Kharkov, an industrial city in the Ukraine that changed hands several times during the war. "We have shown the Ivans we

Jack Ruby

can withstand their terrible winter. It can hold no fear for us again," wrote an SS officer. He was proved wrong.

1943 In Poland during World War II, the Jews of Krakow Ghetto are deported and the ghetto is liquidated.

1950 The U.S. Federal Bureau of Investigation institutes the "10 Most Wanted" list to publicize particularly dangerous fugitives. From March 1950 to May 1998, 454 fugitives appeared on the list; 130 of those were captured.

1964 Jack Ruby, the Dallas, Texas, nightclub owner who killed Lee Harvey Oswald—the accused assassin of President John F. Kennedy—is found guilty of the "murder with malice" of Oswald and sentenced to die in the electric chair. It was the first courtroom verdict to be televised in the United States.

1971 General Hafiz al-Assad is sworn in as president of Syria.

1993 Tiny, landlocked Andorra adopts its first constitution, ending its 715-year-old feudal system of government.

Albert Einstein Born
On this day in 1879, Albert Einstein is born in Württemberg, Germany. Einstein's theories of special and general relativity drastically altered science's view of the universe, and his work in particle and energy theory helped make possible quantum mechanics and, ultimately, the atomic bomb. He received the Nobel Prize in physics in 1921 and immigrated to the United States in 1933, having been deprived of his position in Berlin by the Nazis. In 1939, he agreed to write to President Roosevelt on behalf of a group of scientists who were concerned with American inaction in the field of atomic-weapons research, fearing sole German possession of such a weapon. After World War II, he called for the establishment of a world government that would control nuclear technology and prevent future armed conflict.

Albert Einstein

Julius Caesar

222 B.C. In Rome, March 15 is declared the date when new consuls assume their duties. Because years were designated by the consul's name, March 15 also marked the beginning of each new year until 153 B.C., when the date was shifted to January.

44 B.C. Gaius Julius Caesar, dictator of Rome, is stabbed to death in the Roman Senate by 60 conspirators led by Marcus Junius Brutus and Gaius Cassius Longinus.

933 Henry I of Germany responds to Magyar raids by defeating the barbarians from Hungary in a battle at Riade.

1493 Italian explorer Christopher Columbus's ships Niña and Pinta, having been separated in a storm, arrive at their home port of Palos, Spain, upon return from the New World.

1798 Having occupied Rome in January, France proclaims a Roman Republic, one of several unstable republics that would eventually join to become Italy.

1806 A meteorite lands in France carrying organic carbon-based molecules, suggesting that life existed in the place from which it came.

1812 Russian settlers establish their first California settlement, at the mouth of Russian River.

1820 As part of the Missouri Compromise between the North and the South, Maine is admitted into the Union as the 23rd state. Its entrance as a free state was agreed to by southern senators in exchange for the entrance of Missouri as a slave state.

1870 Three months before his death, English author Charles Dickens completes a series of Farewell Readings at St. James Hall in London.

1892 Voting machines are first authorized for use in New York state. Called Myers' automatic ballot cabinets, the lever-operated machines are still used today.

1892 Jesse W. Reno, of New York, patents the first escalator.

1906 Rolls-Royce Ltd. is officially registered with Charles S. Rolls and F. Henry Royce as directors. In 1904, the two Englishmen had formed a partnership in which Royce produced cars and Rolls sold

Andrew Jackson

> *"Fear not, the people may be deluded for a moment, but cannot be corrupted."*
>
> —Andrew Jackson

them. Success led to the new company.

1907 Finland grants women the right to vote, the first European country to do so.

1909 The 42,000 square-foot Selfridges department store on London's famous Oxford Street opens, with the slogan "Anything from a pin to an elephant." Its founder, Harry Gordon Selfridge, was the son of a shopkeeper from the United States who had made a fortune as a partner in the Marshall Field's department store in Chicago.

1911 Gustave Otto, the son of German internal combustion engine pioneer Nikolaus Otto, organizes Gustav Otto Flugmaschinenfabrik Munchen. Otto's Munich-based aero-engineering firm would later merge with Karl Rapp's firm to form the Bayerische Motoren-Werke, or BMW.

1917 During the February Revolution, Czar Nicholas II, ruler of Russia since 1894, is forced to abdicate the throne by Petrograd insurgents, and a provincial government is installed in his place.

1922 Two weeks after Great Britain unilaterally declared the end of its Egyptian protectorate, Sultan Ahmad Fu'ad becomes King Fu'ad I, the newly independent country's first ruler.

1954 The American group The Chords record "Sh-boom." The song's lighthearted melody and nonsensical lyrics ("Sh-boom, sh-boom, yeah-da-da-da-da-da-da-da-da-da-da-") marked the dawn of "doo-wop" music, which combined *a cappella* harmonies with swinging beats.

1955 American singer Fats Domino records his hit song "Ain't That a Shame," just as rock-and-roll music is breaking into the mainstream. The recording launched the previously obscure Domino to national fame.

1989 General Secretary of the Communist Party Mikhail Gorbachev calls for an end to the Soviet agricultural bureaucracy and the introduction of free-market principles. His dramatic speech indicated that the Soviet Union was suffering serious economic troubles, which eventually led to its collapse in December 1991.

1992 The Republic of Congo adopts a new constitution to "create a new political order, a decentralized State where morality, law, liberty, pluralist democracy, equality, social justice, fraternity, and the general well-being reign."

Nazi occupation of Czechoslovakia (milestone)

597 B.C. Babylonian king Nebuchadnezzar captures Jerusalem and sends Jewish king Johoiachin, along with at least 3,000 of his people, into exile in Babylon.

37 Roman emperor Tiberius, who surprised everyone by rising from his deathbed and calling for food, is smothered to death by a commander of the Praetorian Guard.

455 Valentinian III, hedonistic emperor of Rome, is murdered on Mars Field by two barbarian retainers of Aetius, a patrician who Valentinian had slain with his own hands the previous year.

1190 In York, England, just before Passover, a mob of clergy, barons, and crusaders waiting to follow King Richard the Lion-Heart to the Holy Land besiege more than 150 Jewish residents in Clifford's Tower and later massacre those who do not kill themselves.

1309 Scottish king Robert the Bruce convenes his first Parliament, at St. Andrews.

1792 Gustav III, absolutist king of Sweden, is shot by a former officer of the royal guard at a masquerade ball in Stockholm. He died 13 days later.

1802 The U.S. Military Academy is founded at West

"I once wanted to become an atheist, but I gave up—they have no holidays."

—*Henny Youngman*

Point, New York, in order to train young American men in the theory and practice of military science.

1815 Prince William of Orange ascends the throne of the Kingdom of the Netherlands, a realm manufactured at the Congress of Vienna from Dutch and Belgian territories.

1850 Struggling American writer Nathaniel Hawthorne publishes his novel of adultery and betrayal, *The Scarlet Letter*, winning fame and fortune.

1865 In the waning days of the American Civil War, Union forces under General William T. Sherman brush aside a Confederate attack in the Battle of Averasboro, in North Carolina.

1867 English surgeon Joseph Lister publishes the first of several articles in the medical journal *Lancet* that describe his discovery of antiseptic surgery.

1873 The Scottish Football Association is founded.

1916 During the protracted World War I battle of

The town of Vaux, France, reduced by American artillery during World War I

Verdun, Allied troops repulse five successive German attacks on the town of Vaux. On the same day, a German U-boat torpedoes the Dutch liner *Tubantia* without warning, off Harwich.

1917 In anticipation of renewed attacks along the Somme during World War I, Germany begins a massive withdrawal of its troops to the fortified Hindenburg Line, which was to prove impregnable until late 1918.

1935 Scoffing at the disarmament clauses of the Versailles Treaty, Adolf Hitler reestablishes German conscription and starts building up the country's army, air force, and navy.

1942 In the Philippines during World War II, the Japanese bombard American forts in Manila.

1945 U.S. Marines secure the Pacific island of Iwo Jima after weeks of bitter World War II fighting against an entrenched Japanese force of 21,000. More than 6,000 Marines had been killed in the struggle, along with almost all the Japanese.

1968 During the Vietnam War, an American platoon under the command of Lieutenant William Calley massacres as many as 500 unarmed civilian villagers at My Lai in South Vietnam.

1970 *The New English Bible*, a translation into modern English, is published in Great Britain. The first edition of a million copies sold out within two days.

1975 Toward the end of the Vietnam War, as victorious North Vietnamese troops advance in the Central Highlands, South Vietnamese troops and hundreds of thousands of refugees begin to abandon the region and head for the coast.

1985 American journalist Terry Anderson, covering the Lebanese Civil War for the Associated Press, is kidnapped in Beirut by Islamic militants, who hold him for 2,455 days.

1988 U.S. president Ronald W. Reagan orders more than 3,000 troops to Honduras, claiming that Nicaraguan soldiers had invaded the country. The Honduran government had not called for the American troops and could not confirm that the Nicaraguans had crossed its border.

1995 During civil war in Rwanda, at least 22 of 74 Hutu prisoners die of suffocation in a jail cell built to hold no more than 10.

1996 In Pakistan, an avalanche strikes the Kashmir village of Kel, claiming at least 32 lives.

⚔ **45 B.C.** Julius Caesar wins the Roman civil war by defeating the two sons of his late rival Pompey the Great in the Battle of Munda, in Spain.

▬ **1616** In Holland, cities are given the discretion to decide for themselves whether to admit Jews; those that do must not require Jews to wear identification badges.

⚔ **1776** During the American Revolutionary War, British forces in Boston, threatened by American cannons on Dorchester Heights, evacuate the city and leave behind 200 heavy guns, many small arms, and a large stock of ammunition.

🏴 **1808** In Spain, the Revolt of Aranjuez breaks out, forcing the abdication of Charles IV and then handing French emperor Napoleon the opportunity to make his brother, Joseph Bonaparte, king of Spain.

🇬🇧 **1845** Englishman Stephen Perry patents the rubber band.

🏴 **1846** German astronomer Friedrich Bessel, the first to measure the distance to a star other than the sun (in 1838), dies in Konigsberg, Prussia.

▬ **1862** The U.S. Treasury introduces paper money, "greenbacks," to help finance the American Civil War.

⚔ **1863** In the Battle of Kelly's Ford during the American

> *"Critics don't buy records;*
> *they get 'em free."*
>
> —Nat "King" Cole

MILESTONE

First St. Patrick's Day Parade Held

In New York City, the first parade honoring the Catholic feast day of St. Patrick, the patron saint of Ireland, is held on this day in 1762 by Irish soldiers serving in the British army. Early Irish settlers to the American colonies, many of whom were indentured servants, brought the Irish tradition of celebrating St. Patrick's feast day to America. With the dramatic increase of Irish immigrants to the United States in the mid-19th century, the March 17 celebration became widespread.

St. Patrick

U.S. Treasury greenbacks

Civil War, Union cavalry attack Confederate soldiers along Virginia's Rappahannock River and hold their own for one of the first times in the conflict.

🔬 **1885** In a report to the Pathological Society of London, English physician Frederick Treves makes the first formal description of the deformities of Joseph Merrick, known as the "Elephant Man."

▬ **1898** The USS *Holland*, the world's first practical submarine, makes a 100-minute trial run off Staten Island, New York.

🔬 **1899** For the first time, radio is used to save lives at sea when the German ship *Elbe* uses Marconi's wireless to summon help after running aground on the Goodwin Sands off the coast of southern England.

👠 **1901** The late Dutch artist Vincent van Gogh finally gets the recognition he deserves when the Bernheim-Jeune gallery in Paris hangs 71 of his paintings and causes a sensation across the art world.

▬ **1905** Franklin Delano Roosevelt, who later became the 32nd president of the United States, marries his distant cousin, Eleanor Roosevelt.

1912 On the return leg of Great Britain's ill-fated Scott expedition to the South Pole, Captain Laurence Oates, suffering from frostbite and aware that he is holding up his starving comrades, walks out to his death in a blizzard. Scott recorded his last words: "I am just going outside and may be some time." It was Oates's 32nd birthday.

1916 During World War I, a German U-boat torpedoes the Dutch liner *Palembang* in the North Sea.

1940 German engineer Fritz Todt, designer of the nation's autobahn superhighway system, is appointed minister for weapons and munitions. As such he would create and oversee Adolf Hitler's centralized system of mass slave labor.

1941 During World War II, British destroyers sink two German submarines in defense of an Allied convoy of merchantmen crossing the Atlantic.

1942 American general Douglas MacArthur lands in Australia after his harrowing World War II escape from the Japanese in the Philippines. On the same day, German Nazis in Belarus murder 900 Jews.

1943 The Battle for the Atlantic reaches its climax in the largest convoy battle of World War II, a five-day rout in which 20 German submarines sink 21 well-escorted merchantmen at the loss of just

one U-boat. The battle came one week after another Allied convoy lost 13 merchant vessels.

1949 German automotive engineer Ferdinand Porsche introduces the first car to carry his family name, the Porsche 356, a sports-car version of the Volkswagen he had designed during World War II for Adolf Hitler.

1958 The United States launches its first satellite, *Vanguard I*, equipped with a radio transmitter that broadcasts to a worldwide tracking system.

1959 The American nuclear-powered submarine USS *Skate* surfaces at the North Pole.

1973 American naval pilot John McCain, later a U.S. senator, is released from a North Vietnamese prisoner-of-war camp after more than five years in captivity.

1973 Twenty people are killed in a failed attempt on the life of Cambodian president Lon Nol.

Porche 356 with Ferdinand Porsche Jr., far right, and father Ferdinand

417 Zosimus is consecrated pope in Rome. He died after less than two years of doctrinal conflict during which he freely wielded the power of excommunication against those he perceived as heretics.

978 English king Edward the Martyr is murdered at Corfe Gate in Dorset. His stepmother said he had died falling from his horse, but his body was later found in a shallow grave bearing a stab wound. Nonetheless, his stepbrother, Ethelred the Unready, inherited the throne.

1438 Albert II, archduke of Austria, is elected German king. He died a year later fighting the Turks, but his reforms brought a long period of stability to the region.

1584 Notorious Russian czar Ivan IV, known as Ivan the Terrible, dies, probably of syphilis. During his life, he claimed he had taken the virginity of a thousand women and murdered a thousand of his own illegitimate children.

1766 After four months of widespread protest in America, the British Parliament repeals the Stamp Act, a tax that paid for a standing British army in the colonies. On the same day, Parliament passes the Declaratory Acts, asserting its total legislative power over the colonies.

1768 Laurence Sterne, the Irish author of *Tristram Shandy*, dies in London. He was buried in a pauper's grave, and his body was later exhumed and sold for anatomical studies. However, a student recognized the corpse, which was hastily reburied.

1915 In World War I, Allied forces try to break through the Dardanelles Narrows and open a supply route to Russia. The attack's failure, due in part to an unsuspected drifting minefield that sank or disabled five warships, led to the sacking of First Lord of the Admiralty Winston Churchill.

1921 Its strength weakened by civil war following the revolution, Russia signs the Treaty of Riga, ending hostilities with Poland and giving up a large portion of Belarus.

1924 In the United States, *The Thief of Baghdad* opens to crowds so thick that police form a wedge to escort stars Douglas Fairbanks and Mary Pickford into the theater.

1925 The Great Tri-State Tornado, the worst in U.S. history, cuts a 219-mile path through eastern Missouri,

---

BORN ON THIS DAY

1483
RAPHAEL (RAFFAELLO SANZIO)
Italian painter (*Sistine Madonna; The Marriage of the Virgin*)

1837
GROVER S. CLEVELAND
22nd and 24th U.S. president

1869
NEVILLE CHAMBERLAIN
British prime minister (1937–40)

1886
EDWARD EVERETT HORTON
American actor (*Pocketful of Miracles; Sex and the Single Girl; Cold Turkey*)

1927
GEORGE PLIMPTON
American author (*Paper Lion*) and actor (*Reds; L.A. Story; Good Will Hunting*)

1932
JOHN UPDIKE
American author (*Rabbit, Run; Hugging the Shore; The Witches of Eastwick*)

1936
F. W. DE KLERK
South African president (1989–94)

1938
CHARLIE PRIDE
First African American inducted into the Country Music Hall of Fame ("Kiss an Angel Good Morning"; "When I Stop Leaving I'll Be Gone"; "Burgers and Fries")

1941
WILSON PICKETT
American blues singer ("Mustang Sally"; "In the Midnight Hour"; "Funky Broadway")

"Dreams come true; without that possibility, nature would not incite us to have them."

—John Updike

American colonists celebrate Stamp Act demise

Mexican president Lázaro Cárdenas with oil labor leaders in Tamaulipas state, Mexico

southern Illinois, and southern Indiana, killing 695 people, injuring some 13,000, and causing $17 million in property damage.

1938 Mexican president Lázaro Cárdenas expropriates the holdings of foreign petroleum companies and combines them in a nationalized company, Pemex. Mexicans hailed the move as the reclamation of their rightful property.

1939 Responding to German occupation of Czechoslovakia during World War II, British prime minister Neville Chamberlain angrily announces the end of appeasement. Soon Great Britain joined an alliance with Poland and began preparing for war.

1940 At a World War II meeting in the Alps, German dictator Adolf Hitler tells Italian fascist leader Benito Mussolini that Germany doesn't need help winning the war, but that Italy's assistance is welcome nonetheless. Italy holds back until French defeat is assured, and only then declares war on France and Great Britain.

1941 Prince Paul of Yugoslavia and two top government ministers announce they intend to align their country with Germany as part of the Axis during World War II.

1944 Subhas Chandra Bose arrives in eastern India at the head of his 40,000-strong Indian National Army. Trained and supported by Japan, the army hoped to drive the British from India. Instead, they were driven back to Japanese-held Burma.

1950 In a surprise raid on the communist People's Republic of China, military forces of the Nationalist Chinese government on Taiwan invade the mainland and capture the town of Sungmen, about 200 miles south of Shanghai. The invasion failed after several weeks.

1962 France and the leaders of the Front de Liberation Nationale (FLN) sign a peace agreement to end the seven-year Algerian War, closing 130 years of colonial French rule in Algeria.

1965 Russian cosmonaut Aleksei Leonov pulls himself through an air lock and becomes the first man to walk—or rather float—outside an orbiting spacecraft.

Russian cosmonaut Col. Aleksei Leonov

Annually On this, St. Joseph's Day, the swallows are said to miraculously return to their nesting sites in the Mission of San Juan Capistrano in California.

1227 Ugo di Segni succeeds Honorius as Pope Gregory IX. He established the papal Inquisition, which became infamous for its pursuit, torture, and murder of heresy suspects.

1307 On Palm Sunday, Sir James Douglas, a Scot and a fierce enemy of English rule, makes a third attempt to recover his castle from Robert de Clifford, an Englishman who had seized it. The assault, known as the "Douglas Larder," ended in destruction of the castle.

1604 The first parliament of King James I convenes and proves to be a thorny challenge for the absolutist English king.

1687 French explorer René-Robert Cavelier, Sieur de La Salle, who canoed down the Mississippi River and claimed its entire drainage for France, is murdered in Texas by members of a subsequent expedition.

1792 In India, Governor-general Charles Cornwallis defeats Tipu Sultan, forcing the Mysore ruler to cede half his territory and pay a large indemnity.

1800 In a zoological version of Benjamin Franklin flying

MILESTONE

Tolpuddle Martyrs

On this day in 1834, six agricultural laborers from the English town of Tolpuddle in Dorset are sentenced to seven years in the Australian penal colony for trade union activities. The laborers lived in desperate poverty on wages of nine shillings a week. Their leader, George Loveless, wanted to create a union to give them greater bargaining strength with landowners. The local squire, James Frampton, was determined to stop them and enlisted the support of the Home Secretary, Lord Melbourne. The establishment was keen to quell any sign of revolt, fearing a revolution of the kind that had taken place in France. Frampton created a trumped-up charge based on laws that applied to the Navy, not laborers, and the men were tried in front of a rigged jury headed by the Home Secretary's brother-in-law. Public reaction made the "Tolpuddle Martyrs" into popular heroes and formed the beginning of trade unionism in Great Britain.

Alexander von Humboldt

his kite in a lightning storm, German naturalist Alexander von Humboldt captures electric eels in South America and receives nasty bioelectric shocks while investigating them.

1831 English immigrant Edward Smith robs the City Bank in downtown New York City, marking America's first daylight bank robbery. Smith made off with $245,000 but was caught and sentenced to five years in Sing Sing Prison.

1842 French writer Honoré de Balzac's play *Les Ressources de Quinola* opens to an empty house thanks to a failed publicity stunt. Hoping to create a buzz for the play, the writer circulated a rumor that tickets were sold out. Unfortunately, most of his fans stayed home.

1859 French composer Charles Gounod's masterwork *Faust* debuts in Paris.

1877 The Ottoman Parliament opens in Istanbul. The assembly survived only a year before the sultan eliminated it.

> *"The road to hell is paved with works-in-progress."*
>
> —Philip Roth

1883 African-American inventor Jan Matzeliger patents the lasting machine, the first device to automate the manufacture of shoes.

1916 Eight Curtiss "Jenny" planes of the First Aero Squadron of the U.S. Air Force take off from Columbus, New Mexico, in the first combat air mission in U.S. history. Their goal: to help American troops capture Mexican revolutionary Pancho Villa.

1917 As part of the Samarrah Offensive during World War I, a British brigade takes the Falluja flood-control system near Baghdad, thus preventing Turkish forces from flooding the Euphrates plains and hampering the British advance.

1920 In a 49-35 vote, the U.S. Senate fails to ratify the Treaty of Versailles, and with that rejects the League of Nations and other initiatives pushed on Europe by President Woodrow Wilson. Whether ratification might have prevented World War II is still a matter of controversy among historians.

1931 Hoping to lift Nevada out of Great Depression hard times, the state legislature votes to legalize gambling.

1932 In Australia, the Sydney Harbour Bridge is opened to traffic.

1945 Toward the end of World War II, the commander of the German Home Army, General Friedrich Fromm, is shot by a firing squad for his part in the failed July plot to assassinate Adolf Hitler with a suitcase bomb.

1947 In China's civil war, nationalist forces capture the communist capital, Yan'an, but the victory would soon be reversed.

1978 The U.N. Security Council passes Resolution 425, calling for Israel's withdrawal from Lebanon. Israeli forces, which had entered the country in response to Palestinian raids, were gone by mid-June.

1998 In what Afghanistan's ruling Taliban militia called an accident, an explosion of munitions at a police station in Jalalabad kills more than 40 and injures many more.

71 A total eclipse of the sun plunges Greece into darkness and may have prompted the Greek writer Plutarch to write that the phenomenon "showed us plainly many stars in all parts of the heavens and produced a chill in the temperature like that of twilight."

687 Saint Cuthbert, hermit and bishop of the great Benedictine monastery at Lindisfarne, dies on the islet of Inner Farne, off Northumbria.

1413 English king Henry IV, the first of the Lancastrian line, dies in London and is succeeded by his son, Henry V, who would conquer France during his nine-year reign.

1549 Thomas Seymour, lord high admiral of England and suitor of Princess Elizabeth, is beheaded in London for treason.

1602 The Dutch East India Company is founded by the Dutch government to protect its trade in the Indian Ocean and help in its war against Spain.

1727 English physicist and mathematician Sir Isaac Newton, the leading figure of the 17th-century scientific revolution, dies in London.

1806 The foundation stone of Dartmoor Prison is laid by its creator, Sir Thomas Tyrwhitt. The prison, which features in Sir Arthur Conan Doyle's *The Hound of the Baskervilles,* was built to house French prisoners of war who were being used as cheap labor to build a town planned by Tyrwhitt.

BORN ON THIS DAY

1828
HENRIK IBSEN
Norwegian dramatist (*Peer Gynt; A Doll's House; Hedda Gabler*)

Henrik Ibsen

1904
B. F. SKINNER
American psychologist and theorist of behaviorism

1906
OZZIE NELSON
American musician, actor, and television producer (*The Adventures of Ozzie and Harriet*)

1922
CARL REINER
American actor, writer, and director (*Oh, God!; The Jerk; All of Me; Ocean's Eleven*)

1928
FRED "MISTER" ROGERS
American children's show host (*Mister Rogers' Neighborhood*)

1931
HAL LINDEN
American actor (*Barney Miller*)

1945
PAT RILEY
American basketball coach

1948
BOBBY ORR
American NHL Hall of Fame hockey player

1950
WILLIAM HURT
Academy Award-winning American actor (*Altered States; Broadcast News; Kiss of the Spider Woman*)

1957
SPIKE LEE
American director and independent filmmaker (*Do The Right Thing; Malcolm X; Clockers*)

1815 French emperor Napoleon Bonaparte returns to Paris from exile on the island of Elba and begins his Hundred Days' reign.

1854 American antislavery activists found the Republican Party in order to fight the spread of slavery into the western territories of the United States.

1900 Serbian-American inventor Nikola Tesla receives a patent for the wireless transmission of electricity.

1902 American telephone pioneer Nathan Stubblefield demonstrates the first mobile radio telephone, on a ship in the Potomac River.

1917 U.S. president Woodrow Wilson decides to call a special session of Congress to declare war on Germany, which had just sunk three American merchant ships. On the same day, Germany torpedos the British hospital ship *Asturias* and reports that World War I casualties among its own armed services have reached 4,148,163.

1920 Swiss automaker Bugatti delivers its first luxury car, equipped with a massive, 16-valve racing engine, to a customer in Basel.

1933 The Jews of Vilna, Poland, initiate an anti-Nazi boycott. The idea spread across

---

"The real problem is not whether machines think but whether men do."

—*B. F. Skinner*

British troops on Mandalay Hill

1968 In an analysis of the ongoing Vietnam War, retired U.S. Marine Corps commandant General David Shoup estimates that 800,000 troops would be needed just to defend South Vietnam's population centers and that victory could be achieved only by an invasion of North Vietnam.

1980 In a preamble to eruption, a swarm of minor earthquakes begins beneath the north flank of the American stratovolcano Mount St. Helens, in the Cascade mountains of the American Northwest. Scientists record 47 earthquakes of magnitude 3 or greater within a 12-hour period.

1995 At the height of the morning rush hour in Tokyo, Japan, terrorists from the Aum Shinrikyo religious cult release lethal sarin gas in a subway station, killing 12 and injuring 5,500.

2003 American cruise missiles and planes opened a second war in twelve years against Iraq with an attack against targets in Baghdad, including specific individuals in the Iraqi leadership.

Poland until the country signed its nonaggression treaty with German chancellor Adolf Hitler, which called for an end of all boycott activities.

1944 During World War II, German troops occupy Hungary as the Soviet Red Army makes strong advances toward the Carpathian Mountains. On the same day in the Pacific, Allied troops secure the Emirau Islands, the last step in immobilizing 100,000 Japanese troops in New Britain and New Ireland.

1945 British troops liberate Mandalay, a crucial communications and transportation hub in central Burma, toward the end of World War II.

1952 American actor Humphrey Bogart, who played a series of tough, poker-faced heroes, wins an Oscar for Best Actor in *The African Queen*.

1953 In the wake of Soviet leader Joseph Stalin's death, Nikita Khrushchev nudges aside the heir apparent, Georgi Malenkov, and begins his rise to power.

1956 Tunisia wins full independence from France.

Smokes rises from one of President Saddam Hussein's palaces in Baghdad

630 Eastern Roman emperor Heraclius restores the True Cross to the Church of the Holy Sepulchre in Jerusalem.

1146 In France, St. Bernard of Clairveaux begins agitating for the Second Crusade.

1152 Louis VII, Capetian king of France, repudiates his wife Eleanor for misconduct. She retains control of Aquitaine, however, and soon marries Henry Plantaganet, the next king of England.

1349 A German mob marches into the Jewish quarter of Erfurt, kills more than 100 Jews, and burns many of the homes and shops.

1413 England crowns Henry V, who would win the Battle of Agincourt and make England one of the strongest kingdoms in Europe.

1487 Swiss saint Nicholas of Flue, whose mediation had saved the Swiss Confederation from civil war in 1481, dies in Ranft.

Church of the Holy Sepulchre

MILESTONE

Selma-to-Montgomery March Begins

In the name of African-American voting rights, 3,200 civil rights demonstrators, led by Martin Luther King, Jr., begin a historic march from Selma, Alabama, to the State Capitol at Montgomery on this day in 1965. U.S. Army and National Guard troops were on hand to provide safe passage for the Alabama Freedom March, which twice had been turned back by Alabama state police at Selma's Edmund Pettus Bridge.

Freedom marchers on the Edmund Pettus Bridge

"I can think of nothing less pleasurable than a life devoted to pleasure."
—*John D. Rockefeller III*

1556 Thomas Cranmer, the first Protestant archbishop of Canterbury, is burned at the stake for heresy, on orders of England's Catholic queen Mary.

1591 Pope Gregory XIV prohibits all betting on papal elections, on the length of papal reigns, and on the appointments of cardinals.

1617 Rebecca Rolfe, better known as Pocahontas, dies in England while on a visit with her English husband, the colonist John Rolfe.

1678 The *London Gazette* offers a reward for identifying the writer of an anti-Catholic pamphlet, *An Account of the Growth of Popery*. The author was English writer Andrew Marvell, a member of Parliament, satirist, and poet.

1801 Spain reluctantly gives back the American Louisiana territories to France as the Treaty of San Ildefonso goes into effect.

1804 French emperor Napoleon Bonaparte enacts a new legal framework, the "Napoleonic Code," which gives France its first coherent set of civil and criminal laws since the French Revolution.

1863 Polish patriot Marian Langiewicz, who helped lead an independence insurrection against Russia, flees to

Austria after his short-lived government crumbles.

🇬🇧 **1871** Henry Stanley, the intrepid British-American explorer and journalist, departs from Zanzibar for the interior of Africa in search of fellow explorer David Livingstone.

🔬 **1877** French chemist and microbiologist Louis Pasteur, who proved that microorganisms cause disease, begins work on an anthrax vaccine.

🇬🇧 **1901** Great Britain launches *Discovery*, the ship in which explorer Robert Falcon Scott sailed on his Antarctic voyage of 1901–04.

💥 **1918** The German army launches its last major offensive of World War I, the Second Battle of the Somme, an all-out drive to win the war before American troops land in Europe.

🔬 **1925** Austrian physicist Wolfgang Pauli introduces his famous "exclusion principle," which states that in an atom no two electrons can occupy the same quantum state simultaneously. His work later won him a Nobel Prize.

🎭 **1939** American singer Kate Smith records Irving Berlin's patriotic ballad "God Bless America."

🔬 **1942** In a secret report, American physicists Glenn Seaborg and Arthur Wahl for the first time apply the name "plutonium" to the 94th element.

🇩🇪 **1943** During World War II, a plot by German army officers to assassinate Adolf Hitler fails when the perpetrators cannot find a fuse for the bomb.

🇿🇦 **1960** Afrikaner police fire submachine guns at a group of unarmed black South African demonstrators in Sharpeville, near Johannesburg, killing 69 and wounding 180.

🇺🇸 **1963** Alcatraz Prison, the notoriously harsh, maximum-security facility in California's San Francisco Bay, ceases operation.

1967 During the Vietnam War, the North Vietnamese press reports that Ho Chi Minh has rejected a proposal for peace talks offered by American president Lyndon B. Johnson.

🏆 **1980** U.S. president Jimmy Carter announces the United States' boycott of the Moscow Olympics, in response to the December 1979 Soviet invasion of Afghanistan.

1990 Namibia wins its independence from South Africa and swears in its first president, Sam Nujoma.

1980 Olympic runners in Red Square

1312 Pope Clement V orders suppression of the Knights Templar, ostensibly for immorality and heresy. Templars were members of a religious military order whose power and wealth offended French king Philip IV. Their property was confiscated, many were imprisoned or executed, and their leader was burned at the stake.

1421 In the Hundred Years' War, the Battle of Baugé results in death for the Duke of Clarence, heir to the English throne.

1429 French patriot Joan of Arc dictates letters of defiance to the English. Six weeks later she inspired French forces to defeat English forces besieging Orleans.

1622 Powhatan Indians kill 347 English settlers at Jamestown, Virginia.

1790 Thomas Jefferson becomes America's first secretary of state.

1794 The U.S. Congress outlaws slave trading "from the United States to any Foreign Place or Country," although slavery remains legal in the United States.

1820 U.S. Navy officer Stephen Decatur, the most lauded American naval hero ("Don't give up the ship!") since John Paul Jones, is killed in a duel with a former friend.

> "Never get a mime talking. He won't stop."
>
> —Marcel Marceau

Stephen Decatur

1824 Great Britain's National Gallery is founded when Parliament votes to buy the art collection of merchant John Angerstein at a price of £57,000.

1841 American Orlando Jones patents cornstarch.

1848 Inspired by a wave of republican revolts against monarchies sweeping Europe, Venice declares its independence from Austria.

1873 Spain abolishes slavery.

1895 French inventors Louis and Auguste Lumière give the first public demonstration of the cinematograph, an early movie projector.

1907 Taximeters are installed in cabs in London, England, to indicate the distance traveled and the payment due. Derived from words meaning "price" and "measure," the name of the devices when shortened came to apply to the vehicles: taxis.

1913 Song Jiaoren, who founded the Nationalist, or Guomindang Party, dies in Shanghai from an assassin's bullet. Song's death, shortly after the fall of the Ching dynasty, dimmed hopes of democratic government in China.

1915 Russian forces capture the Austrian fortress of Przemysl, Poland, and are poised to cross the Carpathian mountains into Hungary. The attack stalled, and they were driven back.

1916 Yuan Shikai, first president of the Republic of China and would-be emperor, dissolves his nonexistent empire.

1926 Spain resigns from the League of Nations but later rejoins.

1927 In Shanghai, 600,000 workers participate in a general strike called by the Chinese Communist Party, effectively taking control of the city.

1929 Folksy American humorist Will Rogers signs a contract with Fox to write and star in four films. His fee: $600,000.

1942 In India during World War II, British statesman Sir Stafford Cripps meets with Mohandas Gandhi, hoping to rally the Indian National Congress behind the war effort. Gandhi was leader of the Congress, and wanted a guarantee of independence that Britain would not give. Instead, he was interned for two years as a threat to Indian security.

1945 The Arab League, a regional organization of Arab States, is formed at a meeting in Cairo, Egypt. The founding members are Egypt, Iraq, Jordan, Lebanon, Saudi Arabia, Syria, and Yemen.

1946 At White Sands, New Mexico, the first American-built rocket to leave the atmosphere is launched.

1946 Transjordan, later renamed the Hashemite Kingdom of Jordan, becomes an independent country by a treaty signed in London, England.

1947 In response to public fears and congressional investigations into the rise of communism in the United States, President Harry S. Truman issues an executive decree establishing a sweeping loyalty investigation of federal employees. Although few suspects were turned up, the "Red Scare" only grew as the Cold War intensified.

1958 Mike Todd, inventor of the Todd-AO motion picture system and third husband of Elizabeth Taylor, dies in a plane crash in the Zuni Mountains of New Mexico in the United States.

1960 The laser is patented by American scientists Arthur Schawlaw and Charles Townes.

1967 During the Vietnam War, Thailand grants use of its bases for U.S. bombers flying missions over Vietnam.

Mohandas Gandhi

Patrick Henry

✡ **5 B.C.** Herod, ruler of Galilee, burns alive the rebel Matthias and some companions, as recorded by Flavius Josephus, who also mentions "on the same night there was an eclipse of the Moon."

⚔ **625** Muhammad and a Muslim force of about 1,000 fight an indecisive battle with Meccan forces, damaging the confidence of Muslims in the divine support of their campaign.

✝ **752** Stephen II is chosen to succeed Pope St. Zacharias, but he died two days later of apoplexy.

🎭 **1743** German composer Georg Friedrich Händel's oratorio *Messiah* has its London premiere.

⚔ **1757** Having taken Calcutta, Watson and Clive lead British forces to the capture of Chandernagore, a French possession in India.

1775 Speaking to the second Virginia Convention, American revolutionary Patrick Henry declares his feelings about independence: "I know not what course others may take, but as for me, give me liberty or give me death!"

MILESTONE

Mussolini Founds the Fascist Party

On this day in 1919, Benito Mussolini, an Italian World War I veteran and publisher of socialist newspapers, breaks with the Italian Socialists and establishes the nationalist *Fasci di Combattimento*, named after the Italian peasant revolutionaries. Commonly known as the Fascist Party, Mussolini's new right-wing organization advocated Italian nationalism, had black shirts for uniforms, and launched a program of terrorism and intimidation against its leftist opponents. Initially, Mussolini, who was appointed prime minister at the head of a three-member Fascist cabinet, cooperated with the Italian parliament, but aided by his brutal police organization he soon became the effective dictator of Italy.

Benito Mussolini

"We can lick gravity, but sometimes the paperwork is overwhelming."

—*Wernher Von Braun*

1801 Russian czar Paul I is assassinated by upper-class conspirators angered over his clumsy reforms and his prohibition on travel abroad. He feared foreign ideas and goods, particularly French ones, but his attempt to keep the Russian wealthy from Paris proved fatal.

1806 Having spent a wet and hungry winter on the Pacific Coast, American explorers Lewis and Clark and their men leave Fort Clatsop and head east for home.

⚔ **1815** At the end of the War of 1812, the USS *Hornet* captures and destroys the HMS *Penguin* in a short close-action battle.

1836 The U.S. Mint unveils the latest in coin-making technology—its first steam-powered coin press.

1841 Richard Beard opens Europe's first photographic portrait studio in London, England, offering Daguerreotype portraits. Subjects had to sit still for the one to three minutes needed for each exposure.

1857 The world's first passenger elevator, built by Elisha Otis, goes into service in New York City.

1861 The first horse-drawn tram in London, England,

---

starts operation on Bayswater Road. Its builder: American entrepreneur George Train.

1862 In the American Civil War, Confederate general "Stonewall" Jackson suffers a rare defeat when his attack on Union forces in the Shenandoah Valley fails.

1877 Mormon stalwart John Doyle Lee is executed for his role in the Mountain Meadows Massacre 20 years earlier, in which Mormon settlers slaughtered a wagon train of Arkansas immigrants on the California trail.

1893 Kosher slaughtering is outlawed in Saxony, Germany.

1901 On his 32nd birthday, Philippine rebel leader Emilio Aguinaldo is captured by American forces. He took an oath of allegiance to the United States and retired temporarily on a pension.

1918 "Chinese" Magician Chung Ling Soo, who had amazed audiences for over a decade with his bullet-catching act, is killed on stage in London when a trick gun malfunctions. At the inquest, his true identity was revealed: New York-born Bill Robinson.

1927 In China, Nationalist forces capture Nanking and begin looting foreign properties.

1933 The German Reichstag and Reichsrat pass the Enabling Act, which gives Adolf Hitler's Nazi government dictatorial powers.

1942 During World War II, a British effort to reinforce poorly defended Malta ends in disaster as the Italian Navy sinks four ships carrying fuel oil.

1944 In occupied Italy during World War II, partisans throw a bomb at an SS unit in Rome, killing 33 German soldiers. The next day, the Germans rounded up and murdered 335 Italian civilians in revenge.

1949 Israel signs an armistice agreement with Lebanon.

1961 An American plane is shot down over Laos on a mission to gauge the level of Soviet support to communist Pathet Lao guerrillas.

1962 French president Charles de Gaulle orders all-out war against the Algerian Organisation de l'Armée Secrète, or OAS.

1971 In East Pakistan, on Pakistan National Day, secessionists signal their intentions by raising the Bangladeshi flag. A declaration of independence followed on March 26.

Pakistan National Day

1603 Queen Elizabeth I of England, one of the realm's greatest monarchs, dies in Surrey after a 44-year reign in which England became more unified and distinguished itself in politics, commerce, and the arts.

1721 German musical great Johann Sebastian Bach completes the last of his Brandenburg Concertos.

1765 The British Parliament passes the much-reviled Quartering Act, which requires American colonists to provide temporary housing to British soldiers.

1776 English horologist John Harrison, who invented the first practical chronometer enabling navigators to fix longitude at sea, dies in London.

1794 During the French Revolution, Jacques-René Hebert, who had supported Robespierre during the Reign of Terror, finds the tables turned and his own head—and those of 17 friends—on the guillotine block.

1802 English inventor Richard Trevithick patents the first full-sized road locomotive.

1832 An American mob drags Mormon founder Joseph

John Harrison

BORN ON THIS DAY

1714
CARLO GIOVANNI TESTORI
Italian composer

1874
HARRY HOUDINI
Hungarian-born American magician

Harry Houdini

1887
ROSCOE "FATTY" ARBUCKLE
American vaudeville performer and silent-film actor (*The Gangsters; The Waiters' Picnic; His Wedding Night*)

1911
JOSEPH BARBERA
American cartoonist, producer, and director who teamed with William Hanna (*Tom and Jerry; The Flintstones; The Jetsons; Scooby-Doo; Yogi Bear; Jonny Quest*)

1919
LAWRENCE FERLINGHETTI
American Beat poet ("Constantly Risking Absurdity"; "Wild Dreams of a New Beginning"; "Seascape with Sun and Eagle"; "A Vast Confusion")

1930
STEVE MCQUEEN
American actor (*Papillon; The Great Escape; The Magnificent Seven*)

1932
YURI ANATOLIYEVICH PONOMARYOV
Russian cosmonaut

1937
BOB TILLMAN
American professional baseball player

1953
LOUIE ANDERSON
American comedian and game show host (*Family Feud*)

> *"My brain is the key that sets me free."*
>
> —*Harry Houdini*

Smith from his bed in Ohio, beats him, then tars and feathers him.

1882 German scientist Robert Koch announces the discovery of the tuberculosis bacillus, for which he would later win a Nobel Prize.

1900 American industrialist Andrew Carnegie incorporates his Carnegie Steel Company and soon pockets $25 million—more than half the company's $40 million first-year profit.

1916 A World War I German U-boat mistakes the *Sussex*, a French cross-channel steamer, for a minelayer and torpedoes it, killing 50 passengers and touching off an international crisis.

1917 Emperor Charles of Austria opens secret peace negotiations with the Allies during World War I, suggesting that his country was willing to end hostilities apart from Germany. Italy's recalcitrance eventually scotched the deal.

1921 The Allied reparations committee declares Germany in default of its payments for damages it caused during World War I.

1931 Hindu-Muslim riots of unprecedented scale erupt in north central India during a civil strike called by the Indian National Congress to protest the execution of a militant nationalist.

1933 British scientists Reginald Gibson and Eric Fawcett create polyethylene for the first time by heating ethylene and benzaldehyde under pressure.

1934 The Philippines wins independence from the United States after nearly 50 years of American control.

1939 English actor Basil Rathbone makes his debut as detective Sherlock Holmes, at the premiere of *The Hound of the Baskervilles*, in New York.

1942 American admiral Chester Nimitz is appointed commander in chief of the U.S. Pacific theater during World War II. On the same day, the German Nazis start deporting Slovak Jews to the Auschwitz extermination camp in Poland.

1944 A plane crash kills British general Orde Wingate, leader of the Chindit guerrilla brigade in Burma during World War II. On the same day, U.S. president Franklin D. Roosevelt condemns German and Japanese "crimes against humanity."

1958 Rock star Elvis Presley is officially inducted into the U.S. Army.

1965 To protest American policy in Vietnam, 200 University of Michigan faculty members cancel regular classes and stage a series of rallies and speeches to denounce the war. Similar "teach-ins" followed at university campuses across the country.

1972 The Equal Employment Opportunity Act passes into law in the United States, aimed at ensuring equality of race and gender in the workplace.

1996 American astronaut Shannon Lucid enters the Russian space station *Mir*, thus becoming the first female American astronaut to live in a space station. Her 188-day stay would set a new space endurance record for an American, and a world record for a woman.

1999 NATO warplanes bomb Yugoslavia in response to a new wave of "ethnic cleansing" launched by Serb forces against Kosovar Albanians. The strikes hit Serb military positions, government buildings, and the country's infrastructure.

MILESTONE

Exxon Valdez Runs Aground

On this day in 1989, the worst oil spill in U.S. territory begins when the supertanker *Exxon Valdez*, owned and operated by the Exxon Corporation, runs aground on a reef in Prince William Sound in southern Alaska. An estimated 11 million gallons of oil eventually spilled into the water. Attempts to contain the massive spill were unsuccessful, and wind and ocean currents spread the oil more than 100 miles from its source, eventually polluting more than 700 miles of coastline. Hundreds of thousands of birds and animals were adversely affected by the environmental disaster.

Exxon Valdez *(milestone)*

461 The Italian city of Venice is founded, according to tradition.

1586 Englishwoman Margaret Clitherow, daughter of the sheriff of York and wife of a wealthy butcher, is crushed to death in York for harboring priests. She was later canonized.

1616 English playwright William Shakespeare shakily signs his will, which turned over his property to the male heirs of his elder daughter and bequeathed to his wife his "second-best bed."

1634 The first Maryland colonists arrive at St. Clement's Island, on Maryland's western shore, and found the English settlement of St. Mary's.

1639 Construction begins on America's first canal to provide industrial water power, in Dedham, Massachusetts.

1655 Dutch astronomer, physicist, and mathematician Christiaan Huygens discovers Titan, Saturn's largest satellite.

1712 English botanist Nehemiah Grew, one of the founders of the science of plant anatomy, dies in London.

1807 England establishes the first railway passenger service.

1811 With France cut off from West Indies sugar,

BORN ON THIS DAY

1133
HENRY II
King of England (1154–89)

1867
ARTURO TOSCANINI
Italian conductor

1871
JOHN GUTZON BORGLUM
American sculptor (Mount Rushmore)

1881
BÉLA BARTÓK
Hungarian pianist and composer (*Music for Strings; Percussion and Celesta; Concerto for Orchestra*)

1908
DAVID LEAN
English director (*The Bridge on the River Kwai; Dr. Zhivago; Lawrence of Arabia*)

1920
HOWARD COSELL
American sports announcer

1921
SIMONE SIGNORET
German actress (*Room at the Top; Diabolique; Ship of Fools*)

1934
GLORIA STEINEM
American political activist and writer (*Outrageous Acts and Everyday Rebellions*), who founded *Ms.* magazine

1942
ARETHA FRANKLIN
American rhythm-and-blues singer ("Respect"; "Chain of Fools"; "I Say A Little Prayer"; "Natural Woman"), the first woman to be inducted into the Rock and Roll Hall of Fame

1947
ELTON JOHN
English singer/songwriter ("Goodbye Yellow Brick Road"; "Someone Saved My Life Tonight"; "I'm Still Standing")

"A woman without a man is like a fish without a bicycle."

—*Gloria Steinem*

Emperor Napoleon Bonaparte sets aside 80,000 acres for sugar-beet production, establishes six sugar-beet schools, and orders the construction of 10 sugar-beet factories.

1815 In response to Napoleon Bonaparte's recent return to power, Great Britain, Austria, Prussia, and Russia form a new military alliance pledging to supply 180,000 soldiers each for the fight against the French emperor.

1865 Confederate general Robert E. Lee orders his last attack of the American Civil War, a charge by 11,000 infantry against Fort Stedman, near Petersburg, Virginia. Lee's men were driven off with 3,000 casualties.

1879 Cheyenne chief Little Wolf, who was leading several hundred followers back to their homeland in Montana, surrenders to the U.S. Army and agrees to return to a reservation in Indian Territory.

1901 The first Mercedes is introduced at an auto race in Nice, France.

Rialto Bridge, right, Grand Canal, Venice, Italy,

Little Wolf, Cheyenne chief

🇺🇸 **1911** A one-hour blaze kills 146 garment workers, mostly young female immigrants, at the Triangle Shirtwaist Company in New York City and galvanizes the American public to press for factory reform.

⚔ **1917** In the World War I Battle of Jebel Hamlin, an Anglo-Indian force of 8,000 men tries to encircle 15,000 Turks in Iraq but fails, suffering 1,200 casualties.

⚔ **1918** Germany claims it has taken 45,000 Allied prisoners thus far in the Second Battle of the Somme during World War I.

1941 Yugoslavia casts its World War II lot with the fascists by signing the Tripartite Pact, which allied the Balkan nation with the Axis powers of Germany, Italy, and Japan.

⚔ **1942** During World War II, the Japanese begin daily bombing raids against Allied forces on the strategic island of Corregidor, at the mouth of Manila Bay in the Philippines.

1946 One of the first crises of the Cold War ends as the Soviet Union announces it will withdraw its troops from the oil-rich nation of Iran.

1950 The Somoza family takes control of Nicaragua and will remain in power for the next 40 years, lining its pockets through corrupt government economic ventures and by diverting foreign aid.

1954 The Soviet Union grants "full sovereignty" to East Germany and announces the end of its occupation, but says Soviet troops will remain in the country for security reasons.

1975 King Faisal, the absolute ruler of Saudi Arabia, is assassinated by his nephew and succeeded by his son, Crown Prince Khalid.

1996 The Ukraine raises its minimum wage to $36 a month.

Brothers Amir Khalid and Amir Faisal

752 The second Pope Stephen II is elected and consecrated. The first Stephen II survived only two days, dying before his consecration.

1726 Architect and playwright Sir John Vanbrugh, who designed many of England's greatest houses, dies in London. Referring to his baroque palaces such as Castle Howard and Blenheim, his epitaph reads: "Lay heavy on him, Earth, for he laid many heavy loads on thee."

1799 The United States and Tunis sign a treaty in which the United States buys protection against pirate attacks along the north African (Barbary) coast.

1821 In Canada, the Northwest Company and the Hudson's Bay Company merge and gain exclusive trading rights in the territory for 21 years.

1827 German composer Ludwig van Beethoven dies in Vienna.

1832 The American Fur Company's new steamboat *Yellowstone* departs St. Louis, Missouri, for Montana, opening the era of commercial steam traffic on the Missouri River.

1859 The solar system briefly gains an extra planet when the French amateur

> *"Advice is what we ask for when we already know the answer but wish we didn't."*
>
> —*Erica Jong*

1850
EDWARD BELLAMY
American author (*Looking Backward; The Blind Man's World and Other Stories*)

1874
ROBERT FROST
American poet ("Mending Wall"; "The Road Not Taken"; "Birches")

1911
TENNESSEE WILLIAMS
American playwright (*The Glass Menagerie; A Streetcar Named Desire; Cat on a Hot Tin Roof; The Night of the Iguana*)

1925
JAMES MOODY
American musician and bandleader ("I'm in the Mood for Love")

1930
SANDRA DAY O'CONNOR
First female U.S. Supreme Court justice

1931
LEONARD NIMOY
American actor (*Star Trek*)

1942
ERICA JONG
American author (*Fear of Flying; Fanny; Any Woman's Blues*)

1943
BOB WOODWARD
American journalist who broke the Watergate story with Carl Bernstein for the *Washington Post*

1944
DIANA ROSS
American rock singer ("Touch Me in the Morning"; "Stop in the Name of Love"; "Someday We'll Be Together")

1948
STEVEN TYLER
American rock singer (Aerosmith)

1960
MARCUS ALLEN
American professional football player

astronomer Lescarbault reports seeing an object inside the orbit of Venus. Named Vulcan, the object was later held to be a rogue asteroid.

1864 In the American Civil War, General James B. McPherson assumes command of the Union army of the Tennessee after William T. Sherman is elevated to commander of the Division of the Mississippi, making him the overall leader in the West.

1871 In France, the Communal Assembly takes control of the Paris Commune and the city. Priority reforms include decentralizing national government, separation of church and state, and replacement of the army with a national guard.

1885 Eastman Dry Plate and Film Company in Rochester, New York, begins manufacturing movie film.

1885 The Northwest Rebellion erupts in Manitoba, Canada. Meti settlers objecting to British-style land laws, having captured the store at Duck Lake, kill two "Mounties" and 11 volunteers in the force sent to eject them.

Turkish soldiers during the Balkan War

Egyptian president Anwar el-Sādāt, left, U.S. president Jimmy Carter, center, and Israeli prime minister Menachem Begin.

1886 In an atmosphere of unrest caused by economic depression, workers in Charleroi, Belgium, go on strike, and the government calls in troops to restore order.

1913 In the First Balkan War between the Balkan League and the Ottoman Empire, Bulgarian forces take Adrianople in western Turkey.

1920 American author F. Scott Fitzgerald's first novel, *This Side of Paradise,* is published, launching him to fame and fortune.

1938 Japan passes the National Mobilization Bill, giving the government dictatorial power over economic affairs.

1942 The first transport of Jews arrives at the concentration camp in Auschwitz, Poland, during Adolf Hitler's attempt to rid Europe of Jews during World War II.

1950 Major Oscar Osorio is elected president in El Salvador's first free election since 1931.

1975 During the Tet offensive of the Vietnam War, the city of Hue, in South Vietnam, falls to the North Vietnamese.

1979 At the White House, Egyptian president Anwar el-Sādāt and Israeli prime min-ister Menachem Begin sign the Camp David Accords, ending three decades of hostilities between Egypt and Israel.

1987 Tipped off by an escapee, police in Philadelphia, Pennsylvania, discover the bodies of three women in a basement torture chamber. They were victims of Gary Heidnik, who was later convicted and executed, and who inspired the Buffalo Bill character in Thomas Harris's novel *Silence of the Lambs.*

1992 Cosmonaut Sergei Krikalev returns to Earth after 313 days aboard the *Mir* space station and lands in a new country. While he was in space, the Soviet Union had ceased to exist.

1997 Near San Diego, California, police discover 39 victims of a mass suicide—members of the "Heaven's Gate" cult, who believed that suicide would allow them to leave their bodily "containers" and enter an alien spacecraft hidden behind the Hale-Bopp comet.

Gary Heidnik

⚔ **1351** In the War of Breton Succession, each side picks 30 knights. Then, according to the French chronicler Froissart, "one of them gave a signal and immediately they ran over and fought powerfully all in a pile." The combat determined nothing, but entered legend as the Battle of the Thirty.

🏳 **1794** The U.S. Congress authorizes the creation of a navy.

🏴‍☠ **1802** In the Treaty of Amiens, Great Britain and France conclude a peace that would last less than 14 months.

⚔ **1813** Russian and Prussian forces occupy Dresden, but would be defeated by French general Napoleon Bonaparte weeks later.

⚔ **1836** The Mexican army executes 417 Texas revolutionaries who had surrendered at Goliad. "Remember Goliad" joined "Remember the Alamo" as a battle cry.

🏳 **1841** New York firefighters test the first U.S. steam-powered fire engine. The horse-drawn behemoth was abandoned in part because its clouds of sparks were a fire hazard.

From left, Abraham Lincoln, William Tecumseh Sherman, Philip Henry Sheridan, and Ulysses S. Grant

BORN ON THIS DAY

1746
CARLO BONAPARTE
Corsican attorney, father of Emperor Napoleon I

1844
ADOLPHUS WASHINGTON GREELY
American Arctic explorer

A. W. Greely

1845
WILHELM KONRAD RÖNTGEN
Nobel Prize-winning German physicist who discovered x-rays

1863
SIR HENRY ROYCE
English automobile magnate

1879
EDWARD STEICHEN
American photography pioneer

1899
GLORIA SWANSON
American actress (*The Trespasser; Sadie Thompson; Sunset Boulevard*)

1921
HAROLD NICHOLAS
American dancer (The Nicholas Brothers)

1924
SARAH VAUGHAN
American jazz singer ("Lover Man"; "East of the Sun and West of the Moon"; "Motherless Child")

1942
MICHAEL YORK
English actor (*Cabaret; Murder on the Orient Express; Logan's Run*)

1963
QUENTIN TARANTINO
American director (*Reservoir Dogs; True Romance; Pulp Fiction; Jackie Brown*)

"Whatever is rightly done—however humble—is noble."
—*Sir Henry Royce*

🏳 **1855** American inventor Abraham Gesner gets a patent for a process that derives a flammable oil from coal. He calls the oil kerosene.

🏳 **1865** U.S. president Abraham Lincoln meets with generals Ulysses S. Grant and William T. Sherman at City Point, Virginia, to plot the last stages of the Civil War. Less than four weeks later the Confederacy surrendered.

🔬 **1884** The first long-distance telephone call is made, from Boston, Massachusetts, to New York City.

▬ **1898** In the European rush to force entry into China, Russia extorts a 25-year lease on the Liaodong peninsula and a railway easement from Harbin to two ports on the peninsula.

⚖ **1905** For the first time, fingerprint evidence is used to solve a murder case—the bludgeoning of South London, England, shopkeepers Thomas and Ann Farrow by brothers Alfred and Albert Stratton.

🏳 **1912** Two Japanese cherry trees are planted along the Potomac in Washington, D.C., the first of 3,020 given by Japan to the United States. After World War II, cuttings from Washington's cherry trees were sent back to Japan to restore the Tokyo collection that was decimated by

American bombing attacks during the war.

1925 In England, Cecil Kimber registers his first modified Morris, "Old Number One," the prototype of the enormously popular MG sports car.

1929 Yugoslavia and Greece sign a treaty of friendship.

1931 English writer Arnold Bennett dies of typhoid contracted in Paris.

1941 Two days after Yugoslavia joined the Axis during World War II, a military coup overthrows the government. In response, Germany invaded, and on April 20 occupied Belgrade.

1945 Germany launches the last of their V-2 rockets at England and Belgium, adding almost 200 casualties to the more than 7,000 British and Belgians already killed by the primitive missiles during World War II.

1945 During World War II, Argentina declares war on Germany and Japan.

1952 What many believe to be the best-ever Hollywood musical, *Singin' in the Rain* starring Gene Kelly, premieres at New York's Radio City Music Hall.

1958 Soviet first secretary Nikita Khrushchev replaces Nicolai Bulganin as Soviet premier, becoming the first leader since Joseph Stalin to simultaneously hold the U.S.S.R.'s two top offices.

1964 The Summer Olympics are held in Tokyo,

signaling Japan's postwar recovery in world esteem.

1968 The Indonesian Congress gives General Suharto full presidential powers for a five-year term.

1973 As the last U.S. troops prepare to leave Vietnam toward the end of the Vietnam War, the White House announces that, at the request of Cambodian president Lon Nol, the bombing of Cambodia will continue until communist forces agree to a cease-fire.

1977 In aviation's deadliest accident, two 747 jets collide on the runway at Tenerife Airport in the Canary Islands. A terrorist bomb explosion at the airport on neighboring Gran Canaria had diverted many planes to Tenerife, causing congestion that may have contributed to the crash. Death toll: 582.

Opening day of 1964 Olympic Games

49 B.C. Marcus Tullius Cicero, the Roman statesman, lawyer, and scholar, tells Julius Caesar that he will ask the Roman Senate to oppose Caesar's war against Pompey.

72 Masada, the natural rock fortress in Israel, falls to the Roman army after its defenders take their own lives rather than be sold into slavery.

1629 Austria's Ferdinand II, Holy Roman emperor and a champion of Counter-Reformation, issues the Edict of Restitution, which restores all church lands secularized by Protestant rulers since 1552 and bans Calvinism within the empire.

1776 Spanish explorer Juan Bautista de Anza lands in San Francisco Bay and establishes a settlement with 247 colonists.

1800 The USS *Essex* becomes the first American naval vessel to sail around the Cape of Good Hope in South Africa.

1814 French physician Joseph-Ignace Guillotin, inventor

Tourists visit Masada on the Dead Sea in Israel

"Every new time will give its law."

—*Maxim Gorky*

of the infamous decapitation machine, dies in bed.

1814 The USS *Essex* is captured by British warships during the War of 1812.

1854 In the Crimean War, France and Great Britain declare war on Russia.

1862 In the American Civil War, the Battle of Glorietta Pass ends in defeat for Confederate forces seeking to capture New Mexico and western silver and gold mines.

1898 The German Reichstag passes its First Naval Bill, which called for an expansion of the navy by seven battleships, two heavy cruisers, and seven light cruisers.

1899 The first wireless telegraph message is transmitted between England and Europe by the Italian radio pioneer Guglielmo Marconi.

1900 The British royal family takes delivery of its first motorcar, a Daimler Mail Phaeton.

1905 Cornelius Ehret of Rosemont, Pennsylvania, patents the radio fax, calling it "a system for transmitting intelligence."

1915 A German U-boat torpedoes and sinks a passenger liner, the SS *Falaba*, during World War I.

1917 During World War I, women officially join the British armed forces for the first time with the creation of the Women's Army Auxiliary Corps.

1919 Herbert Hoover, American director of food relief in postwar Europe, urges the Allies to fight communism by making massive deliveries of food to Bolshevik Russia.

1941 At the Battle of Cape Matapan in the Mediterranean during World War II, an outgunned British battle fleet destroys much of Italy's remaining navy, crippling one major battleship and sinking three modern cruisers and two destroyers.

1941 English novelist Virginia Woolf leaves her home at Rodmell in Sussex, and is never seen again. Fearing the onset of madness, aggravated by the events of World War II, she filled her pockets with stones and drowned herself in the River Ouse.

1942 In a daring World War II raid on the French port of St. Nazaire, British commandos ram an explosives-laden destroyer into a dry-dock and destroy many facilities.

1959 China dissolves the Tibetan government headed by the Dalai Lama and installs the Panchen Lama as head of the Tibetan Autonomous Region.

1979 The worst nuclear power accident in American history begins at Pennsylvania's Three Mile Island power plant when a pressure valve fails to close and the reactor core nearly melts down. Within days, more than 100,000 people had fled the area.

1994 In Johannesburg, South Africa, a large demonstration by the Inkatha Freedom Party is fired upon, killing 56 people and injuring 400 others.

Zulu Inkatha Freedom Party supporter taking cover

1188 Holy Roman emperor Frederick Barbarossa, himself a crusader, decrees the protection of Jews under his rule and thus prevents the excessive violence that occurred during previous crusades.

1461 Lancastrians lose the Battle of Towton, in the War of the Roses, and Edward IV secures the English throne. The battle was the bloodiest ever fought on English soil, with a death toll estimated to be as high as 38,000.

1614 *History of the World,* written by English explorer Sir Walter Raleigh while imprisoned in the Tower of London, is published. The unfinished work covered creation to the second century B.C.

Sir Walter Raleigh

1644 During the English civil war, the Royalists commanded by Lord Hopton are defeated by the Parlimentarians under Sir William Waller at the battle of Cheriton in Hampshire.

1797 English social critic Mary Wollstonecraft, an early activist for women's rights, marries William Godwin, the

1561
SANTORIO SANTORIO
Italian physician who designed the clinical thermometer

1616
JOHANN ERASMUS KINDERMANN
German composer

1790
JOHN TYLER
Tenth U.S. president

John Tyler

1867
CY YOUNG
American Hall of Fame baseball player

1918
SAM WALTON
American founder of Wal-Mart stores

1918
PEARL BAILEY
American singer and actress (*Variety Girl; Isn't It Romantic; Carmen Jones; Porgy and Bess*)

1943
JOHN MAJOR
British prime minister (1990–97)

1964
ELLE MACPHERSON
Australian model and actress

1968
LUCY LAWLESS
New Zealand actress (*Xena: Warrior Princess*)

1976
JENNIFER CAPRIATI
American tennis champion

most famous radical reformer of his time. The two were philosophically opposed to marriage, but she was pregnant with a girl: the future Mary Shelley, author of *Frankenstein.*

1806 The U.S. Congress appropriates $30,000 to begin construction of The Great National Pike, also known as the Cumberland Road, the first American highway funded by the national treasury.

1807 The brightest asteroid on record, Vesta 4, is observed for the first time by German astronomer Heinrich Olbers. Vesta is 325 miles in diameter.

1814 The king of Denmark outlaws racial and religious discrimination, allowing Jews to work in any profession.

1847 U.S. troops capture the Mexican fortress of Vera Cruz.

1848 Ice in Lake Erie forms into a dam and cuts off the flow of water out of the lake, causing the Niagara Falls to run dry for more than a day.

1865 The final campaign of the American Civil War begins when Union forces move against Petersburg, Virginia. General Robert E. Lee's outnumbered Rebels soon fled the city, and Lee surrendered on April 9 at Appomattox Court House.

> *"The politician who never made a mistake never made a decision."*
>
> —*John Major*

Grand salute at Vera Cruz

Japanese Set Up Puppet Regime at Nanking

On this day in 1940, Japan establishes its own government in conquered Nanking, the former capital of Nationalist China. In 1937, Japan drummed up a rationale for war against Chiang Kai-shek's Nationalist China (claiming Chinese troops attacked Japanese troops on maneuvers in a so-called autonomous region of China) and invaded northeastern China, bombing Shanghai and carving out a new state, Manchukuo. Nanking was declared by the Japanese to be the center of a new Chinese government, a regime controlled by Wang Ching-wei, a defector from the Nationalist cause and now a Japanese puppet.

Chiang Kai-shek

★ 1867 The Dominion of Canada, not quite an independent country yet, is established by the British North American Act. The first provinces are Ontario, Quebec, New Brunswick, and Nova Scotia.

1879 At Kambula, in northwest Zululand, a force of 2,000 British and Colonial troops under the command of British colonel Henry Evelyn Wood, defeats 20,000 Zulus under king Cetshwayo, turning the tide in favor of the British in the Zulu War.

1885 In his Atlanta, Georgia, backyard, Dr. John Pemberton brews up the first batch of his "brain tonic and intellectual beverage," the cocaine-containing Coca-Cola.

1912 English explorer Robert Falcon Scott writes his last diary entry in the Antarctic, starving to death in a tent only 11 miles from a food depot: "We are getting weaker, of course, and the end cannot be far. It seems a pity, but I do not think I can write more."

1919 Observations of stars during a total solar eclipse show that gravity can bend light rays, supporting a key element of German physicist Albert Einstein's Theory of Relativity.

1945 American general George S. Patton's 3rd Army captures Frankfurt, Germany.

1951 In one of the most sensational trials in American history, Julius and Ethel Rosenberg are convicted of espionage for their role in passing atomic secrets to the Soviets during and after World War II. They were executed in 1953.

1974 The unmanned U.S. space probe *Mariner 10* becomes the first to visit the planet Mercury, sending back close-up images of a celestial body usually obscured because of its proximity to the sun.

Preparations to encapsulate Mariner 10

240 B.C. Halley's Comet reaches perihelion, the nearest point of its orbit to the sun, this week. Chinese observers record seeing a "broom star," the earliest historical record of the comet.

1218 In England, King Henry III proclaims the Yellow Badge Edict, under which every Jew older than seven must wear a yellow identifying badge.

1282 An independence rebellion erupts at Palermo, Italy, and spreads across Sicily. Nearly all resident French were massacred.

1533 Henry VIII divorces his first wife, Catherine of Aragon, after 24 years of marriage. He married five more times before his death 10 years later.

1581 Pope Gregory XIII forbids Catholics to use Jewish doctors.

1649 Oliver Cromwell is appointed commander in chief of British forces sent to put down a rebellion in Ireland. This is accomplished at the cost of many thousands of lives.

1791 The French National Academy defines a meter as one 10-millionth the distance from the equator to the North Pole.

1814 European forces allied against Napoleonic France march triumphantly into Paris, formally ending a decade

---

> *"Laughter is*
> *wine for the soul . . ."*
>
> —*Sean O'Casey*

MILESTONE

President Reagan Shot
On this day in 1981, U.S. president Ronald W. Reagan is shot in the chest outside a Washington, D.C., hotel by a deranged drifter named John Hinckley Jr. The president had just finished addressing a labor meeting and was walking with his entourage to his limousine when Hinckley, standing among a group of reporters, fired six shots at him, hitting Reagan and three of his attendants. Hinckley was then overpowered and pinned against a wall, and Reagan, apparently unaware that he had been shot, was shoved into his limousine by a Secret Service agent and rushed to a hospital.

---

of French domination on the continent.

1840 Beau Brummel, English dandy and trendsetter of his time, dies in France, in self-imposed exile, penniless.

1842 In the first use of ether as a surgical anesthetic, American physician Crawford Long drapes an ether-soaked cloth over a patient's face.

1843 Napoleon Guerin, of New York, patents the mechanical egg incubator.

1849 British India annexes all Sikh territory— primarily the Punjab.

1855 In territorial Kansas's first election, 5,000 "Border Ruffians" from western Missouri force the election of a pro-slavery legislature. Although the number of votes cast exceeded the number of eligible voters, Kansas governor Andrew Reeder reluctantly approved the election to prevent further bloodshed.

1855 By signing a treaty of friendship with British India, Afghanistan acknowledges India's annexation of Peshawar and the Punjab.

1856 The Treaty of Paris ends the Crimean War, forcing Russia to accept the Black Sea as neutral territory. This left Great Britain the major power in the eastern Mediterranean and France the dominant power on the European continent.

1858 H. L. Lipman of Philadelphia, Pennsylvania, patents the concept of attaching an eraser to a lead pencil.

1867 U.S. secretary of state William H. Seward signs a treaty with Russia for the purchase of Alaska for $7 million, roughly two cents an acre. The purchase was ridiculed in Congress and in the press as "Seward's folly," "Seward's icebox," and President Andrew Johnson's "polar bear garden."

1870 The 15th Amendment is formally adopted into the U.S. Constitution. The amendment reads, "the right of citizens of the United States to vote shall not be denied or abridged by the United States or by any State on account of race, color, or previous condition of servitude."

1909 New York City's double-decker Queensboro Bridge, connecting Long Island to the borough of Queens, opens to traffic.

1912 France establishes a protectorate covering most of Morocco.

1917 The Russian provisional government declares its support of an independent Poland defined by land where Poles were the majority population.

1923 Arriving in New York after a 123-day cruise, the *Laconia* becomes the first cruise ship to circle the globe.

1928 In Venice, Italy, Italian pilot Mario de Bernardi tops 300 miles per hour to set a new air-speed flying record, logging 318.62 miles per hour in a Macchi M52bis.

1943 The first musical by Rodgers and Hammerstein, *Oklahoma!*, opens on Broadway.

1947 American inventor Preston Tucker announces his concept for "the Tucker," a rear-engine car with two revolving headlights, one stationary "cyclops" headlight in the middle, and a central steering wheel flanked by two passenger seats. A few Tuckers were built, but the company failed.

1951 The Electronic Control Company runs a 17-hour rigorous acceptance test of UNIVAC, the first commercial computer. After acceptance by the U.S. Census Department, the government ordered five more the following year.

Preston Tucker and the Tucker auto

1282 In Palermo, Sicily, an uprising against the rule of the French Charles of Anjou reaches its height, with the deaths of many French. The revolt had started at Vespers the previous day, and has become known as "Sicilian Vespers."

1492 Spain's Catholic rulers, Ferdinand and Isabella, issue an edict ordering all Jews to convert to Christianity or be expelled from the country. About 40,000 chose exile.

1631 English poet John Donne, perhaps best known for the lines "never send to know for whom the bell tolls; it tolls for thee," dies.

1650 An earthquake destroys much of Cuzco, Peru.

1776 Abigail Adams writes to her husband, future U.S. president John Adams, who at the time is in Congress in Philadelphia, Pennsylvania, drafting laws for independence. She urges him to consider women's rights. "Remember the Ladies. . . . Remember all men would be tyrants if they could."

1796 Johann Wolfgang von Goethe's play *Egmont* premières in Germany.

1831 The Canadian cities of Montreal and Quebec are incorporated.

1836 The first installment of *The Posthumous Papers of the Pickwick Club*, by 24-year-old English writer Charles Dickens, is published under the pseudonym Boz. Originally commissioned as captions for humorous

---

BORN ON THIS DAY

1596
RENÉ DESCARTES
French philosopher, mathematician, and scientist (*La Géométrie*)

René Descartes

1732
JOSEPH HAYDN
Austrian musician and composer (*The Seasons*; "Emperor's Hymn")

1914
OCTAVIO PAZ
Mexican writer and diplomat (*The Labyrinth of Solitude*)

1924
LEO BUSCAGLIA
American author (*Living, Loving and Learning*)

1927
CÉSAR CHÁVEZ
Mexican-American labor leader and activist who organized the first farm workers' union in the United States

1928
GORDIE HOWE
American NHL Hall of Fame hockey player

1934
SHIRLEY JONES
American actress and singer (*Oklahoma!*; *Carousel*; *The Partridge Family*)

1935
HERB ALPERT
American musician ("Taste of Honey"; "This Guy's in Love with You"; "Rise")

1943
CHRISTOPHER WALKEN
American actor (*The Deer Hunter*; *The Dead Zone*; *Joe Dirt*)

1948
AL GORE
U.S. senator and vice-president

"It is not enough to have a good mind. The main thing is to use it well."

—René Descartes

drawings, the whimsical stories soon became popular in their own right.

1840 U.S. president Martin Van Buren strikes a blow for government employees by establishing a 10-hour workday.

1850 The U.S. population is 23,191,876.

1854 In Tokyo, Commodore Matthew Calbraith Perry, representing the U.S. government, signs the Treaty of Kanagawa with the Japanese government, opening the ports of Shimoda and Hakodate to American trade and permitting the establishment of a U.S. consulate in Japan.

1865 In Virginia, fighting at White Oak Road begins the final offensive of the American Civil War. The next day's Battle of Five Forks crushed the Rebel flank and forced General Robert E. Lee to evacuate Richmond and Petersburg.

1880 Wabash, Indiana, becomes the first American community to convert completely to electric street lamps—only four arc lamps powered by a steam engine.

1889 The Eiffel Tower is dedicated in Paris, France. At almost 1,000 feet it was the world's tallest man-made structure. Gustave Eiffel was a

---

The Eiffel Tower

French bridge builder who also designed the framework of the Statue of Liberty.

1896 Chicago inventor Whitcomb L. Judson patents the first zip-type fastener, under the name "clasp locker and unlocker for shoes."

1900 The first car advertisement to run in an American national magazine appears in the American *Saturday Evening Post*. The W. E. Roach Company promised "Automobiles That Give Satisfaction."

1909 Despite outrage over losing what it regarded as its own legacy, Serbia accepts Austria's annexation of Bosnia and Herzegovina.

1909 In Belfast, Ireland, keel blocks are laid for the British passenger liner *Titanic*.

1918 U.S. president Woodrow Wilson signs a law adopting daylight saving time as a fuel-saving measure. Repealed when the war ended, it was reinstated year-round during World War II.

1921 British miners in the midst of a severe postwar depression launch the Great Coal Strike. Railway and transport workers joined the miners for two weeks, but the miners held out until July, when they were offered subsidies and higher wages.

1923 Alma Cummings stays on her feet for 27 hours to win the first U.S. dance marathon.

1930 The Motion Picture Producers and Distributors of America formally adopt the Production Code, which for 30 years imposed strict guidelines on cinematic treatment of sex, crime, religion, violence, and other controversial subjects.

1931 In Nicaragua, a moderate earthquake of 5.6 magnitude kills 2,400 people.

1933 The U.S. Congress establishes the Civilian Conservation Corps, which offered conservation-related jobs to unemployed Americans during the Great Depression.

1939 With an eye on Germany's invasion of Czechoslovakia, Great Britain and France guarantee support of Poland against aggression.

1940 The German auxiliary cruiser *Atlantis*, a converted merchant ship, begins its career as a commerce raider during World War II. Under disguise, the *Atlantis* sank a total of 22 merchant ships before it was sunk by the British cruiser *Devonshire*.

1949 Newfoundland joins the Canadian confederation.

MILESTONE

Dalai Lama Begins Exile

The Dalai Lama, fleeing the Chinese suppression of a national uprising in Tibet, crosses the border into India on this day in 1959, where he is granted political asylum. Tensin Gyatso was designated the 14th Dalai Lama in 1940. At the beginning of the 20th century, Tibet increasingly came under Chinese control, and in 1950, Communist China invaded Tibet. With the beginning of the Cultural Revolution in China, the Chinese suppression of Tibetan Buddhism escalated; the practice of the religion was banned, and thousands of monasteries were destroyed. The exiled Dalai Lama won widespread international support for the Tibetan independence movement, and in 1989 he was awarded the Nobel Peace Prize in recognition of his nonviolent campaign to end Chinese domination there.

The Dalai Lama displays Nobel Peace Prize

1205 Amalric II, king of Cyprus and Jerusalem, dies.

1572 Dutch rebels seize the strategic port of Brielle, in Holland, touching off a successful revolt against Spanish rule.

1700 English pranksters begin popularizing the annual tradition of April Fool's Day by playing practical jokes on one another.

1816 English novelist Jane Austen dismisses a suggestion from the Prince Regent that she write a historical novel by saying, "I could not sit down to write a serious romance under any other motive than to save my life."

1836 English naturalist Charles Darwin, aboard the *Beagle*, arrives at the Cocos (or Keeling) Islands in the Indian Ocean to investigate whether the islands' coral reefs formed atop submerged mountains.

1864 Travelers Insurance Company sells the first-ever travel insurance policy to one James Batterson, who survived his journey and later bought a

The Battle of Five Forks

BORN ON THIS DAY

1578
WILLIAM HARVEY
English physician who discovered the circulation of the blood

1815
OTTO VON BISMARCK
German chancellor
(1866–1890)

1852
EDWARD AUSTIN ABBEY
American painter

1866
FERRUCCIO BUSONI
Italian composer

1868
EDMOND ROSTAND
French poet and playwright
(*Cyrano de Bergerac*)

1873
SERGEI RACHMANINOFF
Russian pianist and composer

Sergei Rachmaninoff

1920
TOSHIRO MIFUNE
Japanese actor (*Rashoman*)

1922
WILLIAM MANCHESTER
American historian and writer
(*Death of a President*)

---

general policy from the same company.

1865 In the waning days of the American Civil War, Union forces cut Confederate supply lines along the Petersburg-Richmond front in Virginia, forcing Southern troops to evacuate both cities and flee westward. The engagement, called the Battle of Five Forks, cost a thousand Union and five thousand Confederate casualties.

1875 The *Times of London* becomes the first newspaper to print a daily weather chart.

1877 American prospector Edward Schieffelin sets off for southern Arizona, where he will discover one of the richest silver veins in the west, the Tombstone Lode, about seventy miles southeast of present Tuscon.

1878 Madame Restell—a supplier of avidly sought-after, mail-order contraceptives—slits her own throat rather than face vice charges under America's prudish Comstock Act.

1889 Chicago inventor Josephine Cockrane markets a primitive version of the dishwasher, which required users to pour boiling water from a tea kettle onto the dishes so they could air dry.

1904 British engineer Henry Royce, dissatisfied with

> *"Growth for the sake of growth is the ideology of the cancer cell."*
>
> —*Edward Abbey*

his Decauville car, produces a 10 hp, 2-cylinder prototype of his own manufacture. Later in 1904 Royce was introduced to Charles Rolls, and two years later the Rolls-Royce Company was founded.

1918 Great Britain forms the Royal Air Force (RAF), an amalgamation of the existing Royal Flying Corps and Royal Naval Air Service. By war's end, the RAF's 300,000 personnel had charge of 22,000 aircraft.

1924 Nazi Party leader Adolf Hitler is convicted of high treason and sentenced to five years in prison for leading an unsuccessful coup called the "Beer Hall Putsch." Hitler served just nine months and used the time to write his autobiography, *Mein Kampf.*

1929 New York inventor Louis Marx introduces the world to the ups and downs of the yo-yo.

1933 Hitler's coalition government begins an assault against German Jews by calling a boycott of Jewish-owned businesses.

1934 Bank robbers Bonnie Parker and Clyde Barrow murder two policemen in Grapevine, Texas.

1942 Japanese troops invade Dutch New Guinea.

1945 Some 50,000 American troops land on the southwest coast of Okinawa and begin a ferocious, twelve-week battle for the strategic island, which was defended by

100,000 Japanese. The battle took the lives of more than 12,000 Americans, more than 90,000 Japanese troops, and at least 100,000 Japanese civilians.

1948 In a precursor to the Cold War's Berlin Blockade, Soviet troops begin stopping U.S. and British military trains traveling through the Russian sector to and from Berlin.

1949 British parliament approves a bill to create Great Britain's first National Parks, 77 years and one month after Yellowstone Park, Wyoming, in the United States, became the world's first National Park. The Peak District became Great Britain's first National Park in December 1950.

1960 The United States launches the world's first weather satellite, *Tiros I.*

1999 The Inuit of the Eastern Arctic gain control of their own homeland as Canada establishes the territory of Nunavut, a vast tract nearly as large as Alaska and California combined.

Nunavut premier Paul Okalik, right, giving a ceremony speech for new territory

MILESTONE

Florida Governor Commits Suicide

Worn down by the stresses of his office, Florida governor John Milton commits suicide on this day in 1865 at his plantation, Sylvania. Milton was a capable governor who valiantly defended his state and supplied provisions to the Confederacy, but by the end of the war much of Florida was occupied by Union forces and the state's finances were depleted. Just before his death, Milton addressed the Florida legislature and said that Yankees "have developed a character so odious that death would be preferable to reunion with them." Milton was 57 when he put a pistol to his head.

🏴 **1234** The outspoken and brilliant scholar Edmund Rich is consecrated as archbishop of Canterbury. He was later canonized St. Edmund of Abington.

1282 Giacomo Savelli, old and crippled, is elected pope and begins a two-year reign in which he clashed with the king of Aragon over the independence of Sicily.

1507 Francis of Paola, founder of an ascetic Roman Catholic order of vegan monks, dies in France. His remains were later dug up and burned by Huguenots.

1513 Spanish explorer Juan Ponce de León sets foot on the Florida coast near present-day St. Augustine and claims the territory for Spain.

🔫 **1517** The Ottoman Empire completes its conquest of Egypt by defeating the Mamluk army at Giza.

1595 The first Dutch trading expedition to the East Indies gets underway as brothers Cornelis and Frederik de Houtman set sail from Amsterdam in command of four merchant ships.

🔫 **1781** The American frigate *Alliance* captures two British privateers, *Mars* and *Minerva*.

1796 A forged Shakespeare play, *Vortigern and Rowena*, flops in London, helping to expose its author, William Henry Ireland, as a fraud.

🔫 **1801** British vice admiral Horatio Nelson raids Copen-

British naval hero Horatio Nelson

hagen harbor and decimates the Danish fleet.

🔫 **1865** In the climax of the American Civil War, Union forces under Ulysses S. Grant overrun Confederate trenches defending the Virginia cities of Petersburg and Richmond. By nightfall Jefferson Davis and the Confederate government had fled and Richmond was ablaze.

🇺🇸 **1879** The first commercial telephone service using toll lines links Springfield and Holyoke, Massachusetts, towns about eight miles apart.

🔬 **1889** American scientist Charles M. Hall patents an inexpensive process for extracting aluminum from its ore.

🔫 **1916** A World War I Zeppelin raid on the east coast of Scotland kills thirteen and injures twenty-four.

🇺🇸 **1917** American president Woodrow Wilson appears before a joint session of Congress and asks for a declaration of war against Germany, warning that "the world must be made safe for democracy." On the same day, a German U-boat sinks the American armed liner *Aztec* off France.

BORN ON THIS DAY

742
CHARLEMAGNE
First Holy Roman emperor (800-814)

1725
GIOVANNI CASANOVA
Italian writer who became famous for his erotic adventures

1798
AUGUST HEINRICH HOFFMAN VON FALLERSLEBEN
German poet whose poem *Deutschland über Alles* became the German national anthem in 1841

1805
HANS CHRISTIAN ANDERSEN
Danish writer of fairy tales

1840
ÉMILE ZOLA
French writer (*Nana; Germinal*)

Émile Zola

1875
WALTER CHRYSLER
American auto manufacturer (Chrysler Corporation)

1891
MAX ERNST
German painter, sculptor who founded Dadaism

1914
SIR ALEC GUINNESS
English actor (*The Bridge on the River Kwai; Star Wars*)

1955
DANA CARVEY
American comedian and actor (*Saturday Night Live; Wayne's World*)

1960
LINFORD CHRISTIE
British athlete, Olympic-gold medalist in 1992

1917 Suffragist and pacifist Jeannette Rankin, the first woman ever elected to the U.S. Congress, takes her seat at the Capitol as a representative from Montana.

1920 American women picket the British embassy in Washington demanding freedom for Ireland.

1935 Scottish physicist Sir Robert Alexander Watson-Watt patents radar for the detection of approaching aircraft.

1941 German general Erwin Rommel and the Afrika Korps resume their advance across Libya, driving the depleted British army back toward Egypt.

1942 German planes begin bombing British submarine and bomber bases on the island of Malta enabling more supply convoys to reach Rommel's army in North Africa.

1943 John Maunchly, a University of Pennsylvania physicist, proposes to build a computer to calculate ballistic missile firing

tables. The result, delivered three years later, was a machine called ENIAC, the world's first electronic computer.

1953 British scientists Francis Crick and James Watson publish the first description of the double-helix structure of DNA, in the journal *Nature*.

1977 Great Britain's Grand National provides two historic firsts: Red Rum becomes the first horse to win the event three times (having won in 1973 and 1974 and come second in 1975 and 1976); and, for the first time, a female jockey is allowed to take part.

1979 Menachem Begin travels to Cairo as the first Israeli prime minister to visit Egypt. The previous year Begin and President el Sādāt of Egypt had been joint recipients of the Nobel Peace Prize.

1982 Argentine troops invade the Falkland Islands, quickly overcoming a small garrison of British marines and triggering a war with Great Britain. The Falklands, which lie 300 miles off the southern tip of Argentina, had been in Great Britain's possession since 1833.

*General Rommel,
standing front
right*

1312 B.C. On this traditional date, the Red Sea is parted for the Israelites fleeing Egypt. By the Hebrew calendar, it was 21 Nissan, 2448.

1559 France, England, and Spain sign the treaty of Cateau-Cambresis, ending 60 years of war.

1692 In Salem, Massachusetts, Sarah Cloyce is accused of witchcraft. Unlike her condemned sister Rebecca Nurse, she was not convicted or executed.

1721 Robert Walpole becomes Great Britain's first prime minister.

1753 Samuel Johnson ("Dr. Johnson") begins work on the second volume of his *Dictionary of the English Language*. The dictionary was published in 1755.

1776 George Washington receives the first honorary Doctor of Law degree conferred by Harvard College.

1811 French forces retreating from Portugal are defeated at Sabugal.

1829 The coffee mill is patented by James Carrington, of Connecticut.

1865 In the American Civil War, the Rebel capital of Richmond, Virginia, falls to Union forces.

1882 Jesse James, one of America's most

M I L E S T O N E

Pony Express Mail Service Begins

On this day in 1860, the first Pony Express mail simultaneously leaves St. Joseph, Missouri, and Sacramento, California, carried by Henry Wallace riding west and John Roff riding east. The Pony Express Company charged $5 for every half-ounce of mail. The mail service captivated the American imagination and helped win federal aid for a more economical overland mail service. It also contributed to the economy of the towns on its route and served the mail-service needs of the American West in the days before the telegraph or an efficient transcontinental railroad. Pony Express mail service was discontinued in October 1861.

Samuel Johnson

notorious outlaws, is shot to death by Robert Ford, a member of his gang who hoped to collect the bounty on Jesse's head.

1885 Gottlieb Daimler is granted a German patent for his one-cylinder, water-cooled engine, a major breakthrough in the design of internal combustion engines.

1917 The U.S. Senate approves the war resolution. Three days later the House followed suit and President Woodrow Wilson declared war on Germany.

1919 Austria's National Assembly passes the Hapsburg Law, requiring all Hapsburgs to leave the country or accept their status as ordinary citizens with no dynastic ambitions.

1919 Norwegian explorer Fridtjof Nansen joins Herbert Hoover in urging the Paris Peace Conference to promote stability in civil war-torn Russia

Pony Express rider (milestone)

> *"I have been under-estimated for decades. I've done very well that way."*
>
> *—Helmut Kohl*

with food distributions rather than military action.

⚖️ **1936** Richard Bruno Hauptmann, convicted in the 1932 kidnapping and murder of the 20-month-old son of aviator Charles Lindbergh, is executed by electrocution.

1941 Iraq's former prime minister Rashid Ali al-Gailani, a supporter of Germany, seizes power in Baghdad. British troops restored the previous government two months later.

1942 Japanese infantry stage a major offensive against Allied troops in Bataan, the peninsula guarding Manila Bay of the Philippine Islands.

1948 U.S. president Harry S. Truman signs into law the Foreign Assistance Act, commonly known as the Marshall Plan. Named after U.S. Secretary of State George C. Marshall, the program channeled more than $13 billion in aid to Europe between 1948 and 1951.

1949 Jordan and Israel sign an armistice putting the West Bank and East Jerusalem, with 500,000 Palestinians, under Jordanian control.

1956 Elvis sings his first RCA recording, "Heartbreak Hotel," on NBC's *Milton Berle Show*. By April 21, the song became Elvis' first No. 1 single.

⚖️ **1957** The American Civil Liberties Union announces it will defend Allen Ginsberg's book *Howl* against obscenity charges. The U.S. Customs Department found it unsuitable for American eyes, but lost the case in court.

1965 The U.S. orbits an experimental space reactor, the *SNAP 10-A*, first nuclear reactor in space. Shut down due to failure after 43 days, it's still up there.

1968 Martin Luther King, Jr. gives his last sermon, in Memphis, Tennessee. "I've been to the mountaintop," he said. "I've looked over, and I've seen the promised land." The next day he was assassinated.

1974 The largest tornado outbreak ever recorded—the "Super Outbreak"—hits 11 U.S. states and southern Canada. In all, 144 tornadoes killed 330 people in two days.

1996 At his small wilderness cabin near Lincoln, Montana, Theodore John Kaczynski is arrested by FBI agents and accused of being the Unabomber, the elusive terrorist blamed for 16 mail bombs that killed three people and injured 23 during an 18-year period.

Theodore John Kaczynski arrested

2094 B.C. Clay tablets from Ur mark the earliest historical reference to a lunar eclipse, calling it a prediction of famine, many deaths, and the murder of the king by his son.

527 Justinian, nephew and adopted son of Byzantine Emperor Justin I, is named co-emperor with the title of Augustus. On the same day, his wife Theodora is crowned Augusta. Four months later, Justin died and Justinian became sole emperor.

1081 Alexius Comnenus, having seized the throne from Nicephorus III, is crowned emperor of the Eastern Roman Empire.

1147 The Prince of Suzdal throws a famous banquet for the Prince of Novgorod-Seversky in Moscow. Recorded in monastic chronicles, the feast became the traditional date for the city's founding.

1284 Alfonso X, Spanish king and astronomer, dies at age 62. He tabulated the movements of the planets, and concluded long before Copernicus that the Ptolemaic model was too complicated.

1798 The HMS *Bounty*, under Captain William Bligh, sets sail from Tahiti and into history. The famous mutiny happened on April 28.

> *"Children's talent to endure stems from their ignorance of alternatives."*
> —*Maya Angelou*

1812 The U.S. declares a 90-day embargo on trade with England, ostensibly to protect America's merchant ships. In fact, President Madison saw British harrassment of American ships as an excuse to enter the War of 1812 and an opportunity for American expansion.

1828 In the Netherlands, Casparus van Wooden patents chocolate milk powder.

1841 Only 31 days in office, William Henry Harrison, the ninth president of the United States, dies of pneumonia at the White House. Vice President John Tyler takes his place the same day.

1850 The city of Los Angeles, then a rowdy cowtown, is incorporated.

1862 Learning quickly from the example of the American armored ships *Monitor* and *Virginia* (formerly *Merrimac*), Great Britain orders the refitting of the 131-gun, wooden-hulled *Royal Sovereign* with armor and turret guns. Within a month, construction also began on Great Britain's first iron-hulled turret-gunned ship.

William Henry Harrison

French soldier in the Somme region

1968 Martin Luther King, Jr. is shot to death at a motel in Memphis, Tennessee. A single shot fired by James Earl Ray from about 200 feet away struck King in the neck. He was 39 years old.

1979 Pakistan's former president and prime minister Zulfikar Ali Bhutto, convicted of ordering the assassination of a political opponent, is hanged.

1981 Susan Brown steers the Oxford crew to victory as the first female cox in the history of the Oxford vs. Cambridge University Boat Race. On the same day, jockey Bob Champion rides racehorse Aldaniti to victory in the Grand National after being told in 1979 that he had just eight months to live.

1871 Mary Potts patents the "Mrs. Potts' Sad Iron," featuring a removable handle allowing one iron to heat while another was being used.

1915 Bell system engineers successfully establish a one-way wireless mobile telephone link between Montauk Point, New York, and Wilmington, Delaware.

1918 During World War I, the Second Battle of the Somme ends. The Germans advanced almost 40 miles toward Paris, inflicted some 200,000 casualties, and captured 70,000 prisoners but suffered nearly as many casualties and exhausted themselves in the process.

1933 By secret decree, Germany establishes the National Defense Council to direct a massive rearmament program.

1949 The North Atlantic Treaty Organization (NATO) is established by 12 Western nations: the United States, Great Britain, France, Belgium, the Netherlands, Denmark, Italy, Luxembourg, Norway, Iceland, Canada, and Portugal.

Martin Luther King, Jr., center, stands on the balcony of the Lorraine Motel

Pocahontas saving Captain John Smith

1464 Anti-Jewish riots break out in Seville, Spain.

1614 In colonial Virginia, Pocahontas marries Jamestown tobacco planter John Rolfe. The union ensured peace for several years between settlers and thirty confederated Indian tribes led by Pocahontas's father.

1753 Parliament founds the British Museum.

1758 Pennsylvania teenager Mary Jemison is kidnapped by Indians from her family's farm. She spent the rest of her long life among the Senecas, and her biography became one of the most popular of the 19th-century captivity stories.

M I L E S T O N E

Howard Hughes Dies

Howard Hughes, one of the richest men to emerge from the American West during the 20th century, dies on this day in 1976 while flying from Acapulco to Houston, Texas. Hughes inherited an estate of nearly a million dollars when his father died. His reputation as an aircraft designer and builder suffered after an ill-fated World War II government-sponsored project to build the Spruce Goose, an immense plane that Hughes claimed would be able to transport 750 passengers. Emaciated and deranged from too little food and too many drugs, Hughes finally became so ill that his aides decided that he needed medical treatment, but Hughes died en route to the hospital.

"Attempt the impossible in order to improve your work."

—Bette Davis

1794 French revolutionary leader Georges Jacques Danton is executed by guillotine. Renowned for his satire, he said, "Be sure you show the mob my head. It will be a long time ere they see its like."

1818 Chilean forces decisively defeat the Spanish army in Chile during the Battle of Maipu, thus winning the South American nation's independence.

1859 British naturalist Charles Darwin sends to his publisher the first three chapters of *Origin of Species*, which laid out his radical evolutionary theory of natural selection.

1862 In the American Civil War, Union General George McClellan falls for an elaborate Confederate ruse and

Anti-Vietnam War protestors march on 6th Avenue in New York City

Josip Broz Tito

besieges Yorktown, Virginia, rather than attack. The numerous artillery pieces that gave him pause were really logs painted black. The siege bought valuable time for the Confederacy's defense of Richmond.

1916 During World War I, British forces launch the First Battle of Kut, a four-week attempt to break the Turkish siege of the Iraqi city where 10,000 British soldiers were trapped.

1923 Just months after being involved in the discovery of the tomb of Tutankhamen in Egypt, the 5th Earl of Carnarvon dies of a mysterious illness, said to be the mummy's curse.

1923 Firestone introduces tires with inflatable inner tubes. The so-called "balloon tires" offered better handling but also ushered in the era of the flat tire.

1927 Fascist Italy signs a "friendship treaty" with Hungary.

1933 In the Hague, the International Court rules that Greenland, the world's largest

island, belongs to Denmark, not to Norway as claimed by the Norwegians. Greenland was granted full self-government in 1981.

1941 German troops invade Yugoslavia.

1942 In the Indian Ocean, Japanese bombers surprise and sink two British heavy cruisers, *Dorsetshire* and *Cornwall*, killing more than 350 sailors. On the same day, Japanese planes bombed the Burmese capital of Madalay, killing two thousand.

1943 German Protestant theologian and Nazi opponent Dietrich Bonhoeffer is arrested and jailed in Berlin.

1945 Yugoslav communist leader Josip Broz Tito signs a "friendship treaty" with the Soviet Union allowing Soviet troops to enter Yugoslavia.

1958 In North America's largest-known nonnuclear commercial explosion, technicians detonate more than 2.75 million pounds of high explosives to destroy the peak of a submerged mountain. The peak, which lay between Vancouver Island and British Columbia, was a navigation hazard that had claimed more than 120 vessels.

1969 A march in New York City to demand an end of the Vietnam War draws 100,000 demonstrators and kicks off a weekend of sit-ins, parades, and other protests across the United States.

1995 Israel launches its first spy satellite, *Ofek 3*.

648 B.C. A total solar eclipse plunges Greece into darkness, prompting the poet Archilochus to write of how Zeuss "made night from mid-day, hiding the light of the shining Sun, and sore fear came upon men."

401 Roman general Flavius Stilicho defeats the Visigoth chieftan Alaric at a battle near modern Pollenza, Italy, forcing the Visigoths to withdraw from the peninsula, for the time being.

1196 William Fitz Osbert, an English crusader who roused London's poor against the city's mayor and aldermen, is hanged in chains at Smithfield, along with nine of his followers.

1199 English king Richard I, known as Coeur de Lion, or the Lion-Heart, is killed by an arrow at the siege of the castle of Chalus (sometimes Chaluz), near Limoges, France.

1327 At a church in Avignon, Petrarch catches a glimpse of his beloved Laura, to whom the obsessed Italian poet would write more than 300 sonnets and other poems.

BORN ON THIS DAY

1483
RAPHAEL (RAFFAELLO SANZIO)
Italian Renaissance painter (*The School of Athens*)

1773
JAMES MILL
Scottish philosopher, father of John Stuart Mill

1866
BUTCH CASSIDY
American outlaw, train robber, and gunfighter

1874
HARRY HOUDINI (ERICH WEISS)
Hungarian-born American magician and escapologist

1882
ROSE SCHNEIDERMAN
American women's rights activist

1884
WALTER HUSTON
Canadian actor (*The Treasure of the Sierra Madre*)

1892
LOWELL THOMAS
American travel journalist

1929
ANDRÉ PREVIN
German-born pianist, composer, and conductor

1937
MERLE HAGGARD
American country music singer ("Okie from Muskogee")

1937
BILLY DEE WILLIAMS
American actor (*Mahogany*)

1943
MARTY PATTIN
American professional baseball player

1520 Italian Renaissance painter Raffaello Santi (or Sanzio), better known simply as Raphael, dies on his birthday, leaving his last work, *Transfiguration*, unfinished.

1593 English lawyer and Congregationalist Henry Barrow is hanged in London for supporting the formation of churches separate and independent from the Church of England.

1609 English navigator and explorer Henry Hudson sails from Holland on the third of his four voyages in search of a short route from Europe to Asia through the Arctic Ocean.

1748 Excavations begin at the ancient Greco-Roman city of Pompeii, which had been destroyed and buried seventeen centuries earlier during an eruption of Mount Vesuvius.

1814 Napoleon Bonaparte, forced to retreat across France to Paris, abdicates and agrees to go into exile on the island of Elba.

1830 American religious leader Joseph Smith establishes the Mormon Church during a small meeting of believers in Fayette Township, New York.

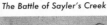

The Battle of Sayler's Creek

> *"Patience is bitter, but its fruit is sweet."*
>
> —*Mahatma Ghandi*

1832 The so-called Black Hawk War erupts in western Illinois as the Sauk leader tries to surrender to U.S. forces along the Mississippi River. The 15-week war led to the virtual annihilation of Black Hawk's people.

1862 One of the bloodiest engagements of the American Civil War, the Battle of Shiloh, opens near Pittsburgh Landing in Tennessee. The two-day battle ended in a major victory for the Union army, which seized Corinth, a crucial rail center.

1865 The Confederacy fights its last major battle of the American Civil War, the Battle of Sayler's Creek, west of Richmond, Virginia. As Confederate general Robert E. Lee watches his men stagger away, he says, "My God, has the army been dissolved?"

1868 Japan's emperor Meiji promulgates the Charter Oath, which paved the way for modernizing the country and establishing a western-style parliamentary constitution.

Will Rogers

1896 The first modern Olympic Games open in Athens before a crowd of 60,000 spectators.

1909 American polar explorer Robert Peary and his party of five men reach what he believes to be the North Pole. Long after Peary's death, navigational errors would be discovered in his log indicating that he had planted his flag perhaps 30 miles short of his goal.

1917 The United States formally enters World War I as the House of Representatives passes a declaration of war on Germany, 373–50.

1930 American humorist Will Rogers begins cracking jokes over CBS radio, as *The Will Rogers Program* makes its debut.

1930 Mahatma Gandhi reaches the end of his 300 mile march across India in protest against the Salt Law, which imposes tax on the production of salt.

1934 The Ford Motor Company introduces whitewall tires as an option on its new vehicles at a cost of $11.25 a set.

1972 American naval and air forces are thrown against a massive North Vietnamese invasion of South Vietnamese (the "Easter Offensive"), hitting troop concentrations and missile emplacements on both sides of the Demilitarized Zone.

Liberated 6-year-old war orphan with a Buchenwald badge on his sleeve

1348 Holy Roman emperor Charles IV establishes Charles University in Prague—the oldest university in central Europe.

1541 Francis Xavier, founder of the Jesuits, leaves Lisbon, Portugal, on his 35th birthday to establish a mission in India.

1720 Britain passes the Declaratory Act, establishing supremacy of the English House of Lords over the Irish parliament.

1739 Notorious highwayman and horse thief Dick Turpin is hanged at York, England.

1794 Three years after a mob burned his home and laboratory in Birmingham, English chemist and discoverer of oxygen Joseph Priestly immigrates to the U.S.

1795 France adopts the meter as a standard measurement.

1805 The Lewis and Clark expedition departs its winter camp among the Mandan Indians in present-day North Dakota. Entering territory "on which the foot of civilized man had never trodden," Lewis proclaimed this day "among the most happy of my life."

1815 Mount Tambora erupts in Indonesia. The most

> *"I usually get my stuff from people who promised somebody else that they would keep it a secret."*
> —Walter Winchell

explosive eruption in the last 10,000 years, it made a crater five miles across and killed some 49,000 people. Its ash cloud caused a year without a summer, remembered in northern countries as "eighteen hundred and froze to death."

1827 Inventor of the friction match, English pharmacist John Walker, makes the first sale of his combustible invention.

1847 Dr. Nathan Cooley administers ether to Fanny Longfellow, wife of the poet, during labor. It was the first obstetric use of anasthesia. On the same day in 1853, Queen Victoria gives birth to Prince Leopold under chloroform.

1862 In the American Civil War, the Battle of Shiloh ends with a Union victory. The cost was high: 13,047 casualties on the Union side, 10,694 on the Confederate—more than all of the war's major battles to that date combined.

1891 American showman Phineas Taylor Barnum dies in Bridgeport, Connecticut. Gravely

The Battle of Shiloh

Herbert Hoover during intercity television demonstration

ill, the 81-year-old showman requested that a New York paper run his obituary before he died so he could enjoy reading it, and the paper obliged.

1914 Canada's Grand Trunk Pacific Railway is completed.

1915 The first coast-to-coast commercial telephone service is established between New York and California. Important calls only: the first three minutes cost $20.70 plus $6.75 for each additional minute.

1917 Panama and Cuba declare war on Germany, thus entering World War I.

1922 Minnesotan Sig Haugdahl obliterates the world land speed record, pushing his Wisconsin Special race car over 180 miles per hour at Daytona Beach, Florida. Lacking official recognition, his speed never made the record books but stood as an unofficial record for over a decade.

1926 Violet Gibson, an Irish woman, shoots Italian dictator Benito Mussolini in the nose. He survived; she was deported.

1927 In the first simultaneous telecast of image and sound, Secretary of Commerce Herbert Hoover reads a speech in Washington, D.C. His voice and image, less than three inches square, were transmitted to a New York audience.

1945 The Japanese battleship *Yamato* is sunk in Japan's counteroffensive in the struggle for Okinawa. Ostensibly the greatest battleship in the world, it was struck by 19 American aerial torpedoes. The death toll among its crew was 2,498.

1951 The U.S. sends armed forces to Iceland at the request of the new nation, which became independent in 1944.

1953 Dag Hammarskjöld, former prime minister of Sweden, is elected secretary-general of the United Nations.

1954 President Dwight D. Eisenhower coins one of the most famous Cold War phrases when he suggests the fall of French Indochina to the communists could create a "domino effect" in southeast Asia.

1959 Scientists at Los Alamos, New Mexico, generate electricity from an atomic reaction for the first time.

1963 A new Yugoslav constitution proclaims Josip Tito president for life of the newly named Socialist Federal Republic of Yugoslavia.

1966 A hydrogen bomb which fell off an American B-52 in February is found intact on the Atlantic sea bed off the coast of Spain.

Elizabeth Dole with Rwandan refugees

Icon of Buddha

563 B.C. According to Buddhist tradition, Gautama Buddha is born in the kingdom of Sakya near the modern India-Nepal border. Son of the king, he was named Prince Siddhartha but gave up wealth and position in his spiritual quest.

1546 The Council of Trent accepts the Latin Vulgate as the official Catholic Bible.

1579 Peasants and townsfolk of Maastricht, in the Netherlands, using guns, explosives, pots of boiling water, and threshing flails, beat back a fierce Spanish assault on the city.

1766 A London watchmaker wins a patent for a fire escape: a basket on a chain, lowered by a pulley mechanism.

1838 The *Great Western*, first steamship capable of carrying commercial cargo and passengers across the Atlantic, leaves England in her maiden voyage.

1861 Austria grants basic political and civil rights to Protestants.

1871 Algerian Sufi leader Sheik al-Haddad, with 120,000

BORN ON THIS DAY

1460
JUAN PONCE DE LEÓN
Spanish conquistador and explorer who discovered Florida

1614
EL GRECO (DOMENIKOS THEOTOCOPOULOS)
Greek-born Spanish painter (*The Burial of Count Orgaz*)

1692
GIUSEPPE TARTINI
Italian violinist and composer

1889
SIR ADRIAN BOULT
English conductor

1892
MARY PICKFORD
Canadian silent-film actress (*Rebecca of Sunnybrook Farm*; *Coquette*)

Mary Pickford

1902
JOSEF KRIPS
Austrian conductor

1923
FRANCO CORELLI ANCONIA
Italian tenor

1940
JOHN HAVLICEK
American Hall of Fame basketball player

1943
MICHAEL BENNETT
American choreographer (*A Chorus Line*)

1946
JIM "CATFISH" HUNTER
American Hall of Fame baseball player

1963
JULIAN LENNON
English singer, son of John Lennon

> *"This thing that we call 'failure' is not the falling down, but the staying down."*
>
> —*Mary Pickford*

troops, joins a holy war and rebellion against French colonial rule. The uprising was suppressed the following January.

1879 A New York dairy introduces the latest in modern milk packaging: glass bottles.

1898 In the dispute between France and England over Egypt, General Herbert Kitchener defeats the Mahdist dervishes on the Atbara River.

1899 In the United States, Martha Place becomes the first woman to be executed in the electric chair.

1907 England and France agree on the independence of Siam (Thailand) but carve out spheres of influence for themselves.

1910 The Los Angeles Motordome, the first motor speedway with a board track, opened near Playa Del Rey, California. On the mile-long, steeply banked circular track, a daredevil could reach speeds up to 100 miles per hour with his hands off the steering wheel.

1917 Two days after declaring war on Germany, the U.S. cuts diplomatic relations with Austria-Hungary.

1920 Portugal joins the League of Nations.

Jomo Kenyatta

1953 Jomo Kenyatta, leader of the Kenyan independence movement, is convicted by Kenya's British rulers of leading the extremist Mau Mau rebellion. An advocate of nonviolence and conservatism, he played little part in the uprising but was imprisoned for nine years. In 1964 Kenyatta became president of newly independent Kenya.

1974 Hank Aaron of the Atlanta Braves hits his 715th career home run, surpassing the record of legendary Babe Ruth.

1989 Soviet nuclear-powered submarine *Komsomolets* catches fire and sinks in the Norwegian Sea with the loss of 42 lives among the 95-person crew.

1992 Palestinian leader Yāsir Arafāt, en route to inspect a PLO training base in Libya, is the only survivor of a plane crash that kills the three-man crew. Palestinians see it as a divine gesture of approval for Arafāt's policies.

1933 Western Australia votes to leave the commonwealth, which did not happen.

1942 As America gears up for world war, the War Production Board orders a halt to all production that was not deemed necessary to the military effort. At the peak of the war, the military used nearly half of the nation's production and services.

1944 Russian forces led by Marshal Fyodor Tolbukhin launch an attack on the German Army in the Crimea, in southern Ukraine. In four days, the attack broke German defensive lines and sent the Germans into retreat.

1947 Astronomers observe a vast sunspot group estimated to cover 7 billion square miles of the sun's surface.

1948 Luang Pibul Songgram becomes elected premier of Siam five months after leading a bloodless coup against the Japanese-friendly government.

1950 India and Pakistan sign the Delhi Pact, reducing tensions but not solving the dispute over Kashmir.

Hank Aaron

243 Mani, an Iranian religious figure who attempted to fuse the teachings of Jesus and Zoroaster, makes his first appearance as a preacher (according to tradition).

837 Halley's Comet makes its closest-known passage to Earth.

1625 The young John Milton, who would become one of England's greatest poets, enters Christ's College in Cambridge at the age of sixteen.

1682 French explorer Rene-Robert La Salle reaches the Gulf of Mexico after a voyage down the Mississippi River. He claimed the entire river basin for France and named it Louisiana.

1747 Scottish Jacobite leader Lord Lovat is beheaded for treason in London.

1859 Samuel Langhorne Clemens, 23, receives his license to pilot steamboats on the Mississippi River. He piloted steamboats until the American Civil War broke out in 1861, then turned to writing and took the pseudonym Mark Twain.

1872 Samuel R. Percy patents powdered milk.

1881 Gunslinger Billy the Kid is convicted of murder-

> *"The interesting thing is how one guy, through living out his own fantasies, is living out the fantasies of so many other people."*
>
> —*Hugh Hefner*

Lee's surrender to Grant at Appomattox Court House (milestone)

ing the corrupt sheriff of Lincoln County, New Mexico, and sentenced to hang.

1905 The first aerial car ferry opens over the ship canal in Duluth, Minnesota, shuttling vehicles and foot passengers across a 393-foot span of water in ten minutes.

1917 In war-torn France, Great Britain opens a spring offensive with attacks on Vimy Ridge and the town of Arras. Among the dead: English poet Edward Thomas.

1918 During World War I, Germany launches "St. George I," a major attack against British positions along the extreme northern front.

1930 The two-way videophone is demonstrated for the first time with a call placed between Bell Laboratories and AT&T headquarters in New York City.

1939 Famed African-American contralto Marian Anderson sings for an audience of 75,000 at the Lincoln Memorial in Washington, D.C. Her concert at Constitution Hall had been cancelled by the Daughters of the American Revolution because of her race.

General MacArthur, left, and General Johnathan Wainwright reunited in 1945

1940 Germany invades neutral Norway and, with the help of local fascists under Vidkun Quisling, quickly captures the coastal cities of Oslo, Bergen, Trondbeim, and Narvik. At the same time, German troops occupy Copenhagen and other Danish cities.

1941 German troops capture the Greek city of Salonika.

1942 American general Jonathan M. Wainwright surrenders to the Japanese at Bataan. His force of 78,000 exhausted troops (66,000 Filipinos, 12,000 American) immediately begins the infamous "Bataan Death March," a 55-mile starvation trek which killed at least 600 Americans and 5,000 Filipinos.

1945 German theologian and outspoken Nazi opponent Dietrich Bonhoeffer is hanged on Hitler's orders at Flossenberg, just days before Allied troops liberate the concentration camp. On the same day, Soviet forces occupy Konigsberg, Germany.

1948 Colombian liberal leader Jorge Gaitan is assassin-

ated in broad daylight in downtown Bogotá, triggering riots that caused an estimated $570 million dollars in property damage.

1962 The Hollywood musical movie, *West Side Story,* an updated Romeo and Juliet tale set in gang-ridden New York City, wins ten Academy Awards.

1963 The U.S. Congress confers honorary American citizenship upon former British prime minister Winston Churchill.

1972 The Soviet Union agrees to arm Iraq in exchange for Iraq's cooperation in political, economic, and military affairs.

1981 The journal *Nature* publishes the longest scientific name in history: the systematic name for human mitochondrial DNA, which runs to 207,000 letters.

1993 At least 100 die in West Bengal, India, as a tornado levels five villages.

1998 More than 118 people die in Mina, Saudi Arabia, as thousands of Muslim pilgrims stampede across a bridge.

Annual Muslim pilgrimage in Mecca

APRIL 10

General Arthur Wellington

1583
HUGO GROTIUS
Dutch jurist, father of international law

1778
WILLIAM HAZLITT
English essayist and critic

1794
COMMODORE MATTHEW CALBRAITH PERRY
American naval commander whose fleet opened Japan to foreign trade

1827
LEW WALLACE
American Civil War general and author (*Ben Hur*)

1829
WILLIAM BOOTH
English founder of the Salvation Army

William Booth

1847
JOSEPH PULITZER
Hungarian-born American publisher

1882
FRANCES PERKINS
American secretary of labor from 1933 to 1945, the first female presidential cabinet member

1929
MAX VON SYDOW
Swedish actor (*Pelle the Conqueror; The Greatest Story Ever Told*)

1932
OMAR SHARIF
Egyptian-born American actor (*Lawrence of Arabia*) and champion bridge player

1941
PAUL THEROUX
American writer (*The Mosquito Coast; O-Zone*)

1302 During his long struggle against the Roman papacy for sovereignty of France, King Philip IV summons the first well-authenticated Estates General, an assembly of clergy, nobility, and town representatives.

1633 Bananas go on sale for the first time in England, at the shop of Thomas Johnson of Snow Hill, London.

1814 British forces under General Arthur Wellington defeat the French army at Toulouse, thus ending the Peninsular War.

1834 A fire at a New Orleans mansion reveals the mistress of the house, Delpine Lalaurie, as a brutal sadist who maintained a torture chamber for brutalizing her slaves.

1849 New Yorker Walter Hunt patents the world's first practical safety pin.

1865 A day after the American Civil War ends, Confederate General Robert E. Lee addresses his army for the last time, explaining that they had been "compelled to yield to overwhelming numbers and resources."

1906 American author William Sydney Porter, writing under the pseudonym O. Henry, publishes his second collection of short stories, which included one of his most beloved tales, *The Gift of the Magi*.

1916 In Paris, the International Olympic Committee announces that the Olympic Games, due to be held this year, will be postponed until World War I is over. The next Games were held in Antwerp, Belgium, in 1920.

1919 British police arrest Indian nationalist leaders Kichloo and Satyapal in Amritsar, triggering riots that kill several Britons.

1919 Emiliano Zapata, leader of peasants and indigenous people who demanded land reform during the Mexican Revolution, is ambushed and killed in Morelos by government forces.

1932 At the second ballot, Paul von Hindenburg wins Germany's presidential election by an uncomfortably narrow margin, having initially dismissed his main rival Adolf Hitler as "that Bavarian corporal."

1933 U.S. president Franklin Roosevelt creates the Civilian Conservation Corps to put thousands of the nation's unemployed young men to work on useful public projects such as

"Fiction gives us a second chance that life denies us."
—Paul Theroux

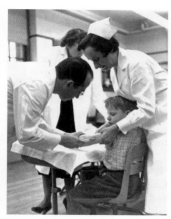

Dr. Jonas Salk innoculating a boy

planting trees, building roads and dams, and fighting forest fires.

1938 A German plebiscite gives Hitler a 99 percent approval rating.

1941 German and Italian military forces in Yugoslavia set up a puppet regime, the Independent State of Croatia, and place fascist insurgents in control. The regime persecuted Serbs, Jews, and others during the war, murdering some 400,000 people, many of whom died at the notorious Jasenovac concentration camp.

1941 While rescuing survivors of a torpedoed Dutch freighter, American destroyer *Niblack* depth-charges a German sub. It was the first action of the war between U.S. and German navies.

1944 The Soviet Red Army recaptures the Ukrainian port city of Odessa.

1944 Two Auschwitz prisoners, Rudolph Vrba and Alfred Wetzler, escape from the death camp and produce a sub-

stantive and highly detailed report which documents the killing process. The report was forwarded to Western intelligence with a request to bomb the camps.

1955 Jonas Salk successfully tests his polio vaccine.

1963 The American submarine *Thresher*, the first of a new class of nuclear-powered submarines, sinks during diving tests off Cape Cod with the loss of all 129 aboard.

1966 English writer Evelyn Waugh, one of the most brilliant satirists of his day, dies in Somerset.

1972 Communist guerrillas in Argentina execute Italian Fiat executive Oberdan Sallustro twenty days after his abduction in Buenos Aires.

1993 Chris Hani, secretary-general of the South African Communist Party, is shot and killed outside his home in a quiet suburb of Johannesburg.

South African Communist leader Chris Hani

1689 Co-sovereigns William and Mary are crowned king and queen of Britain and Ireland.

1713 The Treaty of Utrecht ends the wars of Louis XIV, fixing borders and resolving sovereignty issues on the continent and settling conflicts over colonial possessions in the Americas.

1814 In France, Napoleon Bonaparte abdicates the throne but keeps his title as Emperor, although now he rules only the tiny island of Elba.

1862 During the American Civil War, Fort Pulaski, which guarded the mouth of the Savannah River in Georgia, surrenders after two days of Union bombardment.

1870 While visiting Marathon, Greece, Lord Muncaster of Great Britain is kidnapped by brigands. Muncaster died in a fight between Greek troops and the kidnappers, almost resulting in war with Great Britain.

1888 Henry Ford marries Clara Bryant in Greenfield, Michigan, on her twenty-second birthday. Clara described him to her parents as "quiet, pleasant, keen-minded, and sensible."

1898 U.S. president William McKinley, in the wake of the mysterious destruction of the USS *Maine* in Havana Harbor, caves in to public war

> *"I am at heart,*
> *a gentleman."*
>
> —Marlene Deitrich

Bombardment of Fort Pulaski

fever and asks Congress for authority to wage war against Spain.

1913 Italian Ettore Bugatti first proposed his Bugatti Type 41 Royale. Bugattis were huge hand-crafted luxury cars affordable only for Europe's elite.

1915 *The Tramp*, Charlie Chaplin's third film and first comic masterpiece, is released.

1919 The nascent League of Nations chooses Geneva, Switzerland, for its seat.

1940 Two days after Germany's surprise invasion, Norwegian forces rally, destroying three German cruisers and four troop transport ships.

1942 Rejecting Great Britain's offer of post-war autonomy and unopposed secession, if it comes to that, nationalist leaders in India demand immediate and complete independence. Jawaharlal Nehru, Mohandas Gandhi, and Azad get prison instead, for a few months.

1944 Marlene Dietrich gives the first of many shows for U.S. servicemen overseas. A U.S. citizen since 1939, she worked tirelessly to sell war bonds and entertain troops. She was awarded the Medal of Freedom and named Chevalier of the French Legion of Honor.

1945 The American Third Army liberates the Buchenwald concentration camp near Weimar, Germany. The camp would be judged second only to Auschwitz in the horrors it imposed on its prisoners. Among those saved was Elie Wiesel, winner of the 1986 Nobel Peace Prize.

1957 At Edwards Air Force Base in California, the Ryan X-13 becomes the first jet to take off and land vertically, launching from and returning to a mobile trailer.

1957 Great Britain comes to agreement with Singapore giving the city-state its independence.

1961 The Eichmann trial opens in Jerusalem. Adolph Eichmann, the Nazi war criminal, had been abducted from Argentina, where he lived in hiding after the war. Convicted, he was executed in May 1962.

1967 Tom Stoppard's play *Rosencrantz and Guildenstern Are Dead* premieres at the National Theatre in London.

1970 The Beatles' "Let It Be" hits No. 1 on the pop charts, one day after Paul McCartney formally announced the group's breakup.

Idi Amin, former president of Uganda

1970 *Apollo 13*, the third lunar landing mission, takes off from Cape Canaveral, Florida, carrying astronauts James A. Lovell, John L. Swigert, and Fred W. Haise. Two days later, an oxygen tank exploded and Lovell reported "Houston, we've had a problem here." They made it back alive, barely.

1979 Ugandan dictator and killer Idi Amin flees the Ugandan capital of Kampala as Tanzanian troops and forces of the Uganda National Liberation Front close in. Two days later, Kampala fell and a coalition government of former exiles took power.

1983 Richard Attenborough's film *Gandhi*, starring Ben Kingsley as Gandhi, wins eight Oscars, the greatest number won by a British film to that date.

1986 Halley's Comet comes within 63 million kilometers of Earth but puts on a dim show.

1996 A ban on nuclear arms development and testing is signed by 43 African nations.

1204 In the Fourth Crusade, Venetian and French Crusaders storm and sack Constantinople, which had not been conquered in 900 years.

1606 Great Britain adopts an early form of the Union Jack as its national flag.

1633 Astronomer Galileo Galilei goes on trial for heresy—for believing the Earth revolves around the Sun. Convicted, he spent the rest of his life under house arrest. It took more than 300 years for the Church to admit its error.

1776 The provisional government of North Carolina instructs colonial delegates at the Continental Congress to support a complete break with Great Britain.

1782 Admiral George Rodney leads the British fleet to victory in the Battle of the Saints off Dominica, Great Britain's only major naval victory in the American Revoluntionary War.

1786 In Philadelphia, Pennsylvania, the first charity medical dispensary is established to provide free medicine to the poor.

1818 A new American flag with 13 stripes (the original colonies) and 20 stars (the current number of states) flies over the U.S. Capitol for the first time.

"I would rather be right than be President."

—*Henry Clay*

M I L E S T O N E

IMP Established

Carl Laemmle establishes the Independent Motion Picture Company (IMP) on this day in 1909. Laemmle's studio defied the Motion Picture Patent Company, formed in 1908 by the nine leading film companies to monopolize the fledgling industry. The Patent Company refused to let other companies use their patented film equipment and distributed films only to theater owners who agreed to their terms. Kodak agreed to sell raw film stock only to members of the company, so Laemmle had to buy film stock from overseas. Laemmle fought more than 280 lawsuits from the Patent Company but succeeded in growing his studio.

1824 An act of Parliament establishes free trade between Ireland and Great Britain, devastating the home-based textile industry of southern Ireland.

1829 A landmark in the annals of anasthesia: a woman undergoes a breast amputation under hypnosis.

1829 German naturalist Alexander von Humboldt embarks on a scientific expedition to Siberia as a guest of the Czar. Pampered, guarded, and supervised by Russian nobility, he nonetheless returned with invaluable geographic data about a region unknown to western Europe.

1844 In Washington, D.C., U.S. secretary of state John C. Calhoun signs an annexation treaty with representatives of the Republic of Texas. The Senate rejected the treaty, but Texas became a state the next year.

1861 The American Civil War, the bloodiest four years in American history, begins when Confederate shore batteries

The defense of Fort Sumter

open fire on Union-held Fort Sumter in South Carolina's Charleston Bay. Three days later, U.S. president Abraham Lincoln called for 75,000 volunteer soldiers to quell the Southern "insurrection."

1877 Great Britain annexes the South African Republic, an amalgamation of Boer republics that would become the Crown Colony of Transvaal and later the Province of Transvaal.

1892 George Blickensderfer receives a U.S. patent for his portable type-writer design.

1908 Herbert Henry Asquith takes over as British prime minister and immediately announces two significant new appointments to the Cabinet, both future prime ministers: David Lloyd George as chancellor of the exchequer and "rising star" Winston Churchill as president of the board of trade.

1911 French aviator Pierre Prier makes the first non-stop flight from London to Paris; the journey takes almost four hours.

1945 Franklin D. Roosevelt, the longest-serving president in American history, dies of a cerebral hemorrhage three months into his fourth term. His wife Eleanor cables her sons: "He did his job to the end as he would want you to do."

1955 Ten years after the death of polio victim Franklin D. Roosevelt, scientists announce successful results from field testing of the Salk polio vaccine.

Soviet cosmonaut Yuri Gagarin

1961 Soviet cosmonaut Yuri Alekseyevich Gagarin makes the first successful manned space flight. During his flight aboard the spacecraft *Vostok 1*, the 27-year-old test pilot also became the first man to orbit the planet.

1961 Walt W. Rostow, senior White House specialist on southeast Asia reports to President John F. Kennedy that the time has come for "gearing up the whole Vietnam operation."

1968 A rash of sheep deaths in Utah puzzle health officials. Investigations led to the startling admission by the U.S. Army that it had tested nerve gas in the area.

1980 Liberian president William Tolbert is assassinated by supporters of Master Sargent Samuel Doe. Doe was later elected president in what opponents called a rigged election.

1988 Harvard scientists win a patent for the Harvard Oncomouse, a genetically engineered rodent developed for cancer research.

585 Visigoth prince Hermenegild is beheaded on orders of his father, either for rebellion or for refusing to accept communion from an Arian bishop. He was canonized a thousand years later.

1111 German king Henry V is crowned Holy Roman emperor by Pope Paschal II, whom the king had imprisoned in Rome the previous year.

1534 English Roman Catholics Thomas More and John Fisher jointly refuse to recognize Henry VII's repudiation of papal authority over the English church. Both were later beheaded.

1598 French king Henry IV signs the Edict of Nantes, which ended nearly forty years of religious strife. The edict maintained Roman Catholicism as the state church but gave Protestants religious freedom.

1625 German entomologist Johannes Faber names the "microscope," in a letter to Federigo Cesi, founder of the Italy's scientific society, the Academy of the Lynx.

1742 George Frederick Handel's *Messiah*, Christmas fodder for church choirs throughout the world today, is heard for the first time, in Dublin.

> "A sheltered life can be
> a daring life as well.
> For all serious daring
> starts from within."
>
> —*Eudora Welty*

Tiger Woods Wins First Major

On this day in 1997, in Augusta, Georgia, 21-year-old Tiger Woods wins the prestigious Masters Tournament. It was Woods' first victory in one of golf's four major championships and the greatest performance by a professional golfer in more than a century. By June 1997, Woods was ranked No. 1 in the world. In June 2000, he won his first U.S. Open title. It was the greatest professional golf performance in history. At the age of 24, he was the youngest player ever to win all four major golf titles and just the second to win three majors in a year.

Tiger Woods

George Frederick Handel

1796 The first elephant to set foot in America arrives in New York City from Bengal, India, and immediately impresses the locals by drawing a cork from a bottle with its trunk.

1861 The opening battle of the American Civil War ends with the surrender of Fort Sumter after a thirty-three hour bombardment by Confederate cannons. Neither side lost a man in the battle, and the Union garrison was allowed to leave for the north.

1895 Alfred Dreyfus, a French army officer unjustly condemned for treason, arrives at the infamous penal colony of Devil's Island, off French Guiana.

1918 A German infantry division occupies the Finnish capital of Helsinki.

1919 In India, British troops under General Reginald Dyer surround a large crowd of unarmed nationalist demonstrators in Amritsar and without warning open fire, killing 379 people.

1935 Commercial air service between London and Australia is established.

1939 A U.S. Navy cruiser arrives in Japan to photograph the Japanese battleships *Yamato* and *Musashi*.

1941 Japan and the Soviet Union sign a five-year nonaggression pact. On the same day, Great Britain loses an armed merchant cruiser, *Rajputana*, to a submarine attack in the Denmark Strait between Greenland and Iceland.

1943 America's Jefferson Memorial is dedicated in Washington, D.C., on the 200th anniversary of the third president's birth.

1945 As Allied troops close in on Berlin, Hitler proclaims from his underground bunker that "a mighty artillery" will save the city. Meanwhile, SS and Luftwaffe troops massacre 1,016 people near the German village of Gardelegen by herding them into a barn and setting it on fire.

1958 Harvey Lavan Cliburn, 23, wins the International Tchaikovsky Piano Competition in Moscow, and goes on to fame and fortune as Van Cliburn.

1960 The United States launches its first navigational satellite, the 265-pound *Transit-1B*, to help track submarines and other ships.

1964 Sydney Poitier becomes the first African American to win the Academy Award for Best Actor, for his role as a laborer who helps build a chapel in *Lilies of the Field*.

1966 In an early dissent against U.S. president Lyndon B. Johnson's Vietnam policy, the Southern Christian Leadership Conference issues a statement urging the United States to end the war.

1970 Two days into the third manned mission to the moon, an oxygen tank explodes aboard *Apollo 13*, and the crippled spacecraft begins its harrowing journey back to Earth.

1972 Three North Vietnamese divisions supported by tanks, heavy artillery, and rockets, capture half the city of An Loc, just 65 miles northwest of Saigon.

1990 The Soviet government officially admits responsibility for the 1940 Katyn Massacre, in which Soviet secret police rounded up and murdered 5,000 Polish military officers in the Katyn Forest.

1992 Buckingham Palace announces that Princess Anne has begun legal proceedings to divorce Captain Mark Phillips, her husband of 18 years. The couple had been separated for two and a half years.

Apollo 13 crew, left to right: Fred W. Haise, John L. Swigert, and James A. Lovell aboard the recovery ship USS Iwo Jima

911 Pope Sergius III dies after a turbulent reign, during which he apparently ordered the strangulation of two competing popes (or anti-popes, depending on your point of view) and reputedly fathered an illegitimate son, the future Pope John XI.

1198 Hyacinth Bobo, an elderly cardinal deacon, is consecrated as Pope Celestine III, just a day after his ordination as a priest.

1471 In the English Wars of the Roses, Yorkist king Edward IV wins the Battle of Barnet, a momentous victory over the Lancastrian adherents of Henry VI.

1482 Giovanni Di Fidanza, a leading medieval theologian and minister general of the Franciscan order, is canonized as Saint Bonaventure.

1818 After more than twenty years of research, Yale-educated lawyer Noah Webster publishes his *American Dictionary of the English Language*, one of the first lexicons to include distinctly American words.

Noah Webster

BORN ON THIS DAY

1578
PHILIP III
King of Spain and Portugal
(1598–1621)

1629
CHRISTIAAN HUYGENS
Dutch astronomer who discovered Saturn's rings

1866
ANNE MANSFIELD SULLIVAN
American teacher who taught the blind, deaf Helen Keller to read and write

1889
ARNOLD TOYNBEE
English historian (*A Study of History*)

1904
SIR JOHN GIELGUD
English actor (*Becket; Arthur*)

Sir John Gielgud

1923
ROBERTO DEVICENZO
Argentinean professional golfer

1940
JULIE CHRISTIE
Academy Award-winning Indian-born English actress (*Darling; McCabe and Mrs. Miller*)

1941
PETE ROSE
American professional baseball player who broke Ty Cobb's career record for most hits

1942
DICK BROOKS
American race-car driver

1977
SARAH MICHELLE GELLAR
American actress (*Buffy the Vampire Slayer*)

1832 Brigham Young, a 30-year-old carpenter, is baptized into the Mormon faith. He would later become the second president of the church and lead the Saints to the Salt Lake Valley in Utah.

1849 Hungarian rebels declare independence from the Hapsburg monarchy, triggering a four-month war that crushed the rebellion.

1894 Thomas Edison's kinetoscope, a peep-show machine showing short films of entertainers such as Buffalo Bill, makes its debut in a New York City arcade.

1912 The *Titanic*, running at full speed through the icy North Atlantic, strikes an iceberg, ruptures its hull, and starts to sink. Among those who picked up the liner's distress call: the young David Sarnoff, later founder of NBC.

1915 During World War I, Germany accuses the French of using poison gas near Verdun.

1916 After five months adrift on ice floes, shipwrecked polar explorer Ernest Shackleton and his men land their boats on Elephant Island in the South Shetland Islands.

> *"America is a large, friendly dog in a very small room. Every time it wags its tail, it knocks over a chair."*
>
> —*Arnold Toynbee*

Illustration of the Titanic striking an iceberg

1917 Polish physician Ludwik Zamenhof, creator of the international language Esperanto, dies in Warsaw.

1918 French general Ferdinand Foch is made commander in chief of all Allied armies on the Western Front. On the same day, American military pilots engage in aerial combat for the first time, shooting down two German planes in a dogfight over Toul, France.

1927 The first regular-production Volvo is manufactured in Goteborg, Sweden.

1940 French and British troops land at the Norwegian port city of Narvik in an attempt to oust the Germans, who had landed just five days before.

1941 As Axis troops overrun his country, the Yugoslav king flees to Athens along with his government.

1942 British naval forces use a new radar system to sink a German submarine that had attacked a convoy off the southwest of Ireland. Meanwhile, on the other side of the Atlantic, U.S. Navy destroyer *Roper* sinks another German sub.

1956 The first videotape recorder is demonstrated by its trio of American inventors. The device, the size of a freezer, sold for $75,000.

1988 The Soviet Union agrees to withdraw its beleaguered troops from Afghanistan after more than eight years of fighting Islamic fundamentalist guerrillas.

1993 British archaeologists uncover a 7,000-year-old fishing village on Dalma Island in the United Arab Emirates.

1994 American warplanes over Iraq mistakenly shoot down two helicopters full of international personnel, killing 26.

2000 The NASDAQ posts the biggest drop ever, plummeting 355.49 points and posting a 9.67 percent loss for the day.

1770 In an addendum to a scientific paper, Dr. Joseph Priestly mentions a clever invention, the rubber eraser, and tells readers where to buy one.

1793 The Bank of England issues the first £5 notes.

1811 Twins Chang and Eng arrive in the U.S. from Siam, to be exhibited as a curiosity. Joined at the waist, the "Siamese twins" led to use of the term for others with conjoined bodies.

1861 President Abraham Lincoln, expecting the American Civil War to be a short conflict, calls for 75,000 volunteers to serve for three months.

1865 Abraham Lincoln dies from a bullet wound inflicted the night before by John Wilkes Booth. The president's death came only six days after Confederate general Robert E. Lee surrendered at Appomattox, effectively ending the American Civil War.

1878 A model steam-powered helicopter built by

BORN ON THIS DAY

1452
LEONARDO DA VINCI
Italian artist (*The Last Supper; Mona Lisa*) and inventor

1469
NANAK
First guru of Sikhs

1684
CATHERINE I
Empress of Russia (1725–27)

1741
CHARLES WILLSON PEALE
American artist known for his portraits of Revolutionary War figures

1793
FRIEDRICH STRUVE
German-born astronomer

1800
SIR JAMES CLARK ROSS
Scottish explorer of the Antarctic

1843
HENRY JAMES
American novelist (*The Ambassadors*)

1894
BESSIE SMITH
American blues singer ("Down Hearted Blues"; "Nobody Knows You When You're Down and Out")

1940
JEFFREY ARCHER
British novelist and politician

Italian inventor Enrico Forlanini lifts off and stays in the air for 20 seconds.

1892 General Electric Company is incorporated in New York.

1912 "Unsinkable Molly Brown" wins lasting fame by surviving the sinking of the *Titanic*.

1912 Physicist Albert Einstein refers to time as the "fourth dimension."

1919 Following the British massacre of 379 civilian protesters at Amritsar, India, the province of Punjab is placed under martial law.

1923 Insulin, the new medicine for diabetes, becomes commercially available.

1927 Douglas Fairbanks, Mary Pickford, and Norma and Constance Talmadge become the first celebrities to leave their footprints in cement at Grauman's Chinese Theater in Hollywood. The building was under construction at the time.

The deathbed of U.S. president Abraham Lincoln

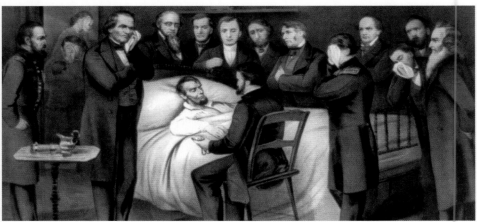

> *"The noblest pleasure is the joy of understanding."*
>
> —*Leonardo da Vinci*

1938 In the Spanish Civil War, rebels under Francisco Franco capture the coastal city of Vinaroz, separating Republican territory in Catalonia from Castile.

1941 Helicopter designer Igor Sikorsky keeps a Vaught-Sikorsky VS-300 in the air for 65 minutes, the first helicopter flight longer than an hour.

1945 Japanese-occupied Laos, with Japanese support, declares independence from France.

1945 British troops liberate Germany's Bergen-Belsen, the first major concentration camp liberated by Allied forces. Conditions were so bad that 28,000 inmates died in the weeks after liberation.

1945 Works of art stolen by the Nazis are found in a mine on the Loser Plateau in Austria. The works included paintings by Michelangelo, Rembrandt, Rubens, da Vinci, and Titian. SS troops were thwarted in their attempts to destroy the entire hoard.

1947 African-American baseball pioneer Jackie Robinson steps onto Ebbets Field to play his first game with the Brooklyn Dodgers.

1959 Four months after leading a successful revolution in Cuba, Fidel Castro arrives in the United States for

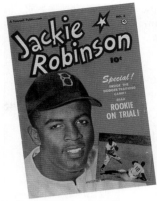

Media coverage of Jackie Robinson

an unofficial visit. Making it clear that he had no intention of meeting with Castro, President Dwight D. Eisenhower went golfing instead.

1961 In a speech at the U.N., Cuban foreign minister Raúl Roa accuses the U.S. and its Latin American allies of plotting an invasion. Two days later, the Bay of Pigs invasion was launched.

1964 The 17.5-mile Chesapeake Bay Bridge, the longest bridge in the world, opens.

1980 French existentialist philosopher Jean-Paul Sartre dies at the age of 74. Sartre, who was an active member of the French Resistance during World War II, refused the Nobel Prize in literature in 1964, saying that he did not want to burden his readers with the weight of such extraneous influences.

1986 In response to a terrorist bombing in Germany, U.S. jets bomb Libyan targets including the personal compound of Libyan leader Muamar Qadhafi, who narrowly escapes death.

MILESTONE

***Titanic* Sinks**

At 2:20 A.M. on this day 1912, the British ocean liner *Titanic* sinks into the North Atlantic Ocean south of Newfoundland, Canada. The massive ship, which carried 2,200 passengers and crew, had struck an iceberg two and half hours before. The RMS *Titanic* failed to divert its course from an iceberg and ruptured at least five of its hull compartments. Then the *Titanic* broke in half, and stern and bow sank to the ocean floor. On September 1, 1985, a U.S.-French expedition located the wreck of the *Titanic* lying on the ocean floor at a depth of about 13,000 feet.

The sinking of the Titanic

1178 B.C. A total eclipse occurs over the Mediterranean, perhaps the one mentioned in Homer's *Odyssey*.

1503 On his fourth and final voyage, near the Isthmus of Panama, Christopher Columbus gives up on finding a passage to Asia and turns his ships for Spain.

1521 Martin Luther, excommunicated by the pope for heresy and summoned to appear before the imperial Diet, is greeted triumphantly by supporters as he arrives in Worms.

1705 Isaac Newton becomes Sir Isaac, the first scientist to be honored with a knighthood. Queen Anne bestowed the honor.

1746 The Battle of Culloden becomes the last major land battle fought in Great Britain. The Duke of Cumberland and an army of loyalist Scots defeated the Jacobite army of 5,000 Highlanders.

MILESTONE

Bernard Baruch Coins the Term "Cold War"

On this day in 1947, multimillionaire and financier Bernard Baruch, in a speech given during the unveiling of his portrait in the South Carolina House of Representatives, coins the term "Cold War" to describe relations between the United States and the Soviet Union. The phrase stuck, and for over 40 years it was a mainstay in the language of American diplomacy. The term Cold War was instantly embraced by American newspapers and magazines as an apt description of the situation between the United States and the Soviet Union: a war without fighting or bloodshed, but a battle nonetheless.

> *"Failure is unimportant. It takes courage to make a fool of yourself."*
> —*Charlie Chaplin*

1789 George Washington, having been elected the first U.S. president, leaves his home at Mount Vernon for inauguration in New York City.

1813 Standardization of parts is specified for the first time in a U.S. government purchase contract for 20,000 military pistols. Any single piece must fit in all 20,000 pistols.

1862 During the American Civil War, the Confederacy starts drafting soldiers. On the same day, President Abraham Lincoln abolishes slavery in the District of Columbia, five months ahead of his Emancipation Proclamation.

1863 During the American Civil War, 12 Union ships loaded with men and sup-

Astronaut John W. Young, commander of Apollo 16, on the lunar surface

Harriet Quimby

plies stage a dramatic nighttime run past heavy Confederate artillery guarding the river town of Vicksburg, Mississippi. The maneuver gave Grant the advantage he sought: Vicksburg fell in July.

1879 Bulgaria adopts its national flag, a red-green-white tricolor.

1881 On the streets of Dodge City, Kansas, famous western lawman and gunfighter Bat Masterson fights the last gun battle of his life. No one died. Masterson turned to newspaper work, and died at his desk in 1921, in New York City.

1883 Paul Kruger, father of the Afrikaner nation, becomes president of the South African Republic.

1883 In Japan's ongoing modernization effort, a new law governing the press provides stiff penalties for libel.

1879 Bernadette of Lourdes, who at age 14 reported a series of visions of the Virgin Mary, dies in a French convent. She was 35.

1912 American aviatrix Harriet Quimby, in her purple satin flying oufit, becomes the first woman to fly across the English Channel.

1917 Vladimir Lenin, leader of the revolutionary Bolshevik Party, returns to Petrograd after a decade of exile to take the reins of the Russian Revolution. One month before, Czar Nicholas II had been forced from power when Russian army troops joined a workers' revolt in Petrograd, the Russian capital.

1943 In Basel, Switzerland, chemist Albert Hoffman accidentally consumes LSD-25, a synthetic drug he had created in 1938 as part of his medicinal research. Inadvertantly, he became the world's first LSD "tripper."

1945 Russian forces launch the battle for Berlin. In addition to some 52,000 Berlin civilians killed by aerial bombing during the war, an additional 100,000 died in the last days.

1947 The worst harbor explosion in U.S. history occurs in Texas when a French freighter loaded with ammonium nitrate fertilizer catches fire and explodes, devastating Texas City and killing nearly 600 people.

1947 Former Auschwitz commandant Rudolph Höss is hanged at Auschwitz. Among his memoirs was his written statement, "History will mark me as the greatest mass murderer of all time."

1972 *Apollo 16*, the fifth U.S. lunar landing mission, lifts off for the moon. The mission returned with more than 200 pounds of moon rocks and loads of data.

858 Pope Benedict III dies after three years as pope.

1521 Martin Luther appears before the Diet of Worms and is asked to repudiate his beliefs. He stalls for time to consider the question.

1524 Italian navigator and explorer Giovanni Verrazano, working for France, discovers New York Harbor.

1790 American statesman, printer, scientist, writer, and humorist Benjamin Franklin dies in Philadelphia, Pennsylvania, at age 84. Franklin helped draft the Declaration of Independence, secured French military and economic aid during the Revolution, and helped negotiate the Treaty of Paris, which formally ended the war with Great Britain.

1792 English navigator George Vancouver sights the west coast of North America and begins his painstaking survey of the coast from San Luis Obispo to Nootka Sound.

The Battle of Cerro Gordo

BORN ON THIS DAY

1837
J. P. (JOHN PIERPOINT) MORGAN
American financier

1870
IAN HAY
Scottish novelist and playwright who coined the phrase "funny peculiar or funny ha-ha?"

1885
ISAK DINESEN (KAREN BLIXEN)
Danish author (*Out of Africa*)

1894
NIKITA KHRUSHCHEV
Soviet premier (1958–64)

1897
THORNTON WILDER
American novelist and playwright (*Our Town; The Bridge of San Luis Rey*)

1903
GREGOR PIATIGORSKY
Russian cellist

1916
SIRIMAVO BANDARANAIKE
Prime minister of Ceylon, the first female prime minister in the world

1918
WILLIAM HOLDEN
American actor (*Sunset Boulevard; Stalag 17*)

1923
HARRY REASONER
American newscaster and journalist (*60 Minutes*)

1810 Pennsylvanian L. M. Norton patents the height of good taste: pineapple cheese.

1847 In the Battle of Cerro Gordo, the first major engagement of the Mexican-American War, 8,500 U.S. troops under Winfield Scott defeat a Mexican force of 12,000 at a mountain pass northwest of Veracruz.

1864 In the American Civil War, 7,000 Confederate soldiers attack the Union garrison in Plymouth, North Carolina, opening the four-day Battle of Plymouth, which ended in a southern victory.

1895 The Sino-Japanese War comes to a formal end with the signing of the Shimonoseki Treaty, which recognized the independence of Korea and granted Formosa to the victorious Japanese.

1897 War breaks out between Greece and the Ottoman Empire over Crete.

1911 American automotive engineer Charles F.

Cuban leader Fidel Castro, lower right, sits inside tank near Playa Girón, Cuba

Kettering patents a self-starter for the Cadillac Car Company.

1917 In the Middle East, three British infantry divisions supported by tanks and a barrage of poison gas shells open the Second Battle of Gaza, a three-day failure that caused 6,444 British casualties.

1919 During postwar chaos in Austria, communists attempt a coup but are put down by a "People's Guard" organized by social democrats.

1929 Baseball great Babe Ruth marries actress Claire Hodgson in a 5 A.M. ceremony.

1935 The League of Nations slaps Hitler's wrist with a formal condemnation of Germany's repudiation of the Versailles Treaty.

1940 American secretary of state Cordell Hull warns the Japanese that the United States

> *"Politicians are the same all over. They promise to build a bridge even where there is no river."*
>
> —Nikita Khrushchev

would oppose any armed attempt to change the status quo in the Dutch East Indies.

1941 Yugoslavia surrenders to Nazi Germany after twelve days of futile resistance. More than 300,000 Yugoslav soldiers were captured.

1942 Imprisoned French general Henri Giraud escapes from a German castle by lowering himself down the castle walls and jumping aboard a moving train bound for France.

1961 The ill-fated Bay of Pigs invasion begins as 1,200 lightly armed, American-backed Cuban exiles wade ashore with the goal of toppling Fidel Castro.

1969 Czech communist leader Alexander Dubcek, who had launched a program of liberal reform, is forced to resign by Soviet occupation forces.

1970 The severely damaged *Apollo 13* spacecraft returns safely to Earth four days after an explosion aborted its mission to land on the moon.

Apollo 13 splashdown

MILESTONE

America Seizes 1,100 Tons of Uranium

On this day in 1945, U.S. Lieutenant Colonel Boris T. Pash commandeers over half a ton of uranium at Strassfut, Germany, in an effort to prevent the Russians from developing an A-bomb. Pash was head of the Alsos Group, organized to search for German scientists in the postwar environment in order to prevent the Russians, previously Allies but now a potential threat, from capturing any scientists and putting them to work at their own atomic research plants. Uranium piles were also rich catches, as they were necessary for the development of atomic weapons.

Pope Julius II

1389 Three thousand Jews are massacred in Prague.

1506 In Rome, Pope Julius II lays the first stone for Saint Peter's Basilica. It took 109 years to build and was the largest church in Christendom until 1989, and is still a major site of pilgrimage.

1521 Martin Luther, chief catalyst of Protestantism, makes a long speech before the Diet of Worms refusing to recant his religious beliefs. He was branded an outlaw and heretic and went into hiding.

1567 The quarrelsome German knight and adventurer Wilhelm von Grumbach is tortured and executed in the marketplace of Gotha, in Germany.

1622 Sir Richard Hawkins, English sailor and adventurer who wrote about Elizabethan life at sea, dies in London at age 62.

1689 Deposed English Catholic king James II, now in

Ireland, calls on the besieged Protestant town of Londonderry to surrender to Irish Catholic forces. He was answered with a sustained barrage of shot and ball, and sat motionless on his horse for hours, just outside range.

1775 Paul Revere makes his famous ride from Boston to Lexington to warn American leaders there that the British were marching toward the Patriot arsenal at Concord.

1797 The French army of the Rhine beats the Austrians at Neuwied, thus ending France's war in Germany.

1864 In the American Civil War, Confederate troops overwhelm a Union wagon train at Poison Springs, Arkansas, and slaughter its wounded black defenders. Confederates couldn't take black prisoners, a Southern newspaper later said, "without a destruction of the social system for which we contend."

1906 The Great San Francisco Earthquake rocks the Bay Area, killing hundreds of people, toppling numerous buildings, and touching off a devastating fire that lasted four days. The quake approached magnitude 8.0 and was recorded as far away as Cape Town, South Africa.

1912 Cunard liner *Carpathia* arrives in New York carrying survivors of the

Ruins of San Francisco after 1906 earthquake

Titanic, which sank three days earlier.

1912 Italy bombards Turkish fortresses along the Dardanelles strait.

1918 The British Parliament passes a bill to draft Irishmen for World War I service, but is soon forced to retract it when the Irish call a general strike.

1919 In the wake of the Amritsar Massacre, Indian nationalist leader Mohandas Gandhi suspends his campaign of civil disobedience.

1942 In the famous Doolittle air raid on Tokyo, sixteen American B-25 bombers under the command of Lieutenant Colonel James H. Doolittle lumber off the deck of the USS *Hornet*, fly 650 miles, and drop their loads over Tokyo. Most of the planes and crew crash-landed safely in China.

1943 Soviet radio propaganda pins the 1940 Katyn Forest Massacre of thousands of Polish Army officers on the German Gestapo. The Soviet Union later admitted (in 1990) the Red Army's culpability.

1955 Visionary physicist Albert Einstein, who revolutionized thought about space, gravity, and time, dies in Princeton, New Jersey, at the age of 76.

1958 American poet Ezra Pound, who had actively supported Mussolini while living in Italy during World War II, is released after thirteen years from a Washington, D.C., hospital for the criminally insane.

1966 Communist China goes public with Mao's Cultural Revolution in an official newspaper proclamation that calls for a "great cultural socialist revolution" against "persons in authority in the Communist Party who have taken the capitalist road."

1974 Red Brigade terrorists kidnap Italian prosecutor Mario Sossi, marking the first time that the left-wing group had struck directly at the Italian government.

1983 A suicide car-bomber destroys the U.S. embassy in Beirut, killing sixty-three people, including seventeen Americans, in a protest against U.S. military presence in Lebanon.

1994 Cricket's batting great Brian Lara, 25, breaks one of the most coveted records in the game, scoring 375 during a game in Antigua.

APRIL 19

69 The Roman senate confirms Vitellius as emperor. He lasted only a few months, until he was murdered by his own soldiers.

1506 Mobs in Lisbon, Portugal, begin three days of killing Jews. Their toll: over 2,000.

1529 A letter representing 14 cities and six Lutheran princes is read in protest of German Emperor Charles V's anti-Lutheran policy. The protesters became known as Protestants, a term eventually applied to most non-Catholic Christians.

1713 Austrian emperor Charles VI issues his Pragmatic Sanction, by which he hoped to settle the matter of succession to the throne by including female descendents.

1770 English navigator Captain James Cook, in search of the legendary Terra Australis Incognita, makes landfall on Australia's east coast. He called it New South Wales, and claimed it for Great Britain.

1775 Seven hundred British troops confront 77 armed American militia men on the common green of Lexington, Massachusetts. In the brief battle, eight Americans died and 10 were wounded. Only one British soldier was injured, but the American Revolution had begun.

1824 George Gordon Byron, English poet and 6th Baron Byron, dies at age 36 in what is now Greece, where he had traveled to support the Greek struggle for independence from Turkey. He became a Greek national hero.

BORN ON THIS DAY

1877
OLE EVINRUDE
Norwegian inventor of the outboard marine engine

1900
RICHARD HUGHES
English author (*A High Wind in Jamica*)

1903
ELIOT NESS
American FBI agent whose "Untouchables" investigated Prohibition-era gangland activities in Chicago

1933
JAYNE MANSFIELD
American actress and sex symbol (*Will Success Spoil Rock Hunter?*)

1935
DUDLEY MOORE
English actor (*Foul Play; 10; Arthur*)

1949
PALOMA PICASSO
Spanish artist and jewelry designer, daughter of Pablo Picasso

1960
FRANK VIOLA
American professional baseball player

1962
AL UNSER JR.
American race-car driver

1968
ASHLEY JUDD
American actress (*Ruby in Paradise; Kiss the Girls; Double Jeopardy*)

"The best car safety device is a rear-view mirror with a cop in it."

—Dudley Moore

1825 Independence leader Juan Antonio Lavalleja arrives in Uruguay with 33 fighters. The date became an important national holiday.

1861 The first blood of the American Civil War is shed when a secessionist mob in slavery-legal Baltimore, Maryland, attacks Massachusetts troops bound for Washington, D.C. Four soldiers and 12 rioters were killed.

1876 A Wichita, Kansas, commission votes not to rehire policeman and legendary gunslinger Wyatt Earp after he beats up a candidate for county sheriff.

1882 Charles Darwin dies of a heart attack in Downe, Kent, England. He was 71.

1902 An earthquake of 7.5 magnitude hits Guatemala; 2,000 die.

1903 In Turkey, an earthquake kills 1,700 people.

The Battle of Lexington

Nazis round up Jews in Warsaw, Poland

1915 During the First World War, French air ace Roland Garros is forced to land with his plane intact. Thus Germany learns about the mechanism that allows a machine gun to fire from behind a propellor. German designer Anthony Fokker used the concept in a plane Allied flyers called the "Fokker Scourge."

1943 In Poland, Waffen SS troops attack Jewish resistance fighters in the Warsaw ghetto. Some 60,000 Jews held out for 28 days. Final death toll: 56,065 Jews, 300 Germans.

1944 Labor leaders in El Salvador call a general strike. General Menéndez fled the country, but before social reforms could gain a toehold, the military installed hard-line General Salvador Castañeda as the new president.

1960 Korean police and soldiers open fire on some 30,000 students and citizens protesting rigged elections, killing 127 and wounding about 1,000. A week later, president Syngman Rhee resigned.

1975 *Aryabhatta*, India's first satellite, is launched from the U.S.S.R.

1993 Near Waco, Texas, the Federal Bureau of Investigation (FBI) launches a tear-gas assault on the compound of the Branch Davidian religious cult, after a tense 51-day standoff. The compound burned to the ground, killing some 80 Branch Davidians, including 22 children.

1995 In Yokohama, Japan, the Aum Shinrikyo religious sect injures 300 in a poison gas attack.

Alfred P. Murrah Federal Building (milestone)

899 B.C. Chinese chroniclers note the "Double Dawn" eclipse, one of the earliest in the historical record.

1164 Antipope Victor IV dies in Tuscany. Having usurped the papacy by armed force and supported by Holy Roman emperor Frederick I, he ruled for five years and was succeeded by antipope Paschal III.

1191 Crusading French King Philip II arrives with his fleet to reinforce the siege of Acre. English King Richard the Lion-Heart joined him three weeks later. Acre fell in July.

1653 Oliver Cromwell dissolves Parliament and expels its members, declaring them "corrupt and unjust men." He set up an appointed "Little Parliament" two months later.

1657 In the War between England and Spain, Admiral Robert Blake destroys a Spanish treasure fleet in the Canary Islands without loss of one English ship.

1689 James II, the former Catholic British king deposed by his Protestant daughter, begins a long, unsuccessful siege of Londonderry, a Protestant stronghold in Northern Ireland.

1775 The day after the battles of Lexington and

M I L E S T O N E

A Massacre at Columbine High School

On this day in 1999, two teenage gunmen kill 13 people in a shooting spree at Columbine High School in Littleton, Colorado. At 11:20 A.M., Dylan Klebold and Eric Harris, dressed in long trench coats, began shooting students outside the school before moving inside to continue their rampage. By the time SWAT team officers finally entered the school at 3:30 P.M., Klebold and Harris had killed 12 fellow students and a teacher and had wounded another 23 people. Turning their guns on themselves, Klebold and Harris then committed suicide.

---

*"The universe is change;
our life is what our
thoughts make it."*

—Marcus Aurelius

Concord, future president James Madison writes, "Of all the enemies of public liberty war is, perhaps, the most to be dreaded."

1832 Congress establishes a park at Hot Springs, Arkansas. Although not named a "national" park, it was the first such reservation in the country. It joined the national park system in 1921.

1841 Edgar Allen Poe's story, *The Murders in the Rue Morgue*, first appears in *Graham's Lady's and Gentleman's Magazine*. The tale is generally considered to be the first detective story.

1859 The Netherlands and Portugal sign an accord dividing islands in the East Indies, including Timor, between them.

1862 Louis Pasteur and Claude Barnard complete the first test of pasteurization, showing that moderate heat could prevent the growth of germs.

1871 Japan establishes its first public postal service, carrying mail between Osaka and Tokyo.

The Vitascope celebrated

suspends performances indefinitely after both her children drown in a freak car accident in Paris. The car stalled and when the chauffeur got out to crank the engine the car ran backward into the Seine. In 1927 Duncan herself was killed in another freak accident: she strangled when her scarf caught in the wheel of her car.

1871 Congress passes the Third Force Act, popularly known as the Ku Klux Act, authorizing President Ulysses S. Grant to use military force to suppress the racist Ku Klux Klan.

1896 A projected movie is shown as a commercial attraction for the first time at Koster and Bial's Music Hall, a vaudeville theater in New York City, using a Vitascope projector.

1902 French scientists Marie and Pierre Curie successfully isolate radioactive radium salts from pitchblende. They shared the 1903 Nobel Prize in physics with colleague A. Henri Becquerel for their work.

1909 Mary Pickford starts her first motion picture job for Biograph Pictures for less than $200 a week. By 1916, the sensational actress would be earning $10,000 a week, plus 50 percent of the profits from her films.

1913 Dancer and choreographer Isadora Duncan

1921 Colombia and the United States sign the Thomson-Urrutia Treaty, by which Colombia recognized the independence of Panama.

1924 The new republic of Turkey adopts a constitution with Islam as the state religion. Four years later, Turkey became a secular republic when the religion clause was removed.

1926 Western Electric and Warner Bros. announce Vitaphone, a process to add sound to movie film.

1931 British MPs give a second reading to a bill proposing to allow cinemas to show films on Sundays, a practice which has hitherto been illegal.

1939 Catholic churches throughout Germany display swastikas to celebrate Adolf Hitler's 50th birthday.

1945 In the Battle of Germany, Russian troops arrive in Berlin.

Columbine High School memorial (milestone)

753 B.C. The city of Rome is founded, according to tradition, by the twins Romulus and Remus, on the site where they had been suckled as orphaned infants by a she-wolf.

43 B.C. Roman statesman and philosopher Marcus Tullius Cicero makes the last of his Philippic orations, which urged the Senate to make war on Mark Antony, who had taken control of Roman affairs in the wake of Caesar's assassination.

1509 English king Henry VII, the first of the Tudor kings, dies and is succeeded by his son Henry VIII.

1697 English settler Hannah Duston returns to a heroine's welcome in Haverhill, Massachusetts, after hatcheting and scalping ten of her Abenaki Indian captors and then making a 100-mile canoe journey.

1836 Texas wins its independence from Mexico in the Battle of San Jacinto, in which Sam Houston's Texas militia surprises and routs the Mexican Army and captures General Santa Anna.

1857 American Alexander Douglas patents an essential Victorian-era undergarment—the bustle.

1878 America gets its first firehouse pole, which was installed in New York City.

1910 American author and humorist Mark Twain dies in Redding, Connecticut.

1918 German flying ace Manfred von Richthofen, a.k.a.

"The Red Baron," is killed by ground fire as he pursues a British airplane deep behind Allied lines. Richthofen, 25, died with 80 victories.

1933 Demonstrating his sympathy for Jews, Danish king Christian X attends the 100th anniversary of the Crystal Synagogue in Copenhagen.

1935 More than 2,000 people are killed by a violent earthquake on the Chinese island of Formosa.

1938 Hitler secretly orders the Wehrmacht to draw up plans for an invasion of Czechoslovakia.

1942 American furniture maker Gustav Stickley, originator of the Mission style, dies in Syracuse, New York, at age 84.

1945 Soviet Red Army forces attack the headquarters of the German High Command, at Zossen, south of Berlin. On the same day, the last Victoria Cross of the war is won by Edward Charlton, for saving the lives of several compatriots trapped in a tank.

Manfred von Richthofen

> *"Nihilism is best done by professionals."*
>
> —Iggy Pop

1953 Aides of U.S. senator Joseph McCarthy demand that more than 30,000 books by "pro-communist" writers be removed from United States Information Service libraries overseas.

1956 Elvis Presley hits the No. 1 spot on the Billboard charts for the first time with "Heartbreak Hotel."

1960 Brazil moves its capital to the brand new city of Brasilia, 580 miles from the coast, to focus attention on the interior of the country.

1962 America's first revolving restaurant, Top of the Needle, in Seattle, Washington, opens with the flip of a remote control switch operated in Palm Beach, Florida, by President John F. Kennedy.

1967 Greek officers led by Colonel Georgios Papadopoulos take power as a military junta.

1968 British right-wing politician Enoch Powell makes his racially controversial "rivers of blood" speech. Arguing against what he sees as high levels of immigration, Powell says: "As I look ahead I am filled with foreboding. Like the Roman, I see the River Tiber foaming with much blood."

1971 Haitian dictator Dr. François "Papa Doc" Duvalier dies at the age of 61. He was elected by popular vote in 1957 but declared himself President for Life and ruled as a ruthless dictator. He was succeeded by his son, Jean-Claude, who was known as "Baby Doc."

1975 In the closing days of the Vietnam War, North Vietnamese troops take Xuan Loc, the last stronghold before Saigon. The victory prompts South Vietnamese president Nguyen Van Thieu to flee to Taiwan.

1983 Great Britain introduces a one-pound coin in three versions, each bearing the head of Elizabeth II on one side, but with a coat of arms (for England), a leek (for Wales), or a thistle (for Scotland) on the reverse.

1994 American astronomer Alexander Wolszczan announces the discovery of three planets orbiting a star in the constellation Virgo.

The Space Needle in Seattle, Washington

> *"Money is the fruit of evil, as often as the root of it."*
>
> —Henry Fielding

1056 A supernova in the Crab nebula fades from the naked eye, causing astrologers the world over to predict dire consequences.

1073 The great reform pope Gregory VII begins his twelve-year reign, in which he attacked various abuses in the church and heatedly contested with Holy Roman emperor Henry IV over lay investiture.

1370 French workmen lay the first stone for the Bastille. Later converted into a prison, the structure was originally part of a fortification to protect Paris from the English.

1500 Portuguese navigator Pedro Alvares Cabral, sailing far to the west during his country's second voyage to India, discovers Brazil and claims it for the Portuguese crown.

1529 Spain and Portugal sign the Treaty of Saragossa, which divided the Pacific Ocean and its territories between the two European powers.

1593 The first Jewish settlers arrive in Amsterdam.

1616 Spanish writer Miguel de Cervantes, author of *Don Quixote*, dies in Madrid.

1793 American president George Washington declares U.S. neutrality in the war

---

MILESTONE

Seduction Is Made Illegal

On this day in 1886, Ohio passes a statute that makes seduction unlawful. Covering all men over the age of 21 who worked as teachers or instructors of women, this law even prohibited men from having consensual sex with women (of any age) whom they were instructing. The penalty for disobeying this law ranged from two to 10 years in prison. On many occasions, women used these laws in order to coerce men into marriage. One man in the middle of an 1867 trial that was headed toward conviction proposed to the alleged victim. The trial instantly became a marriage ceremony.

---

between France and Great Britain.

1823 London fruitseller Robert John Tyers patents inline roller skates.

1838 The first ship to cross the Atlantic solely on steam power, Great Britain's *Sirius*, arrives in New York after an 18-day, 10-hour crossing from Ireland.

1861 In the early days of the American Civil War, Confederate troops sieze the federal arsenal at Fayetteville, North Carolina.

1863 In the American Civil War, Union cavalry under Colonel Benjamin Grierson cut telegraph lines in Macon, Mississippi, during a brilliant, two-week raid that created a diversion for the Union's attack on Vicksburg.

1876 Baseball's National League kicks off its first season with a win for Boston over Philadelphia, 6–5.

Oklahoma land rush

Invasion of Hollandia in New Guinea

1886 At noon, tens of thousands of settlers stream onto a 2 million acre tract of Oklahoma Territory to claim cheap land.

1915 German forces use poison gas for the first time on the Western Front, firing more than 150 tons of chlorine gas at two French divisions during the Second Battle of Ypres.

1944 American troops land in the Hollandia area of New Guinea, touching off a three-month battle that killed nearly 13,000 of the 15,000 Japanese defenders at a cost of 527 GIs.

1945 As Soviet forces close on Berlin, Adolf Hitler admits defeat to his inner circle and says suicide is his only recourse.

1948 In the Palestine Civil War, Zionists capture Haifa.

1954 Anti-communist demagogue Senator Joseph McCarthy begins a televised investigation of the U.S. Army, which he accuses of being "soft" on communism.

1959 The end of the world, according to Florence

Houteff, leader of a reclusive religious sect in Waco, Texas. The sect later morphed into the Branch Davidians, famous for their fiery Waco confrontation with federal agents in 1993.

1968 Shortly after concluding that an American victory in Vietnam was probably impossible, U.S. defense secretary Clark Clifford says the South Vietnamese are now able to "insure their own security."

1972 More than 100,000 Americans protest the Vietnam War in demonstrations throughout the country.

1972 John Fairfax and his girlfriend Sylvia Cook land on Hayman Island off Queensland, Australia, after rowing across the Pacific from San Francisco, a journey lasting 361 days.

2000 Brazilian police fire tear gas and rubber bullets to disband thousands of demonstrators who had assembled to commemorate the European discovery of Brazil as the start of 500 years of oppression and genocide.

Brazilian 500th anniversary riot

1014 Brian Boru, the elderly high king of Ireland, is assassinated by a group of retreating Norsemen shortly after his Irish forces defeated them. Norse power was broken in Ireland forever, but Ireland largely fell into anarchy after Brian's death.

1200 Chinese philosopher Chu Hsi dies. His belief that the key to human perfection lies in the study of ethical principles, shaped Chinese thought for generations.

1509 Two days after the death of his father, Henry VII, 17-year-old Henry VIII is proclaimed king of England. He was crowned in June.

1521 In Spain, the Castilian revolution ends with the defeat of populist comunero forces by an army of the nobility.

1615 Louis XIII orders all Jews out of France and sets the death penalty for any Christians caught sheltering or talking to Jews.

1627 Composer Heinrich Schütz's opera *Dafne* is performed at Torgau, Germany, for the first time. It was the first German-language opera.

1826 In the Greek war of independence, Ottoman forces capture the key Greek fortress of Missolonghi.

1827 At the Royal Irish Academy in Dublin, 21-year-old scientist William Hamilton presents his Theory of Systems of Rays, a work that led to development of the wave theory of light.

William Shakespeare Born on This Day

According to tradition, the great English dramatist and poet William Shakespeare is born in Stratford-on-Avon on this day in 1564. It is impossible to be certain the exact day he was born, but church records show that he was baptized on April 26, and three days was a customary amount of time to wait before baptizing a newborn. Shakespeare's date of death is conclusively known, however: it was April 23, 1616. His plays are performed and read often in more nations than ever before. He captured the full range of human emotions and conflicts with a precision that remains sharp today.

William Shakespeare

"Things won are done, joy's soul lies in the doing."

—*William Shakespeare*

1849 Russian novelist Fyodor Dostoyevsky is arrested with other members of the revolutionary Petrashevsky Circle. He spent eight months in prison and suffered a dramatic release when the group was lined up to be shot, then let go at the last moment.

1850 England's poet laureate William Wordsworth dies in Westmorland at age 80.

1867 William Lincoln of Providence, Rhode Island, patents the Zoetrope, a machine that showed animated pictures by mounting a strip of drawings in a wheel. When viewed through a slit, the drawings appeared to move.

1918 Guatemala declares war on Germany.

1920 Turkish nationalists hold their first parliament, the Grand National Assembly, in Ankara and elect Ataturk Kemal president. Three years later the republic was proclaimed.

1923 British king George V opens the British Empire Exhibition in Wembley. The famous Wembley Stadium was built for the exhibition (its correct title is the Empire Stadium, Wembley) along with exhibition halls known as the Palace of Industry and the Palace of Arts.

1934 Notoriously violent gangster George "Baby Face"

Wall erected for Jewish protection on King George Avenue in Jerusalem during Israel's War of Independence

Nelson, while escaping an FBI raid at Little Bohemia resort in Wisconsin, kills agent H. Carter Baum, saying, "I know you bastards wear bullet-proof vests so I'll give it to you high and low."

1942 In retaliation for the British raid on Lubeck, German bombers launch "Baedeker Raids," killing almost 1,000 English civilians in Exeter and later Bath, Norwick, York, and other "medieval-city centres."

1948 In Israel's War of Independence, the Israeli air force sees its first action. On the same day, the Syrian army is defeated at Deganya—Israel's first important victory in the war.

1949 China's Nationalist government flees its capital, Nanjing, as Communist armies cross the Yangtze River.

1959 During suppression of the Tibetan uprising, China blocks the escape of refugees by sealing the border with India.

1962 The *Ranger IV* satellite is launched from Cape Canaveral, Florida. Its mission: to hit the surface of the moon, which it accomplished three days later.

1975 President Gerald R. Ford declares that American involvement in the Vietnam War is finished—devastating news to the South Vietnamese desperately pleading for U.S. support. The North Vietnamese forces tightened the noose around Saigon.

1981 The first transplant of artificial human skin is performed in Boston, Massachusetts. It promised a breakthrough in the treatment of burns.

1986 Director Otto Preminger, who repeatedly challenged cinema censorship in the United States, dies at 80.

1991 Gerald Ratner, chairman of Ratners, one of Britain's largest retail jewellers, commits financial suicide by publicly describing his goods as "total crap." He went on to say, "We even sell a pair of gold earrings for under a pound, which is cheaper than a prawn sandwich—but I have to say that the sandwich will probably last longer than the earrings."

2000 Islamic radical group Abu Sayyaf abducts 21 people from a Malaysian resort. Holding them on an island in the Philippines, they also seized hostage intermediaries sent to talk to them.

Abu Sayyaf rebel hideout in Sulu Province, the Philippines

🔫 **70** Roman legions break through Jerusalem's middle wall, but are driven back by Jewish defenders.

🟦🟦 **177** April 24 is the traditional date for the beginning of persecution of the Martyrs of Lyons, a group of Christian missionaries from Asia Minor tortured to death in southern Gaul.

🏴󠁧󠁢󠁥󠁮󠁧󠁿 **1066** Halley's Comet appears in the night sky over the English Channel and is interpreted as a harbinger of national disaster. Indeed, William the Conqueror defeated English forces at the Battle of Hastings in October of that year.

🇺🇸 **1800** President John Adams approves legislation to appropriate $5,000 to establish the Library of Congress. The first books were ordered from London. In 1814, British troops burned the Capitol, including the library.

🇺🇸 **1833** Americans Jacob Ebert and George Dulty patent the first soda fountain.

🎭 **1852** In a letter to a friend, French writer Gustave Flaubert describes the writing life: "I love my work with a frenetic and perverse love, as an ascetic loves the hair shirt which scratches his belly."

🔫 **1862** In the dark of night, Union admiral David D. Farragut leads a flotilla past two

> *"Dwelling on the negative simply contributes to its power."*
>
> —*Shirley MacLaine*

Confederate forts guarding New Orleans, on his way to capturing one of the South's major ports.

🏆 **1908** Auto racing legend Ralph DePalma makes his debut in New York. In 25 years, he would rack up nearly two thousand wins, including the Vanderbilt Cup, the Savannah Grand Prix, and the Indy 500.

🔫 **1915** New Zealand and Australian troops land at Gallipoli, for what would become a disastrous attempt to open the Dardanelle Straits. Allied casualties: 300,000.

✈️ **1916** A German naval squadron bombards the English coast at Yarmouth and Lowestoft.

🟦🟦 **1916** On Easter Monday in Dublin, the Irish Republican Brotherhood, a secret organization of Irish nationalists, launches the so-called Easter Rebellion. Britain soon crushed the rebellion but unrest continued and in 1922 most of Ireland won independence.

🟦🟦 **1920** At the Conference of San Remo, called by the Allies to divide up the former

Ralph DePalma pulls his car across the finish line at the 1912 Indianapolis 500

Clarence Darrow, left, and William Jennings Bryan, opposing attorneys at the "Monkey Trial"

Ottoman Empire, Britain gets the mandate for Palestine. Palestinian Arabs called it the "year of catastrophe."

⚖️ **1922** Colin Ross is hanged in Australia for the rape and murder of 13-year-old Alma Tirtsche. He was one of the first criminals in Australia convicted on the basis of forensic evidence.

⚖️ **1925** In defiance of a Tennessee state law that forbids the teaching of evolution theory in public schools, teacher John Scopes conducts a lesson on the subject. The resulting "Scopes Monkey Trial" drew global attention.

🎭 **1934** Laurens Hammond patents the first organ without pipes or reeds.

🇺🇸 **1936** A group of firemen responding to an alarm in Camden, New Jersey, become subjects in the first unplanned television broadcast event—a forerunner of live TV news coverage.

🇬🇧 **1953** Winston Leonard Spencer Churchill, the British leader who guided Great Britain and the Allies through the crisis of World War II, is knighted by Queen Elizabeth II.

🔬 **1962** The first coast-to-coast telecast by satellite takes place. Signals from California were bounced off the orbiting weather balloon Echo I and received in Massachusetts.

1965 President-for-life Sukarno orders the seizure of all foreign-owned property in Indonesia.

1970 China launches its first space satellite, the *Dong Fang Hong*, or *The East Is Red*—also the name of that favorite old tune of the people, which the device broadcast from orbit.

🎭 **1974** American entertainer Bud Abbott, half of the famous Abbott and Costello comedy team dies, penniless, after an 8-year battle with the IRS over back taxes.

Indonesia's first president, Sukarno

795 During a procession in Rome, Pope Leo III is attacked by assailants attempting to blind him and cut out his tongue. Leo escaped the city, but returned in the autumn with an escort provided by his protector, Charlemagne.

1464 During the English Wars of the Roses, the Yorkists crush the Lancastrians in the Battle of Hedgeley Moor.

1790 British writer Daniel Defoe publishes *The Life and Strange Adventures of Robinson Crusoe*, which was based on the true story of Alexander Selkirk, a Scottish sailor shipwrecked off the west coast of South America.

1792 The guillotine is used for the first time, in Paris, to execute highwayman Nicolas Jacques Pelletier.

1831 Davy Crockett is glorified in a New York play called *The Lion of the West*, the first of many books, plays, movies, and television shows to idolize the Tennessee frontiersman.

Robinson Crusoe and his man Friday

BORN ON THIS DAY

1214
LOUIS IX
King of France (1226–70)

1284
EDWARD II
King of England (1307–27)

1599
OLIVER CROMWELL
Puritan lord protector of England (1653–58)

1792
JOHN KEBLE
English clergyman and poet after whom Keble College, Oxford, is named

1873
WALTER DE LA MARE
English poet

1874
GUGLIELMO MARCONI
Italian inventor who pioneered development of the radio

1908
EDWARD R. MURROW
American broadcast journalist (*Person to Person*)

1918
ELLA FITZGERALD
American jazz singer celebrated for her interpretations of Gershwin and Cole Porter songs

1940
AL PACINO
Academy Award-winning American actor (*The Godfather; Scarface; Scent of a Woman*)

1849 A Canadian mob burns the Parliament building in Montreal. Canada subsequently moved its capital to Ottawa.

1859 Construction of the Suez Canal begins with the swing of a pickaxe at Port Said, Egypt. It would take ten years to complete the 101-mile canal connecting the Mediterranean and Red Seas.

1881 The modern era of German anti-Semitism is ushered in with a petition signed by 250,000 Germans asking the government to bar foreign Jews.

1898 The United States declares war on Spain.

1901 New York becomes the first American state to require automobile license plates and issues a grand total of 954 sets the first year.

1925 Italian automaker Alfieri Maserati wins the Targa Florio with his first car, the Tipo 26.

1926 Former Cossack cavalryman Colonel Ali Reza Khan, who deposed the Shah in 1925 to become prime minister of Persia (now Iran), has himself crowned Shah at the Royal Palace in Tehran.

> *"A great many people think they are thinking when they are merely rearranging their prejudices."*
>
> —*Edward R. Murrow*

"Revolution of the Flowers" coup

📺 **1935** The first round-the-world telephone call is placed by one telephone executive in New York to another seated just fifty feet away.

⚔️ **1945** American and Russian armies link up near Berlin, prompting a 324-gun salute in Moscow and causing New York City crowds to burst into song and dance in Times Square.

🕊️ **1945** International representatives convene in San Francisco to write the charter for the United Nations.

🏆 **1956** Boxer Rocky Marciano (born Rocco Francis Marchegiano) announces that he is to retire from the ring. He turned professional in 1947 and retired with a record of 49 wins from 49 bouts. He had been world heavyweight champion since 1952.

🏆 **1959** Italian-American auto racing great Mario Andretti makes his debut by driving the family 1948 Hudson to victory at his hometown track in Nazareth, Pennsylvania.

🏴󠁧󠁢󠁥󠁮󠁧󠁿 **1959** The first known AIDS patient checks into an English hospital where he dies several months later. Two decades after his death, his condition was diagnosed from tissue samples.

🇺🇸 **1964** U.S. president Lyndon B. Johnson puts General William Westmoreland in charge of all American military forces in Vietnam.

⚔️ **1972** North Vietnam's "Easter Offensive" nearly cuts South Vietnam in two as Hanoi's 320th Division attacks Kontum in the Central Highlands.

🏴 **1974** In Portugal, the "Revolution of the Flowers," a coup led by Francisco da Costa Gomes, topples the nation's dictatorship of Macrelo Caetano.

⚔️ **1982** In the Falklands War, British forces retake South Georgia Island from Argentina.

🎭 **1995** American actress Ginger Rogers, best known as the dancing partner of Fred Astaire in 10 films, dies at age 83.

🇨🇳 **1999** Ten thousand adherents of the Falun Gong spiritual movement stage an unauthorized demonstration in Beijing.

Falun Gong demonstration in Beijing, China

APRIL 26

1478 In the Cathedral of Florence, assassins stab two Medici brothers, killing one and wounding the other, in an attempt to overthrow the powerful family. The attack was backed by the city's archbishop and launched with the knowledge of Pope Sixtus IV.

1655 Dutch West India Company directors refuse to ban Jews from New Amsterdam, future site of New York City, and specify further that no trade restrictions may be placed upon them.

1777 During the American Revolution, 16-year-old New York patriot Sybil Ludington rides through the night rousing local militiamen to defend the region's arsenal in Danbury, Connecticut.

1804 Thousands of meteorite fragments shower the French town of L'Aigle, proving even to the most ardent skeptics that stones could come from outer space.

1807 Russia and Prussia form an alliance to force France out of the German states.

1828 Russia declares war on the Ottoman Empire.

1848 English explorer-naturalists Alfred Russel Wallace and Henry Walter Bates sail for the Amazon.

1862 In a letter to her editor, American poet Emily Dickinson remarks that though she has heard of Walt Whitman she has not read any of his work, because she had been told that his poems were "disgraceful."

BORN ON THIS DAY

1711
DAVID HUME
Scottish social scientist and author (*Treatise of Human Nature*)

1785
JOHN JAMES AUDUBON
American naturalist and artist

1798
FERDINAND VICTOR EUGÈNE DELACROIX
French painter

1888
ALEKSANDR MIKHAILOV
Russian astronomer

1893
ANITA LOOS
American author (*Gentlemen Prefer Blondes*)

1895
RUDOLF HESS
German Nazi Party deputy

1900
CHARLES FRANCIS RICHTER
American seismologist

1914
BERNARD MALAMUD
American author (*The Fixer; The Natural*)

1917
SAL MAGLIE
American professional baseball player

1933
CAROL BURNETT
American actress and comedian (*The Carol Burnett Show*)

1947
DONNA DE VARONA
American Olympic swimmer

"A wise man proportions his belief to the evidence."
—David Hume

1865 Union soldiers corner Abraham Lincoln's assassin, John Wilkes Booth, in a Virginia barn and shoot him. He dies three hours later and is secretly buried in the floor of the Old Penitentiary in Washington, D.C. On the same day, Confederate forces under General Joseph Johnston surrender.

1882 British scientific great Charles Darwin is buried at Westminster Abbey with full ecclesiastical honors.

1882 On a lax day at the U.S. Patent office, inventor John Sutliff is granted a patent for his perpetual motion machine.

1915 In World War I's secret Treaty of London, Italy agrees to switch sides in exchange for Austro-Hungarian territory, German African territory, and a large sum of money.

1915 Union of South African troops under General Louis Botha defeat German

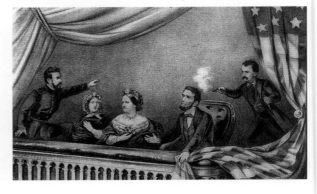

Assassination of President Abraham Lincoln by John Wilkes Booth

German president Paul von Hindenburg, left, and Chancellor Adolf Hitler

1954 Mass testing of the Salk polio vaccine begins in the United States.

1961 American Robert Noyce patents the integrated circuit.

1972 In the midst of North Vietnam's "Easter Offensive," U.S. president Richard Nixon announces the withdrawal of another 20,000 American troops.

1986 The world's worst nuclear power plant accident occurs at the Chernobyl plant in the Soviet Union when an explosion blows the lid off a reactor vessel. Fifty tons of radioactive material billowed into the atmosphere, thirty two people die within days, thousands more over the long run, and millions of acres of forest and farmland are contaminated.

1994 South Africa holds its first multiracial parliamentary elections and elects former political prisoner Nelson Mandela president in a landslide.

forces at Riet and Treckkopje in German Southwest Africa.

1916 Great Britain and France begin secret negotiations for the post-war dismemberment of the Middle East.

1921 The first broadcast weather report in the United States airs from station WEW in St. Louis, Missouri.

1925 German field marshal Paul von Hindenburg is elected second president of Germany's Weimar Republic.

1936 The population of the Irish Free State is 2,968,420.

1937 Germany takes advantage of the Spanish Civil War to test its powerful new air force with a raid on Guernica that killed or wounded a third of the undefended town's 5,000 inhabitants.

1952 During night exercises in the mid-Atlantic, the American destroyer *Hobson* collides with the aircraft carrier *Hornet* and sinks with the loss of 176 lives.

MILESTONE

Lucille Ball Dies
Comedienne Lucille Ball dies at age 78 on this day in 1989. She and husband Desi Arnaz transformed television, creating the first long-running hit situation comedy. Ball was an actress whose movie roles didn't fully showcase her talent. Frustrated, she turned to radio and starred as a ditzy wife in *My Favorite Husband* from 1948 to 1951. CBS decided to launch the popular series on the relatively new medium of TV. *I Love Lucy* became one of the most popular television shows in history. She died of congestive heart failure following an open-heart surgery earlier in the month.

Nelson Mandela casting his vote in South Africa's first all-race elections

APRIL 26   **237**

Johannes Kepler

4977 B.C. According to Johannes Kepler, the universe was created on this day.

711 Moslem invaders under Tarik invade southern Spain. At the later battle of Xeres, they defeated Roderick, last of the Visigoth kings.

1521 After traveling three-quarters of the way around the globe, Portuguese navigator Ferdinand Magellan is killed by a poison arrow during a tribal skirmish on Mactan Island in the Philippines.

1650 In the English Civil War, Scottish forces under the Marquess of Montrose are defeated at Carbisdale, Scotland. Montrose, betrayed, was executed in May.

1667 Blind, impoverished poet John Milton sells the copyright to his great work *Paradise Lost* for a mere 10 pounds. Once printed, it was immediately hailed as a masterpiece.

1727 Russian Empress Catherine I orders expulsion of all Jews from the Ukraine.

1773 The British Parliament passes the Tea Act,

MILESTONE

Tragedy on the Mississippi

On this day in 1865, just days after the end of the Civil War, the worst maritime disaster in American history occurs when the steamboat *Sultana*, carrying 2,100 passengers, explodes and sinks in the Mississippi River, killing all but 400 of those aboard. The Mississippi, with its dikes and levees damaged by four years of war, stood at flood stage, and most of those who died were drowned in the surging river. All but 100 of those killed were Union veterans, and most were Yankee survivors of Andersonville and other brutal Confederate prisoner of war camps.

Explosion of steamboat Sultana

---

giving the East India Company a monopoly on the American tea trade. Seeing this as another example of taxation tyranny, colonists later organized the Boston Tea Party—an early act of defiance in the American independence movement.

1805 In the First Barbary War, U.S. agent William Eaton leads a small force of U.S. Marines and Berber mercenaries against Tripoli's port city of Derna. The resulting successful action is celebrated in the phrase "to the shores of Tripoli," in the U.S. Marine Corps song.

1813 Zebulon Pike, explorer of the Rocky Mountains, and for whom Pikes Peak was named, dies in York (modern Toronto, Canada) during a battle in the War of 1812. American forces captured York, but abandoned it within days.

1871 The American Museum of Natural History opens in New York City.

1887 Philadelphia surgeon George Thomas Morton performs the first appendectomy.

> *"Labor disgraces no man, but occasionally men disgrace labor."*
>
> —Ulysses S. Grant

1898 Five months after imposition of a hut tax, the people of Sierra Leone stage a general uprising against British rule. On the same day in 1961, Britain grants independence to the West African country.

1921 In the aftermath of World War I, the reparations commission declares that Germany must pay 132 billion gold marks.

1972 During the Hue offensive, North Vietnamese troops move to within 2.5 miles of Quang Tri. South Vietnamese forces suffered their highest casualties of any week in the war.

1978 Afghan president Sardar Mohammed Daoud is overthrown and murdered in a coup led by procommunist rebels. The resulting turmoil led to Soviet military intervention two years later.

1981 Xerox introduces the first computer with a mouse and a point-and-click interface, but it failed to catch on, perhaps because of the price: $16,500.

1995 The U.S. Air Force Space Command announces that the Global Positioning System satellite array is complete and fully operational.

1939 As war clouds gather, Great Britain institutes military conscription for men 20 to 21 years of age.

1941 The German army enters Athens, signaling the end of Greek resistance.

1960 Togo becomes independent from France. Its first president is Sylvanus Olympio.

North Vietnamese infantry attacking

66 Roman forces under General Florus sack Jerusalem.

70 Having been driven back earlier, Roman legions under Titus retake Jerusalem's middle wall and destroy it.

1686 Isaac Newton presents to the Royal Society in London the first volume of his masterpiece, *Philosofiæ Naturalis Principia Mathematica*. The work detailed the Newtonian laws of motion.

1770 British explorer Captain James Cook arrives at Botany Bay, Australia.

1789 Three weeks after leaving Tahiti, mutineers led by master's mate Fletcher Christian seize the HMS *Bounty*. Tyrant Captain William Bligh and 18 loyal sailors were set adrift in a small boat, and the *Bounty* sailed off in search of paradise.

1796 Italy admits defeat by Napoleon Bonaparte at the armistice of Cherasco, and is forced to abandon its alliance with Austria.

1817 By the Rush-Bagot Agreement, the United States and Great Britain agree to limits on naval forces in the Great Lakes region.

1897 The Chickasaw and Choctaw, two of the so-called Five Civilized Tribes who had

for years been exiled to Indian Territory in Oklahoma, agree under pressure to abolish tribal government and communal ownership of land. The other tribes soon followed, throwing all of Indian Territory open to white settlement.

1903 A strong earthquake kills 2,200 in Turkey.

1919 A committee led by U.S. president Woodrow Wilson presents The Covenant of the League of Nations in its final form.

1925 American poet T. S. Eliot, already recognized as a major poet, accepts a position as editor at Faber and Faber publishers, which allows him to quit his job as a bank clerk.

1932 A vaccine for yellow fever is announced during a meeting at the American Societies for Experimental Biology in Philadelphia, Pennsylvania.

1936 King Fu'ad of Egypt dies and is replaced on the throne by his son Faruq.

1945 "Il Duce," Benito Mussolini, and his mistress, Clara Petacci, are shot by Italian partisans who had captured the couple as they

Left to right, David Lloyd, of Great Britain, Vittorio Orlando, of Italy, Georges Clemenceau, of France, and U.S. president Woodrow Wilson

> "Until I feared I would lose it, I never loved to read. One does not love breathing."
>
> —Harper Lee

attempted to flee to Switzerland. Hauled in a truck to Milan, the bodies were hung upside down in public for revilement by the masses.

1945 Sweeping into Po Valley, British and American forces crush German resistance in northern Italy.

1947 Norwegian anthropologist Thor Heyerdahl leaves Peru aboard his balsa raft *Kon Tiki*, bound for Polynesia. He covered the distance of 4,300 miles in 101 days.

1952 General Dwight D. Eisenhower gives up his post as supreme commander of NATO's military forces to campaign for the U.S. presidency.

1955 Ex-model Ruth Ellis goes on trial at the Old Bailey for the murder of her lover, race-car driver David Blakely. She was found guilty and, on July 13, became the last woman in Great Britain to be hanged.

1955 Civil war erupts in Saigon, South Vietnam, between Bing Xuyen rebels and government troops. The rebels were forced from the city after five days of fighting.

1965 To prevent what he claims will be a "communist dictatorship," President Lyndon B. Johnson sends more than 22,000 U.S. troops to restore order in the Dominican Republic, an act widely condemned in Latin America.

1967 Boxing officials yank Muhammed Ali's world boxing title for refusing military service.

1969 Charles de Gaulle resigns as president of France following defeat, in a national referendum, of his proposals for constitutional reform.

1988 Three Italian fighter jets collide during an air show over Ramstein Air Force Base in Germany and crash into the crowd of spectators. Seventy were killed.

Three Italian jets collide over Ramstein Air Force Base in Germany

West Point, from above Washington Valley

■■ **1109** Hugh of Cluny, French Benedictine abbot under whose direction medieval monasticism reached its peak, dies at Cluny. He was canonized in 1120.

■ **1428** Le Loi becomes king of Vietnam, in Dong Do, now Hanoi.

■■ **1429** French peasant girl Joan of Arc, 17, breaks the English siege of Orleans during the Hundred Years' War.

■■ **1699** In Paris, the French Academy of Science holds its first public meeting, at the Louvre.

■ **1812** The U.S. Military Academy at West Point, originally created as a school for military engineers, is reorganized around a four-year military science curriculum.

■ **1854** The first African-American college, Ashmun Institute (later Lincoln University), is founded in Chester County, Pennsylvania, to train students in theology, science, and the classics.

⚔ **1861** In the American Civil War, Union troops take formal possession of New Orleans, a severe blow to the Confederacy that soon opened 400 miles of the lower Mississippi River to the Yankees.

MILESTONE

Duke Ellington Gets Medal of Freedom

On this day in 1969, jazz musician, composer, arranger, and bandleader Duke Ellington receives the Presidential Medal of Freedom on his 70th birthday. His hits range from jazz classics to religious suites. He won countless honors, awards, and honorary degrees and continued to travel and perform for most of his life. In 1965, the music jury of the Pulitzer Prize Committee unanimously recommended Ellington for a special award, but the Advisory Board declined the jury's recommendation. While the rejection sparked accusations of racism, the 66-year-old Ellington simply responded, "Fate doesn't want me to be too famous too young."

Duke Ellington

> *"I merely took the energy it takes to pout and wrote some blues."*
>
> —*Duke Ellington*

🎭 **1875** American writer Henry James publishes one of his first books, *Transatlantic Sketches*, a collection of travel pieces.

▬ **1898** The first American cancer lab is established, in New York State.

⚔ **1918** The Battles of the Lys, one of two major German spring offensives, is suspended south of Ypres after opening a wide breach along the British front. On the same day, the Germans overthrow the Ukrainian government and install one more to their liking.

▬ **1925** The U.S. National Academy of Sciences elects its first woman member, histologist Florence Rena Sabin.

▬ **1933** Russian communist Nikolay Yezhov is named to the government's central Purge Commission. As chief of the Soviet security police (1936–38), he would administer the most severe, ruthless, and widespread phase of Stalin's purges.

⚔ **1942** Survivors of the Bataan Death March stagger into Camp O'Donnell, in the Philippines. At least 600 Americans and 5,000 Filipinos died during the ordeal. On the same day, the Japanese captured Lashio, the Burma Road's southern terminus, cutting off supplies to Allied troops in China.

1944 In the Pacific, an American naval task force of twelve aircraft carriers begins a two-day bombing raid of Japanese shipping at Truk.

1945 As shells rain down around his Berlin bunker, Adolf Hitler marries longtime mistress Eva Braun.

1945 Dachau, the first Nazi concentration camp and site of countless heinous crimes against its inmates, is liberated by the U.S. Army. Appalled by what they find, Americans execute at least two groups of SS guards.

1946 Japan's wartime premier, Hideki Tōjō, is indicted for war crimes by an international tribunal.

1949 The retiring president of the Royal Academy is heckled as he describes modern art as "silly daubs," ridiculing artists such as Picasso, Matisse, and Henry Moore.

1952 A U.S. federal district court rules that President Harry S. Truman's seizure of the nation's steel industry is unconstitutional.

1963 Reform-minded president of the Dominican Republic Juan Bosch pushes through a constitution that alienates landowners, the Catholic Church, industrialists, and the military (which toppled him five months later).

1975 As North Vietnamese troops close in on Saigon, U.S. forces begin a massive helicopter evacuation of 1,000 Americans and 6,000 Vietnamese from the South Vietnamese capital.

1980 English film director and master of suspense Sir Alfred Hitchcock dies at the age of 80, having received the American Institute's Lifetime Achievement Award a year earlier and been knighted a mere four months before his death.

1981 English lorry-driver Peter Sutcliffe, known as the Yorkshire Ripper, admits to attacking and killing 13 women over a four year period. He had already pleaded guilty to the attempted murder of seven other women.

1992 An all-white, suburban Los Angeles jury acquits four police officers in the beating of black motorist Rodney King, thus triggering three days of rioting.

1993 In Costa Rica, gunmen release nineteen Supreme Court justices and their five assistants after the government refuses to pay a $20 million ransom.

1998 Brazil sets aside 25 million acres of the Amazon rain forest, an area the size of Great Britain, for conservation.

Looting during the Los Angeles riots

463 B.C. A total eclipse of the sun over Thebes prompts Greek poet Pindar to write, "O star supreme, reft from us in the daytime! Why has thou perplexed the power of man and the way of wisdom by rushing forth on a darksome track?"

89 B.C. During Rome's Social War, Lucius Sulla sacks the Italian coastal city of Stabiae, which had thrown its lot against Rome the previous year.

59 A total eclipse of the sun casts Italy into temporary darkness. Pliny witnessed it. The historian Tacitus later embellished the event: "A woman gave birth to a snake. Another was killed by a thunderbolt in her husband's embrace. Then the sun was suddenly darkened and the fourteen districts of the city were struck by lightning."

311 Ailing Roman emperor Galerius, fearing that his disease was caused by the wrathful God of the Christians he had so ruthlessly persecuted, issues an edict tolerating the new religion, then dies.

1367 Pope Urban V leaves Avignon, France, on an ultimately unsuccessful attempt to reestablish the papacy at the Vatican in Rome.

1439 Richard Beauchamp, fifth earl of Warwick,

> *"Politics is not a bad profession. If you succeed there are many rewards. If you disgrace yourself, you can always write a book."*
> —Ronald W. Reagan

BORN ON THIS DAY

1602
WILLIAM LILLY
English astrologer, author, and almanac compiler

1662
MARY II
Queen of Great Britain and Ireland (1662–94)

1777
KARL FRIEDRICH GAUSS
German mathematician and astronomer

1870
FRANZ LEHÁR
Slovakian composer

1883
JAROSLAV HASEK
Czech author (*The Good Soldier Schweik*)

1909
JULIANA
Queen of the Netherlands who abdicated this day in 1980

1910
AL LEWIS
American actor (*The Munsters*)

1912
EVE ARDEN
American actress (*Mildred Pierce; Our Miss Brooks*)

1923
PERCY HEATH
American jazz musician

1933
WILLIE NELSON
American singer/songwriter ("Blue Eyes Crying in the Rain"; "Crazy; "Georgia on My Mind")

1945
MICHAEL J. SMITH
American astronaut

Michael J. Smith

---

dies in France. The knight, hero, and diplomat had served under three English kings: Henry IV, Henry V, and Henry VI.

1494 Christopher Columbus drops anchor at Cuba during his second voyage to the New World.

1632 Johann Tilly, Bavarian general and commander of the Catholic League in Germany during the Thirty Years' War, is killed defending Bavaria from the Swedes.

1671 Austria executes four Hungarians involved in the Wesselenyi Conspiracy, a plot to overthrow the Hapsburg dynasty in Hungary.

1789 George Washington is sworn in as the first president of the United States, in New York City.

1798 The U.S. Navy is established by an act of Congress.

1803 Terms for the Louisiana Purchase are agreed to between France and the United States. The $15 million land deal doubled the area of the United States by adding the territory between the Mississippi and the Rocky Mountains.

1897 British physicist Joseph John Thomson announces the discovery of the electrons (which he called corpuscles), to a disbelieving audience at the Royal Institution in London.

1918 German forces intervening in the Finnish Civil War take the city of Viborg.

1939 World's Fair poster

1932 The Irish Dail votes 77 to 71 to abolish the oath of loyalty to the British monarch, previously sworn by all Irish MPs. Dail president Éamon de Valera said, "Unlike the British Dominions we have never freely admitted that our right to sovereign independence derives from a British statute."

1939 The New York World's Fair opens on 1,200 acres at Flushing Meadow Park in Queens, featuring futuristic technologies such as FM radio and fluorescent lighting.

1945 Burrowed into his Berlin bunker, Adolf Hitler commits suicide by swallowing cyanide and shooting himself with his service revolver. His body and that of Eva Braun are then cremated.

1945 In Southeast Asia, Allied forces under Admiral Lord Louis Mountbatten finish off the Japanese 15th, 28th, and 33rd armies after inflicting 347,000 Japanese casualties.

1975 The Vietnam War ends as North Vietnamese troops occupy the presidential palace in Saigon and South Vietnamese general Duong Van Minh surrenders.

1982 U.S. president Ronald W. Reagan pledges American support for Great Britain in the Falklands crisis, describing the Argentinian invaders as "aggressors" and Great Britain as "our closest ally" but stating that there would be no direct American involvement in any fighting.

1998 The Malaysian government announces that the city of Kuala Lumpur will be hosed down from skyscrapers in an attempt to clear hazardous smog caused by immense forest fires on Borneo.

Air pollution shrouds Kuala Lumpur

Franconi's Hippodrome in New York City

1497 Italian navigator John Cabot sets sail in search of a westward route to Asia under letters patent from King Henry VII of England. Cabot landed on June 24, 1497 to claim North America for England.

1507 During his three years at the Augustinian monastery at Erfurt, German religious reformer Martin Luther is ordained a priest.

1519 Italian artist Leonardo da Vinci dies at Cloux, France.

1670 King Charles II of England, Ireland, and Scotland charters the Hudson Bay Company.

1853 Franconi's Hippodrome, an arena for circus games, opens at Broadway and 23rd Street in New York City. The gala opening featured a chariot and ostrich race as the main attraction.

1863 Confederate general Thomas "Stonewall" Jackson is accidentally wounded by his own troops in the American Civil War. He died eight days later.

1885 The first edition of one of the most endearing American magazines, *Good Housekeeping*, is published. By

MILESTONE

Loch Ness Monster Sighted

Although accounts of an aquatic beast living in Scotland's Loch Ness date back 1,500 years, the modern legend of the Loch Ness Monster is born when a sighting makes local news on this day in 1933. The newspaper *Inverness Courier* related an account of a local couple who claimed to have seen an enormous animal rolling and plunging on the surface. A famous 1934 photograph seemed to show a dinosaur-like creature with a long neck emerging out of the murky waters, leading some to speculate that "Nessie" was a solitary survivor of the long-extinct plesiosaurs.

1966 the magazine, founded by businessman Clark W. Bryan and later purchased by the Hearst publishing company, had reached a circulation of 5.5 million readers.

1887 Hannibal W. Goodwin of Newark, New Jersey, applies for a patent for celluloid photographic film, the material from which movies are shown.

1926 A drawing is faxed across the Atlantic for the first time. It was a sketch of Ambassador Alanson Bigelow Houghton, sent from London, England, to New York City.

1932 American comedian Jack Benny debuts in his own radio show on the NBC Blue Network. His beginning salary was $1,400 per week.

1941 The U.S. Federal Communications Commission grants the first commercial television licenses to 10 stations, authorizing them to begin broadcasting the following July 1.

1945 All German armed forces in Austria and Italy surrender to the Allies.

What some say is the Loch Ness Monster (milestone)

> *"Age is strictly a case of mind over matter. If you don't mind, it doesn't matter."*
>
> —*Jack Benny*

1949 American playwright Arthur Miller wins a Pulitzer Prize for *Death of a Salesman*.

1952 A new era of passenger flight is born as a de Havilland Comet leaves London for Johannesburg in the first scheduled jet airline service.

1960 Caryl Chessman, a convicted sex offender, is executed in the California gas chamber at San Quentin. Although he killed no one, Chessman was convicted under the "Little Lindbergh law," which permits the death penalty for crimes less serious than murder.

1964 U.S.-born British politician Nancy Astor dies at the age of 84. Her husband Waldorf Astor was elected MP for Plymouth, and when he was elevated to the House of Lords, Nancy took over his seat to become the first female MP to sit in the House of Commons.

1965 The "Early Bird" satellite is used to send television pictures across the Atlantic for the first time.

1974 Film production gets under way on the movie *Jaws* at Martha's Vineyard in Massachusetts. Production for the celluloid thriller took 120 days, while costs soared from the projected $3.5 million to $8 million.

1974 Former vice-president Spiro Agnew, earlier convicted of crimes during his service under President Richard M. Nixon, is disbarred by the Maryland Court of Appeals, preventing him from practicing law anywhere in the United States.

1982 During the Falklands War, a Royal Navy submarine controversially sinks the Argentine battleship *General Belgrano*. The Argentine government described the attack as "a treacherous act of armed aggression," while British prime minister Margaret Thatcher described it as the removal of "a very obvious threat to British forces."

1990 The path to ending apartheid in South Africa is widened as the government of South Africa and the African National Congress open their first formal talks toward this goal.

1994 Nelson Mandela is officially declared the president of South Africa in the country's first free democratic election.

Nelson Mandela celebrates his victory

BORN ON THIS DAY

1660
ALESSANDRO SCARLATTI
Italian composer, father of composer Domenico Scarlatti

1729
CATHERINE THE GREAT
German-born Empress of Russia

1859
JEROME K. JEROME
English author (*Three Men in a Boat*)

1860
THEODOR HERZL
Hungarian-born journalist, founder of the Zionist movement

1887
VERNON CASTLE
British dancer

1892
MANFRED FREIHERR VON RICHTHOFEN "THE RED BARON"
German WWI fighter pilot who was leader of the "Flying Circus" squadron

1895
LORENZ HART
American composer, lyricist: half of famous team of (Richard) Rodgers and Hart

1903
BENJAMIN SPOCK
American pediatrician, author (*Common Sense Book of Baby Care*)

1904
BING CROSBY
American singer, actor (*Pennies from Heaven; Holiday Inn; The Bells of St. Mary's*)

1925
JOHN NEVILLE
British actor (*The Adventures of Baron Munchausen*)

1935
LINK WRAY
American musician

1936
ARNOLD GEORGE DORSEY
English singer better known as Englebert Humperdinck

1937
LORENZO MUSIC
American actor, cartoon voice of "Garfield"

1494 Italian-born Spanish explorer Christopher Columbus sights the island of Jamaica on a voyage from Spain. Spanish colonists settled the island 15 years later, although the British took it in 1655.

1802 Washington, D.C., now the United States' capital, is incorporated as a city.

1810 English poet Lord Byron swims the Hellespont in one hour and 10 minutes. Known today as the Dardanelles, this 40-mile-long body of water separates Asian and European Turkey.

1915 British chancellor of the exchequer David Lloyd George announces that Great Britain's three main enemies in World War I are "Germany, Austria and Drink," after allegations that heavy drinking by munitions workers was slowing down the supply of arms to troops on the Western Front.

1916 The British execute Irish nationalist Padraic Pearse and two companions for their roles in the Easter Uprising.

1921 West Virginia becomes the first U.S. state to impose a sales tax. Today, such taxes are almost universal among American states.

1933 Mrs. Nellie Ross becomes the first female director of the U.S. Mint.

1937 American author Margaret Mitchell's popular novel about the American Civil War, *Gone With the Wind*, wins the Pulitzer Prize. Published in 1936, it became one of the best-selling novels of all time.

M I L E S T O N E

Excel Announced

On this day in 1985, Microsoft unveiled its plans for a new spreadsheet for the Apple Macintosh. At the time, Microsoft was known primarily as a company that produced operating systems. In 1982, the company had started publishing word processing and other types of programs, and it had quickly become one of the largest suppliers of Macintosh software. The new product, called Excel, was a badly needed business application for the Mac. Spreadsheets had quickly become a "killer app"—software so compelling that it drove people to buy machines to run it—when VisiCalc, the first spreadsheet, was released in December 1979.

1939 American singers Patti, Maxine, and LaVerne Andrews (the Andrews Sisters) record "The Beer Barrel Polka" for Decca Records. It became a major hit.

1944 The United States ends the rationing of most grades of meat, a policy launched as a conservation measure when World War II began.

1948 The U.S. Supreme Court decides that deed covenants prohibiting the sale of real estate to African Americans or other minorities are legally unenforceable.

1948 American playwright Tennessee Williams wins the Pulitzer Prize for *A Streetcar Named Desire*.

1949 British parliament introduces the Ireland Bill. The Bill was passed on its second reading on May 11, recognizing the Republic of Eire.

1952 An airplane sets a new first: landing at the geographical location of the North Pole.

1957 Brooklyn Dodgers owner Walter O'Malley announces he will move his baseball team from New York to Los Angeles, California, after private investors agree to build a new stadium for the team in Chavez Ravine.

David Lloyd George

> *"The cock may crow, but it's the hen that lays the egg."*
>
> —*Margaret Thatcher*

Jimi Hendrix

1965 The lead element of the 173rd Airborne Brigade ("Sky Soldiers") departs from Okinawa, Japan, for South Vietnam. It was the first U.S. Army combat ground unit committed to the Vietnam War.

1968 The United States and North Vietnam agree to begin formal talks in Paris, France, toward ending the Vietnam War. No agreement was reached, except on the site for talks.

1969 Guitar legend Jimi Hendrix is arrested in Toronto for possession of heroin. Hendrix died the following year after mixing barbiturates and alcohol.

1971 Planning to shut down the U.S. capital, protestors against the Vietnam War begin four days of demonstrations in Washington, D.C.

1979 Conservative Party leader Margaret Thatcher becomes Britain's first female prime minister as the Tories oust the incumbent Labor government in parliamentary elections.

1978 "Sun Day," a quasi-holiday extolling the virtues of solar energy, attracts thousands of people to events across the United States.

1986 An unmanned U.S. Delta rocket loses main engine power on its launch, forcing safety officers to destroy it by remote control.

1989 Palestinian Liberation Organization leader Yāsir Arafāt states that the PLO charter calling for the destruction of Israel has been "superseded" by a declaration urging peaceful coexistence of the Palestinian and Israeli states.

1991 The American TV soap opera *Dallas* airs its last episode. The show broke ratings records in 1980 when 83.6 million viewers breathlessly watched to see who shot villainous oil baron J. R.

1999 President Bill Clinton meets at the White House with Japanese prime minister Keizo Obuchi, the first U.S. visit by a Japanese premier in 12 years.

President Bill Clinton and first lady Hillary welcome Japanese prime minister Keizo Obuchi and wife Chizuko

1471 In the Wars of the Roses, the Yorkists, led by Edward IV, defeat the Lancastrians at the Battle of Tewkesbury, finally destroying any resistance on behalf of the deposed king Henry VI. Edward IV never had to fight again to defend his crown, though the dynastic struggle resumed after his death in 1483.

1626 Dutch colonist Peter Minuit arrives on the island of Manhattan in what is today New York City. In one of history's most spectacular bargains, he bought the island for $24 from resident Indians.

1776 Rhode Island declares its freedom from England, two months before the signing of the Declaration of Independence.

1780 One of Great Britain's most prestigious horse races, the Epsom Derby, is run for the first time (at Epsom in Surrey). It is said that the name of the derby was decided by the toss of coin between the race's founders, Charles Bunbury and the Earl of Derby: Bunbury had the consolation that his horse *Diomed* was the first winner.

1864 The Army of the Potomac embarks on the biggest campaign of the American Civil War, crossing the Rapidan River, precipitating the climactic Battle of the Wilderness that would nearly end the war.

> *"Be ashamed to die until you have won some victory for humanity."*
>
> —*Horace Mann*

BORN ON THIS DAY

1655
BARTOLOMMEO CRISTOFFORI
Italian harpsichord-maker and inventor of the piano

1796
HORACE MANN
American educator, often called the father of public education in the United States

1825
THOMAS HENRY HUXLEY
English social scientist, humanist

Thomas Henry Huxley

1827
JOHN HANNING SPEKE
English explorer who discovered Lake Victoria and the source of the Nile

1909
HOWARD DASILVA
American actor

1919
HELOISE
Author, columnist ("Hints from Heloise")

1926
MILTON "MILT" THOMPSON
American NASA test pilot, chief engineer

1928
HOSNI MUBARAK
President of Egypt

1929
AUDREY HEPBURN
Academy Award-winning Belgian actress (*Roman Holiday; Breakfast at Tiffany's; My Fair Lady*)

1936
MANUEL BENITEZ PEREZ
"EL CORDOBES"
Spanish bullfighter

1959
RANDY TRAVIS
American country singer

1916 Reacting to a demand of U.S. president Woodrow Wilson during World War I, Germany agrees to limit its submarine warfare, averting a diplomatic break with America.

1920 The Symphony Society of New York stages a concert at the Paris Opera House in France. It was the first American orchestra to make a European tour.

1932 In Chicago, Illinois, crime boss Al Capone is convicted not for the murders of which he is suspected, but on charges of federal income tax evasion. He was sentenced to 11 years in prison.

1945 German forces in the Netherlands, Denmark, and northwest Germany agree to surrender terms in World War II.

1948 *The Naked and the Dead*, the first novel of 25-year-old American author Norman Mailer, is published. It was considered one of the best World War II stories.

1954 Princeton and Yale meet at the Racquet and Tennis Club in New York City in the

The Army of the Potomac

Freedom Rider bus in flames near Anniston, Alabama

first American intercollegiate tennis match ever held.

1959 In the United States, the National Academy of Recording Arts and Sciences announces the winners of the first Grammy Awards. Henry Mancini won the Best Album award for *The Music from Peter Gunn,* and Perry Como and Ella Fitzgerald were rated the best male and female vocalists of the year.

1961 U.S. secretary of state Dean Rusk reports that Viet Cong forces in South Vietnam have grown to 12,000 men and that they kidnapped or killed more than 3,000 persons in 1960. President Kennedy said the United States was considering sending troops to the area.

1961 A group of "Freedom Riders" leaves Washington, D.C., for New Orleans, Louisiana, to challenge segregation laws on buses and in bus terminals.

1964 For the first time, the Pulitzer Prize jury decides not to award winners in the areas of fiction, drama, and music.

1970 Gunfire by Ohio National Guard troops kills four Kent State University students and wounds 11 others during a demonstration protesting President Richard M. Nixon's announcement that he had ordered U.S. troops into Cambodia during the Vietnam War.

1977 English journalist David Frost interviews former president Richard M. Nixon in the first of four TV programs. The interviews offered the first major explanations by Nixon of the events leading up to his resignation of the U.S. presidency.

1980 Marshal Tito (Josip Broz), communist leader of Yugoslavia since 1945, dies at the age of 88 in Belgrade. He led Yugoslavia on a course that combined dogmatic allegiance to Marxism and an independent relationship with the Soviet Union during his 35-year service.

1982 During the Falklands War, Royal Navy destroyer HMS *Sheffield* is sunk by an Argentinian Exocet missile. *Sheffield* was the first major British warship to be lost in 37 years.

MILESTONE

Margaret Thatcher Sworn In

Margaret Thatcher, leader of the Conservative Party, is sworn in on this day in 1979 as Britain's first female prime minister. She was the first woman president of the Oxford University Conservative Association, and in 1950 she ran for Parliament in Dartford. In 1959, she was elected as the Conservative MP for Finchley, a north London district. She rose rapidly in the ranks of the Conservative Party and in 1967 joined the shadow cabinet, sitting in opposition to Harold Wilson's ruling Labour cabinet. With the victory of the Conservative Party in 1970, Thatcher became secretary of state for education and science.

Margaret Thatcher, first woman prime minister

1809 Mary Kies of South Killingly, Connecticut, becomes the first woman to be issued an American patent. Her invention: a technique to weave straw with silk and thread.

1821 French emperor Napoleon Bonaparte dies in exile on the island of St. Helena in the Atlantic.

1847 The American Medical Association is organized in Philadelphia, Pennsylvania.

1862 Outnumbered three to one, Mexican general Ignacio Zaragoza's troops defeat Napoleon Bonaparte's invading French army at Puebla. Cinco de Mayo ("Fifth of May") is today one of Mexico's most cherished holidays.

1877 Sioux Indian chief Sitting Bull leads a band of followers from the United States to Canada a year after the Battle of the Little Big Horn, in which his warriors massacred every member of U.S. Army general George Custer's 7th Cavalry. After four years in frustrated exile, the chief led 187 of his followers back to the United States and died in 1890.

1891 Carnegie Hall (then named Music Hall) holds its opening night in New York City.

1900 *The Billboard*, a magazine for the music and entertainment industries, begins weekly publication in the United States. Later, the name was shortened to *Billboard*.

1936 American actress Bette Davis wins the Academy

BORN ON THIS DAY

1352
RUPRECHT
Roman Catholic German king

1813
SØREN KIERKEGAARD
Danish philosopher

1818
KARL MARX
Prussian author, social scientist, founder of communism

1830
JOHN BATTERSON STETSON
American hat manufacturer after whom the cowboy hat is named

1849
HAMBLETONIAN
American trotting horse, greatest standard-bred horse

1867
NELLIE BLY (ELIZABETH COCHRANE SEAMAN)
American journalist

1883
CHARLES BENDER
Professional baseball player who is the only Native American in the Hall of Fame

Charles Bender

1920
JOHN HIDALGO MOYA
Architect, designer of the Skylon Tower at Niagara Falls

1926
ANN B. DAVIS
American actress (*The Brady Bunch*)

1934
"ACE" CANNON
American saxophonist

1943
MICHAEL PALIN
English comedian (*Monty Python's Flying Circus*)

Award for Best Actress for her role in *Dangerous*.

1936 Edward Ravenscroft of Glencoe, Illinois, receives a patent for the screw-on bottle cap with a pour lip.

1941 Emperor Haile Selassie returns to Addis Ababa, the capital of Ethiopia, after an absence of five years. Also known as Abyssinia, the country was occupied by Italy on this same date five years earlier.

1945 A Japanese balloon bomb explodes on Gearhart Mountain in Oregon, killing a pregnant woman and five children. It was the only fatal attack of its kind on continental U.S. soil during World War II.

1955 The Federal Republic of Germany (West Germany) is born as the United States, Great Britain, and France end their military occupation begun at the end of World War II. The move gave Germany the right to rearm.

1955 Mixing baseball and ballet, the musical *Damn Yankees* opens in New York City. It ran for 1,019 performances.

1956 In Los Angeles, California, Jim Bailey becomes the first runner to break the four-minute mile in the United States. His time: 3:58.6.

> *"Reason has always existed, but not always in a reasonable form."*
>
> —*Karl Marx*

British SAS atop Iranian embassy

former Nazi concentration camp at Belsen with a visit to the Bitburg war cemetery, which contains the graves of 49 SS soldiers.

1988 Eugene Antonio Marino becomes the first African-American Roman Catholic bishop. He was installed as archbishop of the diocese in Atlanta, Georgia.

1989 A federal judge orders sweeping changes in the FBI's promotion system, months after he found that the American law enforcement bureau had discriminated against Hispanic employees.

1994 Michael Fay, an American teenager charged with vandalism, is given four strokes with a cane on the buttocks as punishment in Singapore.

1995 In Oklahoma City, Oklahoma, rescue workers end their search for bodies after a bomb explosion that killed 168 people at the Murrah Federal Building. Timothy McVeigh was later convicted and executed for the crime.

1961 Astronaut Alan B. Shepard becomes America's first space traveler in a 15-minute suborbital flight in a capsule launched from Cape Canaveral, Florida.

1973 A crowd of 56,800 pays $309,000 to see Led Zeppelin at Tampa Stadium in Florida. It was the largest paying audience ever for a single musical act, topping even the Beatles' 55,000-fan, $301,000 performance earlier.

1980 Great Britain's elite special forces squadron, the SAS, carries out a daring 11-minute raid on the Iranian embassy in London, killing four of the five terrorists who had taken over the building six days earlier and rescuing 19 hostages. One hostage had already been killed by the terrorists and one was killed during the raid.

1981 Imprisoned Irish Catholic militant Bobby Sands dies after a hunger strike that lasted 66 days. His death touched off widespread rioting in Belfast as sympathizers clashed with British Army troops.

1985 U.S. president Ronald W. Reagan provokes anger by following a visit to the

Murrah Federal Building in Oklahoma City after car bombing

General James E. Longstreet on horseback

1835 James Gordon Bennett publishes the first edition of the *New York Herald*.

1864 During the American Civil War, Confederate general James E. Longstreet is seriously wounded by the fire of his own troops on the second day of fighting in the Battle of the Wilderness.

1876 English artist Thomas Gainsborough's painting *Duchess of Devonshire* is removed from 100 years of obscurity and sold at auction in London for 10,000 guineas, the highest price ever paid for a work of art up to then. The painting was stolen a few weeks later, then recovered in a bizarre case involving a thief named Adam Worth, on whom the character of Dr. Moriarty, nemesis of detective Sherlock Holmes, was patterned.

1889 With the just-completed Eiffel Tower dedication as its major attraction, the Paris Exposition formally opens in France.

1915 Playing for the Boston Red Sox, American baseball great Babe Ruth hits his first major-league home run. The "Sultan of Swat" hit 714 round-trippers before he retired, as a New York Yankee, in 1935.

1916 The captain of the U.S. battleship *New Hampshire,* off the coast of Virginia, calls naval commanders in Washington, D.C., as the first successful test of the radio-telephone as a wartime communications option.

1925 The first transpacific fax is sent from Honolulu, Hawaii, to New York City via radio and telephone. It was also the first transcontinental fax.

1939 California author John Steinbeck is awarded the Pulitzer Prize for his novel *The Grapes of Wrath*, the fictional account of a Depression-era Oklahoma farm family that moves west in search of a better life. The author of many best-selling works of fiction and nonfiction, Steinbeck was awarded the Nobel Prize in 1962. He died in New York in 1968.

1942 Lieutenant General Jonathan Wainwright surrenders all U.S. troops in the Philippines to the Japanese during World War II. The last American bastion in the Philippines to resist Japanese occupation was on the island of Corregidor.

"My doctor told me to stop having intimate dinners for four—unless there are three other people."

—*Orson Welles*

1952 Italian nursery education pioneer Dr. Maria Montessori dies in the Netherlands at the age of 81. Montessori was Italy's first female physician, and she developed a system of education based on spontaneity of expression, self-discovery, and freedom from restraint.

1954 A British medical student, Roger Bannister, is the world's first person to break the notorious barrier of the four-minute mile. Running for the Amateur Athletic Association, he made history in 3 minutes, 59.4 seconds. He later earned a medical degree from Oxford and was knighted for his athletic skills by Queen Elizabeth II.

1955 American actress Grace Kelly meets her future husband, Prince Rainier of Monaco, while in the principality on a photo shoot for a French fashion magazine. The two were married less than a year later.

1957 U.S. senator John F. Kennedy of Massachusetts is awarded the Pulitzer Prize for his book *Profiles in Courage*.

1957 American playwright Eugene O'Neill wins a Pulitzer Prize for his play *Long Day's Journey Into Night*.

1959 American actor Raymond Burr wins the Best Actor in a Dramatic Series Emmy for his portrayal of the crime-solving attorney Perry Mason. Launched in 1957, the television show ran nine years.

1960 Princess Margaret of Great Britain marries Anthony Armstrong-Jones, a commoner, in London's Westminster Abbey. They were divorced in 1978.

1974 West German chancellor and 1971 Nobel Peace Prize winner Willy Brandt resigns after it is discovered that his aide Gunther Guillaume is an East German spy.

MILESTONE

***Hindenburg* Explodes**
On this day in 1937, the *Hindenburg*, the largest airship ever built and the pride of Nazi Germany, bursts into flames while touching a mooring mast in Lakehurst, New Jersey, on a flight from Frankfurt, Germany. Thirty-six passengers and crew members died in the accident. At over 800 feet long, the *Hindenburg* is still the largest aircraft ever to have flown. More like an ocean liner than an airplane, the *Hindenburg* boasted a promenade deck where passengers could sightsee, a smoking lounge, and passenger cabins. The disaster in Lakehurst was likely caused by the ignition of the ship's volatile hydrogen gas by static electricity. While later designs used safer helium gas, the commercial airship industry never recovered from this tragedy.

The Hindenburg (milestone)

1763 "Pontiac's Rebellion" begins when a group of Native American warriors under Ottawa chief Pontiac attack the British force at Detroit. Pontiac finally signed a treaty with the British in 1766.

1769 George Washington brings a package of resolutions before the Virginia House of Burgesses attacking the "taxation without representation" policy of the American colonies' mother country, England. This policy and others ultimately led to the launch of the War of Independence in 1776.

1789 The first U.S. inaugural ball is held in New York, honoring President and Mrs. George Washington.

1864 In the American Civil War the Army of the Potomac, commanded by General Ulysses S. Grant, moves south after a bloody battle with Confederate troops in the Wilderness forest. Neither side gained a clear victory, although the Confederates inflicted more casualties than Grant's forces and, while outnumbered, held off the Yankees.

1867 Alfred Nobel files a British patent for dynamite. In 1875, he went on to invent gelignite. Both were intended

---

MILESTONE

First Hit By a Coed Group

"Monday, Monday," by the Mamas and the Papas, hits the top of the charts on this day in 1966. This was the first musical quartet to include two men and two women. Almost all previous groups that topped the charts were single-sex groups, like the Supremes and the Chiffons, or the Beatles and the Beach Boys. A few male groups sported a token woman singer (like Ruby and the Romantics), but the Mamas and the Poppas were the first group to feature fully balanced coed vocals.

"A minute's success pays the failure of years."

—*Robert Browning*

for engineering applications. As a committed pacifist, Nobel hoped that his explosives would provide such a deterrent to war that they would bring peace to mankind. In his will he endowed the annual Nobel Prizes, awarded to those who have "conferred the greatest benefit on mankind" in five categories, including peace.

1896 Dr. H. H. Holmes, one of America's first well-known serial killers, is hanged in Philadelphia, Pennsylvania. He reportedly killed more than 200 victims and hid their remains on his property.

1912 In New York City, Columbia University approves final plans for awarding the first Pulitzer Prize, established by publisher Joseph Pulitzer.

1915 The unarmed Cunard liner *Lusitania* is torpedoed and sunk by a German U-boat, with the loss of over 1,000 lives. Those killed included more than 100 Americans, a fact that is thought to have hastened American involvement in World War I.

Lusitania in New York Harbor

1939 Germany and Italy announce a military and political alliance known as the Rome-Berlin Axis. Japan later would join the two countries as a partner in World War II.

1941 American bandleader Glenn Miller and his orchestra record "Chattanooga Choo Choo" for RCA Victor Records.

1945 German general Alfred Jodl signs the unconditional surrender of all German forces at Reims in France toward the end of World War II. General Walter B. Smith signed for the Allies. Jodl was convicted of war crimes in the Nuremburg trials and hanged.

1951 The International Olympic Committee admits Russia to the 1952 Olympic Games.

1954 Ho Chi Minh's forces decisively defeat the French at Dien Bien Phu in northwest Vietnam after a 57-day siege. The victory marked the end of French colonial rule in French Indochina (Vietnam) and made possible the division of the country into two states, north and south of the 17th parallel.

1958 American pianist Van Cliburn signs an artist's contract with RCA Victor Records.

China's foreign minister Tang Jiaxuan surveys Chinese embassy bombing damage

1960 Leonid Brezhnev, one of Nikita Khrushchev's most trusted aides, is picked as chairman of the Presidium of the Supreme Soviet, the Soviet equivalent to the U.S. presidency. Four years later, he would take control of the Soviet Union.

1963 The communications satellite *Telstar II* is launched by the United States.

1973 Journalists Carl Bernstein and Bob Woodward are awarded the Pulitzer Prize for their investigation of the Watergate cover-up.

1999 NATO jets strike the Chinese embassy in Belgrade, Yugoslavia, killing three people and injuring 20. U.S. president Bill Clinton calls it a "tragic mistake."

Hernando de Soto

1541 Spanish explorer Hernando de Soto discovers the Mississippi River.

1794 Antoine-Laurent Lavoisier, the French chemist who identified oxygen, is guillotined in Paris by the Revolution Convention.

1846 American general Zachary Taylor defeats a detachment of the Mexican Army in the first major battle of the Mexican War at Palo Alto and Resaca de la Palma. The victory forced Mexican troops across the Rio Grande to Matamoros, protecting the newly annexed state of Texas.

1886 Dr. John S. Pemberton sells the first Coca-Cola at Jacob's Pharmacy in Atlanta, Georgia. A bookkeeper, Frank Robinson, coined the soft drink's name; his handwriting is the one used in the "Coke" trademark.

1903 French Post-Impressionist painter Paul Gauguin dies in Tahiti.

1914 W. W. Hodkinson creates the American film company Paramount Pictures. After several mergers and many production company and theater acquisitions, Paramount became

MILESTONE

Soviets to Boycott L.A. Olympics

Citing fears for the safety of its athletes in what it considered a hostile and anti-communist environment, the Soviet government announces a boycott of the 1984 Summer Olympic Games to be held in Los Angeles, California, on this day in 1984. Although the Soviets had cited security concerns, the boycott was more likely the result of strained Cold War relations due to America's generous aid to Muslim rebels fighting in Afghanistan—and payback for the U.S. boycott of the 1980 Moscow Olympic Games. A number of other Soviet Bloc countries and Cuba followed suit in boycotting the Los Angeles Games.

USA MEDALISTS

President Ronald Reagan and Mrs. Nancy Reagan with USA Olympic medalists.

one of Hollywood's most powerful studios. It was acquired by Viacom in 1994.

1921 Sweden abolishes capital punishment, being among the first European powers to do so. Most others would follow suit.

1927 Former French fighter pilot Charles Nungesser is killed in an attempt to fly from Paris to New York, less than two weeks before Charles Lindbergh makes the first solo nonstop transatlantic flight (in the opposite direction, from New York to Paris).

1939 A Hollywood, California, racetrack first uses a new invention of Clay Puett in widespread use today—the electric starting gate. The push of one button automatically opened the gates, letting the horses run; the entire set of gates then wheeled off the course.

1939 In the build-up to World War II, Pope Pius XII asks representatives of Germany, France, Great Britain, and Poland to come to the Vatican for peace talks.

1942 During World War II, the Battle of the Coral Sea ends

> *"A politician is a man who understands government and it takes a politician to run a government. A statesman is a politician who's been dead ten or fifteen years."*
>
> —*Harry S. Truman*

when the U.S. Pacific fleet turns back a Japanese force headed for Port Moresby, New Guinea.

1958 U.S. vice president Richard M. Nixon is shoved, booed, and spat upon by anti-American protesters during a visit to Lima, Peru.

1959 *One Man's Family,* a popular American radio show dating back to 1932, airs for the final time. It completed 3,256 episodes altogether.

1961 New Yorkers pick the "Mets" as a new name for the National League baseball franchise that is scheduled to begin play at the Polo Grounds the following year.

1972 During the Vietnam War, U.S. president Richard M. Nixon announces that he has ordered the mining of major North Vietnamese ports to prevent the flow of arms to communist forces fighting South Vietnamese and Americans in the south.

1973 Armed members of the American Indian Movement surrender to federal authorities after a 71-day siege of Wounded Knee in South Dakota, site of the infamous massacre of 300 Sioux by the U.S. 7th Cavalry in 1890. The massacre was the final battle of the 19th-century Indian wars.

1978 American "Son of Sam" serial killer David Berkowitz pleads guilty in New York to killing six people.

1980 The World Health Organization announces that smallpox has been successfully

eradicated as a disease of humans.

1984 In London, the Thames Flood Barrier is officially opened by Queen Elizabeth II, who describes this remarkable feat of engineering as the Eighth Wonder of the World—a title already claimed for the Brooklyn Bridge, which was opened on May 24, 1883.

1985 In the United States, the first ill-fated cans of New Coke roll out of Coca-Cola bottling and canning plants.

1988 Stella Nickell is convicted on two counts of murder in Seattle, Washington, for putting cyanide in Excedrin capsules in an effort to kill her husband. Instead, two persons died after buying Excedrin poisoned by Nickell in Seattle stores. She received two 90-year sentences.

1989 Former U.S. president Jimmy Carter, leading an international team overseeing Panama's elections, declares that the armed forces were defrauding the opposition party from victory.

Robert C. Goizueta, chairman of the board and chief executive officer of Coca-Cola Co., left with Donald R. Keough, president

MAY 9

1502 Italian-born Spanish explorer Christopher Columbus sails from Cadiz, Spain, on his fourth and last voyage to the New World.

1671 Thomas Blood, an Irish adventurer better known as "Captain Blood," is captured in attempting to steal the Crown Jewels from the Tower of London. He became a celebrity in England and died in 1680.

1754 The first American newspaper cartoon is published, in the *Pennsylvania Gazette*. It depicted the disunited state of the British colonies as a snake chopped into eight pieces representing the eight colonies. The message: "Join or Die."

1825 The first gaslit theater in America, the Chatham Theater, opens in New York City.

1868 Reno is the official name chosen for a town in northwestern Nevada, after General Jesse Lee Reno, a Union officer in the American Civil War.

1887 William Cody ("Buffalo Bill") opens his Wild West show in London, England, giving Queen Victoria and her

General Jesse Lee Reno

subjects their first look at real American cowboys and Indians.

1914 President Woodrow Wilson proclaims a new holiday in the United States: Mother's Day.

1926 American polar explorer Richard E. Byrd and copilot Floyd Bennett claim they flew this day over the North Pole from Spitzbergen, Norway. In 1966, evidence emerged to suggest that they may have been 150 miles short of the Pole.

1936 Italian dictator Benito Mussolini appears on the balcony of the Palazzo Venezia to boast of his conquest of Ethiopia, which he calls Abyssinia, saying: "Italy at last has her empire . . . It is a fascist empire because it bears the indestructible sign of the will and power of Rome."

1945 Hermann Goering, Adolf Hitler's designated successor and commander of the Nazi German *Luftwaffe* air force during World War II, is taken prisoner by the U.S. 7th Army in Bavaria. Charged with war crimes in the Nuremburg trials, he committed suicide in his jail cell.

1955 West Germany formally joins the North Atlantic Treaty Organization 10 years after its defeat in World War II.

> *"A static hero is a public liability. Progress grows out of motion."*
> —*Richard E. Byrd*

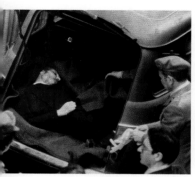

Prime Minister Aldo Moro's body found

1962 The English rock group The Beatles sign their first recording contract. The band would play for EMI Parlophone.

1969 William Beecher, military correspondent for the *New York Times,* publishes a front-page article reporting that American military aircraft have begun secret bombing of Cambodia during the Vietnam War.

1970 An estimated 100,000 young people, mostly from college campuses, demonstrate near the White House in Washington, D.C., against the Vietnam War.

1974 On July 30, the U.S. House of Representatives Judiciary Committee begins impeachment hearings against President Richard M. Nixon, voting to impeach him on three counts. Facing impeachment proceedings, Nixon resigned the presidency on August 8.

1976 West German terrorist leader Ulrike Meinh of of the Red Army Faction, also known as the Baader-Meinhof gang, is found dead in her cell in Stammheim high security prison, having committed suicide.

1978 The body of former Italian prime minister Aldo Moro is found, riddled with bullets, in the back of a car in central Rome. He had been kidnapped by Red Brigade terrorists on March 16 after a shootout.

1980 A Liberian freighter rams the Sunshine Skyway Bridge over Tampa Bay, Florida, collapsing a 1,400-foot span. Thirty-five motorists died in the accident.

1994 South Africa's newly elected parliament formally installs Nelson Mandela as the country's first black president.

1995 U.S. president Bill Clinton arrives in Moscow for a summit meeting with Russian president Boris Yeltsin.

1995 The city of Kinshasa, Zaire, is placed under quarantine after an outbreak of the dreaded Ebola virus.

1995 The United States returns the first boatload of Cuban refugees to their homeland, a move protested by the Cuban-American community.

Cuban residents demonstrating against President Clinton's immigration policy in New Havana area of Miami, Florida

1749 The tenth and final volume of English author Henry Fielding's novel *Tom Jones* is published. It tells the humorous story of the attempts of an illegitimate but charming Englishman to win the hand of his neighbor's daughter.

1774 Louis the XVI ascends the throne of France.

1775 Ethan Allen and his Green Mountain Boys capture the British-held fortress at Ticonderoga, New York, in the American Revolutionary War.

1863 General Thomas J. "Stonewall" Jackson, colorful Confederate soldier, dies of wounds and pneumonia after losing his arm to friendly fire in the Battle of Chancellorsville during the American Civil War.

1872 Victoria Claflin Woodhull becomes the first woman nominated to be president of the United States. She was chosen by the National Woman Suffrage Association in New York City.

1898 The city of Omaha, Nebraska, adopts a law allowing vending machines. A permit costs $5,000.

1924 J. Edgar Hoover is promoted to director of the U.S. Federal Bureau of Investigation. He remained in office until his death in 1972.

1927 The Hotel Statler in Boston, Massachusetts, installs headsets in 1,300 rooms. It was the first time a hotel offered broadcasts from radio stations.

BORN ON THIS DAY

1760
CLAUDE JOESPH ROUGET DE LISLE
Composer of "La Mareillaise," which was to become the French national anthem

1838
JOHN WILKES BOOTH
American actor, assassin of Abraham Lincoln

John Wilkes Booth

1850
SIR THOMAS LIPTON
Scottish Lipton Tea producer

1864
LÉON GAUMONT
French film pioneer

1888
MAX STEINER
Austrian composer of film music (*Gone with the Wind; Casablanca*)

1899
FRED ASTAIRE
American dancer, actor (*Shall We Dance; Royal Wedding; Finian's Rainbow*)

1909
MOTHER MAYBELLE CARTER
American country music singer and musician

1915
DENIS THATCHER
Husband of British prime minister Margaret Thatcher

1943
JAMES EARL CHANEY
American civil rights activist

1955
HOMER SIMPSON
Animated character (*The Simpsons*)

1960
BONO
Irish singer (*U2*)

"The greatest lesson in life is to know that even fools are right sometimes."

—*Winston Churchill*

1933 Chancellor Adolf Hitler's Nazis stage massive public book burnings across Germany.

1940 Winston Churchill, first lord of the Admiralty, replaces Neville Chamberlain as British prime minister. He would guide Great Britain through the remaining days of World War II.

1941 Rudolf Hess, Nazi German dictator Adolf Hitler's deputy, parachutes into Scotland during World War II, claiming he is on a peace mission. He ended up with a life sentence in Spandau, Germany, near Berlin, where he died of an apparent suicide in 1987.

1945 Soviet troops enter Prague, the last European capital to be liberated at the end of World War II.

1954 The American musical group Bill Haley and the Comets releases "Rock Around the Clock," the first rock-and-roll number to top the charts. The song started out slowly but became a hit when it was used in the movie *The Blackboard Jungle.*

1968 Preliminary peace talks toward ending the Vietnam War begin in Paris.

1977 American actress Joan Crawford, who won an Oscar for her role in the film *Mildred Pierce,* dies.

1978 Princess Margaret of Great Britain and the Earl of Snowdon announce they are divorcing after 18 years of marriage.

1981 François Mitterand is elected president of France at the third attempt, becoming the country's first socialist president.

1984 The International Court of Justice in the Hague, Netherlands, rules that America should cease military action against the Sandinista government in Nicaragua.

1989 Panamanian general Manuel Antonio Noriega announces his government is nullifying the country's elections. The opposition insisted they won by a 3-to-1 margin.

1990 The government of the People's Republic of China announces the release of 211 people arrested during the massive protests held in Beijing's Tiananmen Square in June 1989.

Students demonstrate at U.S. embassy in Beijing, China

1994 Illinois executes convicted serial killer John Wayne Gacy for the murders of 33 young men and boys.

1999 China breaks off talks on arms control with the United States and permits demonstrators to hurl stones at the U.S. embassy in Beijing to protest NATO's bombing of the Chinese embassy in Yugoslavia.

Burning of books in Berlin, Germany

1647 Dutch settler Peter Stuyvesant arrives in New Amsterdam to become governor. The colonial city would later become New York.

1812 Spencer Perceval, prime minister of Great Britain since 1809, is shot to death in London by a demented businessman, John Bellingham. Though deemed insane, the assassin was executed a week later.

1816 The American Bible Society is formed in New York City.

1858 Minnesota, the "Land of 10,000 Lakes," is admitted to the Union as the United States' 32nd state.

1864 J. E. B. Stuart, one of the Confederate Army's most colorful generals, is fatally wounded at the Battle of Yellow Tavern near Richmond, Virginia, during the American Civil War. His death seriously affected the operations of the South's commander, General Robert E. Lee.

1900 Boxer James J. Jeffries knocks out James J. Corbett, known as "Gentleman

General J. E. B. Stuart, right

1811
CHANG & ENG BUNKER
Famous Chinese Siamese twins

1888
IRVING BERLIN
Russian-born composer ("God Bless America"; "White Christmas"; "There's No Business Like Show Business")

Irving Berlin

1889
PAUL NASH
English painter, official war artist during World War I.

1904
SALVADORE DALÍ
Spanish artist (*The Persistence of Memory; Meditative Rose*)

1905
MARJORIE SYKES
English peace activist

1912
FOSTER BROOKS
American comedian and actor

1924
JACKIE MILBURN
British professional soccer player

1927
MORT SAHL
Canadian comedian and political satirist

1932
VALENTINO
Italian fashion designer

1933
LOUIS FARRAKHAN
American Nation of Islam minister who initiated the Million Man March

1940
BUTCH HARTMAN
American race-car driver

Jim," in the 23rd round, winning the American heavyweight boxing title. Corbett had beaten Jeffries previously.

1910 Glacier National Park is established in Montana.

1927 The Academy of Motion Picture Arts and Sciences is founded in the United States. It was several years later, however, that the first of its famous "Oscars" was awarded.

1927 Francis Davis files one of five patents for a system of hydraulic power steering for motor vehicles. General Motors took out a license to use the invention but the Great Depression and then World War II meant that the technology was not applied to passenger cars until 1951, by Chrysler.

1940 Passengers on the Bermuda-bound steamer S.S. *President Roosevelt* watch the opening ceremonies of the New York World's Fair in the world's first shore-to-ship TV broadcast.

1942 William Faulkner publishes *Go Down, Moses,* one of his greatest collections of short stories. All were based on Faulkner's observations in his native state of Mississippi. Some of these Yoknapatawpha County stories led to his receiving the Nobel Prize in literature in 1949 and the National Book Award in 1951.

> *"When your house is on fire you can't be bothered with the neighbors."*
>
> —*Gary Kasparov*

1943 In World War II, U.S. forces land on the island of Attu in the Aleutian chain of Alaska. Nineteen days later, the island was taken from the Japanese by the United States.

1944 Allied forces begin a major World War II assault on the Gustav Line, a German defensive line drawn across central Italy just south of Rome. This attack was launched not only to take the capital but to release thousands of American troops in Italy to the cross-channel assault that became known as D-Day.

1946 The first packages from the relief agency Cooperative for American Remittances to Europe arrive at Le Havre, France. CARE was a major resource for rehabilitating war-torn Europe.

1947 B. F. Goodrich announces the development of the tubeless tire in Akron, Ohio.

1949 Israel is admitted to the United Nations as its 59th member.

1969 During the Vietnam War, U.S. and South Vietnamese forces fight North Vietnamese troops for Ap Bia Mountain (Hill 937). Because of heavy casualties suffered by both sides, the American media dubbed the mountain "Hamburger Hill."

1981 Reggae singer Bob Marley dies of cancer in Miami. In 1965, Marley formed the band the Wailers with Peter Tosh and "Bunny" Livingstone, recording such classics as "No Woman, No Cry," "I Shot the Sheriff," and "Exodus."

1985 A flash fire sweeps a jam-packed soccer stadium in Bradford, England, killing more than 50 people.

1985 American race-car driver Duane "Pancho" Carter grabs the pole position for the Indianapolis 500 auto race with a historic speed of 212.583 miles per hour in four qualifying laps for the upcoming Memorial Day race.

1987 Klaus Barbie, former Nazi Gestapo chief of German-occupied Lyon, France, goes on trial more than four decades after the end of World War II. While serving a life sentence for 177 war crimes against humanity, he died in prison in 1991.

1989 In a move to preserve its threatened elephant population, Kenya announces it will seek a worldwide ban on the ivory trade.

1998 India sets off three underground atomic blasts, its first nuclear tests in 24 years.

Wildlife rangers stack elephant ivory in Nairobi, Kenya

1831 Edward Smith, the first indicted bank robber in the United States, is sentenced to five years' hard labor. He served it on the "rock pile" at Sing Sing Prison in Ossining, New York.

1847 The odometer, an instrument to measure distance traveled, is invented by pioneer William Clayton while crossing the American plains as part of the movement of Mormons from Illinois to Utah.

1864 During the Battle of Spotsylvania Court House in the American Civil War, Union and Confederate troops engaged in a bloody, 20-hour battle at close quarters in ankle deep mud during a rainstorm. The nightmarish fight ended in a stalemate at the log breastworks that became known as the "Bloody Angle."

1870 Manitoba enters the Canadian Confederation as a province.

1903 Cameraman H. J. Miles captures the visit to San Francisco of President Theodore

---

BORN ON THIS DAY

1812
EDWARD LEAR
English illustrator, poet, champion of the limerick ("The Owl and the Pussycat")

1820
FLORENCE NIGHTINGALE
English health activist and nurse

1828
DANTE GABRIEL ROSSETTI
English poet and painter

1842
JULES MASSENET
French composer

1889
OTTO FRANK
Father of German diarist Anne Frank

1907
KATHARINE HEPBURN
American actress (*The Philadelphia Story; The Lion in Winter; On Golden Pond*)

1924
ANTHONY JOHN HANCOCK
English comedian better known as Tony Hancock (*Hancock's Half Hour*)

1925
LAWRENCE PETER "YOGI" BERRA
American Hall of Fame baseball player

1948
STEVE WINWOOD
English singer/songwriter

1968
TONY HAWK
American professional skateboarder

Roosevelt. It was one of the first movie documentaries, called actualities, shown in nickelodeons across the United States.

1908 Nathan Stubblefield obtains a patent for wireless voice transmission. He had demonstrated the instrument in 1902 in Fairmont Park in Philadelphia, Pennsylvania.

1917 A horse named Omar Khayyam becomes the first imported horse to win the Kentucky Derby. The prize: $49,070.

1925 A radio station in Philadelphia, Pennsylvania, broadcasts the first all-star program featuring film actors and actresses. Among the voices heard were those of Lillian Gish and Marion Davies.

1932 The body of Charles Lindbergh Jr., kidnapped son of Charles and Anne Morrow Lindbergh, is found in a wooded area in Hopewell, New Jersey. A handyman, Bruno Hauptmann, was later arrested for the crime, tried, and executed.

1943 Axis forces in North Africa surrender after advances by U.S. and British troops during World War II.

1949 The Soviet Union lifts an 11-month blockade of West Berlin, Germany. The

Battle of Spotsylvania Court House

> *"In theory there is no difference between theory and practice. In practice, there is."*
>
> — *Yogi Berra*

U.S. stamp commemorating Berlin airlift

United States and Great Britain had already made the blockade ineffective with a massive airlift of supplies to the citizens of West Berlin.

1950 The American Bowling Congress abolishes its white-only membership restriction after 34 years.

1955 New York passengers crowd aboard "The El," an elevated train system, for the last time. The trip was from Chinatown to the Bronx.

1957 American race-car driver A. J. Foyt earns his first auto-race victory in Kansas City, Missouri. He later became a four-time winner of the Indianapolis 500—in 1961, 1964, 1967, and 1977.

1957 Fourteen people are killed in Italy when a race car driven by the Spanish Marquis de Portago runs into the crowd during the grueling Mille Miglia ("Thousand Miles") motor race.

1961 U.S. vice president Lyndon B. Johnson meets with South Vietnamese president Ngo Dinh Diem in Saigon, promising him additional military aid in fighting the communists. After Johnson became president he escalated the Vietnam War, eventually committing more than 500,000 troops to Vietnam.

1964 American singer Barbra Steisand wins the Grammy Award for Best Female Vocalist for *The Barbra Streisand Album*.

1967 English poet John Masefield dies. Poet Laureate since 1930, perhaps his most famous lines were: "I must go down to the sea again, to the lonely sea and the sky, /And all I ask is a tall ship and a star to steer her by . . ."

1975 Communist forces in Cambodia capture the American freighter *Mayaguez* and its crew, touching off an international incident.

1982 Security guards in Fatima, Portugal, overpower a Spanish priest armed with a bayonet who was trying to reach Pope Paul II.

1995 During a stopover in the Ukraine, U.S. president Bill Clinton visits Babi Yar, the site where more than 30,000 Kiev Jews were massacred by the Nazis in 1941, during World War II.

President Clinton, center, First Lady Hilary Clinton, and Rabbi Bleich at the Menorah memorial in Kiev, Ukraine

1568 A confederacy of Scottish Protestants defeats the 6,000 Catholic troops of Mary, Queen of Scots, in the Battle of Landside in the southern suburb of Glasgow. The queen fled to Cumberland, England, and sought the protection of Queen Elizabeth I.

1767 Mozart's opera *Apollo et Hyacinthus* premieres in Salzburg.

1787 Royal Navy Captain Arthur Phillip sets sails for Botany Bay, Australia, with the first fleet of eleven ships of criminals sentenced to transportation. The fleet arrived on January 26, 1788, and Sydney was founded as a penal colony.

1821 Samuel Rust of New York City patents the first practical printing press in America.

1864 A Confederate prisoner of the American Civil War, who died at a local hospital, is buried on the Arlington House grounds on the Potomac River opposite Washington, D.C. His was the first burial in what is now Arlington Cemetery.

1898 American inventor Thomas Edison sues American Mutoscope and Biograph Pictures, claiming that the studio

Custis-Lee Mansion (Arlington House)

BORN ON THIS DAY

1717
EMPRESS MARIA THERESA
Queen of Hungary and German empress

1828
JOSEPHINE ELIZABETH BUTLER
British social reformer

1842
ARTHUR SULLIVAN
English composer (Gilbert and Sullivan) (*Pirates of Penzance*; "Onward Christian Soldiers")

1856
PETER HENRY EMERSON
English-American photographer, first to promote photography as an independent art

1882
GEORGES BRAQUE
French painter

1907
DAME DAPHNE DU MAURIER
English novelist (*Rebecca; The Birds*)

1923
BEATRICE ARTHUR
American actress (*The Golden Girls*)

1931
JIM JONES
Self-styled American minister who poisoned over 900 followers in Guyana, an act known as the Jonestown Massacre

1941
RITCHIE VALENS
Venezuelan-born singer ("La Bamba"; "Donna"; "Come On Let's Go!")

1950
STEVIE WONDER
American singer/songwriter ("Superstition"; "My Cherie Amour"; "Signed, Sealed, Delivered")

1961
DENNIS "THE WORM" RODMAN
American professional basketball player

1977
SARA DeCOSTA
Goalie for the gold-medal-winning American Women's Hockey team, 1998

"Communism was just an idea. Just pie in the sky."

—Boris Yeltsin

infringed on his patent for the Kinetograph movie camera.

1915 During World War I, South African prime minister General Louis Botha, personally leading his troops in the field, captures the territory of German South West Africa.

1915 Less than a week after the sinking of the *Lusitania*, King George V severs ties with his cousin the German Kaiser of the Order of the Garter. In 1917 he went further by renouncing his German surname and replacing it with the name Windsor.

1917 Three peasant children near Fatima, Portugal, claim they have seen a vision of the Virgin Mary.

1918 The United States issues its first airmail stamps. They pictured an airplane that on some stamps was erroneously printed upside down, making it a collector's item.

1924 German actress Marlene Dietrich and Rudolf Sieber are married. The match lasted more than 50 years.

1935 Carl C. Magee of the Dual Parking Meter Company files a patent for an improved version of his delightful invention, the parking meter (first patented in December 1932). The world's first parking meters were installed in Oklahoma

---

MOVE's headquarters after police bombing

City, Oklahoma, two months after this patent application.

🎭 **1938** American musician Louis Armstrong and his orchestra record "When the Saints Go Marching In" for Decca Records. The song remains a New Orleans jazz favorite.

🇺🇸 **1954** U.S. president Dwight D. Eisenhower signs the St. Lawrence Seaway Development Act into law.

1958 Vice President Richard M. Nixon is attacked by an angry crowd in Caracas, Venezuela, as an expression of outrage over America's Cold War policies, particularly its refusal to give Latin American countries more economic aid. Nixon was unharmed but left Venezuela ahead of schedule.

🇬🇧 **1982** The EEC calls for a ban on the use of rubber bullets by British forces in Northern Ireland.

🇺🇸 **1985** The radical group named MOVE holds a violent demonstration in Philadelphia, Pennsylvania. Police dropped an explosive onto the group's headquarters, starting a fire that killed 11 people.

🇺🇸 **1989** U.S. president George H. Bush calls on Panama's people and its defense forces to overthrow its dictatorial military leader, General Manuel Antonio Noriega.

1990 Two U.S. airmen are shot to death in the Philippines as the two governments prepare for talks concerning American bases on the islands. The revolutionary New People's Army claimed responsibility for the killings.

🔬 **1991** American company Apple announces an improved version of the Macintosh system called System 7.0. It let all Macintosh users share files in a network without the intervention of a server.

🇺🇸 **1998** U.S. president Bill Clinton orders harsh sanctions against India for launching a second round of nuclear tests despite worldwide criticism.

1999 Russian lawmakers open hearings on whether president Boris Yeltsin should be impeached. Five charges against Yeltsin were rejected, including his instigation of the Chechen War.

Pope John Paul II in St. Peter's Square just before assassination attempt (milestone)

1264 English king Henry III is defeated by Simon de Montfort at the Battle of Lewes. The terms of surrender saw Henry's son Prince Edward held captive as a guarantee of the king's good behavior and left de Montfort effectively in control of the country—a significant step on the road to English democracy.

1610 French king Henri IV is assassinated by the religious fanatic François Ravaillac.

1643 Louis XIV becomes king of France at age four upon the death of his father, Louis XIII.

1804 An expedition led by Meriwether Lewis and William Clark leaves St. Louis, Missouri, on a mission to explore the American Northwest from the Mississippi River to the Pacific Ocean. The exploration group included 28 men and one woman—a Native American named Sacajawea.

1842 English poet Alfred, Lord Tennyson, publishes a volume called *Poems*, which includes works like "Ulysses" and "Morte d'Arthur" and is considered his best work to date. He continued writing and publishing poetry until his death in 1892.

1862 Adolphe Nicole of Switzerland patents the chronograph, a timepiece by which split-second timing of sporting events can be done.

> *"Knowledge comes, but wisdom lingers."*
> —Alfred, Lord Tennyson

BORN ON THIS DAY

1686
GABRIEL DANIEL FAHRENHEIT
German physicist who invented the mercury thermometer and gave his name to a scale of temperature

1727
THOMAS GAINSBOROUGH
English painter

1884
CLAUDE DORNIER
German aircraft designer

1885
OTTO KLEMPERER
German conductor and composer

1897
SIDNEY BECHET
American jazz musician

1921
RICHARD DEACON
American actor (*The Dick Van Dyke Show; Mister Ed*)

1925
PATRICE MUNSEL
American singer who performed as a diva at the Metropolitan Opera at age 17

1926
ERIC MORECAMBE
English comedian (*Morecambe and Wise*)

1940
SIR CHAY BLYTH
British yachtsman, first westward solo circumnavigator of the globe, first to row across the Atlantic from America to Ireland (with John Ridgway)

1944
GEORGE LUCAS
American movie producer (*Star Wars; Raiders of the Lost Ark; American Graffiti*)

1952
DAVID BYRNE
American singer/songwriter (Talking Heads)

1969
CATE BLANCHETT
Australian actress (*Elizabeth; The Shipping News; Lord of the Rings*)

1874 McGill University of Montreal, Canada, and Harvard meet at Cambridge, Massachusetts, in the first college football game to charge admission. It was also the first time goalposts were used on the playing field.

1878 American inventor Robert A. Chesebrough registers the trademark name for Vaseline, a brand of petroleum jelly.

1897 In Philadelphia, Pennsylvania, John Philip Sousa's stirring march "The Stars and Stripes Forever" is played for the first time in public. U.S. president William McKinley attended the event to commemorate the unveiling of a statue of George Washington.

1904 The first Olympic Games to be held in the United States open in St. Louis, Missouri.

1913 American philanthropist John D. Rockefeller establishes the Rockefeller Foundation with a gift of $100,000,000 to promote the worldwide well-being of mankind.

John Philip Sousa

1943 Leaders of the United States and Great Britain meet in Washington, D.C., during World War II to approve and plot out Operation Pointblank, a joint bombing offensive against Germany from British air bases. The operation was intended to set the stage for one fatal blow to bring the Nazis to their knees. Ironically, on the opening day of the campaign the Germans shot down 74 British planes.

1948 In Tel Aviv, Jewish Agency chairman David Ben-Gurion proclaims the state of Israel. The new nation, which established the first Jewish state in 2,000 years, ended British colonial rule.

1955 The Soviet Union and seven of its European satellites sign a treaty establishing the Warsaw Pact in Poland, a mutual defense organization that put the Soviets in command of the armed forces of the member states.

1969 During the Vietnam War, President Richard M. Nixon proposes a phased, mutual withdrawal of major portions of the United States' forces and South Vietnamese troops in South Vietnam over a 12-month period. The communists' proposal and Nixon's counter-offer were diametrically opposed, and the peace talks stalled.

1970 Allied military officials announce that 863 South Vietnamese were killed in the Vietnam War between May 3 and May 9. It was the second-highest weekly death toll for that nation.

1989 Peronist candidate Carlos Saul Menem wins the presidential election in Argentina.

1990 Soviet president Mikhail Gorbachev declares that the republics of Estonia and Latvia have no legal basis for moving toward independence.

1993 American companies Softkey Software and WordStar International announce they will merge. The WordStar word processor, released in 1979, sold nearly one million copies.

1995 Myrlie Evers-Williams is sworn in to head the National Association for the Advancement of Colored People (NAACP). She pledged to lead the American civil rights organization away from its recent internal troubles and toward leadership as a political and social force.

1999 U.S. president Bill Clinton finally makes telephone contact with Chinese president Jiang Zemin, who had refused previous calls. Clinton told the Chinese leader he hoped the two countries could repair the damage caused by the recent U.S. bombing of the Chinese embassy in Belgrade, Yugoslavia.

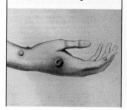

Hand of a Gloucestershire milkmaid showing cowpox blisters from which Edward Jenner developed smallpox vaccination techique

Myrlie Evers-Williams, chairman of the NAACP's Board of Directors

1602 English navigator Bartholomew Gosnold discovers Cape Cod on the Atlantic coast of present-day Massachusetts.

1718 The world's first machine gun is patented by English inventor James Puckle, a London lawyer.

1756 England declares war on France in America, beginning a global conflict that would become known as the Seven Years' War. The conflict ended with the Treaty of Paris in 1763, but the French, bitter over their large colonial losses in the war, later sided with the patriots in the American Revolutionary War.

1856 When law enforcement agencies are unable to keep order in the lawless Gold Rush boomtown of San Francisco, California, a group of angered residents form a second vigilance committee to combat robberies and other crimes. Some offenders were summarily hanged, others were escorted out of town.

1864 Students from the Virginia Military Institute take part in the Battle of New Market during the American Civil War, part of a prolonged offensive designed to take Virginia out of the war. The Confederates, badly outnumbered, pressed the 271 cadets—some no older than 15—into service. Nine were killed and many were wounded.

1886 The American author of at least 800 poems, Emily Dickinson dies in Amherst, Massachusetts. All but five of the poems remained unpublished until after her death.

MILESTONE

Twenty Million Bugs
On this day in 1981, the twenty millionth Volkswagen Beetle manufactured throughout the world rolled off the assembly line at the Volkswagen de Mexico assembly plant in Puebla, Mexico. Production of the car in Wolfsburg, Germany, had ceased in 1978 after 16.5 million Beetles had been produced. The car was also produced in Brazil until 1986, but today the only place in the world still making the original Volkswagen Beetle is the Puebla plant. No other car has sold as many units while remaining essentially the same model throughout its history. In 1991, the Volkswagen Beetle was proclaimed the Car of the Century by a panel of 100 automotive jurists from 37 nations.

"It is a man's world, and you men can have it."
—*Katherine Anne Porter*

1941 During World War II, the jet-propelled Gloster-Whittle E 28/39 aircraft flies successfully over Cranwell, England, in the first test of an Allied aircraft using jet propulsion. The turbojet was designed by Frank Whittle, an aviation engineer and pilot, generally regarded as the father of the jet engine.

1941 American baseball player Joe DiMaggio begins his memorable major-league hitting streak, which would last 56 games.

1942 Gasoline rationing goes into effect in 17 U.S. states as an economy measure during World War II. Sales were limited to three gallons per week for nonessential vehicles.

1942 A U.S. congressional bill establishing the U.S. Women's Auxiliary Army Corps becomes law. It granted women official military status, enabling them to serve in noncombat positions. It was not until 1978, however, that women were allowed to become regular U.S. Army members.

1948 Israel is attacked by Jordan, Syria, Egypt, Iraq, and Lebanon just hours after gaining independence from Great Britain.

Joe DiMaggio

1953 World heavyweight boxing champion Rocky Marciano knocks out former champ "Jersey" Joe Walcott at Chicago Stadium to collect his 44th boxing victory. He did it in two minutes, 25 seconds of the first round.

1957 Great Britain drops its first hydrogen bomb, on Christmas Island in the Pacific.

1958 The Oscar-winning movie musical *Gigi,* based on Colette's novel, opens at New York City's Royale Theater. Starring Maurice Chevalier and Leslie Caron, two of its hit tunes were, "Thank Heaven for Little Girls" and "I Remember It Well."

1963 Astronaut Gordon Cooper is launched into space aboard *Faith 7,* on the longest American space mission to that date. During 34 hours in space, Cooper completed 22 orbits, landing safely in the Pacific Ocean on May 16.

1967 During the Vietnam War, U.S. Marine forces just south of the Demilitarized Zone in Vietnam are pounded by heavy fire from North Vietnamese artillery. More than 100 Americans were killed or wounded.

1970 U.S. president Richard M. Nixon awards the Medal of Honor to Sergeant John L. Levitow, the only enlisted airman to receive the medal in the Vietnam War and one of only four enlisted airmen ever to receive this highest decoration since World War II. Although seriously wounded, Levitow had managed to save the lives of several crew members by throwing himself on an activated magnesium flare.

1970 In the Netherlands, the International Olympic Committee announces that South Africa will be barred from the 1972 Olympic Games in Munich as part of international pressure against the South African apartheid system.

1972 Governor George Wallace of Alabama is shot by 21-year-old Arthur H. Bremer during the U.S. presidential campaign and is permanently paralyzed from the waist down. He continued to campaign from his hospital room and wheelchair but lost his third-party bid for the presidency in the end. Wallace died in 1998.

1988 Soviet troops begin their withdrawal from Afghanistan eight years after their intervention in that country. The attempt to build up the communist Afghanistan government cost the Soviets dearly, with an estimated 15,000 troops dead and an enormous bite on the Soviet treasury.

1999 Russian president Boris Yeltsin beats his Communist Party foes to defeat an impeachment vote in the Russian parliament.

Arthur H. Bremer, center

1643 In the English Civil War, a Royalist army led by Sir Ralph Hopton defeats a Parliamentarian army in the Battle of Stratton, despite being outnumbered almost 2 to 1. The result was that the Royalists were able to consolidate their position in the southwest of England.

1717 Famous for his classical tragedies, French writer François-Marie Arouet (better known as Voltaire) is imprisoned in the Bastille in Paris for his satirical attacks on politics and religion. After a year in the French prison, he continued his epistles and was forced to flee to England.

1770 Louis, the French dauphin, marries Marie Antoinette, daughter of Austrian archduchess Maria Theresa and Holy Roman emperor Francis I, at Versailles. Four years later, when King Louis XV died, they were crowned King Louis XVI and queen of France.

1811 At the Battle of Albuera in Spain, an Anglo-Spanish-Portuguese force under the command of Marshal Beresford defeats a French army attempting to lift the siege of Badajoz. Casualties were high, and Wellington said, "another such battle would ruin us."

1861 Tennessee is officially admitted to the Confederacy, opening the door for its alliance with the southern rebels in the American Civil War.

1862 Frenchman Jean Joseph Etienne Lenoir builds the first gas-fueled internal combustion engine.

MILESTONE

Unborn Baby Theft

On this day in 1975, Norma Jean Armistead checks herself into Kaiser Hospital in Los Angeles, California, with a newborn that she claims to have given birth to at home. Examining doctors were confused when it appeared that Armistead hadn't actually given birth. The mystery was soon solved when a 28-year-old woman turned up dead in her Van Nuys apartment. The baby she was carrying, and expected to give birth to shortly, had been cut from her body. Doctors quickly pieced the evidence together and Armistead was arrested for murder. Armistead was convicted and sent to prison for life.

Poster of the 1869 Cincinnati Reds baseball team

"There is nothing new except what has been forgotten."

—Marie Antoinette

1863 The Union Army defeats the Confederate Army in the Battle of Champion's Hill in the American Civil War, sealing the fate of Vicksburg, Mississippi, which fell to General Ulysses S. Grant's forces on July 4.

1868 The U.S. Senate fails to convict President Andrew Johnson of high crimes and misdemeanors by a single vote in the first impeachment proceedings begun by the House of Representatives.

1869 The Cincinnati Reds, American baseball's first all-professional team, plays its first game.

1888 Inventor Emile Berliner, a German immigrant to the United States, demonstrates the first modern phonograph record. This flat, grooved device was easier to duplicate than the cylindrical recorder developed by Thomas Edison.

1897 In the United States, Stuart Blackton and Albert E. Smith of the newly formed Vitagraph film company shoot their first film, *The Burglar on the Roof*. Warner Brothers purchased the pioneering studio in 1925.

1925 Arthur Atwater Kent calls his wife, Mabel Lucas Kent, in a car in Philadelphia, Pennsylvania, as he flies in the blimp *The Los Angeles*. It was history's first air-to-ground telephone call.

1938 The first animal breeding society is organized in New Jersey.

1943 The Warsaw Ghetto uprising ends as Nazi soldiers gain control of Warsaw's Jewish ghetto in World War II. Disease and starvation had killed thousands every month in the enclave following the German occupation. The uprising claimed many thousands of Warsaw Jews, compared to the loss of about 300 German soldiers.

1960 Russian leader Nikita Khrushchev lashes out at the United States and President Dwight D. Eisenhower at a summit meeting in Paris. The reason for the Soviet's ire: the Russian downing of an American U-2 spy plane, whose pilot was captured.

1965 Ninety-five U.S. servicemen are injured and 25 die when a bomb accidentally explodes on a military airplane at the Bien Hoa air base near Saigon in the Vietnam War. Four South Vietnamese were also killed.

1968 In Paris, recent student demonstrations for educational reform, hospitalizing hundreds, escalate to a general nationwide strike. Leftists calling for economic and political reform idled millions and shut down newspapers and transportation, bringing France to the brink of a radical-left revolution.

1968 Donald E. Ballard, a U.S. Navy corpsman, is awarded the Medal of Honor for heroism in the Vietnam War. He had covered a live hand grenade with his body, protecting his fellow soldiers. Although the grenade did not go off, it was considered an act of valor worthy of the nation's highest combat award.

1969 The U.S. nuclear submarine *Guitarro* sinks in San Francisco Bay off California.

1975 Junko Tabei of Japan, becomes the first woman to reach the summit of Mount Everest, the highest mountain in the world. The mountain was first ascended in May 1953 by a party that included Edmund Hillary of New Zealand and Sir John Hunt.

1995 Japanese police arrest cult leader Shoko Asahara and charge him with poisoning a Tokyo subway with nerve gas one month earlier.

Junko Tabei at summit of Mount Everest

1792 The New York Stock Exchange is founded by 24 brokers, signing a two-sentence contract called the Buttonwood Agreement. This took place under a button-wood tree on what today is Wall Street.

1814 Norway's constitution is signed, providing for a limited monarchy.

1849 A fire in St. Louis, Missouri, destroys more than 400 buildings and 24 steamships.

1863 The Union Army defeats the Confederates on the Big Black River in a major campaign of the American Civil War, driving them into Vicksburg, Mississippi. A total of 1,752 Confederate troops were killed, wounded, or captured, compared to the Yankees' 279.

1875 Aristides wins the first Kentucky Derby at the Louisville Jockey Club. Fourteen of the 15 jockeys were African Americans.

1876 Nikolaus August Otto files a British patent for the first four-stroke internal combustion engine, published as GB 2081/1876 (and later, in

---

MILESTONE

Brown v. Board of Education

In a major civil rights victory on this day in 1954, the U.S. Supreme Court hands down a unanimous decision in *Brown v. Board of Education of Topeka*, ruling that racial segregation in public educational facilities is unconstitutional. The historic decision, which brought an end to federal tolerance of racial segregation, specifically dealt with Linda Brown, who had been denied admission to her local elementary school in Topeka, Kansas, because of the color of her skin. In an opinion written by Chief Justice Earl Warren, the nation's highest court ruled that the separate but equal doctrine was unconstitutional.

NAACP attorneys in the Brown v. Board of Education *from left are: Special Counsel Thurgood Marshall, Louis Redding, and U. Simpson Tate*

"Progress is man's ability to complicate simplicity."

—Thor Heyerdahl

America and Germany, as US 178023 and DE 532). It was not the first internal combustion engine but it was a vast improvement on Luxembourg-born French engineer Étienne Lenoir's engine of 1859.

1877 The first interstate telephone call, from New Brunswick, New Jersey, to New York City is answered by Alexander Graham Bell.

1877 The first telephone switchboard burglar alarm is installed by Edward T. Holmes of Boston, Massachusetts.

1885 The fearless Apache Indian chief Geronimo, the last Native American to surrender to the United States, breaks out of an Arizona reservation for the second time. For 30 years he and his followers had resisted attempts of white Americans to take away their homeland.

1939 King George VI and Queen Elizabeth of Great Britain arrive in Quebec. It was

---

Refugees carrying water containers near the Rwandan border at the Benaco Refugee Camp in Tanzania

Geronimo, Apache chief

the first visit to Canada by reigning British sovereigns.

1939 A New York City radio station, WNBT-TV, telecasts the first fashion show seen on TV. It originated at the Ritz-Carleton Hotel in Manhattan.

1943 The *Memphis Belle,* one of a group of American bombers based in Great Britain in World War II, flies its 25th mission over Europe, the first B-17 to complete that many combat flights.

1943 British Wing Commander Guy Gibson leads the RAF's famous "Dam Busters" raids on the Mohne and Eder dams in the German Ruhr valley.

1970 Norwegian ethnologist and adventurer Thor Heyerdahl sets out from Morocco in a papyrus sailing craft named *Ra II,* attempting to prove that Mediterranean civilizations in ancient times could have sailed to America. The raft completed the 4,000-mile transatlantic voyage to Barbados in 57 days.

1974 Five hundred police in Los Angeles, California, surround a home in Compton to rout a group of terrorists known as the Symbionese Liberation Army. The SLA earlier had kidnapped newspaper heiress Patty Hearst, but she was not in the home at the time. The raid left six SLA members dead.

1987 Thirty-seven American sailors die when an Iraqi warplane attacks the U.S. Navy frigate *Stark* in the Persian Gulf. Both the United States and Iraq called the attack a mistake.

1994 The United Nations Security Council approves a peacekeeping force and an arms embargo for Rwanda in the wake of violence in that nation.

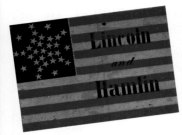

Campaign banner for Lincoln and Hamlin

1804 Napoleon Bonaparte is proclaimed emperor of France by the French Senate.

1860 In Chicago, Illinois, the Republican National Convention nominates Abraham Lincoln for president and Hannibal Hamlin of Maine for vice president. A Kentucky-born former Whig representative, Lincoln went on to win the presidency. One month after his March 1861 inauguration the American Civil War began. Lincoln's antislavery views were a major reason for the secession of southern states.

1863 Union general Ulysses S. Grant surrounds Vicksburg, the last Confederate stronghold on the Mississippi River during the American Civil War, after a 180-mile march and five battles.

1898 In *Plessy v. Ferguson,* the U.S. Supreme Court rules seven to one that a Louisiana law providing for "separate but equal accommodations for the white and colored races" on railroad cars is constitutional. The decision stood until 1954, when a later Supreme Court struck down that ruling in the *Brown v. Board of Education* case of Topeka, Kansas.

BORN ON THIS DAY

1798
ETHAN ALLEN HITCHCOCK
American major general (*Union volunteers*)

1872
BERTRAND RUSSELL
English philosopher, mathematician, and Nobel Prize winner

Bertrand Russell

1883
WALTER GROPIUS
German-born American architect

1897
FRANK CAPRA
Academy Award-winning Italian-born director (*It Happened One Night; Mr. Smith Goes to Washington; It's a Wonderful Life*)

1909
FRED PERRY
English-born American tennis player, the first player to win all four major titles

1911
BIG JOE TURNER
American singer ("Shake Rattle and Roll")

1912
PERRY COMO
American singer ("Dream Along with Me"; "Don't Let the Stars Get in Your Eyes")

1914
PIERRE BALMAIN
French fashion designer

1919
DAME MARGOT FONTEYN
English ballerina

1920
POPE JOHN PAUL II
264th pope of the Roman Catholic Church, the first Polish pope

---

"Common looking people are the best in the world: that is the reason the Lord makes so many of them."
—Abraham Lincoln

1899 The first Hague Peace Conference opens in the Netherlands.

1908 The U.S. Congress adopts a law making the phrase "In God We Trust" obligatory on certain American coins. The motto dated back to the Civil War in the early 1860s, when religious feelings were stirred throughout the nation.

1914 The *Mariner* becomes the first cargo-carrying steamboat to pass through the Panama Canal.

1927 The new Grauman's Chinese Theater, named for its Asian-influenced décor, opens in Hollywood, California. The first movie shown there was Cecil B. DeMille's *The King of Kings.* As a later tradition, more than 180 film stars placed their hand and footprints in cement in the front of the theater.

1943 Nazi dictator Adolf Hitler launches Operation Alaric, the German occupation of Italy, during World War II. So secret that Hitler communicated the order only verbally, the campaign was designed to assure German control should Italy surrender or switch its allegiance to the Allies.

1944 The Polish Corps, part of a multinational Allied 8th Army offensive in southern Italy during World War II, finally pushes into Monte Cassino as

---

the final battle to break German field marshal Albert Kesselring's defensive Gustav Line nears its end.

1951 The United Nations moves into a permanent home in New York City, vacating temporary quarters in Lake Success, New York.

1953 American Jacqueline Cochran becomes the first woman to break the sound barrier, flying a North American F-86 Canadair over California.

1977 The right-wing Likud Party is voted into power in Israel, with Menachem Begin as prime minister.

1980 A massive volcanic eruption of Mount St. Helens in southwestern Washington devastates 210 square miles of wilderness, leaving 57 dead or missing. The volcano had erupted periodically during the past 4,500 years, the last active period being between 1831 and 1857.

M I L E S T O N E

India Joins the Nuclear Club

On this day in 1974, in the Rajasthan Desert, India successfully detonates its first nuclear weapon, a fission bomb similar in explosive power to the U.S. atomic bomb dropped on Hiroshima, Japan. The test fell on the traditional anniversary of the Buddha's enlightenment, and Indian Prime Minister Indira Gandhi received the message, "Buddha has smiled" from the exuberant test-site scientists after the detonation. The test, which made India the world's sixth nuclear power, broke the nuclear monopoly of the five members of the U.N. Security Council—the United States, the Soviet Union, Great Britain, China, and France.

Anne Boleyn

🇬🇧 **1536** Convicted of adultery, Anne Boleyn, second wife of King Henry VIII of England, is beheaded.

1588 Bent on a conquest of England, a massive fleet known as the Spanish Armada sets sail from Lisbon, Portugal, intending to get control of the English Channel to invade Great Britain from the Netherlands. By the time its 130 ships and 30,000 men reached the English coast after storm delays, the English were ready, and the "invincible armada" was beaten back.

1643 The Duc d'Enghien leads the French to victory against the supposedly invincible Spanish Army in the Battle of Rocroi.

1749 The Ohio Company is granted a charter of several hundred thousand acres of land around the forks of the Ohio River by King George II of England to promote the westward settlement of American colonists from Virginia. France had claimed the entire Ohio River Valley in the previous century, but English fur traders and settlers disputed these claims.

1796 Calling for penalties for people hunting or destroying

BORN ON THIS DAY

1795
JOHNS HOPKINS
American philanthropist who founded Johns Hopkins University

1800
SARAH PEALE
American artist

1858
ROLAND NAPOLEON BONAPARTE
French officer

1861
HELEN PORTER MITCHELL
Australian soprano better known as Dame Nellie Melba (after her native city of Melbourne)

1879
VISCOUNT AND VISCOUNTESS ASTOR
American-born British MPs born on the same day: Waldorf Astor was elected MP for Plymouth, and when he was elevated to the House of Lords his wife Nancy Astor took over his seat to become the first female MP to sit in the House of Commons

1890
HO CHI MINH
Vietnamese patriot, North Vietnamese leader during the wars against the French and Americans after World War II

1915
POL POT
Cambodian dictator and mass murderer

1925
MALCOLM X
Black nationalist and civil rights activist

1935
DAVID HARTMAN
American television personality

1939
FRANCIS SCOBEE
Commander of the ill-fated U.S. space shuttle *Challenger*

1945
PETER TOWNSHEND
English rock musician (The Who)

1952
JOEY RAMONE
American singer (The Ramones)

---

game within Indian territory, the first U.S. game law is approved.

🇺🇸 **1836** Indians of the Comanche, Kiowa, and Caddo tribes in Texas kidnap nine-year-old Cynthia Ann Parker and kill her family. Cynthia was adopted by the Comanches and was loved and treated well, eventually marrying a young warrior and bearing him three children. Twenty-five years later the Texas Rangers attacked her village, killing the warrior and capturing Cynthia and her daughter. She lived only seven more unhappy years with a people she no longer understood.

1864 A Confederate attack against Union forces ends 12 days of fighting near Spotsylvania in the American Civil War. Northern forces under General Ulysses S. Grant lost 18,000 troops, compared to the South's 33,000. The heaviest fighting of the war was yet to come.

🇬🇧 **1897** Irish author Oscar Wilde is released from jail after two years of hard labor. He had been convicted of homosexuality, then a crime in Great Britain. A brilliant writer of many famous works, he fled to Paris after his imprisonment and died three years later of acute meningitis.

🇺🇸 **1928** A frog jumps three feet, four inches—higher than 49

"If we don't stand for something, we may fall for anything."

—*Malcolm X*

NORAD main command center

competitors—to win the first frog-jumping contest in Calaveras County, California. Writer Mark Twain inspired the event during California's gold-rush days.

1935 T. E. Lawrence, known as Lawrence of Arabia, dies in a hospital in Clouds Hill, Dorset, England, where he had been taken after being critically injured in a motorcycle accident five days earlier. All Great Britain mourned the passing of this legendary war hero, author, and archaeological scholar.

1958 Canada and the United States jointly establish the North American Air Defense Command (NORAD).

1964 The U.S. State Department says it has found 40 Soviet microphones hidden in the American embassy in Moscow.

1967 The Soviet Union ratifies a treaty banning nuclear weapons in outer space, joining several dozen other nations, including the United States and Great Britain.

1977 In Nairobi, Kenya, president Jomo Kenyatta announces a ban on big game hunting as part of a drive to conserve wildlife.

1999 The U.S. Justice Department alleges that John Demjanjuk was the Nazi death-camp guard known as "Ivan the Terrible" and renews its campaign to revoke his U.S. citizenship.

John Demjanjuk's military service pass

Vasco da Gama standing in rowboat

1498 Arriving at Calicut on the Malabar coast, Portuguese explorer Vasco da Gama becomes the first European to reach India via the Atlantic Ocean or Mediterranean.

1506 Christopher Columbus, the great Italian explorer, dies without realizing the extent of his achievements. His serendipitous discovery of the New World would help make Spain the wealthiest, most powerful nation on Earth.

1830 The *Baltimore American* becomes the first newspaper to publish timetables when it prints one for the Baltimore & Ohio Railroad.

1856 Edward Hughes of Louisville, Kentucky, receives a patent for his telegraph ticker, the first ticker to print successfully.

1861 The Confederate capital is moved from Montgomery, Alabama, to Richmond, Virginia, during the American Civil War.

1862 President Abraham Lincoln signs into law the Homestead Act, allowing men and women over age 21 to

claim 160 acres from the public domain. Stimulating farm development in the United States, the act required that landowners cultivate their new property, build a barn or house on it, and live there for five years; then, for a $10 fee, it became theirs for good.

1873 American inventor Levi Strauss secures the necessary patents to make canvas pants with copper rivets reinforcing the stress points. Ever after, his popular line of pants would be known simply as "Levis."

1902 The United States ends its occupation of Cuba.

1916 American artist Norman Rockwell's first cover on *The Saturday Evening Post* is published. It depicts a boy having to care for a baby sibling while his buddies play ball, one of many themes by Rockwell that tugged at the heartstrings.

1930 A San Francisco newspaper reports that a University of California committee has awarded $1,500 for research on a "nagging, embarrassing, burning, itching" problem—athlete's foot.

1932 American aviator Amelia Earhart takes off from

Cruiser Brooklyn leaving Havana, Cuba

> *"Nothing so fortifies a friendship as a belief on the part of one friend that he is superior to the other."*
>
> —Honoré de Balzac

Newfoundland on a flight to Ireland. She was the first woman to fly the Atlantic solo.

1939 Pan American Airways begins regular transatlantic air service with a flight by the *Yankee Clipper* from Port Washington, New York, to Europe.

1940 The German Army reaches the English Channel on the northern French coast in its move for domination of Europe during World War II. With Nazi tanks in sight of England, British prime minister Winston Churchill ordered security measures beefed up in Great Britain.

1956 The United States drops a hydrogen bomb over the Pacific atoll of Bikini in the Pacific, the first airborne test of an improved hydrogen device.

1961 A busload of civil rights demonstrators called Freedom Riders is attacked by a white mob in Montgomery, Alabama. The federal government dispatched U.S. marshals to restore order.

1969 In the Vietnam War, U.S. and South Vietnamese troops capture Hill 937 after 10 bloody assaults. The spot had no strategic value and was abandoned soon after.

1978 Mavis Hutchinson becomes the first woman to run across America. The fifty-three-year-old jogged the 3,000 miles in 69 days.

1980 The people of Quebec vote to remain part of Canada in a referendum called by the provincial government, the Parti Québécois, on the subject of independence.

1983 A car bomb explodes outside the South African Air Force headquarters in Pretoria, killing at least 16 people and injuring nearly 200. The attack is blamed on the African National Congress (ANC).

1990 An Israeli opens fire on a group of Palestinian laborers south of Tel Aviv, killing seven. The gunman was caught and later sentenced to life in prison.

1995 As a security measure, U.S. president Bill Clinton orders a two-block section of Pennsylvania Avenue fronting the White House permanently closed to motor vehicles.

A skater rolls past the White House on Pennsylvania Avenue

1471 The deposed king Henry VI is murdered in the Tower of London. Henry had been kept alive by Edward IV to prevent an uprising in the name of Henry's son but when the prince was killed at the Battle of Tewkesbury (May 4) there was no longer any political need to keep Henry alive.

1539 Indians kill Estevan, a black slave who was the first non-Indian to visit the pueblo lands of the American Southwest. As a guide to the party of Fray Marcos de Niza, who had been searching for legendary cities of gold, Estevan apparently alienated the Pueblo Indians by using the paraphernalia of a Plains Indian medicine man as well as demanding women and treasure.

1542 Spanish conquistador Hernando de Soto dies on the banks of the Mississippi River in present-day Louisiana. So that Indians would not know of his death, thus unmasking de Soto's claim of divinity, the explorer's men buried his body in the river.

1819 The first bicycles in the United States roll along the streets of New York City. They

Hernando de Soto on his death bed

BORN ON THIS DAY

427 B.C.
PLATO
Greek philosopher (*Utopia*)

1471
ALBRECHT DURER
German Northern Renaissance artist

1688
ALEXANDER POPE
English poet

1780
ELIZABETH FRY
British Quaker minister, prison reformer, and nurse

1844
HENRI ROUSSEAU
French Post-Impressionist painter

1898
ARMAND HAMMER
American industrialist who founded the Occidental Petroleum Co.

1904
THOMAS "FATS" WRIGHT WALLER
American jazz pianist ("Ain't Misbehavin'")

1909
SISTER MARIA INNOCENTIA HUMMEL
German kindergarten art teacher whose work was inspiration for the famous Hummel figurines

1917
RAYMOND BURR
Canadian actor (*Perry Mason; Ironside*)

1921
ANDREI SAKHAROV
Physicist who produced the first Soviet atomic bomb and hydrogen bomb, and who later became a human rights activist

1924
PEGGY CASS
American comedienne

1944
JANET DAILEY
American romance novelist

1944
MARY ROBINSON (NÉE BOURKE)
First female president of Ireland

1952
MR. T (LAWRENCE TUREAUD)
American actor (*The A Team*)

---

were called swift walkers at that time.

1832 The U.S. Democratic Party holds its first national convention, in Baltimore, Maryland.

1840 New Zealand is declared a British colony.

1881 The U.S. Lawn Tennis Association is formed in New York City.

1906 Louis H. Perlman of New York City receives a patent for a demountable tire rim. It was similar to those used on today's cars, but wider.

1910 An estimated 500,000 people line the streets of London to witness the funeral procession of King Edward VII, who died on May 6.

1923 Stanley Baldwin is elected prime minister of Great Britian after the resignation of Andrew Bonar Law, who has been diagnosed with throat cancer.

1924 Ten-year-old Bobbie Franks is abducted and killed in Chicago in what begins one of the most sensational murder cases in U.S. history. Two brilliant, wealthy students, Nathan Leopold and Richard Loeb, were convicted of the crime, which turned out to be a "thrill killing" to test if they could literally get away with murder. Both went to prison.

> *"To err is human, to forgive is divine."*
>
> —*Alexander Pope*

Mustafa Dirani, Lebanese guerrilla leader

🏆 **1950** A former mechanic, Argentina's Juan Manuel Fangio, wins the first of 24 Grand Prix auto-racing victories, at Monaco. Fangio's skills on the racing circuit made him a hero in his native country and gave him a reputation of being the most talented race-car driver who ever lived.

🎭 **1959** Inspired by the life of American stripper Gypsy Rose Lee, the musical *Gypsy* opens on New York City's Broadway.

1932 American aviator Amelia Earhart lands in Ireland to become the first female to fly nonstop across the Atlantic, duplicating Charles Lindbergh's feat five years to the day earlier.

1940 A "special military unit" in Germany murders more than 1,500 mentally ill hospital patients in East Prussia during World War II. The killings were part of the Nazis' program to exterminate anyone considered "unfit."

1942 Destined for gas-chamber extinction during World War II, 4,300 Jews are deported from the town of Chelm in Poland to the Nazi death camp at Sobibor. On the same day, the German firm of IG Farben sets up a factory just outside Auschwitz, Poland, to take advantage of Jewish slave laborers in that equally infamous concentration camp.

🎭 **1945** In a romance that may have begun when they co-starred in the movie *To Have and Have Not,* American actors Humphrey Bogart and Lauren Bacall marry. They shared many screen credits before Bogart died of cancer in 1957.

1968 The final word is heard from the U.S. nuclear-powered submarine *Scorpion,* which disappeared in the Atlantic with 99 men aboard. The wreckage was later found on the sea floor 400 miles southwest of the Azores.

💥 **1982** During the Falklands War, British troops go ashore at San Carlos Water and establish a bridgehead, the first step toward reclaiming the Falklands from Argentinian forces which had invaded the islands on April 2.

🎭 **1988** The Royal Shakespeare Company's stage adaptation of Stephen King's novel *Carrie* closes at the end of a disastrous Broadway run lasting less than a week.

1991 A suicide bomber assassinates former Indian prime minister Rajiv Gandhi during national elections.

1994 Mustafa Dirani, a Shiite Muslim guerrilla leader, is abducted by Israeli commandos in Lebanon's eastern mountains.

Red Cross poster

1455 In the English Wars of the Roses, the Duke of York's forces clash with King Henry VI's Lancastrian army in the first Battle of St. Albans, 20 miles northwest of London. The king was defeated by his cousin Richard of York in this opening engagement of the 30-year Wars of the Roses, so named because roses of different colors were the badges of the opposing forces.

1761 The first life insurance policy in America is issued in Philadelphia, Pennsylvania. What a name it had: the Corporation for Relief of Poor and Distressed Presbyterian Ministers and of the Poor Distressed Widows and Children of Presbyterian Ministers.

1819 The *Savannah*, sailing from its namesake home port of Savannah, Georgia, departs on the first transatlantic crossing by a steam-powered vessel. It arrived in Liverpool, England, on June 20.

1849 Future U.S. president Abraham Lincoln receives a patent for a floating dry dock.

1856 Southern congressman Preston Brooks savagely beats Northern senator Charles Sumner with a cane in the halls of the U.S. Congress

---

MILESTONE

A Thousand Pioneers Head West on the Oregon Trail

The first major wagon train to the northwest departs from Elm Grove, Missouri, on the Oregon Trail on this day in 1843. Although U.S. sovereignty over the Oregon Territory was not clearly established until 1846, American fur trappers and missionary groups had been living in the region for decades. Dozens of books and lectures proclaimed Oregon's agricultural potential, piquing the interest of American farmers. The first overland immigrants to Oregon, intending primarily to farm, came in 1841 when a small band of 70 pioneers left Independence, Missouri.

"I don't know the key to success, but the key to failure is trying to please everybody."

—Bill Cosby

in a debate over the expansion of slavery. Other congressmen subdued Brooks, who became an instant hero in the South, receiving many replacement canes.

1868 Seven members of the Reno gang get away with $98,000 in loot in the "Great Train Robbery" near Marshfield, Indiana.

1900 A. DeVilbiss Jr. of Toledo, Ohio, patents a pendulum-type computer scale used for produce.

1900 A pneumatic piano player, a pianola, is patented by Edwin S. Votey in Detroit, Michigan. The battery-powered device could attach to any piano.

1900 The Associated Press is incorporated in New York. A nonprofit news cooperative, it is still in business today.

The covered wagon of the great western migration (milestone)

1939 Germany and Italy sign the "Pact of Steel," agreeing to a military and political alliance that would give formal birth to the Axis powers in Europe. A little over three months later, Germany attacked Poland, launching World War II.

1944 American and British aircraft launch a systematic World War II bombing raid on railroads in Germany and elsewhere in northern Europe, dubbed "Operation Chattanooga Choo Choo."

1947 The U.S. Congress approves the Truman Doctrine, an economic and military assistance package for Greece and Turkey in the aftermath of World War II.

1955 The popular radio program of American comedian Jack Benny goes off the air for the last time after more than two decades. The TV version of the show ran from 1950 to 1965.

1964 U.S. secretary of state Dean Rusk accuses North Vietnam of initiating aggression in South Vietnam. In a Washington, D.C., speech, he said that withdrawal of American forces would "cause grievous losses to the free world."

1966 Bill Cosby wins the Emmy for Best Actor for his TV series *I Spy*. He was the first African-American actor to star in a regular dramatic television series.

1969 As a dress rehearsal for the real lunar landing to follow, the lunar module of U.S. *Apollo X* flies to within nine miles of the moon's surface.

1970 After pressure from Home Secretary James Callaghan, the Cricket Council withdraws an invitation to the South African cricket team to tour England. The move was part of growing international condemnation of South Africa's apartheid system.

1972 The island nation of Ceylon gains a new name: the Republic of Sri Lanka.

1972 U.S. president Richard M. Nixon arrives in Moscow for a summit meeting with Soviet leaders. Although he had visited the Soviet capital as vice president, this was the first visit to the U.S.S.R. by an American president. The two superpowers reached several agreements, the most important being the groundwork for a joint space flight in 1975 and the Strategic Arms Limitation Treaty.

1999 Wearing blue-and-silver gowns, Columbine High School seniors in Littleton, Colorado, march in single file in a graduation ceremony. It's a day of mixed emotions; the celebration was also a day of remembrance of the victims of a recent massacre on the school campus.

Columbine senior Lisa Kreutz at graduation

1430 The Burgundians capture French military leader Joan of Arc and sell her to the English.

1533 The marriage of King Henry VIII of England to Catherine of Aragon is annulled.

1701 The notorious English privateer William Kidd, popularly known as Captain Kidd, is hanged for piracy and murder in London. For years, stories of buried treasure involving Kidd attracted treasure seekers around the world.

1788 South Carolina, the colony originally named in honor of Charles I of England, becomes the eighth U.S. state to ratify the Constitution.

1827 A school to "relieve parents of the laboring classes from the care of their children" is established in New York City. It was America's first nursery school.

1865 Celebrating the end of the Civil War, the costliest war in American history in terms of casualties, the Army of the Potomac marches in victory along Pennsylvania Avenue in Washington, D.C. Only weeks before, mourners had watched Abraham Lincoln's funeral cortege pass along the same thoroughfare.

1873 The Northwest Mounted Police force of Canada (the "Mounties") is established.

1876 American baseball player Joe Borden of Boston pitches the first no-hit game in National League history.

MILESTONE

New York Public Library Dedicated
In a ceremony presided over by President William Howard Taft on this day in 1911, the New York Public Library, the largest marble structure ever constructed in the United States, is dedicated in New York City. Occupying a two-block section of Fifth Avenue between 40th and 42nd streets, the monumental *beaux-arts* structure took 14 years to complete at a cost of $9 million. The day after its dedication, the library opened its doors to the public, and some 40,000 citizens passed through to make use of a collection that already consisted of more than one million books.

New York Public Library

1900 For fighting for the Union cause in the American Civil War, sergeant William Harvey Carney becomes the first African American to be awarded the Congressional Medal of Honor 36 years later. Wounded in battle, he was discharged with disability in 1864.

1910 The American Mutograph and Biograph company releases *Ramona*, a film based on Helen Jackson's novel examining the treatment of Native Americans.

1915 Italy declares war on Austria-Hungary in World War I.

1922 *Abie's Irish Rose* opens at the Fulton Theater in New York City. It's estimated that 50 million people have attended one of the 2,327 performances of the play somewhere in the world.

1923 The Crow Indian scout Curley, the last man on the U.S. Army side to see General George Custer and his 7th Cavalry alive in the Battle of Little Big Horn, is buried at the National Cemetery at the Big Horn battlefield in Montana. Custer's entire army was killed in the skirmish.

1934 Their Midwest crime spree finally over, infamous American bank robbers Clyde Barrow and Bonnie Parker are shot to death by Texas and Louisiana state police as they drive a stolen car near Bienville

> *"The test of democracy is freedom of criticism."*
> —David Ben-Gurion

Bonnie Parker and Clyde Barrow

1945 Heinrich Himmler, chief of Adolf Hitler's SS, assistant chief of the Gestapo, and architect of the Nazis' extermination of German Jews, swallows cyanide to commit suicide in a Luneberg, Germany, prison one day after his capture.

1949 Soviet premier Joseph Stalin lifts the Berlin Blockade. A 10-month American airlift of goods kept 2.5 million Berliners from starvation and freezing, at the expense of 78 U.S. airmen's lives. The airlift made West Berlin a symbol of resistance to communism.

1960 Israeli prime minister David Ben-Gurion announces that Nazi war criminal Adolf Eichmann has been seized in Argentina by Israeli agents.

Parish, Louisiana. Police said that the pair had attempted to flee; more likely the reason for the fusillade was that Bonnie and Clyde had killed five policemen.

1941 Captain Lord Louis Mountbatten, second cousin of King George IV of Great Britain, is thrown into the Mediterranean when his destroyer, HMS *Kelly*, is sunk off Crete by German dive bombers during World War II. Mountbatten swam safely ashore to take command of the rescue operation.

1967 U.S. Representative James J. Howard reads a letter to the House of Representatives that claims almost all Americans killed in the Vietnam War battle for Hill 881 died as a result of their new M-16 rifles jamming. The Defense Department later corrected the admitted deficiencies, and the M-16 became a popular weapon.

The Army of the Potomac in Washington, D.C.

1543 Polish astronomer Nicolaus Copernicus dies in what is now Frombork, Poland. He was the first to propose that Earth and the other planets revolve around the sun. He also noted that Earth turns daily on its axis, accounting for the changing seasons as the axis shifts.

1830 The first passenger railroad in America begins service. It ran from Baltimore to Elliotts Mills, Maryland.

1859 French composer Charles Gounod's "Ave Maria" is sung in public for the first time, by Madame Caroline Miolan-Carvalho.

1864 Union general Ulysses S. Grant's troops pummel Robert E. Lee's Army of Northern Virginia in a critical engagement of the American Civil War along the North Anna River. By the ceaseless pounding, Grant hoped to prevent Lee from retooling his forces.

1881 The Canadian ferry *Princess Victoria* sinks near London, Ontario, killing some 200 people.

1903 The death of French race-car driver Marcel Renault and his riding mechanic in the Paris-to-Madrid race and a second deadly crash bring to an end the era of city-to-city races in Europe. Almost every race, started in 1897, cost at least one life, including drivers and spectators.

MILESTONE

Brooklyn Bridge Opens

After 14 years and 27 deaths while being constructed, the Brooklyn Bridge over the East River is opened on this day in 1883, connecting the great cities of New York and Brooklyn for the first time in history. Thousands of residents of Brooklyn and Manhattan Island turned out to witness the dedication ceremony, which was presided over by President Chester A. Arthur and New York governor Grover Cleveland. Designed by the late John A. Roebling, the Brooklyn Bridge was the largest suspension bridge ever built to that date. The Brooklyn Bridge was dubbed the eighth wonder of the world.

A grand display of fireworks at the opening of the Brooklyn Bridge

---

1929 *The Cocoanuts*, the first film to star the American comedians Marx Brothers, opens at the Rialto Theater in Los Angeles, California.

1941 Germany's largest battleship, *Bismarck*, sinks the battle cruiser HMS *Hood*, in the North Atlantic near Iceland during World War II. The *Hood*, Great Britain's largest battle cruiser at 41,200 tons and capable of speeds of 31 knots, was the pride of its fleet.

1943 Dr. Josef Mengele, who would earn the nickname "the Angel of Death," arrives at the Auschwitz concentration camp in Poland to begin his systematic killing of Jewish prisoners by injecting thousands with everything from petrol to chloroform in his "medical studies." Mengele fled to South America at the end of World War II and assumed the name of a former Nazi. He died of a stroke while swimming in 1979.

1958 In the United States, the United Press International news service results from a merger of the United Press and International Press Service.

> *"He not busy being born is busy dying."*
>
> —Bob Dylan

1964 Senator Barry Goldwater, while running for the U.S. presidency, gives an interview in which, detractors would claim, he suggests the use of atomic bombs in North Vietnam to defoliate forests and destroy other targets. After a storm of protest, Goldwater said the suggestion was not his but one by competent military commanders that he had merely passed along.

1964 A controversial decision by the referee of a soccer match between Argentina and Peru sparks a riot that leaves more than 100 people dead and over 500 injured.

1974 American jazz great Duke Ellington dies at age 75 after a lifetime of performing music from pop tunes to jazz classics, ballets, film scores, and religious suites. He received the Presidential Medal of Freedom in 1969.

1974 *The Dean Martin Show* is seen for the last time on American television. It was aired for nine years in a variety of formats.

1976 Boxer Muhammad Ali defeats Richard Dunn in Munich with a knockout to retain the world heavyweight boxing title which he had regained in 1974.

1976 Transatlantic Concorde air service to Washington, D.C., is opened by Great Britain and France.

1989 American corporation Xerox announces it will seek licensing fees from computer companies using graphical user interfaces. One target of the move was Apple, which used some of Xerox's inventions in its user-friendly Macintosh computers.

1990 A bomb explodes in a car in Oakland, California, injuring two members of the Earth First! militant environmental movement. No charges were filed against them, although authorities believed they carried the bomb themselves.

1993 American software giant Microsoft introduces a new operating system, Windows NT ("New Technology"). The 32-bit operating system was unveiled during a war among Microsoft Windows, IBM's OS/2, and Apple's Macintosh.

1994 A U.S. court sentences four men convicted of the bombing of the World Trade Center in New York City to 240 years each in prison.

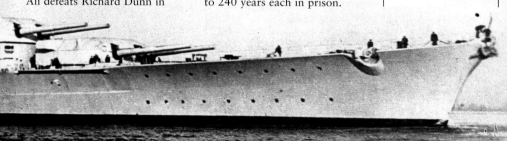

1787 Fifty-five state delegates meet in Philadelphia, Pennsylvania, to compose a new United States constitution. Ratified several years earlier, the Articles of Confederation provided for a loose confederation of the states, with Congress, on paper, responsible for affairs of national concern but in practice given no authority for their enforcement.

1790 Congress enacts the first American copyright protection law. The law was signed by President George Washington six days later. Copyright was for 14 years and renewable only by living filers.

1793 Father Stephen Theodore Badin becomes the first Catholic priest to be ordained in the United States, in a ceremony in Baltimore, Maryland. He was appointed to the Catholic mission in Kentucky.

1810 Argentina begins a revolt against Spain.

1861 President Abraham Lincoln suspends the writ of habeas corpus during the American Civil War, suspending certain civil rights. The U.S. Supreme Court ruled Lincoln's act unconstitutional but the president defied the ruling, saying the suspension was needed to put down the rebellion in the South.

1862 Confederate general Thomas "Stonewall" Jackson wins a significant victory in the American Civil War in a battle in Shenandoah Valley, with 17,000 troops under his command. The victory cemented his reputation as one of the greatest generals of all time.

BORN ON THIS DAY

1803
RALPH WALDO EMERSON
American essayist and poet

Ralph Waldo Emerson

1847
JOHN ALEXANDER DOWIE
Scottish-born evangelist, "Elijah the Restorer"

1865
JOHN RALEIGH MOTT
American organizer of the YMCA

1878
BILL "BOJANGLES" ROBINSON
American dancer

1886
PHILIP MURRAY
Scottish-born American labor leader who founded Congress of Industrial Organizations

1889
IGOR SIKORSKY
Russian engineer who developed the first successful helicopter

1923
JOHN WEITZ
German-born author and fashion designer

1926
MILES DAVIS III
American jazz trumpet player

1927
ROBERT LUDLUM
American author (*The Bourne Identity; The Osterman Weekend*)

1939
SIR IAN McKELLEN
English actor (*Gods and Monsters; Lord of the Rings*)

1944
FRANK OZ
English puppeteer who created the Muppets

1963
MIKE MYERS
Canadian comedian and actor (*Saturday Night Live; Wayne's World; Austin Powers*)

"A hero is no braver than an ordinary man, but he is braver five minutes longer."

—*Ralph Waldo Emerson*

1927 The era of American automaker Henry Ford's popular Model T comes to an end as the "Tin Lizzie" rolls off the assembly line for the last time. It was replaced by the Model A, a more modern car.

1927 American aviator Charles Lindbergh's pioneering flight from New York City to Paris, France, is featured in the *Movietone News*, shown for the first time at the Sam Harris Theater in New York.

1935 Jesse Owens of Ohio State University breaks two world sprint records, ties a third, and breaks a long-jump world record at a meet in Ann Arbor, Michigan. The *New York Times* called it "the greatest day in the history of track."

1944 Stuart Perry of New York City gets a patent on the gasoline engine.

1944 Germany launches Operation Knights Move in World War II, an attempt to seize Yugoslav partisan leader Marshal Tito. Tito escaped a massive invasion by Nazi parachute drops and glider troops.

1944 During a World War II revolt at the Nazi extermination camp at Auschwitz, in Poland, hundreds of fleeing Hungarian Jews are killed.

1946 King Abdullah Ibn Ul-Hussein is proclaimed the new

USS Iowa gun turret explosion

the worst domestic air crash in U.S. history.

1982 During the Falklands War, British container ship *Atlantic Conveyor* is destroyed by Argentine Exocet missiles, and the Royal Navy destroyer HMS *Coventry* is bombed.

1990 A congressional report finds a troubled sailor was probably the cause of an April 19, 1989, blast aboard the battleship USS *Iowa* that killed 47 servicemen.

monarch as Transjordan (now Jordan) becomes a kingdom.

1963 The Organization of African Unity in Addis Ababa, Ethiopia, is founded.

1967 Scottish soccer team Glasgow Celtic beat Milan to become the first British team to win the European Cup.

1968 The communists launch their third major assault of the year against Saigon in the Vietnam War. The target was Cholon, the Chinese section of the South Vietnamese capital. The Viet Cong launched this offensive to influence the Paris peace talks in their favor.

1968 A part of the Jefferson National Expansion Memorial in St. Louis, Missouri, the Gateway Arch is dedicated.

1977 The Chinese communist government lifts a decade-old ban on the writings of William Shakespeare, more evidence the country's Cultural Revolution is over.

1979 American Airlines Flight 191 crashes on takeoff at Chicago O'Hare Airport, killing all 271 aboard as well as causing some ground casualties. It was

Martin Luther

1521 German church reformer Martin Luther is banned by the Edict of Worms because of his writings and religious beliefs.

1637 An allied Puritan and Monhegan force under English captain John Mason attacks a Pequot village in Connecticut, killing 500 Indian men, women, and children. Thus began the Pequot War, which nearly annihilated this Indian tribe.

1703 English diarist Samuel Pepys dies. Pepys's diaries gave a vivid account of 17th-century life, including court intrigue and accounts of the Great Plague (1665–66) and the Fire of London (1666).

1864 President Abraham Lincoln signs an act establishing the Montana Territory, in an effort to add free territories to the Union during the American Civil War. Little happened in Montana, however, until the 1850s, when gold was discovered there.

1865 Confederate general Edmund Kirby Smith becomes the last southern general to surrender during the American

---

BORN ON THIS DAY

1689
LADY MARY WORTLEY MONTAGU
English essayist, feminist, and eccentric

1759
MARY WOLLSTONECRAFT GODWIN
English writer, mother of Mary Shelley

1799
ALEXANDER PUSHKIN
Russian poet

1822
EDMOND DE GONCOURT
French novelist in whose name the annual Prix Goncourt for fiction is awarded

Edmond de Goncourt

1835
EDWARD PORTER ALEXANDER
American brigadier general of artillery (Confederate Army)

1886
AL JOLSON (BORN ASA YOELSON)
American entertainer who starred in the first "talkie" (*The Jazz Singer*)

1907
JOHN "DUKE" WAYNE
Academy Award-winning American actor (*Stagecoach; True Grit; Rio Grande*)

1910
LAURANCE S. ROCKEFELLER
American conservationist, CEO of Chase Manhattan Bank

1948
STEVIE NICKS
American singer/songwriter (Fleetwood Mac)

1951
SALLY RIDE
Astronaut who was the first American woman in space

1964
LENNY KRAVITZ
American singer/songwriter

Civil War. He was the last surviving full Confederate general until his death in 1893.

1897 Irish horror writer Bram Stoker's classic vampire tale *Dracula* is offered for sale in London. It told the story of a Transylvanian vampire and his English victims.

1913 The Actors' Equity Association is organized in the United States.

1915 English poet Julian Grenfell is killed on the Western Front. He wrote the lines: "And he is dead who will not fight / And who dies fighting has increase."

1940 During World War II, U.S. president Franklin D. Roosevelt appeals for support from the Red Cross to help French and Belgian citizens suffering the effects of the German drive to the northern coast of France and the English Channel.

1954 American pianist Liberace performs in a three-hour one-man concert in New York City's Madison Square Garden, drawing an audience of 16,000. This nearly broke the previous box-office draw of 18,000 set by Polish pianist Ignacy Jan Paderewski.

1960 The U.S. ambassador to the United Nations charges that the Soviet Union has committed acts of espionage at the U.S. embassy in Moscow

> *"Life is too short for a long story."*
> —Lady Mary Wortley Montagu

by placing listening devices there. The charges were an attempt to deflect Soviet criticism concerning an American U-2 spy plane shot down over the Soviet Union earlier in the month.

1965 Australia joins in the Vietnam War by sending 800 troops. At the same time, neighboring New Zealand announces it will commit an artillery battalion to the cause.

1969 A successful eight-day dress rehearsal for the first moon landing ends as U.S. *Apollo 10* astronauts return to Earth.

1971 An estimated 1,000 North Vietnamese capture the strategic rubber-plantation town of Seoul, driving out 2,000 South Vietnamese as U.S. air strikes support the Allied forces. The victory gave the communists control of sections of strategically important routes 7 and 13 leading into South Vietnam as well as access to military equipment and supplies during the Vietnam War.

1976 Outgoing prime minister Harold Wilson's resignation honors list, leaked in advance, provokes an angry reaction in parliament. Wilson was famous for his trademark raincoat, and among the controversial honors was a life peerage for Sir Joseph Kagan, manufacturer of Gannex raincoats.

1977 New York City police arrest George Willig, the "Human Fly," but not before he manages to use a window washer's rig to scale 110 stories of the World Trade Center. The feat took Willig 3 hours. (His fine: $1.10.)

1981 American attorney S. Pal Asija, a programmer and patent lawyer, receives a patent for software. Previously, software was protected only by copyright, making it easy for competitors to steal software ideas. This patent set a legal precedent for software patent rights.

1981 A U.S. Marine jet crashes onto the flight deck of the aircraft carrier USS *Nimitz* off Florida, killing 14 people.

1991 All 223 people aboard die when a Lauda Air Boeing 767 crashes in Thailand.

1994 U.S. president Bill Clinton, in renewing trade privileges for China, says his administration will no longer link Chinese trade status with its human rights record.

1994 American pop singer Michael Jackson and Lisa Marie Presley, daughter of Elvis, are married in the Dominican Republic.

U.S. ambassador to the U.N. Henry Cabot Lodge explaining the listening devices

MAY 27

1647 The first recorded American execution of a "witch" takes place in Salem, Massachusetts.

1703 Czar Peter I founds the city of St. Petersburg as the new Russian capital. Peter the Great's sweeping military, political, economic, and cultural reforms made Russia a major European power.

1831 Comanche Indians kill colorful trapper/explorer Jedediah Smith as he rides alone on the Santa Fe Trail. Smith was one of the leading "mountain men" hired by eastern companies seeking the fur trapping and trading opportunities that led to opening up the far West.

1863 U.S. chief Supreme Court justice Roger B. Taney issues *Ex parte Merryman*, which challenged the authority of President Lincoln and the military to suspend the writ of habeas corpus in Maryland. The case involved a vocal secessionist, John Merryman, who had been arrested in Cockeysville. Although the military continued to arrest sympathizers of the South, Taney's ruling led to a softening of the policy. Merryman was never brought to trial and the treason charges were dropped.

MILESTONE

Golden Gate Bridge Opens

San Francisco's Golden Gate Bridge, a stunning technological and artistic achievement, opens to the public after five years of construction on this day in 1937. On opening day, some 200,000 bridge walkers marveled at the 4,200-foot-long suspension bridge, which spans the Golden Gate Strait at the entrance to San Francisco Bay and connects San Francisco and Marin County. On May 28, the Golden Gate Bridge opened to vehicular traffic. At 4,200 feet, it was the longest bridge in the world until the completion of New York City's Verrazano Narrows Bridge in 1964.

"Profit and morality are a hard combination to beat."

—Hubert Humphrey

1896 A tornado strikes St. Louis, Missouri, and East St. Louis, Illinois, killing 255 people.

1909 Alva J. Fisher files a patent application for the first electric washing machine, manufactured by the Hurley Machine Company of Chicago, Illinois. Two years earlier the German Henkel company had produced the first washing powder, named *Persil*® from its active ingredients perborate and silicate.

1924 Jules Stein founds the Music Corporation of America in Chicago, Illinois, which books bands into clubs and dance halls. After a series of mergers and changes over the years, it became Universal Studios in 1996.

1926 The citizens of Hannibal, Missouri, erect the first bronze statue of the literary characters for which their town was noted, including Huck Finn and Tom Sawyer.

1933 Walt Disney's cartoon *Three Little Pigs*, featuring

298   *Golden Gate Bridge San Francisco, California (milestone)*

the song "Who's Afraid of the Big Bad Wolf?" is released. It was the most popular animated cartoon up to that time.

1936 The Cunard ocean liner *Queen Mary* leaves England on its maiden voyage.

1940 During World War II, units from Germany's SS Death's Head division battle British troops just 50 miles from the French port of Dunkirk, where trapped British soldiers await evacuation across the English Channel to England. Ninety-nine British Expeditionary troops, after agreeing to surrender, were brutally gunned down. Two survived.

1941 Avenging the sinking of HMS *Hood,* pride of the British Navy, British warships sink Germany's battleship *Bismarck* in the North Atlantic during World War II. More

than 2,000 German sailors died in the action.

1964 Jawaharlal Nehru, the first prime minister of independent India, dies.

1965 U.S. warships from the 7th Fleet launch a series of major raids against communist targets in central South Vietnam, augmenting the vital role of U.S. carrier raids in the Vietnam War.

1971 Sweden discloses that it has been providing assistance to the Viet Cong in the Vietnam War, insisting that it included no military aid but $500,000 worth of medical supplies.

1971 At St. Andrews, golfers representing Great Britain and Ireland beat the United States to win the Walker Cup for the first time since 1938.

1972 U.S. president Richard M. Nixon and Soviet president Leonid Brezhnev meet in Moscow to sign the Strategic Arms Limitation Treaty, the most far-reaching attempt yet to control nuclear weapons.

1533 The marriage of King Henry VIII and Anne Boleyn is declared valid by the Archbishop of Canterbury, Thomas Cranmer.

1754 A Virginia militia under Lieutenant Colonel George Washington defeats a French reconnaissance party in southwestern Pennsylvania, killing 10 French soldiers and losing only one soldier of its own. The skirmish was the opening round of the French and Indian War, the last and most important colonial conflict between British and American colonists and the French and American Indians.

1863 The first African-American regiment in the American Civil War, the 54th Massachusetts infantry, leaves Boston for combat in the South.

1890 Elijah Jefferson Bond, Charles Kennard, and William Maupin, all of Baltimore, Maryland, file a patent for the Ouija® board. The patent was eventually published as US 446054 and GB2451/1891.

1902 Owen Wister publishes his novel *The Virginian*, the first serious "western" in American publishing.

1922 Otto Krueger conducts the Detroit News Orchestra, the first known

> *"The soul is nurtured by want as much as by plenty."*
>
> —*Thomas Moore*

BORN ON THIS DAY

1371
JOHN THE FEARLESS
Duke of Burgundy

1738
DR. JOSEPH IGNACE GUILLOTIN
French physician, inventor of the guillotine

1759
WILLIAM PITT
Youngest-ever British prime minister (elected in 1783 at the age of 24)

1779
THOMAS MOORE
Irish poet, lyricist ("Irish Melodies"; "Lalla Rookh"; "Loves of the Angels")

1908
IAN FLEMING
English author of the James Bond spy novels

1910
T-BONE WALKER
American blues musician ("T-Bone Shuffle"; "Call It Stormy Monday (But Tuesday's Just as Bad)")

1912
PATRICK WHITE
Australian novelist, winner of the 1973 Nobel Prize in literature

1934
DIONNE QUINTUPLETS (ANNETTE, CÉCILE, ÉMILIE, MARIE, YVONNE)
First known set of surviving quintuplets, these Canadian girls were treated as a side show and lived in a virtual museum

1936
BETTY SHABAZZ
American civil rights leader, wife of Malcolm X

1944
RUDOLPH GIULIANI
Former mayor of New York City

1944
GLADYS KNIGHT
American singer (Gladys Knight and the Pips)

1945
JOHN FOGERTY
American singer/songwriter (Credence Clearwater Revival)

The first "western" novel

radio orchestra, on the WWJ radio station, owned by the *Detroit News*.

1925 AT&T's New York office sends a fax containing a stethogram and electrocardiogram to a doctor in Chicago, Illinois. It was the first such long-distance medical fax.

1929 The first movie with sound and color, Warner Brothers' Technicolor *On With the Show*, debuts at New York City's Winter Garden.

1937 Neville Chamberlain becomes prime minister of Great Britain.

1940 During World War II, King Leopold III of Belgium accepts an unconditional surrender demand from the invading Germans after 18 days of ceaseless Nazi bombardment. His request for an armistice was rejected, and his refusal to flee the country led to his imprisonment in his palace.

1954 English-born filmmaker Alfred Hitchcock's 3-D thriller *Dial M for Murder* opens at New York City's Paramount Theater.

1957 The National Academy of Recording Arts and Sciences, the organization that sponsors the Grammy awards each year, is formed.

1961 The *London Observer*, a British newspaper, launches a campaign calling for release of all persons imprisoned for peaceful expression of their beliefs. At specific issue was a group of students in Portugal jailed for toasting to "freedom" in a restaurant.

1970 English soccer captain Bobby Moore rejoins the national World Cup squad in Mexico, having been held in Colombia for two days accused of stealing from a jewelry shop. The judge who released Moore told him, "I hope it goes well for you and that you score many goals."

1972 The Duke of Windsor, who abdicated his throne as king of England in 1936 to marry divorcée Wallis Warfield Simpson, dies in Paris at age 77.

1977 A fire in the Beverly Hills Supper Club in Southgate, Kentucky, kills 165 people.

1982 Made popular through Agatha Christie's mystery novel *Murder on the Orient Express*, the train of the same name is reborn with a 26-hour trip across Europe after a long respite.

1984 U.S. president Ronald W. Reagan leads a funeral in Arlington National Cemetery in Virginia for an unknown serviceman killed in the Vietnam War. The remains

were later identified and removed to a cemetery in St. Louis, Missouri, for reburial.

1985 Old Coca-Cola Drinkers of America is founded in an effort to bring back the original-formula Coca-Cola to replace the New Coke foisted on the nation by the Atlanta-based company. As a result, Classic Coke was born.

1987 Matthias Rust, a 19-year-old amateur pilot from West Germany, takes off from Helsinki, Finland, flies through more than 400 miles of Soviet air space, evades Soviet air defenses, and lands his small plane in Moscow's Red Square. The incident caused embarassment in Soviet military security circles.

1999 Viktor Chernomyrdin, Russia's envoy to the Balkans, meets with Slobodan Milosevic and declares the Yugoslav president the key to a peace plan in Kosovo, despite his indictment for war crimes.

John Steinbeck

Former Russian prime minister Viktor Chernomyrdin, left, shakes hands with Yugoslav president Slobodan Milosevic

1765 "If this be treason, make the most of it!" American patriot Patrick Henry exclaims in denouncing the Stamp Act in Virginia's House of Burgesses.

1790 Rhode Island becomes the 13th and last original English colony to ratify the U.S. Constitution.

1844 When voting for a Democratic presidential candidate deadlocks at the Democratic National Convention in Baltimore, Maryland, James K. Polk's name is entered as the first "dark horse" candidate. He went on to win the nomination on the ninth ballot and, eventually, the presidency.

1848 Wisconsin becomes the 30th state of the U.S. union. The "Badger State" got this name from Wisconsin lead mines called badgers.

1864 Union troops end some of the bloodiest days of the American Civil War when the Confederate troops of General Robert E. Lee successfully defend Cold Harbor, Virginia, against the foolish attack of Union general Ulysses S. Grant in a slaughter nearly unmatched in the war.

1910 Claiming a $10,000 prize, aviator Glenn Curtiss beats a train on a race from Albany, New York, to New York City.

> *"Conformity is the jailer of freedom and the enemy of growth."*
> —*John F. Kennedy*

BORN ON THIS DAY

1630
CHARLES II
King of England, Ireland, and Scotland

1736
PATRICK HENRY
American revolutionary patriot who said, "Give me liberty, or give me death!"

1874
GILBERT KEITH CHESTERTON
English journalist, poet, critic, and novelist

1892
ALFONSINA STORNI
Argentine poet

1903
BOB HOPE
English-born American comedian

1917
JOHN FITZGERALD KENNEDY
35th U.S. president

1932
PAUL EHRLICH
German biologist, author who helped form Zero Population Growth, a group advocating a limit of two children per family

1939
AL UNSER SR.
American race-car driver

1956
LATOYA JACKSON
American singer

1958
ANNETTE BENING
American actress (*The Grifters; The American President; American Beauty*)

1914 The British ocean liner *Empress of Ireland* collides with the Norwegian freighter *Storstad*, drowning 1,012 of its 1,477 passengers and crew as it sinks in the gulf of Canada's St. Lawrence River.

1932 A group of 1,000 American World War I veterans arrive in Washington, D.C., as the "Bonus Expeditionary Force" marches to demand passage of a veterans' payment bill for their military service.

1942 During World War II, Nazi German dictator Adolf Hitler orders all Jews in occupied Paris, France, to wear an identifying yellow star on the left side of their coats. This form of isolation was not the first for the Jews, who endured such humiliation by Catholics throughout the history of the papal states.

1942 "White Christmas," a recording by American singer Bing Crosby, is released by Decca Records. The biggest-selling single of all time, it is still played frequently each Christmas season.

1943 American artist Norman Rockwell's portrait of "Rosie the Riveter" appears on

World War I Veteran's Bonus marchers parade past the White House

Pope John Paul II with Queen Elizabeth II

the cover of the *Saturday Evening Post*. It was a tribute to women on the home front working in defense plants in World War II.

1951 Actress and singer Fanny Brice, who rose from her roots as the poor daughter of Jewish immigrants in New York City to become one of America's best-loved comediennes, dies at age 60.

1962 Buck (John) O'Neil becomes the first African-American coach in major-league baseball when he accepts a job with the Chicago Cubs.

1972 The United States and the Soviet Union issue a joint communiqué following summit talks between President Richard M. Nixon and General Secretary Leonid Brezhnev. Despite differing views on U.S. involvement in Vietnam, the communiqué indicated, the two countries hoped that the thawing of relations between them would continue.

1973 Tom Bradley is elected as Los Angeles's first African-American mayor. He defeated incumbent Sam Yorty.

1979 Mary Pickford, known as "America's Sweetheart," dies at the age of 86. One of Hollywood's first true movie stars, in later years she became a powerful movie producer and co-founder of United Artists studios.

1982 Pope John Paul II visits Canterbury Cathedral as part of the first visit to Great Britain by any Pope since 1531. The last visit came before Henry VIII established the Church of England in defiance of the Catholic church.

1983 A Rembrandt painting worth £1 million is stolen from the Dulwich Picture Gallery in south London.

1985 Thirty-five people die in a riot that broke out between British and Italian spectators during soccer's European Cup Final at the Heysel Stadium in Brussels, Belgium.

1990 Peru is struck by an earthquake that claims 56 lives.

Edmund P. Hillary of New Zealand, left, and Tenzing Norgay of Nepal (milestone)

MILESTONE

Men Reach Everest Summit

At 11:30 A.M. on this day in 1953, Edmund Hillary of New Zealand and Tenzing Norgay, a Sherpa of Nepal, become the first explorers to reach the summit of Mount Everest, which at 29,035 feet above sea level is the highest point on Earth. The two, part of a British expedition, made their final assault on the summit after spending a fitful night at 27,900 feet. News of their achievement broke around the world on June 2, the day of Queen Elizabeth II's coronation, and Britons hailed it as a good omen for their country's future.

MAY 30

1431 French patriot and martyr Joan of Arc is burned at the stake in Rouen, having been found guilty of heresy and sorcery by an ecclesiastical court of the Inquisition. She was declared Blessed in 1908 and canonized in 1920.

1536 English king Henry VIII marries his third wife Jane Seymour just 11 days after the execution of his second wife Anne Boleyn for adultery. Seymour had been a lady-in-waiting to both of the king's previous wives and died in 1537 twelve days after giving birth to his son Edward (later Edward VI).

1539 Spanish explorer Hernando de Soto lands in Florida.

1593 English playwright Christopher Marlowe, 29, is stabbed to death in a brawl over a bar tab. Marlowe is best known for *Dr. Faustus*.

Faustus *theatre advertisement*

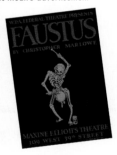

BORN ON THIS DAY

1672
PETER I (PETER THE GREAT)
Russian Czar, Emperor of Russia

1835
ALFRED AUSTIN
Poet laureate of England

Alfred Austin

1903
COUNTEE CULLEN
American poet (*Black Christ and Other Poems*)

1909
BENNY GOODMAN
American jazz clarinetist and bandleader

1912
JOSEPH STEIN
American playwright (*Fiddler on the Roof; Enter Laughing*)

1926
CHRISTINE JORGENSEN
American pioneer transsexual

1927
CLINT WALKER
American actor (*Cheyenne*)

1946
CANDY LIGHTNER
American political activist who founded Mothers Against Drunk Drivers (MADD)

> *"Is life worth living? Yes, so long as there is wrong to right."*
>
> —*Alfred Austin*

1783 Benjamin Towne publishes the *Pennsylvania Post*, the first daily newspaper in the United States.

1806 Future U.S. president Andrew Jackson kills Charles Dickinson, a lawyer regarded as one of the best pistol shots in the area, in a duel in Logan County, Kentucky. Jackson, who participated in several duels, challenged Dickinson, who allegedly slandered Jackson's wife, Rachel, as a bigamist.

1848 W. G. Young of Baltimore, Maryland, patents the first ice-cream freezer.

1854 Nebraska and Kansas are established as American territories.

1862 The Confederates abandon the city of Corinth, Tennessee, in the American Civil War. Although the city was lost to the Union Army, General Pierre Beauregard's Confederate Army and their hope in the west remained intact.

Cologne, Germany, in 1921

1868 General John A. Logan of the Grand Army of the Republic proclaims the first Memorial Day to honor those who died in defense of their country. The holiday was known to some as "Decoration Day," because early mourners honored Civil War dead by decorating their graves with flowers.

1883 In New York City, a stampede occurs on the Brooklyn Bridge after a rumor spreads that the famous structure is in danger of collapsing; 12 people are crushed to death.

1896 A Duryea motor wagon driven by Henry Wells from Springfield, Massachusetts, collides with a bicycle ridden by Evylyn Thomas of New York City (where the accident occurred). It was the first recorded American auto accident.

1911 Ray Harroun is the winner of the first long-distance auto race at Indianapolis, Indiana.

1922 U.S. chief justice William Howard Taft dedicates the Lincoln Memorial in Washington, D.C.

1942 The medieval city of Cologne, Germany, is pounded by 1,500 tons of bombs dropped by 1,000 British bombers, killing

Earthquake damage in Kol, Afghanistan

469 and leaving hundreds homeless, a devastating blow to German morale during World War II.

1943 During World War II, American troops wrest the island of Attu in the Aleutian island chain from the Japanese.

1958 Unidentified soldiers killed in World War II and Korea are buried in Arlington National Cemetery in Virginia.

1967 Biafra proclaims its independence after years of suppression by the military government of Nigeria. As separate nations, the two countries went to war the following July, and Biafra was forced to surrender to Nigerian authorities.

1998 A powerful earthquake rocks northern Afghanistan, killing up to 5,000 people.

MAY 31

1759 Bowing to pressure from religious groups, Pennsylvania lawmakers adopt a law forbidding the performance of plays in the state. The fine for violating the edict was 500 English pounds.

1809 Austrian composer Franz Joseph Haydn dies in Vienna.

1880 The first national bicycle society in the United States, the League of American Wheelmen, is formed in Newport, Rhode Island.

1889 The town of Johnstown, Pennsylvania, is nearly wiped off the map as heavy rain and a neglected dam combine to cause one of the worst floods in American history. More than 2,209 people die.

1895 John Harvey Kellogg of Battle Creek, Michigan, files a U.S. patent for "flaked cereals and process of preparing same," published in April 1896 as U.S. 558393.

1902 Great Britain and the Boer states sign the Treaty of Vereeniging, officially ending

People stand atop houses among ruins after Johnstown flood

MILESTONE

Seinfeld Premieres
The sitcom *Seinfeld* debuts on this day in 1990. On July 5, 1989, the pilot for this comedy series, called *The Seinfeld Chronicles,* aired. In May 1990, the program launched, featuring Jerry Seinfeld as a thirty-something stand-up comic and his group of wacky friends, including chronic worrywart George, eccentric neighbor Kramer, and quirky ex-girlfriend Elaine. The show wasn't an instant hit but gradually gained popularity. The program hit first place in the 1994–95 season. The show aired its last episode on May 14, 1998, and 76 million viewers tuned in to watch.

the three-year-old Boer War. The war originated when gold and diamonds were discovered, igniting old animosities between the Boers and British.

1907 The new "Paris cabs" arrive in New York City. They are the city's first taxis.

1910 The Union of South Africa is founded.

1916 British and German fleets meet in the World War I Battle of Jutland, off Denmark.

1937 Mary, Mona, Roberta, and Leota Keys receive degrees from Baylor University in Waco, Texas. They are the first quadruplets to complete college.

1941 During World War II, a 22,000-man German parachute invasion of the Mediterranean island of Crete ends with the evacuation of the last of its Allied defenders. Defending the island cost 1,742 Allied land soldiers and another 2,265 sailors lost in the sinking of nine warships.

1957 American playwright Arthur Miller is convicted of contempt of Congress for refusing to denounce writers with alleged Communist views to the House of Representatives Un-American Activities Committee.

1962 In the first execution to take place in the state of

"He most honors my style who learns under it to destroy the teacher."
—*Walt Whitman*

1965 Indianapolis 500 winner Jim Clark

Israel, former SS officer Adolf Eichmann is hanged near Tel Aviv for his war crimes.

1965 As part of Operation Rolling Thunder, U.S. planes bomb an ammunition depot at Hoi Jan, west of Hanoi, in the Vietnam War. The operation continued until October 1968, when it was halted under increasing domestic and political pressures.

1965 Scottish Formula One world champion racing driver Jim Clark becomes the first non-American driver since 1916 to win the Indianapolis 500.

1970 During the Vietnam War, about 75 communist soldiers who had seized key outposts in the city of Dalat, 145 miles northeast of Saigon, slip past 2,500 South Vietnamese troops who had surrounded their positions and escaped.

1977 After three years of construction, the trans-Alaska oil pipeline, running from Prudhoe Bay to Valdez, is completed.

1985 John Sculley, president of the American computer company Apple, removes co-founder Steve Jobs from his job

as head of the Macintosh unit. Sales of Macintosh computers had fallen far below expectations in their first year, despite fanfare by Apple, leading to a feud between the two men.

1988 U.S. president Ronald W. Reagan and Soviet leader Mikhail Gorbachev end a summit meeting in Moscow on notes of both frustration and triumph. While Reagan came across in the "Great Communicator" style for which he was famous, Gorbachev blocked attempts on arms limitations and progress toward human rights.

1990 U.S. president George H. Bush and his wife, Barbara, welcome Soviet president Mikhail Gorbachev in a ceremony at the White House. Talks on German reunification followed the greeting.

1994 The United States announces it will no longer aim nuclear missiles at targets in the former Soviet Union.

1999 The treason trial of Kurdish rebel leader Abdullah Ocalan opens in Turkey. Ocalan was convicted and sentenced to death.

Abdullah Ocalan in front of Turkish flag

1495 Exchequer rolls in Scotland record that distilled whiskey has been produced for the first time, by Friar John Cor.

1533 Anne Boleyn is crowned queen of England, four months after she, already carrying Henry VIII's child, secretly became his second wife.

1638 An earthquake rocks Plymouth, Massachusetts. It was the first time colonists in the New World had observed this phenomenon.

1774 The port of Boston, Massachusetts, is closed by the British, one of the Coercive Acts imposed in the aftermath of the Boston Tea Party (December 16, 1773), in which American colonists' protests of British taxation turned violent.

1779 During the American Revolutionary War, Benedict Arnold's anger at being court-martialed over procedural irregularities leads him to plot with the British to capture the military complex at West Point, New York, and its leader, George Washington. Although his plot was discovered and foiled, his name became synonymous in the United States with treachery.

1831 Scottish explorer James Ross determines the position of the North Magnetic Pole on the west coast of the

> *"I've been on a calendar, but never on time."*
> —Marilyn Monroe

1801
BRIGHAM YOUNG
American Mormon church leader

1878
JOHN MASEFIELD
English poet ("Christmas Eve at Sea"; "Sea Fever"; "Trade Winds")

1907
SIR FRANK WHITTLE
English air commodore and developer of the first successful jet engine

1921
NELSON RIDDLE
American musical conductor

1926
ANDY GRIFFITH
American actor (*The Andy Griffith Show; Matlock*)

1926
MARILYN MONROE
American actress (*Gentlemen Prefer Blondes; The Misfits; Some Like It Hot*)

1928
GEORGI T. DOBROVOLSKY
Russian cosmonaut

1930
EDWARD WOODWARD
English actor (*The Wicker Man; Breaker Morant; The Equalizer*)

1934
PAT BOONE
American singer ("April Love"; "Love Letters in the Sand")

1935
JAMES GEORGE
American weightlifter who won an Olympic silver medal in 1960 and the bronze in 1956

1938
COLLEEN McCULLOUGH
Australian author (*Tim; The Thorn Birds*)

1939
CLEAVON LITTLE
American actor (*Vanishing Point; Blazing Saddles*)

1947
RON WOOD
English rock musician (Rolling Stones)

1974
ALANIS MORISETTE
Canadian singer/songwriter ("Thank U"; "Ironic")

Sojourner Truth

Boothia Peninsula in Canada's Northwest Territory.

1843 Freed slave Sojourner Truth leaves New York to act for the first time as conductor on the Underground Railroad. Harriet Beecher Stowe, best known as the author of *Uncle Tom's Cabin*, dubbed her a "Libyan Sybil" in an article about the network that escorted fugitive slaves north.

1861 In a gesture symbolizing the breakdown of communications between North and South that would shortly lead to the Civil War, the United States and the Confederacy simultaneously suspend mail interchange.

1868 Navajo who have been displaced to a reservation in New Mexico plead with Governor Sherman to return them to their homelands. He presents a prepared document that grants this wish, but reduces the size of their lands.

1888 California, a state that would become identified with earthquakes, installs its first seismograph.

1900 The Boxers, whose Chinese name translates literally as "Fists of Righteous Harmony," conquer the city of Tientsin, China, in a rebellion targeting foreigners and Chinese Christians.

1904 Three French officers are arrested in connection with the Dreyfus Affair as, a decade after it began in October 1894, the tide begins to turn for the young French Jew who, on the basis of handwriting analysis, had been accused and convicted of delivering military documents to the Germans. Both Alfred Dreyfus and novelist Émile Zola, who came to his defense by publishing the blistering article "J'Accuse" in the popular press, spent time in prison before the verdict was overturned in 1906.

1915 German zeppelins bomb London, England, for the first time, causing extensive fires as World War I impacts urban civilian life.

1916 The introduction of the U.S. National Defense Act increases the strength of the National Guard to 450,000.

1916 The west coast of the United States is hit by its first major labor disruption when 4,000 dock workers walk off their jobs in San Francisco, California.

1920 The first international exposition of Dadaism, a cynical art movement whose iconic image is the *Mona Lisa with Moustache* presented by French artist Marcel Duchamp, opens at a gallery in Berlin, Germany. Work by German artist George Grosz is featured, but Grosz positioned himself at the entrance wearing placards

that proclaimed, "Art is dead. This is the new machine art."

1921 Race riots in Tulsa, Oklahoma, kill 85 people and destroy a 30-block section of a central African-American neighborhood.

1944 The British Broadcasting Service sends the first coded message to the French Resistance, signaling that the World War II D-Day invasion is imminent.

1981 The first English-language newspaper is published in mainland China.

2001 The king and queen of Nepal, along with seven other members of the royal family, are slain in the palace by Crown Prince Dipendra, who then mortally wounds himself.

Nepal's King Gyanendra and Queen Komal

1835 American showman P. T. Barnum takes his circus on its first U.S. tour.

1851 Maine joins a trend by outlawing the consumption of alcohol. This ban, promoted by a growing temperance movement and Prohibition politicians, would culminate in the 1919 passage of the 18th Amendment to the U.S. Constitution, which prohibited the manufacture, sale, or transport of alcoholic beverages.

1857 American James Gibbs patents a chain-stitch single-thread sewing machine, one of the technological advances that drove the Industrial Revolution.

1873 Work begins on the first line of San Francisco's famous cable car system. Designed by English-born engineer Andrew Smith Hallidie, the first train ran less than two months later. Today the cable car is a major tourist attraction and one of the emblems of the city.

1896 The world's first patent for a radio communications device is filed in Britain by Guglielmo Marconi, the Italian-born inventor. His wireless telegraph apparatus marked the beginning of the fields of radio and telecommunications.

1897 Rumors that writer Samuel Clemons had died at the age of 61 were squelched with publication in the *New York Journal* of the kind of quip that earned "Mark Twain" his

"Nobody's interested in sweetness and light."
—Hedda Hopper

BORN ON THIS DAY

1491
HENRY VIII
King of England (1509–47)

1740
THE MARQUIS DE SADE (DONATIEN ALPHONSE FRANÇOIS)
French author (*Justine; Juliette*)

1835
SAINT PIUS X
Roman Catholic pope (1903–14)

1840
THOMAS HARDY
English poet, novelist (*Return of the Native; Jude the Obscure*)

1850
JESSE BOOT, BARON TRENT OF NOTTINGHAM
English philanthropist and businessman who founded Britain's largest chain of drug stores

1857
SIR EDWARD ELGAR
English composer ("Pomp and Circumstance"; "Enigma Variations")

1890
HEDDA HOPPER
American gossip columnist

1904
JOHN WEISSMULLER
American Olympic swimmer and actor (*Tarzan*)

1920
JOHNNY SPEIGHT
English comedy writer, creator of the bigoted Alf Garnett (*Till Death Us Do Part*) and his American alterego Archie Bunker (*All in the Family*)

1930
CHARLES "PETE" CONRAD JR.
American astronaut

1944
MARVIN HAMLISCH
American composer famous for his film scores (*The Spy Who Loved Me; Sophie's Choice; A Chorus Line*)

1946
LASSE HALLSTRÖM
Swedish movie director (*The Cider House Rules; Chocolat; The Shipping News*)

1953
CRAIG STADLER
American golfer

---

reputation for succinct humor: "The report of my death was an exaggeration."

1905 President Theodore Roosevelt opens the Lewis & Clark Centennial Exposition in Portland, Oregon. A century earlier, the pair had explored the western regions of North America. Their travels, from St. Louis, Missouri, to the source of the Missouri River and along the Columbia River to its mouth at the Pacific, bolstered U.S. claims to the "Oregon country."

1917 Boston Braves catcher Hank Gowdy becomes the first major-league baseball player to leave his team and enlist in the U.S. Army as the United States prepares to enter World War I.

1918 The destroyer *Ward* is launched 17.5 days after its construction began, setting a record for shipbuilding as the United States bolsters the Allies in World War I.

1925 As various expeditions reach and explore Earth's

Hank Gowdy

Frank Hawks

poles, Canada claims all land between Alaska and Greenland.

🇺🇸 **1930** New model cars make motoring increasingly accessible, and 100,000 Americans register for new driver's licenses.

🇺🇸 **1933** A new record flying time between Los Angeles, California, and New York City is set by Frank Hawks: 13 hours, 26 minutes.

🏆 **1935** American baseball great Babe Ruth retires after 22 major-league seasons. Ruth retired holding nearly every important batting record, including a career total of 714 home runs. He played for the Boston Red Sox, New York Yankees, and Boston Braves from 1914 to 1935.

1944 During World War II, the Allies move air power to the Russian front; en route, 130 Flying Fortresses drop bombs on Hungary and Romania. Allied troops were conspicuously active near Pas-de-Calais, as Operation Cover hoped to convince the Germans that it would be the site of their D-Day invasion.

🇮🇹 **1946** Italians vote for a republican form of government, ending their ineffective monarchy and repudiating the Fascist regime that had led the country through World War II.

🇮🇳 **1947** After escalating violence between Hindus and Muslims had erupted into riots and caused thousands of deaths in the two years since the All-India Congress had failed to reach accord on ministers, the new government convinces Great Britain that partition of India along religious lines is necessary. Viceroy Louis Mountbatten announced a plan to create the independent Muslim state of Pakistan and allow Hindus to be the ruling majority in the rest of India.

🇵🇱 **1979** Pope John Paul II becomes the first pontiff to visit a communist country when he visits his Polish homeland and is welcomed by cheering throngs.

Queen Elizabeth II at coronation ceremony

JUNE 3

1539 Hernando de Soto claims the peninsula now called Florida for the king of Spain.

1770 Gaspar de Portola and Father Junipero Serra officiate at the founding of the Mission San Carlos Borromeo de Carmelo (de Monterey), expanding the network of administrative centers and religious communities up the California coast.

1861 In the first land battle of the American Civil War, the Union Army defeats the Confederates at Philippi, West Virginia.

1875 French composer Georges Bizet dies at the age of 36, following a heart attack the previous evening. He believed his famous opera *Carmen* (the inspiration for the musical *Carmen Jones* which used Bizet's music) to be a total failure. Prima Donna Mme. Galli-Marié, performing the title role at the time the heart attack occurred, reported a vision of Bizet and a sudden pain in her chest.

1900 The International Ladies' Garment Workers Union is founded. From Jewish girls who labored in tenements on New York City's Lower East Side in the 19th century to Thai immigrants held in virtual slavery in Los Angeles, California, sweatshops a century later, women have held a dispropor-

"I wouldn't be caught dead marrying a woman old enough to be my wife."
—*Tony Curtis*

BORN ON THIS DAY

1761
HENRY SHRAPNEL
British army officer and inventor of the shrapnel shell

1771
REVEREND SYDNEY SMITH
English clergyman, essayist, and gourmet

1808
JEFFERSON DAVIS
President of the Confederate States of America (1861–65)

1832
CHARLES LE COCQ
French composer ("La Fille de Madame Angot"; "Le Coeur et la Main")

1864
RANSOM ELI OLDS
American automobile and truck manufacturer

1865
GEORGE V
King of England (1910–36)

1877
RAOUL DUFY
French painter

1906
JOSEPHINE BAKER
American-born dancer, singer, and Parisian night club owner

1925
TONY CURTIS
American actor (*Some Like It Hot*; *Operation Petticoat*; *The Great Race*)

1926
ALLEN GINSBERG
American Beat Generation poet (*Howl*; *Kaddish*; *The Sunflower Sutra*)

1942
CURTIS MAYFIELD
American singer/songwriter ("Gypsy Woman"; "People Get Ready")

1946
PENELOPE WILTON
English actress (*Cry Freedom*; *Carrington*; *Iris*)

1947
MICHAEL BURTON
American Olympic swimmer

1951
DENIECE WILLIAMS
American soul singer

Children working in the garment industry

tionate number of jobs in U.S. clothing manufacturing.

1918 The U.S. Supreme Court rules that child labor laws are unconstitutional.

1922 Norwegian explorer Roald Amundsen—who was the first to sail the Northwest Passage and was credited with discovery of the South Pole 10 years earlier—leaves Seattle, Washington, on an expedition that will include long periods of planned drift across the North Pole.

1923 Italian premier Benito Mussolini signs a bill allowing Italian women to vote in municipal elections.

1924 Austrian author Franz Kafka (*Metamorphosis*; *The Trial*) dies at the age of 40, never having seen his major works published.

1934 The Nazi government falls afoul of the Vatican, which reprimands it for encouraging cremation, a practice the Roman Catholic Church condemns as "pagan."

1935 The French ocean liner *Normandie* crosses the Atlantic in record time, less than four days, reclaiming the title from the German ship *Bremen* by traveling at an average speed of nearly 30 knots. By 1970, passengers on the Concorde supersonic airplane could make the same trip in less than five hours.

1937 The Duke of Windsor, former British king Edward VIII, marries American Wallis Warfield Simpson, whose divorce from her second husband is not yet finalized. The king had requested permission for a morganatic marriage, which would exclude his wife and potential heirs from some royal privilege and the line of accession, but he chose to abdicate the British throne when that request was not granted.

1938 The colorful paintings of the Fauves, a French term meaning "wild things," that identified an international modern art movement, as well as sculpture, books, and paintings by German Expressionists, are confiscated and destroyed as "degenerate" art by Nazi Germans. They felt that the art not only expressed a degraded

The Duke and Duchess of Windsor

sensibility, but had the power to corrupt the general populace.

1940 Two hundred planes of the German Reich strafe Paris during World War II, dropping 1,100 bombs on the capital.

1942 As its civilians and cultural centers are targeted by German bombs and its military casualties continue to mount during World War II, Great Britain announces its government will take over the nation's coal mines.

1946 Nearly a decade before Rosa Parks would refuse to relinquish her seat at the front of a Montgomery, Alabama, bus, the U.S. Supreme Court rules that segregation of public transportation is illegal.

1948 A 200-inch reflecting telescope named for George Ellery Hale, who was instrumental in its design but died before its fabrication was complete, is installed at Palomar Observatory, north of San Diego, California.

1949 The richest gold field in South Africa is discovered in the Orange Free State.

1960 The research plane *North American X-15A* is flown to a record height of 136,500 feet by Air Force major Robert White, who would push the same vehicle to a record speed of 4,093 miles per hour on November 9, 1961.

1975 Brazilian soccer legend Pelé signs to play with the New York Cosmos of the North American Soccer League. His three-year, $7 million contract is the most lucrative in pro sports to that time.

740 B.C. Chinese observers record the occurrence of a total solar eclipse.

1792 Captain George Vancouver claims Puget Sound for the British Crown.

1814 The Restoration monarchy is established in France. Its charter recognized the rights to liberty, equality, property, and freedom of religion—even though the state sponsored Catholicism.

1892 The Sierra Club is founded to "make the mountains glad," in the words of Scottish-born American environmentalist John Muir, who would serve as the organization's president until his death in 1914. Muir's identification with the Sierra Club, which now has 70,000 members, made it the dominant force in the grassroots American environmental movement. "He was a great factor in influencing the thought of California and the thought of the entire country," opined President Theodore Roosevelt, who worked with Muir to "secure the preservation of these great natural phenomena."

1912 Massachusetts passes the first minimum-wage law in the United States. By 1923, 14

John Muir

other states and the District of Columbia had followed suit.

1912 Fires in Constantinople, Turkey, destroy 1,000 buildings.

1914 Great Britain is paralyzed by strikes as mine and railroad unions join construction workers on picket lines.

1918 Just days after the first U.S. troops joined the Allies fighting World War I in Europe, the confrontation reaches American territory. The port of New York was closed after nine ships off the Atlantic coast were sunk by German U-boats, and German mines were discovered in Delaware Bay.

1919 The 19th Amendment to the U.S. Constitution, which grants American women the right to vote, passes the Senate 56–25 and is sent to the states for ratification.

1927 The United States defeats Great Britain to capture the first Ryder Cup. The event became a biennial competition between top golfers from the two countries. In 1979, the team from Great Britain was expanded to include golfers from across Europe.

1929 American inventor George Eastman, a major figure in developing the technology to make photography a popular medium, demonstrates a

> *"Taking joy in life is a woman's best cosmetic."*
>
> —Rosalind Russell

Technicolor movie at his studio in Rochester, New York.

1934 President Franklin D. Roosevelt asks the U.S. Congress to allocate $525 million to mitigate the effects of drought that is turning the nation's breadbasket into the Dust Bowl.

1939 The ocean liner SS *St. Louis,* which sailed from Europe with 900 Jewish refugees among its passengers, is denied permission to dock at Florida ports. After it was also turned away from Cuba, it returned to Europe; many of the Jewish passengers, whose plight was ignored by the United States, perished in Nazi war camps during World War II.

1942 The Japanese suffer heavy losses during the Battle of Midway Island, a turning point in the Pacific in World War II.

1945 Kobe, Japan, is firebombed during World War II. Between March, when tens of thousands were killed in the firebombing of Tokyo, and July, when air raids battered Japan, the war in the Pacific reached a horrific crescendo.

1953 During tests in the Nevada desert, the U.S. military detonates an atomic device with twice the power of the one dropped on Hiroshima, Japan, during World War II.

1965 The English rock group Rolling Stones release "Satisfaction," one of their most enduring hits.

1966 Growing opposition to U.S. involvement in the Vietnam War is expressed in a political ad, signed by 6,400 prominent Americans and published in the *New York Times.*

1972 Angela Davis, an African-American militant, is acquitted by an all-white jury in San Jose, California, on charges stemming from a 1970 shootout in a California courtroom. Her trial drew international attention because of the weakness of the prosecution's case and the obvious political nature of the proceedings.

1974 Media reports calculate that 250,000 people have been killed in Uganda since Idi Amin took power.

1980 Ice hockey's most accomplished player, Gordie Howe, retires as the sport's all-time leader in goals, assists, points, and games played. Howe was 52 when he finally hung up his skates. He had scored 801 goals in 1,767 games in 32 seasons for the Detroit Red Wings and Hartford Whalers.

Gordie Howe

1455 French poet François Villon fatally wounds a priest in a street battle and is banned from Paris.

1783 The Montgolfier brothers of France become the first men to make a successful ascent in a hot-air balloon. Ballooning was then a branch of aviation, not sport, but its spectator appeal and competitions for height and distance maintained interest in the field long after it had lost its technological standing.

1849 Denmark becomes a constitutional monarchy. On this day in 1953, it adopted a new constitution.

1862 The Treaty of Saigon grants France control of three southern provinces of Vietnam, or "Cochin China." The Treaty of Hué, signed June 6, 1884, brought the northern provinces, or "Tonkin," under French control. Ten days later the Treaty of Cambodia established French sovereignty in that part of Indochina, at least on paper.

1875 A quarter-century after gold was discovered in California, the Pacific Stock Exchange opens, linking the new states in the West with the nation's financial center on Wall Street in New York City.

> *"Virtue is more to be feared than vice, because its excesses are not subject to the regulation of conscience."*
>
> —*Adam Smith*

BORN ON THIS DAY

1723
ADAM SMITH
Scottish philosopher and author (*The Wealth of Nations*)

1798
ALEXEY FYODOROVICH L'VOV
Russian Composer

1819
JOHN COUCH ADAMS
English mathematician and astronomer who determined the existence of the planet Neptune

1883
JOHN MAYNARD KEYNES
English economist who gave his name to a branch of economics

1884
DAME IVY COMPTON BURNETT
English novelist (*Elders and Betters; Parents and Children*)

1887
RUTH BENEDICT
American anthropologist and author (*Patterns of Culture*)

1898
FEDERICO GARCÍA LORCA
Spanish poet and dramatist (*When Five Years Pass; The Gypsy Ballads; Poet in New York*)

1900
DENNIS GABOR
Hungarian inventor of holography and three-dimensional laser photography

1919
AKEO WATANABE
Japanese conductor

1932
CHRISTY BROWN
Irish author (*My Left Foot; Shadow on Summer; Background Music: Poems*)

1934
BILL MOYERS
American journalist, television show host, and cultural commentator

1939
MARGARET DRABBLE
English novelist and biographer (*A Natural Curiosity; The Witch of Exmoor*)

World War I poster

1917 The U.S. draft boards announce that 9.5 million American men have been registered to serve in the armed forces. President Woodrow Wilson's urgent appeal for 70,000 volunteers to help end World War I in Europe started the build-up of the armed forces, but the United States had to end its reliance on a volunteer corps and required men between ages 21 and 31 to register. Seventy-two percent of the American men who fought in the war were draftees.

1933 The United States abandons the gold standard, which backed its currency values with reserves of bullion, thereby reversing the policies that President Grover S. Cleveland had promised would rescue America from the severe economic depression of 1893. The gold standard had also dominated debate in the 1896 presidential campaign, in which William Jennings Bryan trounced William McKinley in oration ("Crucify this nation on a cross of gold") but lost the election.

1933 To protest the Nazi repression of modern artists,

---

which the Nazis branded as "degenerate," Italian musician Arturo Toscanini boycotts a German music festival where he had been scheduled to perform.

1940 As World War II increases demand for essential resources, tires molded from synthetic rubber are exhibited in Akron, Ohio, a cradle of the U.S. tire industry.

1944 Rome, the "Eternal City," is rescued from the Fascists during World War II. Although the city had little strategic significance, it was the first European capital to be liberated, and it emerged from its ordeal largely intact, in part because the retreating German Army ignored Adolf Hitler's orders to blow up bridges across the Tiber.

1947 U.S. secretary of state George C. Marshall outlines his plan to rebuild Europe in the aftermath of World War II.

1961 Laws that ban communist activity in the United States and require American workers to swear anticommunist oaths are legal, the Supreme Court opines.

1963 British Secretary of War John Profumo resigns after revelations that he lied to the House of Commons about his affair with alleged prostitute Christine Keeler.

1965 The U.S. State Department acknowledges for the first time that American troops are engaged in combat duty in Vietnam.

1967 The Six-Day War, which will change political boundaries and alliances in the Middle East, is initiated by Israel. The Israeli air raids, bombing airfields in Egypt, Syria, Jordan, and Iraq, destroyed 400 aircraft on the ground.

1972 The number of American men and women posted on combat duty in the Vietnam War is tallied at 63,700, the lowest number in the seven years since the government first acknowledged that U.S. troops served in this capacity.

1975 The Suez Canal in Egypt, which had been closed since the Six-Day War with Israel in 1967, reopens to international shipping.

1978 More than 100,000 political prisoners held in Chinese prisons since a crackdown in 1957 have been released, according to the current government.

1981 The U.S. Centers for Disease Control and Prevention announce that five gay men in Los Angeles have been diagnosed with a rare form of cancer. Later these were recognized as the first cases of Acquired Immune Deficiency Syndrome.

Israeli troops enter Gaza City

1523 The Swedish National Day commemorates the date in history when Gustavus I became the fledgling nation's first king.

1816 In the United States, New England experiences a 10-inch snowfall during the "year without summer," as weather patterns continue to be disrupted in the aftermath of the eruption of the Tamboura volcano, which occupies most of a small island just east of Bali. A series of volcanic eruptions from 1812 to 1815 threw off so much ash and sulfuric gas, which was carried in the stratosphere around the globe, that it blocked sunlight from penetrating to Earth.

1838 Little had gone well in the relationship between Europeans and Cherokees since Spanish explorer Hernando de Soto first encountered the tribe in 1540, but the forced emigration of the Cherokee to the "Indian Territory" (in present-day Oklahoma) was one of the more barbaric acts of cultural and territorial imperialism. Of the 800 Cherokee loaded onto boats in Tennessee in the first group to be shipped west, slightly more than half reached Fort Coffee three weeks later; many escaped en route, but extreme heat and drought that summer added to the horrible toll on the Cherokee.

1844 The Young Men's Christian Association is formed in London, England, under the leadership of George Williams. The movement was inspired by the poor social conditions of the time, caused by the growth of cities during the industrial revo-

"I only regret that I have but one life to lose for my country."

—Nathan Hale

lution. The first American YMCA was opened in Washington, D.C., in 1853. Williams was knighted by Queen Victoria in 1894.

1882 A cyclone hits Bombay, India, and drowns 108,000 people.

1882 Henry W. Seely registers a patent for an electric iron in New York.

1892 Benjamin Harrison becomes the first sitting U.S. president to attend a major-league baseball game. He watched the Washington Senators knock off the Cincinnati Reds in 11 innings. In 1910, William Howard Taft became the first president to throw out the first ball, a ceremony that traditionally kicks off the baseball season in April.

1896 Frank Samuelson and George Harpo leave New York to row across the Atlantic. They arrived in France fifty-four days later.

1908 France's National Assembly decrees that divorce will be automatically granted at the conclusion of a three-year separation.

1912 The largest 20th-century volcanic eruption alters the configuration of the Katmai Peninsula, the southwestern landmass on the Gulf of Alaska, dumping 33 cubic kilometers of tephra into the surrounding area.

✈ **1942** Japanese troops overcome two islands, Kiska and Attu, in the Aleutian chain, as their World War II assault in the Pacific reaches its height.

✈ **1944** During the D-Day invasion that helped end World War II in Europe, 150,000 troops from the Allied Expeditionary Forces storm the beaches of Normandy, France.

✈ **1944** U.S. planes resume bombing the Japanese mainland for the first time since 1942.

1963 Ayatollah Ruhollah Khomeini is among 30 Moslem religious leaders arrested after a riot in Tehran that was intended to topple the regime of Iranian shah Mohammed Reza Pahlavi.

1966 Racial tensions in the United States mount as

D-Day landing on the coast of France

James Meredith lying wounded

black activist James Meredith, leading a campaign for voter registration, is shot by a white sniper on a Mississippi highway five days after 2,400 people attended a conference on civil rights sponsored by President Lyndon B. Johnson, which was held at the White House.

1984 In attempting to seize control of the Golden Temple of Amritsar, a Sikh holy site in Punjab, Indian troops gun down more than 300 people in a bloody massacre.

MILESTONE

The Ashmolean Opens

The Ashmolean, the world's first university museum, opens in Oxford, England, on this day in 1683. At the time of the English Restoration, Oxford was the center of scientific activity in England. In 1677, English archaeologist Elias Ashmole donated his collection of curiosities to Oxford University, whose directors planned the construction of a building to display the items permanently. The displays were organized so that the university could use the collections for teaching purposes, and the museum was regularly opened to the public. It remains open to this day, free of charge, as Great Britain's oldest museum.

1494 As Spain and Portugal vie for dominance in sea exploration and rush to claim the lands they "discover," Pope Alexander VI grants Spain exclusive right to all lands south and west of a point 100 leagues west of the Azores. The Treaty of Tordesillas refined the line of demarcation and moved it 270 leagues farther west.

1576 Martin Frobisher sets sail on behalf of England, which lags far behind Portugal and Spain in exploring and establishing trade routes in a world whose horizons have been expanded by seafaring pioneers.

1654 Louis XIV, the "Sun King" who would create the magnificent palace at Versailles, is crowned in France.

1776 Richard Henry Lee of Virginia addresses the Continental Congress in Philadelphia, Pennsylvania, stating, "These United Colonies are and of right ought to be free and independent States." A committee of five was appointed to draft a declaration of independence, which was prepared by Thomas Jefferson and adopted less than a month later.

1864 Abraham Lincoln accepts his second nomination as U.S. Republican presidential candidate.

> *"We are each other's harvest; we are each other's business; we are each other's magnitude and bond."*
>
> —*Gwendolyn Brooks*

BORN ON THIS DAY

1502
POPE GREGORY XIII
Spanish pontiff who introduced the modern calendar

1761
JOHN RENNIE
Scottish engineer who designed London's Waterloo, Southwark, and London bridges

1778
GEORGE BRYAN "BEAU" BRUMMEL
English dandy

1825
RICHARD D. BLACKMORE
English author (*Lorna Doone*)

1848
PAUL GAUGUIN
French Post-Impressionist painter (*Vision After the Sermon; Where Do We Come From? Where Are We? Where Are We Going?*)

1893
J. B. MORTON
English humorist known as "Beachcomber"

1896
ROBERT MULLIKEN
Nobel Prize-winning American chemist and physicist

1909
VIRGINIA APGAR
American physician, developed the Apgar Score System method of evaluating newborns' need for medical care

1917
GWENDOLYN BROOKS
American Pulitzer Prize-winning poet (*Annie Allen; The Bean Eaters*)

1917
DEAN MARTIN
American singer, actor, and comedian (*The Dean Martin Show*)

1922
ROCKY GRAZIANO
American heavyweight boxer

1940
TOM JONES
Welsh singer ("It's Not Unusual"; "What's New Pussycat?")

1958
PRINCE
American singer/songwriter ("Little Red Corvette"; "Purple Rain"; "When Doves Cry")

Richard Henry Lee

1866 Chief Seattle, the Suquamish leader reputed to have given one of the great speeches on ecology, dies a century before that famous text would be penned by screenwriter Ted Perry. Chief Seattle had given a speech in 1854 before 1,000 tribal people gathered to meet the U.S. government's agent for Indian affairs, but he spoke in the Salish language and the only English record of its contents was made many years later. In 1855, Chief Seattle signed a treaty selling the area that now bears his name to the United States.

1887 The monotype machine, a breakthrough in typesetting that mechanizes creation of full-line printing templates, is patented by Tolbert Lanston in Washington, D.C.

1905 Norway and Sweden dissolve the political union that had linked their fates since 1814.

1913 Hudson Stuck, a longtime Episcopalian missionary in Alaska, plants the American flag at the summit of Mount McKinley. His was judged the first credible claim to scale the highest point, at 20,500 feet, on the American continent, in part because he was recognized as an accomplished mountaineer who had climbed in the highest peaks of the Alps and Rockies.

1914 The first ship passes through the locks on the Panama Canal.

1922 A British expedition reaches 26,800 feet on Mount Everest, the highest altitude recorded to date.

1926 At his death, Catalan architect Antoni Gaudí leaves Barcelona's landmark cathedral, La Sagrada Familia, unfinished.

1929 The Vatican, the seat of Roman Catholicism, which had long had a troubled relationship with its host country, Italy, is granted sovereignty when the Lateran Treaty takes effect.

1930 Gallant Fox wins the U.S. horse race the Belmont Stakes in New York, following victories in the Kentucky Derby and the Preakness. Sportswriter Charles Halton coined the phrase

Israeli soldiers celebrate at the wailing wall

"Triple Crown" to describe the feat, previously accomplished only once, by Sir Barton in 1919.

1930 The trendsetting newspaper *The New York Times* begins to capitalize the word "Negro" when it appears in its pages.

1939 King George VI and Queen Elizabeth become the first reigning British monarchs to visit England's former colonies, the United States.

1955 *$64,000 Question* premieres on American television, giving a new phrase to the English language.

1965 The U.S. Supreme Court removes restrictions on prescribing and selling birth control pills, which had been approved by the FDA five years earlier.

1966 Ronald W. Reagan makes the transition from Hollywood stardom to politics by winning the Republican nomination for governor of California.

1967 Israeli troops occupy Old Jerusalem during the Six-Day War.

1980 Bjorn Borg of Sweden becomes the first man to win six French Open tennis titles.

1997 In the United States, a report issued by the National Institutes of Health links diet and consumption of specific foods to many kinds of cancer.

1999 Indonesia's first democratic election in 44 years includes candidates from 40 political parties.

632 Muhammad ibn Abdallah, who was born in Mecca about 570 and founded the religion of Islam, dies after making a farewell pilgrimage from Medina to Mecca. Muhammad became the prophet of Allah, the supreme and sole deity of the faith, who conveyed the divine scripture that was later collected in the Koran ("recitations").

1374 English author Geoffrey Chaucer is appointed Comptroller of Customs and Subsidy of Wools. His salary of 10 pounds per year permitted him to write *The Canterbury Tales,* an unfinished, often bawdy, poem of 17,000 lines in which pilgrims tell tales of 14th-century life.

1405 The Archbishop of York, Richard Scrope, is beheaded for his siding with the Earl of Northumberland in a rebellion against King Henry IV. Scrope was the first British bishop to be executed.

1783 The Lakagigar volcano in southern Iceland begins an eight-month eruption that would cover 220 square miles in lava. Deaths attributed to the eruption total 9,350, some from famine that followed the spread of a deadly blue haze over the island (and much of Europe and parts of Asia), destroying crops and causing livestock to starve.

1865 Sir Joseph Paxton, the English architect and engi-

> *"The truth is more important than the facts."*
>
> —Frank Lloyd Wright

The Jungle by Upton Sinclair

neer who designed the Great Exhibition's "Crystal Palace," dies at the age of 64. On the same day in 1882, another British engineer who pioneered the use of iron structures dies: John Scott Russell, the Scottish designer of the first fully ironclad battleship.

1906 Following publication of American author Upton Sinclair's novel *The Jungle,* which described unsanitary conditions in meatpacking plants in Chicago, Illinois, the government requires inspection of such manufacturing facilities.

1912 Carl Laemmle founds Universal Studios, the first major producer of motion pictures in the United States.

1918 Nova Aquila, which is called the brightest nova since Kepler's of 1604, is discovered by Portuguese astronomer Alfredo Pereira.

1920 Italians riot when the price of bread, regulated by the government, is raised.

1927 Oliver Lodge, a professor at Oxford University in England, asserts that biologists will one day be able to manufacture synthetic protoplasm with which to control and humanely manage the future evolution of human life.

1928 Australian aviator Sir Charles Kingford Smith pilots the first flight over the Pacific.

1929 Great Britain gains its first ever woman cabinet minister when Prime Minister Ramsay MacDonald appoints Margaret Bondfield as Minister of Labour.

1934 U.S. president Franklin D. Roosevelt outlines his New Deal objectives: providing security for home ownership, jobs, and a financial cushion for old age.

1942 U.S. general Dwight D. Eisenhower is appointed commander of the European theater of war operations during World War II.

1966 The six-year-old American Football League

agrees to merge with the long-established National Football League beginning with the 1970 season. The merger also set up an annual championship game that would become known as the Super Bowl.

1973 After single-handedly ruling Spain for 34 years, Generalissimo Francisco Franco appoints a president, Admiral Luis Blanco, but his totalitarian system of government would still isolate the major portion of the Iberian Peninsula.

1996 China detonates a nuclear device underground, three weeks before a comprehensive test ban treaty would come into effect.

2002 American tennis player Serena Williams defeats her sister Venus in the final of the French Open, earning her second Grand Slam tournament title. The Williams sisters ended the season ranked numbers one and two in the world, a tennis first for sisters.

Serena Williams, right, and sister Venus at the French Open finals

> *"Most gentlemen don't like love; they just like to kick it around."*
>
> —Cole Porter

68 Nero, emperor of Rome, commits suicide.

1534 Jacques Cartier, supported by François Premier, the king who brought the Italian Renaissance to France, sails into the Saint Lawrence River, establishing a benchmark of French interests in North America.

1822 The first patent for false teeth is registered in the United States by Charles Graham.

1869 Charles Hires sells root beer, a soda with a distinctive woody taste, for the first time in Philadelphia, Pennsylvania.

1898 China leases Hong Kong's New Territories to Great Britain for 99 years in a treaty that stipulates that the former Crown Colony of Hong Kong will revert to Chinese ownership at its conclusion.

1899 American boxer James J. Jeffries wins the world heavyweight boxing title, defeating Bob Fitzsimmons. Jeffries outweighed Fitzsimmons 206 pounds to 167, but Fitzsimmons had been successful in earlier fights against bigger men. The heavyweight division in those days was as low as 150 pounds; today, heavyweights must weigh at least 191 pounds.

1901 The New York Giants rap out thirty-one hits in a victory over the Cincinnati Reds. It is the second-most hits ever by one team in a game, two short of the current record set in 1932 by the Cleveland Indians.

1920 The latest U.S. census ranks New York the nation's largest city with 5.6 million residents, followed by Chicago, Illinois, and Philadelphia, Pennsylvania. For the first time, the population of Los Angeles, California, surpasses that of San Francisco.

1934 *The Thin Man*, a film based on the novel by American author Dashiell Hammett, debuts in New York.

1940 Norway surrenders to Germany during World War II.

1947 The Missouri River rises above its banks, initiating flooding in Missouri, Illinois, and Iowa. By the end of the month, when the Mississippi River reached its highest recorded crest in St. Louis, midwestern farmlands had suffered damage estimated at $160 million.

1951 The last groups of Nazis convicted of war crimes during World War II are hanged at Nuremberg, Germany.

1966 Martin Luther King, Jr. spearheads the effort to continue registering Mississippi voters, which was the focus of James Meredith's activities when he was gunned down by a sniper's bullet a few days earlier.

James J. Jeffries

Crown Prince Naruhito and Masako Owada

1969 The vaccine to prevent rubella ("German measles") is licensed in the United States.

1978 American boxer Larry Holmes wins the World Boxing Council heavyweight championship with a 15-round split decision over Ken Norton in Las Vegas, Nevada. Several international organizations now name "world" champions. In recent years, some boxers have "unified" these titles, that is, been named champion by several organizations; however, occasionally there are several "world" title holders at one time.

1978 The Church of Jesus Christ of Latter-day Saints, or the Mormon faith, which then claimed 4.2 million members, reverses a 148-year-old policy that excluded African-American men from its priesthood.

1983 British prime minister Margaret Thatcher leads her Conservative Party to a landslide victory, ensuring her another five-year term. Thatcher's popularity had been in serious decline until the Falklands conflict of 1982, but the victory there, combined with the poor media image of the Labour opposition, gave the Conservatives the biggest Commons majority in 37 years.

1988 Korean students demanding reunification of the two Koreas and withdrawal of American troops take to the streets in such numbers that 60,000 policemen armed with tear gas are dispatched to regain control of Seoul.

1991 A U.N. weapons-inspection team charged with overseeing the destruction of nonconventional weapons arrives in Baghdad, Iraq.

1993 Japanese crown prince Naruhito, 33, weds Harvard-educated Masako Owada, 29, in formal ceremonies whose traditions have evolved over a millennium.

1610 Dutch settlers from New Jersey cross the Hudson River to form the first European settlement on Manhattan Island.

1719 The battle of Glenshiel in Scotland puts an end to the second rebellion aimed at putting James Francis Edward Stuart, the "Old Pretender," on the throne. Government ships had destroyed the Jacobite supply base at Eilean Donan Castle, and with Spanish support hampered by bad weather, the rebellion melted away.

1752 American inventor Benjamin Franklin's kite is struck by lightning, leading him to develop theories of electricity.

1791 The British Parliament passes the Canada Act, which divides the country at the Ottawa River into Upper Canada (chiefly British) and Lower Canada (predominantly French). Those of French ethnic heritage formed the largest segment of the Canadian population, then estimated at 140,000 of French descent, 110,000 British, 50,000 native peoples in settled areas, and less than 10,000 people of African descent.

1829 The first Oxford and Cambridge boat race, which would become an annual sporting event from 1856, is won by Oxford in 14 minutes, 30 seconds. The race was run on the Thames from Hambledon lock

"Be a first-rate version of yourself, not a second-rate version of somebody else."

—*Judy Garland*

BORN ON THIS DAY

1688
JAMES EDWARD STUART
Son of British king James II, the "Old Pretender" who led a rebellion to restore the Catholic succession in 1715

1819
GUSTAVE COURBET
French Realist painter (*Self-portrait at Ste. Hagie; The Sleepers; The Burial at Ornans*)

Gustave Courbet

1895
HATTIE MCDANIEL
Singer and actress (*Judge Priest; Gone with the Wind*) who was the first African American to win an Academy Award

1904
FREDERICK LOEWE
German-born American composer who collaborated with Jay Lerner (*Brigadoon; Paint Your Wagon; My Fair Lady*)

1911
TERENCE RATTIGAN
English playwright (*The Winslow Boy; The Browning Version; The Deep Blue Sea*)

1914
SAUL BELLOW
Pulitzer and Nobel Prize-winning Canadian author (*Herzog; Humboldt's Gift*)

1921
PRINCE PHILIP MOUNTBATTEN
Duke of Edinburgh, husband of Elizabeth II

1922
JUDY GARLAND
American singer and actress (*The Wizard of Oz; Meet Me in St. Louis; Judgment at Nuremburg*)

1923
ROBERT MAXWELL
British newspaper publisher who stole from pension funds and died at sea under mysterious circumstances in 1991

Joseph Conrad

to Henley Bridge. The first race on the modern course, from Putney Bridge to Mortlake in London, was run in 1845.

1848 The first telegraphic link between New York City and Chicago, Illinois, is made functional.

1865 German composer Richard Wagner's opera *Tristan und Isolde* premieres in Munich.

1869 The first shipment of frozen beef is unloaded at the harbor in New Orleans, Louisiana.

1878 Polish-born Joseph Conrad arrives in England as a deck hand on the Polish freighter *Mavis* and steps ashore at Lowestoft, knowing little of the English language. Before the turn of the century he had written one of the great books of English literature, *Heart of Darkness*, which was followed the next year by *Lord Jim*.

1909 A Cunard Line ship wrecked off the Azores, the S.S. *Slavonia*, sends an SOS by Morse Code, the first civilian emergency use of this signal.

1911 China estimates its population at 451 million.

1925 Tennessee schools adopt a biology textbook that denies the theory of evolution.

1934 Italian dictator Benito Mussolini is in the stands to watch host nation Italy defeat Czechoslovakia in the second competition of soccer's quadrennial World Cup championship.

1935 Alcoholics Anonymous, a 12-step program of self-monitoring and group support to overcome dependence on alcohol, is formed in New York.

1940 Italy joins World War II on the side of the Germans, declaring war on France and Great Britain.

1944 The French town of Oradour-sur-Glane is destroyed by SS troops, perhaps in reprisal for the killing of an SS officer. The men of the town were shot, while women and children were locked into the church, which was set on fire. Only 7 of the 700-plus inhabitants survived, and the town has been left in ruins as a memorial.

1948 American test pilot Chuck Yeager exceeds the speed of sound, flying over the Southern California desert in a Bell XS-1 plane.

1955 Taiwan welcomes American air bases, which will be used to provide surveillance of "communist China."

1956 Although the Summer Olympics won't get underway until October in Melbourne, the equestrian competition begins in Stockholm, Sweden. A horse quarantine forced the events to be moved out of Australia.

1963 In a speech at American University, President John F. Kennedy vows to "make the world safe for diversity," beginning the process of détente with the Communist bloc.

1963 A Buddhist monk, Quang Duc, sets fire to himself in the center of Saigon to protest the South Vietnamese government's treatment of Buddhists, focusing attention worldwide on the conflict in Vietnam.

1967 A U.N.-brokered cease-fire ends the Six-Day War between Arabs and Israelis, in which Israel took control of Arab territories many times the size of the nation itself. Although the war was brief, casualties were estimated at 100,000.

1990 The Civic Forum, headed by dissident writer Vaclav Havel, wins the first free election in Czechoslovakia in 40 years.

Communist memorial removed from Czechoslovakia with free elections

1488 King James III of Scotland is stabbed to death by a nobleman disguised as a priest. The killing followed the Battle of Sauchieburn between the unpopular king and his son, who became King James IV.

1495 The second voyage of Italian-born Spanish explorer Christopher Columbus, which entailed 17 caravels and 1,500 men to establish settlements in the lands he had visited on his first voyage, returns to Spain after a nearly two-year journey.

1509 King Henry VIII of Britain takes Catherine of Aragon, widow of his brother, as his first of six brides.

1644 A letter of this date, written by Italian scientist Evangelista Torricelli, describes his invention of the barometer.

1770 One of the most successful of a generation of British navigators, Captain James Cook sails to the South Pacific to observe the Transit of Venus. He then explored New Zealand and Australia before running aground on Australia's Great Barrier Reef.

1859 The Comstock silver lode is discovered in Nevada.

1895 Charles A. Duryea is granted the first U.S. patent for a gas-powered automobile.

1919 The powerful horse Sir Barton captures the U.S. horse race the Belmont Stakes,

> **"Fatigue makes cowards of us all."**
> —Vince Lombardi

M I L E S T O N E

The Quest for the Northwest Passage

This day marks two significant events in the search for a northwest passage between the Atlantic and Pacific oceans. In 1517, the first British expedition to find a route brings Sir Thomas Pert to Hudson Bay. Much later, in 1845, perhaps the most famous expedition set sail under the command of Sir John Franklin. His ships HMS *Terror* and HMS *Erebus* were last seen by a fishing vessel off the coast of Baffin Island. The fate of the expedition captured the public imagination, and several missions were sent to discover their fate and bring back any survivors. When public interest—and government funds—waned, Lady Jane Franklin funded an expedition that set out in 1858 to find her husband. On King William Island, a note was found in a stone cairn, saying that Sir John had died on June 11th, 1847. No survivors were ever found.

---

becoming the first horse to win the Kentucky Derby, Preakness Stakes, and Belmont Stakes in one year. The feat would later be called the Triple Crown.

1927 American aviator Charles Lindbergh is welcomed as a hero in Washington, D.C.; in his speech he cites the need to develop airports.

1939 The U.S. polo team defeats Great Britain for the 25th year in a row in the International Cup competition.

1943 U.S. president Franklin D. Roosevelt asks the Italians to overthrow dictator Benito Mussolini on the same day that the island of Pantelleria, the last Axis position in the Sicilian Strait, yields to the Allies in World War II.

1948 World War II ordnance continues to claim victims as 150 people are killed when the Danish steamer *Kobenhavn* hits a mine in the North Sea and sinks.

1950 American golfer Ben Hogan caps a remarkable comeback from a devastating auto accident to capture his second consecutive U.S. Open title.

U.S. president Calvin Coolidge welcomes Charles A. Lindbergh in Washington, D.C.

Ben Hogan

Doctors had thought Hogan would not walk again, let alone play golf, but he proved them wrong and battled back to the course to continue one of golf's greatest careers.

1959 The U.S. postmaster general bans importation of English author D. H. Lawrence's novel *Lady Chatterley's Lover*. It still reached bookshelves in the United States, however, being printed by Grove Press. A district court later ruled it not obscene.

1963 Lines are drawn in the defining struggles for civil rights in America. Martin Luther King, Jr. is arrested for attempting to integrate restaurants in Florida; Governor George Wallace tries to thwart the registration of African-American students at the University of Alabama; and in a speech, President John F. Kennedy brands segregation as morally wrong, concluding, "It is time to act."

1968 The massive shield volcano on Fernandina Island in the Galápagos spews out enough lava in its eruption that the caldera floor drops more than 1,000 feet when it is over. Few people lived on these islands 600 miles off the coast of Ecuador, but their diversity of plant and animal life caused Darwin to ponder the origins of species when he visited them in 1835.

1979 John Wayne, the star of *Stagecoach, True Grit, Rooster Cogburn,* and dozens more western films, dies of cancer at the age of 72.

1985 Karen Ann Quinlan, who had been comatose but was breathing with life-support systems, dies at age 31. Her plight galvanized the right-to-die movement, which seeks to limit medical intervention and honor wishes expressed by individuals before they become mortally ill or incapacitated.

1986 The U.S. Supreme Court upholds the 1973 decision in *Roe v. Wade* that legalized abortion.

2001 Timothy McVeigh, who was convicted of unapologetically masterminding the bombing of the Oklahoma City federal building in 1995, is executed by lethal injection at the prison in Terre Haute, Indiana.

Death-penalty protester at McVeigh execution

1665 When, after more than a half-century on Manhattan, Dutch settlers abandon their village of New Amsterdam, English colonists quickly rename the settlement New York.

1776 The American colony of Virginia adopts a Declaration of Rights. Beginning with the assertion "That all men are by nature equally free and independent," it later formed the basis for part of the Declaration of Independence and the U.S. Bill of Rights.

1792 English captain George Vancouver circumnavigates the island that marks the entrance to Puget Sound and today bears his name, while sailing along the northern Pacific Coast of the American continent. Passage of the Canada Act six months earlier had granted Great Britain hegemony in northern regions and France authority in the

---

MILESTONE

Philippine Independence Declared

During the Spanish-American War, Filipino rebels led by Emilio Aguinaldo proclaim the independence of the Philippines after 300 years of Spanish rule on this day in 1898. By mid-August, Filipino rebels and U.S. troops had ousted the Spanish, but Aguinaldo's hopes for independence were dashed when the United States formally annexed the Philippines as part of its peace treaty with Spain. In 1935, the Commonwealth of the Philippines was established with U.S. approval, and Manuel Quezon was elected the country's first president. On July 4, 1946, the United States granted full independence to the Republic of the Philippines.

> *We all live with the objective of being happy; our lives are all different and yet the same."*
>
> —Anne Frank

south. A Spanish expedition had beat Vancouver to the Northwest, but it abandoned its claims to the region in a treaty in 1790.

1867 The Austro-Hungarian Empire forms. It recognized two independent states joined by a common monarch and granted legal equality to Jews within the domain.

1897 A magnitude 8.7 earthquake, one of the most severe events ever recorded, strikes Assam, India, causing devastation of 9,000 square miles of the subcontinent.

1909 Japanese workers who walked off their jobs at

Queensboro Bridge, Roosevelt Island, New York

Hawaiian sugar plantations are charged with inciting disorder.

1909 The Queensboro Bridge, linking the boroughs of Manhattan and Queens in New York City, opens.

1925 With a $600,000 gift from the Rockefellers, The Metropolitan Museum of Art in New York City acquires the complex of European architectural fragments known as the Cloisters, in which its medieval holdings will be displayed.

1928 In a precursor of the Wall Street Crash of 1929, five million shares are traded on the New York Stock Exchange as values plummet.

1931 American gangster Al Capone, who recently spent a year in prison on weapons charges, is arrested with 68 of his mob for breaking Prohibition laws.

1938 Dikes on the Yellow River burst, killing 150,000 Chinese in the ensuing floods.

1942 Russia and Japan agree to extend most-favored-nation status to each other; the Japanese value the first year's trade at 30 million yen.

1944 The dreaded V-1 pilotless "flying bomb," which the Germans have been developing during World War II, makes its first appearance over London, England. Nicknamed the "Doodlebug"

Babe Didrikson Zaharias

by the British, the deadly device, which carried a ton of explosives and flew at 370 miles per hour, killed more than 2,500 Londoners by the month's end.

1947 Golfer Babe Didrikson Zaharias becomes the first American to win the British Amateur Ladies' Championship. Along with her prowess on the links, Zaharias won Olympic gold in track (in 1932) and was considered by most experts to be the greatest female athlete of all time.

1955 A horrific crash during the LeMans endurance auto race in France spews fiery debris into the stands, killing 82 spectators and injuring another 78.

1964 Nelson Mandela is sentenced to life imprisonment by the South African government, which is attempting to retain privileges granted whites under the apartheid system.

1964 The popularity of the English rock group The Beatles has spread worldwide: 300,000 fans greet them on their arrival at Adelaide Airport in Australia.

1978 David Berkowitz, who as the self-proclaimed Son of Sam terrorized New Yorkers one summer with sniper attacks on young lovers in cars, is sentenced to 25 years to life for each of six counts of murder.

Marquis de Lafayette

1744 Rhode Island becomes the first colony to ban trafficking in human beings within its borders, ending its importation of slaves.

1777 Marquis Marie Joseph de Lafayette, who served as the French government's on-site liaison for its secret support of American revolutionary efforts, arrives in New York. Six months later, France's role was formalized by the signature of treaties of commerce and alliance.

1804 Meriwether Lewis and William Clark, who at the behest of U.S. president Thomas Jefferson set out on an 8,000-mile round-trip journey from St. Louis, Missouri, to the Pacific, encounter massive waterfalls on the Missouri River that force them to carry their boats and equipment 18 miles overland. Detouring around that site, now known as Great Falls, Montana, took the expedition a month, but such surprises were routine in venturing into unexplored wilderness.

1837 Just as the first colonists left Great Britain seek-

BORN ON THIS DAY

40
GNAEUS JULIUS AGRICOLA
Roman general who conquered Wales and Northern England

1752
FANNY BURNEY
English novelist (*Evelina; The Wanderer*) and playwright (*A Busy Day; The Woman Hater*)

1865
WILLIAM BUTLER YEATS
Irish poet and dramatist (*The Lake Isle of Innisfree; Lapis Lazuli; Easter, 1916*)

1881
LOIS WEBER
First American female film director (*The Heiress; It's No Laughing Matter; White Heat*)

1888
ELISABETH SCHUMANN
German soprano

1892
BASIL RATHBONE
South African-born English actor (*Tower of London; Sherlock Holmes and the Secret Weapon*)

1893
DOROTHY L. SAYERS
English novelist and creator of the detective Lord Peter Wimsey (*The Nine Taylors; Gaudy Night*)

1913
RALPH EDWARDS
American television personality (*This Is Your Life*)

1915
JOHN DONALD BUDGE
American tennis player, the first person to hold all four major championship titles at the same time

1935
CHRISTO
Bulgarian artist (*Valley Curtain; Running Fence; Wrapped Reichstag*)

1943
MALCOLM MCDOWELL
English actor (*A Clockwork Orange; Tank Girl*)

1949
J. P. BORDELEAU
Canadian professional hockey player

---

ing freedom to practice the religion of their choice, missionaries for the Mormon church, one of the religions developed in America, leave Kirtland, Ohio, to proselytize in England.

1888 The U.S. Congress creates the Department of Labor.

1909 Lieutenant Ernest Shackelton arrives back in London, England, after a two-year Antarctic expedition that reached the south magnetic pole and surpassed the records set by his fellow countryman Robert F. Scott in 1902–04. Roald Amundsen would place the Norwegian flag on the South Pole in December 1911. Scott would reach the same location a month later, but his entire party would perish in the mission.

1917 The first U.S. troops to be sent to the European front in World War II leave New York harbor.

1929 Florenz Ziegfield signs a contract with MGM Studios to produce American movie musicals.

1935 American boxer James Braddock defeats Max Baer to win the world heavyweight boxing championship.

1941 The Petain government of France, which is headquartered in Vichy because

---

"Baseball changes through the years. It gets milder."

—Babe Ruth

Babe Ruth at Yankee stadium

German soldiers have claimed possession of Paris during World War II, announces that 12,000 Jews in France have been sent to concentration camps for hindering French-German cooperation.

1946 For the first time, a transcontinental round-trip flight is completed in one day, from California to Maryland and back.

1948 Just months before his death from throat cancer, the great American baseball star Babe Ruth says good-bye to fans in an emotional ceremony at Yankee Stadium in New York City.

1949 The University of California, which has become an equalizing platform for success among the state's many racial, social, and political groups, establishes a policy requiring all faculty to sign oaths asserting that they do not ascribe to communist ideals or the Communist Party.

1950 South Africa's White Assembly, representing only 20 percent of the country's population, votes to establish segregated districts for blacks and whites, which becomes the legal basis of apartheid.

 1957 A replica of the *Mayflower* duplicates the original ocean crossing from England in a 54-day sail to Plymouth, Massachusetts.

1958 China's first atomic reactor begins operating.

1966 The U.S. Supreme Court issues its "Miranda" ruling, which requires police making an arrest to inform a suspect of his rights—to have a lawyer present during questioning, to remain silent, and to otherwise not incriminate himself.

1971 François Mitterand is named head of the French Socialist Party, a position that would carry him to the country's presidency within 10 years.

1971 The *New York Times* begins publishing the Pentagon Papers, a confidential report on U.S. involvement in Vietnam, which had been leaked to the press by Daniel Ellsberg.

1983 The U.S. spacecraft *Pioneer 10,* which had traveled in space for 11 years, becomes the first man-made object to leave the solar system.

Illustration of Pioneer 10 in orbit

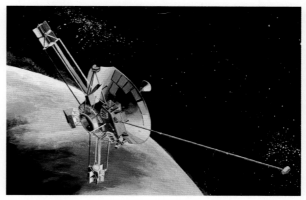

Betsy Ross sewing U.S. flag and George Washington standing alongside

1642 The first compulsory education law is passed by the Massachusetts Bay Colony.

1662 After the restoration of the English monarchy, Sir Harry Vane, a Parliamentary leader during the Civil War, is beheaded for treason.

1775 The Army of the United States is founded, as colonists prepare to take up arms against Great Britain. The next day, George Washington was appointed the army's commander in chief.

1777 The Continental Congress adopts the Stars and Stripes as the national flag of the fledgling United States, to replace the British Grand Union flag. This date becomes Flag Day on modern American calendars.

1834 Isaac Fischer Jr., a handyman in Springfield, Vermont, receives a patent for sandpaper.

1846 A group of settlers in Sonoma proclaim the State of California, hoisting a flag with a brown bear, four years before California joined the United States. The bear, which symbolized the fierce independence of

MILESTONE

Defeat for the Royalists at Naseby

In one of the key battles of the English Civil War, Oliver Cromwell's New Model Army decisively defeats the Royalists under Charles I and Prince Rupert of the Rhine at Naseby in Northamptonshire. The New Model Army had been created by Parliament at the end of the previous year, and this was their first major engagement. The New Model Army was the first British force to wear red coats, a part of the uniform that remains in ceremonial use to this day. The crushing defeat of the Royalists marked the end of the first stage of the Civil War, and was an important step toward Cromwell's ultimate victory.

Oliver Cromwell

settlers who would also stand their ground, was retained on the official state flag, which also features the Sierra Nevada, center of the gold rush that had been California's impetus to statehood.

1881 John McTamanny Jr. of Cambridge, Massachesetts, produces a mechanical system that will play prerecorded songs and is granted a patent for the player piano.

1900 The Hawaiian Republic becomes the U.S. Territory of Hawaii.

1901 A boat rams and sinks a Staten Island ferry. The disaster caused five fatalities and enough public uproar that New York City demanded to take over the boat link, creating the Municipal Ferries, which today transport 70,000 people daily.

1909 Dr. Anna Shaw of New York issues a call for suffragettes to form an alliance. This more militant phase in the push to extend the franchise to women in the United States will yield success in 1920 with ratification of the 19th Amendment to the U.S. Constitution.

1917 General John Pershing and his staff arrive in Paris, France, to set up U.S. headquarters for World War I.

1922 Warren G. Harding becomes the first U.S. president

> *"Silence is argument carried out by other means."*
>
> —Ernesto (Che) Guevara

General Pershing, third from right, on his arrival at the railroad station in Paris, France

to be heard on radio when his speech dedicating the Francis Scott Key memorial is broadcast in Baltimore, Maryland.

1941 To ensure that U.S. financial institutions are not inadvertently aiding the Axis powers during World War II, President Franklin D. Roosevelt orders all Italian and German assets to be frozen.

1943 The Supreme Court rules that it is unconstitutional for state or municipal governments to require schoolchildren to recite the pledge of allegiance to the American flag if so doing conflicts with their religious beliefs.

1954 Over spirited public objections, U.S. president Dwight D. Eisenhower signs a bill adding the words "under God" to the pledge of allegiance.

1972 The U.S. Environmental Protection Agency bans the use of the insecticide DDT, which had been implicated in polluting the water table and endangering many species.

1982 Argentina surrenders to Great Britain, ending the war over the Falkland Islands.

1982 Israeli tanks cut off Muslim West Beirut, trapping leaders of the Palestinian Liberation Organization.

1983 Repeated demonstrations against President Augusto Pinochet draw 100,000 Chileans to the streets as citizens protest against his government. Pinochet clung to power until 1988.

President of Chile, Augusto Pinochet

763 B.C. Assyrians, the native people of today's Iran, record on a clay tablet the occurrence of a total solar eclipse.

1300 Dante Alighieri becomes prior of Florence, one of six members of the Italian city's governing board. He is remembered not for his short tenure in that position, but for writing *The Divine Comedy*.

1381 In England, the Peasants' Revolt, which had seemed on the verge of success, is crushed when William Walworth, the Mayor of London, attacks its leader Wat Tyler, who is beheaded soon afterward.

1520 Pope Leo X threatens to excommunicate Martin Luther, the Augustinian friar who in 1517 launched the Protestant Reformation, which challenged the exclusive authority of the Roman Catholic Church to define doctrines and practices.

1775 George Washington is appointed commander of the armed forces of the rebellious American colonies. Native Americans,

Pope Leo X, center

BORN ON THIS DAY

1330
EDWARD THE BLACK PRINCE
Prince of Wales (1343–76)

1789
JOSIAH HENSON
African-American escaped slave and preacher, held to be the model for Uncle Tom in *Uncle Tom's Cabin*

1815
HABLOT KNIGHT BROWNE
English illustrator of stories by Charles Dickens under the pen-name "Phiz"

1843
EDVARD GRIEG
Norse composer ("Peer Gynt Suites"; "The Hall of the Mountain King"; "Mountain Song Piano Concerto")

1894
ROBERT RUSSELL BENNETT
American composer ("Abraham Lincoln Symphony") and arranger (*Oklahoma!*)

1914
YURI ANDROPOV
Soviet leader (1983–84)

1932
MARIO CUOMO
Governor of New York (1983–95)

1937
WAYLON JENNINGS
American country singer ("Luckenbach, Texas"; "Are You Sure Hank Done It Thisaway"; "Ain't Livin' Long Like This")

1954
JIM BELUSHI
American comedian and actor (*The Principal*; *K-9*)

1958
WADE BOGGS
American professional baseball player

1963
HELEN HUNT
Academy Award-winning American actress (*Mad About You*; *As Good as It Gets*; *Cast Away*)

1964
COURTNEY COX
American actress (*Friends*; *Ace Ventura: Pet Detective*; *Scream*)

who feared further incursions of the settlers into their lands, generally sided with the British in the American Revolutionary War.

1785 Two French balloonists die in the world's first fatal aviation accident.

1804 The 12th Amendment to the U.S. Constitution, which deals with the manner of electing the president, is ratified.

1846 The Oregon Treaty is signed by the United States and Great Britain, establishing the 49th parallel as the U.S. boundary with what is now Canada. American farmers settled in the Willamette Valley to the south, and itinerant British fur traders hunted in the northern wilderness.

1864 Arlington National Cemetery in Virginia, which would become the final resting place of many who fought in America's wars, is created to receive the remains of those who perished in the American Civil War.

1896 A tsunami wave rolls over a Shinto festival at Sanriku, Japan, leaving 27,000 dead and 9,000 injured.

1900 Polish-born pianist Ignace Paderewski, who attained the pinnacle of his fame before American audiences, donates $10,000 to establish an annual fund for an

> *"You campaign in poetry. You govern in prose."*
>
> —*Mario Cuomo*

outstanding original work by an American composer.

1919 Sixteen hours and 27 minutes after leaving Newfoundland, Captain John Alcock and Lieutenant Arthur Whitten-Brown land at Clifden in Ireland, becoming the first people to fly nonstop across the Atlantic. Their plane was a modified Vickers Vimy World War I bomber.

1934 Great Smoky Mountain National Park, which consists of 800 square miles of land that contains more types of trees than all the forests of Europe combined, is dedicated. Logging and pulpwood companies owned 85 percent of this forest by the 1920s, when the U.S. government began acquiring it for preservation.

1940 Having marched into Paris, the Nazi Germans now capture Le Havre (a major port on the English Channel), the fortress at Verdun, and assault the Maginot Line during World War II.

1944 The first World War II test raids by U.S. B-29 Superfortress bombers on Japanese urban areas are con-

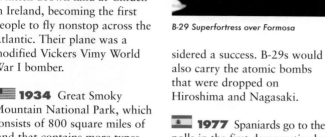
B-29 Superfortress over Formosa

sidered a success. B-29s would also carry the atomic bombs that were dropped on Hiroshima and Nagasaki.

1977 Spaniards go to the polls in the first democratic elections there since 1936, electing a Democratic Center Coalition government under Adolfo Suarez.

1980 American golfer Jack Nicklaus wins his fourth U.S. Open championship, setting a record with a score of 272.

1991 After a 600-year dormancy, Mount Pinatubo erupts, covering the Philippines in ash and sending a cloud of dust across the Pacific.

Filipino tribesmen in the ash from erupting Mount Pinatubo

JUNE 16

1487 The bid by Lambert Simnel to take the throne of England from Henry VII ends at the Battle of Stoke in Nottinghamshire. Simnel had claimed that he was the lawful successor to Richard III.

1507 Mary, Queen of Scots, is imprisoned in Lochleven Castle by noble troops commanded by her brother. She abdicated in favor of her son, who became King James VI, but languished in prison for nearly a year before escaping to England in May 1508.

1716 English poet Alexander Pope publishes his translation of *The Iliad*, which is praised for its language but criticized for straying too far from the Homeric verse.

1815 The Duke of Wellington's forces defeat the French under Marshal Ney at the battle of Quatre-Bras. Wellington's next military engagement was to provide his famous victory at Waterloo.

1858 Abraham Lincoln, in accepting the Republican nomination for U.S. senator from Illinois, articulates his antislavery position: "A house divided against itself cannot stand."

1879 *HMS Pinafore*, musical theater by Gilbert and Sullivan, debuts at the Bowery Theatre in New York.

> *"You can take a horse to water, but a pencil must be lead."*
>
> —*Stan Laurel*

The CAPTAIN and SWEET LITTLE BUTTERCUP.

H.M.S. PINAFORE

HMS Pinafore poster

1884 The first roller coaster in America opens at Coney Island, Brooklyn, a beachside playground for metropolitan New York.

1903 The Ford Motor Company, which in the early years of motoring would put more Americans into their first cars than any other firm, is incorporated.

1904 Irish author James Joyce meets Nora Barnacle, the chambermaid at a Dublin hotel who would become his wife. He accompanied her on a long stroll through the city, an event on which he would pattern *Ulysses*, in which Leopold Bloom's day-long excursions throughout Dublin are intended to suggest a modern parallel to the Homeric odyssey.

1909 Glenn Curtiss, the Wright Brothers' fiercest competitor in flight and arch rival in aviation technology, who founded the first commercial aviation company in the United

States in 1907, sells an airplane for $5,000.

1933 In the aftermath of the stock-market crash and the ensuing Great Depression, Congress creates the Federal Deposit Insurance Corporation, which guarantees Americans that their principal deposited in a licensed bank would never again be lost.

1937 The Marx Brothers' *A Day at the Races* premieres in Los Angeles, California.

1940 Prime Minister Winston Churchill offers France a declaration of permanent union with Great Britain. Because Prime Minister Paul Reynaud could not rally support for this proposal, he resigned and Marshal Henri Pétain formed a government that made every concession to mollify the rampaging Third Reich armies during World War II.

1947 Pravda, the Russian news agency, denounces the Marshall Plan for European rebuilding in the aftermath of World War II.

1952 *Anne Frank: Diary of a Young Girl* is published in the United States.

1958 Imre Nagy, the former prime minister of Hungary, is hanged after a secret trial. Nagy had come to power following an uprising in 1956 that was crushed by Soviet military force.

1961 When the Russian Ballet arrives in Paris, France, Rudolf Nureyev defects, seeking asylum in the United States.

1968 Lee Trevino becomes the first Spanish-American golfer to win a major American title when he captures the U.S. Open.

1977 Leonid Brezhnev becomes president of the Soviet Union.

1987 Bernhard Goetz, who shot four African-American youths who attempted to rob him on the New York City subway, is acquitted of all charges except gun possession.

1989 Four golfers shoot holes-in-one on the same hole (the sixth) on the same day of the U.S. Open, played in Atlanta, Georgia.

1995 Salt Lake City, Utah, is chosen by the International Olympic Committee to host the 2002 Winter Games. The city had first made a bid to host a Winter Olympics in 1966.

1998 The American Film Institute publishes its list of the Top 100 American Films of the 20th Century. The list was criticized as a commercialization of the institution's role as caretaker of film art, but its popular success led the AFI to issue similar tabulations of film criteria.

Valentina Tereshkova

Court officers escort Bernhard Goetz, center with glasses, from courthouse

1579 English explorer Sir Francis Drake lands on the coast of California and heads north.

1775 The Battle of Bunker Hill, one of the opening salvos of the American Revolutionary War, inflicts severe troop losses on the British, who would ultimately drive the Colonial troops from their entrenchments defending Boston, Massachusetts.

1789 A National Assembly is formed in France by commoners in their quest for a political voice.

1837 American inventor Charles Goodyear receives his first patent for rubber. Vulcanization, or treating crude rubber chemically to enhance its elasticity, strength, and stability, permitted the substance to be bonded to a tire structure.

1885 The Statue of Liberty, a gift from the people of France, arrives in New York harbor aboard the ship *Isere*.

The Battle of Bunker Hill

MILESTONE

Watergate Burglars Arrested

In the early morning hours of this day in 1972, five men are arrested for breaking into the Democratic National Committee headquarters at the Watergate, an office-hotel-apartment complex in Washington, D.C. Three of the men were Cuban exiles, one was a Cuban-American, and the fifth was James W. McCord Jr., a former CIA agent. That day, the suspects, who said they were anticommunists, were charged with felonious burglary and possession of implements of crime. On June 18, however, it was revealed that McCord was the salaried security coordinator for President Richard M. Nixon's reelection committee.

The head is 10 feet wide from ear to ear and the elevated right arm, holding the torch, is 42 feet long. Until 1899, "Lady Liberty" was New York City's tallest structure.

1917 The eruption of Mount Lassen in northern California—to this date the only volcano in the 48 contiguous states to blow since colonists had arrived in North America—ends five years after it began on May 30, 1912. The next volcanic event on the continent would not occur until 1980, when Mount St. Helens erupted in Washington.

1928 American aviator Amelia Earhart is the first woman to cross the Atlantic in an airplane, on a flight piloted by Wilmer Stultz. She became the first woman to fly solo across the Atlantic in 1932 and across the Pacific three years later.

1944 The island of Iceland, for nearly a millennium the stepchild of Denmark and a steppingstone in Viking journeys across the north Atlantic, is proclaimed an independent republic at Thingvallir, where its Althing, or parliament, had met annually throughout the island's recorded history.

1946 Japanese emperor Hirohito is spared the ignominy of a war-crimes trial, in part because U.S. general Douglas

> *"Everybody's got soul. Everybody doesn't have the same culture to draw on, but everybody's got soul."*
>
> —*James Brown*

MacArthur feels that he is a unifying force who will help stabilize the country as it rebuilds from its defeat in World War II.

1947 The publishing world mourns the loss of Maxwell Perkins, one of the greatest American literary editors. In the course of more than 25 years at Scribner's, the Harvard graduate cut Thomas Wolfe's unwieldy manuscript for *Look Homeward Angel* to its published form and worked with many luminaries of the 1920s and 1930s, including F. Scott Fitzgerald and Ernest Hemingway.

1950 The world's first kidney transplant is performed in Chicago, Illinois.

1956 Golda Meir becomes foreign minister of Israel.

1962 American golfer Jack Nicklaus wins his first pro tournament and first major tournament by defeating Arnold Palmer to win the U.S. Open. It was the first of what would become a record 20 major-tournament wins by Nicklaus.

1963 The U.S. Supreme Court bans required reading of the Lord's Prayer and the Bible in public schools.

1966 The Tennessee Valley Association awards a contract for the world's largest

President Boris Yeltsin, left, with President George H. Bush

nuclear power plant to General Electric.

1967 China gains thermonuclear power, becoming the fourth nation to have the ability to build a hydrogen bomb.

1971 A reversion treaty releases Okinawa, the southernmost group of islands in the Japanese chain, from occupation by the United States that began at the end of World War II.

1992 U.S. president George H. Bush and Russian president Boris Yeltsin sign a breakthrough arms reduction treaty that is intended to cut long-range nuclear arsenals by two-thirds.

1994 After failing to surrender to prosecutors to face two counts of murder in the slaying of his former wife, O. J. Simpson leads police on a 60-mile odyssey across Southern California freeways before he is arrested in his own driveway.

Hirohito

1746 A group of book-sellers in London, England, contracts with Samuel Johnson to write his 40,000-word dictionary, for which he would be paid 1,575 pounds sterling.

1778 Fifteen thousand British troops under Sir Henry Clinton evacuate Philadelphia, the former U.S. capital. The British position there had become untenable after France's entrance into the war on the side of the Americans.

1812 The United States declares war on Great Britain, in part to discourage British support of Canadian natives who were opposed to expansion on the western frontier.

1873 For attempting to vote in the 1872 U.S. presidential election, suffragist Susan B. Anthony is fined $100, which she never pays.

1911 In New York City, American actress Sarah Bernhardt ends a 35-week tour of U.S. and Canadian theaters.

1918 "Retreat, hell! We just got here," responds an American marine colonel urged to back off the Allied counter-attack on World War I's western front. In fact, the first U.S. troops had arrived in Europe a year earlier, with 50,000 more joining the ranks each month. The American doughboys brought Allied infantry ranks to par with Germany's 1.5 million riflemen, but the casualties on both sides were staggering.

1923 Mount Etna, which towers over eastern Sicily as the last active volcano in Europe,

---

MILESTONE

Napoleon Meets His Waterloo

Napoleon Bonaparte's dreams of military conquest of Europe finally come to an end on this day in 1815. The diminutive Corsican had installed himself as dictator of France in 1799, and had begun a campaign of conquest in 1803. Forced to abdicate in 1814, he escaped from captivity on the island of Elba and returned to power. At Waterloo in Belgium, though, he finally met his match in the English Duke of Wellington, assisted by forces under the command of the Prussian marshal Blücher. Napoleon's army lost 25,000 men, with 10,000 killed on the British side, leading Wellington to remark "Nothing except a battle lost can be half so melancholy as a battle won." Napoleon retreated to France, and was again forced to abdicate. A train station in London is named in honor of the battle—ironically, it is here that trains from France and Belgium now arrive through the Channel Tunnel.

Napoleon Bonaparte

World War I poster

erupts, causing 30,000 to flee their homes.

1932 In Italy, two men are executed for their part in a plot to assassinate Benito Mussolini.

1933 Parents who do not adhere to the Nazi program for the education of their children may lose them, German chancellor Adolf Hitler warns, adding, "We shall rear them as needful for the Fatherland."

1940 In a radio address, Prime Minister Winston Churchill urges perseverance, asking beleaguered Britons to endure the ordeal of World War II so future generations could only conclude, "This was their finest hour."

1942 British prime minister Winston Churchill

"A lie gets halfway around the world before the truth has a chance to get its pants on."

—*Sir Winston Churchill*

arrives in Washington, D.C., to discuss war strategy with U.S. president Franklin D. Roosevelt.

1954 Relentless investigations into the private lives of American citizens, as well as scathing critiques of government institutions and their staffs, which Senator Joseph McCarthy presented as an effort to rout out communism in U.S. society, climax in 35 days of televised hearings.

1958 In a break with centuries of tradition, Prince Akihito, the future emperor of Japan, is allowed to choose his own wife.

1959 Arkansas state laws that permit schools to be closed rather than integrated are voided by a federal court.

1960 Arnold Palmer wins the U.S. Open golf tournament with one of the greatest final-round comebacks ever. Palmer trailed leaders by seven strokes entering the final round, but he posted a 65 to win by two strokes.

1973 The U.S. stock market struggles to regain the momentum that carried it through the 1960s: the Dow Jones average closes at 875, its lowest level since late 1971.

1983 Astronaut Sally K. Ride boards the seventh U.S. space shuttle mission, Challenger I, to become the first American woman in space.

2000 American golfer Tiger Woods wins the U.S. Open golf tournament by a record fifteen strokes, finishing 12 under par. It was the most dominating performance in the history of golf's major tournaments, and it cemented Woods's place among the sport's all-time greats.

Sally K. Ride

JUNE 19

240 B.C. Greek geographer and mathematician Eratosthenes estimates the circumference of Earth.

1586 English colonists desert the colony on Roanoke Island they had named Virginia in honor of Elizabeth I, "the Virgin Queen," sailing for home after two years of deprivation and fear.

1846 The first recorded baseball game is played on the Elysian Fields in Hoboken, New Jersey, between the Knickerbocker Athletic Club and the New York Nines. New York won 23–1.

1862 Slavery is outlawed in all United States territories.

1865 All slaves in Texas are freed.

1867 Austrian archduke Maximilian, who had been

Elysian Fields, Hoboken, New Jersey

MILESTONE

First Nickelodeon Opens
On this day in 1905, Pittsburgh, Pennsylvania, showman Harry Davis opens the world's first nickelodeon, showing a silent film called *The Great Train Robbery*. The storefront theater boasted 96 seats and charged only five cents. Nickelodeons soon spread across the country, typically featuring live vaudeville acts as well as short films. By 1907 some two million Americans had visited a nickelodeon, and the storefront theaters remained the main outlet for films until they were replaced around 1910 by large modern theaters. Inventors in Europe and the United States, including Thomas Edison, had been developing movie cameras since the late 1880s.

> *"What is freedom of expression? Without the freedom to offend, it ceases to exist."*
>
> —*Salman Rushdie*

named emperor of Mexico by an international debt-collecting expedition when it took possession of Mexico City in June 1863, is executed by his subjects. Under pressure from the United States, Napoleon III had withdrawn his support for Emperor Maximilian, who refused to abdicate.

1915 "Hail California," conducted by Camille Saint-Saëns, is heard for the first time at the Panama-Pacific Exposition in San Francisco.

1925 British archaeologists discover a primitive human skull that bears a close resemblance to the Neanderthal man discovered earlier in Europe, in a cave at Tabgha near Jerusalem.

Joe Louis knocked out by Max Schmeling

1941 Germany and Italy expel U.S. diplomats during World War II.

1941 American boxer Joe Louis defeats Billy Conn in a famous fight at the Polo Grounds in New York City. Conn, a former lightweight moving up in class, was ahead late in the fight, but went for a knockout and was himself knocked out in the 13th round.

1943 Joseph Goebbels, the Nazi German minister of propaganda during World War II, announces that Berlin is now free of Jews.

1945 During civil war in China, Communist Party chairman Mao Zedong refuses an offer from nationalist leader Chiang Kai-shek to negotiate. The disagreement between the authoritarian, right-wing Chiang and the communist Mao led to civil war in China, hard on the heels of the end of World War II.

1948 The U.S. Congress enacts peacetime selective service for the first time, requiring all men between the ages of 19 and 25 to register for the draft.

1953 Julius and Ethel Rosenberg, who were convicted of conspiring to pass U.S. atomic secrets to the Soviets, are executed at Sing Sing Prison in New York.

1961 Great Britain's empire in the Middle East continues to shrink as it removes Kuwait's protectorate status but pledges military aid to the oil-rich nation. Six days later, Iraq claimed sovereignty over the country.

1926 Twenty thousand Native Americans commemorate the 50th anniversary of the battle at Little Bighorn, Montana, in which Colonel George Custer and his entire party were killed.

1933 France grants Russian revolutionary Leon Trotsky political asylum.

1934 American author Nathaniel West publishes the second of his three novels in a career cut short by a car crash in 1940. *A Cool Million* offers a sardonic look at the rags-to-riches Horatio Alger ideal of American society and furthered the reputation created by *Miss Lonelyhearts*, which had earned its author early critical acclaim.

1935 President Franklin D. Roosevelt suggests overhauling the U.S. tax code to prevent the accumulation of great wealth in the hands of a few, proposing an inheritance tax and higher levies on big fortunes.

1936 The great American heavyweight champion Joe Louis suffers the first defeat of his boxing career, losing to German fighter Max Schmeling.

Great Seal of the United States

1756 A group of prisoners from the British garrison at Calcutta are imprisoned in a cell 14 feet wide and 18 feet long, known at the time as a "black hole," many of them dying during the night. One survivor claimed that of 146 prisoners in the cell, 123 died, but in probability both figures were considerably lower.

1782 The U.S. Congress approves the Great Seal of the United States, which displays an American bald eagle hold-

MILESTONE
Boxer Rebellion Begins in China

On this day in 1900, in response to widespread foreign encroachment upon China's national affairs, Chinese nationalists launch the so-called Boxer Rebellion in Beijing. The nationalists occupied Beijing, killed several Westerners, and besieged the foreign legations in the diplomatic quarter of the city. The Boxers soon grew powerful. As the Western powers and Japan organized a multinational force to crush the rebellion, the siege of the Beijing legations stretched into weeks, and the diplomats, their families, and guards suffered through hunger and degrading conditions as they fought to keep the Boxers at bay.

"It isn't what they say about you, it's what they whisper."

—*Errol Flynn*

ing an olive branch and a bundle of 13 arrows in its feet and a banner reading *E Pluribus Unum* ("Out of many, one") in its beak.

1791 French king Louis XVI and his family attempt to flee the country, seeking protection of loyalist troops. They were recognized and returned to Paris, where in mid-September the king would swear an oath of allegiance to the Constitution of 1791, which transferred to an assembly the rights to initiate laws and abolished the aristocracy.

1837 Queen Victoria, whose long reign would define

The trans-Alaska pipeline in Alaska

a period of British culture, assumes the throne on the death of her uncle, William IV.

1863 West Virginia, the part of Virginia that remained loyal to the Union cause, becomes the 35th state during the American Civil War.

1898 During the Spanish American War, the U.S. cruiser *Charleston* captures the island of Guam, which was then a Spanish territory and today remains an American protectorate in the Pacific.

1919 Rather than sign a peace treaty with the Allies after World War I, German chancellor Philipp Scheidemann resigns.

1944 During World War II, the Japanese lose 400 planes and three aircraft carriers in the Battle of the Philippine Sea.

1947 The United States loans Iraq $25 million over 15 years to purchase surplus military equipment.

1961 Gamal Abdel Nasser, president of the United Arab Republic (a union of Egypt and Syria), approves a plan to move the ancient temple of Abu Simbel above floodwaters created by construction of the Aswan Dam, a billion-dollar power and water project.

1963 In an attempt to reduce the potential for mutual annihilation by improving communications, the United States and Soviet Union agree to install "hot lines" that will instantly activate a secured telephone line between the nations' leaders.

Jim Hines at the XIX Summer Olympic

1966 French president Charles de Gaulle, on a state visit to Russia, confides that he envisions a "Europeanized Europe," free of American and Soviet domination.

1967 Boxer Muhammad Ali is stripped of his heavyweight title after being convicted of draft evasion during the Vietnam War. Ali refused to join the U.S. Army based on beliefs from his Islamic faith. He famously said, "I ain't got no quarrel with the Vietcong."

1968 American sprinter Jim Hines became the first man to run 100 meters in less than 10 seconds, setting a world record of 9.95 seconds.

1977 The oil pipeline linking Prudhoe Bay above the Arctic Circle and Valdez on Alaska's southern coast, which is expected to transport 10 percent of the oil consumed daily in the United States, begins operation.

1980 American boxer Sugar Ray Leonard is defeated for the first time in his career, losing his welterweight championship bout to Roberto Duran of Mexico.

Galileo

1633 Italian astronomer Galileo, whose celestial research was published in 1632 as *Dialogue concerning the two chief world systems,* is commanded by the Inquisition to "abjure, curse, and detest" his Copernican heliocentric views.

1814 The United Kingdom of Netherlands, which includes present-day Holland and Belgium, is created as buffer to France. Prince William of Orange became King William I and served in that capacity for a quarter century, although Belgium, inspired by the French Revolution, declared its independence in 1830 and deposed him.

1824 With repeal of the Combination Acts by Parliament, workers in Great Britain can organize—but not strike, because the use of threats or violence is prohibited. As a result, unions of such skilled workers as printers and engineers were created.

MILESTONE

U.S. Constitution Ratified

On this day in 1788, New Hampshire becomes the ninth and last state needed to ratify the Constitution of the United States, thereby making the document the law of the land. By 1786, defects in the post-Revolutionary War Articles of Confederation had become apparent, such as the lack of central authority over foreign and domestic commerce. Congress endorsed a plan to draft a new constitution, and on May 25, 1787, the Constitutional Convention convened at Independence Hall in Philadelphia. On September 17, 1787, after three months of debate moderated by convention president George Washington, the new U.S. constitution was signed.

"Freedom is what you do with what's been done to you."

—Jean-Paul Sartre

1834 American inventor Cyrus Hall McCormick patents the reaping machine, which would industrialize farming of certain staple crops and become the foundation of International Harvester, a supplier of farm machinery worldwide.

1854 The first act of bravery to be rewarded with a Victoria Cross is committed by Mate Charles Lucas, who throws a live shell overboard from HMS *Hecla* seconds before it explodes. Lucas received the medal, which is awarded for exceptional bravery by military personnel in wartime, at the first investiture in June 1857.

1893 Visitors to the World Columbian Exposition in Chicago, Illinois, are privileged to ride the world's first Ferris wheel.

U.S. Marines on Okinawa

1919 The captured German fleet, at Scapa Flow in Orkney, is scuttled on the instructions of Admiral Reuter, who claims that orders from the start of World War I prohibited him from surrendering a single vessel.

1926 The fiftieth Wimbledon Tennis Tournament opens in England, with Prince Albert, Duke of York, a contender in the doubles matches.

1932 The U.S. federal government has borne much of the cost of creating an interstate highway system, and now it begins collecting tax from those who use this infrastructure. Drivers began paying a penny per gallon of gas into federal coffers.

1943 French Resistance leader Jean Moulin is betrayed and captured by Germans during World War II, who torture him before executing him on July 7.

1945 The United States claims victory in the campaign to control Okinawa, the island chain 300 miles south of the main Japanese islands, ending the bloodiest land battle of World War II in the Pacific after nearly three months of fierce combat. The Japanese lost 100,000 men.

1948 *The Gathering Storm*, the first volume of for-

Arthur Miller

mer British prime minister Winston Churchill's series on World War II history, is published by Houghton-Mifflin.

1949 To prevent further fighting between black and white youths, the mayor of St. Louis, Missouri, proposes that pools and playgrounds in the city be segregated.

1954 The American Cancer Society presents research data that shows smokers over the age of 50 have a 75 percent higher mortality rate than persons their age who do not smoke.

1955 *Summertime*, starring American actress Katharine Hepburn, premieres in Hollywood, California.

1956 Pulitzer Prize–winning American playwright Arthur Miller, appears before the House Committee on Un-American Activities. He refused to implicate others in communist activities.

1535 John Fisher, the bishop of Rochester, is beheaded by English king Henry VIII. Fisher had spoken out against the powers Henry had taken for himself as head of the church in England, and been imprisoned for his pains. Hearing that the pope had made Fisher a cardinal, Henry angrily said he would send Fisher's head to Rome to have the Cardinal's mitre placed on it.

1679 The rebellion by the Scottish Covanenters, outraged by King Charles II's reintroduction of bishops in their country, was put down by the duke of Monmouth at the Battle of Bothwell Bridge.

1839 Elias Boudinot, editor of the newspaper published for eight years by the Cherokee, Chief Major Ridge, and his son John are murdered for signing The New Echota Treaty of 1835, by which Cherokee lands east of the Mississippi were ceded to the U.S. government, which would replace them with "Indian Territory" in present-day

John Ridge, left, and Chief Major Ridge

MILESTONE

Nazi Germany Becomes a One-Party State

Hitler effectively assumes absolute power in Germany on this day in 1933 with the banning of all opposition parties. Although the Social Democrats had won the second-largest number of seats in the election of March 23rd, in which the Nazis had failed to win an absolute majority, the last of their deputies were thrown out of the Reichstag on the grounds that they were "subversive and inimical to the state." The National party would shortly be absorbed into the Nazis, and the few remaining non-Nazi deputies provided no opposition.

"He has Van Gogh's ear for music."

—*Billy Wilder*

Oklahoma and relocate the Cherokee there. The treaty was signed by fewer than 100 representatives of the estimated 18,000 Cherokees. Tribal law decreed the death penalty for anyone who transferred Cherokee lands without approval of the majority.

1900 The Wallace Collection, one of the preeminent collections of art and armor accumulated by individuals—in this case, three generations of a noble British family—is opened to the public at the Hertford House in London.

1907 Wine scandals that introduced violent clashes in France are addressed as lawmakers in the *Chambre des Deputes* approve stiff penalties for fraud.

1910 The first commercial passengers to ride in a zeppelin board the airship *Deutschland*.

1918 During World War I, French troops under the command of General Charles Mangin halt the German Army's advance 45 miles from Paris.

1918 Molla Bjurstedt wins her record fourth straight U.S. Lawn Tennis Association title.

1922 American swimmer Johnny Weissmuller breaks four world records in one day at a meet in Hawaii. After winning gold medals in the 1928 and 1932 Olympics, Weissmuller earned greater

1944 American servicemen are offered unprecedented educational opportunities to compensate them for their efforts in World War II, as President Franklin D. Roosevelt signs the G.I. Bill of Rights.

1970 The mounting death toll of the Vietnam War continues to effect social change in the United States: President Richard M. Nixon signs a bill allowing 18-year olds to vote—the same age when men must register for the draft.

1981 Mark David Chapman pleads guilty to the murder of English musician John Lennon. The former Beatle, renowned as one of the greatest musicians of the modern era, was shot at close range as he crossed the courtyard of his apartment building on Central Park West in New York City.

1990 A massive earthquake along the Iranian-Russian border leaves 40,000 people dead and 100,000 injured and devastates towns throughout the region.

Mark David Chapman

Adolf Hitler, center, in Paris, France

fame playing Tarzan in a series of movies.

1931 In the first public effort to bring Italian crime bosses to justice, 131 Mafiosi are sentenced to life terms by a Roman court.

1933 A waterway connecting the Great Lakes to the Mississippi River system and its tributaries creates a maritime link between the United States' northern border and the Gulf of Mexico.

1940 Eight days after German troops overran Paris during World War II, France signs an armistice, granting Nazi dictator Adolf Hitler a stunning, demoralizing victory.

1941 German Armies, estimated at three million men with their allies from Italy, Romania, Hungary, and Finland, invade the Soviet Union during World War II. The hostilities would soon stretch along a 2,000-mile front, from the Baltic to the Black Sea.

1683 William Penn, founder of the Pennsylvania colony and city of Philadelphia, signs a friendship treaty with Delaware chief Tammany. Penn tried to develop cordial relations with Native Americans, while aggressively trading his supplies for their land.

1868 American inventor Christopher Latham Sholes is granted a patent for a device he calls a "type-writer."

1900 Sacré Coeur, the modern Catholic basilica whose white dome on the slopes of Montmartre can be seen all across Paris, is consecrated.

1905 The Wright brothers' third heavier-than-air craft, "Flyer no. 3," is launched. It was the first plane to travel in a consistent linear pattern but the last the American aviation pioneers would design before Wilbur Wright's prize-winning 77-mile flight on New Year's Eve, 1908.

1931 American aviator Wiley Post and Australian navigator Harold Gatty leave Roosevelt Field on New York's Long Island on the first successful round-the-world flight in a single-engine plane. They logged 15,474 miles, flying via Newfoundland to England, then staying north, across Siberia, Alaska, and Canada, before returning to New York eight days, 15 hours, and 51 minutes later.

1938 Marineland, the first aquarium in the United States, opens in Florida. Marine science captured the popular imagination as aquariums were built as tourist attractions in many communities at the end of the 20th century.

1947 The Taft-Hartley Bill, which gives the federal government more leverage in regulating union activities, is passed, overturning U.S. president Harry S. Truman's veto. Still in effect today, it allows the federal government to prohibit strikes that are likely to cripple the economy, requires either side to give 60 days notice of a possible strike or lockout, and bans the use of union funds for political activities.

1967 American runner Jim Ryun lowers his world record in the mile to 3:51.1.

1969 Chief Justice Earl Warren, who led one of the most liberal phases of the U.S. Supreme Court, resigns his seat. Warren Burger became the new leader of the chief judicial office in the United States, shifting the court to the right.

MILESTONE

Nasser Elected President

On this day in 1956, 99.95 percent of Egyptian voters mark their ballots to elect Gamal Abdel Nasser as the first president of the Republic of Egypt. Nasser was the only presidential candidate on the ballot. Voters also approved his new constitution. Nasser was a consistently popular leader during his 18 years in power. His economic policies and land reforms improved the quality of life for many Egyptians, and women were granted many rights during his tenure. His ascendance ended 2,300 years of rule by foreigners, and his independent policies won him respect not just in Egypt but throughout the world.

"Good manners will open doors that the best education cannot."

—*Clarence Thomas*

William Penn's treaty with the Indians, when he founded Pennsylvania

1972 The Higher Education Act of 1972 is signed into law by U.S. president Richard M. Nixon. It included Title IX, which bars sexual discrimination in sports and other activities and greatly increases participation in women's collegiate sports. Also on the presidential agenda that day was a conversation with H. R. Haldeman on using the CIA to thwart the FBI's investigation of the break-in at Democratic headquarters in the Watergate complex.

1985 A bomb planted aboard an Air India jet downs the plane in the Irish Sea, killing 329 people.

1985 Eric Heiden wins the first U.S. Pro Cycling Championship, a 156-mile race. Heiden turned to cycling after winning five gold medals in speed skating at the 1980 Winter Olympics.

1986 The U.S. Justice Department supports a policy that employees may be terminated because they have tested positive for HIV, the virus that causes AIDS.

1988 The worst drought in 50 years is the result of the "green-house effect," a NASA scientist reports to the U.S. Congress. He asserted that the increased consumption of fossil fuels, which release carbon dioxide that traps the sun's radiation, is causing global climate change. If temperatures continue to increase, the effects on weather patterns could be cataclysmic; polar ice caps could melt, raising sea levels.

1993 The Canadian Senate ratifies the North Atlantic Free Trade Agreement, which mutually prohibits import or export taxes or quotas on goods produced in Canada, the United States, and Mexico.

1993 Forty-eight years of U.S. military presence in Berlin comes to an end when the Stars and Stripes are lowered at Templehof Air Base.

1995 Pocahontas, who became the first Native American woman to marry a colonist when she wed John Rolfe in 1614, is the subject of a Disney animated film.

1996 U.S. sprinter Michael Johnson breaks a 17-year-old world 200-meter record, setting the new mark at 19.68 seconds. Amazingly, only two months later at the Summer Olympics at Atlanta, he beat even that mark, setting the new standard at 19.32 seconds.

1996 Desmond Tutu, who worked tirelessly to improve conditions for non-whites in South Africa and focus the attention of the world on the racist policies of the National Party, retires as archbishop of Cape Town. He won the Nobel Peace Prize in 1984.

Michael Johnson

JUNE 24

Discovery of America by John Cabot

1497 John Cabot, a wealthy Italian merchant who had spent only two years in England before following Columbus's course to the land of the Great Khan, comes ashore at Cape Breton Island in northern Newfoundland. He claims this section of eastern Canada for England.

1509 Henry VIII is crowned king of England. On this day in 1540, he divorced Anne of Cleves, who had served as his fourth wife for less than six months.

1859 A bloody battle between Austria and France at Solferino in Italy leads to the creation of an international humanitarian institution. Jean Henri Dunant, a Swiss philanthropist, was inspired by the suffering of the wounded to create the International Red Cross.

"To be positive is to be mistaken at the top of one's voice."
—Ambrose Bierce

1887 Anna Puacz, who as Ganna Walska would work 40 years creating a 37-acre botanical treasure in Santa Barbara, California, is born in Poland. Madame Walska achieved a certain reputation on the opera stage, bolstered in part by the encouragement of one of her wealthy husbands, Harold McCormick, heir to the International Harvester fortune, who purchased the Théâtre des Champs Elysées and commissioned many Erté costumes to support her career. But she left her greatest legacy by putting her six husbands behind her and dedicating her wealth and talents to creating theme gardens of exotic plants on the Montecito estate she had purchased for $40,000 in 1941, which she left to the public.

1894 An international agreement that the Olympic games will resume in modern competition is signed.

1900 Oliver Lippincott becomes the first motorist in America's Yosemite National Park. Lippincott would start a trend with his visit, as motorists increasingly chose to drive to National Parks, avoiding the more time-consuming train and coach rides.

1910 The Japanese Army invades Korea.

1911 John McDermott becomes the first American-born player to win the U.S. Open golf tournament. Held since 1895, the Open had always been won by English or Scottish golfers.

1916 "America's sweetheart," Mary Pickford, becomes the first Hollywood star to sign a seven-figure movie contract.

1939 Brazil steps into the breach created three weeks earlier, when the United States and Cuba denied port access to Jewish passengers on the ocean liner *St. Louis*, and welcomes 3,000 other German Jews as immigrants.

1949 *Hopalong Cassidy,* the first American western programming on television, begins broadcasting on NBC.

1951 Peter Walker becomes the first British driver in 16 years to win the Le Mans endurance auto race. Drivers race over the French course for 24 hours.

1953 Jacqueline Bouvier and then-Massachusetts senator John Fitzgerald Kennedy announce their engagement in Newport, Rhode Island. Their "storybook" romance later fueled comparisons of the Kennedy presidency to Camelot.

Moshe Dayan

1964 The Federal Trade Commission announces that health warnings must be printed on all packages of cigarettes manufactured in the United States. Twenty-eight years later to the day, the U.S. Supreme Court ruled that printing government health warnings on cigarette packaging does not protect cigarette companies from paying damages in legal actions brought against them.

1970 The Gulf of Tonkin Resolution, which had given President Lyndon B. Johnson unusual war powers in the modern era and, in the view of many citizens, helped escalate U.S. involvement in the Vietnam War, is repealed by a Senate vote of 81–10.

1981 Moshe Dayan announces that Israel has the capacity to make an atomic bomb.

1983 Frenchman Laurent Fignon wins the Tour de France bicycle race.

British prime minister Robert Peel

1483 Richard, duke of York and protector of the young English king Edward V, who is his nephew, takes steps to secure the crown for himself. Edward's stepbrother Lord Richard Grey and another uncle, Anthony Woodville, the first Earl Rivers, were executed on Richard's order, who would assume the crown as Richard III the next day.

1672 The Society of Friends, popularly known as Quakers, hold their first colonial meeting in Sandwich, Massachusetts.

1846 British prime minister Robert Peel succeeds in repealing the Corn Laws, protectionist rules aimed at keeping the price of British grain artificially high. Poor harvests, combined with the disastrous potato famine in Ireland, made the repeal an urgent necessity, but many landowners in Peel's Conservative party were strongly opposed to the measure, and forced Peel to resign four days later.

1857 French poet Charles-Pierre Baudelaire publishes his definitive free-form verse, *Les Fleurs*

MILESTONE

Kim Campbell Takes Office

In Ottawa, Kim Campbell is sworn in as Canada's 19th prime minister, becoming the first woman to hold the country's highest office on this day in 1993. In 1986 she was elected to the British Columbia legislature, and two years later Prime Minister Brian Mulroney appointed her minister of Indian affairs. She became the first female to hold the office of Canadian attorney general and proved instrumental in the movement to increase gun control. In 1993, Campbell was appointed minister of national defense and veterans' affairs. Mulroney announced his resignation, and Campbell was encouraged to run for the Conservative Party leadership.

General Custer's last charge

du Mal. He and his publisher were promptly condemned for "offending public morals."

1868 The southeastern states—Florida, Georgia, North Carolina, South Carolina, Alabama, and Louisiana—are readmitted to the United States after the American Civil War.

1876 In the Battle of Little Bighorn, Montana, Sioux Indians commanded by Chief Crazy Horse defend their encampment against troops led by Lieutenant Colonel George Armstrong Custer, who is among 200 U.S. casualties.

1921 Jock Hutchison becomes the first American golfer to win the British Open golf tournament.

1938 Federal law sets the U.S. minimum wage at 40 cents an hour.

1941 The Soviets bomb Helsinki during World War II, causing Finland to declare war the next day.

1941 General Dwight D. Eisenhower, who would serve as U.S. president during the placid postwar years, takes over command of American troops in the European war.

1950 The Korean War erupts when North Korean troops cross the 38th parallel at many points, taking possession of Seoul before the end of June.

> *"All great work is preparing yourself for the accident to happen."*
>
> —*Sidney Lumet*

1951 CBS television broadcasts in color for the first time, but the four-hour special program cannot be seen in American homes, which lack color-receiving systems. CBS itself only has four such sets at its headquarters, among three dozen spread throughout its network.

1952 The Olympic torch is lit in the Temple of Zeus in Athens, Greece.

1959 The first commercially produced hovercraft makes its maiden flight from Cowes on the Isle of Wight in the UK. The invention of British electronic engineer Sir Christopher Cockerell, the SR-N1 hovered nine inches above the surface of the sea, traveling on a cushion of air. Developed from original experiments with two tin cans and a vacuum cleaner, hovercraft have proved their value for ferry services and military transportation.

1961 American sprinter Frank Budd sets a new world record in the 100-yard dash, breaking the tape at 9.2 seconds at a meet in New York City.

1962 The U.S. Supreme Court rules 5–4 that the nondenominational prayer allowed in New York State schools is unconstitutional because it violates the separation of church and state.

1969 American tennis player Pancho Gonzales defeats Charley Passarell in a singles match at Wimbledon, England, that takes 5 hours and 12 minutes (and 112 games) to complete, the longest singles match ever at the tournament.

1977 Doctors in Great Britain release results of a study that indicates women who smoke experience symptoms of menopause earlier that those who do not use tobacco.

1978 Argentina defeats the Netherlands 3–1 to win the World Cup soccer championship.

SR-N1 hovercraft

JUNE 26

Francisco Pizarro

1483 Richard III usurps the English throne from his twelve-year-old nephew, who "disappeared" after being confined to the Tower of London, from which his skeleton would be exhumed 200 years later. Richard's tumultuous two-year rule ended when he was killed in battle with Henry, earl of Richmond, who became King Henry VII. His crown was supposedly found dangling from a rosebush, symbolizing that the 40-year civil war, called the Wars of the Roses because it was perpetuated by enmity between the houses of York (white rose) and the Lancaster (red rose), ends with his death.

1541 Francisco Pizarro, the Spanish conquistador who explored and conquered Peru, murdering the Inca king Atahualpa, is killed by his followers after feuding.

1754 Canadian Anthony Henday, an employee of the Hudson Bay Company, sets off with a party of Cree Indians to explore the interior regions of northern North America, reaching present-day Alberta.

1794 Lighter-than-air aviation is applied to warfare for the first time when a bal-

Pearl S. Buck

"What is new is only new to us."
—Pearl S. Buck

loon is used for reconnaissance, and French Army captain Coutelle directs troops from a tethered hydrogen balloon at the Battle of Fleurus.

1797 American Charles Newbold is granted a patent for a cast-iron plow, but his device is regarded with suspicion by farmers who fear the effects of iron implements on the soil.

1870 The Boardwalk in Atlantic City, New Jersey, welcomes summer visitors to its shorefront attractions.

1905 Some 20,000 Jewish residents of Lodz, one of the cultural centers of Poland, flee the czar's aggressions. The rise of revolutionary political parties and assassinations, as well as heavy casualties and defeats in Asian wars, have plagued the Russians this year.

1907 American author Samuel Clemens, who writes under the pen name Mark Twain, receives an honorary doctorate from Oxford University.

1917 The first troops of the American Expeditionary Forces arrive in Europe to aid the Allies in ending the carnage of World War I.

1918 "Big Bertha," the 400-millimeter German howitzer that has killed 800 Parisians, again bombards Paris with shells weighing 1,750 pounds during World War I.

1925 British actor Charlie Chaplin communicates masterfully without saying a word in *The Gold Rush,* which has its Los Angeles, California, premiere.

1945 The charter of the United Nations is signed by representatives of 50 nations meeting in San Francisco, California. This international federation replaced the League of Nations, which had failed to attain the promise intended in its creation at the conclusion of World War I. Hitler's New Order and Japan's militant doctrine of Asia for Asians had both been repudiated by World War II.

1948 In his final fight, American heavyweight champion Joe Louis rallies to stop Jersey Joe Walcott in the 11th round. The lackluster fight drew jeers from the Yankee Stadium crowd in New York City, and Louis announced his retirement in his dressing room after the fight, ending a great ring career.

1948 The Berlin Airlift begins, delivering tons of food and supplies each day until September 30, 1949, peaking at 12,940 tons delivered in 1,398 sorties on April 16. Berlin, Germany, was isolated by Soviet premier Joseph Stalin's troops, who had cut rail connections to the outside and now shut off water and power.

1959 The St. Lawrence Seaway, which links the Great Lakes with the Atlantic Ocean, is officially opened by Queen Elizabeth II of Great Britain and U.S. president Dwight D. Eisenhower.

1963 U.S. president John F. Kennedy electrifies Europeans as he stands before the Berlin Wall and announces, *"Ich bin ein Berliner,"* suggesting that all people must become engaged in ending the political division of the German people that has persisted since World War II.

1971 New York City's Central Park is the scene of the largest demonstration to date demanding gay rights, or the cessation of discrimination based on the sexual orientation of individuals.

1972 Mexican boxer Roberto Duran wins his first world championship, the lightweight title, by defeating Ken Buchanan.

1975 The International Whaling Commission bans the hunting of finback whales, one of five species it claims is on the verge of extinction. Japan and

Russia, which hunt whales for food, refused to comply with a U.N.-sanctioned moratorium on commercial whaling in 1972. The focus on preserving whales is but one aspect of a growing environmental movement that has been spurred by the alarming rate of species extinction since 1900.

Finback whale

Joshua Slocum

1743 George II, the last British king to command an army in battle, leads English, Austrian, and Hanoverian forces to victory over the French at the battle of Dettingen.

1787 English historian Edward Gibbon, who has spent 25 years on his massive *History of the Decline and Fall of the Roman Empire,* completes his manuscript.

1844 Mormon founder Joshua Smith is led from an Illinois jail and shot dead by unknown assailants.

1898 Joshua Slocum becomes the first man to circumnavigate the world solo when he lands in Rhode Island. He sailed his sloop *Spray* more than 46,000 miles around the globe.

1905 The captain and officers of the *Potemkin,* Russia's most powerful battleship in the Black Sea fleet, are killed and tossed overboard at Odessa harbor when the crew mutinies.

1918 A parachute that deploys on command saves a German pilot, the first successful use of this aviation safety device.

1922 The first Newbery Medal for excellence in children's literature is presented to Hendrik Van Loon for *The Story of Mankind.* Among the books awarded this prestigious prize in the past decade are *Shiloh* (P. R. Naylor, 1992); *The Giver* (L. Lowry, 1994); and *Holes* (L. Sachar, 1999).

1925 A secret cache of $3 million is discovered in the home of Prince Felix Youssoupoff, one of the oldest and wealthiest members of the former Russian royal families, who apparently hoped to outlive the communist regime.

1929 Color television technology is first demonstrated in New York.

1940 The British Empire, alarmed by the growing Japanese presence in the South Pacific, which threatens Australia, asks the United States for military aid in that area.

1940 The confirmed presence of German submarines in U.S. waters, as well as attacks on civilian vessels in the English Channel, cause President Franklin D. Roosevelt to declare emergency powers to control shipping vessels approaching the U.S. coast and in American ports.

> *"I long to accomplish a great and noble task; but it is my chief duty to accomplish small tasks as if they were great and noble."*
>
> —Helen Keller

President Kennedy in New Ross, Ireland

1944 Deportations since May 15 to the concentration camp at Auschwitz, Poland, are counted at 475,000 people, for many their final destination.

1949 Former prime minister of Great Britain Winston Churchill's *Their Finest Hour* is published in London.

1954 The world's first nuclear generator begins producing power in the Soviet Union, which 25 years later would experience the worst potential hazards of this technology when the Chernobyl plant suffered a meltdown that contaminated thousands of miles surrounding the site.

1957 An earthquake claims 1,200 lives in Russia, but humanitarian efforts are rebuffed and, in the name of protecting national security, no other details are released.

1963 John Fitzgerald Kennedy, the first Catholic and Irish American to be elected president of the United States, honors his family homeland with a visit.

1978 *Seastat I*, the first oceanographic satellite, is launched by the United States.

1982 The U.S. space shuttle *Columbia* carries its first commercial and military payloads.

1986 Irish citizens place Catholic morals above civil liberties in voting to uphold the nation's ban on divorce.

1988 American boxer Mike Tyson needs only 91 seconds to win a heavyweight bout over Michael Spinks, the fourth-shortest such fight ever.

1993 New York Mets pitcher Anthony Young sets a dubious American major-league record with his 24th consecutive loss.

1999 American skateboarder Tony Hawk pulls off the first-ever "front-side 900" (an aerial somersault off the lip of a halfpipe in which he makes two and a half rotations with the board at his feet) during the X Games Best Trick competition in San Francisco, California.

Skateboarder Tony Hawk

1609 Samuel de Champlain, who had founded the French settlement at Quebec in 1608, sets off with a party of 11 Frenchmen and Algonquin and Huron Indians, following the Richelieu River to the lake that now bears his name.

1762 Catherine II ascends the throne of Russia, which she would rule until 1796, earning her the sobriquet Catherine the Great by modernizing and centralizing power, expanding Russia's territory and influence into Europe and Asia, and exploring the coastline of North America.

1820 Scientists disprove the popular belief that the tomato is poisonous.

1838 Queen Victoria, who had ruled the British Empire for a year since the death of her uncle, is crowned in Westminster Abbey.

1888 Robert Louis Stevenson, the Scottish author of the great seafaring tale *Treasure Island,* leaves San Francisco, California, on his first voyage to the South Seas. He settled in Samoa, where he died in 1894.

1894 The U.S. Congress establishes a workers' holiday, now called Labor Day and celebrated the first Monday in September.

1921 A coal miners' strike in Great Britain is settled

"I base most of my fashion taste on what doesn't itch."

—*Gilda Radner*

MILESTONE

Milestones of World War I

This day marks events that both triggered and finally ended "the War to End All Wars." In 1914, Gavrilo Princip, a Serbian student, shoots dead the heir to the Austro-Hungarian throne, Archduke Franz Ferdinand, who is visiting Sarajevo in Bosnia. Princip told police he was taking revenge for oppression of Serbs. Austria-Hungary declared war against Serbia at the end of July, with Germany backing Austria and Russia aligning itself behind Serbia. Five years to the day later, after more than ten million deaths, the Treaty of Versailles is signed, officially putting an end to the bloodiest human conflict yet seen. The reparations demanded of Germany, however, created economic conditions and resentment in which Hitler's extremist policies later flourished.

---

after three months, ensuring that the privations suffered by the English during World War I will not soon be revisited upon them.

1928 Swedish-born star Greta Garbo's $5,000 per week salary at MGM film studios is renewed by American movie producer Louis B. Mayer.

1928 American jazz musician Louis Armstrong and the Hot Five record "West End Blues."

1942 All Jews in France over the age of six are required to wear a yellow Star of David armband following German occupation during World War II.

1947 At talks in Europe, Russian minister V. M. Molotov rejects one of the basic premises of the Marshall Plan: the Soviets do not believe that European unity should be a precondition of American aid for rebuilding the war-damaged economy and infrastructure.

1947 The University of California at Berkeley wins the first College World Series baseball

Archduke of Austria Franz Ferdinand and wife Sophie in Sarajevo (milestone)

Malcolm X

championship. The Golden Bears beat Yale 8–7 in the final. Playing first base for Yale was future president George H. Bush.

1951 *Amos 'n' Andy,* which had amused radio audiences but angered blacks who objected to its racist portrayal of characters played by white actors, premieres on CBS television.

1957 Secretary of State John Foster Dulles says the United States will never recognize "Red China," which he characterizes as a temporary government.

1958 Although he is only 17, Brazilian soccer star Pelé leads his team to the first of three World Cup soccer championships he would help them win in his matchless career.

1964 Malcolm X forms the Organization for Afro-American Unity.

1965 During the Vietnam War, U.S. president Lyndon B. Johnson orders the first ground troops into Vietnam.

1969 As a prelude to the first U.S. manned space flight, NASA puts a 16-pound monkey into orbit.

1971 The U.S. Supreme Court rules 8–1 to prohibit reimbursement of taxes or any other form of federal funding for parochial, or church-based, schools.

1972 Stung by the outpouring of protest and criticism over his handling of the Vietnam War, U.S. president Richard M. Nixon vows that no new draftees will be sent to Vietnam.

1996 The Citadel, an elite military school in South Carolina with a 153-year history, votes to admit female students.

1997 American boxer Evander Holyfield is declared the winner of a heavyweight fight against Mike Tyson after Tyson bites off the top of Holyfield's ear and is disqualified.

1998 On an official visit to China, U.S. president Bill Clinton criticizes the country's human rights record. His comments were covered live on Chinese television and radio, to the chagrin of his hosts.

Citadel freshmen Petra Lovetinska, left, and Jeanie Mentavlos

Mission Dolores

🎭 **1613** The Globe Theatre in London, England, catches fire and burns to the ground during a performance of Shakespeare's *Henry VIII*.

1767 The British parliament passes the Townshend Revenue Acts, which impose duties on processed products including glass, paint, paper, and tea imported by the American colonies. The duties were to pay salaries of resident tax collectors, but colonists organized boycotts and protests, leading to the repeal of all but the tea tax in April 1770.

1776 Mission Dolores is founded at San Francisco, California.

1854 The United States pays Mexico $10 million in the Gadsden Purchase, acquiring parts of Arizona and New Mexico.

🎭 **1854** English author Charlotte Brontë, who portrayed the social restrictions and subtle interactions among men and women in 19th-century England, marries curate Arthur

---

BORN ON THIS DAY

1805
HIRAM POWERS
American Neoclassical sculptor (*Psyche; The Greek Slave*)

1858
GEORGE WASHINGTON GOETHALS
American engineer who oversaw the building of the Panama Canal

1861
WILLIAM JAMES MAYO
American surgeon, co-founder of the Mayo Clinic

1900
ANTOINE DE SAINT-EXUPÉRY
French aviator and author (*The Little Prince*)

1901
NELSON EDDY
American actor and singer (*Rose-Marie; Phantom of the Opera*)

1908
LEROY ANDERSON
American composer ("Sleigh Ride")

1910
FRANK LOESSER
American lyricist ("Two Sleepy People") and composer (*Guys and Dolls*)

1912
JOHN TOLAND
Pulitzer Prize-winning American author (*Adolf Hitler; The Battle of the Bulge; But Not in Shame: The Six Months After Pearl Harbor*)

1919
SLIM PICKENS
American actor (*Blazing Saddles; Dr. Strangelove*)

1941
KWAME TURE (STOKELEY CARMICHAEL)
American civil rights activist

1949
DAN DIERDORF
American professional football player and sports announcer

1956
PEDRO GUERRERO
Dominican-born American professional baseball player

1963
ANNE-SOPHIE MUTTER
German violinist

Bell Nicholls over her father's objections.

🏆 **1902** Marcel Renault (founder of the Renault car manufacturing company) wins an auto race from Paris, France, to Vienna, Austria, completing the 800-mile journey in 15 hours, 22 minutes.

1904 The Prohibition Party meets in Indianapolis, Indiana, to nominate the aptly named Silas C. Swallow as its presidential candidate. Without Swallow at the helm, the party's mandate becomes federal law when the 18th Amendment takes effect on January 29, 1919.

🏆 **1909** The first American transcontinental auto race concludes. The drivers traveled from New York City to Seattle, Washington, in 23 days. Auto manufacturers sponsored the event, whose finish was part of the Alaska-Yukon-Pacific Exposition.

1909 The modern skyline of New York City begins to take shape when plans for the 909-foot Equitable Life Building are unveiled.

🔬 **1916** American timber merchant William E. Boeing, who had recently incorporated Pacific Aero Products, sees one of his aircraft fly for the first time. In its early phase Boeing (as the company was called after 1917) was

> *"The first need of a free people is to define their own terms."*
>
> —*Kwame Ture*

Displaced European Jews in a DP camp

known for warplanes, including the B-17 bomber, which was dominant in World War II air battles. In the immediate postwar period, Boeing took the lead in developing commercial jetliners, from its 707 to the "wide-bodied" 747 that doubled passenger and cargo capacities when it entered commercial use in 1970.

1925 A powerful earthquake levels much of Santa Barbara, California. The city was recast in its present form as new codes restricted building height and the Spanish style, best articulated in the landmark County Courthouse, becomes its signature architecture. To promote a harmonious architecture, the city offers free Spanish-revival plans to those who apply for building permits.

1926 The fascist government adds an extra hour to the Italians' workday in order to increase economic efficiency.

1946 The resettlement of Jewish people displaced by the Holocaust of World War II to Palestine is disrupted when British authorities arrest 2,700 local Jews in a campaign to stamp out terrorism.

1949 Dutch troops pull out of Jakarta, the capital of the United States of Indonesia, a federation of 16 states that had been brokered by the United Nations.

1949 The South African government, whose white constitution contrasts with the ethnic makeup of the nation it rules, bans mixed-race marriage.

1950 In perhaps the biggest upset in soccer history, the United States defeats England in a World Cup game, 1–0. America would not win another World Cup game until 1994.

1956 With a leap of 7 feet, 5/8 inches, Charles Dumas became the first high jumper to clear the 7-foot barrier.

1990 Fernando Valenzuela of the Los Angeles Dodgers and Dave Stewart of the Oakland Athletics become the first players in American major-league baseball history to throw no-hitters on the same day.

1992 The U.S. Supreme Court upholds the principle that abortion is a constitutional right, but it places certain restrictions on the judgment rendered in *Roe v. Wade*.

Abortion activists demonstrate in front of the U.S. Supreme Court Building

Hernán Cortés before Montezuma

⚔ **1097** The Battle of Nicaea is one of the turning points of the First Crusade, as the Muslim capital of Asia Minor falls to combined Byzantine Greek and crusading forces. The call to join the Christian campaign had emptied whole villages in France as some 30,000 people joined five loosely organized campaigns, financed by the papacy, to recover holy places in the Middle East.

🍁 **1520** Aztec emperor Montezuma II is killed, but various sources ascribe his death to different parties: some assert that he was killed by other Aztecs; others claim he was stabbed by Spaniards in the party of Hernán Cortés.

🇬🇧 **1837** The British parliament ends the use of the pillory as a means of punishment. The device—a hinged board in which the miscreant's head and hands were locked—had been in use since the middle ages. Famous victims of the undignified punishment included Daniel Defoe, author of *Robinson Crusoe.*

🎭 **1857** English author Charles Dickens gives the first public reading of *A Christmas*

MILESTONE

Daredevil Crosses Niagara Falls on Tightrope

Jean-François Gravelet, a Frenchman known professionally as Émile Blondin, becomes the first daredevil to walk across Niagara Falls on a tightrope on this day in 1859. Some 5,000 spectators witnessed the feat, which was performed 160 feet above the Niagara gorge just downriver from the Falls. Blondin crossed a cable about two inches in diameter and 1,100 feet long with only a balancing pole to protect him from plunging into the dangerous rapids below. It was the first in a series of famous Niagara tightrope walks performed by The Great Blondin from 1859 to 1860.

Bobby Jones

> *"It's not the load that breaks you down, it's the way you carry it."*
>
> —*Lena Horne*

Carol at St. Martin's Hall in London. Following his death at age 58, he was buried in Poet's Corner of Westminster Abbey and was eulogized by Queen Victoria as a man with "a large, loving mind and the strongest sympathy with the poorer classes."

🇺🇸 **1892** A strike is called against Carnegie Steel, which reopens its plant in Homestead, Pennsylvania, with non-union workers, including southern blacks. As a result of the failed action, Amalgamated Union lost clout with American steelworkers.

1908 As the sun set over the Tunguska River in Central Siberia, herders in the sparsely populated area witnessed the approach of a giant fireball with a trail that stretched 800 kilometers behind it in the night sky. Once the huge object impacted Earth with 2,000 times the force of the atomic bomb that leveled Hiroshima, it would be noted around the globe. When Russia's chief meteorologist gained access to the remote site years later, he found trees felled in a radial pattern by the blast over an area of more than 1,500 square kilometers, and 1,000 square kilometers that burned in the subsequent fires.

🇺🇸 **1914** A U.S. congressional resolution declares that the tribal government of the Cherokee nation no longer exists, leaving individual Cherokees without any representatives on the federal level and in a region that had not yet become a state.

1915 German submarines sink the civilian ocean liner *Armenian*, flouting U.S. and British protests of torpedoes that sank the Cunard line's *Lusitania* a month earlier.

1930 American golfer Bobby Jones wins the British Open on his way to capturing the Grand Slam, then made up of the U.S. and British Opens and Amateurs.

1934 Hitler orders the killing of leaders of the S.A. storm troopers and others in what will become known as the "Night of the Long Knives." Nazi head of propaganda Josef Goebbels claimed that Ernst Roehm and others were plotting to overthrow Hitler. In reality it rid the party of its more radical, socially progressive forces.

1936 American author Margaret Mitchell's *Gone with the Wind* is published by Macmillan. Fifty thousand copies were sold on one day in October, making it the world's fastest-selling novel to date.

1936 The 40-hour workweek becomes federal law in the United States.

1971 Russians, who have pushed the envelope of the space race since the 1950s, are stunned to find three cosmonauts dead within the capsule of *Soyuz 11* upon its return to Earth.

1974 The mother of American civil rights leader Martin Luther King, Jr. is slain by a 21-year-old gunman as she plays the organ for services at Ebenezer Baptist Church in Atlanta, Georgia.

1985 The hijacking of a TWA flight from Athens, Greece, which hopscotched across the Middle East, landing and departing again in various airports, ends 17 days after it began when the 39 surviving American hostages are freed in Beirut, Lebanon.

Shiite Moslem at door of hijacked TWA

JULY 1

96 Two Egyptian legions hail Vespasian, a Roman general, as the emperor of Rome, following the corruption and mismanagement of government by Vitellius.

1097 After six hours of fierce fighting, the Crusaders defeat the Turks at Dorylaeum in the first great battle of the First Crusade. Although the Crusaders were driven back during the initial hours, a relief force, led by Raymond of St. Giles and Adhémar, eventually appeared and forced the Turks to flee.

1200 Sunglasses made of rock crystal are first demonstrated in China during the Ming dynasty.

1535 Sir Thomas More goes on trial in England, charged with treason for his refusal to subscribe to the Act of Supremacy. The act impugned the pope's authority and made Henry VIII the head of the English Church.

1543 England and Scotland sign the Peace of Greenwich, providing for the marriage of Prince Edward Tudor and Mary, Queen of Scots.

1776 The first vote on the American Declaration of Independence is taken, in Philadelphia, Pennsylvania.

> *"There is only one step from the sublime to the ridiculous."*
>
> —*Napoleon Bonaparte*

1798 Napoleon Bonaparte conquers Alexandria, Egypt.

1840 The first prepaid postal stamps are issued in Great Britain. Their use spread rapidly throughout the world.

1858 A paper by English naturalist Charles Darwin outlining his theory of evolution and natural selection is read before the Linnaean Society in London.

1863 The largest military conflict in North American history begins when Union and Confederate forces collide at Gettysburg, Virginia. The epic battle, which lasted three days, would come to be viewed as the turning point of the American Civil War.

1867 The Dominion of Canada is officially recognized as an independent entity by Great Britain with the passage of the British North America Act.

1890 Two thousand Census Bureau clerks begin the daunting task of tallying the results of the United States' 11th census, aided for the first time by mechanical calculating devices invented by 29-year-old

Theodore Roosevelt and the Rough Riders

Confederate charge at Gettysburg

Herman Hollerith. Hollerith later founded the Tabulating Machine Company, which eventually became IBM.

1898 Theodore Roosevelt and his volunteer cavalry, the Rough Riders, help secure a U.S. victory in the Battle of Santiago, the decisive battle of the Spanish-American War.

1903 The first Tour de France bicycle race begins.

1916 The British launch a massive offensive with 100,000 soldiers against German forces in the Somme River region of France during World War I. By the end of the day, 20,000 British soldiers were dead and 40,000 wounded. It's the single heaviest day of casualties in military history.

1939 Roy Plunkett of Kinetic chemicals (a subsidiary of DuPont) files a patent application for Teflon®.

1942 A turning point in World War II in North Africa, the Battle of El Alamein begins.

1949 France grants independence to Republic of Vietnam.

1968 The Nuclear Nonproliferation Treaty is signed by the United States, Britain, the Soviet Union, and 58 other nations.

1994 After 27 years in exile, Palestinian Liberation Organization chairman Yāsir Arafāt returns to Palestinian land by driving from Egypt into Gaza.

1997 After 156 years of British colonial rule, Hong Kong is returned to China in a ceremony. While a few thousand Hong Kong citizens protested the turnover, it was otherwise celebrated peacefully.

Governor Chris Patten holds folded British flag in final ceremony before the turnover of Hong Kong to China

1298 In Germany, an army under Albert of Austria defeats forces led by Adolf of Nassau. Adolf was elected king over Albert (son of Rudolf I of Hapsburg) out of fear over the growing power of the Hapsburgs. He sought to strengthen his rule through territorial expansion and an alliance with England and France to halt French encroachment on German territory. The alliance never worked, and Adolf was deposed in favor of Albert.

1625 Under command of Ambrogio Spinola, the Spanish Army takes Breda, Spain, after nearly a year of siege. As part of the Thirty Years' War, the siege was an attempt to prevent the triumph of Protestant forces that would side with Holland and threaten Spain's remaining position in the southern Netherlands.

1644 Oliver Cromwell's "Roundheads" crush Prince Rupert's Royalists at the Battle of Marston Moor in their first major defeat of the English Civil War.

1747 Marshal de Saxe leads the French forces, allied with Prussia against Austria in the War of the Austrian Succession, to victory over an Anglo-Dutch force in Holland at the Battle of Lauffeld. Marshal de Saxe was the great-grandfather of novelist George Sand.

> *"When dealing with the insane, the best method is to pretend to be sane."*
>
> —*Hermann Hesse*

MILESTONE

President Garfield Shot

On this day in 1881, U.S. president James Garfield is shot in the back by crazed assassin Charles Guiteau. Guiteau claimed he shot Garfield out of revenge, having written a deranged speech for the president (which was never read) and not been rewarded with the ambassadorship to France for doing so. President Garfield did not die immediately, but instead lived for eleven weeks while doctors tried to find the bullet lodged in his back. Because antiseptic procedures now standard were not practiced at the time, the probing by many unwashed fingers resulted in an infection that ultimately caused Garfield's death. The president's incapacitation sparked a constitutional crisis when the Cabinet divided over whether Vice President Chester Arthur should assume the role of president or merely act in Garfield's stead. Later, the twenty-fifth amendement declared that the vice president will assume power in such situations.

1809 Alarmed by the growing encroachment of whites squatting on Native American lands, the Shawnee chief Tecumseh calls on all Indians to unite and resist.

1819 British Parliament passes the Factory Act, which prohibits the employment of children under nine in textile factories and allows children under 16 to work a maximum of 12 hours a day.

1850 American inventor B. J. Lane patents the gas mask.

1853 The Crimean War begins when the Russian army crosses the Pruth River and invades Turkey.

1858 Russian serfdom on imperial lands is banned by Czar Alexander II.

1864 American baseball player Bill "Candy" Cummings pitches the first curve ball.

1900 Count Ferdinand von Zeppelin flies his first airship from Lake Constance near Friedrichshafen, Germany.

President James Garfield shot by Charles Guiteau (milestone)

Stephen Hawking in Beijing, China

1917 The first phone call from an airplane is received at Langley Field, Virginia.

1921 The first prizefight offering a million-dollar purse is broadcast from Jersey City, New Jersey. Jack Dempsey knocked out George Carpentier in the fourth round.

1928 The first regularly scheduled telecasts designed to be received by the American public are broadcast using a technique called "Radiovision."

1934 The Fox Film Corporation negotiates a new contract with six-year-old Shirley Temple. The contract raised her salary from $150 a week to $1,000 a week, with a $35,000 bonus for each film. Under this contract, Temple became one of the most popular actresses of her day.

1937 American aviator Amelia Earhart disappears. With navigator Frederick Noonan, she was attempting to fly around the world when they lost their bearings over the Pacific Ocean. No trace of Earhart or Noonan was ever found.

1938 American tennis player Helen Wills Moody claims a record by winning her eighth Wimbledon women's singles title.

1940 German dictator Adolf Hitler orders that plans be drawn for an invasion of England during World War II.

1947 Rejecting the Marshall Plan as an attempt to contain growing Soviet influence, Soviet foreign minister V. M. Molotov walks out of a meeting with representatives of the British and French governments.

1947 An object crashes to Earth near Roswell, New Mexico, giving rise to speculation that it was an alien spacecraft.

1964 U.S. president Lyndon B. Johnson signs the Civil Rights Act into law.

1976 Following the Vietnam War, North and South Vietnam become one country with Hanoi as the capital.

1992 Physicist Stephen Hawking breaks British publishing records with *A Brief History of Time*. The book explained the latest theories on the origins of the universe in a language that could easily be understood by ordinary educated people.

1994 Former communist president Ramiz Alia is sentenced by an Albanian court to nine years in jail on charges of abuse of power and violating citizens' rights.

Washington taking command of the army

1775 George Washington draws his sword at Cambridge Common in Massachusetts, rides out in front of the American troops, and formally takes command of the Continental Army.

1790 In France, the Marquis of Condorcet proposes that women be granted civil rights.

1819 The first bank in the United States, The Bank for Savings, opens for business in New York City. The first day's deposits totaled $2,807.

1861 The Pony Express makes its first trip to San Francisco, California, with letters from New York City.

1863 On the third day of the Battle of Gettysburg, Confederate general Robert E. Lee's last attempt at breaking the Union line ends in disastrous failure, bringing the most decisive battle of the American Civil War to an end.

1898 After a three-year journey, Canadian-born Captain Joshua Slocum completes the first solo circumnavigation of the world in his fishing boat *Spray* when he reaches Newport, Rhode Island.

1898 The United States defeats the Spanish fleet in the harbor of Santiago, Cuba, during the Spanish-American War.

1920 William Tilden becomes the first American tennis player to win the men's singles title at Wimbledon.

1928 John Logie Baird demonstrates the world's first color television transmission in his studio in London, England.

1938 The *Mallard*, a steam locomotive, sets a world speed record in Great Britain: 126 miles per hour.

1940 British naval forces destroy the French fleet at Mers-el-Kebir, a port in Algeria, in order to prevent Germany from co-opting French ships to use in a World War II invasion of Britain.

1940 The legendary American comedy duo Bud Abbott and Lou Costello debut with their network radio show on NBC.

1945 The first American passenger car built since the February 1942 World War II shutdown is driven off the assembly line at the Ford Motor Company plant in Detroit, Michigan.

1946 Legendary show-business partners Jerry Lewis and Dean Martin meet for the first time, in Atlantic City, New Jersey.

> *"I think age is a very high price to pay for maturity."*
>
> —Tom Stoppard

Jackie Robinson at Hall of Fame induction

1954 Almost nine years after World War II, Great Britain ends food rationing.

1957 Nikita Khrushchev takes control in the Soviet Union by orchestrating the ouster of his most serious opponents from positions of authority in the Soviet government. Khrushchev's action delighted the United States, which viewed him as one of the more moderate figures in the communist government of Russia.

1962 Jackie Robinson is inducted into the National Baseball Hall of Fame, the first African American to be so honored.

1962 French president Charles de Gaulle declares Algeria an independent state after 132 years of French rule.

1976 Israeli commandos rescue 103 hostages in a raid on Entebbe Airport in Uganda. The hostages had been taken from an Air France airliner hijacked by pro-Palestinian guerrillas.

1986 Russian-born Mikhail Baryshnikov, arguably the world's greatest ballet dancer,

becomes a U.S. citizen at Ellis Island, in New York Harbor.

1988 In the Persian Gulf, the U.S. Navy cruiser *Vincennes* shoots down an Iranian passenger jet that it mistakes for a hostile Iranian fighter aircraft. Two missiles were fired from the American warship, the aircraft was hit, and all 290 people aboard were killed. Minutes before Iran Air flight 655 was shot down, the *Vincennes* had engaged Iranian gunboats that shot at its helicopter.

1990 Wheelchair-users block London's New Oxford Street in protest of the lack of assistance given to disabled people on public transport.

1992 Belgian defense minister Leo Delcroix announces that compulsory military conscription will end in Belgium in 1994.

1993 General Raoul Cedras signs a plan developed by the United Nations to restore democracy to Haiti.

Mourners in the streets of Tehran for victims of Iran Air flight 655

1054 The brightest known supernova (now called the Crab Nebula) begins shining. Recorded by Chinese and Japanese astronomers, it was visible in the daytime sky for 23 days.

1631 The world's first employment agency, the Bureau d'Adresse, is established in Paris, France.

1653 Oliver Cromwell, frustrated with members of the British Parliament who had not passed political or religious tests, dismisses its members. He replaced them with a select group of committed Puritans in what became known as "The Barebones Parliament," named after Praise-God Barebone, a London merchant. It also failed.

1817 In the United States, construction begins on the Erie Canal to connect Lake Erie and the Hudson River. The canal contributed greatly to the financial well-being of New York City, opened up eastern markets to Midwest farms, and allowed for immigration to that region and the establishment of several large cities.

1845 Writer and naturalist Henry David Thoreau goes to live in a shack adjacent to Walden Pond, Massachusetts. The journal he wrote of his encounters with nature became

---

MILESTONE

U.S. Declares Independence

In Philadelphia, Pennsylvania, on this day in 1776 the Continental Congress adopts the Declaration of Independence, which proclaims the independence of the United States of America from Great Britain and its king. The declaration came 442 days after the first volleys of the American Revolution were fired at Lexington and Concord in Massachusetts and marked an ideological expansion of the conflict that would eventually encourage France's intervention on behalf of the Patriots. On August 2, the declaration was signed. In 1783, with the signing of the Treaty of Paris with Great Britain, the U.S. formally became a free and independent nation.

---

the basis for *Walden,* one of the most important works of American literature.

1848 Karl Marx and Friedrich Engels publish *The Communist Manifesto.*

1855 Walt Whitman self-publishes the first edition of *Leaves of Grass,* containing a dozen poems. It became what is generally considered the most influential volume of poems in the history of American literature.

1863 The Confederacy is split down the Mississippi River when General John C. Pemberton surrenders to Union general Ulysses S. Grant at Vicksburg during the American Civil War.

1865 The first edition of *Alice in Wonderland,* written by English mathematician Lewis Carroll, is published.

1879 A British colonial force smashes the Zulu army at Ulundi, the last great battle of the Anglo-Zulu War. The war was provoked by Great Britain's fear that a self-reliant Zulu kingdom would be a threat to

Declaration of Independence in Congress (milestone)

"Opportunities are usually disguised as hard work, so most people don't recognize them."

—*Ann Landers*

Mars Pathfinder

its plan of bringing various British colonies, Boer republics, and independent African groups under common control.

1883 "Buffalo Bill" Cody creates the first Wild West show, at North Platte, Nebraska.

1884 France presents the United States with the Statue of Liberty, commemorating the French and American revolutions.

1886 The first American rodeo is held at Prescott, Arizona.

1886 The first scheduled passenger train with transcontinental service reaches Port Moody, British Columbia.

1895 "America the Beautiful" is first published as a poem.

1903 The first transpacific telegraph cable is inaugurated, running between Honolulu, Midway, Guam, and Manila. U.S. president Theodore Roosevelt sent the first message.

1906 Ethiopia is granted independence by Great Britain, France, and Italy.

1987 Klaus Barbie, the Nazi "butcher of Lyon," receives a lifetime jail sentence in France for crimes against humanity during World War II.

1997 NASA's Mars *Pathfinder* becomes the first U.S. spacecraft to land on Mars in more than two decades. The craft used parachutes to slow its approach to the Martian surface and then deployed air bags to cushion its impact. Images transmitted from the spacecraft were put on the Internet this same day.

Statue of Liberty

1294 Pietro di Murrone, a pious hermit, is elected as Pope Celestine V. He was so besieged by the political, social, and religious challenges of the position that just five months later he became the first pope to resign, for which he was imprisoned by his successor, Boniface VIII.

1295 Scotland and France sign the "Auld Alliance" against England—one of the world's oldest mutual defense treaties.

1643 The first documented instance of a tornado is recorded in Essex County, Massachusetts.

1687 The Royal Society in England publishes Isaac Newton's *Principia,* one of the most important publications in the history of science. It states Newton's three laws of motion and the universal law of gravitation.

1811 Simón Bolívar declares Venezuela's independence from Spain.

1841 Thomas Cook opens the world's first travel agency, in Leicester, England. The agency specialized in organizing trips for the Temperance Society, which was opposed to alcoholic beverages.

1859 American captain N. C. Brooks discovers the Midway Islands.

1861 The first large-scale engagement of the American Civil War is fought in southwestern Missouri, signaling an escalation in the hostilities between the North and South.

Salvation Army poster

1865 In London, England, revivalist preacher William Booth and his wife, Catherine, establish the Christian Mission, later known as the Salvation Army. Determined to wage war against the evils of poverty and religious indifference with military efficiency, they modeled their organization after the British Army, labeling uniformed ministers as "officers" and new members as "recruits."

1892 Although born a slave, African-American inventor Andrew Beard is issued a patent for a rotary engine.

1921 Jury selection begins in the trial of Chicago White Sox players, including "Shoeless" Joe Jackson, Buck Weaver, and Eddie Cicotte, accused of throwing the World Series.

1933 Fritz Todt is appointed general inspector for German highways and is assigned to build a comprehensive autobahn system. The autobahns became the envy of the industrialized world and a source of both anxiety and awe for Europeans.

> *"There are three roads to ruin: women, gambling and technicians. The most pleasant is with women, the quickest is with gambling, but the surest is with technicians."*
>
> —*Georges Pompidou*

1942 Ian Fleming becomes the first graduate of a training school for spies in Canada, known as "Special 25." The training proved invaluable to the creation of his fictional spy, James Bond.

1945 Due to British desire for rapid social reform, Winston Churchill, despite having led Great Britain through World War II, is defeated in the general election.

1950 The United States engages the North Koreans for the first time in the Korean War, and Private Kenneth Shadrick of Skin Fork, West Virginia, becomes the first U.S. serviceman to die in that war.

1950 Israel passes the "Law of Return," which guarantees all Jews worldwide free and automatic citizenship if they choose to immigrate to that country.

1951 English-born William Shockley, working at Bell Telephone Labs, announces the invention of the junction transistor. The invention heralded a revolution in radio, television, and computer circuitry.

1977 Pakistan's army, led by General Mohammad Zia ul-Haq, overthrows the government of Zulfikar Ali Bhutto in a bloodless coup.

1989 Former Reagan Administration White House aide Oliver North is fined $150,000 for his role in the Iran-Contra scandal.

American paratroopers comb over a village near Sunchon, North Korea

JULY 6

1189 England's Richard I ("The Lion-Heart") becomes king after his father, Henry II, dies.

1483 England's Richard III is crowned king. Although tradition notes his evilness (perpetuated by Shakespeare's play), much of this reputation was the result of propaganda by the Tudors to justify Henry VII's usurpation of the crown.

1519 After making some well-placed bribes, Charles of Spain becomes Holy Roman emperor.

1536 After having discovered the St. Lawrence River in Canada, Jacques Cartier returns to France.

1553 Mary I becomes the first queen to rule autonomously in England. Her persecution of Protestants resulted in the nickname "Bloody Mary."

1699 New York businessman-turned-pirate Captain William Kidd is captured in Boston and extradited to England.

1770 The Russians destroy the entire Ottoman fleet at the Battle of Cesme.

1785 Congress names U.S. currency the "dollar" and adopts a decimal coinage system.

> *"In the practice of tolerance, one's enemy is the best teacher."*
>
> —*Dalai Lama*

1854 In the United States, the Republican Party is officially created in Jackson, Michigan.

1858 Lyman Blake of Abington, Massachusetts, patents the shoe-manufacturing machine.

1862 Writing under the name of Mark Twain, American author Samuel Clemens begins publishing news stories in the Virginia City *Territorial Enterprise.*

1885 French scientist Louis Pasteur applies the first successful antirabies vaccine to Joseph Meister, a boy who had been bitten by an infected dog.

1886 The public gets its first taste of malted milk, thanks to Horlick's of Wisconsin.

1907 In England, the world's first purposely built motor-racing track opens at Brooklands, Surrey.

1908 American explorer Robert Peary's expedition departs New York City and heads for the North Pole.

1912 During the Olympic Games in Stockholm, Sweden, American Jim Thorpe gains fame as the world's greatest athlete.

Louis Pasteur

Lawrence of Arabia

When the King of Sweden paid him this tribute, Thorpe replied, "Thanks, King."

1917 Arab forces led by Englishman T. E. Lawrence ("Lawrence of Arabia") capture the port of Aqaba from the Turks during World War I.

1919 A British dirigible lands in New York after 108 hours in the air, becoming the first airship to cross the Atlantic Ocean.

1923 The Union of Soviet Socialist Republics is formed.

1928 *The Lights of New York*, the first all-talking feature film, premieres in New York City.

1942 In Nazi-occupied Holland during World War II, 13-year-old Jewish diarist Anne Frank and her family are forced to take refuge in a secret sealed-off area of an Amsterdam house. After the war, Anne's diary was discovered undisturbed in the hiding place and in 1947 was translated into English and published. *The Diary of Anne Frank* became an instant bestseller and was eventually translated into more than 30 languages.

1945 Nicaragua is the first nation to officially accept the United Nations Charter.

1946 FBI agents arrest George "Bugs" Moran. Once one of the biggest organized-crime figures in America, his criminal career took an abrupt downturn after the infamous St. Valentine's Day Massacre in Chicago, Illinois, 1929, in which his top gunmen were slaughtered by rival Al Capone's henchmen.

1957 Althea Gibson wins the Wimbledon women's singles tennis title, the first African American to do so.

1957 Fifteen-year-old Paul McCartney attends a church picnic in the village of Woolton, near Liverpool, England, where he meets 16-year-old John Lennon. Lennon had formed a band called the Quarrymen, which was playing at the picnic.

1988 The Piper Alpha oil platform explodes in the British sector of the North Sea, killing 167 people. It became the world's worst offshore accident.

Smoke pours out of the Piper Alpha oil platform in the North Sea

JULY 7

1456 Joan of Arc is posthumously acquitted of various crimes, including heresy and witchcraft, by Charles II in recognition of her service to France.

1585 King Henri III and Duke De Guise sign the Treaty of Nemours. As a result, French Huguenots lose all their freedoms.

1802 The first comic book, *The Wasp*, created by Robert Rusticoat, is published in Hudson, New York.

1807 The first of the Treaties of Tilsit are signed between France and Russia. They became allies and divided Europe between them.

1815 With French general Napoleon Bonaparte defeated at Waterloo, the victorious Allies march into Paris.

1846 Commander J. D. Sloat of the U.S. Navy raises the American flag in Monterey, annexing California after the surrender of a Mexican garrison.

"Belief gets in the way of learning."
—Robert A. Heinlein

1863 U.S. lieutenant colonel Christopher "Kit" Carson leaves Santa Fe with his troops, beginning his campaign against the Indians of New Mexico and Arizona. Although a famed "mountain man," Carson was responsible for waging a destructive war against the Navajo Indians.

1876 Jesse James, the most notorious train robber of the American West, holds up the Missouri-Pacific train and robs it of $15,000. James and his gang came to typify the dangers of the 19th-century frontier as portrayed in motion pictures.

1908 The Great White Fleet, sixteen new American Atlantic Fleet battleships painted all white except for gilded scrollwork on their bows, leaves San Francisco to circumnavigate the globe and project American sea power.

Four images of Jupiter and the luminous night-side impact of fragment W of comet Shoemaker-Levy 9

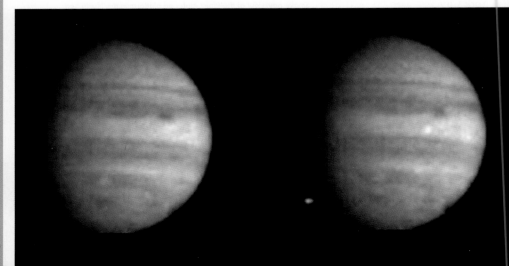

Saint Frances Xavier Cabrini

1920 A U.S. naval seaplane flies 95 miles guided exclusively by radio signals. This was the first time an airplane relied on radio signals for navigation.

1925 South Africa recognizes Afrikaans as one of its official languages, along with English and Dutch.

1937 The Peel Report, published in Great Britain as part of a commission to investigate the situation in Palestine, recommends separate Arab and Jewish states.

1942 Heinrich Himmler, architect of Nazi German dictator Adolf Hitler's program to exterminate Europe's Jewish population, begins to perform medical experiments on women in the Auschwitz concentration camps in Poland.

1943 During World War II, Nazi German dictator Adolf Hitler makes his V-2 missile program a major priority.

1946 Italian-American educator Mother Frances Xavier Cabrini becomes the first American citizen to be canonized as a saint by the Catholic Church.

1952 On her maiden voyage, the ocean liner *United States* make the fastest-ever crossing of the Atlantic to date.

1989 Compact discs outsell vinyl albums for the first time.

1992 The comet Shoemaker-Levy 9 is torn into at least 23 pieces by Jupiter's gravitational forces. The eventual collision of the pieces into Jupiter was an event never before directly observed.

1994 Northern Yemeni forces gain total control of Aden, crushing a bid to recreate an independent state.

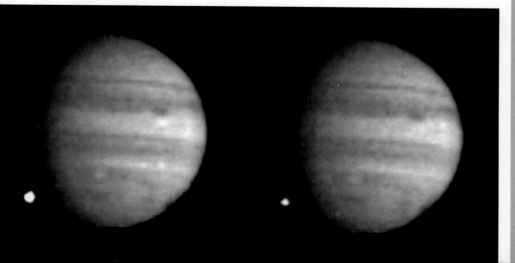

■■ 52 B.C. Julius Caesar conquers a fishing village called Lutetia Parisiorum, occupied by the Parisii (Gauls). Under Roman rule, it acquired considerable importance and was eventually renamed "Paris." As such, this is the date that is usually associated with the founding of Paris.

1497 Portuguese navigator Vasco da Gama sails from Lisbon in search of a sea route to India, which he discovers by sailing around the southern tip of Africa. As a result of his trip, Portuguese king Emmanuel I conferred on him the title of admiral of the Indian Ocean.

1608 Samuel de Champlain establishes the first French settlement at Quebec, Canada.

1663 The British crown grants a charter to the American colony of Rhode Island's Roger Williams guaranteeing freedom of worship.

1709 The Swedish empire comes to an end when Peter the Great defeats Charles XII at Poltava, in the Ukraine.

1776 The Liberty Bell rings out from the tower of

Liberty Bell

1838
COUNT FERDINAND GRAF VON ZEPPELIN
German military officer who invented rigid dirigibles

Count Ferdinand Graf von Zeppelin

1839
JOHN D. ROCKEFELLER
American capitalist who founded the Standard Oil company

1898
ALEC WAUGH
British novelist (*Island in the Sun*)

1908
NELSON A. ROCKEFELLER
American politician, governor of New York

1913
WALTER KERR
American Pulitzer Prize-winning drama critic

1915
CHARLES HARD TOWNES
American physicist who developed lasers

1946
CYNTHIA GREGORY
American ballerina

1949
WOLFGANG PUCK
Austrian-born chef, television personality, and cookbook author (*Modern French Cooking for the American Kitchen; Pizza, Pasta and More!*)

1951
ANJELICA HUSTON
Academy Award-winning American actress (*Prizzi's Honor; Crimes and Misdemeanors; The Addams Family*)

1952
JACK LAMBERT
American professional football player

Commodore Matthew Calbraith Perry

Philadelphia's Pennsylvania State House (now known as Independence Hall), summoning American citizens to the first public reading of the Declaration of Independence, by Colonel John Nixon.

1800 Dr. Benjamin Waterhouse administers the first cowpox vaccination (to prevent smallpox) in the United States to his son, Daniel.

● ■■ 1853 Commodore Matthew Calbraith Perry, representing the U.S. government, sails into Tokyo Bay, Japan, with a squadron of four vessels. Under threat of attack, the Japanese accepted letters from President Millard Fillmore, making the United States the first Western nation to establish relations with Japan in two centuries.

1856 The machine gun is patented by Charles E. Barnes of Lowell, Massachusetts.

■■ 1881 The first ice-cream sundae is served by Edward Berner of Two Rivers, Wisconsin. It was so named because he offered it only on Sundays.

1884 The National Society for the Prevention of Cruelty to Children (NSPCC) is founded in the United States. The London Society for the Prevention of Cruelty to Children (later the English NSPCC) and the Royal Scottish Society for the Prevention of Cruelty to Children are founded in the same year.

1889 The first issue of the *Wall Street Journal* hits the stands in New York City.

1892 The American Psychological Association is founded by psychologist G. Stanley Hall, president of Clark University. Hall regarded childhood and adolescence as the human analog of Charles Darwin's theory of evolution.

1905 The mutinous crew of the Russian battleship *Potemkin* surrender. In June, sailors on the battleship had protested against the serving of rotten meat. The captain ordered that the ringleaders be shot, but the firing-squad refused to carry out the order. The mutiny helped move forward the Russian revolution that overthrew the czar.

1918 American novelist Ernest Hemingway, working as an American Red Cross ambulance driver, is severely wounded while carrying a companion to safety on the Austro-Italian front during World War I.

"There are three periods in life: youth, middle age, and how well you look."
—*Nelson A. Rockefeller*

1922 Trumpet player Louis Armstrong leaves his hometown of New Orleans, Louisiana, taking a train to Chicago, Illinois. He had been invited to play with King Oliver's famous jazz band. Playing with Oliver, Armstrong became one of the most influential figures of the jazz era, popularizing the instrumental solo as a fundamental ingredient of jazz.

1936 Civil war erupts in Spain as Generalissimo Francisco Franco leads a military rebellion in response to national elections in which the Popular Front (consisting of socialists and communists) was victorious.

1960 American pilot Francis Gary Powers is charged with espionage by the Soviet Union after it shoots down his U-2 spy plane.

1989 Carlos Saul Menem is inaugurated as president of Argentina. It's the country's first transfer of power from one democratically elected civilian leader to another in 60 years.

MILESTONE

First Americans Killed in South Vietnam
On this day in 1959, Major Dale R. Ruis and Master Sergeant Chester M. Ovnand become the first Americans killed in the American phase of the Vietnam War when guerrillas strike a Military Assistance Advisory Group compound in Bien Hoa, 20 miles northeast of Saigon. The group had arrived in South Vietnam on November 1, 1955, to provide military assistance. The organization consisted of U.S. Army, Navy, Air Force, and Marine Corps personnel who provided advice and assistance to the Ministry of Defense, Joint General Staff, corps and division commanders, training centers, and province and district headquarters.

Ernest Hemingway, front third from right, standing with ARC men and women in Milan, Italy

118 Hadrian, Rome's new emperor, formally enters the city. He was generally vigorous and judicious in his reign, but ruthless on the issue of Palestine, where he forbade Jews from entering Jerusalem.

1595 A revelation leads German astronomer Johannes Kepler to describe a geometrical model of the cosmos, which he incorporates in his first book, *Cosmic Mystery*. The book caught the attention of Danish astronomer Tycho Brahe, who invited Kepler to join his team in Prague.

1789 The French National Assembly declares itself the Constituent Assembly and begins to prepare a French constitution in Versailles.

1816 At the Congress of Tucuman, Argentina declares its independence from Spain.

1846 Shortly after the Mexican War begins, U.S. captain John Montgomery sails his warship into the bay just off the village of Yerba Buena. Meeting no resistance, he raised the American flag in the central plaza. The following year, the Americans renamed the village San Francisco.

1872 New England sea captain John F. Blondel patents the doughnut cutter. His invention became a favorite among

> *"May you live as long as you want and not want as long as you live."*
>
> —Tom Hanks

Captain John Montgomery

bakers because of the efficiency and speed with which it could give the dough its typical ring shape.

1877 The All England Croquet and Lawn Tennis Club begins its first lawn tennis tournament at Wimbledon, then an outer suburb of London. Twenty-one amateurs showed up to compete.

1887 The first paper napkins are introduced by John Dickenson at an annual dinner for paper manufacturers at the Castle Hotel in Hastings, England.

1893 Dr. Daniel Hale Williams performs the world's first successful open-heart surgery without using anesthesia, in Provident Hospital in Chicago, Illinois.

1900 The British Parliament establishes the Commonwealth of Australia, uniting the separate colonies under one federal government. The new Commonwealth officially comes into being on January 1, 1901.

1910 Archeologists discover a tablet created in A.D. 94 chronicling the fall of Jerusalem.

1922 American swimmer Johnny Weissmuller is the first person to swim the 100 meters freestyle in less than one minute. He ultimately won five Olympic gold medals and set 51 world records. Weissmuller would later become Hollywood's "Tarzan of the Jungle."

1925 Twenty-two-year-old Oonagh Keogh becomes the first female member of a stock exchange when she's admitted to the floor of the Dublin Stock Exchange.

1926 *The Son of the Sheik*, starring Rudolph Valentino, opens in U.S. theaters. Although the silent film was a splendid romantic adventure, it was Valentino's last. He died two months later.

1935 The torture chamber of Ivan the Terrible is unearthed in Moscow, Russia. He was the grand duke of Moscow and first adopted the title of czar in 1547. Ivan was infamous for cruelties in his later years, when he was prone to fits of rage and suspected conspiracies everywhere.

The Enigma coding machine

Peter Thomson

1941 During World War II, British cryptologists break the secret German "Enigma" code. Enigma was the Germans' most sophisticated coding machine. Originally employed for business purposes, the German Army adapted the machine and considered its encoding system unbreakable.

1947 Princess Elizabeth, 21, and Greek prince Lieutenant Philip Mountbatten, 26, later Queen Elizabeth II and Prince Philip, Duke of Edinburgh, announce their engagement.

1954 Australian golfer Peter Thomson, 24, becomes the youngest player to win the British Open.

> *"The regularity of a habit is generally in proportion to its absurdity."*
>
> —*Marcel Proust*

1460 During the Wars of the Roses, fought between the rival dynasties of Lancaster and York, English king Henry VI is captured at the Battle of Northampton. The consequence of Henry's defeat was the Act of Settlement, which made the Duke of York heir to the throne in place of the Lancastrian Prince of Wales.

1553 Lady Jane Grey is proclaimed Queen of England at the age of 15, after the death of Edward VI, primarily on the basis of her Protestant piety and learning. Edward, a Protestant, could not bring himself to leave the throne to his Catholic sister, Mary. Nine days later, however, Mary claimed the throne with great popular support, and Jane was imprisoned and subsequently executed.

1778 French king Louis XVI declares war on England in support of the American Revolution.

1790 The U.S. House of Representatives votes to locate the national capital on a site along the Potomac River.

1892 The world's first concrete-paved street is built in Bellefountaine, Ohio.

1900 "His Master's Voice," one of the most famous trademarks in the world, is registered with the U.S. Patent Office. Created for the Victor Recording

---

MILESTONE

Monkey Trial Begins

On this day in 1925 in Dayton, Tennessee, the Monkey Trial begins with John Thomas Scopes, a high school science teacher, accused of teaching evolution in violation of a Tennessee state law. The law made it a misdemeanor punishable by fine to "teach any theory that denies the story of the Divine Creation of man as taught in the Bible, and to teach instead that man has descended from a lower order of animals." Scopes conspired with George Rappalyea to get charged with this violation. After his arrest they enlisted the aid of the American Civil Liberties Union to organize a defense.

Victor Recording Company logo

Company (later RCA Victor), the logo shows a dog looking into the horn of a gramophone.

1919 President Woodrow Wilson delivers the Treaty of Versailles to the U.S. Senate and personally urges its ratification.

1920 Man o' War defeats John P. Grier in one of America's greatest horse races. Man o' War set a time of 1 minute, 49⅕ seconds in the 1⅛ mile event, a world record.

1925 TASS, the official news agency of the Soviet Union, is established.

1940 The Germans begin the first in a series of World War II bombing raids against Great Britain, known as the Battle of Britain, which lasts three and a half months.

1943 During World War II, the Allies begin their invasion of Axis-controlled Europe with landings on the island of Sicily, off mainland Italy. Encountering little resistance from the demoralized Sicilian troops, 150,000 Allied troops went ashore within three days.

1958 England installs its first parking meter.

1962 *Telstar 1,* the world's first commercial communications satellite, is launched from Cape Canaveral, Florida, at about 4:30 A.M. By 7:30 A.M. it had relayed its first telephone call, from the chairman of AT&T in Maine to Vice President Lyndon B. Johnson. Also on this day, the satellite relays the first transoceanic satellite test telecast, from Andover, Maine, to various points in Europe and the United States.

1984 Former Nigerian transport minister Umaru Dikko, who had sought political asylum in Great Britain after a military coup in Nigeria, is found drugged in a crate at Stansted Airport as an attempt to forcibly return him to Nigeria was foiled.

1987 In Auckland harbor in New Zealand, the *Rainbow Warrior* sinks after French agents in diving gear plant a bomb on the hull of the vessel. The *Rainbow Warrior,* the flagship of international conservation group Greenpeace, had been preparing for a protest voyage to a French nuclear test site in the South Pacific.

1991 Boris N. Yeltsin is inaugurated as the first democratically elected president in Russian history.

1992 Panamanian leader Manuel Noriega is convicted by a U.S. federal judge of drug and racketeering charges and is sentenced to 40 years in prison.

1997 In London, England, scientists say that DNA from a Neanderthal skeleton supports a theory that humanity descended from an "African Eve" 100,000 to 200,000 years ago.

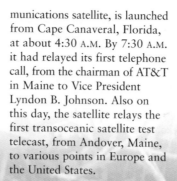

Three children in a London suburb sitting next to the remains of what was once their home, after German bombing

1533 Pope Clement VII excommunicates England's king Henry VIII when Henry decides to divorce Catherine of Aragon in order to marry Anne Boleyn.

1656 Coming from Barbados, Englishwomen Ann Austin and Mary Fisher become the first Quakers to immigrate to the American colonies when they land at Massachusetts Bay Colony. Shortly after arriving, however, their liberal teachings enraged the Puritan colonial government, and they were jailed and eventually deported to Barbados.

1776 Captain James Cook sails from Portsmouth, England, seeking a passage around the north coast of America from the Pacific.

1807 U.S. vice president Aaron Burr fatally shoots Alexander Hamilton. Hamilton came to detest Burr, whom he regarded as a dangerous opportunist. When Burr ran for the vice presidency in 1796, Hamilton launched a series of public attacks against him. Burr resolved to restore his reputation by challenging Hamilton to

---

BORN ON THIS DAY

1274
ROBERT THE BRUCE
King of Scotland (1328–29)

1754
THOMAS BOWDLER
British physician, and literary censor of Shakespeare

1767
JOHN QUINCY ADAMS
Sixth U.S. president (1825–29)

1899
E. B. (ELWYN BROOKS) WHITE
American author (*Stuart Little; Charlotte's Web*)

1920
YUL BRYNNER
Russian-born actor (*The King and I; The Ten Commandments; The Magnificent Seven*)

1934
GIORGIO ARMANI
Italian fashion designer

1950
BONNIE POINTER
American singer (The Pointer Sisters)

1953
LEON SPINKS
American Olympic and heavy-weight champion boxer

1959
SUZANNE VEGA
American singer/songwriter ("Tom's Diner"; "Luka"; "Oh Suzanne")

"Analyzing humor is like dissecting a frog. Few people are interested and the frog dies of it."
—*E. B. White*

a duel, or an "affair of honor," as it was known.

1914 American baseball great Babe Ruth debuts in the major leagues as a pitcher for the Boston Red Sox, making $2,900 in his rookie season.

1938 *Mercury Theater on the Air* debuts on American air waves. Featuring Orson Welles, the show is best remembered for its 1938 radio broadcast of *The War of the Worlds*, a science-fiction drama about a Martian invasion in Grovers Mill, New Jersey. The program sparked panic among listeners who believed it was a real news broadcast.

1945 After World War II, the Soviet Union promises to hand power over to British and U.S. forces in West Berlin. Although the division of Berlin into zones of occupation was seen as a temporary postwar expedient, the dividing lines quickly became permanent and a symbol for Cold War tensions.

1950 In Great Britain, puppets Andy Pandy, Teddy, and Looby Loo first appear on television. The episodes were rerun for more than 25 years.

1950 Frank Sinatra makes his London debut with a sell-out show at the London Palladium. Sinatra had recently overtaken Bing Crosby as the

---

Aaron Burr and Alexander Hamilton duel at Weehawken, New Jersey

Skylab in orbit at the end of its mission

highest paid singer in the United States.

🏆 **1962** American scuba-diver Fred Baldasare becomes the first person to swim the English Channel underwater.

🏳️ **1964** In the United States, the first 7-11 convenience store opens its doors. Its name derives from its extended hours: from 7 A.M. to 11 P.M.

🎭 **1971** Andrew Lloyd Webber's musical *Jesus Christ Superstar* has its first American stage performance, in Pittsburgh, Pennsylvania.

🏳️ **1974** More than 6,000 life-sized terra-cotta figures of warriors are unearthed by Chinese archeologists near the ancient Chinese capital of Xian. The three-acre burial site had been created about 206 B.C. to guard the tomb of the first Ch'in emperor.

🏳️ **1977** The Reverend Dr. Martin Luther King, Jr. is posthumously awarded the Presidential Medal of Freedom for his work in advancing civil rights in the United States.

🔬 **1979** Skylab, America's first space station, comes crashing

down five years after the last manned mission ended. It made a spectacular return, showering debris over the Indian Ocean and Australia. No one was injured.

🏳️ **1981** In the United States, Neva Rockefeller becomes the first woman ordered to pay alimony to her former husband.

🔬 **1985** American surgeon Dr. H. Harlan Stone uses zippers rather than stitches on 28 patients, thinking zippers would facilitate reopening if internal bleeding followed the initial operations. The zippers were eventually replaced with permanent stitches.

🏆 **1986** Maricica Puica of Romania sets a women's world record by running 2,000 meters (approximately 1.25 miles) in 5 minutes, 28.69 seconds. Also on this day, Ingrid Kristiansen of Norway runs 10,000 meters (approximately 6.25 miles) in a world-record 30 minutes, 13.74 seconds.

🏳️🏳️ **2000** Palestinians and Israelis open peace talks at Camp David, Maryland.

U.S. president Bill Clinton, Israeli prime minister Ehud Barak, left, and Palestinian leader Yásir Arafát, right, at Camp David, Maryland

526 St. Felix IV begins his reign as pope. Felix was particularly interested in issues concerning the nature and efficiency of grace and published several canons on the issue of grace and free will.

1389 King Richard II of England appoints Geoffrey Chaucer, who would later become famous for *The Canterbury Tales,* to the position of chief clerk of the king's works in Westminster. Chaucer, the middle-class son of a wine merchant, served as a page in an aristocratic household during his teens and was associated with the aristocracy for the rest of his life.

1630 In the American colonies, New Amsterdam's governor buys Gull Island from Native Americans and renames it Oyster Island. It later became known as Ellis Island.

1679 British king Charles II ratifies the Habeas Corpus Act. Regarded as the great writ of liberty, it doesn't judge the guilt or innocence of a person, but whether the actual act of imprisonment was unlawful.

1690 At the Battle of the Boyne, Protestant forces led by King William III defeat the Roman Catholic army of James II. The victory led to the Protestant domination in northern Ireland.

1794 Horatio Nelson, later Admiral Lord Nelson, loses

> *"Men have become the tools of their tools."*
> —Henry David Thoreau

100 B.C.
JULIUS CAESAR
Roman emperor

1730
JOSIAH WEDGEWOOD
British pottery designer and manufacturer

1817
HENRY DAVID THOREAU
American naturalist, pacifist, and author (*Walden*)

Henry David Thoreau

1854
GEORGE EASTMAN
American philanthropist and inventor of the Kodak camera

1884
AMEDEO MODIGLIANI
Italian painter and sculptor (*Reclining Nude*)

1895
OSCAR HAMMERSTEIN II
American lyricist who worked with Richard Rodgers

1904
PABLO NERUDA
Chilean Nobel Prize-winning poet

1908
MILTON "UNCLE MILTIE" BERLE
American comedian

1917
ANDREW WYETH
American landscape painter (*Hoffman's Slough; Corner of the Woods; Far From Needham*)

1934
VAN CLIBURN
American piano virtuoso

1937
BILL COSBY
American comedian and actor (*The Bill Cosby Show*)

King William III

his right eye at the siege of Calvi in Corsica.

1817 Dannybrook, County Cork, Ireland, hosts the first recorded flower show.

1817 The "Laufmaschine" (running machine), one of the predecessors of the modern bicycle, is demonstrated for the first time by inventor Baron Karl Drais von Sauerbronn of Germany. It was made entirely of wood and was propelled by pushing one's feet against the ground.

1843 In the United States, the leader of the Mormon Church, Joseph Smith, sanctions the practice of polygamy as a result of a divine revelation.

1861 Wild Bill Hickok begins to establish his reputation as a gunfighter after he coolly shoots three men during a shootout in Nebraska.

1862 President Abraham Lincoln signs into law a measure calling for the awarding of a U.S. Army Medal of Honor.

1870 John W. Hyatt Jr. and Isaiah S. Hyatt of Albany, New York, are awarded a patent for a process by which celluloid is produced.

1906 French artillery officer Alfred Dreyfus is finally pardoned and restored to his rank and regiment. He was falsely accused of treason in a famous trial (often called "The Dreyfus Affair") that smacked of anti-Semitism rather than actual guilt.

1912 *Queen Elizabeth* becomes the first foreign-made film to premiere in the United States.

1920 U.S. president Woodrow Wilson presides over the official opening of the Panama Canal.

1943 The Battle of Kursk during World War II, one of the greatest clashes of armor in military history, comprising 900 Russian and 900 German tanks, takes place as the German offensive is stopped in a devastating battle, marking the turning point on the Eastern front in the Russians' favor. When it was over, 300 German tanks, and even more Russian ones, were strewn over the battlefield.

1944 Britain's Royal Air Force becomes the first air force to use jet aircraft.

1954 American singer Elvis Presley, 19, signs a recording contract with Sun Records. He simultaneously quits his day job at the Crown Electric Company.

1957 The U.S. surgeon general, Leroy E. Burney, reports a direct link between smoking and lung cancer.

1960 The first Etch-A-Sketch goes on sale. More than 50 million units would be sold during the next 25 years.

1960 *Echo I* is launched by the United States. It was the first passive satellite (essentially a giant balloon) used to bounce radio and TV signals around the world.

1962 At the Marquee Club in London, England, the Rolling Stones give their first public performance.

1977 The U.S. space shuttle *Enterprise* completes its first free-flight test.

Enterprise and crew members Fred Haise, left, and C. Gordon

JULY 13

1568 Alexander Nowell, dean of St. Paul's Cathedral in London, England, perfects a way to bottle beer. He discovered the concept of bottle-conditioning after leaving his beer at his favorite fishing spot.

1787 The U.S. Congress enacts the Northwest Ordinance, permitting the Northwest Territory to become three to five states with a total population of 60,000.

1832 American explorer Henry Schoolcraft discovers the source of the Mississippi River.

1836 John Ruggles of Thomaston, Maine, receives patent No. 1 from the U.S. Patent Office, under a new system for numbering patents. Before this time, there had been 9,957 non-numbered patents issued. Ruggles received his patent for a traction wheel used in locomotive steam engines.

1837 Britain's Queen Victoria becomes the first monarch to live in the 600-room Buckingham Palace.

1861 Union general George B. McClellan distinguishes himself by routing Confederates under General Robert Garnett at Carrick's Ford in western Virginia, during the American Civil War. The battle ensured Yankee control of the region, secured the Union's east-west railroad connections, and set in motion the events that

"Everybody is ignorant, only on different subjects."

—*Will Rogers*

would lead to the creation of West Virginia.

1865 American newspaper publisher and editor Horace Greeley advises a reader to "Go west, young man."

1875 The first cash-carrier system (the forerunner of the pneumatic tube) is patented by David Brown of Lebanon, New Jersey. It was a basket moved by a wire, a pail, and pulleys.

1878 The Treaty of Berlin signals a continuing dissolution of the Ottoman Empire. The Caucasus was given to Russia, and Bosnia and Herzegovina went to Austria. Romania became an independent nation, and Great Britain had the right to occupy Cyprus.

1882 After three days of firing by battleships, the British succeed in destroying forts built by the Arab Pasha threatening the Suez Canal.

1917 A vision of the Virgin Mary appears to the children of Fatima, Portugal.

Horace Greeley

Frank Sinatra with the Harry James band

1919 The British dirigible R-34, commanded by Major George H. Scott, lands in Norfolk, England, to become the first lighter-than-air craft to make a two-way transatlantic voyage. The airship departed Edinburgh on July 2, arriving in New York on July 6 before making the return flight.

1925 The Ziegfeld Follies burlesque musical revue, looking for a last-minute replacement for W. C. Fields, who went home to attend his mother's funeral, picks a struggling unknown comedian named Will Rogers.

1930 The first soccer World Cup begins in Montevideo, Uruguay. Uruguay beat Argentina, 4–2, in the final to become the first World Champions over 13 other competing nations.

1938 Massachusetts Television Institute opens a "television theater" in Boston, the first theater of its kind. The institute charged 25 cents for admission and some 200 people attended the first show. The auditorium was fitted with a 9-by-12-inch black-and-white television screen, which relayed images of singers, musicians, and dancers who were performing in a studio above.

1939 American singer Frank Sinatra makes his recording debut with the Harry James band, singing "Melancholy Mood" and "From the Bottom of My Heart."

1977 New York City experiences a 25-hour blackout, the first such blackout in a major city anywhere in the world.

Lady Diana, left, Prince Charles, and Bob Geldof at Live Aid concert (milestone)

1099 During the First Crusade, Christian knights from Europe capture Jerusalem after seven weeks of siege and begin massacring the city's Muslim and Jewish populations.

1682 English musician Henry Purcell is appointed organist of Chapel Royal, London. Best remembered for his baroque compositions, Purcell is England's best-known 17th-century composer.

1798 Congress passes the Sedition Act, which makes it a crime to publish scandalous, false, or malicious writings about the U.S. government.

1811 The English poet Lord Byron returns to England after touring Europe and the Near East for two years. His travels inspired his first highly successful work, *Childe Harold's Pilgrimage*. The poem brought Byron almost instant public acclaim, and his taste, manners, and fashion all become widely imitated.

1853 The first U.S. World's Fair opens in Crystal Palace, New York.

MILESTONE

Bastille Day

On this day in 1789 French revolutionaries and mutinous army troops storm the Bastille, a state prison and royal fortress that had come to symbolize the tyranny of the Bourbon monarchs. This action signaled the beginning of the French Revolution, in which King Louis XVI was overthrown and tens of thousands of people, including the king and his wife, Marie Antoinette, were executed. Bastille Day is celebrated each year on this day to commemorate the end of monarchy and the ascendance of the idea that absolute power was not the exclusive right of the king as God's representative, but rather that the right and power to govern resided in the people themselves. This idea had been expressed throughout the eighteenth century by French philosophers, and the revolutionary acts of the day marked the beginning of the First Republic in France.

1865 English climber Edward Whymper leads the first team to reach the summit of the Matterhorn in the Alps.

1867 Swedish explosives manufacturer Alfred Nobel first demonstrates his invention, dynamite, at Merstham Quarry in Redhill, Surrey.

1881 American outlaw William H. Bonney ("Billy the Kid") is shot by his former friend Patrick Floyd Garrett.

1914 Dr. Robert H. Goddard of Worcester, Massachusetts, is granted the first patent for a liquid-fueled rocket design.

1933 In Germany, all political parties except the Nazi Party are outlawed.

1938 English director Alfred Hitchcock signs a contract with David O. Selznick to direct movies in Hollywood. His first American film, *Rebecca*, starring Laurence Olivier and Joan Fontaine, was released in 1940 and won Academy Awards for Best Picture and Best Cinematography.

1946 Dr. Benjamin Spock's *The Common Sense Book of Baby and Child Care* is published. The book, which prescribed treatment of children based on affection and respect,

---

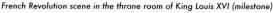

French Revolution scene in the throne room of King Louis XVI (milestone)

"When I was a little boy, they called me a liar, but now that I am grown up, they call me a writer."

—Isaac Bashevis Singer

became America's second best-seller of all time, after the Bible.

🏆 **1951** Citation becomes the first horse to earn more than $1,000,000 in his career when he wins the Hollywood Gold Cup at Hollywood Park in Inglewood, California.

1955 Volkswagen introduces the Karmann-Ghia, creating an "image car" to accompany its plain but reliable "Bugs" and "Buses." Sales climbed steadily through the 1960s, but Volkswagen found that the Bug had increased in popularity, especially in the U.S. market, and executives decided to abandon the Karmann-Ghia, which was last produced 1974.

1957 The famous American comedy team of Bud Abbott and Lou Costello end their partnership.

1958 King Faisal of Iraq is assassinated, along with his entire household and his prime minister, in a coup by army officers led by General Abdul Karim Kassem. The coup resulted in Iraq's becoming a republic.

1959 The first nuclear warship is launched, the 14,000-ton cruiser USS *Long Beach.*

1963 Relations between the Soviet Union and China reach the breaking point as the two governments engage in an angry ideological debate about the future of communism. China was unhappy with the Soviet Union's policy of cooperation with the West. On this day, the Soviet government issued a stinging rebuttal, saying "peaceful coexistence" between

communist and capitalist nations was essential in the atomic age.

1964 U.S. military intelligence publicly charges that North Vietnamese regular army officers were commanding and fighting in so-called Viet Cong forces in the northern provinces. This marked a major change in the tempo and scope of the war in South Vietnam and resulted in President Lyndon B. Johnson committing U.S. combat troops.

1972 Antiwar radio broadcasts made in Hanoi by actress Jane Fonda during the Vietnam War are referred to as "distressing" by the U.S. State Department.

1972 Jean Westwood is chosen head of the Democratic Party's National Committee, becoming the first woman to hold this position in either of the two major parties.

1976 Jimmy Carter wins the U.S. Democratic presidential nomination by a substantial margin at the party's convention in New York City.

Jane Fonda in North Vietnam

Pope Innocent III

971 Bishop Swithun is buried, according to his wishes, outside the west door of the minster in Winchester, England, so that "the sweet rain of heaven may fall upon [his] grave." When the minster was enlarged, Swithun's grave was opened on this day in order to re-inter the remains. It rained and continued to rain for 40 days, giving rise to the legend that if it rains on St. Swithun's Day, it will rain for a further 40 days.

1205 Pope Innocent III creates Church doctrine making all Jews liable to perpetual servitude and subjugation because of their crucifixion of Jesus.

1662 Charles II grants a charter to establish the Royal Society in London, England.

1783 In France, the first successful steamboat, the *Pyroscaphe*, makes a trial run on the River Saone.

1795 Written in 1792 by Rouget De Lisle, "La Marseillaise" is officially adopted as the French national anthem.

1806 Zebulon Pike, the U.S. Army officer who in 1805 led an exploring party in search of the source of the Mississippi River, sets off with a new expedition to seek out the headwaters of the Arkansas and Red rivers and to investigate Spanish settlements in New Mexico. The information he provided about Kansas and Colorado was a great impetus for future U.S. settlement.

1815 British oarsmen row Napoleon Bonaparte from his last home in France to HMS *Bellerophon*, where he surrenders to Captain Frederick Maitland, thinking he might be allowed to live as an exile in Britain. He was then transferred to HMS *Northumberland*, but didn't touch land until he arrived on St. Helena, his final place of exile.

1862 The ironclad CSS *Arkansas* battles with Union ships on the Mississippi River during the American Civil War, severely damaging three. The encounter changed the complexion of warfare on the Mississippi and helped to reverse Confederate fortunes on the river in the summer of 1862. The *Arkansas* was similar in design and appearance to the more famous CSS *Virginia* (*Merrimac*).

1869 Hippolyte Mège-Mouriérs of Paris receives a patent for margarine, originally created for use by the French navy.

"Writing is like getting married. One should never commit oneself until one is amazed at one's luck."

—*Iris Murdoch*

🏆 **1912** Led by athlete Jim Thorpe, the U.S. Olympic team wins more medals than any other nation at the Olympic Games in Stockholm, Sweden.

🏴 **1912** The British National Insurance Act goes into effect.

🔬 **1913** Franz Schneider of Germany files a patent application for synchronized machine-gun fire from an aircraft, allowing machine guns to fire safely between the blades of the propellers.

🇺🇸 **1916** Pacific Aero Products, which will be renamed the Boeing Company, is founded in Seattle, Washington, by William Boeing.

🇺🇸 **1922** The duck-billed platypus first arrives in America, direct from Australia. It was exhibited at the Bronx Zoo in New York City.

🇺🇸 **1933** Aviator Wiley Post, flying a Lockheed Vega called *Winnie Mae,* leaves New York for the first solo flight around the world. The trip took 7 days, 18 hours, and 49¹/₂ minutes.

🇺🇸 **1939** American aviator Clara Adams is the first woman to complete a round-the-world flight.

🇨🇿 **1949** Czechoslovakian-born Jaroslav Drobny, a Wimbledon tennis champion for only two weeks, defects to the West.

🔬 **1954** The first Boeing 707 jetliner takes off from Seattle, Washington.

🇺🇸 **1965** The U.S. Congress passes a law requiring a health warning on all cigarette packages.

🔬 **1965** The unmanned U.S. spacecraft *Mariner 4* passes over Mars at an altitude of 6,000 feet and sends back to Earth the first close-up images of the red planet.

Gianni Versace

Wiley Post climbs out of Winnie Mae after his first solo flight around the world

622 The traditional start of the Islamic Era, this day marks the occasion when a persecuted Muhammad fled from Mecca to Medina.

1212 The Battle of Las Navas de Tolosa takes place, establishing the rule of Christian kings on the throne of Spain.

1429 Joan of Arc leads the French Army in the successful Battle of Orleans. This battle marked the height of her fortunes.

1439 Kissing is outlawed in England in an attempt to halt the spread of the Plague.

1769 Father Junípero Serra, a Spanish Franciscan missionary, founds the first Catholic mission in California on the site of present-day San Diego. After Serra blessed his new outpost of Christianity in a high mass, the royal standard of Spain was unfurled over the mission, which he named San Diego de Alcala.

1790 The District of Columbia, or Washington, D.C., is established as the permanent location of the U.S. government.

1867 Reinforced concrete is patented in France by Joseph Monier, a Parisian gardener who made garden pots and tubs of concrete reinforced with an iron mesh.

1926 The American magazine *National Geographic*

> *"There are no small parts. Only small actors."*
>
> —*Ginger Rogers*

1486
ANDREA DEL SARTO
Italian painter (*Portrait of a Young Man; Pietà; The Sacrifice of Isaac*)

1723
SIR JOSHUA REYNOLDS
English portrait painter and first president of the Royal Academy

1821
MARY BAKER EDDY
American religious leader and founder of Christian Science

1872
ROALD AMUNDSEN
Norwegian explorer who discovered the South Pole; first man to sail through the Northwest Passage

1907
ORVILLE REDENBACHER
American popcorn gourmet and tycoon

1907
BARBARA STANWYCK
American actress (*Ladies of Leisure; Night Nurse; So Big*)

1911
GINGER ROGERS
American actress and dance partner of Fred Astaire

1942
MARGARET JEAN SMITH COURT
Australian tennis player and winner of 66 Grand Slam events

1948
PINCHAS ZUKERMAN
Israeli-born violinist and orchestra conductor

prints the first underwater color photographs. The pictures were taken off the Florida Keys.

1942 French police arrest nearly 14,000 Jewish men, women, and children in Paris as part of a German roundup of the Jewish community during World War II. After three days, they were deported to the concentration camp at Auschwitz, Poland.

1945 The United States conducts an atomic bomb test at its research facility in Los Alamos, New Mexico. The official development began with the establishment of the Manhattan Project in August 1942, which brought together scientists from the United States, Great Britain, and Canada. The project proceeded with urgency, since it was rumored that Nazi Germany had also embarked on a similar program.

1948 The *Vickers Viscount*, the world's first turbine-propeller aircraft, makes its maiden flight in Australia.

1950 The final of soccer's World Cup in Rio de Janeiro, Brazil, is watched by the largest crowd in sporting history— 199,854. Uruguay defeated Brazil.

Scientists and workmen rig first atomic bomb to 100-foot tower

Senator Barry Goldwater accepts the Republican presidential nomination

1951 American author J. D. Salinger's only novel, *The Catcher in the Rye,* is published by Little, Brown. The book, about a confused teenager disillusioned by the adult world, was an instant hit and would be taught in high schools for half a century. Fame did not agree with Salinger, who retreated to a hilltop cabin in Cornish, New York, but he continued to publish stories periodically.

1956 American circus performer Emmett Kelly, after 50 years of portraying the clown Weary Willy, does his last show under the canvas tent for Ringling Brothers, Barnum & Bailey Circus. It was also the last time the circus performed under canvas.

1964 In his acceptance speech for the Republican presidential nomination in San Francisco, U.S. senator Barry M. Goldwater says "extremism in the defense of liberty is no vice" and "moderation in the pursuit of justice is no virtue."

1967 Five thousand people attend a rally in London's Hyde Park demanding, "Legalize Pot in 1967."

1969 At 9:32 A.M., local time, *Apollo 11,* the first U.S. lunar landing mission, is launched from Cape Canaveral, Florida, on a historic journey to the surface of the moon. The Apollo program was a costly and labor-intensive endeavor, involving an estimated 400,000 engineers, technicians, and scientists, and costing $24 billion (about $100 billion in today's dollars).

1977 Shaun Cassidy achieves his only No. 1 song on the U.S. singles chart with "Da Doo Ron Ron."

1979 Saddam Hussein becomes president of Iraq.

1981 After 23 years of familiarity with the name "Datsun," Nissan executives in Japan decide to change the name of their cars to "Nissan."

1990 The Soviet Union drops its objection to a united Germany's membership in NATO.

709 B.C. The earliest confirmed recording of a solar eclipse is made in China.

1453 The Battle of Castillon takes place between France and England. The battle, which the English lost, signaled the end of the Hundred Years' War.

1790 Thomas Saint of London, England, patents the first sewing machine, although it doesn't appear ever to have been manufactured.

1821 Spain cedes Florida to the United States as part of a deal to cancel $5 million in debts.

1841 The first issue of *Punch* is published in London, England. The magazine came into being at a time of great bitterness, particularly toward the political systems of the day, and met the need for a humorous, family-oriented publication. *Punch* was published continuously until 1992. It was then bought and revived in 1996 by Mohamed Al Fayed, the owner of the famous London department store Harrods.

1861 The U.S. Congress authorizes the printing of paper money for the first time, primarily to assist in financing the Civil War. These "Demand Notes" were replaced a year later by "Legal Tender Notes," which were the predecessors of today's "Federal Reserve Notes."

1862 National cemeteries are authorized by the U.S. government. Arlington National Cemetery, located just outside Washington, D.C., in Virginia, is one of the most honored in the country.

1868 The city of Edo is replaced by Tokyo City as Japan's capital.

1913 Film audiences are introduced to the pie-in-the-face routine, recorded in the American silent film *A Noise from the Deep*. Mabel Normand hit Fatty Arbuckle in the face with a pie.

1917 The British royal family changes its name from "Saxe-Coburg-Gotha" to "Windsor."

1920 American author Sinclair Lewis finishes his now-famous novel *Main Street*.

1938 Doug "Wrong Way" Corrigan leaves Floyd Bennett Field in New York for

"Whatever you may look like, marry a man your own age—as your beauty fades, so will his eyesight."
—*Phyllis Diller*

Los Angeles, California. He landed his 1929 Curtiss Robin monoplane about 28 hours later in Ireland, at Dublin's Baldonnel Field.

1945 The final "Big Three" meeting between the United States, the Soviet Union, and Great Britain takes place toward the end of World War II. The discussions dealt with issues relating to postwar Europe and plans to deal with the ongoing conflict with Japan. By the time the meeting began, U.S. and British suspicions concerning Soviet intentions in Europe were intensifying.

1958 Paleontologists Louis and Mary Leakey discover one of the oldest hominid skulls in the Olduvai Gorge, northern Tanzania. Originally named *Zinjanthropus* (East African Man), the skull was later renamed *Australopithecus boisei*. The Leakeys estimated the skull to be 1.75 million years old.

1964 Donald Campbell, the son of Great Britain's most prolific land-speed record holder, Sir Malcolm Campbell, drives the Proteus Bluebird to a four-wheel, gasoline-powered land-speed record with two identical runs of 403 miles per hour at Lake Eyre, South Australia.

1968 The Beatles' animated film *Yellow Submarine*

Anastasio Somoza

premieres in London, England. In the movie's psychedelic fantasy, The Beatles save Pepperland from the evil Blue Meanies.

1979 Following a civil war in Nicaragua to protest brutally repressive acts, President Anastasio Somoza resigns and flees into exile in Miami, Florida.

1989 The American B-2 stealth bomber gets its first test flight at Edwards Air Force Base in California.

1990 Iraqi president Saddam Hussein gives a Revolutionary Day speech that claims Kuwait stole oil from Iraq.

1990 Seven nations negotiating German reunification reach agreement in Paris on Poland's permanent border, clearing the way for the merger of East and West Germany.

Walt Disney in front of Sleeping Beauty Castle on opening day at Disneyland

64 A fire erupts in Rome and when the flames finally die out more than a week later, nearly two-thirds of the city is destroyed. Some speculated that Emperor Nero had ordered the burning, but he was away in Antium when the fire began. According to later Roman historians, Nero blamed Christians for the fire and launched the first Roman persecution of them in response.

1536 In England, the authority of the pope is declared void by an act of Parliament.

1768 The *Boston Gazette* publishes "The Liberty Song," the first American patriotic song.

1853 The first North American international railroad is opened, as trains begin running between Portland, Maine, and Montreal, Quebec.

1863 During the American Civil War, "Negro troops" of the 54th Massachusetts Infantry Regiment under Colonel Robert G. Shaw assault fortified Confederates at Fort Wagner, South Carolina. Colonel Shaw and half of the 600 men in the regiment were killed.

1870 The Vatican Council proclaims the dogma of papal infallibility in matters of faith and morals.

1872 Great Britain introduces the concept of voting by secret ballot.

1877 American inventor Thomas Edison invents the carbon telephone transmitter for

---

MILESTONE

Hitler Publishes *Mein Kampf*

On this day in 1925, seven months after being released from Landsberg jail, Nazi leader Adolf Hitler publishes the first volume of his personal manifesto, *Mein Kampf.* Dictated by Hitler during his nine-month stay in prison, *Mein Kampf,* or *My Struggle,* was a bitter and turgid narrative filled with anti-semitic outpourings, disdain for morality, worship of power, and the blueprints for his plan of Nazi world domination. The autobiographical work soon became the bible of Germany's Nazi Party. In the early 1920s, the ranks of Hitler's Nazi Party swelled with resentful Germans who sympathized with the party's bitter hatred.

Mein Kampf opened with words "Das Wort" (the Word)

Western Union and has other first successes with recording and storing the sounds of the human voice.

1909 One hundred sixteen people are killed in an earthquake in Greece.

1921 In France, Albert Calmette and Camille Guerin administer the first BCG vaccination against tuberculosis.

1925 The American Automobile Association declares women drivers to be as competent as men.

1934 British king George V opens the Mersey Tunnel, the longest underwater tunnel to date.

1935 Emperor Haile Selassie of Abyssinia (Ethiopia) speaks to his parliament in Addis Ababa about an imminent attack by Italy, saying that it is better to die for freedom than to live as a slave.

1936 The Spanish Civil War begins as a revolt by right-wing Spanish military officers in Spanish Morocco and spreads to mainland Spain.

King George V

Abalone is illuminated on the sunken Titanic

1942 The world's first jet-powered flight is made by the German Messerschmitt Me 262 prototype fitted with two Junkers 109-004A turbojet engines, piloted by Fritz Wendel.

1947 U.S. president Harry S. Truman signs the Presidential Succession Act. The act designated the speaker of the house as next in line to the presidency after the vice president, followed by the Senate president pro tempore, then by members of the cabinet. In 1792, the Senate president pro tempore was next in line after the vice president, and in 1886 Congress changed that to place cabinet officers as first in line.

1960 Production begins on American actress Marilyn Monroe's final film, *The Misfits*.

1968 The Intel Corporation, where the microchip would be invented, is incorporated in the United States.

1969 After leaving a party on Chappaquiddick Island, U.S. senator Edward "Ted" Kennedy of Massachusetts drives off a bridge into a tide-swept pond. Kennedy escaped, but his passenger, Mary Jo Kopechne, did not.

1969 John Fairfax of England becomes the first person to row solo across the Atlantic Ocean as he arrives in Fort Lauderdale, Florida.

1976 Fourteen-year-old Romanian gymnast Nadia Comaneci stuns those watching the Olympics by executing a perfect score of "10" from the judges. This was the first perfect score ever recorded on the uneven parallel bars.

1980 India launches its first satellite, *Rohini*.

1986 The remains of RMS *Titanic* are seen by the world for the first time as videotapes of the British luxury liner are released by researchers from Woods Hole Oceanographic Institution in Massachusetts.

> *"There are two kinds of marriages—where the husband quotes the wife and where the wife quotes the husband."*
>
> —*Clifford Odets*

2781 B.C. The first known Egyptian calendar, created in the XII Dynasty is presumed to begin.

1545 The *Mary Rose*, the pride of English King Henry VIII's battle fleet, keels over and sinks. More than 700 lives were lost.

1553 Mary Tudor is proclaimed queen of England.

1799 During Napoleon Bonaparte's Egyptian campaign, a soldier discovers a black basalt slab inscribed with ancient writing near Rosetta, a town about 35 miles north of Alexandria. The stone contained passages written in Greek, Egyptian hieroglyphics, and Egyptian demotic. The Greek passage noted that the three scripts were all of identical meaning. The "Rosetta Stone" thus held the key to solving the riddle of hieroglyphics.

1821 George IV is crowned king of the United Kingdom of Great Britain and Ireland. His wife, Caroline, from whom he had separated, traveled from Italy to claim her rights but was prevented from attending the coronation.

1837 English civil engineer Isambard Kingdom Brunel's *Great Britain*, the first Atlantic liner built of iron, is launched.

> *"I don't want to make money. I just want to be wonderful."*
>
> —*Marilyn Monroe*

MILESTONE

Pennsylvania Passes Censorship Laws

On this day in 1911, Pennsylvania becomes the first state to pass laws censoring movies. From their debut as peep shows in penny arcades and vaudeville attractions, movies were viewed with suspicion by authorities wishing to safeguard American morals. As early as 1909, movie producers had submitted to censorship, allowing the Board of Censorship in New York, for example, to review new films. The Pennsylvania laws were the first specifically allowing censorship by a government body. In 1915, the U.S. Supreme Court upheld such laws. Fearing increased government censorship, studios began working together to censor their own films.

1843 Amelia Jenks Bloomer, an American social reformer against sex discrimination and advocating temperance and women's suffrage, introduces a new form of female dress, which is eventually named "bloomers."

1848 In Seneca Falls, New York, the first women's rights convention ever held in the United States convenes, with almost 200 women in attendance. It was organized by Lucretia Mott and Elizabeth Cady Stanton, who met at the 1840 World Anti-Slavery Convention in London, England. As women, they were barred from the convention floor, and this was the impetus for their founding of the movement.

1870 France declares war on Prussia, heralding the beginning of the Franco-Prussian War.

1879 "Doc" Holliday commits his first murder, killing a man for shooting up his New Mexico saloon. Despite his formidable reputation as a deadly gunslinger, Holliday engaged in only eight shootouts during his life, and it has only been verified that he killed two men.

Lucretia Mott, left and Elizabeth Cady Stanton, right

1898 Novelist Émile Zola flees France after being convicted of libel against the French Army in the notorious Dreyfus affair. Zola wrote an inflammatory newspaper letter, entitled "J'Accuse," exposing a military cover-up regarding Captain Alfred Dreyfus, who had been accused of espionage in 1894 and sentenced in a secret military court-martial.

1903 The first Tour de France cycle race, created by journalist Henri Desgrange, ends in Paris. Maurice Garin was the first to cross the finish line, two hours and 49 minutes ahead of his nearest rival.

1935 The first American automatic parking meter, the Park-O-Meter invented by Carlton Magee, is installed in Oklahoma City, Oklahoma, by the Dual Parking Meter Company. Twenty-foot spaces were painted on the pavement, and a parking meter that accepted nickels was planted in the concrete at the head of each space.

1941 British prime minister Sir Winston Churchill first displays the two-finger "V for Victory" hand signal.

1945 The USS *Cod* saves 51 sailors from a Dutch submarine. It remains the only international submarine-to-submarine rescue to take place.

1946 American actress Marilyn Monroe takes her first screen test and is signed to her first contract with Twentieth Century-Fox Studios. The first of her 29 films was *Scudda-Hoo! Scudda-Hay!*

1949 Singer Harry Belafonte begins recording for Capitol Records. Capitol didn't believe that Belafonte was "commercial enough," but he eventually signed with RCA Victor and had a highly productive career.

1956 Responding to the Egyptian government's unceasing attacks on Western colonialism and imperialism, the United States withdraws its financial aid to Egypt for construction of the Aswan Dam on the Nile River.

1962 A U.S. antimissile missile makes the first successful interception of an intercontinental ballistic missile.

Winston Churchill holds up two fingers to make V-sign for victory

1402 Mongol warrior Tamerlane (who claimed to be a descendant of Genghis Khan), looking to expand his domain, leads a massive force of Tartars and defeats and captures the sultan of the Ottoman Empire at the Battle of Angora (now Ankara, Turkey).

1654 Following the signing of the Anglo-Portuguese Treaty, Portugal is placed under English control.

1715 The British Riot Act goes into effect. The act prohibited assemblages of more than 12 people. If larger groups assembled, they were read the Riot Act, which called upon them to disperse.

1773 Scottish settlers arrive for the first time at Nova Scotia, Canada.

1810 Colombia declares its independence from Spain.

1869 American author Mark Twain's book *The Innocents Abroad* is published, recounting his journey to Europe and the Holy Land. It became a bestseller.

Sitting Bull

BORN ON THIS DAY

1304
FRANCESCO PETRARCH
Italian poet

1844
JOHN SHOLTO DOUGLAS
Eighth marquis of Queensberry and British boxing patron

1873
ALBERTO SANTOS-DUMONT
Brazilian aviation pioneer

1889
JOHN REITH
First director-general of the British Broadcasting Corporation

1903
OLAV V
King of Norway and first royal Olympic gold medalist (yachting)

1919
SIR EDMUND HILLARY
New Zealand explorer who was one of the first men to climb Mount Everest

1933
NELSON DOUBLEDAY JR.
American publisher and owner of the New York Mets

1938
NATALIE WOOD
American actress (*Rebel Without a Cause; West Side Story; Splendor in the Grass*)

1938
DIANA RIGG
Tony Award-winning English actress

1942
PETE HAMILTON
American race-car driver

1947
CARLOS SANTANA
Mexican musician ("Evil Ways"; "Black Magic Woman"; "Oye Como Va")

1956
PAUL COOK
British musician (Sex Pistols)

1957
DONNA DIXON
American actress (*Bosom Buddies; Doctor Detroit; Spies Like Us*)

1871 The English Football Association Challenge Cup Competition, better known today as the FA Cup, is established. The first final, played in 1872, saw the Wanderers beat the Royal Engineers 1-0 and was watched by a crowd of 2,000.

1881 Five years after General George A. Custer's infamous defeat at the Battle of Little Bighorn, Hunkpapa Teton Sioux leader Sitting Bull surrenders to the U.S. Army, which promises amnesty for him and his followers. Sitting Bull had been a major leader in the 1876 Sioux uprising that resulted in the death of Custer and 264 of his men at Little Bighorn.

1910 The Christian Endeavor Society of Missouri campaigns to ban all motion pictures depicting kissing between nonrelatives.

1917 Serbs, Croats, and Slovenes agree to the Pact of Corfu, forming a union called Yugoslavia.

1940 The American magazine *Billboard* publishes its first "Music Popularity Chart." The first No. 1 hit was "I'll Never Smile Again" by the Tommy Dorsey Orchestra, on which Frank Sinatra sang vocals. From then on, *Billboard* published its list of top sellers once a week.

"There are several good protections against temptaion, but the surest is cowardice."

—*Mark Twain*

Women's Army Corps poster

1942 The first detachment of the U.S. Women's Army Auxiliary Corps begins basic training at Fort Des Moines, Iowa. It would become informally known as the WACs.

1944 As German dictator Adolf Hitler studies a map during a meeting at the Wolf's Lair Headquarters in Rastenburg, East Prussia during World War II, a bomb placed under the conference table by a top officer of the Wehrmacht explodes. Hitler survived, thousands of officers were arrested, tortured, and executed.

1948 President Harry S. Truman institutes the first peacetime draft in the history of the United States, underlining the urgency of his administration's concern about a possible military confrontation with the Soviet Union.

1954 The French sign an armistice with the Vietminh, ending French involvement in Vietnam and separating it into North and South.

1956 Tunisia's independence is recognized by France.

1957 British prime minister Harold Macmillan coins a famous phrase, saying: "Let us be frank about it. Most of our people have never had it so good."

1960 The Soviet Union successfully recovers two dogs as part of its space program. They were the first living creatures to return from a space flight.

1962 The world's first passenger hovercraft service opens. Operated by British United Airways, it provided a link across Dee estuary between Rhyl, North Wales, and Wallasey in Cheshire.

1965 Owen Finlay Maclaren, a former aeronautical engineer and test pilot who worked on the design of the Spitfire undercarriage, files a patent for the Maclaren® folding baby buggy.

1965 Great Britain's House of Lords unexpectedly approves a bill to abolish hanging, which becomes law on November 8.

1985 Treasure hunters find the Spanish galleon *Nuestra Senora de Atocha*, which sank 40 miles off the coast of Key West, Florida, in 1622. They also discovered her cargo of $400 million in coins and silver ingots, the biggest underwater jackpot in history.

Pendant found at the wreck site of the Nuestra Senora de Atocha

Neil Armstrong

365 Alexandria, Egypt, is hit by an earthquake. Approximately 50,000 die.

1667 The Peace of Breda ends the Second Anglo-Dutch War, and the Dutch territory of New Netherlands (New York state) falls into English hands.

1711 The year-long Russo-Turkish War ends as Russia and Turkey sign the Treaty of Pruth.

1733 The first honorary Doctor of Law degree in the United States is granted to John Winthrop by Harvard College in Cambridge, Massachusetts.

1773 Pope Clement XIV issues the politically based brief *Dominus ac redemptor noster,* which officially dissolves the Society of Jesuits. This left important gaps in Catholic education and foreign missions.

MILESTONE

Rigolly and Campbell Set Speed Records

On this day in 1904 Louis Rigolly, driving a fifteen-liter Gobron-Brillie on the Ostend-Newport road in Belgium, becomes the first man to break the 100 mile per hour barrier in a car by raising the landspeed record to 103.55 miles per hour. On the same day in 1925, Sir Malcolm Campbell is first to beat the 150 miles per hour mark when he drives his Sunbeam to a two-way average of 150.33 miles per hour at the Pendine Sands in Wales.

1831 Belgium breaks from the Netherlands to become an independent kingdom and crowns Leopold I its first king.

1836 The first Canadian railroad opens, running between Laprairie and St. John, Quebec.

1861 In the Battle of Bull Run, the first major land battle of the American Civil War, Union forces endure a loss of 3,000 men while the Confederates suffer 2,000 casualties. The scale of this bloodshed horrified the U.S. government in Washington, which was now faced with an uncertain military strategy in quelling the "Southern insurrection."

1865 In what may be the first true western showdown, in Springfield, Mississipi, Wild Bill Hickok has a quarrel with Dave Tutt, a former Union soldier. The two agreed to a duel the next day and confronted each other from opposite sides of the town

The Battle of Bull Run

Sir Francis Chichester

square. Tutt drew his revolver and fired a shot that went wild, then Hickok shot Tutt with a bullet through the chest.

1873 American outlaw Jesse James and his gang pull off their first train robbery. Their downfall started in 1876 when, after killing two people and failing to secure any money in an attempted bank robbery, they lost several members. A reward eventually tempted one of the gang, Robert Ford, who caught James off guard and killed him.

1886 Elzear Alexandre Taschereau, 66, archbishop of Quebec, becomes the first Canadian to be made a cardinal in the Catholic Church.

1904 The Trans-Siberian railway is finally completed. It took 13 years of effort to lay the 4,607 miles of track.

> *"Always do sober what you said you'd do drunk. That will teach you to keep your mouth shut."*
>
> —*Ernest Hemingway*

1946 U.S. lieutenant James J. Davidson becomes the first pilot to take off and land a jet aircraft from a ship-based launching platform.

1959 A U.S. District Court judge in New York City rules that D. H. Lawrence's novel *Lady Chatterley's Lover* is not pornographic.

1960 England's Sir Francis Chichester sets a new record of 40 days for a solo Atlantic crossing when he lands in New York in his yacht *Gypsy Moth II*.

1968 American Arnold Palmer becomes the first golfer in history to make one million dollars in career earnings.

1969 *Apollo XI* astronauts Neil Armstrong and Edwin "Buzz" Aldrin lift off from the moon and return to the command module piloted by Michael Collins. The astronauts left behind a plaque reading, "Here men from the planet Earth first set foot upon the moon, July 1969 A.D. We came in peace for all mankind."

1970 After 11 years, the Aswan High Dam across the Nile River in Egypt is completed. The dam ended the cycle of flood and drought in the Nile River region and exploited a tremendous source of renewable energy, but it had several negative environmental impacts.

1974 The U.S. House Judiciary Committee approves two Articles of Impeachment against President Richard M. Nixon for his possible involvement in the Watergate affair.

1298 The English army—using longbows for the first time—routs Scottish rebels, including William Wallace, at the battle of Falkirk.

1587 Following Sir Walter Raleigh's failure to establish a colony in the New World, John White delivers 177 colonists to Roanoke Island off North Carolina to establish a second colony. The colony vanishes under mysterious circumstances.

1598 English playwright William Shakespeare's *The Merchant of Venice* is entered on the Stationers' Register. Although the entry licensed its printing, the first version of the play would not be published for another two years.

1604 Bishop Bancroft and King James I of England and VI of Scotland develop a set of 14 instructions to the translators of a new version of the Bible. The instructions were designed to ensure that the work would be a Protestant Bible and biblical names be as close as possible to the original. The new translation would be called the King James Version.

1793 Alexander Mackenzie, after whom Canada's Mackenzie River is named, becomes the first European to cross the Rocky Mountains and reach the Pacific Ocean. A young Scotsman engaged in the fur trade out of Montreal, Mackenzie made his epic journey across the continent without any of the governmental financial backing and support given to Americans Meriwether Lewis and William Clark more than a decade later,

Aleksandr Kerensky

when they made the first overland journey across the United States to the Pacific coast.

1893 Wellesley College professor Katharine Lee Bates writes the poem "America the Beautiful" in Colorado Springs, Colorado, having been inspired by the view from Pike's Peak.

1894 The first automobile road race takes place in France over a distance of 78 miles from Paris to Rouen. Count De Dion breaks the record average speed of 13.6 miles per hour during this race.

1916 A bomb hidden in a suitcase explodes during a World War I "Preparedness Day" parade on Market Street in San Francisco, California. The bomb killed 10 people and wounded 40.

1917 Aleksandr Kerensky becomes prime minister of the Russian provisional government following the overthrow of the czar. His failure to deal with economic problems and his insistence on remaining in World War I led to his overthrow by the Bolsheviks later that year.

1933 American aviator Wiley Post completes his attempt to become the first to fly solo around the world.

1934 John Dillinger, America's "Public Enemy No. 1," is killed in a hail of bullets by federal agents. In a fiery bank-robbing career that lasted just over a year, Dillinger and his associates robbed 11 banks for more than $300,000 and killed seven police officers and three federal agents.

1942 In World War II Poland, the deportation of Jews from the Warsaw ghetto begins, as thousands are rounded up and transported to a newly constructed extermination camp at Treblinka.

1944 The Bretton Woods Conference in New Hampshire creates the International Monetary Fund. The IMF was created to maintain a stable system of buying and selling currencies so that payments in foreign money could take place between countries in a smooth manner. It actually began operation in 1946, with 39 member countries.

1960 United States-owned sugar factories in Cuba are nationalized.

1963 English sculptor Frank Dobson dies. Dobson was part of the "London Group," which included Eric Gill, Jacob Epstein, and Roger Fry. His best-known works were *Cornucopia*, *The Man Child*, and *Morning*.

1965 The comedy *Till Death Us Do Part* debuts on England's BBC-TV. The popular show was the forerunner of the American *All in the Family*.

1975 The U.S. House of Representatives and the U.S. Senate vote to restore the American citizenship of Confederate general Robert E. Lee.

1981 Turkish extremist Mehmet Ali Agca is sentenced by a Rome court to life in prison for an assassination attempt on Pope John Paul II.

1982 Twenty-two hundred couples are married in the biggest wedding ceremony in history. The Reverend Sun Myung Moon of the Unification Church performed it in New York City.

> *"I'm like old wine. They don't bring me out very often, but I'm well preserved."*
> —Rose Fitzgerald Kennedy

The Reverend Sun Myung Moon sprinkles holy water over married couples

776 B.C. The first Olympic Games open in Olympia, Greece.

636 The Byzantine Empire loses control of most of Palestine to Arabs.

1715 The first lighthouse in America is authorized to be built at Little Brewster Island, Massachusetts.

1798 French general Napoleon Bonaparte captures Alexandria, Egypt.

1827 The first swimming school in the United States opens in Boston, Massachusetts. Famous former students include John Quincy Adams and John James Audubon.

1829 William Austin Burt of Michigan patents the first typewriter.

1848 Protesting slavery as well as U.S. involvement in the Mexican War, American author Henry David Thoreau refuses to pay his $1 poll tax and is casually arrested and jailed. When told he could leave the next day, he angrily objected. Leo Tolstoy and Mohandas Gandhi later read his written account of the experience, and it persuaded them to advocate civil disobedience.

1888 Scottish veterinary surgeon John Boyd Dunlop files a patent for the pneumatic tire after fitting his son's tricycle with tires made from lengths of garden hose filled with water. The family doctor suggested filling the tires with air instead of water, and so the first pneumatic cycle tire was born. Dunlop's patent was

Londoners sleep on stopped escalators of a subway station during the German bombing blitz

later invalidated by the discovery that another Scotsman, Robert Thompson, had patented a pneumatic tire in 1845. Thompson's invention had been used only for horse-drawn carriages and since forgotten.

1903 The first Ford Model A is delivered to its owner, Dr. Ernst Pfenning of Chicago, Illinois. The car cost $850 and was able to reach a speed of 30 miles per hour.

1914 Following the killing of Archduke Francis Ferdinand by a Serb assassin, Austria-Hungary issues an ultimatum to Serbia.

1940 The German "Blitz" of World War II begins with all-night air raids on London, England.

1945 French marshal Henri Petain, who had headed the Vichy government—which

> *"As man draws nearer to the stars, why should he not also draw nearer to his neighbor?"*
> —*Lyndon B. Johnson*

became a German tool during World War II—is charged with treason. He was condemned to death, but his sentence was later commuted.

1952 Egypt's "Society of Free Officers" seizes control of the government in a coup staged by Colonel Gamal Abdal Nasser. King Farouk, whose rule had been criticized for its corruption and failures in the first Arab-Israeli war, abdicated power.

1956 U.S. lieutenant colonel Frank K. Everest becomes the fastest man alive when his Bell X-2 rocket plane reaches the speed of Mach 2.87 (about 1,900 miles per hour), almost three times the speed of sound.

1962 The *Telstar* satellite sends the first major live television broadcast between the United States and Europe.

1962 Australia's Dawn Fraser becomes the first woman to swim 100 meters in under one minute.

1964 U.S. president Lyndon B. Johnson launches his "War on Poverty." Aimed at nothing less than eradicating poverty, it met with only modest results.

1967 English cyclist Tommy Simpson dies in intense heat during the 13th stage of the Tour de France. In 1962 he had been the first Briton ever to wear the yellow leader's jersey.

1973 After U.S. president Richard M. Nixon refuses to turn over tapes and documents possibly involved in the Watergate scandal, special prosecutor Archibald Cox serves subpoenas on the White House.

1984 The first resignation of a Miss America occurs when 21-year-old Vanessa Williams, the first African-American winner in the pageant's history, relinquishes her title as nude photos of her are printed in *Penthouse* magazine.

1986 England's Prince Andrew, fourth in line to the British throne and the duke of York, marries commoner Sarah Ferguson in Westminster Abbey in front of a global television audience of 300 million.

1996 The U.S. women's gymnastics team wins its first Olympic gold medal. The win was clinched by a dramatic vault from 18-year-old Kerri Strug, who made the vault with a badly sprained ankle.

1997 Serbian president Slobodan Milosevic is sworn in as president of the Federal Republic of Yugoslavia.

2000 At 24 years of age, American golfer Tiger Woods wins the British Open to become the youngest player to win the career "Grand Slam" of golf (The Masters, PGA Championship, U.S. Open, and British Open). He was also the first to win all four majors since American Jack Nicklaus's victory in 1966.

Kerri Strug

1216 Cencio Savelli is consecrated Pope Honorius III. While serving for 11 years, he confirmed two well-known religious orders: the Dominicans (1216) and the Franciscans (1223).

1487 The citizens of Leeuwarden Neth in the Netherlands rebel against a ban on foreign beer.

1534 In the name of King François I of France, explorer Jacques Cartier takes possession of mainland Canada.

1567 During her imprisonment at Lochleven Castle in Scotland, Mary, Queen of Scots, is forced to abdicate in favor of her one-year-old son, later crowned King James VI of Scotland and, in 1603, James I of England. In 1587, she was beheaded for treason.

1673 English astronomer Edmund Halley, for whom the famous comet is named, enters Queen's College, Oxford, as an undergraduate.

1683 The first German settlers leave for the United States.

1701 The administrator in French North America, Antoine de la Mothe Cadillac, founds a fur-trading post, which he names Font-Pontchartain du Détroit. The name is eventually shortened to Detroit.

> *"All generalizations are dangerous, even this one."*
>
> —*Alexandre Dumas*

MILESTONE

O. Henry Released from Prison

William Sydney Porter, otherwise known as O. Henry, is released from prison on this day in 1901, after serving three years in jail for embezzlement from a bank in Austin, Texas. He went to jail and began writing stories to support his young daughter. After his release, Porter moved to New York and worked for *New York World*, writing one short story a week from 1903 to 1906. In 1904, his first story collection, *Cabbages and Kings*, was published. His second, *The Four Million*, contained one of his most beloved stories, *The Gift of the Magi*.

William Sydney Porter (O. Henry)

1704 English admirals Sir George Rooke and Sir Cloudesley Shovel capture Gibraltar from Spain.

1758 In the American colonies, George Washington is admitted to the Virginia House of Burgesses.

1797 Admiral (later Lord) Nelson suffers the wound that leads to the loss of his right arm during an assault on Santa Cruz de Tenerife.

1847 After 17 months and many miles of travel, Brigham Young leads 148 Mormon pioneers into Utah's Valley of the Great Salt Lake. Gazing over the parched earth of the remote location, he declared, "This is the place." Within days, Young and his companions began building the future Salt Lake City at the foot of the Wasatch Mountains.

1883 The first man to swim the English Channel, Matthew Webb, drowns while trying to swim the rapids below Niagara Falls.

1911 The Lost City of the Incas, Vilcapampa (now called Machu Picchu), is discovered by American explorer Hiram Bingham. It is where the last Incan Emperors found refuge from the Spanish conquistadors.

1923 The Treaty of Lausanne, which settled the boundaries of modern Turkey, is concluded in Switzerland. Turkey gave up all claims to non-Turkish territories it had won during World War I.

1929 U.S. president Herbert Hoover proclaims the Kellogg-Briand Pact, renouncing war as an instrument of foreign policy.

1933 The first successful lung removal operation is performed by Dr. W. F. Reinhoff Jr. in Baltimore, Maryland.

1936 The British General Post Office inaugurates a telephone Speaking Clock service, and 248,828 calls were made in the first week.

1938 American bandleader Artie Shaw first records "Begin the Beguine." Shaw, a dedicated clarinet player, turned professional in his teens. The record rocketed him to international fame.

1943 The heaviest British bombing raids so far during World War II set the entire city of Hamburg on fire, killing 42,000 German civilians. During two raids within 24 hours, 2,326 tons of bombs were dropped, creating a "firestorm," a word that entered the language for the first time as a result of this event. The bombing was followed up with further devastating air raids on the city by the Royal Air Force and United States Air Force on August 3.

1948 The Soviets blockade Berlin, Germany, from the west.

1949 Novelist and Nobel laureate Thomas Mann returns to his homeland of West Germany after years in exile. Mann spoke against the Nazis from as early as 1929, left for Switzerland in 1933, and settled in the United States in 1936. He broadcast anti-Hitler speeches to Germany over the BBC during World War II, returning to Switzerland in 1947 and Germany in 1949.

1982 The International Whaling Commission votes for a total ban on commercial whaling.

Ancient Inca city Machu Picchu in the Andes mountains

1261 Constantinople is recaptured by Emperor Michael VIII. This reestablishes the Byzantine Empire, although on a much reduced scale.

1554 Mary I of England makes an unpopular marriage to Philip II of Spain, a devout Catholic. Mary's attempts to restore Catholicism to England resulted in harsher and harsher persecution of Protestants. Eventually more than 300 were burned at the stake as heretics, earning her the nickname "Bloody Mary."

1593 King Henri IV of France converts from being a Protestant to a Roman Catholic.

1775 Maryland issues currency depicting King George III of Great Britain and Ireland trampling the Magna Carta.

1814 George Stephenson of England demonstrates his first steam locomotive, called "Blucher."

1853 California Rangers claim a $6,000 reward by

MILESTONE

Dylan Goes Electric

Folk singing legend Bob Dylan changed the face of folk—and rock—music forever when he appeared on this day in 1965 at the Newport Folk Festival. Forsaking his acoustic guitar for an electric guitar, and backed by the Paul Butterfield Blues Band, Dylan launched into a raucous rendition of "Maggie's Farm" and in doing so outraged his fans and many other folk singers. His change eventually moved rock and folk music closer together, and he brought with him into the world limelight a number of musicians who played behind him, such as Al Kooper, Paul Butterfield, and The Band.

Bob Dylan

---

bringing in the severed head of outlaw Joaquin Murrieta. In the early months of 1853, a wild band of desperadoes began terrorizing Calaveras County in central California. Law officers believed the shadowy Murrieta led the outlaws, although confusion abounded since there were at least four desperadoes named Joaquin in the territory.

1866 Ulysses S. Grant is elevated to the rank of a full (four-star) general of the U.S. Army. He was the first American officer to reach that rank.

1871 Perforated wrapping paper is patented by Seth Wheeler of Albany, New York.

1909 French aviator Louis Blériot is the first person to fly across the English Channel. His aircraft was a 28-horsepower wooden monoplane tied together with piano strings. It weighed only 45 pounds and had a wingspan of just 23 feet.

1917 Mata Hari (Margaretha Geertruida Zelle), the archetypal seductive female spy, is sentenced to death in

---

Starting the motor for Louis Blériot's cross-channel flight

> *"Success is the space one occupies in the newspaper. Success is one day's insolence."*
>
> —Elias Canetti

France for spying on Germany's behalf during World War I.

1943 Benito Mussolini, fascist dictator of Italy, is voted out of power by his own Grand Council and arrested upon leaving a meeting with King Vittorio Emanuele, who tells Il Duce that World War II is lost.

1945 Meeting in Potsdam during World War II, Allied leaders call on Japan to surrender or face "prompt and utter destruction."

1956 The Italian ocean liner *Andrea Doria* and the Swedish ocean liner *Stockholm* collide in a heavy Atlantic fog. Fifty-one passengers and crew were killed in the collision but, miraculously, all 1,660 on the *Andrea Doria* were rescued before it sank the next morning.

Lance Armstrong

1994 Israeli prime minister Yitzhak Rabin and King Hussein of Jordan sign a declaration that ends their 46-year state of war.

1999 Having overcome cancer, Lance Armstrong becomes the first cyclist on an American team to win the Tour de France.

2000 A supersonic Air France Concorde jet crashes on takeoff from Paris, killing all 113 people on board. It was the first crash of the supersonic passenger jet.

Benjamin Franklin

657 Mu'awiyah, an early Islamic leader and founder of the great Umayyad dynasty of caliphs, defeats Caliph Ali in the Battle of Siffin in Mesopotamia. He restored unity to the Muslim empire and made Damascus its capital.

1529 Francisco Pizarro of Spain receives a royal license from the queen "to discover and conquer Peru."

1579 English explorer Sir Francis Drake leaves San Francisco to cross the Pacific Ocean.

1745 The first recorded women's cricket match takes place at Gosden Common near Guildford, Surrey, England.

1775 The U.S. postal system is established by the 2nd Continental Congress, with Benjamin Franklin as its first Postmaster General.

1779 A silver medallion, the first decoration to a foreign national, is awarded by the U.S. Congress to Lieutenant Colonel François Louis Treisseidre de Fleury. De Fleury commanded part of the American attack that captured the British flag at

BORN ON THIS DAY

1796
GEORGE CATLIN
American author and painter of Native American scenes

1856
GEORGE BERNARD SHAW
Irish Nobel Prize-winning dramatist (*Pygmalion*)

1875
CARL GUSTAV JUNG
Swiss founder of analytic psychology

1894
ALDOUS HUXLEY
English author (*Brave New World*)

1902
GRACIE ALLEN
American comedienne (*The George Burns and Gracie Allen Show*)

1908
SALVADOR ALLENDE
Chilean president (1970–73) who became the world's first democratically elected Marxist president

1922
BLAKE EDWARDS
American writer and movie director (*10; Victor/Victoria*)

1922
JASON ROBARDS JR.
American actor (*All the President's Men; Julia*)

1928
STANLEY KUBRICK
American movie director (*Dr. Strangelove or: How I Learned to Stop Worrying and Love the Bomb; 2001: A Space Odyssey; A Clockwork Orange*)

1943
MICK JAGGER
English rock singer (Rolling Stones)

1956
DOROTHY HAMILL
American Olympic gold medal winning figure skater

1959
KEVIN SPACEY
American actor (*Glengarry Glen Ross; The Usual Suspects; American Beauty*)

Stony Point, New York, during the Revolutionary War.

1788 British colonists settle Sydney, Australia.

1835 The first sugar cane plantation in Hawaii starts.

1847 The Republic of Liberia, formerly a colony of the American Colonization Society, declares its independence. Under pressure from Great Britain, the United States hesitantly accepted Liberian sovereignty, making the West African nation the first democratic republic in African history.

1847 In Dover, New Hampshire, Moses Garrish Farmer builds the first miniature train that children can ride.

1869 The Disestablishment Bill is passed in England, officially dissolving the Church of Ireland. Organized opposition coined one of longest words in the English language as a result: antidisestablishmentarianism.

1878 American outlaw Black Bart robs his last stagecoach. Wearing a flour sack over his head, he stole a safe box with $400 and a passenger's diamond ring and watch. When the empty box was recovered, a taunting poem signed "Black Bart" was found inside. This wasn't the first

> *"Experience is not what happens to a man; it is what a man does with what happens to him."*
>
> —Aldous Huxley

time he had robbed a stagecoach and left a poem for the police; however, it was the last time he got away with it.

1887 Polish doctor L. L. Zamenhof publishes the first book in Esperanto. Created with the idea of promoting peace and understanding among cultures, Esperanto was an artificial language for use between people who speak different native languages.

1920 The 19th Amendment to the U.S. Constitution is ratified, granting women the right to vote.

1923 Scottish inventor John Logie Baird files his patent for a "system of transmitting views, portraits, and scenes by telegraphy or wireless telegraphy," now better known as television.

1941 In retaliation for the Japanese occupation of French Indochina during World War II, U.S. president Franklin D. Roosevelt seizes all Japanese assets in the United States.

1945 A few weeks before the defeat of Japan in World War II, Winston Churchill is forced to resign as British prime minister following his party's electoral defeat by the Labour Party. It was the first general election held in Britain in more than a decade.

1953 Fidel Castro begins revolt against the regime of Fulgencio Batista. The attack, on an army barracks in eastern Cuba, was unsuccessful, but Castro finally ousted Batista in 1959.

1956 The Suez Crisis begins when Egyptian president Gamal Abdel Nasser nationalizes the British- and French-owned Suez Canal, hoping to charge tolls that would pay for construction of a massive dam on the Nile River.

1971 *Apollo 15* is launched from Cape Kennedy, Florida, for a fourth lunar landing and the debut of the lunar rover.

Lunar rover during the Apollo 15 mission

MILESTONE

FBI Founded

On this day in 1908, the Federal Bureau of Investigation (FBI) is born when U.S. Attorney General Charles Bonaparte orders a group of newly hired federal investigators to report to the Department of Justice. When the Department of Justice was created in 1870 to enforce federal law and coordinate judicial policy, it had no permanent investigators on its staff. Seeking to form an independent and more efficient investigative arm, 10 former Secret Service employees were hired to join an expanded Office of the Chief Examiner. The date when these agents reported to duty is celebrated as the genesis of the FBI.

1214 During the Battle of Bouvines, Philip II Augustus of France wins a decisive victory over a coalition of the Holy Roman emperor Otto IV, King John of England, and others. The victory enhanced the power and the prestige of the French monarchy in Europe.

1245 Excommunicated on charges of sacrilege, Holy Roman emperor Frederick II is deposed by Pope Innocent IV and the First Council of Lyons.

1540 Thomas Cromwell is executed for treason. Principal adviser to King Henry VIII of England, he arranged a marriage between the king and Anne of Cleves to secure German allies against the Catholic Holy Roman emperor Charles V. But Anne was unattractive and the alliance failed, and Cromwell was blamed for both misfortunes.

1586 English explorer Sir Walter Raleigh brings the first tobacco from Virginia to England.

1694 The Bank of England is founded as a commercial institution by act of Parliament.

1775 Benjamin Church becomes the first surgeon general of the American Continental Army.

1784 *Courier De L'Amérique* becomes the first French newspaper to be published in the United States.

1789 The Department of Foreign Affairs is created by the U.S. Congress. The agency

---

MILESTONE

Insulin Isolated in Toronto

At the University of Toronto, Canadian scientists Frederick Banting and Charles Best successfully isolate insulin—a hormone they believe could prevent diabetes—for the first time. Within a year, the first human sufferers of diabetes were receiving insulin treatments, and countless lives were saved from what was previously regarded as a fatal disease. On this day in 1921, Banting and Best successfully isolated insulin from canine test subjects, produced diabetic symptoms in the animals, and then began a program of insulin injections that returned the dogs to normalcy.

John Dillinger

---

later was renamed the State Department.

1794 Maximilien Robespierre, the architect of the French Revolution's Reign of Terror, is overthrown and arrested. Robespierre encouraged the execution, mostly by guillotine, of more than 17,000 people. The day after his arrest, he was guillotined before a cheering mob in the Place de la Révolution in Paris.

1866 The laying of the Atlantic Cable is successfully completed, allowing transatlantic telegraph communication to commence. An earlier attempt to establish a transatlantic telegraph cable in 1858 was only moderately successful and service was quickly abandoned.

1900 The H. J. Heinz Company, the maker of tomato ketchup, is incorporated in the United States.

1923 John Dillinger joins the U.S. Navy to avoid charges of auto theft, marking the beginning of America's most notorious criminal's career. Years later, Dillinger's reputation was forged in a single 12-month period, during which he robbed more banks than had Jesse James and became the most wanted fugitive in the nation.

1940 American cartoonist Chuck Jones's Bugs Bunny first appears on the silver screen in *A Wild Hare*. As in many future installments, *A Wild Hare* featured Bugs as the would-be dinner for frustrated hunter Elmer Fudd.

> *"Happiness is made up of those tiny successes. . . . And if you don't collect all these tiny successes, the big ones don't really mean anything."*
>
> —*Norman Lear*

1943 Joseph Stalin, premier and dictator of the Soviet Union, issues Order No. 227, the "Not One Step Backward" order, in light of German advances during World War II. The order declared, "Panic makers and cowards must be liquidated on the spot. Not one step backward without orders from higher headquarters!"

1944 The United States regains possession of Guam from the Japanese and completes its liberation during World War II.

1949 The world's first jet-propelled airliner, the British De Havilland Comet, makes its maiden flight. It held 40 passengers.

1953 After three years of a bloody and frustrating war, the United Nations, the People's Republic of China, North Korea, and South Korea agree to an armistice, bringing the Korean War to an end.

1954 The British government agrees with Egyptian leader Colonel Nasser that British troops will pull out of Suez by the end of 1956.

1955 After 17 years of occupation by troops from four different countries, Austria regains its sovereignty.

1960 Republicans nominate Vice President Richard M. Nixon for president at their national convention in Chicago, Illinois.

1974 Russian ballet dancer Mikhail Baryshnikov makes his U.S. debut in a performance of *Giselle* with the American Ballet Theater in New York City.

1984 English actor James Mason dies in Lausanne at the age of 75. A respected theatre actor, Mason also appeared in films including *Odd Man Out* and *The Shooting Party*.

1990 Belarus declares its independence from the Soviet Union.

1993 Two weeks shy of her 14th birthday, China's Fu Mingxia becomes the second-youngest gold medalist in Olympic history as she wins the women's 10-meter platform diving event.

Fu Mingxia

1540 King Henry VIII of England marries Catherine Howard, his fifth wife.

1586 Sir Thomas Harriot introduces potatoes to Europe, which he brought to Britain from Colombia.

1588 Britain begins its defeat of the Spanish Armada. This marked the decline of Spain and the ascent of Britain for world supremacy.

1615 On his seventh voyage to the New World, French explorer Samuel de Champlain discovers Lake Huron.

1717 Prussian king Frederick William I creates compulsory education for all children ages 5 to 12.

1809 The British, under Sir Arthur Wellesley (who became the Duke of Wellington), defeat the French at the Battle of Talavera, southwest of Madrid, Spain.

1835 King Louis Napoleon of France survives an assassination attempt by Giuseppe Maria Fleschi. Fleschi rigged 25 guns together and fired them simultaneously with the pull from a single trigger.

1858 William Herschel, of the Indian Civil Service at Jungipur, makes the first use of fingerprints as a means of iden-

> *"Becoming number one is easier than remaining number one."*
>
> —Bill Bradley

Smoke billows from the Empire State Building after a B-25 bomber crashed into upper floors

tification by taking the print of Rajyadhar Konai on the back of a contract. He went on to establish a fingerprint register.

1864 Confederates under General John Bell Hood make a third attempt to break General William T. Sherman's hold on Atlanta during the American Civil War. Like the first two, this attack failed, destroying the Confederate Army of Tennessee's offensive capabilities.

1914 Austria-Hungary declares war on Serbia, and World War I begins.

1914 Harry Fox introduces a new dance, the foxtrot, at New Amsterdam Roof Garden in New York City.

1920 Mexican revolutionary leader Francisco Pancho Villa surrenders to the Mexican government.

1932 President Herbert Hoover orders the U.S. Army under General Douglas MacArthur to evict by force the Bonus Marchers from the nation's capital. The marchers were a group of 20,000 World

War I veterans, in desperate financial straits, seeking promised cash payments for their veterans' bonus certificates. MacArthur's men set the marchers' camps on fire, and the veterans were driven from the city.

1933 The singing telegram is introduced. The first person to receive it was American singer Rudy Vallee, on his 32nd birthday.

1945 In a ringing declaration indicating that America's pre-World War II isolation was truly at an end, the U.S. Senate approves the charter establishing the United Nations. In the years to come, the United Nations would be the scene of some of the most memorable Cold War confrontations between the United States and the Soviet Union.

1945 A B-25 bomber crashes into the 79th floor of the fog-shrouded Empire State Building in New York City, killing more than a dozen people.

1976 An earthquake measuring between 7.8 and 8.2 on the Richter scale flattens Tangshan, a Chinese industrial city with about one million people. An estimated 242,000 were killed, making the earthquake one of the deadliest in recorded history, surpassed only by the 300,000 who died in the 1737 Calcutta earthquake and the 830,000 thought to have perished in 1556 in China's Shaanxi province.

1976 Captain Elden W. Joersz, U.S.A.F., travels 2193.16 miles per hour in a Lockheed SR-71. This is the record for the fastest a human has gone within Earth's atmosphere.

1977 The 799-mile trans-Alaska pipeline goes into full operation.

United States Air Force SR-71 refueling

Nathaniel Bacon

1030 Norwegian king Olav Haraldsson is killed in the Battle of Stiklestad (near what is now Trondheim) attempting to recover his throne from the Danes. During his reign, he used harsh methods to convert Norwegians to Christianity. It was only after his death that Norway embraced Christianity and Olav Haraldsson was declared a saint.

1565 Mary, Queen of Scots, marries her cousin Henry Stuart (Lord Darnley).

1676 Nathaniel Bacon is declared a rebel by Virginia governor William Berkley for assembling frontiersmen to protect the settlers from Native Americans.

1751 The first International World Title Prize Fight takes place in Harlston, Norfolk, England. Jack Slack of England beat Jean Petit of France in 25 minutes.

1776 Silvestre de Escalante and Francisco Dominguez, two Spanish Franciscan priests, leave Santa Fe, New Mexico, for an epic

journey through the Southwest to convert as many of the native inhabitants as possible to the Catholic faith. The two were the first to extensively explore the Great Basin country, and Escalante's written account of the expedition became an essential guide for future explorers.

1845 The oldest surviving yacht club in the United States, the New York Yacht Club, is founded.

1848 At the height of the potato famine in Ireland, a nationalist revolt against British rule is crushed by a government police detachment in Tipperary. The nationalists had planned to declare an independent Irish republic, but they lacked support from the Irish peasantry, who were occupied entirely with surviving the famine.

1858 The first commercial treaty between the United States and Japan is signed, allowing U.S. citizens to live anywhere in Japan.

1874 Major Walter Copton Wingfield of England receives U.S. patent no. 685 for a game that he calls "sphairstike," or "lawn tennis."

1907 In England, Sir Robert Baden Powell organizes a summer camp for boys, leading to the foundation of the Boy Scouts the following year.

1921 Adolf Hitler becomes president of Germany's National Socialist (Nazi) Party.

1927 The first "iron lung" is installed at New York City's Bellevue Hospital.

> *"We are not permitted to choose the frame of our destiny. But what we put into it is ours."*
>
> —*Dag Hammarskjöld*

1935 *Seven Pillars of Wisdom* is published. The book, an account of the Arab Revolt, is rated as one of the classics of war literature and was written by T. E. Lawrence, better known as Lawrence of Arabia.

1936 In the United States, RCA shows the first real television program, which consists of dancing, a fashion show, a film on locomotives, a monologue from *Tobacco Road,* and a comedy.

1938 Jenny Kammersgaad of Denmark becomes the first person to swim the Baltic Sea.

1940 Orson Welles films the first scene of *Citizen Kane.* He co-wrote, produced, directed, and starred in the movie, his first foray into film. In 1998, it topped the American Film Institute's list of America's 100 Greatest Movies.

1947 ENIAC, one of the world's first digital computers, is turned back on after receiving a memory implant, a rudimentary storage capacity, which it lacked. Owned by the U.S. Army, the machine had been shut off on November 9, 1946. After it was rebooted, it remained in service until October 2, 1955.

1981 Nearly one billion television viewers in 74 countries witness the marriage of Prince Charles, heir to the British throne, and Lady Diana Spencer, a young English schoolteacher. Married at St. Paul's Cathedral in the presence of 2,650 guests, the couple's romance was the envy of the world.

1989 Javier Sotomayer of Cuba is the first to clear eight feet in the high jump, for a world record set at the Caribbean Championship in San Juan, Puerto Rico.

Prince Charles and his bride, the Princess of Wales, after their wedding

657 St. Vitalian begins his reign as Pope. He succeeded in establishing a good relationship with Constantine IV, which created peace between Rome and Constantinople.

1419 Anti-Catholic Bohemian Hussites, followers of executed church reformer Jan Hus, storm the town hall in Prague and throw Catholic councilors out of windows.

1626 Naples, Italy, is hit by an earthquake and 10,000 people are killed.

1760 The end of London, England, as a walled city takes place as three of its gates are sold for scrap.

1787 The French parliament refuses to approve a more equitable land tax for parts of India under its control. This eventually led to the "freedom movement" and the first war of Indian Independence against the French.

1792 The French national anthem, "La Marseillaise," is first sung, in Paris.

1839 African slaves take over the Spanish slave ship *Amistad* and kill most of the Spanish on board. Two months later, the boat was found off the coast of New York. The U.S. Supreme Court, in a case argued by former U.S. president

> *"You can't build a reputation on what you are going to do."*
>
> —Henry Ford

BORN ON THIS DAY

1511
GIORGIO VASARI
Italian painter, architect, and art historian

1818
EMILY BRONTË
English author (*Wuthering Heights*)

1857
THORSTEIN VEBLEN
American economist and author (*The Theory of the Leisure Class*)

1863
HENRY FORD
American auto manufacturer who pioneered the assembly line

Henry Ford

1880
ROBERT RUTHERFORD MCCORMICK
American journalist, editor, and publisher (*Chicago Tribune*)

1898
HENRY MOORE
Castlefordian sculptor whose work graces the Time-Life building in London, England, the UNESCO building in Paris, France, and Lincoln Center in New York City

1909
CYRIL NORTHCOTE PARKINSON
English political scientist, historian, and author (*Parkinson's Law; The Pursuit of Progress*)

1939
PETER BOGDANOVICH
American movie director (*The Last Picture Show; What's Up, Doc?; Paper Moon; Mask*)

1941
PAUL ANKA
Canadian singer/songwriter ("Diana"; "Put Your Head on My Shoulder"; "Puppy Love")

1945
DAVID SANBORN
American saxophonist

John Harvey Kellogg

John Quincy Adams, stated the Africans were free men and women, were never citizens of Spain, and were not guilty of murder for the deaths of the crewmen during the takeover.

1894 Corn flakes are invented by brothers Will Keith Kellogg and Dr. John Harvey Kellogg. Dr. Kellogg was the superintendent and his brother, the business manager of a hospital and health spa in Battle Creek, Michigan. They stressed healthful living and had their patients on a strict diet without caffeine, meat, alcohol, or tobacco.

1898 *Scientific American* carries the first magazine automobile ad. Urging readers to "dispense with a horse," the ad was placed by the Winton Motor Car Company of Cleveland, Ohio.

1900 The British Parliament passes legislation that outlaws child labor in mines, encourages the enhancement of safety for railroad workers, and creates workmen's compensation to cover illness.

1918 French captain Sarret makes the first-ever parachute jump from a plane, from a height of 800 feet.

1923 New Zealand claims the Ross Dependency. The large, wedge-shaped part of Antarctica was originally claimed by the United Kingdom when whalers became interested in the Ross Sea region. The Dependency was handed over to New Zealand through an official British Order-in-Council.

1932 Walt Disney releases his first color cartoon, *Flowers and Trees*, made in Technicolor.

1936 American author Margaret Mitchell sells film rights for *Gone with the Wind* to MGM. Film magnate David O. Selznick had balked at Mitchell's asking price of $50,000, which was more than any studio had ever paid for rights to a first novel. He gave in, however, just before the book was released.

1943 During World War II, Nazi German dictator Adolf Hitler learns that Axis ally Italy is buying time before negotiating surrender terms with the Allies in light of Benito Mussolini's fall from power.

1946 The first rocket to attain 100 miles of altitude is launched from White Sands, New Mexico.

1956 The phrase "In God We Trust" is adopted as the U.S. national motto. Although originally stamped on coins during the Civil War, it was officially adopted in response to the growing influence of the Soviet Union.

1966 England beats West Germany, 4–2, to win soccer's World Cup final at Wembley Stadium in London, England.

1971 The U.S. spacecraft *Apollo 15* lands at Mare Imbrium on the moon.

1974 The U.S. House Judiciary Committee votes to impeach President Richard M. Nixon for his defiance of subcommittee subpoenas in the Watergate cover-up.

1975 Thirty-five nations begin a summit meeting in Helsinki, Finland, in which they agree to respect boundaries established after World War II and abide by the rule of international law. The meeting established a foundation for more fruitful U.S.-Soviet relations in later years, including dramatic breakthroughs in nuclear arms control.

1988 King Hussein of Jordan dissolves his country's lower house of Parliament, half of whose members were from the Israeli-occupied West Bank.

Soviet general secretary Leonid Brezhnev shakes hands with U.S. president Gerald Ford at the summit in Helsinki, Finland

1485 *Morte d'Arthur*, by English author Sir Thomas Malory, is published. In the source book for the legend of King Arthur, Malory wrote the tale of knightly love and chivalry while in prison for armed assault and rape.

1498 During his third voyage to the New World, Italian explorer Christopher Columbus arrives at an island he'll name Trinidad.

1602 Charles, Duc de Biron, is executed for conspiring against Henri IV of France.

1703 English author Daniel Defoe is put in the pillory for seditious libel, due to the publication of his pamphlet "The Shortest Way with Dissenters." The pamphlet was an attack on High Churchmen, written as if from the High Church point of view but extending arguments to the point of foolishness. It wasn't until he was nearly 60 that Defoe began writing fiction. In 1719, his *The Life and Strange Adventures of Robinson Crusoe* was published.

1777 After offering help to the rebelling American colonists, 19-year-old French nobleman the Marquis de Lafayette is made a major-general in the Continental Army.

1792 The cornerstone for the U.S. Mint, the first official

> *"A kind and compassionate act is often its own reward."*
>
> —*William Bennett*

Washington and Lafayette at Valley Forge

building of the federal government, is put in place in Philadelphia, Pennsylvania.

1812 Venezuela falls to Spain a year after declaring independence, and its leader, Francisco de Miranda, is arrested.

1891 Great Britain declares that territories from Southern Africa up to the Congo are within its sphere of influence.

1912 In the first movie censorship regulation to go into effect, the U.S. government prohibits movies and photos of prize fights.

1922 Ralph Samuelson rides the world's first water skis, at Lake City, Minnesota.

1928 The MGM lion logo appears for the first time, introducing the studio's first talking picture, *White Shadows on the South Seas*.

1941 Hermann Goering, writing under instructions from Nazi German dictator Adolf Hitler during World War II, orders Reinhard Heydrich, SS general and Heinrich Himmler's number-two man, to submit as soon as possible a general plan for the mass, systematic extermination of Jews in "all the territories of Europe under German occupation."

1945 Pierre Laval, the puppet leader of Nazi-occupied Vichy France, surrenders to American authorities in Austria at the end of World War II. Extradited to France, he was convicted of treason by the High Court of Justice in a sensational trial. Condemned to death, he attempted suicide by poison but was nursed back to health in time for his execution on October 15, 1945.

1954 A six-year U.S. research program in Los Angeles, California, discovers that smog is caused by the chemical reaction of sunlight on auto and industrial emissions.

1954 An Italian team led by Ardito Desio makes the first ascent of the world's second-highest peak, Mount Godwin-Austen (K2).

1955 At the age of 17, Marilyn Bell of Toronto, Canada, becomes the youngest person to swim the English Channel.

1960 In the United States, Elyah Muhammad, leader of "Nation of Islam," calls for an African-American state.

1964 *Ranger 7*, an unmanned U.S. lunar probe, takes the first close-up images of the moon—4,308 in total—before it impacts with the lunar surface northwest of the Sea of the Clouds. The images were 1,000 times as clear as anything ever seen through Earth-bound telescopes.

1964 In a news conference, U.S. secretary of state Dean Rusk admits there are differences between the United States and South Vietnam on the issue of extending the war into North Vietnam, but claims agreement on the general conduct of the war. He stated that U.S. warnings to communist China and North Vietnam indicated total U.S. commitment.

1965 Cigarette advertisements are banned from British television.

1969 U.S. spacecraft *Mariner 6*, coming to within 2,000 miles of the planet Mars, transmits the first pictures of the red planet.

1975 Teamsters Union president Jimmy Hoffa is reported missing in Detroit, Michigan.

1991 U.S. president George H. Bush and Soviet president Mikhail S. Gorbachev sign the long-range Strategic Arms Reduction Treaty (START), the first treaty to mandate nuclear weapons reductions by these two countries.

Last Minuteman II missile silo imploded in accordance with START

1137 In France, King Louis VI dies and is succeeded by his son Louis VII, who will launch the Second Crusade.

1291 The communities of Uri, Schwyz, and Unterwalden form an alliance known as the Swiss Confederation to protect themselves against the Austrian House of Hapsburg. The anniversary of this founding has been celebrated as National Day in Switzerland since 1891.

1498 Italian explorer Christopher Columbus sets foot on the American mainland for the first time, at the Paria Peninsula in present-day Venezuela. Thinking it an island, he christened it Isla Santa and claimed it for his patron country, Spain.

1715 What is possibly the oldest annual sporting event in the world begins in London as Thomas Doggett, an Irish comedian and theater owner, organizes a rowing race to mark the anniversary of George I's accession to the throne. The winner's trophies, a coat and badge, were created with money Doggett left in his will.

1740 "Rule Britannia" is sung for the first time, as part of composer Thomas Arne's masque *Alfred*, at a party for the third birthday of the Prince of Wales's daughter Augusta.

1774 English minister and scientist Joseph Priestley discovers oxygen.

> *"Life's a voyage that's homeward bound."*
> —Herman Melville

BORN ON THIS DAY

10 B.C.
CLAUDIUS
Roman emperor (41–54)

1744
JEAN BAPTISTE DE LAMARCK
French naturalist who developed a forerunner of the theory of evolution

1770
WILLIAM CLARK
American explorer (Lewis and Clark expedition)

1779
FRANCIS SCOTT KEY
American attorney and poet who composed the lyrics for the "Star-Spangled Banner"

1818
MARIA MITCHELL
Astronomer who was the first woman elected to the American Academy of Arts and Sciences and the first American woman to become a professor of astronomy

1819
HERMAN MELVILLE
American author (*Moby-Dick; Billy Budd*)

1843
ROBERT TODD LINCOLN
Son of U.S. president Abraham Lincoln who was once rescued from a train accident by Edwin Booth, brother of President Lincoln's assassin

1916
JAMES HILL
American film producer (*The Unforgiven; Vera Cruz*)

1930
LIONEL BART
English composer and writer of musicals (*Oliver*)

1930
GEOFFREY HOLDER
Trinidad-born dancer and actor

1936
YVES ST. LAURENT
French fashion designer

1942
JERRY GARCIA
American rock musician (The Grateful Dead)

Joseph Priestley

1778 Hamburg, Germany, becomes the site of the world's first savings bank.

1790 The first U.S. census is completed. It showed a population of 3,939,326, with Virginia the most populous state with 747,610 inhabitants.

1793 France becomes the first country to use the metric system of weights and measures.

1798 Napoleon Bonaparte's conquest of the Middle East is thwarted when the British fleet under Lord Nelson defeats the French fleet at the Battle of the Nile, at Aboukir Bay, Egypt.

1831 The new London Bridge is opened by King William IV and Queen Adelaide of Great Britain and Ireland. It replaced the old bridge completed in 1209 and lasted nearly 140 years before it was sold and rebuilt in Arizona.

1834 Great Britain passes the Abolition Act, in which slavery is declared unlawful throughout the British Empire. The act was the result of a combination

---

of slave revolts, humanitarian concerns, and growing industrialization. Approximately 770,280 slaves were freed.

1864 During the U.S. Civil War, Union general Ulysses S. Grant appoints General Philip Sheridan commander of the Army of the Shenandoah. Within a few months, Sheridan drove a Confederate force from the Shenandoah Valley and destroyed nearly all possible sources of Rebel supplies.

1873 English inventor Andrew Smith Hallidie successfully tests the first cable car he designed for the city of San Francisco, California.

1894 The first Sino-Japanese War starts, the result of a dispute concerning the control of Korea.

1939 Bandleader Glenn Miller records "In the Mood," which becomes one of the most famous songs performed by an American artist.

1941 The Willys Truck Company successfully answers the U.S. Army's call for a fast, lightweight all-terrain vehicle to be built in just 49 days. The new truck was christened the "Jeep."

1943 A Japanese destroyer rams an American PT boat, No. 109, slicing it in two. Two crewmen were killed but 11 survived, including Lieutenant John F. Kennedy, who would later become president of the United States.

1943 The groundbreaking ceremony in Oak Ridge, Tennessee, for the first uranium 235 production plant takes place. Uranium 235 was needed to build the atomic bomb.

1944 Thirteen-year-old German Jew Anne Frank makes the last entry in her diary, which she kept for two years while hiding with her family to escape the Nazi concentration camps during World War II.

1944 During World War II, an advance Soviet armored unit reaches the eastern suburb of Warsaw, prompting 40,000 Poles in the city to launch a major uprising against the Nazis.

1953 *Shane*, considered by many critics to be the greatest American western movie ever made, is released by Paramount Pictures.

1956 The Salk polio vaccine becomes available to the American public. As a result, the incidence of polio in the United States began to decline radically.

1972 The first article exposing the American Watergate scandal is printed by the *Washington Post*.

American troops climb over a sandbag revetment in France (milestone)

216 B.C. Hannibal defeats the Romans at the Battle of Cannae, and, as a result, most of southern Italy allies itself with him.

47 B.C. Roman general Julius Caesar beats Pharnaces III of Pontus with such ease that he reports his victory with the words *"Veni, vidi, vici"* ("I came, I saw, I conquered").

1100 English king William II, known as William Rufus, is killed by an arrow while hunting in the New Forest. Dismissed at the time as an accident, later historians believe William may have been assassinated, possibly by his successor, Henry I.

1552 Religious freedom is given to Lutherans in Germany when the Treaty of Passau revokes the Augsburg Interim of 1548.

1610 English explorer Henry Hudson enters what is known today as Hudson Bay, in Canada.

1718 The Quadruple Alliance is formed by Great Britain, the Netherlands, France, and the Holy Roman Empire against Spain, which sought to nullify the peace settlement after the War of Spanish Succession.

1769 The area now known as Los Angeles, California, is first noted as a likely place for a large settlement by Spanish explorer Gaspar de Portola and Juan Crespi, a Franciscan priest. They came upon the area while exploring north of San Diego, and were

---

MILESTONE

Hitler Becomes Führer
With the death of German president Paul von Hindenburg, Chancellor Adolf Hitler becomes absolute dictator of Germany under the title of Führer ("Leader") on this day in 1934. The German Army took an oath of allegiance to its new commander-in-chief, and the last remnants of Germany's democratic government were dismantled to make way for Hitler's Third Reich. Hitler was appalled by Germany's defeat in World War I, which he blamed on enemies within—chiefly German communists and Jews—and was enraged by the punitive peace settlement forced on Germany by the victorious Allies.

> *"Life is not a having and a getting, but a being and a becoming."*
>
> —*Myrna Loy*

impressed by the fertile land around a river that would provide water for irrigation.

1802 In France, Napoleon Bonaparte is declared "Consul for life."

1830 The last Bourbon king of France, Charles X, abdicates after a revolution to protest his rigid control of the press, his dissolution of a newly elected chamber, and his restrictions on the right to vote.

1858 The British Parliament passes the India Bill, which transferred the government of India from the East India Company to the Crown.

1861 During the U.S. Civil War, Congress passes the first income tax to raise revenues for the war effort. Although

Adolf Hitler, left, and his aides in Nuremberg, Germany (milestone)

never enacted, it was an important fiscal innovation that paved the way for growth of the government in the 20th century.

1865 *Alice's Adventures in Wonderland* by English author Lewis Carroll (the pen name of Charles Dodgson) is published, but is quickly withdrawn due to bad printing. Only 21 copies of the first edition survive.

1870 The world's first tube railway opens in London, traveling under the Thames near the site of the later Tower Bridge. Earlier underground trains had been built by the "cut and cover" method where a trench is dug and then roofed over.

1881 In the United States, the Federation of Organized Trades and Labor Unions is formed. It will later be renamed the American Federation of Labor.

1909 The U.S. Army accepts delivery of the first military airplane, which was built by the Wright Brothers.

1926 American actors John Barrymore and Mary Astor star in the first film demonstrating the Vitaphone system for combining picture and sound for movies.

1939 German-born American physicist Albert Einstein writes to U.S. president Franklin D. Roosevelt, urging "watchfulness and, if necessary, quick action" on the part of the United States in atomic research. Einstein, a lifelong pacifist whose work helped make possible early atomic research, feared that Nazi Germany had begun work on an atomic bomb.

John Dean III

1945 The Potsdam Conference between the Soviet Union, the United States, and Great Britain concludes after two weeks of intense and sometimes acrimonious debate. The conference failed to settle most of the important issues at hand—including the fate of postwar Germany after World War II—and thus helped set the stage for the Cold War.

1971 During the Vietnam War, the administration of U.S. president Richard M. Nixon officially acknowledges that the CIA is maintaining a force of 30,000 "irregulars" fighting the Communist Pathet Lao in Laos.

1974 John Dean III, counsel to U.S. president Richard M. Nixon, is sentenced for his part in the Watergate cover-up to one to four years in prison.

1990 Iraqi forces invade Kuwait, capturing Kuwait City within hours and establishing a provincial government there. By annexing Kuwait, Iraq gained control of 20 percent of the world's oil reserves.

"The greatest mystery of all is the human heart, and that is the mystery with which all good novelists are concerned."

—P. D. James

1347 The French city of Calais surrenders to Edward III of England in the Hundred Years' War.

1460 During his invasion of England, King James II of Scotland is accidentally killed by an exploding cannon in the siege of Roxburgh Castle.

1678 Robert LaSalle builds the first ship in America, the *Griffon*.

1769 The La Brea Tar Pits in Los Angeles, California, are first noted by Franciscan friar Father Juan Crespi in his diary.

1778 La Scala opera house opens in Milan, Italy.

1795 Notorious English highwayman Jerry Abershaw is hanged on Kennington Common in south London.

1846 Abraham Lincoln is elected to the U.S. House of Representatives.

1858 English explorer John Speke discovers Lake Victoria, the source of the Nile River.

1861 The last installment of English author Charles Dickens's serialized novel *Great Expectations* is published.

MILESTONE

Columbus Sets Sail

On this day in 1492 Christopher Columbus sets sail from the Spanish port of Palos. The Italian explorer was in command of three ships—the *Santa Maria*, the *Pinta*, and the *Niña*—on a journey to find a western sea route to China, India, and the fabled gold and spice islands of Asia. Columbus's journey took him to Teneriffe in the Canary Islands for a brief stop. A volcano erupted upon their departure from Teneriffe, an ill omen to some crewmembers. Columbus kept a double logbook so his sailors would not know the real distance they had traveled out of sight of land on their voyage. The discoveries they would make would not be fully understood for decades afterward, but Europe and the New World were both changed profoundly.

Christopher Columbus

Firestone tire advertisement

1900 The Firestone Tire & Rubber Company is established in Akron, Ohio, with only 12 employees.

1914 France is drawn into World War I as Germany declares war on its neighbor.

1916 Great Britain hangs Irish nationalist Sir Roger Casement for treason because of his attempts to get Germany to support Irish independence.

1921 John Macready performs the first crop dusting from an airplane in order to kill caterpillars in a grove in Troy, Ohio.

1933 The world-famous Mickey Mouse watch is first sold. The price of the timepiece was $2.75. Today, an original watch sells for hundreds of dollars.

1941 Although the United States has not yet entered World War II, gasoline rationing begins in eastern parts of the nation.

1943 During World War II, U.S. general George S. Patton slaps and verbally abuses Private Charles Herman Kuhl at an army hospital in Sicily, accusing him of cowardice. General Dwight D. Eisenhower later ordered Patton to apologize.

⚖ **1948** In hearings before the House Un-American Activities Committee, Whittaker Chambers, a self-professed former member of the Communist Party, accuses former U.S. state department official Alger Hiss of being a communist and a spy for the Soviet Union. Hiss was eventually convicted of perjury.

🎭 **1955** Irish playwright Samuel Beckett's *Waiting for Godot*, famously described by critic Vivian Mercier as a play in which "nothing happens, twice," is performed for the first time, in London, England. Though the play is now considered a classic, half the audience walked out.

🔬 **1958** The U.S. submarine USS *Nautilus* accomplishes the first undersea voyage to the geographic North Pole. The world's first nuclear submarine, the *Nautilus* dived at Point Barrow, Alaska, and traveled nearly 1,000 miles under the Arctic ice cap to reach the top of the world.

🟥 **1960** Niger gains independence from France. Part of the once powerful Islamic Sokoto Empire, it was annexed by France at the end of the 19th century.

🎭 **1963** The English rock group The Beatles play in The Cavern in Liverpool for the last time before leaving for a tour of the United States.

🎭 **1971** In the United States, English rock musician and former Beatle Paul McCartney forms a new band called Wings.

🔬 **1977** American company Radio Shack introduces the TRS-80 computer, generally recognized as the first completely assembled computer and the first affordable computer available at retail. The $599.95 system featured a black-and-white monitor, cassette tape storage, four kilobytes of RAM, and a Z80 eight-bit 1.77-megahertz processor.

🇺🇸 **1981** Tired of working clock-busting shifts on "obsolete" equipment, 13,000 members of the U.S. Professional Air Traffic Controllers Organization walk off the job. President Ronald W. Reagan fired 11,500 strikers on August 5, a tactic emboldening employers to take a more aggressive stance against union activity.

Nuclear-powered submarine USS Nautilus

1265 In England during the Second Barons' War (a war between King Henry III and his barons), the Royalists under Prince Edward defeat the Barons under Simon de Montfort at the Battle of Evesham.

1578 The Portuguese are defeated in their attempted invasion of Morocco at the Battle of Alcazarquivir. King Sebastian of Portugal was killed, as were the king of Fez and the Moorish pretender to the throne of Fez.

1693 Champagne is invented by the monk Dom Perignon, who lives at the Benedictine Abbey of Hautvillers in the region of Champagne, in northern France.

1704 A joint Anglo-Dutch force attacks and captures the Spanish city of Gibraltar during the War of the Spanish Succession.

1735 Freedom of the press is established in the United States as John Peter Zenger, publisher of the *New York Weekly Journal*, wins an acquittal against libel charges placed by British royal governor William Crosby. Crosby tried to censor Zenger's attacks on the Crown.

1753 George Washington, a young Virginia planter, becomes a Master Mason, the highest basic rank in the secret fraternity of freemasonry. Washington was 21 years old and would soon command his first military operation as a major in the Virginia colonial militia.

1789 The Constituent Assembly in France abolishes all feudal privileges and rights during the French Revolution.

MILESTONE

Nelson Mandela Arrested

Nelson Mandela, South African lawyer and campaigner against the injustices of his country's regime, is arrested on this day in 1962. He would remain a prisoner for nearly 30 years, finally being released on February 11, 1990. Mandela, in conflict with the white-controlled government for much of his life, was apprehended by security police for inciting strikes and having illegally left the country, and was sentenced to five years in prison. During his sentence, he was further charged with sabotage and sentenced to life imprisonment. Following his release, he became the country's first democratically elected president in 1994.

"The more we study the more we discover our ignorance."

—*Percy Bysshe Shelley*

1845 The first package tour is organized by Thomas Cook—a printer from Leicester in England who had arranged trail trips to Temperance galas. The tour took in Liverpool, Caernarfon, and Mount Snowdon.

1892 In Fall River, Massachusetts, Andrew and Abby Borden are found bludgeoned to death in their home. The Bordens lived with their two unmarried daughters, Emma and Lizzie. Since Lizzie was the only person besides the housekeeper who was present when the bodies were found, suspicion soon fell upon her in what became a sensational case. But she was never convicted, and the murders remain unsolved.

1914 Britain declares war as Germany invades its neutral neighbor, Belgium. The news brought cheering crowds

to Buckingham Palace, though it is doubtful that King George V shared their enthusiasm—German Kaiser Wilhelm II was his first cousin, as was Russian Czar Nicholas II, ruler of Britain's ally.

1914 President Woodrow Wilson formally proclaims the neutrality of the United States as World War I breaks out. However, that position was soon compromised by Germany's attempted quarantine of the British Isles and when several U.S. ships traveling to Great Britain were damaged or sunk by German mines.

1922 Every telephone in the United States and Canada goes dead as switchboards and switching stations are shut down for one minute in memory of the device's inventor, Alexander Graham Bell, who had died two days before.

1936 In Greece, Ioannis Metaxas sets up the dictatorial Fourth of August Regime.

1953 U.S. president Dwight D. Eisenhower warns that the situation in Asia is

Burned-out car of murdered civil rights workers

becoming "very ominous for the United States." Eisenhower made specific reference to the need to defend French Indochina from the communists.

1957 Juan Fangio wins his last auto race and captures the world auto-racing championship for the fourth consecutive year. Fangio, born in Argentina and of Italian descent, won the world championship a record five times, as well as capturing 24 Grand Prix titles.

1964 The remains of three American civil rights workers are found on this day in 1964. Michael Schwerner, Andrew Goodman, and James Chaney had been helping to organize civil rights efforts in Mississippi on behalf of the Congress of Racial Equality. Nineteen men were indicted in December by the U.S. Justice Department for violating the civil rights of the murdered men.

1305 Sir William Wallace, Scottish hero and champion of Scottish independence, is captured by the English after being betrayed by Sir John Menteith, governor of Dumbarton. Wallace was later tried for treason and executed.

1529 King Francis I of France and Holy Roman emperor Charles V sign the Treaty of Cambrai. The treaty called for Francis to renounce his claim to Italy and for Charles to renounce his claim to Burgundy.

1570 A group of Spanish Jesuits led by Fray Batista Segura arrive at the Chesapeake Bay area to convert the Native Americans.

1583 Sir Humphrey Gilbert founds the first English colony in North America at St. John's, Newfoundland, in Canada.

1716 At the battle of Peterwardein, Darnad Ali Pasha suffers a devastating blow as 40,000 Austrians led by Prince Eugene of Savoy defeat his 150,000 Turks. More than 30,000 Turks died.

1775 The *San Carlos* becomes the first Spanish ship to enter San Francisco Bay in California.

> *"All lovely things will have an ending, All lovely things will fade and die; And youth, that's now so bravely spending, Will beg a penny by and by."*
>
> —*Conrad Aiken*

BORN ON THIS DAY

1624
WILLIAM
First black child born in English America (Jamestown colony)

1749
THOMAS LYNCH
American congressman who signed the Declaration of Independence

1811
AMBROISE THOMAS
French composer (*Hamlet; Le Comte de Carmagnola; Mognon*)

1850
GUY DE MAUPASSANT
French author (*Boule de Suif; Bel-Ami*)

1860
JOSEPH CAREY MERRICK
British victim of Proteus Syndrome; who was known as the "Elephant Man"

1860
LOUIS WAIN
English artist and caricaturist

1889
CONRAD AIKEN
American Pulitzer Prize-winning poet

1906
JOHN HUSTON
American director (*The African Queen; The Misfits; Prizzi's Honor*)

1910
JACQUETTA HAWKES
Archaeologist and writer, wife of J. B. Priestley

1911
ROBERT TAYLOR
American actor (*Billy the Kid; Johnny Eager*)

1930
NEIL ARMSTRONG
American astronaut, first man to set foot on the moon

1946
LONI ANDERSON
American actress (*WKRP in Cincinnati*)

1962
PATRICK EWING
American professional basketball player

Admiral Farragut on U.S. Navy recruitment poster

1850 South Australia, Tasmania, and Victoria are granted representative governments by the Australian Government Act.

1858 The first transatlantic telegraph line is completed. The cable, which stretched more than 1,950 miles and was laid as deep as two miles under the Atlantic Ocean, established transatlantic telegraph communication. However, its weak signal was insufficient for regular communication, and service ended on September 1. A more powerful cable was laid in 1866.

1861 Flogging is abolished in the U.S. Army.

1864 During the American Civil War, Union admiral David Farragut issues the order, "Damn the torpedoes! Full speed ahead!" as he leads his flotilla through the Confederate defenses at Mobile, Alabama. The fall of Mobile Bay was the first in a series of successes that secured the reelection of President Abraham Lincoln.

1882 The Standard Oil Company of New Jersey is established as part of John D. Rockefeller's oil empire, Standard Oil Trust. The Trust became the first great monopoly in American history, eventually acquiring 90 percent of the world's oil-refining capacity before it was ordered to dissolve in 1892.

1884 The cornerstone for the Statue of Liberty is laid at Bedloe's Island (now known as Liberty Island), New York. On October 28, 1886, U.S. president Grover S. Cleveland accepted the actual statue as a gift to the United States from the people of France.

1914 The British Expeditionary Force is mobilized the day after war was declared against Germany.

1921 The *New York World* publishes the cartoon "On the Road to Moscow," by Rollin Kirby. It became the first cartoon ever awarded a Pulitzer Prize.

1947 German automotive engineer Ferdinand Porsche is released from a French prison. Porsche had been arrested as a suspected Nazi collaborator by U.S. and French occupation authorities after World War II and was held in custody for two years. He is best known for the automobile that bears his name.

1950 U.S. swimmer Florence Chadwick swims the English Channel in 13 hours, 23 minutes, breaking the previous record by more than an hour.

1953 In Panmunjom, Korea, Operation Big Switch—an exchange of prisoners of war between the North Koreans, Chinese, and the U.N. Command—takes place toward the end of the Korean War.

1963 Representatives of the United States, the Soviet Union, and Great Britain sign the Nuclear Test Ban Treaty, which prohibits the testing of nuclear weapons in outer space, underwater, or in the atmosphere.

1963 American race-car driver Craig Breedlove sets a world auto-speed record of 407.45 miles per hour.

1974 U.S. president Richard M. Nixon admits he withheld information about the Watergate break-in.

1991 Sergei Bubka of the Soviet Union sets a pole-vault record of 20 feet, $1/4$ inch in Malmö, Sweden.

1992 U.S. federal civil rights charges are filed against four white Los Angeles police officers who were acquitted by a California court in the videotaped beating of Rodney King, a black motorist. Two of the officers were later convicted.

Operation Big Switch

Marilyn Monroe

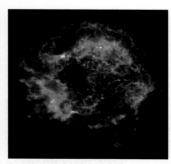

X-ray image of the Cassiopeia supernova

1181 A supernova is observed by Chinese and Japanese astronomers in the constellation Cassiopeia. Modern equipment now reveals it to be a neutron star rotating 15 times per second.

1497 Explorer John Cabot returns to Bristol, England, after discovering what is now Newfoundland.

1600 France's Henry IV invades Savoy after negotiations break down over Saluzzo, which had been controlled by Savoy since 1588.

1661 Holland sells Brazil to Portugal for eight million guilders (today, approximately $20 million in U.S. currency).

1726 Emperor Karel VI and Czarina Catherine the Great sign the Treaty of Vienna, whereby Russia put 30,000 troops at the disposal of her allies in return for support in a possible war with the Ottoman Empire.

1762 The sandwich is born as inveterate gambler the Earl of Sandwich calls for a piece of beef between two slices of bread, so that he can eat without leaving the card table.

MILESTONE

Hiroshima Devastated by Atomic Bomb

At 8:15 A.M., the U.S. Army Air Corps Superfortress *Enola Gay* drops an atomic bomb, code-named "Little Boy" on the Japanese city of Hiroshima. Seventy thousand people are killed almost instantaneously, and as many more will die from the aftereffects of the world's first nuclear bombing. The atom bomb had been developed in the United States, prompted by fears that Hitler was working on such a device. Though the dropping of this bomb, and another three days later on Nagasaki, brought about the end of World War II, many historians argue that it also ignited the Cold War.

"The secret of staying young is to live honestly, eat slowly, and lie about your age."

—Lucille Ball

1774 English religious leader Ann Lee, founder of the United Society of Believers in Christ's Second Coming, arrives in New York. Her society became known as the Shaker Movement.

1787 In Philadelphia, Pennsylvania, delegates to the Constitutional Convention begin debating the first complete draft of the proposed Constitution of the United States.

1806 German emperor Francis II officially dissolves the Holy Roman Empire, which was formed in 962. Although it was intended to be a continuation of the ancient Roman Empire, it had long ago ceased to be a major political power.

Allied correspondent in the rubble of Hiroshima (milestone)

1824 Simón Bolívar defeats the Spanish at the battle of Junin, northwest of Lima, in the Peruvian War of Independence.

1825 After nearly 300 years of Spanish rule, Bolivia becomes an independent republic.

1859 The first known advertising slogan, "Worth a guinea a box," appears in an advertisement for Beecham's Pills in the English newspaper the *St. Helen's Intelligencer*.

1889 The Savoy Hotel is opened in London, England.

1890 The first execution by electrocution is carried out at Auburn Prison in New York on William Kemmler, who had been convicted of murdering his lover with an ax. Electrocution as a means of execution was first suggested in 1881 by Dr. Albert Southwick.

1918 The Second Battle of the Marne ends during World War I. The last German attack on the Western Front, it resulted in approximately 100,000 German casualties.

1926 American magician Harry Houdini stays underwater for 91 minutes inside a compartment that supposedly has only enough air to keep someone alive for six minutes.

1932 In the United States, Richard Hollingshead Jr. first registers his patent for the drive-in movie theater. The patent was declared invalid in 1950, however, and as a result, thousands of drive-ins appeared on the American landscape,

Harry Houdini

reaching a high of more than 4,000 in 1958.

1940 During World War II, Italy invades British Somaliland, starting the Battle of North Africa.

1942 Queen Wilhelmina of the Netherlands becomes the first reigning queen to address a joint session of the U.S. Congress, saying that despite the Nazi occupation, her country's motto was "No surrender."

1962 After 307 years within the British Commonwealth, Jamaica becomes an independent dominion.

1990 Alleging rampant government corruption, President Ghulam Ishaq Khan of Pakistan dismisses Prime Minister Benazir Bhutto.

1991 English computer scientist Tim Berners-Lee releases files describing his experimental World Wide Web project on the Internet.

1498 Italian explorer Christopher Columbus arrives in the Caribbean on his third expedition for Spain. He was forced to carry convicts as colonists, as the novelty of the New World was wearing off.

1575 Spanish troops lay siege to Oudewater, Holland. The town eventually fell after resisting for several weeks, and all but three inhabitants were killed.

1782 U.S. general George Washington creates the Purple Heart. Originally called the "Badge for Military Merit," it consisted of a purple, heart-shaped piece of silk, edged with a narrow binding of silver, with the word "Merit" stitched across the face in silver.

1789 The U.S. Congress establishes the War Department (now called the Department of Defense).

1794 Irate farmers in Pennsylvania rise up against a federal tax on liquor and stills. In what was called "The Whiskey Rebellion," the farmers torched tax collectors' homes, as well as tarred and feathered revenue officers. President George Washington called 12,900 federal troops from surrounding states to forcefully usher the farmers back to their homes.

1821 The sudden death of Caroline of Brunswick, the uncrowned queen of

---

MILESTONE

U.S. Satellite Photographs Earth

From the Atlantic Missile Range in Cape Canaveral, Florida, the U.S. unmanned spacecraft *Explorer 6* is launched into orbit around Earth on this day in 1959. The spacecraft, commonly known as the Paddlewheel satellite, featured a photocell scanner that transmitted a crude picture of the planet's surface and cloud cover from a distance of 17,000 miles—the first photograph ever taken of Earth from a U.S. satellite. The photo, received in Hawaii, took nearly 40 minutes to transmit. Released by NASA in September, it depicted a crescent shape of part of the planet in sunlight.

Modern-day Purple Heart

"If you want to get across an idea, wrap it up in a person."

—*Ralph Bunche*

Great Britain, leads to rumors of poisoning. The estranged wife of George IV had been refused entry to Westminster Hall at the king's coronation the previous month.

1840 The British Parliament bans the employment of boys to climb inside chimneys to clean them.

1861 During the U.S. Civil War, Thaddeus Lowe becomes the first man to fly professionally for the American military as he performs reconnaissance over Confederate forces in a balloon.

1888 A patent for the revolving door is issued to Theophilus Van Kannel of Philadelphia, Pennsylvania.

1912 Former U.S. president Theodore Roosevelt is nominated for the presidency by the Progressive Party, a group of Republicans dissatisfied with the renomination of President William Howard Taft. Also known as the Bull Moose Party, the Progressive Party called for the direct election of U.S. senators, women's suffrage, reduction of the tariff, and many social reforms.

1915 Driving a Peugeot, Italian Dario Resta breaks the 100-miles-per-hour speed barrier while winning the 100-mile Chicago Cup Challenge Race at the Maywood Board Speedway in Illinois. His average speed was 101.86 miles per hour.

1942 The U.S. 1st Marine Division begins Operation Watchtower, the first U.S. Pacific offensive of World War II, by landing on Guadalcanal, one of the Solomon Islands.

1944 The world's first program-controlled calculator, a mechanical machine popularly called the Harvard Mark I, is dedicated at Harvard University in Boston, Massachusetts. It weighed five tons, stored 72 numbers, and could perform three additions or subtractions per second as well as calculate logarithms or perform trigonometry.

1947 The balsa wood raft *Kon Tiki* runs aground on the Tuamotu Archipelago 101 days and 4,300 miles after leaving Peru. Led by Thor Heyerdahl, the six-man expedition attempted to prove that pre-Incan Indians could have colonized the Polynesian islands simply by drifting on ocean currents.

1949 A British Gloster Meteor fighter sets a new record for the longest flight by a jet aircraft: 12 hours, 3 minutes.

Final edition of the Washington Star

1960 In Africa, Ivory Coast gains independence from France.

1964 The U.S. Congress overwhelmingly approves the Gulf of Tonkin Resolution, giving President Lyndon B. Johnson nearly unlimited powers to oppose "communist aggression" in Southeast Asia.

1981 In the United States, the *Washington Star* ceases operation after 128 years of publication. The *Washington Post* thus became the only daily newspaper to serve the nation's capital.

1981 One million members of Solidarity, the Polish trade union headed by Lech Walesa, go on strike to protest the country's economic crisis and food shortages.

1992 To raise funds to repair fire damage at Windsor Castle, tickets are sold for a tour of Buckingham Palace. It was the first time the public got to see inside the London home of Queen Elizabeth II.

117 Following the death of his father, Trajan, Hadrian becomes emperor of Rome.

1549 The Anglo-French War begins as French king Henry II declares war on England with the intention of retaking Boulogne.

1570 In France, the third Civil War ends with the peace of St. Germain-en-Laye. The Huguenots were granted amnesty and were given La Rochelle and Cognac as places of refuge.

1576 Danish astronomer Tycho Brahe begins work in his observatory at Uraniborg. The observatory was the first such structure of its kind ever built.

1709 Father Bartolomeu de Gusmao of Portugal makes the first known ascent in a hot-air balloon.

1758 During the Seven Years' War, British troops plunder the French town of Cherbourg.

1786 Dr. Michael Gabriel Piccard and Jacques Balmat of France become the first to climb Mont Blanc, the highest mountain in western Europe.

1844 In the United States, Brigham Young is chosen to lead the Mormons following the murder of the movement's founder, Joseph Smith.

> *"I have no riches but my thoughts. Yet these are wealth enough for me."*
>
> —Sara Teasdale

BORN ON THIS DAY

1763
CHARLES BULFINCH
First American professional architect

1866
MATTHEW HENSON
American explorer who made a North Pole expedition in 1908–09 with Robert Peary

1876
CHARLES HAMILTON
English author who, under the pseudonym Frank Richards, created the rotund schoolboy Billy Bunter

1879
EMILIANO ZAPATA
Mexican revolutionary and peasant leader

1884
SARA TEASDALE
American poet who won the first Pulitzer Prize in 1918 (*Love Songs*)

1899
RUSSELL MARKERT
American choreographer who founded and directed the Radio City Music Hall Rockettes

1901
ERNEST LAWRENCE
Nobel prize-winning nuclear physicist

1907
BENNY CARTER
American jazz musician

1919
DINO DE LAURENTIIS
Italian movie producer (*Ragtime; Hannibal*)

1922
ESTHER WILLIAMS
American swimmer and actress

1932
MEL TILLIS
American singer/songwriter ("Coca Cola Cowboy"; "Lying Time Again"; "Blind in Love")

1937
DUSTIN HOFFMAN
Academy Award-winning American actor (*The Graduate; Tootsie; Rain Man*)

1854 American manufacturer Smith & Wesson patents metal bullet cartridges.

1860 The queen of the Sandwich Islands (Hawaii) becomes the first queen to visit the United States when she arrives in New York City.

1876 American inventor Thomas Edison receives a patent for the mimeograph machine, an automated device for creating multiple copies of a document. Four years later, Edison received a second patent for an improved model. The mimeograph machine preceded the electronic copier and was used through the early 1970s.

1899 The refrigerator is patented by A. T. Marshall of Brockton, Massachusetts.

1900 The United States defeats Great Britain in the first Davis Cup Tennis Tournament. The tournament was inaugurated in a lawn tennis match in Boston, Massachusetts.

1906 Cambridge beats Harvard by two lengths in an international University boat race on the Thames.

Liliuokalani, queen of the Sandwich Islands

The Ku Klux Klan marches down Pennsylvania Avenue past the Treasury Building

MILESTONE

The Great Train Robbery
One of the most famous robberies of all time takes place in England on this day in 1963. A mail train of the General Post Office, en route from Glasgow to London, was ambushed near Mentmore in Buckinghamshire. A gang of fifteen masked men escaped with a large sum of cash—exactly how much wasn't at first clear. An initial police press conference put the haul at a quarter of a million pounds, provoking disbelief in some quarters. In fact the true figure was vastly more—£2,631,784—of which less than a seventh has ever been recovered. Ten men were jailed in 1964. Ronnie Biggs, among others, later escaped and fled abroad, returning to Britain—and to prison—in 2001. The train driver, Jack Mills, who was attacked with an iron bar during the robbery, never fully recovered, and died in 1970.

1907 The British-engineered Rolls-Royce Silver Ghost passes its 15,000-mile official trial with flying colors, showing off its seven-liter engine and four-speed overdrive gearbox. It was this trial that made the "Ghost's" reputation and allowed it to be called "The Best Car in the World." A total of 6,173 Silver Ghosts were produced.

1911 The newsreel becomes a standard feature at American movie screenings when the French film company Pathé begins releasing weekly black-and-white broadcasts to theaters. Newsreels became increasingly important sources of information during the two world wars.

1925 The largest-ever Ku Klux Klan rally takes place in Washington, D.C. Approximately 40,000 Klansmen paraded down Pennsylvania Avenue.

1940 The Battle of Britain begins with the first of several high-intensity air raids by German bombers.

1945 The Soviet Union officially declares war on Japan, pouring more than one million Soviet soldiers into Japanese-occupied Manchuria, in northeastern China, to take on the 700,000-strong Japanese army during World War II.

1974 In an evening televised address, President Richard M. Nixon becomes the first president in American history to resign. With impeachment proceedings underway against him for his involvement in the Watergate affair, Nixon was bowing to pressure from the public and Congress to leave the White House.

1983 In Guatemala, President Rias Montt is overthrown in a coup led by Defense Minister General Oscar Humberto Mejia, who would eventually become head of state.

1995 Saddam Hussein's regime in Iraq is shaken when two of his daughters and their husbands, along with several senior army officers, defect.

Money from the Great Train Robbery found in a London phone booth

⚔ **480 B.C.** The Persians defeat King Leonidas of Sparta and 10,000 Greeks at the Battle of Thermopylae.

⚔ **48 B.C.** Roman general Julius Caesar defeats his one-time friend, Pompey, in Greece. When Pompey fled to Egypt, Caesar followed but found he had been murdered. It was this event that prompted Caesar to meet Cleopatra.

⚔ **378** In one of the most decisive battles in history, a large Roman army is defeated by horse-mounted Visigoths at the Battle of Adrianople in present-day Turkey. Two-thirds of the Roman army were overrun and slaughtered. The Visigoth victory left the Eastern Roman Empire nearly defenseless and established the supremacy of cavalry over infantry that would last for the next millennium.

1483 Pope Sixtus IV celebrates the first mass in Rome's Sistine Chapel, which was named in his honor.

⚔ **1757** During the French and Indian War, Fort William Henry on Lake George is taken

---

BORN ON THIS DAY

1593
SIR IZAAK WALTON
English author and fishing expert (*The Compleat Angler*)

1631
SIR JOHN DRYDEN
England's first official poet laureate

1686
BENEDETTO MARCELLO
Italian composer

1757
THOMAS TELFORD
Scottish civil engineer who created many canals, roads, villages, and bridges, notably the Menai bridge in Wales

1875
ALBERT KETÈLBY
English composer ("In a Monastery Garden")

1896
JEAN PIAGET
Swiss pioneer developmental psychologist and zoologist

1902
ZINO (RENÉ) FRANCESCATTI
French concert violinist

1957
MELANIE GRIFFITH
American actress (*Shining Through; Working Girl*)

1965
PHILIP LARKIN
English poet (*This Be the Verse; High Windows; Church Going*)

"God has two dwellings: one in heaven, and the other in a meek and thankful heart."

—*Izaak Walton*

by the Marquis Joseph de Montcalm. James Fenimore Cooper would later incorporate this battle into his novel *The Last of the Mohicans.*

1778 Captain James Cook of England passes through the Bering Strait in search of the Northwest Passage.

1792 The French Legislative Assembly calls for revolution and the removal of King Louis XVI.

1831 The inaugural run of the first U.S. steam locomotive train takes place between Albany and Schenectady, New York.

1842 The Webster-Ashburton Treaty between the United States and Great Britain is signed, establishing the boundary between the United States and Canada from the east coast to the Great Lakes.

1854 American philosopher Henry David Thoreau publishes *Walden.*

1870 In Great Britain, the Elementary Education Act is passed, giving compulsory free education to every child between the ages of five and 13.

1892 Thomas Edison receives a U.S. patent for the two-way telegraph, which allowed operators to send messages

---

The La Creazion fresco, by Michaelangelo, in Rome's Sistine Chapel

Snow White and the Seven Dwarfs poster

simultaneously over one wire. The American inventor had already patented the device in Great Britain, France, Italy, Austria-Hungary, and Russia.

1902 A year after the death of his mother, Queen Victoria, 64-year-old Edward VII is crowned king of Great Britain and Ireland at Westminster Abbey in London, England. The coronation had originally been scheduled for June 26, but had to be postponed as the king required an emergency appendectomy.

1910 The first electric washing machine is patented by A. J. Fisher of Chicago, Illinois.

1930 Betty Boop makes her debut in American cartoonist Max Fleischer's animated *Dizzy Dishes*.

1934 American filmmaker Walt Disney presents his animators with an outline of the first full-length animated film, *Snow White and the Seven Dwarfs*.

1942 Indian Nationalist leader Mohandas K. Gandhi is arrested by the British after starting the "Quit India" movement.

1945 A second atom bomb is dropped on Japan by the United States, at Nagasaki, resulting in Japan's unconditional surrender in World War II.

1965 After seceding from Malaysia, Singapore becomes an independent republic within the English Commonwealth.

1969 Five people are killed in film director Roman Polanski's home in Hollywood, California, including Polanski's pregnant wife, Sharon Tate, by members of a cult who scrawled a message in blood on the walls. The city of Los Angeles was in a state of panic until the leader of the cult Charles Manson, was identified and arrested.

1971 Northern Ireland detains hundreds of guerrilla suspects and begins a policy of internment without trial. Over 20 died in the riots that followed.

1972 NASA awards Rockwell International the contract to construct the U.S. space shuttle.

Guitarist Jerry Garcia, right, and drummer Mickey Hart of the Grateful Dead (milestone)

⚔ **955** King Otto I of Germany prevents a possible invasion by defeating the Magyars (Hungarians) at the Battle of Lechfeld.

🏴 **1498** King Henry VII of England rewards John Cabot for the discovery of Canada with 10 pounds (approximately $15.75 in current U.S. dollars).

1519 Portuguese explorer Ferdinand Magellan's five ships set sail to circumnavigate the Earth. On the same day in 1990, the U.S. *Magellan* spacecraft landed on Venus.

⚔ **1557** At the Battle of Saint Quentin during the Spanish-French Wars, the French lose more than 14,000 men when they try to block a Spanish army under Count Egmont. The Spaniards lost just 50 men.

⚔ **1627** Cardinal Richelieu of France begins what will be a 14-month siege of the Huguenot fortress at La Rochelle.

1628 The vast Swedish warship *Vasa* is sunk at the start of its maiden voyage. The ship, with its 164-foot mast, remained on the sea bed until 1961, when it was raised so well preserved that—ironically—it could float.

1664 The Peace of Vasvar is signed, whereby the Ottomans restore their authority in

> *"Words without actions are the assassins of idealism."*
>
> —*Herbert Hoover*

MILESTONE

Smithsonian Institution Created

After debate about how best to spend a bequest left to the United States by an obscure English scientist, President James Knox Polk signs the Smithsonian Institution Act into law on this day in 1846. In 1829, James Smithson died in Italy, leaving a will stating that in the event his only nephew died without any heirs, Smithson's estate would go to the nation to found, at Washington, D.C., under the name of the Smithsonian Institution, an establishment for the increase and diffusion of knowledge. His nephew did indeed die without heirs, and in 1836 Congress authorized acceptance of Smithson's gift.

James Knox Polk

Frederick Douglass

Transylvania (now Austria) following Hapsburg efforts to intervene.

🔬 **1675** The foundation stone of the Royal Observatory is laid at Greenwich in London, England, by order of King Charles II. John Flamsteed was the first Astronomer Royal.

🇺🇸 **1776** Thomas Jefferson, Benjamin Franklin, and John Adams suggest the adoption of *"E Pluribus Unum"* ("Out of many, one") as the motto for the Great Seal of the United States.

🎵 **1787** Austrian composer Wolfgang Amadeus Mozart completes *Eine Kleine Nachtmusik*.

🇫🇷 **1792** King Louis XVI of France is arrested after a mob storms the Tuileries in Paris.

🇺🇸 **1863** In the U.S., Frederick Douglass pushes President Lincoln for full equality for Union "Negro troops."

🏴 **1889** Dan Rylands, of Yorkshire, England, patents the screw-top bottle.

🔬 **1889** The skeleton of a mammoth that was 36 feet long

and stood 15 feet high is found in St. James, Nebraska.

1893 Testing begins on German engineer Rudolf Diesel's prototype engine. It was commercially produced four years later.

1895 English conductor Henry Wood leads the first Promenade Concert at Queen's Hall in London.

1897 The oldest automobile club, the Automobile Club of Great Britain and Ireland, later known as the Royal Automobile Club, is founded by C. Harrington Moore and Frederick R. Simms.

1904 During the Russo-Japanese War, the Russian fleet takes heavy losses when the Japanese fleet blocks their escape from Port Arthur in the Battle of the Yellow Sea.

1907 The greatest automobile race in history takes place. Stretching 8,000 miles, this race from Beijing, China, to Paris, France, lasted for 62 days and was won by Prince Borghese of Italy. Driving like a madman across Asia and Europe, the prince encountered brush fire, got stuck in a swamp, and was pulled over by a policeman in Belgium who refused to believe that he was racing, rather than merely speeding.

1913 The second Balkan War ends as Bulgaria and the Balkan Allies, Greece, Serbia, Montenegro, and Romania, sign the Treaty of Bucharest.

1920 Following World War I, Turkey and the Allied powers sign the Treaty of

Sevres. As a result, Turkey gave up much of the land ruled by the Ottoman Empire.

1921 Future U.S. president Franklin D. Roosevelt is diagnosed with polio.

1949 U.S. president Harry S. Truman signs the National Security Bill, which establishes the Department of Defense. As the Cold War heated up, the department became the cornerstone of America's military effort to contain the expansion of communism.

1977 Panama and the United States reach an agreement to transfer the Panama Canal to Panama by the year 2000.

1985 In the United States, pop singer Madonna's album *Like a Virgin* is certified with sales of five million copies. It's the first solo album by a female artist to be so certified.

1995 In the United States, Timothy McVeigh and Terry Nichols are indicted for the Oklahoma City bombing on April 19 that killed 168 people.

President Franklin D. Roosevelt holds his black Scottie, Fala, alongside his caretaker's granddaughter

1492 Spanish-born Rodrigo de Borja is proclaimed pope. Known as Alexander VI, he was suspected of buying out church officials to obtain the papacy. Although charged with corruption by historians, he had a policy of tolerance toward Jews.

1587 English explorer Sir Walter Raleigh lands in North Carolina on his second expedition to the New World.

1711 The first Royal Ascot race meeting is held in England. The race course was created by Queen Anne, who had bought the land near the village of East Cote for £558. At the first meeting, horses competed for the 100-guinea Her Majesty's Plate. Ascot, now held in June, is famous for the lavish millinery worn by women who attend.

1712 The Treaty of Aargau is signed in Switzerland, guaranteeing Protestant superiority over Catholic cantons.

1772 An explosive eruption blows 4,000 feet off the top off Papandayan, a volcano in Java, Indonesia. Three thousand people were killed.

1860 The United States' first successful silver mill begins operations near Virginia City, Nevada.

1863 Cambodia becomes a French protectorate.

MILESTONE

Watts Riot Begins

In the Watts neighborhood of Los Angeles, California, racial tension reaches a breaking point after two white policemen scuffle with a black motorist suspected of drunken driving on this day in 1965. Spectators gathered to watch the arrest and were angered by what they believed to be an incident of racially motivated abuse by the police. A riot soon began and spread over a 50-square-mile area of South Central Los Angeles. With the assistance of thousands of National Guardsmen, order was restored on August 16. The violence left 34 dead, 1,032 injured, nearly 4,000 arrested, and $40 million worth of property destroyed.

National Guardsmen stand guard in Los Angeles

"Boasting of glory does not make glory, and singing in the dark does not dispel fear."
—*King Hussein*

1866 Newport, Rhode Island, becomes home to the world's first roller-skating rink.

1877 American astronomer Asaph Hall discovers the two moons of Mars.

1885 In the United States, $100,000 is raised for the pedestal of the Statue of Liberty.

1906 Eugene Augustin Lauste of Paris, France, patents the first talking motion picture.

1909 Finding itself in trouble off Cape Hatteras, North Carolina, the U.S. ocean liner *Arapahoe* is the first to use the distress call S.O.S.

1924 The first newsreel of U.S. presidential candidates is taken in Washington, D.C.

1934 A group of federal prisoners classified as "most dangerous" arrives at Alcatraz Island off California, the first civilian prisoners to be housed on this 22-acre rocky outcrop situated 1.5 miles offshore in San Francisco Bay. Although some three dozen have attempted, no prisoner is known to have successfully escaped "The Rock."

1942 In Russia during World War II, Dimitri Shostakovich's Seventh Symphony, the *Leningrad Symphony,* is first performed. Many members of the orchestra were on leave from the Eastern Front and some performed in military uniform.

1943 German forces begin a six-day evacuation of the Italian island of Sicily, having been beaten back by the Allies, who invaded the island in July. The Germans had maintained a presence in Sicily since the earliest days of World War II, but with the arrival of U.S. general George S. Patton and his 7th Army and British general Bernard Montgomery and his 8th Army, they could no longer hold their position.

1952 Prince Hussein is proclaimed the king of Jordan after his father, King Talal, is declared unfit to rule on grounds of mental illness. Hussein was the third constitutional king of Jordan and a member of the Hashemite dynasty, said to be in direct line of descent from the Prophet Muhammad. He died in 1999 as the 20th century's longest-serving executive head of state.

1954 A formal peace ends more than seven years of fighting between the French and communist Viet Minh in Indochina.

1966 A treaty is signed in Jakarta ending three years of hostilities between Malaysia and Indonesia.

1968 In England, The Beatles launch their new record label, Apple.

1972 The last U.S. ground combat unit in South Vietnam, the Third Battalion, 21st Infantry, departs for the United States. The unit had been guarding the U.S. air base at Da Nang during the Vietnam War.

1985 Rudolf Povarnitsin of the Soviet Union sets a new world high-jump record of 7 feet, 10 inches.

1993 U.S. president Bill Clinton signs an executive order endorsing the "Brady Bill" for handgun control and bans the import of semiautomatic assault-style handguns. On this day in 1995, he bans all U.S. nuclear tests.

Federal penitentiary on Alcatraz Island in San Francisco Bay, California

Grouse

"The public is always right."

—*Cecil B. DeMille*

Annually The British grouse-shooting season opens today, running until December 10. The "Glorious Twelfth," as it is known, sees a race to get the first birds from the grouse moors of Scotland and northern England to restaurant tables in London.

1099 Crusaders defeat the Egyptians at Ascalon on the Palestine coast during the First Crusade.

1332 Superior forces under David, king of Scotland, are defeated by disinherited Scottish barons under Edward Baliol at the Battle of Dupplin.

1450 Charles VII's conquest of Normandy is completed as the English surrender Cherbourg during the Hundred Years' War.

1508 Spanish explorer Juan Ponce de León lands in Puerto Rico.

1530 In Italy, Florence is restored to the Medicis after a siege of 10 months.

1658 The first police force in the United States is established in New Amsterdam (now New York).

1676 In colonial New England, King Philip's War comes to an end when Philip, chief of the Wampanoag Indians, is assassinated. This ended the Native American presence in the region and inaugurated a period of unimpeded colonial expansion.

1687 During the Ottoman Wars, the Turks under Mohammed IV are decisively beaten by the Austrians under Louis of Baden and the Hungarians in the Battle of Mohacz.

1759 At the Battle of Kunersdorf in the Seven Years' War, the Russians under General Soltikov and the Austrians under General Landon defeat 40,000 Prussians under Frederick the Great.

1822 Lord Castlereagh, the Tory foreign secretary in the British government, commits suicide by cutting his throat with a penknife. He had been suffering from an increasingly severe mental illness—shortly before he died he said "My mind, my mind, is, as it were, gone."

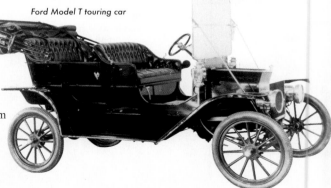

Ford Model T touring car

1851 In New York City, Isaac Singer patents the revolutionary double-treadle sewing machine.

1865 English surgeon Joseph Lister is the first to use disinfectant during an operation. The mouthwash brand Listerine was named for him.

1877 American inventor Thomas A. Edison reputedly finishes his first phonograph, which utilizes a tin-foil-wrapped cylinder. The first sound recording was "Mary Had a Little Lamb."

1908 Henry Ford's first Model T, affectionately known as the "Tin Lizzie," rolls off the assembly line in Detroit, Michigan. The Model T revolutionized the automotive industry by providing an affordable, reliable car for the average American.

1938 Nazi dictator Adolf Hitler institutes the Mother's Cross, to encourage German women to have more children, to be awarded each year on August 12, Hitler's mother's birthday. A gold medal was awarded to women with seven children, a silver to women with six, and a bronze to women with five.

1941 U.S. president Franklin D. Roosevelt and British prime minister Winston Churchill meet in Newfoundland to confer on issues ranging from support for Russia to threatening Japan to post-World War II peace. Chief among their declarations was a promise to strive for a postwar world free of "aggrandizement, territorial or other." This document would be called the Atlantic Charter and would comprise the founding principles of the United Nations.

1960 *Echo I*, the world's first experimental communications satellite, is launched from Cape Canaveral, Florida.

1961 In an effort to stem the tide of refugees attempting to leave East Berlin, the communist government of East Germany begins building the Berlin Wall to divide East and West Berlin.

1992 The United States, Mexico, and Canada agree to form a free-trade zone (later known as the North American Free Trade Agreement, or NAFTA). It became the world's largest single trading bloc.

2000 The Russian military submarine *Kursk* and its crew sink in the Barents Sea as a torpedo explodes in one of the sub's forward compartments.

Construction of the Berlin Wall while soldiers stand guard

1521 After a three-month siege, Spanish forces under Hernán Cortés capture Tenochtitlán, the capital of the Aztec empire. Cortés's men leveled the city and captured Cuauhtémoc, the Aztec emperor. This victory marked the fall of the Aztec empire. Cuauhtémoc, Cuitláhuac's successor as emperor, was taken prisoner and later executed, and Cortés became the ruler of a vast Mexican empire.

1587 Manteo, of the Croatoan tribe in North Carolina, becomes the first Native American to be converted to Protestantism and baptized into the Church of England.

1624 In France, Cardinal Richelieu is named as first chief minister of finance by King Louis XIII.

1642 Dutch mathematician and physicist Christiaan Huygens discovers the Martian south polar cap.

1704 The Battle of Blenheim is fought during the War of the Spanish Succession. A combined British, German, and Dutch army defeated French and Bavarian forces.

1784 The English parliament accepts the India Act. A

Cardinal Richelieu portraits

1422
WILLIAM CAXTON
First English printer (*Histories of Troy*)

1655
JOHANN CHRISTOPH DENNER
German inventor of the clarinet

1792
QUEEN ADELAIDE
Queen consort of British king William IV, for whom the capital of South Australia is named

Queen Adelaide

1802
NIKOLAUS LENAU HUNGARY
German poet ("Faust"; "Die Albigenser")

1818
LUCY STONE
American pioneer of women's rights

1820
SIR GEORGE GROVE
English engineer and musicologist

1879
JOHN IRELAND
English composer and teacher of Benjamin Britten ("The Forgotten Rite"; "Sarnia")

1888
JOHN LOGIE BAIRD
Scottish inventor of the television

1907
SIR BASIL SPENCE
Scottish architect who designed the new Coventry Cathedral replacing the medieval one destroyed by Nazi bombing

1912
BEN HOGAN
American golf champion

1927
FIDEL CASTRO (RUZ)
Cuban political leader

---

dual policy between the East India Company and the Crown to control India, the act was successful for 75 years.

1788 Prussia joins with the English and Dutch to form the Triple Alliance, whose aim was to stop the spread of the Russo-Swedish War.

1814 The Dutch formally cede the Cape of Good Hope to the British.

1868 Earthquakes in Peru and Ecuador kill 25,000 and cause $300 million in damage.

1876 German composer Richard Wagner's entire Ring Cycle (*Der Ring des Nibelungen*) is first performed, at Bayreuth, Bavaria.

1907 The first American taxicab takes to the streets of New York City. Motorized taxis had begun appearing on the streets of Europe in the late 1890s. The taxi was named after the taximeter, a device that automatically records the distance traveled or time consumed and is used to calculate the fare. The term "cab" originated from the cabriolet, a one-horse carriage let out for hire.

1910 English nurse Florence Nightingale dies at the age of 90. Famous for her work in the Crimean War, she had also pioneered the use of statistics in analyzing casualty num-

> *"Drama is life with the dull bits cut out."*
>
> —*Alfred Hitchcock*

bers, inventing an early form of the pie chart.

1912 St. Joseph's College in Philadelphia, Pennsylvania, is granted the first experimental radio license.

1914 Carl Wickman of Hibbing, Minnesota, creates the first bus line in the United States, called Greyhound.

1915 A bullet fired by a German sniper enters the barrel of the rifle held by English soldier Private W. J. Smith, who had been about to shoot at the sniper. The rifle was badly damaged, but Private Smith was unharmed.

1918 The British government recognizes the state of Czechoslovakia.

1924 Floods in China have left as many as 50,000 people dead, with two million more homeless.

1942 American filmmaker Walt Disney's classic animated film *Bambi* premieres at Radio City Music Hall in New York City.

1960 The Central African Republic and Chad proclaim their independence from France.

1986 The U.S. Congress approves President Ronald W. Reagan's request for $100 million to aid the Nicaraguan contra rebels in their guerilla war against the Sandinista government.

1996 The U.S. *Galileo* space probe sends data indicating there may be water on Jupiter's moon Europa, suggesting the possible existence of a primitive form of life.

Illustration of Galileo spacecraft approaching another of Jupiter's moons, Io, left

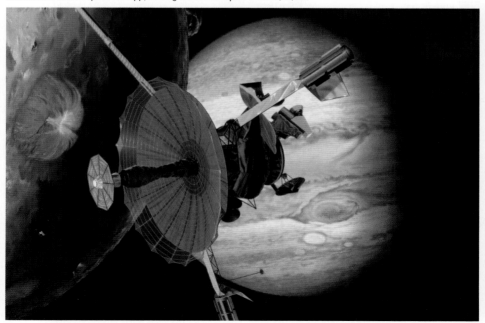

1040 Macbeth murders King Duncan of Scotland and takes the throne.

1281 Mongol emperor of China Kublai Khan's fleet disappears in a typhoon near Japan.

1385 At the battle of Aljubarrota, Portuguese forces stop an invasion by John I of Castille, thus securing independence for Portugal.

1678 William of Orange leads a surprise attack against the French army near Mons. The French rallied, however, and repulsed William, who lost several thousand men.

1733 The War of Polish Succession begins. It was caused by rival claims to the throne of Poland upon the death of Augustus II by his son Augustus III and Polish nobleman Stanislaw Leszczynski.

1782 The South American country of Suriname outlaws the selling of slave mothers without their babies.

1784 On Kodiak Island, Russian fur trader Grigory Shelikhov founds Three Saints Bay, the first permanent Russian settlement in Alaska. The European discovery of Alaska came in 1741, when a Russian expedition led by Danish navigator Vitus Bering sighted the Alaskan mainland.

1834 Nineteen-year-old American Richard Henry Dana, author of the highly popular book *Two Years Before the Mast*, an autobiographical account of the abuse endured by seamen, begins his stint at sea.

BORN ON THIS DAY

1777
HANS CHRISTIAN OERSTED
Danish physicist for whom a unit of magnetic field strength is named

1863
ERNEST THAYER
American poet ("Casey at the Bat")

1867
JOHN GALSWORTHY
English Nobel Prize-winning author (*The Forsyte Saga*)

1903
JOHN RINGLING NORTH
American circus director

1931
FREDERIC RAPHAEL
English playwright and novelist (*Personal Terms; Old Scores; A Double Life*)

1941
DAVID CROSBY
American rock musician (Crosby, Stills, Nash, and Young)

1945
STEVE MARTIN
American actor, comedian, and author (*The Jerk; Picasso at the Lapin Agile*)

1950
GARY LARSON
American cartoonist ("The Far Side")

"A man of action forced into a state of thought is unhappy until he can get out of it."

—*John Galsworthy*

1834 The Poor Law Amendment Act is passed in Great Britain. The Act essentially required that the government provide all able-bodied people financial assistance unless they entered a workhouse.

1880 One of Europe's Gothic masterpieces, Cologne Cathedral in Germany, is finally completed. Construction started in 1248.

1898 After a three-month blockade of Manila Bay, U.S. forces capture Manila during the Spanish-American War.

1900 During the Boxer Rebellion, an international force featuring British, Russian, American, Japanese, French, and

The Cologne Cathedral in Germany

German troops relieves the Chinese capital of Beijing after fighting its way 80 miles from the port of Tientsin. The Chinese nationalists besieging Beijing's diplomatic quarter were crushed, and the Boxer Rebellion effectively came to an end.

1908 Folkestone, Kent, England, witnesses the world's first international beauty contest at the Pier Hippodrome. The winner was Nellie Jarman from East Molesey in Surrey.

1923 The American comic strip *Felix the Cat* debuts.

1925 American sculptor Gutzon Borglum first proposes the monumental Mount Rushmore in South Dakota, with figures honoring U.S. presidents Washington, Jefferson, Lincoln, and Theodore Roosevelt. Borglum's son, James, would complete the project in 1941, eight months after his father's death.

1932 Italian radio pioneer Guglielmo Marconi completes work on the world's first short-wave radio.

1935 The U.S. Social Security Act is passed.

1936 The first Olympic basketball competition takes place at the games in Berlin, Germany. The United States defeated Canada, 19–8.

1945 An official announcement of Japan's unconditional surrender to the Allies in World War II is made public to the Japanese people. More than 1,000 Japanese soldiers stormed the Imperial

Lech Walesa

Palace in an attempt to find the proclamation and prevent its being transmitted to the Allies.

1959 The first telecast of Earth from outer space is transmitted. The satellite *Explorer 6* sent pictures showing 20,000 square miles of Earth.

1962 Italian and French workers complete the road tunnel under Mont Blanc after three and a half years of digging.

1979 The Fastnet yacht race, a major international sporting event held in the waters between southern Ireland, Wales, and England, is hit by devastating Atlantic storms, killing 14 people.

1980 Workers in Gdansk, Poland, seize the Lenin Shipyard and demand pay raises and the right to form a union free from communist control. The massive strike also saw the rise to prominence of labor leader Lech Walesa, who would be a key figure in bringing an end to communist rule in Poland.

"If you think you can do a thing or think you can't do a thing, you're right."

—Henry Ford

1057 At the Battle of Lumphanan, King Macbeth of Scotland is slain by Malcolm Canmore, whose father, King Duncan I, was murdered by Macbeth 17 years earlier.

1658 The League of the Rhine, an alliance between several small German states and France, is established after French king Louis XIV failed to be elected Holy Roman emperor. It was a defense against the reestablishment of Hapsburg domination sought by Holy Roman emperor Leopold I.

1684 The Truce of Ratisbon, guaranteeing peace for 20 years, is signed between France and the Holy Roman Empire.

1744 An invasion of Saxony by King Frederick II of Prussia starts the second Silesian War.

1805 The American Lewis and Clark expedition crosses the Continental Divide in what is now Montana.

1824 The African country of Liberia is founded by freed American slaves.

Poster of Polish war hero Józef Pilsudski

1843 The Tivoli Gardens open in Copenhagen, Denmark.

1848 M. Waldo Hanchett of Syracuse, New York, receives a patent for the dental chair.

1852 Croquet is introduced to the United States from England. It became quite popular as a social event, rather than an athletic one, as it allowed men and women to compete together.

1867 Great Britain passes the Second Reform Act, which doubles the electorate by extending suffrage to all urban men owning or renting property valued at more than 10 pounds sterling.

1877 American inventor Thomas Edison suggests the use of "Hello" when answering the telephone, instead of "Ahoy," as suggested by its inventor, Alexander Graham Bell.

1899 Henry Ford resigns as a chief engineer at the Detroit Edison Company to concentrate on automobile production. After turning to automobiles full time, he would revolutionize the American automotive industry with the Model T and the modern assembly line.

1914 The Panama Canal is inaugurated with the passage of the U.S. vessel *Ancon,* a cargo and passenger ship.

1918 In the wake of the Bolshevik Revolution, the United States severs diplomatic relations with Russia.

1920 Polish Marshal Józef Piłsudski crushes Soviet troops and blocks their march on Western Europe during the Battle of Warsaw.

1938 The ocean liner *Queen Mary* beats its own record for crossing the Atlantic, returning to England from the United States in three days, 23 hours, and 58 minutes.

1939 MGM's *The Wizard of Oz* has its premiere at Grauman's Chinese Theater in Hollywood, California.

1944 The Allied forces of World War II land in southern France to open up a second front after the Normandy landings in June.

V-J Day celebration in Times Square

1945 V-J Day is proclaimed by the Allies, after Japan agrees to surrender unconditionally in World War II.

1947 Great Britain's first nuclear reactor, at Harwell in Oxfordshire, begins operation.

1947 The Ferrari makes its racing debut, in Pescara, Italy, placing second.

1969 The Woodstock Music and Art Fair opens in upstate New York. Nearly half a million people converged on the concert site. Despite rain and mud, the audience enjoyed nonstop performances by singers like Janis Joplin and Joe Cocker, as well as bands like The Grateful Dead and Jefferson Airplane.

AUGUST 16

1513 Under Henry VIII of England, English and German forces defeat the French in what was called "The Battle of the Spurs."

1743 English boxer Jack Broughton establishes the earliest code of rules for the sport.

1775 The heart of Paul Whitehead, a leading member of the Hellfire Club, is interred in the mausoleum on Wycombe Hill in southern England, by the club's founder Francis Dashwood, Lord le Despencer. The club, known to its members as the Knights of St. Francis, was believed at the time to indulge in satanic orgies.

1777 In an important American victory during the American Revolution, patriots led by General John Stark defeat the British at the Battle of Bennington.

1780 During the American Revolution, the British, led by General Charles Cornwallis, defeat the Americans led by General Horatio Gates at Camden, New Jersey.

1812 During the War of 1812, American general William Hull surrenders Fort Detroit and his army to the British without a fight. Hull, a 59-year-old veteran

William Hull

of the American Revolution, had lost hope of defending the settlement after seeing the large English and Indian force gathering outside Detroit's walls. The general was also preoccupied with the presence of his daughter and grandchildren inside the fort.

1819 In what became known as the Peterloo Massacre, a crowd gathers on St. Peter's Field in Manchester, England, to demand parliamentary reforms. But troops, including veterans of the Battle of Waterloo, are called in to dispatch the crowd and 11 people are killed.

1829 Chang and Eng Bunker, the original Siamese twins, arrive in Boston, Massachusetts, to be exhibited in the United States.

1841 President John Tyler, a former Whig ally, vetoes a bill that would have established the Second Bank of the United States. The move sparked a riot outside the White House, as incensed—and drunk—members of the Whig Party bombarded the White House with stones, fired their guns in the air, and burned Tyler in effigy. The outburst still stands as the most violent demonstration ever held outside the White House.

1898 American inventor Edwin Prescott patents the roller coaster.

"Poor is the man whose pleasures depend on the permission of another."
—Madonna

Wreckage of a Nazi plane

1914 Revolutionaries and bandits Emiliano Zapata and Pancho Villa gain control of northern Mexico.

1923 American company Carnegie Steel establishes the eight-hour day for its workers, instead of the previous 12-hour shifts.

1928 The Soviet Union makes military service obligatory.

1931 During a major flood in China, 10 million people are left homeless and more than a million are thought to have drowned.

1937 Harvard University in Cambridge, Massachusetts, becomes the first school to institute graduate study courses in traffic engineering and administration.

1940 During World War II, 45 German aircraft are shot down over England.

1960 The Island of Cyprus becomes a republic, led by Archbishop Makarios.

1966 The Declaration of Bogotà is signed. It called for the economic integration of Latin America and for nonintervention in the internal affairs of Latin American states.

1966 The House Un-American Activities Committee investigates Americans who have given aid to the Viet Cong, with a view toward introducing legislation to make such activities illegal.

1977 The king of rock 'n' roll, Elvis Presley, dies at the age of 42 in Memphis, Tennessee.

1999 The Russian Parliament confirms Vladimir Putin as Russia's fifth prime minister since early 1998.

Flowers for Elvis Presley at Forest Hills Cemetery in Memphis, Tennessee

MILESTONE

George Carmack Discovers Klondike Gold

Sometime-prospector George Carmack stumbles across gold on this day in 1896 while fishing along the Klondike River in the Yukon. His discovery in that region sparked the last great western gold rush, but it was pure chance that he made it. Carmack was not a particularly serious prospector. He had traveled to Alaska in 1881, drawn by the reports of major gold in the Juneau area, but failing to make a significant strike, he headed north into the isolated Yukon Territory. Carmack got rich from his discovery, reportedly taking a million dollars worth of gold out of his claims.

1424 During the Hundred Years' War, the English defeat the Scots and French at the Battle of Verneuil.

1560 Roman Catholicism is abolished by the Scottish estates.

1563 Although he's only 13 years old, King Charles IX of France is declared an adult.

1585 In the Dutch War of Liberation, Spanish forces take Antwerp after a 14-month siege.

1743 The Peace of Abo is signed, ending the Russo-Swedish War that started in 1741.

1807 Laughing spectators watch the maiden voyage of Robert Fulton's steamboat from the banks of New York City's Hudson River. Few people expected the boat to work and doubters called it "Fulton's Folly." Yet soon Fulton's steamboat, the *Clermont,* was carrying passengers and freight on a regular schedule.

1812 The Russians, retreating to Moscow, are defeated by Napoleon's army at the battle of Smolensk.

1833 The Canadian ship *Royal William* begins her journey from Nova Scotia to the Isle of Wight, becoming the first

> *"When choosing between two evils, I always like to try the one I've never tried before."*
>
> —Mae West

MILESTONE

Natural Disaster Devastates Turkey

On this day in 1999 an earthquake measuring 7.8 on the Richter scale strikes northwestern Turkey, home to one-third of the country's population and half its industry, at 3 A.M. Centered on the town of Izmit, the quake killed thousands instantly as their homes collapsed on them. All told, more than 17,000 people were killed, damage totaling $6.5 billion affected over 70,000 buildings, making the quake one of the most devastating of the 20th century. Tragically, another earthquake, measuring 7.2, hit Turkey less than three months later.

---

steamship to cross the Atlantic entirely under its own power.

1835 The wrench is patented by American inventor Solyman Merrick of Springfield, Massachusetts.

1850 Denmark cedes the Gold Coast of Africa to Great Britain.

1859 The first airmail in the United States, sent by balloon, takes off from Lafayette, Indiana.

1862 In Minnesota, desperate Dakota Indians attack white settlements along the Minnesota River. With crops destroyed by cutworms, many Dakota families faced starvation and couldn't convince traders to extend credit. Four Dakota warriors stole eggs from a white settlement and, during an argument, killed five settlers. Sensing they would be attacked, Dakota leaders seized the initiative.

1877 Though only a teenager at the time, William Bonney ("Billy the Kid")

Battle between Dakota Indians and settlers

wounds Arizona blacksmith Frank "Windy" Cahill, who dies the next day. Cahill was the famous outlaw's first victim.

1879 Ferdinand de Lesseps of France forms the Panama Canal Company.

1896 Mrs. Bridget Driscoll's skull is crushed by a motor car at the Crystal Palace in London, making her the first pedestrian to be killed in an automobile accident.

1903 American philanthropist Joseph Pulitzer makes a donation of one million dollars to Columbia University and starts the Pulitzer Prizes.

1915 Charles F. Kettering of Detroit, Michigan, patents the electric automobile self-starter. Kettering, along with Edward A. Deeds, founded Delco (Dayton Engineering Laboratories Company), which would later become a subsidiary of General Motors. The Cadillac was the first car to use the electric starter.

1940 Nazi German dictator Adolf Hitler orders a complete blockade of Great Britain.

1943 U.S. general George S. Patton and his 7th Army arrive in Messina several hours before British field marshal Bernard L. Montgomery and his 8th Army, winning the unofficial "Race to Messina" and completing the Allied conquest of Sicily.

1945 After 350 years of Dutch occupation, Indonesia declares its independence. Achmed Sukarno became the first president of the new republic, but it was only after several years of fighting that Indonesia was actually granted independence by the Netherlands.

1962 East German guards gun down Peter Fechter, a young man trying to escape across the Berlin Wall, into West Berlin, and leave him to bleed to death. It was one of the ugliest incidents to take place at one of the ugliest symbols of the Cold War.

1978 The *Double Eagle II* completes the first transatlantic balloon flight when it lands in a barley field near Paris, France, 137 hours after lifting off from Preque Isle, Maine.

1994 Riots ensue as King Letsie III of Lesotho dissolves the country's first democratically elected government, which had been operating for 20 years.

1996 Ruth Perry becomes Africa's first female head of state when she is chosen by a meeting of West African leaders to chair Liberia's ruling council.

Peter Fechter's body carried away by East German border guards

King Philip II of Spain

1274 Edward I is crowned king of England.

1289 Pope Nicholas IV publishes the decree *Supra montem*. It confirmed the third order of St. Francis, a middle state between the cloister and the world for those who wished to follow in the saint's footsteps but were debarred by marriage or other ties from entering either the first or second order.

1564 Spanish King Philip II joins the Council of Trent of the Roman Catholic Church, which was called to meet the crisis of the Protestant Reformation.

1590 John White, governor of the Roanoke Island colony in present-day North Carolina, returns from a supply trip to England to find the settlement deserted. There was no trace of the 100 or so colonists left behind, and no sign of violence. Among the missing was Virginia Dare, White's granddaughter and the first English child born in America, whose third birthday was on this day.

1686 Italian astronomer Giovanni Domenico Cassini reports seeing a satellite orbiting Venus.

1759 At the Battle of Lagos Bay, the French fleet is defeated by the British under the command of Admiral Boscawen.

1825 Alexander Gordon Laing, a Scottish explorer, becomes the first European to reach Timbuktu, now in Mali.

1868 During an eclipse, French astronomer Pierre Janssan discovers helium in the sun's spectrum.

1900 Frenchman Constantin Perskyi coins the word "television" during a presentation at the Paris International Electricity Conference.

1905 American attorney Newell S. Wright files to register the Cadillac crest as a trademark. The insignia has adorned Cadillac's luxury car ever since.

1914 President Woodrow Wilson issues his Proclamation of Neutrality, aimed at keeping the United States out of World War I.

1920 The 19th Amendment to the U.S. Constitution, guaranteeing women the right to vote, is ratified by Tennessee, giving it the two-thirds majority of state ratification needed to make it the law of the land.

1929 Austria bans the classic World War I novel *All Quiet on the Western Front*.

1932 Jim Mollison, a Scottish aviator, makes the first westbound transatlantic solo flight. He flew from Portmarnock, Ireland, to New Brunswick, New Jersey.

James H. Meredith

Genghis Khan, the Mongol leader who forged an empire stretching from the east coast of China to the Aral Sea, dies on this day in 1227 during a campaign against the Chinese kingdom of Xi Xia. Born as Temujin in about 1162, he grew into a feared warrior and a charismatic figure. After his wife was kidnapped by a rival tribe, he organized a military force to defeat the tribe. Successful, he then turned against other clans and tribes and set out to unite the Mongols by force. He was granted the title Genghis Khan, meaning Universal Ruler.

> *"The ear of the leader must ring with the voices of the people."*
> —*Woodrow Wilson*

1961 The Berlin Wall is completed, dividing East and West Germany.

1963 James H. Meredith, the first African American to attend the University of Mississippi, graduates with a degree in political science. His enrollment was met with deadly riots, and he subsequently attended class under heavily armed guard.

1943 *A Tree Grows in Brooklyn*, Betty Smith's novel about life in the slums of Brooklyn, New York, is published.

1958 Russian-born American author Vladimir Nabokov's controversial novel *Lolita* is published in the U.S.

1991 Hard-line elements of the Soviet government and military attempt a coup against President Mikhail Gorbachev. The attempt signified a decline in Gorbachev's power and influence, while one of his most ardent opponents, Boris Yeltsin, emerged with more power than ever.

Mikhail Gorbachev, left, and Boris Yeltsin

1071 During the Battle at Manzikert, an important town of ancient Armenia, the Seljuk Turks, under Persian Sultan Alp Arslan, rout the troops of Byzantine emperor Romanus IV, an event that resulted in the fall of Asia Minor to the Seljuks.

1263 King James I of Aragon (also known as James the Conqueror) censors Hebrew writing.

1399 King Richard II of England surrenders to the forces of the Duke of Hereford in a squabble over Richard's ability to rule and his confiscation of Hereford's inheritance. Richard abdicated and Hereford became King Henry IV.

1477 Maximilian I, son of Holy Roman emperor Frederick III, acquires the Burgundian possessions in the Netherlands and France when he marries Mary of Burgundy.

1561 After spending 13 years in France, Mary, Queen of Scots, arrives in Scotland to assume the throne.

1587 Sigismund III, son of John of Sweden, is elected

MILESTONE

Federico García Lorca Shot Dead

Spanish poet, novelist, and playwright Federico García Lorca is shot to death by right-wing Falangists in Granada, after being forced to dig his own grave on this day in 1936. Lorca was one of Spain's foremost writers of the twentieth century, best known abroad for his plays such as *Blood Wedding*, *Yerma*, and *The House of Bernada Alba*. The reasons for his murder are unclear: although he was anti-fascist by inclination and his work displayed a certain social conscience, he was largely an unpolitical figure. His family, though, were known as supporters of the leftist Popular Front, and his brother-in-law, the mayor of Granada, had been executed not long before. Lorca was one of the first, and most celebrated, victims of the Spanish Civil War, his career cut tragically short at the age of 38.

King of Poland. Although he sought a union of Poland with Sweden, he inadvertently created a war between the two countries.

1692 Four men and one woman are convicted of witchcraft and hanged in Salem, Massachusetts.

1772 In Sweden, Gustav III seizes control of the government and restores the full power of the monarchy. The monarchy had been subordinate to parliament since 1720.

1812 During the War of 1812, the U.S. Navy frigate *Constitution* defeats the British frigate *Guerrière* in a furious engagement off the coast of Nova Scotia. Witnesses claimed that the British shot bounced off the *Constitution*'s sides as if it were made of iron rather than wood. By the war's end, "Old Ironsides" had destroyed or captured seven more British ships, providing a tremendous boost in morale for the American republic.

1839 French artist and inventor Louis Daguerre announces the first process to allow an image to be chemically fixed as a permanent picture. His invention, the beginning of photography, would become known as the daguerreotype.

1848 Though gold was discovered in California in

Frigate battle of the War of 1812, between the Constitution and Guerrière

> *"The function of leadership is to produce more leaders, not more followers."*
>
> —*Ralph Nader*

January, the news didn't make it to the East Coast until this day, when the *New York Herald* announces the rush is on.

1856 Gail Borden of Brooklyn, New York, patents his process for producing condensed milk. Borden's became one of the largest dairy-product companies in the world.

1886 Author Joseph Conrad, born Jozef Teodor Konrad Korzeniowski in Poland, becomes a British citizen. Conrad joined the merchant marines at age 17, and his many harrowing adventures at sea set the scenes for much of his fiction. His best-known books include *Lord Jim, Nostromo, The Secret Agent,* and *Heart of Darkness.*

1909 A dirt track is opened for the testing of automobiles in Indianapolis, Indiana. It would later become the Indianapolis Speedway.

1919 Afghanistan declares independence from the United Kingdom. Afghan ruler Amanollah introduced several social reforms, including the removal of women's veils and the establishment of coeducational schools. Many religious and tribal leaders opposed these reforms.

1927 Henry and Edsel Ford drive the 15 millionth Model T off the assembly line at the Highland Park plant in Michigan, officially ending Model T production.

1934 The first All-American Soap Box Derby is held in Dayton, Ohio. The event was eventually moved to Akron because of its hilly terrain. To this day, children from throughout the United States and from several foreign countries arrive in Akron each year with their home-built racers.

1934 Adolf Hitler, already chancellor, is also elected president of Germany in an unprecedented consolidation of power in the short history of the republic.

1953 The Iranian military, with the support of the U.S. government, overthrows the government of Premier Mohammed Mosaddeq and reinstates the Shah of Iran.

1960 In the Soviet Union, captured American U-2 pilot Francis Gary Powers is sentenced to 10 years imprisonment for his confessed espionage.

1996 Consumer advocate Ralph Nader, calling for an alternative to the two mainstream U.S. political parties, accepts the presidential nomination of the Green Party, in Los Angeles, California.

Ralph Nader

636 The Byzantines attempt to drive Muslims out of Syria but are thwarted at the Battle of Yarmuk.

1667 English poet John Milton's *Paradise Lost,* an epic poem about the fall of Adam and Eve, is published.

1741 Danish explorer Vitus J. Bering and his crew become the first Europeans to reach Alaska. The Bering Strait was named after him.

1833 With just three months before the election, U.S. president James Tyler withdraws his renomination candidacy. He became the first chief executive in U.S. history not to seek reelection.

1882 Russian composer Peter Ilych Tchaikovsky's *1812 Overture* has its premiere in Moscow.

1908 King Leopold of Belgium gives the Congo, which he held as a private possession, to the Belgian State.

1910 U.S. lieutenant Jacob Fickel fires a rifle at a target on the ground from an

Peter Tchaikovsky

BORN ON THIS DAY

1561
JACOPO PERI
Italian composer widely regarded as having created the first opera

1778
BERNARDO O'HIGGINS
Chilean revolutionary known as the "Liberator of Chile"

1785
OLIVER HAZARD PERRY
U.S. Naval hero

1833
BENJAMIN HARRISON
23rd U.S. president, grandson of 9th president William H. Harrison

1860
RAYMOND POINCARÉ
French president and prime minister

1890
H. P. (HOWARD PHILLIPS) LOVECRAFT
American author of macabre fiction

1901
SALVATORE QUASIMODO
Nobel Prize-winning Italian poet

1908
AL LOPEZ
American Hall of Fame baseball manager

1918
JACQUELINE SUSANN
American author (*Valley of the Dolls*)

1931
DON KING
American boxing promoter

1944
RAJIV GHANDI
Prime minister of India (1989–91)

1946
CONNIE CHUNG
American television newscaster

1948
ROBERT PLANT
English rock singer (Led Zeppelin)

1948
TOM BANKS
American professional football player

"Learning carries within itself certain dangers because out of necessity one has to learn from one's enemies."

—*Leon Trotsky*

airplane over Brooklyn, New York. It was the first time a gun was fired from an aircraft.

1914 During World War I, the German Army captures Brussels while the Belgian army retreats to Antwerp.

1922 The first Women's Olympic Games are held in Paris, France, with athletes from five countries, after it was found that women's track and field events were to be excluded from the 1924 Olympic Games. The name was changed to the World Games after the International Olympic Committee complained, and the sports eventually became part of the regular Olympics.

1940 During the Battle of Britain in World War II, Prime Minister Winston Churchill tells Parliament, "Never in the field of human conflict was so much owed by so many to so few."

1940 Leon Trotsky, the Russian revolutionary living in exile in Mexico, is attacked by a hired assassin, dying the following day.

1941 Nazi German dictator Adolf Hitler gives the go-ahead to develop the V-2 missile during World War II.

1942 Chemists led by American Glenn T. Seaborg

Soviet tanks in Prague, Czechoslovakia

isolate a visible amount of plutonium for the first time.

1944 The Americans and British capture 50,000 Germans from the 7th Army at Falaise-Argentan Gap, west of Paris, during World War II.

1946 The German armed forces, the *Wehrmacht,* is ordered disbanded by the Allies after World War II.

1949 Hungary adopts a Soviet-style constitution and is renamed the Hungarian People's Republic.

1964 U.S. president Lyndon B. Johnson signs the Economic Opportunity Act, a $1 billion antipoverty measure.

1968 Approximately 200,000 Warsaw Pact troops and 5,000 tanks invade Czechoslovakia to crush the "Prague Spring," a brief period of liberalization in the communist country. Czechoslovakians protested the invasion with public demonstrations and other nonviolent tactics, but were no match for the Soviet tanks.

1974 In the wake of President Richard M. Nixon's resignation, the U.S. Congress reduces military aid to South Vietnam from $1 billion to $700 million. This was one of several actions that signaled the North Vietnamese that the United States was backing away from its commitment to South Vietnam during the Vietnam War.

1977 The U.S. spacecraft *Voyager II* is launched on the first mission to explore the outer planets on a "Grand Tour" before leaving the solar system.

1980 The U.N. Security Council condemns an Israeli declaration that all of Jerusalem is its capital.

1986 U.S. Postal Service employee Patrick Henry Sherril kills 14 co-workers and injures six others, then kills himself in a post office in Edmonton, Oklahoma.

1991 The Republic of Estonia declares its immediate and full independence from the Soviet Union.

Saigon newspaper reporting President Nixon's resignation

1581 The Arizona/New Mexico area is claimed for Spain by Francisco Chamuscado.

1680 Pueblo Indians drive out the Spanish and take over Santa Fe, New Mexico.

1808 British troops led by Arthur Wellesley, who will later become the duke of Wellington, defeat the French at the Battle of Vimiero during the Iberian Peninsular War.

1810 Using the name Charles John, one of French emperor Napoleon Bonaparte's generals, Marshall Bernadotte, is elected crown prince of Sweden.

1841 John Hampton of New Orleans, Louisiana, patents Venetian blinds.

1858 Senator Stephen Douglas of Illinois and Abraham Lincoln, a former U.S. representative from Illinois, begin the first of seven famous public encounters on the issue of slavery. During the Lincoln-Douglas debates, Lincoln argued against the spread of slavery while Douglas maintained that each territory should have the right to decide the issue for itself.

Lincoln and Douglas debate poster

DU PAGE COUNTY CENTENNIAL
LINCOLN ★ DOUGLAS
DEBATE
AUGUST · 27TH
WEST CHICAGO

BORN ON THIS DAY

1165
PHILIP II AUGUSTUS
King of France (1179–1223)

1660
HUBERT GAUTIER
French engineer who wrote the first book on bridge building

1754
WILLIAM MURDOCH
Scottish engineer who pioneered the use of coal gas for lighting

1765
WILLIAM IV
King of England (1830–37)

1872
AUBREY BEARDSLEY
English Art Nouveau illustrator

1896
CAPTAIN ALBERT BALL, VC
British World War I flying ace who, at the time of his death in 1917, had won more honors for bravery than anyone of his age

1904
WILLIAM "COUNT" BASIE
American bandleader and pianist

1930
PRINCESS MARGARET
Sister of Queen Elizabeth II of Great Britain

1932
MELVIN VAN PEEBLES
American author, filmmaker, and playwright (*Sweet Sweetback's Baadasssss Song*)

1933
DAME JANET BAKER
English mezzo-soprano

1936
WILT CHAMBERLAIN
American Hall of Fame basketball player

1938
KENNY ROGERS
American singer and actor ("Coward of the County"; "The Gambler")

1962
MATTHEW BRODERICK
American actor (*Biloxi Blues; Glory; The Producers*)

1863 A vicious guerrilla war in Missouri spills over into Kansas and precipitates one of the most appalling acts of violence during the American Civil War. One hundred fifty men in the abolitionist town of Lawrence were murdered by a notorious band of southern partisans led by William Quantrill.

1883 The trial of American outlaw Frank James begins in Gallatin, Missouri. It was held in an opera house in order to accommodate the crowd of spectators. Discouraged by the murder of his brother Jesse the previous spring, Frank decided to turn himself in, hoping that his considerable public popularity would win him a short sentence. The jury found him not guilty.

1903 America's first transcontinental auto race, stretching from New York City to San Francisco, California, is won by Tom Fetch and M. C. Karrup. They both drove Model F Packards, traveling an average of 80 miles per day for 51 days.

1911 In perhaps the most brazen art theft of all time, Vincenzo Peruggia walks into the Louvre in Paris, France, heads straight for the *Mona Lisa,* removes it from the wall, hides it beneath his clothes, and escapes. Peruggia was arrested in November 1913, when he attempted to retrieve a hefty ransom. The painting was unharmed.

> *"Nobody roots for Goliath."*
> —*Wilt Chamberlain*

The Mona Lisa

1951 In the United States, the construction order is given for the world's first atomic submarine, the *Nautilus*.

1961 Jomo Kenyatta, leader of the Kenyan independence movement, is released by British authorities after nearly nine years of imprisonment and detention. Kenyatta became prime minister when Kenya achieved independence two years later.

1963 South Vietnamese forces attack Buddhist pagodas, damaging many and arresting 1,400 Buddhists.

1983 Benigno Aquino, leader of the Filipino opposition to the repressive Marcos regime, is gunned down by an assassin at Manila airport.

1986 Gas belching from a volcanic lake in Cameroon kills more than 1,700 people.

1912 Arthur R. Eldred of Oceanside, New York, is the first boy to attain the rank of Eagle Scout—the highest rank possible in the Boy Scouts of America.

1935 American jazz clarinet player Benny Goodman performs at the Palomar Theater in Los Angeles, California. Broadcast nationally, the concert drew an enormous audience and is frequently credited with kicking off the "swing era."

1936 The British Broadcasting Corporation makes its first television broadcast.

1941 In Paris, 5,000 Jews are taken into detention at the Drancy detention camp, a holding center for people condemned to deportation.

1944 Representatives from the United States, Great Britain, the Soviet Union, and China meet at Georgetown in Washington, D.C., to formulate the principles of an organization that would provide collective security on a worldwide basis—the United Nations.

MILESTONE

Hawaii Becomes 50th State

The United States receives its crowning star when President Dwight D. Eisenhower signs a proclamation admitting Hawaii into the Union as the 50th state on this day in 1959. He also issued an order for an American flag featuring 50 stars arranged in staggered rows. The new flag became official on July 4, 1960. During World War II, Hawaii became firmly ensconced in the American national identity following the surprise Japanese attack on Pearl Harbor in December 1941. In March 1959 the U.S. government approved statehood for Hawaii, and in June the Hawaiian people voted by a wide majority to accept admittance into the United States.

President Eisenhower displays the new 50-star flag (milestone)

1138 The English defeat the Scots at Cowton Moor in the Battle of the Standard. It was so named because banners of various saints were carried into battle.

1485 In the last major battle of the War of the Roses, King Richard III of England is defeated and killed at the Battle of Bosworth Field by Henry Tudor, the earl of Richmond. The crowning of Henry as King Henry VII inaugurated the rule of the house of Tudor over England, a dynasty that would last until Queen Elizabeth I's death in 1603.

1567 The Duke of Alba, sent to reestablish Spanish authority in the Netherlands, begins a reign of terror as military governor.

1582 King James VI of Scotland, son of Mary, Queen of Scots, is seized by William

MILESTONE

International Red Cross Founded

The Geneva Convention of 1864 for the Amelioration of the Condition of the Wounded and Sick of Armies in the Field is adopted by 12 nations meeting in Geneva, Switzerland. The agreement, advocated by humanitarian Jean-Henri Dunant, called for nonpartisan care to the sick and wounded in times of war and provided for the neutrality of medical personnel. It also proposed the use of an international emblem to mark medical personnel and supplies. In honor of Dunant's nationality, a red cross on a white background—the Swiss flag reversed—was chosen. In 1901, Dunant was awarded the first Nobel Peace Prize.

"If you want to lift yourself up, lift up someone else."

—Dorothy Parker

Ruthven in a complicated struggle over whether Scotland should ally itself with France (favored by James) or England (favored by Ruthven).

1642 The English Civil War begins between the supporters of Charles I (Royalists or Cavaliers) and of Parliament (Roundheads) as Charles brands Parliament and its soldiers as traitors.

1715 Handel's "Water Music" is performed for the first time, to accompany British king George I's procession by barge along the Thames.

1770 Captain James Cook of England claims Australia for the British crown.

A statue of King George III is demolished as rebellion breaks out in the American colonies

1775 King George III of England officially recognizes the American Revolution when he proclaims the American colonies to be in a state of open rebellion.

1831 Believing himself chosen by God to lead his people out of slavery, Nat Turner launches a bloody slave insurrection in Southampton County, Virginia, that would lead to the deaths of 60 whites. Turner, with seven followers, planned to rally hundreds of slaves and capture the county armory at Jerusalem, Virginia. He was eventually caught and hanged.

1851 The U.S. schooner *America* bests a fleet of Great Britain's finest ships in a race around England's Isle of Wight. The ornate silver trophy was later donated to the New York Yacht Club on condition that it forever be placed in international competition.

1906 The first Victrola record player is manufactured by the Victor Talking Machine Company of Camden, New Jersey. Hand cranked with a horn for a speaker, it sold for $200.

1910 Japan annexes Korea.

1922 Michael Collins, the Irish Sinn Fein leader who had negotiated the treaty that led to the creation of the Irish Free State, is gunned down in an ambush near Cork by militant nationalists.

1941 During World War II, Nazi German troops reach the outskirts of Leningrad,

Soviet Red Army defending Leningrad

Russia, the start of a siege that would last more than two years.

1942 Brazil becomes the only South American country to send combat troops into Europe during World War II as it declares war on the Axis powers.

1947 The Mormon Tabernacle Choir is organized in the United States.

1950 Abdel Rehim of Egypt wins the first swimming race across the English Channel. He crossed it in 10 hours, 50 minutes.

1986 In the United States, the Kerr-McGee Corporation settles a 10-year-old nuclear contamination lawsuit by agreeing to pay the estate of the late Karen Silkwood, a former employee, $1.38 million.

1992 Hurricane Andrew strikes the Florida coast, with damage estimated at $7.3 billion, making it the most costly hurricane in U.S. history.

410 The Visigoths sack Rome, signaling the end of the Roman Empire.

1305 William Wallace, who fought for Scottish independence against English king Edward I, the "Hammer of the Scots," is put on trial for treason. In his defiant defense, Wallace said that he could never have been a traitor to Edward because he was never his subject. Found guilty, Wallace was hanged and drawn and quartered.

1609 Italian astronomer Galileo demonstrates his telescope for the first time.

1617 London, England, creates the first one-way streets. Seventeen narrow and congested lanes were specified to regulate the "disorder and rude behavior of Carmen, Draymen and others using Cartes."

1793 France creates the first national military conscription, drafting all unmarried men between ages 18 and 25.

1833 Great Britain abolishes slavery in its colonies around the world.

1839 During the Opium War with China, the British occupy Hong Kong.

1850 More than 1,000 people attend the first U.S. national women's rights convention, held in Worcester, Massachusetts.

> *"Character is power."*
> —*Booker T. Washington*

BORN ON THIS DAY

1754
LOUIS XVI
Last king of France (1774–92)

1849
W. E. HENLEY
English poet (*England, My England*) and critic, who co-wrote four plays with Robert Louis Stephenson (*Deacon Brodie; Admiral Guinea*)

1900
ERNST KRENEK
Austrian composer

1911
CARL DOLMETSCH
English early music expert and manufacturer of recorders

1912
GENE KELLY
American dancer and actor (*Brigadoon; Singin' in the Rain; That's Dancing*)

1917
TEX WILLIAMS
American singer and actor (*Rustler's Ransom; Cactus Caravan*)

1934
SONNY JURGENSEN
American Hall of Fame football player

1942
PATRICIA MCBRIDE
American ballerina

1944
ANTONIA NOVELLO
Puerto Rican-born American physician, the first woman and first Hispanic appointed U.S. surgeon general

1945
BOB PECK
English actor (*Edge of Darkness; Slipstream; Jurassic Park*)

1946
KEITH MOON
English rock musician (The Who)

1947
WILLY RUSSELL
English playwright (*Educating Rita; Blood Brothers; Shirley Valentine*)

1951
LISA NAJEEB HALABY (QUEEN NOOR)
Widow of King Hussein of Jordan

Booker T. Washington

1852 *Uncle Tom's Cabin* is published. Written by first-time American novelist Harriet Beecher Stowe, it became a runaway bestseller.

1889 The first ship-to-shore wireless message to be received in the United States is "Sherman is sighted." The message was sent by U.S. Lightship No. 70, off San Francisco, California, to announce the arrival of the troopship *Sherman*.

1900 The National Negro Business League is formed by Booker T. Washington in Boston, Massachusetts.

1904 The grip-tread snow tire chain for automobiles is patented in the United States.

1913 The statue of *The Little Mermaid* is unveiled in Copenhagen, Denmark. Based on the story by Hans Christian Andersen, it was donated by brewer Carl Jacobsen and became a famous symbol of the city.

1914 Japan enters World War I as the Emperor declares war on Germany.

1914 During World War I, German troops kill more than

600 people in the Belgian town of Dinant, then sack and burn the town.

🏆 **1922** A car named "Chitty Chitty Bang Bang," driven by Count Louis Zborowski at 73.1 miles per hour, wins the first Southsea Speed Carnival in England. The name reappeared as the title of Ian Fleming's book about a magical car, which became a movie in 1968 and a hit stage musical in 2002.

👣 **1926** The funeral of world-wide movie heart-throb Rudolph Valentino, in New York, draws vast crowds. The flocks of mostly female mourners, some of them hysterical, extended over eleven blocks. One woman was reported to have shot herself on hearing the news of his death.

💥 **1942** Six hundred German bombers strike Stalingrad. The seven-month Battle of Stalingrad was one of the most important of World War II because Soviet forces were able to stop the advance of the Axis troops. During the siege, about two million people were killed.

🏆 **1942** Francisco Segura of Ecuador becomes the first South American player to win a major U.S. grass-court tennis tournament (the Longwood Bowl at Brookline, Massachusetts).

🇷🇴 **1944** King Michael of Romania dismisses Prime Minister Ion Antonescu, leaving the country free to abandon the Axis powers in favor of the Allies.

🇺🇸 **1950** Members of the U.S. Army Organized Reserve Corps are involuntarily called to active duty to fight in the Korean War.

🏁 **1961** The Western powers place tanks and troops along the Berlin Wall as East Germany imposes new curbs on travel between West and East Berlin.

🔬 **1966** U.S. *Lunar Orbiter 1* takes the first photograph of Earth from the moon.

🔬 **1977** Bryan Allen wins the Kremer Prize for the first human-powered flight. He pedaled the *Gossamer Condor* for at least a mile at Schafter, California. The aircraft was made of thin aluminum tubes covered with plastic and weighed just 70 pounds.

👣 **1979** Russian ballet star Aleksandr Godunov defects to the United States after a performance in New York City. He became the first dancer to defect from the prestigious Bolshoi Ballet.

M I L E S T O N E

Nonaggression Pact Sparks World War II

On this day in 1939, in an event that leads directly to the outbreak of World War II, Germany and the Soviet Union sign a nonaggression pact, stunning the world, given their diametrically opposed ideologies. The pact basically called for the carving up of parts of Eastern Europe while leaving each other alone in the process. The most immediate effect was the partitioning of Poland, which Germany invaded on September 1, leading to the declaration of war by Britain. Supporters of Bolshevism around the world were outraged that Joseph Stalin would enter into any kind of league with the fascist dictator Adolf Hitler. The pact was broken in June 1941 when Germany invaded Russia, bringing the Soviets into the war on the side of the Allies.

Soviet commissar for foreign affairs Vyacheslav Mikhailovich Molotov as he signs the German-Soviet nonaggression pact with Communist Party leader Joseph Stalin behind him, second from right (milestone)

1456 Volume two of the famed Gutenberg Bible comes off the press, completing a two-year publishing project.

1572 King Charles IX of France, under the sway of his mother, Catherine dé Medici, orders the assassination of Huguenot Protestant leaders in Paris, setting off an orgy of killing that results in the massacre of tens of thousands of Huguenots across France.

1690 India's largest city, Calcutta, is founded when Job Charnock establishes a trading post at the West Bengali village of Kalikata for the English East India Company.

1780 King Louis XVI of France ends torture as a means to get suspects to confess.

1814 During the War of 1812, British forces overwhelm American militiamen at the Battle of Bladensburg, Maryland, and march unopposed into Washington, D.C. They set the city aflame in revenge for the burning of Canadian government buildings by U.S. troops earlier in the war. The White House, a number of federal buildings, and several private homes were destroyed.

1821 Spanish viceroy Juan de O'Donojú signs the Treaty of Córdoba, which approves a plan

> *"The only reason they come to see me is that I know that life is great—and they know I know it."*
>
> —*Clark Gable*

BORN ON THIS DAY

1113
GEOFFREY PLANTAGENET
French conqueror of Normandy

1591
ROBERT HERRICK
English poet ("Gather Ye Rosebuds")

1724
GEORGE STUBBS
English painter, chiefly of horses (*Whistlejacket; A Horse Affrighted*) who wrote and illustrated *The Anatomy of the Horse*

1759
WILLIAM WILBERFORCE
British politician and humanitarian who was instrumental in bringing about the end of slavery in the British Empire

1787
JAMES WEDDELL OSTEND
English Antarctic explorer

1872
SIR MAX BEERBOHM
British caricaturist and author

1890
JEAN RHYS
West Indies-born English author (*Wide Sargasso Sea*)

1899
JORGE LUIS BORGES
Argentinean author (*In Praise of Darkness; The Book of Imaginary Beings*)

1903
GRAHAM SUTHERLAND
English painter and designer whose portrait of Churchill was so hated by its subject that Lady Churchill had it burned

1929
YĀSIR ARAFĀT
Egyptian-born Palestinian leader

1936
A. S. BYATT
English novelist (*Possession; Still Life; The Virgin in the Garden*)

1958
STEVE GUTTENBERG
American actor (*Cocoon; Three Men and a Baby*)

1961
CAL RIPKEN JR.
American professional baseball player

to make Mexico an independent constitutional monarchy.

1847 The English publishing firm of Smith, Elder, & Co. receives the manuscript for *Jane Eyre, an Autobiography,* by Currer Bell. Three years later, Charlotte Brontë revealed she was the author.

1853 In Saratoga Springs, New York, chef George Crum invents potato chips.

1857 The New York branch of the Ohio Life Insurance and Trust Company goes bankrupt and plunges the United States into the Panic of 1857. As a result of rampant overspeculation in railroad and real estate securities, 4,923 businesses closed before the end of the year.

1869 Cornelius Swarthout of Troy, New York, patents the waffle iron.

1903 Lou Dillon becomes the first American racehorse to break the two-minute-mile barrier with a time of one minute, 58.5 seconds.

1909 The first concrete is poured for the Panama Canal.

Louis "Lepke" Buchalter in handcuffs

Sir Alexander Fleming

developed a purified form of penicillin, the first antibiotic agent against bacterial infections.

1953 The British colonial government of Kenya calls on Mau Mau guerrilla fighters, in a murderous uprising against British rule, to surrender. The British arrested hundreds, among them Jomo Kenyatta, who went on to become Kenya's first prime minister.

1963 American swimmer Don Schollander becomes the first to swim the 200-meter freestyle in less than two minutes. His time was one minute, 58.4 seconds.

1968 France explodes a hydrogen bomb, becoming the world's fifth nuclear power.

1991 The Ukraine declares its independence from the Soviet Union.

1995 In the most publicized software release in history, Microsoft's Windows 95 software goes on sale, selling some seven million units within six weeks.

1921 During the Turkish War of Independence, the Battle of the Sakarya River begins between Greece and Turkey. The Turks were victorious after three weeks of fighting.

1932 American aviator Amelia Earhart becomes the first woman to fly nonstop across the United States.

1938 American actor Clark Gable reluctantly agrees to play Rhett Butler in David O. Selznick's film *Gone with the Wind*. He hesitated to take the role because he feared the production's high profile would set impossible expectations for any actor playing the romantic lead. The studio, MGM, persuaded him with a generous bonus.

1939 Louis "Lepke" Buchalter, head of the American crime syndicate Murder, Incorporated, gives himself up to New York newspaper columnist Walter Winchell. Winchell turned the underworld leader over to the FBI.

1940 Expanding on the work of Sir Alexander Fleming, Oxford professors Howard Florey and Ernst Chain report in the British medical journal *The Lancet* that they have

Japanese shoppers in Tokyo checking out Microsoft's Windows 95

325 The first General Council of Nicaea (in modern-day Turkey) establishes the doctrine of the Holy Trinity and attempts to standardize the date of Easter.

1580 Spanish forces defeat the Portuguese at the Battle of Alcantara. As a result, Portugal is secured for Spain.

1718 The city of New Orleans, Louisiana, is founded. It was named in honor of the duke of Orleans of France.

1770 Thomas Chatterton, a 17-year-old poet and literary forger, commits suicide, becoming a literary and artistic icon, immortalized in verse by Wordsworth and in paint by Henry Wallis.

1804 Alice Meynell of England becomes the first woman jockey.

MILESTONE

The Liberation of Paris
After more than four years of Nazi occupation, Paris, France, is liberated on this day in 1944 by the French Resistance, the French 2nd Armored Division, and the U.S. 4th Infantry Division. General Dietrich von Choltitz, commander of the German garrison, defied an order by Adolf Hitler to blow up Paris's landmarks and burn the city to the ground before its liberation. General Eisenhower, keen to avoid an all-out battle for the city, had initiated Resistance operations, such as a police strike and the seizure of the Police Prefecture, before sending in the French forces. General de Gaulle entered the city on the evening of the 25th with the words "Vive Paris."

"To govern is always to choose among disadvantages."
—*Charles de Gaulle*

1825 Uruguayan revolutionaries declare their nation's independence from Brazil. A war ensued, but British diplomats mediated a settlement leading to the creation of an independent Uruguay in 1828.

1829 Mexico refuses U.S. president Andrew Jackson's offer to buy Texas.

1837 The production process for galvanized iron is patented by Henry William Crawford of London, England.

1875 Matthew Webb, an English Merchant Navy captain, becomes the first known person to successfully swim

American troops near the Arc de Triomphe after liberation of Paris, France (milestone)

unaided across the English Channel. Captain Webb accomplished the grueling 21-mile crossing, which actually entailed 39 miles of swimming because of tidal currents, in 21 hours, 45 minutes.

1883 France, under the terms of the Treaty of Hué, assumes the protectorate over Annam and Tonkin (now in Vietnam).

1910 Walden W. Shaw and John D. Hertz form the Walden W. Shaw Livery Company in Chicago, Illinois, which later became the Yellow Cab Company. The first yellow cab hit the streets in 1915, and its distinctive color became the company's trademark.

1919 The world's first scheduled international airline flight takes off, between London, England, and Paris, France.

1920 In Antwerp, Belgium, Ethelda Bleibtrey becomes the first woman to win an event for the United States in Olympic competition as she sets a 100-meter freestyle swim world record of one minute, 13.6 seconds.

1926 The classic American film *Beau Geste*, starring William Powell, opens. The silent film about three brothers in the French Foreign Legion was remade three times. It was based on the novel by English author Percival Christopher Wren.

1940 Lithuania, Latvia, and Estonia become part of the Soviet Union.

1941 Stalin orders the destruction of one of the Soviet Union's greatest engineering achievements, the Lenin-Dueproges dam, to hamper invading Nazi forces. The dam, which had been completed in 1932 with much work carried out by American engineers, supplied power for the industries of the Ukraine.

1945 John Birch, an American missionary to China before World War II and a captain in the U.S. Army during the war, is killed by Chinese communists days after the surrender of Japan, for no apparent reason. In the 1950s, Robert Welch would create an organization called the John Birch Society, pronouncing Birch "the first casualty in the Third World War between Communists and the ever-shrinking Free World."

1993 Egyptian cleric Sheik Omar Abdel-Rahman is indicted by a U.S. federal grand jury on charges of terrorist activities, including the planning of the 1993 bombing of the World Trade Center in New York City.

Sheik Omar Abdel-Rahman

Michelangelo

⚔ **55 B.C.** Britain is invaded by Roman forces under Julius Caesar.

⚔ **1346** During the Hundred Years' War, King Edward III's English army annihilates a French force under King Philip VI at the Battle of Crécy in Normandy. The battle, which saw an early use of the deadly longbow by the English, marked the decline of the mounted knight in European warfare and the rise of England as a world power.

🎭 **1498** Italian artist Michelangelo is commissioned to create the *Pietà*.

▌▌ **1789** France's National Assembly adopts the Declaration of the Rights of Man.

⚔ **1813** As Napoleon Bonaparte begins his successful push at Dresden, Germany, the French, under Marshal Macdonald, stumble onto a marginally larger Allied Prussian army, under Marshal Gebhart Leberecht von Blücher. In the Battle of Katzbach the French lost 15,000 men, while Blücher had an estimated 4,000 casualties, placing the French in a precarious strategic position.

MILESTONE

19th Amendment Adopted

The 19th Amendment, guaranteeing women the right to vote, is formally adopted into the U.S. Constitution on this day in 1920. The amendment was the culmination of more than 70 years of struggle by woman suffragists. Its two sections read simply: "The right of citizens of the United States to vote shall not be denied or abridged by the United States or by any State on account of sex and Congress shall have power to enforce this article by appropriate legislation." The movement was founded by women who were politically active through their work in the abolitionist and temperance movements.

"Life is not so bad if you have plenty of luck, a good physique and not too much imagination."

—Christopher Isherwood

● **1858** The Treaty of Edo is signed, opening up Japan to British trade and residency.

🔬 **1858** The first news dispatch sent by commercial telegraph is received by the *New York Sun*. It announced that Great Britain and France had signed a peace treaty with China.

🏳 **1873** The first public-school kindergarten in the United States is authorized in St. Louis, Missouri.

☪ **1896** The Ottoman Bank in Constantinople is attacked by Armenian revolutionaries. Six thousand Armenians died in the resulting three-day battle.

🎭 **1907** At an aquatic park in San Francisco, California, American magician Harry

Chicago policemen confront demonstrators in Chicago, Illinois

Houdini is placed underwater while attached to a 75-pound ball-and-chain and escapes in 57 seconds.

1932 The U.S. government announces a temporary halt on foreclosures of first mortgages on homes during the Great Depression.

1939 The first televised major-league baseball game is shown on station W2XBS. Red Barber announced the game between the Cincinnati Reds and the Brooklyn Dodgers at Ebbets Field in Brooklyn, New York.

1940 Retaliating against World War II attacks on London, England, the Royal Air Force bombs Berlin, Germany, for the first time.

1945 At the end of World War II, Japanese envoys receive instructions for their subsequent surrender onboard the U.S. battleship *Missouri* on September 2.

1957 The Soviet Union says it has successfully tested an intercontinental ballistic missile. The announcement caused great concern in the United States and started a national debate over the "missile gap" between the United States and Russia.

1968 During the Democratic National Convention in Chicago, Illinois, thousands of antiwar demonstrators take to the streets to protest American involvement in the Vietnam War. At the most violent convention in U.S. history, police and National Guardsmen clashed with protesters. The Chicago police beat hundreds of people, including innocent bystanders.

1978 Cardinal Albino Luciani of Venice, Italy, is elected as Pope John Paul I, but he serves only 33 days before dying of a heart attack.

1985 The Yugo automobile, manufactured in Yugoslavia, is introduced to the U.S. market. The car quickly became infamous for its poor quality and was the punch line of many jokes.

1991 The Soviet Congress votes to disband its government and form a new interim government.

1992 The United States, France, and Great Britain institute a "no-fly zone" over the southern third of Iraq to protect Iraqi Shiite Muslims.

1997 F. W. de Klerk, South Africa's last white president before the democratic elections of 1994, resigns as leader of the opposition National Party.

1998 Lybian leader Colonel Gaddafi agrees to hand over the two chief suspects in the bombing of Pan Am flight 103 over Lockerbie for trial under Scottish law in the Netherlands.

F. W. de Klerk

"Worry not that no one knows of you; seek to be worth knowing."

—*Confucius*

413 B.C. During the Peloponnesian War, the Athenian fleet is attempting to withdraw after a defeat by Sparta when an eclipse of the moon occurs. Considering it a sign from the gods, the Athenians stayed. But the delay proved fatal and the fleet was eventually trapped.

1601 The first Dutch exploration of the New World is completed by Olivier van Noort.

1660 Because of English poet John Milton's attacks on King Charles II, his books are burned in London.

1664 New Amsterdam is renamed New York as 300 English soldiers take the town from the Dutch. The name honors King Charles II's brother James, the duke of York.

1667 The first recorded U.S. hurricane strikes Jamestown, Virginia.

1776 During the American Revolution, British forces under General William Howe defeat Patriot forces under General George Washington at the Battle of Brooklyn in New York. However, Howe failed to

BORN ON THIS DAY

551 B.C.
CONFUCIUS (K'UNG FU-TZU)
Chinese philosopher

1871
THEODORE DREISER
American author (*An American Tragedy; Sister Carrie*)

1877
CHARLES STEWART ROLLS
British aviation pioneer and auto manufacturer, co-founder of Rolls-Royce

1886
ERIC COATES
English composer ("The Dam Busters' March"; "By the Sleepy Lagoon")

1899
C. S. FORESTER
English author, creator of Captain Horatio Hornblower

1908
SIR DONALD BRADMAN
Australian cricketer, the first to receive a knighthood

1908
LYNDON BAINES JOHNSON
36th president of the United States

1910
MOTHER TERESA (AGNES GONXHA BOJAXHIU)
Yugoslavian missionary of Calcutta, India, who won the Nobel Peace Prize in 1971

1916
MARTHA RAYE
American comedienne and actress

1929
IRA LEVIN
American author (*Rosemary's Baby; The Boys from Brazil*)

1950
CYNTHIA POTTER
American champion diver, the only woman to have won 28 championship titles

follow the advice of his subordinates and storm the redoubts at Brooklyn Heights, and on August 29, Washington ordered a brilliant retreat to Manhattan by boat, saving the Continental Army from capture.

1783 Frenchman Jacques Alexandre César Charles launches the first practical hydrogen balloon.

1859 Edwin Drake strikes oil at 69 feet near Titusville, Pennsylvania—the world's first successful oil well.

1883 The world's largest explosions occur on the Indonesian volcanic island of Krakatoa. Heard 2,000 miles away, the explosions threw five cubic miles of earth 50 miles into the air, created tidal waves up to 120 feet high, and killed 36,000 people.

1894 The U.S. Congress passes the nation's first graduated income tax as part of the Wilson-Gorman Tariff Act, but the Supreme Court declares it unconstitutional.

1896 In a dispute over who is rightly the sultan of Zanzibar, the British protectorate loses to England in the shortest war on record: 38 minutes.

Calvin Coolidge, Herbert Hoover, and Frank B. Kellogg, standing, with representatives of the governments who have ratified the Treaty for Renunciation of War (Kellogg-Briand Pact), in the East Room of the White House

1904 Newport, Rhode Island, imposes the first jail sentence for a speeding violation. This was a harsh sentence, as traffic laws were still relatively new. The first traffic code had only been implemented in 1903, when New York introduced a two-page book of regulations.

1910 The first radio broadcast from an airplane in flight is transmitted. The message was sent from a plane over Sheepshead Bay, New York.

1913 The first aerobatic maneuver in an airplane takes place in Kiev as Lieutenant Peter Nestrov of the Imperial Russian Air Service performs a loop.

1917 American director John Ford's first feature-length film, *Straight Shooting*, is released. A former actor and stuntman, Ford won Academy Awards for Best Director for *The Informer, The Grapes of Wrath, How Green Was My Valley,* and *The Quiet Man.* In 1973 he received the Medal of Freedom from President Richard M. Nixon.

1928 Sixty nations meeting in Paris, France, sign the Kellogg-Briand Pact, which outlaws war in favor of the peaceful settlement of disputes.

Christa McAuliffe

1953 The movie *Roman Holiday,* introducing Belgian actress Audrey Hepburn in her first major role, opens. She won an Oscar for Best Actress.

1966 English yachtsman Sir Francis Chichester begins the first around-the-world solo sea voyage.

1972 During the Vietnam War, U.S. warplanes bomb Haiphong Harbor in North Vietnam for the first time.

1979 British statesman Earl Mountbatten of Burma is assassinated by an IRA bomb in his fishing boat off the coast of southern Ireland.

1984 President Ronald W. Reagan announces that the first "citizen astronaut" to fly aboard the space shuttle will be a schoolteacher. Christa McAuliffe, the teacher who was eventually chosen, died in the *Challenger* disaster in January 1986.

1609 English navigator Henry Hudson discovers Delaware Bay.

1619 Ferdinand II is elected Holy Roman emperor. His attempts to eradicate Protestantism led to the Thirty Years' War.

1830 The steam locomotive *Tom Thumb*, the first of its kind built in America, is demonstrated in Baltimore, Maryland.

1837 Pharmacists William Perrins and John Lea of Worcester, England, begin the commercial production of Worcestershire sauce.

1849 Venice, under siege since July 20 after proclaiming independence against Austrian rule, surrenders to the Austrians.

1850 German composer Richard Wagner's *Lohengrin* is performed for the first time.

1867 The Midway Islands, located in the Pacific Ocean, are annexed by the United States.

1879 King Cetshwayo, the last great ruler of Zululand, is captured by the British following his defeat in the British-Zulu War. He was subsequently sent into exile. Cetshwayo's defiance of British rule in southern Africa led to Great Britain's invasion of Zululand in 1879.

> *"Excellence is rarely found, more rarely valued."*
> —*Johann Wolfgang von Goethe*

BORN ON THIS DAY

1749
JOHANN WOLFGANG VON GOETHE
German author (*Faust; Stella*)

1774
ELIZABETH ANN BAYLEY SETON
First American Catholic saint

1833
SIR EDWARD BURNE-JONES
British painter, one of the Pre-Raphaelites (*Cupid and Psyche; Saint George and the Dragon; King Cophetua and The Beggar Maid*)

1878
GEORGE HOYT WHIPPLE
American astrophysicist who won the Nobel Prize in 1934

1897
CHARLES BOYER
French actor (*Gaslight; Casino Royale; Barefoot in the Park*)

1906
SIR JOHN BETJEMAN
English poet who became Poet laureate in 1972 (*"A Subaltern's Love Song"; "Myfanwy"*)

1919
BEN AGAJANIAN
American professional football player

1926
DONALD O'CONNOR
American actor and dancer (*Singin' in the Rain*)

1951
JOEL YOUNGBLOOD
American professional baseball player

1957
DANIEL STERN STAMFORD
American actor (*Breaking Away; Diner; City Slickers*)

1958
SCOTT HAMILTON
American figure-skating champion

1965
SHANIA TWAIN
Canadian pop singer/songwriter (*"Man! I Feel Like a Woman"; "That Don't Impress Me Much"*)

"Tomatina" tomato fight in Bunol, Spain

1883 American John J. Montgomery makes the first controlled flight in a glider. He flew 603 feet at a height of 15 feet at Wheeler Hill, California.

1884 The first known photograph of a tornado is taken 22 miles southwest of Howard, South Dakota.

1907 Nineteen-year-old Jim Casey borrows $100 from his friend Claude Ryan and starts a local delivery service, called the American Messenger Company. By the 1920s, the company's growing fleet of trucks had been painted dark brown for a professional appearance, and it soon became known as United Parcel Service. Today, UPS provides delivery service to more than 185 countries and territories.

1914 In the battle of Heligoland Bight, the first major naval engagement of World War I, the British Royal Navy sinks three German cruisers.

1914 Austria-Hungary declares war on Belgium, drawing the neutral state into World War I.

1922 The Autodromo, an automobile-racing track, is opened in Monza, Italy. Set in a busy industrial center along the Lambro River, this famed track, with its elliptical shape and concrete banked curves, is said to be the fastest in the world.

1932 As the town of Bunol, Spain, had banned bull-fighting, the city's newly established Tomato Throwing Festival takes its place.

1941 More than 23,000 Hungarian Jews are murdered by the German Gestapo in the occupied Ukraine during World War II.

1961 Excavations at Fishbourne in Sussex reveal spectacular Roman mosaics from a palace built during the first century A.D. The finds are the earliest Roman mosaics discovered in Great Britain.

1964 The first weather satellite capable of providing nighttime cloud photos is launched. The satellite transmitted some 27,000 pictures of hurricanes and typhoons before it stopped working in September.

1966 Soviet newspapers report that North Vietnamese pilots are training in a secret Soviet air base to fly supersonic interceptors.

1972 At the Summer Olympics in Munich, Germany, American swimmer Mark Spitz captures the first of his seven gold medals. He completed the 200-meter butterfly in 2 minutes, $7/10$ of a second, a new world record.

1973 Princess Anne becomes the first member of the British royal family to visit Soviet Russia.

1978 Donald Vesco sets a motorcycle speed record. He topped out at 318 miles per hour while riding a Kawasaki motorcycle at Utah's Bonneville Salt Flats.

1984 In the United States, the American pop singing group The Jacksons' "Victory Tour" breaks the record for concert ticket sales, passing the 1.1 million mark in only two months.

1986 Convicted for his role in a Soviet spy ring, retired U.S. Navy warrant officer Jerry A. Whitworth is sentenced to 365 years in prison.

1994 Tiger Woods, at age 18, becomes the youngest winner in the history of the U.S. Amateur Golf Championship.

Dr. Martin Luther King, Jr. (milestone)

1350 At the Battle of Winchelsea during the Hundred Years' War, a Spanish fleet entering the English Channel to support the French is defeated by the English.

1475 Edward IV of England signs the Truce of Picquigny, agreeing to withdraw his invading army from France in return for gold and a yearly pension.

1526 During the Turkish-Hungarian War, 30,000 Hungarians are defeated by more than 100,000 Turks at the Battle of Mohacz.

1533 Atahuallpa, the 13th and last emperor of the Incas, dies by strangulation at the hands of Francisco Pizarro's Spanish conquistadors. His execution marked the end of 300 years of Inca civilization.

1756 The Seven Years' War starts when Frederick II of Prussia, on learning of a Franco-Austrian alliance, invades Saxony.

1758 The first Indian reservation is established by the New Jersey legislature on a tract of 1,600 acres.

Frederick II of Prussia

BORN ON THIS DAY

1632
JOHN LOCKE
English philosopher

1780
JEAN-AUGUSTE-DOMINIQUE INGRES
French painter (*Oedipus and the Sphinx; Madame Moitessier*)

1809
OLIVER WENDELL HOLMES
American physician and author (*The Chambered Nautilus*)

Oliver Wendell Holmes

1862
MAURICE MAETERLINCK
Belgian poet and playwright (*Pelléas et Mélisande*)

1915
INGRID BERGMAN
Swedish actress (*Casablanca; Spellbound; Notorious*)

1920
CHARLIE PARKER JR.
American jazz saxophonist

1923
SIR RICHARD ATTENBOROUGH
English actor (*The Great Escape; Jurassic Park*)

1939
WILLIAM FRIEDKIN
American director (*The Brink's Job; The Exorcist*)

1948
CHARLES D. WALKER
American astronaut

1959
MICHAEL JACKSON
American pop singer ("Billie Jean"; "Thriller"; "Smooth Criminal")

1962
CARL BANKS
American professional football player

1820 The Portuguese rebellion against the Regency begins in Oporto, leading to a democratic constitution under King John VI.

1831 English physicist Michael Faraday successfully demonstrates his electrical transformer, at the Royal Institution in London.

1835 John Batman buys 600,000 acres of land from Australian Aborigines. The land was officially named Melbourne, after the British prime minister, Lord Melbourne, and would eventually become Australia's second-largest city.

1842 The Treaty of Nanking is signed by the British and Chinese, ending the Opium War and ceding Hong Kong to Great Britain.

1862 The U.S. Bureau of Engraving and Printing is created. The original "money factory" had a staff of six who separated bills that were produced by private companies. The bureau started printing its own notes in 1863 and by 1887 had assumed full responsibility for producing the nation's currency.

1882 The England cricket team is defeated on home soil for the first time, by Australia, provoking a mock obituary for English cricket in the *Sporting Times*: "the body will be

---

"The actions of men are the best interpreters of their thoughts."

—*John Locke*

Glenn Curtiss at the wheel of his plane June Bug

🏆 **1909** The world's first air race, held in Rheims, France, is won by American aviator Glenn Curtiss.

🇺🇸 **1945** U.S. general Douglas MacArthur is named the supreme commander of Allied Powers in Japan.

⚫ **1949** The Soviet Union successfully detonates its first atomic bomb, code name "First Lightning." The explosion, at 20 kilotons, was roughly equal to that of "Trinity," the first U.S. atomic bomb.

1949 Yugoslavian prime minister Tito asks the United States for a loan to aid the country in resisting a Soviet blockade.

1991 The Communist Party's 75-year control of the Soviet Union ends as the Supreme Soviet, the parliament of the Soviet Union, suspends all party activities.

M I L E S T O N E

First Motorcycle Patented

The world's first motorcycle, made by German engineer Gottlieb Daimler, is patented on this day in 1885. The two-wheeled vehicle gained immense popularity after 1910, when it was used heavily by all branches of the armed forces during World War I. The motorcycle's popularity lagged during the Great Depression, but came back with a vengeance after World War II and remains high today. Associated with a rebellious image, the vehicle is often used for high-speed touring and sports competitions.

---

cremated and the ashes taken to Australia." England beat Australia during their next tour, and the team was presented with the ashes of one of the bails, creating the annual Ashes competition.

🏆 **1885** The first American prizefight is held under the Marquis of Queensberry Rules. John L. Sullivan defeated Dominick McCaffery in six rounds in Cincinnati, Ohio.

🇺🇸 **1896** According to legend, a chef of Li Hung-Chang, China's ambassador to the United States, creates chop suey while in New York.

Moscow pupils take a break on a toppled statue of Stalin

Cleopatra

30 B.C. Cleopatra, queen of Egypt and lover of Julius Caesar and Mark Antony, takes her own life following the defeat of her forces against Octavian, the future first emperor of Rome.

1146 European leaders convene to outlaw the crossbow in the hope that, by banning the weapon, wars will end. But crossbows continued to be used until firearms replaced them in the 16th century.

1645 Chief Oratamin of the Hackensack Indians negotiates a peace treaty with the Dutch at New Amsterdam (later known as New York), ending conflict in the area.

1682 William Penn sails from England to America, where he will establish the colony of Pennsylvania.

1781 A fleet of 24 French ships defeat the British at the Battle of Chesapeake Capes in the American Revolutionary War.

1881 Clement Adler of Germany patents the first stereo system.

BORN ON THIS DAY

1748
JACQUES-LOUIS DAVID
French Neoclassical painter
(*Death of Marat*)

1797
MARY WOLLSTONECRAFT SHELLEY
English author (*Frankenstein*)

1871
ERNEST RUTHERFORD
New Zealand-born English physicist who won the Nobel Prize in chemistry in 1908 for discovering the atomic nucleus

1896
RAYMOND MASSEY
Canadian actor (*The Desert Song; East of Eden*)

1917
DENIS HEALEY, LORD HEALEY OF RIDDLESDEN
British Labour politician, chancellor of the exchequer in the 1970s

1918
TED WILLIAMS
American Hall of Fame baseball player who was the last man to bat over .400

1919
KITTY WELLS
American country singer

1922
REGINA RESNIK
American opera singer

1943
JEAN-CLAUDE KILLY
French Olympic champion skier

> *"Life is obstinate and clings closest where it is most hated."*
>
> —*Mary Wollstonecraft Shelley*

1884 The first match with boxing gloves takes place as American boxer Jack Dempsey wins the middleweight title.

1901 In Scotland, Hubert Cecil Booth patents the vacuum cleaner, which he created by reversing the action of a dust-blowing machine.

1914 One of history's great military disasters, the World War I Battle of Tannenberg, ends after the Germans crush the Russian Second Army, which lost 30,000 troops.

1918 Soviet leader Vladimir Lenin is shot twice by Fanya Kaplan, a member of the Social Revolutionary party. Lenin was seriously wounded but survived. The assassination attempt set off a wave of reprisals by the Bolsheviks against the Social Revolutionaries and other

German soldiers in trenches in World War I

political opponents. Thousands were executed as Russia fell deeper into civil war.

1922 "Tiger Rag," one of the world's most familiar American ragtime jazz tunes, is recorded by the New Orleans Rhythm Kings.

1935 U.S. president Franklin D. Roosevelt's Revenue Act is passed into law. Aptly referred to as the Wealth Tax Act, the legislation increased taxes on rich citizens and big business while lowering taxes for small businesses. While it hardly paved the way for a wholesale redistribution of wealth, the act did seek to rectify imbalances in the American economy.

1939 Great Britain begins to evacuate thousands of children from the cities into the country in preparation for expected German bombing. World War II began four days later.

1941 The last railroad link between Leningrad and the rest of the Soviet Union is severed by German forces.

1945 U.S. general Douglas MacArthur lands in Japan to organize the post-World War II Japanese government.

1962 The Caribbean islands of Trinidad and Tobago gain independence from Great Britain.

1963 A 24-hour-a-day hot line between Moscow and Washington, D.C., goes into effect. The hot line was supposed to help speed communication between the governments of the United States and the Soviet Union to prevent the possibility of an accidental war.

1967 The U.S. Senate confirms Thurgood Marshall as Supreme Court justice. He was the first African American to hold such position.

1969 BBN, the company contracted by the U.S. Defense Department to build networking machines as the backbone of ARPANET, the Internet's precursor, ships its first machine to the University of California at Los Angeles. Over the next several months, the company would ship several more machines, and the beginnings of the Internet would be established.

1973 The hunting of elephants and the trade in ivory are banned in Kenya.

1979 In the first recorded event of its kind, a comet collides with the sun. The collision released an energy amount equal to that of 1 million hydrogen bombs.

On Challenger's middeck, Guion Bluford exercises on the treadmill (milestone)

1422 King Henry V of England dies of dysentery and is succeeded on the throne by his nine-month-old son, who is named Henry VI.

1823 During the Battle of the Trocadero, Ferdinand VII is restored to the throne of Spain as a French army enters Cadiz and ends a Liberal uprising.

1864 During the American Civil War, General William T. Sherman launches the attack that finally secures Atlanta, Georgia, for the Union and seals the fate of Confederate general John Bell Hood's army, which is forced to evacuate the area.

1876 Sultan Murad V of Turkey is deposed after suffering mental collapse and is succeeded by his brother, Abdul Hamid II.

1888 English prostitute Mary Ann Nichols, the first victim of London serial killer "Jack the Ripper," is found murdered and mutilated in Whitechapel's Buck's Row. The East End of London saw four more victims of the murderer during the next few months, but no suspect was ever found.

1902 Mrs. Adolph Landenburg of Saratoga Springs, New York, introduces the split skirt for riding horseback.

1907 The Anglo-Russian Convention is signed in St. Petersburg, settling differences between England and Russia over Afghanistan, Persia, and Tibet.

1935 President Franklin D. Roosevelt signs an act prohibiting the export of U.S. arms to belligerents.

BORN ON THIS DAY

12 B.C.
CALIGULA (GAIUS CAESAR)
Third Roman emperor (37–41)

1811
THÉOPHILE GAUTIER
French writer and art critic

1821
HERMAN VON HELMHOLTZ
German physicist and physiologist

1834
AMILCARE PONCHIELLI PADERNO
Italian composer

1870
MARIA MONTESSORI
Italian educator who was the first woman to attend medical school and first female doctor in Italy

Maria Montessori

1885
DuBOSE HEYWARD
American author whose novel *Porgy* provided the basis for the musical *Porgy and Bess*

1897
FREDRIC MARCH
American actor (*Death Takes a Holiday; A Star Is Born; The Buccaneer*)

1903
ARTHUR GODFREY
American musician, entertainer, and comedian (*The Arthur Godfrey Show*)

1908
WILLIAM SAROYAN
Pulitzer Prize-winning American playwright (*The Time of Your Life; The Human Comedy*)

1918
ALAN JAY LERNER
American lyricist and songwriter (*My Fair Lady; Camelot*)

1939 Despite threats of British and French intervention, Nazi German leader Adolf Hitler signs an order to attack Poland. That evening, Nazi SS troops wearing Polish uniforms staged a phony invasion of Germany, which Nazi propagandists publicized as an unforgivable act of aggression. Hitler expected appeasement from Great Britain and France, but Germany was told to withdraw by September 3 or face war with the Western democracies.

1951 The first 33-rpm long-playing record is introduced by the German company Deutsche Grammophon.

1955 The world's first solar-powered automobile, designed by William G. Cobb, is demonstrated at the General Motors Powerama in Chicago, Illinois.

1955 U.S. secretary of state John Foster Dulles openly supports South Vietnamese president Ngo Dinh Diem's position in refusing to hold "national and general elections" to reunify the two Vietnam states. Although called for by the Geneva Accords of July 1954, both parties realized that if the elections were actually held, the more populous North would probably reunite Vietnam under the Communist banner.

> *"If men had to have babies, they would only ever have one each."*
>
> —*Princess Diana*

Newspaper vendor in London announcing Nazi German invasion of Poland

1975 The former president of the Teamsters Union, James Hoffa, is reported missing in Detroit. No trace of him has ever been found.

1976 A few showers of rain bring relief to Great Britain, basking in the century's hottest summer so far. Water shortages had led to a ban on the use of garden hoses and householders being asked to place bricks in their toilet cisterns to reduce consumption.

1977 Prime Minister Ian Smith of Rhodesia, espousing racial segregation, wins the general election with 80 percent of the white electorate's vote.

1978 In the United States, William and Emily Harris, founders of the Symbionese Liberation Army, plead guilty to the 1974 kidnapping of newspaper heiress Patricia Hearst.

1980 The Gdansk agreement between shipyard workers and the Polish government is signed. The agreement led to the creation of the Solidarity Movement and gave workers the right to strike and to organize their own union.

1985 Richard Ramirez, the notorious "Night Stalker" who murdered at least a dozen people, is captured and nearly killed by a mob in East Los Angeles, California, after being recognized from a photograph shown both on television and in newspapers.

1986 English sculptor Henry Moore dies at the age of 88. Famous for his semi-abstract monumental bronze figures, Moore had also been a war artist during World War II, producing a series of drawings of life in British air-raid shelters.

1991 The number of republics seeking to secede from the Soviet Union increases to ten as Uzbekistan and Kirghizia declare their independence.

1994 Russia ends half a century of military presence on German soil with a ceremony presided over by German chancellor Helmut Kohl and Russian president Boris Yeltsin.

Young girl pays tribute outside Westminster Abbey

891 German king Arnulf crushes the Vikings at the Dyle River, north of Brussels, thus putting a stop to their raids up the Rhine.

1159 Pope Adrian IV, the only Englishman ever to attain the papacy, dies in Anagni, Italy.

1181 Pope Lucius III begins a four-year reign, during which the former Cistercian monk founds the medieval inquisition. It condemned heretics and turned them over to civil authorities for burning.

1422 Henry VI, nine months old, becomes king of England. Within six weeks he also inherited the crown of France.

1695 During the War of the Grand Alliance, English forces capture the strategic French city of Namur after a costly siege. The English lost 18,000 men, the French defenders, 9,000.

1715 French king Louis XIV, "The Sun King" who ruled during one of France's most brilliant periods, dies at Versailles.

1773 The first volume of poetry published by an African American appears in England: Phillis Wheatley's

---

BORN ON THIS DAY

1791
LYDIA SIGOURNEY
American author (*Traits of the Aborigines of America; Letters to Young Ladies*)

1854
ENGELBERT HUMPERDINCK
German composer (*Hansel and Gretel*)

1866
JAMES JOHN "GENTLEMAN JIM" CORBETT
American world heavyweight boxing champion (1892–97)

1875
EDGAR RICE BURROUGHS
American author (*Tarzan of the Apes; The Lost Continent*)

1900
DON WILSON
American television announcer and actor (*The Jack Benny Show*)

1907
WALTER REUTHER
American labor union leader, president of the United Auto Workers (1946–70)

1923
ROCKY MARCIANO
American boxer who retired undefeated as the world heavyweight champion

1923
YVONNE DE CARLO
American actress (*The Munsters*)

1935
SEIJI OZAWA
Chinese-born Japanese symphony conductor (Boston Symphony Orchestra)

1939
LILY TOMLIN
Emmy Award-winning American comedienne and actress (*The Search for Intelligent Life in the Universe*)

"If you're not big enough to lose, you're not big enough to win."

—*Walter Reuther*

Poems on Various Subjects, Religious and Moral.

1807 Former U.S. vice president Aaron Burr is acquitted of treason, on a technicality. He had plotted to seize American and Spanish territory in the West and to establish an independent republic.

1836 Missionary Narcissa Whitman arrives in the area of present-day Walla Walla, Washington, with her husband, Marcus, and becomes one of the first Anglo-American female settlers west of the Rockies.

1857 In Southeast Asia, a French amphibious force launches an invasion of Vietnam with an attack on the port city of Tourane (modern-day Danang).

1865 English physician Joseph Lister performs the first antiseptic surgery.

1870 During the Franco-German War, Prussian forces decisively defeat the French Army in the Battle of Sedan, capturing Napoleon III himself

Yokohama, after the great earthquake of 1923

Napoleon III

and marching on toward Paris. The loss quickly led to the fall of the Second French Empire.

1914 The passenger pigeon, *Ectopistes migratorius,* officially becomes extinct as the last-known survivor of the species dies at the Cincinnati Zoo in Ohio.

1916 Bulgaria declares war on Romania.

1923 In Japan, a 7.9-magnitude earthquake destroys Yokohama and most of Tokyo, killing at least 142,000 people and demolishing the homes of 2.5 million more.

1950 The first thorough-bred Porsche is completed in Zuffenhausen, Germany.

Though a previous car had borne the Porsche name, the 1950 model was the first to sport a Porsche engine.

1959 English-born American actress Elizabeth Taylor inks a $1 million deal to make *Cleopatra* for Twentieth Century Fox. It was the costliest film to date.

1960 Pennsylvania Railroad workers go on strike for the first time in the company's 114-year history.

1966 French president Charles de Gaulle denounces U.S. policy in Vietnam and urges the withdrawal of American troops.

1969 Libyan Army captain Muammar al-Qaddafi, 27, leads a bloodless coup against King Idris, abolishes the monarchy, and begins building his anti-Western dictatorship.

1983 A Korean Airlines passenger jet that had strayed into Russian air space is shot down by Soviet warplanes, killing 269 passengers and crew.

1985 The wreck of the British luxury liner *Titanic* is discovered on the floor of the North Atlantic 73 years after it struck an iceberg and sank 400 miles west of Newfoundland.

German invasion of Poland

🔫 **490 B.C.** The Greeks rout the Persians at the Battle of Marathon and, according to tradition, send a trained runner named Pheiddipides back to Athens with the good news. His 26-mile jaunt, which exhausted and killed him, inspired the modern marathon.

🔫 **31 B.C.** In fleet action during the Roman Civil War, Octavian defeats Antony and Cleopatra in the Battle of Actium, fought off the Greek coast.

🔫 **1192** The Third Crusade ends as English king Richard the Lion-Heart and Islamic sultan Saladin sign a peace treaty that allows pilgrims access to holy sites in Muslim-held Jerusalem.

🏴 **1666** The Great Fire of London in England begins with a blaze at the house of the king's baker that spreads across the city, eventually destroying 13,000 houses, 90 churches, and many public buildings. Just 16 people died.

🏴🇺🇸 **1752** England and its American colonies use the Julian calendar for the last time, dropping it in favor of the Gregorian one. Eleven days

"Man's loneliness is but his fear of life."
—Eugene O'Neill

(September 3–13 inclusive) vanished as the calendar was adjusted forward so that September 14 followed September 2.

🇺🇸 **1775** The first American warship, the *Hannah*, is commissioned at Marblehead, Massachusetts, with George Washington acting as christener-in-chief.

🇺🇸 **1789** The United States Treasury is established.

🇫🇷 **1792** The French Revolution's "First Terror" begins as an armed band attacks and kills a group of prisoners. In all, some 1,200 prisoners would die during the September Massacres, which were carried out because of fears that inmates might rise in a counterrevolutionary plot.

🏴 **1834** Indefatigable English engineer Thomas Telford, who oversaw construction of 1,000 miles of roads and 1,200 bridges, reaches the end of his own road and dies in London.

⚖️ **1885** White miners in Rock Springs, Wyoming, attack Chinatown, killing 28 people, wounding 15 others, and driving hundreds more out of town.

🔫 **1898** In Africa, an Anglo-Egyptian force under General Horatio Kitchener decimates the Sudanese Mahdist army and captures the important Nile River city of Omdurman. Future British prime minister

The massacre of Chinese at Rock Springs, Wyoming

Winston Churchill was involved in the cavalry charge of the 21st Lancers.

🇬🇧 **1908** Lionized English polar explorer Captain Robert Scott marries Kathleen Bruce in the Hampton Court Palace.

⚔️ **1914** Japan lays siege to the German-held Chinese port and naval base of Tsingtao, pitting 23,000 men and 142 guns against the garrison of 6,000.

🎌 **1930** French aviators complete the first nonstop airplane flight from Europe to the United States aboard the dubiously named aircraft *Pointe d'Intérrogation (Question Mark).*

🎭 **1931** American crooner Bing Crosby debuts in his first radio show, *15 Minutes with Bing Crosby,* on CBS.

⚔️ **1940** During World War II, the United States gives Great Britain 50 overage destroyers for use against German U-Boats in return for long-term leases on British naval bases.

⚔️ **1942** On the Egyptian front during World War II, British forces stop German general Erwin Rommel's drive toward Egypt.

⚔️ **1943** During World War II, Allied troops surprise the Germans with a small landing on the heel of Italy and quickly capture the ports of Taranto and Brindisi.

⚔️ **1944** U.S. naval aviator Lieutenant George H. Bush, later president of the United States, is shot down and rescued while attacking Chichi Jima, an island off the coast of Japan, during World War II.

⭐ **1945** Vietnamese communist leader Ho Chi Minh copies from the American Declaration of Independence as he proclaims Vietnamese independence: "All men are born equal; the Creator has given us inviolable rights, life, liberty, and happiness!"

🎭 **1946** American playwright Eugene O'Neill premieres his last Broadway play, *The Iceman Cometh,* considered by many to be his finest work.

🎭 **1969** The last regular-season episode of *Star Trek* airs, but the American sci-fi cult program would gain eternal life, or so it seems, in reruns.

⭐ **1969** Ho Chi Minh, Vietnamese communist leader and father of the nation's independence movement, dies of a heart attack in Hanoi.

🔬 **1993** The United States and Russia agree to combine efforts in outer space by sharing *Mir* while jointly designing and building a new international space station.

Japanese surrender aboard the USS Missouri *(milestone)*

590 Gregory I becomes pope. Among his many accomplishments, the Gregorian chant is perhaps the best known.

1189 Richard the Lion-Heart is crowned King of England at Westminster Abbey.

1260 The Mamluks save their empire by defeating Mongol invaders at Ayn Jalut in Palestine.

1650 English general Oliver Cromwell defeats Charles II at Dunbar, Scotland.

1651 Cromwell again routs the Royal Army, this time at Worcester. Charles II barely escaped.

1658 Oliver Cromwell dies, having ruled England for almost five years as Lord Protector, a post to which he was appointed in December 1653. After the restoration of the monarchy, Cromwell's body was disinterred from Westminster Abbey and hanged at Tyburn gallows.

1777 The American flag, with 13 red and white stripes and 13 stars in a circle on a blue background, is flown in battle for the first time during a Revolutionary War skirmish at Cooch's Bridge, Maryland.

1803 In his notebook, English chemist John Dalton, who proposed the atomic theory of matter, uses atomic symbols for the first time.

1855 American general William Harney and 700 soldiers attack a Sioux village in Nebraska, killing 100 men, women, and children despite

---

MILESTONE

Treaty of Paris Signed

The American Revolution formally comes to an end when representatives of the United States, Great Britain, Spain, and France sign the Treaty of Paris on this day in 1783. The British recognized American independence. Under the terms of the treaty, Britain also agreed to remove all of its troops from American soil. New borders were also established for the United States, which included all land from the Great Lakes to Florida, and from the Atlantic Ocean west to the Mississippi River. For its part, America agreed to allow British troops to leave, to pay all debts to Britain, and not to persecute loyalists still in America.

"I hate television. I hate it as much as peanuts. But I can't stop eating peanuts."

—*Orson Welles*

Chief Little Thunder's offer of immediate surrender. It earned the general his nickname, "Squaw Killer Harney."

1861 In the early days of the American Civil War, Confederate general Leonidas Polk commits a major political blunder by marching his troops into the neutral state of Kentucky. In response, the Unionist legislature invited federal troops into the state, and the Union gained important strategic positions.

1871 Japan and China sign the Treaty of Tianjin.

1895 What many regard as the first professional game of American football is played in Pennsylvania by the Latrobe YMCA and the Jeannette Athletic Club. Latrobe won.

1900 At the city's annual Labor Day parade, Charles Wisner shows off a home-built prototype automobile, the first car built in Flint, Michigan. Eight years later, W. C. Durant consolidated Flint's various small manufacturers into the General Motors Company.

Anwar el-Sādāt

1902 American author Sarah Orne Jewett is tossed from a carriage on her 53rd birthday and badly injured, virtually ending her writing career. Jewett's works include *Deephaven, The Country of the Pointed Firs, A Country Doctor, A White Heron,* and *The Tory Lover.*

1933 Police in Darwin, Australia, make an urgent request to the government for police reinforcements to deal with Aboriginal unrest in Arnhem Land, where Aborigines have murdered five Japanese and a policeman.

1935 At the Bonneville Salt Flats in Utah, famed English speed demon Malcolm Campbell blows through the 300-miles-per-hour barrier to set a new land-speed record of 301.13 miles

per hour in his Campbell Rolls-Royce Railton *Blue Bird.*

1937 In New York City, Orson Welles produces, directs, and stars in *Les Misérables,* the first radio play to be produced by the fledgling Mercury Theater group.

1939 The first and only Yugoslavian Grand Prix is held at Kalemagdan Park in Belgrade. The winner: Italian champion Tazio Nuvolari.

1939 Following Nazi dictator Adolf Hitler's World War II invasion of Poland, Great Britain and France declare war on Germany. The first casualties were 112 civilians aboard the British ocean liner *Athenia,* sunk by a German submarine.

1943 During World War II, Allied forces cross the Strait of Messina from Sicily to launch the invasion of Italy.

1950 A U.S. Military Assistance Advisory Group of 35 men arrives in Saigon, Vietnam, to assist in the war against communism.

1981 In a period of four days, Egyptian police arrest more than 1,500 critics of Anwar el-Sādāt's government and outlaw the Muslim Brotherhood. A month later, Sādāt was assassinated.

422 Pope Boniface I dies in Rome. His four-year reign was marked by schism and his strong support for St. Augustine.

476 By traditional reckoning, the Roman Empire comes to an end when German general Odoacer deposes the usurper Romulus Augustulus, generally considered the last of the Western Roman emperors.

925 Athelstan, first king of all the English, is crowned at Kingston-upon-Thames. He ruled at the height of Anglo-Saxon power.

1260 The armies of Siena and Florence meet on the Hill of Montaperti, outside Siena. An act of treachery brought defeat to thousands of Florentines. Dante, in the *Inferno,* placed the traitor Bocca in the ninth circle of Hell.

1554 Franciscan monk Cornelio da Montalcino is burned alive in Rome for having converted to Judaism.

1568 English playwright William Shakespeare's father is elected high bailiff of Stratford-upon-Avon.

1609 Aboard his tiny ship, the *Half Moon,* English explorer Henry Hudson arrives at the wilderness island of Manhattan.

1781 Felipe de Neva founds Los Angeles, California. The city's full name: *El Pueblo de Nuestra Señora la Reina de los Angeles de Porciuncula.*

1864 In the American Civil War, the Union cavalry finally catches up with feared

For almost 30 years he had fought the whites who invaded his homeland, but Geronimo, the wiliest and most dangerous Apache warrior of his time, finally surrenders in Skeleton Canyon, Arizona, on this day in 1886. Operating in the border region around Mexico's Sierra Madre, southern Arizona, and New Mexico, Geronimo and his band of 50 warriors had succeeded in keeping white settlers off Apache lands for decades. Although they had successfully evaded U.S. Army generals George Crook and Nelson Miles, further resistance seemed increasingly pointless—there were too many whites and too few Apaches.

Geronimo

The Half Moon

Confederate cavalry leader John Hunt Morgan, who is shot and killed at his headquarters in Greenville, Tennessee.

1870 French emperor Napoleon III having been captured by Prussia in the Franco-German War, his empire is overthrown and the Third Republic is proclaimed.

1879 Great Britain and France restore dual control of Egypt to protect their investments in the Suez Canal.

1882 The Edison Electric Illuminating Company fires up its first central generator, supplying current to about 800 light bulbs in New York.

1888 American inventor George Eastman patents the Kodak camera, the first to use roll film instead of glass plates.

> *"Never insult an alligator until you've crossed the river."*
> —Cordell Hull

Users sent the entire camera to Kodak for processing.

🇺🇸 **1894** Fed up with sweatshop working conditions, some 12,000 tailors protest in New York, but achieve only limited results.

🏆 **1913** American champion boxer Jack Johnson, who is visiting Great Britain for a series of fights, is seriously injured when his car is hit by a London taxi.

🇮🇳 **1920** In a special five-day session, the Indian National Congress defines its aim as the nonviolent attainment of self-rule and approves Mohandas Gandhi's noncooperation movement, a boycott of foreign goods.

🏆 **1928** American George Wood sets the first official water-speed record— 92.838 miles per hour— in the *Miss America VI* on the Detroit River.

🇦🇷 **1939** Argentina declares neutrality in World War II.

🇺🇸 **1940** U.S. secretary of state Cordell Hull warns Japan that aggression in southeast Asia would stir bad feelings in America.

⚔ **1940** The destroyer *Greer* becomes the first U.S. vessel fired on in World War II when a German submarine shoots torpedoes at it,

First Kodak girl

and misses. The German commander mistakenly thought the *Greer* had dropped depth charges at the sub.

🇺🇸 **1957** Governor Orval Faubus calls up the National Guard to keep nine African-American students out of all-white Central High School in Little Rock, Arkansas. He succeeded, until President Dwight D. Eisenhower sent in federal troops.

🇺🇸 **1957** American automaker Ford proclaims "E-day" in celebration of its new Edsel. The unpopular Edsels were produced for only three years.

🇺🇸 **1958** The United States declares its readiness to send American forces to aid Chinese Nationalist troops defending the islands of Quemoy and Matsu from communist attack.

🇺🇸 **1959** The Labor Reform Act is passed by the U.S. Congress. A revision of the Taft-Hartley Act, its main purpose was to protect rank-and-file union members from dishonest union officials.

🏆 **1972** U.S. swimmer Mark Spitz wins his seventh gold medal at the 1972 Summer Olympics in Munich, Germany.

⚔ **393** Roman emperor Theodosius launches the Battle of Frigidus in order to crush a pagan revolution in France led by Arbogast, a Roman general who had seized power in Gaul.

🇬🇧 **1666** With London still smoldering from the Great Fire, English architect Sir Christopher Wren begins working on a plan to rebuild the city.

🇬🇧 **1682** England's last executions for witchcraft dispatch three alleged sorceresses.

🇺🇸 **1774** The first Continental Congress convenes in Philadelphia, Pennsylvania, to respond to British Parliament's enactment of the Coercive Acts, which had established British military rule in Massachusetts, granted immunity to British officials, and forced American colonists to house British troops.

⚔ **1778** During the American Revolutionary War, British forces assault and burn to the ground the deep-water port town of New Bedford, Massachusetts, which had harbored American privateers.

⚔ **1781** The Battle of Virginia Capes, the decisive naval battle of the American Revolutionary War, opens outside Chesapeake Bay between French and British ships. The French victory three days later stranded British forces under General Charles Cornwallis on the Yorktown peninsula, in Virginia.

"You can't fake listening. It shows."

—Raquel Welch

Fridtjof Nansen

🇫🇷 **1792** During the French Revolution, Paris elects Maximilien Robespierre to head a delegation to the National Convention.

🇫🇷 **1793** The Reign of Terror begins in France, with Maximilien Robespierre at the head of the revolution's infamous Committee of Public Safety. More than 300,000 people were arrested over the following year, and 17,000 were executed.

🇺🇸 **1863** During the American Civil War, the American foreign minister to Great Britain warns the British government that war between the two nations could erupt if Britain goes ahead with plans to send two ironclad ships to the Confederacy.

🇺🇸 **1877** Crazy Horse, the Oglala Sioux chief who helped defeat U.S. general George Custer at the Little Bighorn, is bayoneted by guards forcing him into a prison cell.

🇺🇸 **1879** At the outset of a disastrous American expedition to the North Pole, George Washington De Long's ship, the *Jeannette,* is trapped in pack ice off Wrangel Island, in the East Siberian Sea. The ship sank after 21 months in the ice; De Long and most of his crew died trying to reach help in Siberia.

1882 New Yorkers celebrate the first Labor Day. It became a U.S. national holiday in 1894.

1882 During his first Arctic expedition, Norwegian explorer Fridtjof Nansen and five other skiers reach the top of Greenland's expansive ice cap and begin their descent to the west coast.

1889 Striking London dock workers force employers to the bargaining table in a major victory that would revitalize Great Britain's trade-union movement.

1905 The Russo-Japanese War officially ends with the signing of the Treaty of Portsmouth, which cedes Russian territory to Japan along with railway and port rights in Manchuria.

1914 The Battle of the Marne, the first major Allied victory of World War I, begins just 30 miles northeast of Paris. The six-day counterattack saved the French capital, threw back the Germans, and killed or wounded 100,000 soldiers.

1915 Russian czar Nicholas II fires his popular commander in chief during World War I and takes supreme command himself, even though he had no previous wartime command experience.

1930 Two New York men complete their 7,180-mile auto trip to Los Angeles, California, and back, having made the entire journey driving a 1929 Ford Model A in reverse.

1958 Russian author Boris Pasternak's novel *Dr. Zhivago,* banned in his own country, makes its debut in the United States. It won the Nobel Prize the same year.

1969 During the Vietnam War, U.S. Army lieutenant William Calley is charged with six counts of premeditated murder for his role in the My Lai massacre of 109 Vietnamese civilians the previous year.

1997 Mother Teresa, founder of a Roman Catholic congregation of women dedicated to the poor and destitute of India and winner of a Nobel Peace Prize, dies in Calcutta.

Mother Teresa

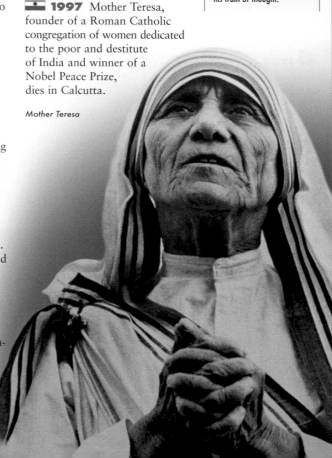

1492 Italian-born explorer Christopher Columbus sails west from the Canary Islands during his first voyage to North America.

1522 The first circumnavigation of the world is completed as the haggard remnant of Portuguese explorer Ferdinand Magellan's five-ship fleet returns to Spain after setting sail three years before. Just 22 of 270 men and a single ship, the *Vittoria*, survived the ordeal. Magellan himself was murdered in the Philippines in April 1521.

1634 During the Thirty Years' War, the Holy Roman Empire and Spain rout the Swedish Army in the pivotal Battle of Nordlingen, ending Sweden's domination of southern Germany.

1720 Italian composer Domenico Scarlatti debuts his serenata *Contesa delle Stagioni* at the Portuguese royal palace in Lisbon.

1781 During the American Revolutionary War, British forces under the traitorous Benedict Arnold attack and burn New London, Connecticut, a deep-water privateering base.

1844 American explorer John C. Fremont, following in the footsteps of many fur trappers, arrives at the shores of the Great Salt Lake.

1847 American writer, abolitionist, and recluse Henry David Thoreau leaves his shack on Walden Pond in Massachusetts and moves in with poet Ralph Waldo Emerson and his family.

MILESTONE

Vehicles of War

The first tank prototype is given its first test drive on this day in 1915. Several European nations had been working on the development of a shielded, tracked vehicle that could cross the uneven terrain of World War I trenches, but Great Britain was the first to succeed. The tanks made their first authoritative appearance at the Battle of Cambrai in 1917, when 474 British tanks faced German tanks for the first time and managed to break through the German lines during World War I. The Allies began using the vehicles in increasing numbers throughout the rest of the war. Afterward, European nations continued

---

1861 During the early months of the American Civil War, Union troops under General Ulysses S. Grant bloodlessly capture Paducah, Kentucky, to control the mouth of the Tennessee River.

1879 Great Britain's first telephone exchange opens, on Lombard Street in London.

1900 An electric car sets a new speed record, streaking over a five-mile track in Newport, Rhode Island, in 10 minutes, 20 seconds, for an average speed of more than 29 miles per hour.

1901 U.S. president William McKinley is mortally wounded at the Pan-American Exposition in Buffalo, New York, when anarchist Leon Czolgosz steps forward to shake hands and then shoots him twice at point-blank range.

1920 In the first prizefight broadcast on radio, American boxer Jack Dempsey knocks out Billy Miske in the third round.

1941 Reacting to an Allied oil embargo during World

Assassination of President McKinley

War II, the Japanese high command decides that war against the United States and Great Britain is probably inevitable. On the same day, the Nazis force 40,000 Jews into the Vilnius ghetto, in Lithuania.

🏆 **1943** The youngest baseball player to appear in an American League game, Carl Scheib, pitches for the Philadelphia Athletics at age 16 years, 8 months, 5 days.

💥 **1944** During World War II, British intelligence intercepts a Japanese message indicating that Italian guerrillas are widening the scope of their activities against German occupation.

🏳 **1945** U.S. president Harry S. Truman outlines a post–World War II economic recovery plan.

🏳 **1966** South African prime minister Hendrik Verwoerd, architect of the country's apartheid system, is stabbed to death in Cape Town by parliamentary messenger Dmitri Tsafendas.

🏳 **1969** Radio Hanoi announces Ho Chi Minh's successor: a committee of four competent government and military officials.

🏳 **1972** An attempt to rescue Israeli Olympic athletes from Arab terrorists ends in a disastrous firefight in which all nine hostages, five terrorists, and one German policeman are killed.

> *"We are the prisoners of ideas."*
> —*Ralph Waldo Emerson*

Princess Diana's funeral procession

🏳 **1972** In South Vietnam, President Nguyen Van Thieu abolishes popular elections.

🏆 **1975** In New York, Czech tennis star Martina Navratilova asks for political asylum. She became a U.S. citizen in 1981.

☪ **1975** A 6.8-magnitude earthquake strikes Turkey, killing 2,312.

● **1976** A Soviet Air Force pilot lands a MiG-25 fighter jet in Japan and asks for asylum in the United States.

🏳 **1983** In Moscow, Soviet officials admit that military chiefs gave the order to attack the Korean Airlines passenger jet which overflew Soviet airspace on September 1.

🏴 **1997** Great Britain mourns Princess Diana at her funeral in Westminster Abbey in London.

1191 During the Third Crusade, Richard the Lion-Heart's forces rout Saladin's army at Arsuf.

1303 Guillaume de Nogaret, advisor to French king Philip, breaks into Pope Boniface VIII's palace in central Italy and arrests him to prevent publication of a papal bull excommunicating Philip.

1695 The English government bans Irish Catholics from teaching, sending children to other countries for education, having guns, or owning horses worth more than £5.

1706 Eugene, Prince of Savoy, Austrian field marshal and one of history's great military stategists, conquers Turin, and with it most of northern Italy.

1776 During the American Revolutionary War, a man-powered submersible craft attempts to attach a time bomb to the hull of a British warship in New York Harbor. The submariner made contact, but was unable to attach his bomb. It was the first use of a submarine in warfare.

1778 Shawnee Indians launch a siege of Daniel Boone's Kentucky settlement, Boonesborough.

1812 French general Napoleon Bonaparte defeats

> *"A person is a person because he recognizes others as persons."*
>
> —*Desmond Tutu*

MILESTONE

Guillaume Apollinaire Arrested for Stealing the *Mona Lisa*

On this day in 1911, French poet Guillaume Apollinaire is arrested and jailed on suspicion of stealing Leonardo da Vinci's *Mona Lisa* from the Louvre museum in Paris. Known for his support for extreme avant-garde art movements, Apollinaire's mysterious background and radical views led authorities to view him as a dangerous foreigner and prime suspect in the heist. No evidence surfaced, and he was released after five days. Apollinaire went on to produce experimental works, and he coined the term "surrealist" to describe his play *The Breasts of Tiresias*. Vincenzo Peruggia was eventually arrested for the crime and the painting was recovered.

Russian forces under General Kutuzov in the bloody Battle of Borodino, opening the way to Moscow only 70 miles farther east.

1813 "Uncle Sam," the personification of the U.S. government, is born as a newspaper in Troy, New York, uses the term for the first time in print.

1822 Dom Pedro, prince regent of Brazil, declares Brazilian independence from Portugal. Later he was proclaimed emperor of Brazil and crowned Pedro I.

1838 Grace Darling, the 22-year-old daughter of a lighthouse-keeper in the Farne Islands off the coast of Northumberland, sets out with her father in a rowboat to rescue the passengers and crew of a steamer wrecked in a storm and becomes a national heroine.

1860 Italian patriot Giuseppe Garibaldi conquers Naples and declares himself "Dictator of the Two Sicilies."

1864 In preparation for his march to the sea during the American Civil War, Union

Daniel Boone protecting his family

Bishop Desmond Tutu

general William T. Sherman orders residents of Atlanta, Georgia, to evacuate the city.

1876 Attempting a bold daytime robbery of the First National Bank of Northfield, Minnesota, the James–Younger gang suddenly finds itself surrounded by angry armed townspeople intent on protecting their savings. Jesse and Frank James escaped, but their gang was nearly wiped out.

1892 John L. Sullivan falls to "Gentleman" Jim Corbett in the first world heavyweight title fight under the Queensberry Rules held in New Orleans, Louisiana.

1899 In America's first automobile parade, more than a dozen motorcars decorated with hydrangeas, streamers, lights, and Japanese lanterns roll through Newport, Rhode Island.

1901 The Boxer Protocol lays out the punishment of China for the Boxer Rebellion: a huge indemnity, an apology to the Western powers, destruction of all defensive forts, and broad trade concessions.

1914 During World War I, British troops from Nigeria invade the German colony of the Cameroons. The Germans ultimately abandoned the colony.

1921 Margaret Gorman, of Washington, D.C., becomes the first-ever Miss America.

1926 Hollywood movie studios close for the day to honor the funeral of heart-throb Italian-born American actor Rudolph Valentino, who had died after ulcer surgery in August at the age of 32.

1933 In Iraq, King Ghazi succeeds his father, King Faisal. He became popular as a champion—although an ineffective one—of Arab nationalism.

1940 Three hundred German bombers raid London, England, in the first of 57 consecutive nights of World War II bombing. The London "blitz" would continue until May 1941.

1950 Having earlier approved the use of force to repel the North Korean invasion of South Korea, the U.N. Security Council rejects a Soviet resolution that would condemn the American bombing of North Korea.

1986 Bishop Desmond Tutu becomes the archbishop of Cape Town, two years after winning the Nobel Peace Prize for his nonviolent opposition to apartheid in South Africa. He was the first black to head South Africa's Anglican Church.

BORN ON THIS DAY

1533
ELIZABETH I
Queen of England
(1558–1603)

1836
SIR HENRY CAMPBELL-BANNERMAN
Scottish statesman, liberal
British prime minister
(1905–08)

1860
GRANDMA MOSES (ANNA MARIE
ROBERTSON)
American artist

1887
EDITH SITWELL
English poet (*Song of the Cold;
Gardeners and Astronomers*)

1900
TAYLOR CALDWELL
American author (*Dear and
Glorious Physician; Devil's
Advocate; Captains and the
Kings*)

1909
ELIA KAZAN
Academy Award-winning
Turkish-born American movie
producer (*Gentleman's
Agreement; On the Waterfront*)

1914
JAMES ALFRED VAN ALLEN
American physicist who discovered and named the two radiation belts surrounding Earth

1917
LEONARD CHESHIRE
English philanthropist and
founder of the Cheshire Homes
for the sick

1930
SONNY ROLLINS
American jazz saxophonist

1932
JOHN PAUL GETTY JR
American philanthropist

1936
BUDDY HOLLY
American singer/songwriter
("Peggy Sue"; "Every Day";
"Maybe Baby")

1429 During her unsuccessful attempt to recover Paris from English occupiers, French military leader Joan of Arc is wounded outside the Saint-Honoré Gate.

1504 Italian sculptor Michelangelo's *David* is unveiled in the Florence town square.

1565 Ottoman forces besieging Malta withdraw after four months, defeated by the epic heroism of the island's defenders, members of the Knights Hospitalers.

1680 Don Antonio de Otermin, the Spanish governor of New Mexico, writes to his superiors describing a bloody Pueblo Indian uprising as "the lamentable tragedy, such as has never before happened in the world, which has occurred in this miserable kingdom."

1760 In the French and Indian War (the American side of the Seven Years' War), Montreal surrenders to British forces, and France loses all claims to Canada.

1798 A French force that invaded Ireland in support of Irish independence surrenders at Bullinamuck.

1810 The Pacific Fur Company's ship, the *Tonquin*, leaves New York bound for the

> *"The trouble with telling a good story is that it invariably reminds the other fellow of a dull one."*
>
> —Sid Caesar

1157
RICHARD I, THE LION-HEART
King of England (1189–99)

1830
FRÉDÉRIC MISTRAL
French poet, winner of the Nobel Prize in literature (1904)

1841
ANTONÍN DVOŘÁK
Czech composer and violinist (*New World Symphony*)

1886
SIEGFRIED SASSOON
English poet and author (*The Old Huntsman; Counter-Attack; Memoirs of an Infantry Officer*)

1889
ROBERT A. TAFT
U.S. senator and presidential candidate

Robert A. Taft

1900
CLAUDE PEPPER
U.S. senator

1921
SIR HARRY SECOMBE
Welsh actor, singer, and comedian (*The Goon Show*)

1922
SID CAESAR
American comedian and actor (*Your Show of Shows; It's a Mad, Mad, Mad, Mad World*)

1925
PETER SELLERS
English actor (*Lolita; The Pink Panther; What's New, Pussycat?*)

1932
PATSY CLINE
American country singer ("Crazy"; "Walkin' After Midnight"; "I Fall to Pieces")

1933
MICHAEL FRAYN
English playwright (*Noises Off; Copenhagen*)

Northern Pacific Railroad poster

coast of Oregon. As the first American merchant ship to visit the far west, the *Tonquin* hoped to establish a fur trade in the land explored by Lewis and Clark.

1831 Polish hopes for independence are crushed when Russian forces capture Warsaw.

1863 During the American Civil War, a small Confederate force thwarts a Union invasion of Texas at the mouth of the Sabine River on the Texas–Louisiana border.

1883 The United States' second transcontinental rail line, the Northern Pacific, is completed.

1892 The Pledge of Allegiance, written by Francis Bellamy to honor the American flag, is first published, in *Youth's Companion* magazine.

1900 Packing 130-mile-per-hour winds, a hurricane and storm surge strike Galveston, Texas, destroying most of the city and killing more than

8,000 people—the worst natural disaster in American history.

1928 The first U.S. cross-country airmail service begins operating between San Francisco, California, and New York.

1938 American patent analyst Chester Carlson files his own patent, describing a photocopier that would simplify his job of copying patent specifications by hand. The first truly practicable photocopier was not built until 20 years later.

1941 During World War II, German forces begin the siege of Leningrad, Russia, a grueling 872-day battle.

1943 U.S. general Dwight D. Eisenhower announces the surrender of Italy to the Allies during World War II. Nazi dictator Adolf Hitler reacted with Operation Axis, the German occupation of Italy.

1944 Germany lobs a V-2 ballistic missile at Paris, France, the first of 1,100 such weapons launched against Allied targets in Europe during the next seven months of World War II.

1945 U.S. troops land in Korea to begin their post–World War II occupation of the southern part of that nation, one month after Soviet troops entered northern Korea to begin their own occupation. Intended as a temporary measure, the partition of Korea became permanent.

1950 In the Korean War, North Korean forces achieve their farthest advance, holding most of the Korean peninsula.

United Nations forces clung to a beachhead at Pusan.

1951 The Treaty of Peace with Japan is formally signed. Western occupation ended in April, and Japan regained its national sovereignty.

1953 Continental Trailways offers the first transcontinental express bus service in the United States. The 3,154-mile ride from New York City to San Francisco, California, took 89 hours and cost $56.70.

1974 U.S. president Gerald R. Ford pardons his disgraced predecessor, Richard M. Nixon, for any crimes he may have committed while in office.

1998 American baseball player Mark McGwire, playing for the St. Louis Cardinals, hits his 62nd home run of the season, breaking Roger Maris's former one-season record of 61. McGwire finished the season with 70 home runs.

Mark McGwire

SEPTEMBER 9

3 Gaius Caesar, grandson and heir apparent of Roman emperor Augustus, is wounded in battle while attacking the city of Artagira, in Armenia.

1087 King William I, Norman conqueror of England, dies at age 60 near Rouen while putting down challenges to his authority in France.

1499 Portuguese navigator Vasco da Gama returns to Lisbon after the first of his three voyages to India, which opened up the sea route to the East and launched a new era in world history.

1513 English king Henry VIII's northern army routs the Scots, killing James IV of Scotland and more than 10,000 of his subjects at the Battle of Flodden near Branxton, Northumberland.

1668 French comic playwright Jean Baptiste Poquelin Molière first stages *L'Avare,* his stark comedy about a pathological miser.

1781 In the Battle of Eutaw Springs, American revolutionaries force British troops to withdraw to Charleston, South Carolina, thus further isolating the British Army at Yorktown.

1798 Charles Cornwallis, British viceroy of Ireland, turns back a French invasion of the Emerald Isle.

1845 British bare-knuckle boxing champ Benjamin Caunt is defeated by Bendigo (William Thompson) in the 93rd round.

"Everyone thinks of changing the world, but no one thinks of changing himself."
—*Leo Tolstoy*

1850 California, part of the United States for just two years, becomes the nation's 31st state.

1863 Union troops under General William Rosecrans capture Chattanooga to end a brilliant and largely bloodless American Civil War campaign for control of south central Tennessee.

1883 The world's first hot dog stand opens in St. Louis, Missouri.

1893 First Lady Frances Folsom Cleveland, wife of U.S. president Grover S. Cleveland, gives birth to a daughter, Esther, in the White House.

1896 Norwegian explorer Fridtjof Nansen returns from his last Arctic expedition, a

Ralph Nader testifies before a Senate Government Operations Subcommittee (milestone)

three-year adventure by ship (the *Fram*), dogsled, and kayak that had led him farther north than any previous explorer.

🏆 **1901** Drivers set off on the first long-distance car race, a 464-mile course from New York City to Buffalo, New York. The race lasted five days, with the winner posting an average speed of 15 miles per hour.

🎭 **1910** Alice B. Toklas, lifelong companion of American poet Gertrude Stein, moves into Stein's home in Paris, France, permanently.

▬ **1918** On World War I's Eastern Front, anarchy reigns in Petrograd, Russia, as Bolsheviks massacre the bourgeoisie and threaten to execute British officials.

🎌 **1919** In Boston, Massachusetts, police walk off the job to begin the infamous Boston Police Strike; criminals loot the city.

⚔️ **1922** Turkish forces under Mustafa Kemal recapture Izmir, in western Turkey, after its Greek occupiers make a panicked naval evacuation. Murder, mayhem, and fire followed.

🎌 **1939** American journalist Alicia Patterson and her wealthy third husband, Harry F. Guggenheim, launch the New York City tabloid *Newsday*.

🎌 **1940** The U.S. Navy contracts to build 210 ships, including a dozen aircraft carriers and seven battleships.

⚔️ **1943** Allied troops land in the Gulf of Salerno, Italy, during World War II and drive toward the cities of Salerno and Taranto.

🎌🎌 **1944** During World War II, French general and statesman Charles de Gaulle returns to Paris from exile in Algiers, Algeria, and begins setting up a provisional government. On the same day in the Pacific, American naval warplanes strike Japanese shipping at Mindanao, the Philippines.

🎭 **1956** American rock singer Elvis Presley makes his first television appearance on *The Ed Sullivan Show* and becomes a household name, singing "Don't Be Cruel" and "Hound Dog."

⚖️ **1971** In an escalation of the events of the previous day, hundreds of inmates riot at New York's Attica prison, taking 39 guards and other employees hostage.

Inmates of Attica State Prison during riots

1224 Franciscan monks first arrive in England.

1401 The reconstruction of the Japanese imperial palace at Kyoto is completed.

1419 The pro-English Duke of Burgundy is killed in the presence of Charles, 16-year-old heir to the French throne. The assassination took place just six weeks after the pair had concluded a friendship pact.

1526 Turkish sultan Suleyman I briefly occupies Buda, Hungary, but would soon depart with more than 100,000 captives.

1547 At the Battle of Pinkie, an English army under Edward Seymour defeats the Scots in order to enforce a marriage contract between Henry VII's 10-year-old son and Mary, Queen of Scots. Vanquished in battle, the Scots bundled five-year-old Mary off to France to avoid the union.

1608 In colonial America, English adventurer John Smith is elected council president of Jamestown after having directed survival efforts during the settlement's difficult first year.

1623 Ottoman sultan Mustafa I, ineffectual in the face of lawlessness and revolution, is deposed.

1763 The first issue of *Freeman's Journal*, a radical Irish newspaper, goes to press.

1813 In the first unqualified defeat of a British naval squadron by an American force, American captain Oliver Hazard Perry's flotilla of nine

---

MILESTONE

The Guillotine Falls One Last Time

At Baumetes Prison in Marseille, France, Hamida Djandoubi, a Tunisian immigrant convicted of murder, becomes the last person executed by guillotine on this day in 1977. The guillotine first gained notoriety during the French Revolution when physician and revolutionary Joseph-Ignace Guillotin won passage of a law requiring all death sentences to be carried out by means of machine. Guillotin and his supporters viewed decapitating machines as more humane than other execution techniques. A highwayman became the first person in Revolutionary France to be executed by this method. In September 1981, France outlawed capital punishment altogether, thus abandoning the guillotine forever.

"A classic is a book that doesn't have to be written again."

—*Carl Van Doren*

ships beats six British warships in the Battle of Lake Erie during the War of 1812. The victory forced the British to evacuate Detroit and relinquish control of the American Northwest.

1815 Shipworkers in Wheeling, Virginia, lay the keel for the first double-decker steamboat, the *Washington*.

1846 The hand-cranked sewing machine is patented by Elias Howe of Spencer, Massachusetts.

1861 During the early months of the American Civil War, Union troops force Confederates from the bluffs overlooking Carnifex Ferry on Virginia's Kanawha River. The victory gave the North control of the Kanawha Valley. Combatants included two future U.S. presidents: Rutherford B. Hayes and William McKinley.

Oliver Hazard Perry standing on the front of a boat at the Battle of Lake Erie

Drums of gasoline in 1945 headed for the war effort land on Luzon

1863 Union cavalry cross the Arkansas River, beat Confederate troops in the Battle of Bayou Fourche, and occupy Little Rock during the American Civil War.

1897 British police make the first drunk-driving arrest.

1913 The Lincoln Highway opens as the first paved, coast-to-coast highway in the United States.

1919 Austria signs the Treaty of Saint-Germain. It formally marked the end of the Hapsburg monarchy and forbade the union of Austria and Germany.

1921 The world's first controlled-access highway, part of Germany's autobahn system, opens near Berlin.

1923 Ireland is admitted into the League of Nations.

1931 American mobster Charles "Lucky" Luciano has rival gang boss Salvatore Maranzano murdered and begins forming a national crime syndicate.

1933 American comic Jimmy Durante premieres his popular radio show, *The Jimmy Durante Show,* which would run for 17 years.

1939 As Nazi German dictator Adolf Hitler's armies overrun Poland, a British Expeditionary Force lands in France during World War II. On the same day, Canada declares war on Germany.

1940 British bombers indiscriminately drop their loads over Berlin, in retaliation for World War II German raids on London that would become known as "the Blitz."

1942 Wartime rationing of gasoline begins in the United States.

1963 After a quick tour of Vietnam, a pair of American advisors tell President John F. Kennedy that the South Vietnamese are making progress in their war against the Vietcong but that the Diem regime is near collapse. Kennedy says, "You two did visit the same country, didn't you?"

1990 Pope John Paul II consecrates the world's biggest Christian church, the basilica of Our Lady of Peace at Yamoussoukro, capital of Côte d'Ivoire (Ivory Coast).

1998 In Northern Ireland, Unionist leader David Trimble and Sinn Fein leader Gerry Adams meet for private talks. This was the first time that Unionist and Sinn Fein leaders had met one-to-one since the partition of Ireland in 1922.

🔫 **1297** At the Battle of Stirling Bridge, Scottish patriot William Wallace defeats an English army under the command of John de Warenne and Hugh de Cressingham.

🏴 **1382** Louis I, king of Hungary and Poland, dies. Poland chose his nine-year-old daughter Jadigwa as their ruler, and crowned her two years later.

🏴 **1581** A Royal Charter establishes the Levant Company to pursue trade between England and the Ottoman.

🔫 **1697** Austria defeats the Ottomans at the Battle of Zenta.

🔫 **1709** In the War of Spanish Succession, France loses the Battle of Malplaquet, but the Anglo-Dutch-Austrian allies suffer far greater casualties.

🔫 **1714** James Fitzjames, duke of Berwick, storms

BORN ON THIS DAY

1700
JAMES THOMSON
Scottish poet ("The Seasons"; "Liberty"; "The Castle of Indolence")

1862
O. HENRY (WILLIAM SYDNEY PORTER)
American short-story author ("The Gift of the Magi"; "The Last Leaf")

1877
JAMES JEANS
British physicist and author (The New Background of Science; Through Space and Time; Science and Music)

1885
D. H. LAWRENCE
English author (Lady Chatterley's Lover; Sons and Lovers)

1902
JIMMIE DAVIS
Governor of Louisiana and Country Music Hall of Fame songwriter ("You Are My Sunshine")

1917
JESSICA MITFORD
English-born American journalist and author (The American Way of Death; Kind and Usual Punishment: The Prison Business)

1932
VALENTINO
Italian fashion designer

1935
GHERMAN TITOV
Russian cosmonaut who was the second man in space

> "A straw vote only shows which way the hot air blows."
> —O. Henry

Barcelona, taking the last Catalan stronghold against King Philip V. Berwick was an English nobleman who served France in the early 1700s.

🔫 **1777** General George Washington throws his ragged army against the British at Brandywine Creek near Wilmington, Delaware, during the American Revolutionary War. British forces under General Charles Cornwallis crushed the Americans, who were lucky to escape in a semblance of order.

🇺🇸 **1789** U.S. president George Washington appoints stalwart Federalist Alexander Hamilton to be the first secretary of the treasury.

🔫 **1798** Following Napoleon Bonaparte's occupation of Egypt, Ottoman sultan Selim III declares war on France.

🔫 **1814** During the Battle of Plattsburg on Lake Champlain in the War of 1812, a newly built U.S. fleet destroys a British squadron. The victory saved New York from possible invasion and helped lead to the conclusion of peace negotiations in Belgium.

Firefighters dwarfed by debris at the World Trade Center in New York City (milestone)

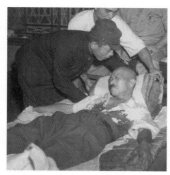
General Hideki Tōjō after suicide attempt

🏆 **1903** The world's oldest major motor speedway, the Milwaukee Mile, opens at the Wisconsin State Fair Park.

1914 Portugal, allied with England, sends a reinforcing expedition to its colonies in Africa.

1914 After a successful French counterattack, the First Battle of the Marne ends with German armies in retreat after it had appeared that Nazi-controlled Paris would surely fall. The battle spoiled German plans for a quick conquest of France during World War I.

1945 Following Japan's surrender in World War II, former prime minister Hideki Tōjō attempts suicide. He survived and was later hanged for war crimes.

1952 In Kenya, the Mau Mau rebellion breaks out against British rule.

1973 Chile's armed forces stage a coup against President Salvador Allende, the first democratically elected Marxist leader in Latin America. Allende died, and Augusto Pinochet Ugarte was installed as president.

1841 U.S. president John Tyler's entire cabinet, except for Secretary of State Daniel Webster, resigns over what in modern times would be called his bipartisan politics.

1847 "Oh! Susanna," American composer Stephen Foster's first big hit, is performed for the first time in a Pittsburgh, Pennsylvania, saloon.

1855 In the Crimean War, the 11-month Siege of Sevastopol comes to an end, as Russian forces destroy their own fortifications, sink their own ships, and abandon the city.

1857 Mormon pioneers, stoked by religious zeal and hostility from decades of public abuse and federal interference, murder 120 emigrants at Mountain Meadows, Utah.

1213 Simon de Montfort defeats Raymond VI at the Battle of Muret, taking from him the countship of Toulouse.

1351 In the early stages of the Hundred Years' War, French king John II signs a truce with England. It did not hold.

1683 Hapsburg forces led by John III Sobieski break the siege of Vienna, severely damaging Turkish influence in Eastern Europe.

1759 During the French and Indian War, British general James Wolfe lands 4,000 soldiers at a secret path beneath the French fortress of Quebec, Canada, which would fall the next day.

1772 A French court in Aix executes effigies of the Marquis de Sade and his servant Latour, convicted in absentia of sexual abuse.

1793 Maryland forbids commerce with Philadelphia, Pennsylvania, during an outbreak of yellow fever. It was the first quarantine of an American city.

1846 English poet Elizabeth Barrett elopes with poet Robert Browning after a short

Robert and Elizabeth Barrett Browning

BORN ON THIS DAY

1812
RICHARD MARCH HOE
American inventor who built the first successful rotary printing press

1818
RICHARD JORDAN GATLING
American inventor of the Gatling gun

1829
CHARLES DUDLEY WARNER
American essayist and novelist who, with Mark Twain, wrote *The Gilded Age*

1852
HERBERT HENRY ASQUITH
English statesman, liberal prime minister of Britain (1908–16)

1880
H. L. MENCKEN
American journalist and iconoclast

1888
MAURICE CHEVALIER
French singer, dancer, and actor (*Love in the Afternoon; Gigi; Can-Can*)

1892
ALFRED A. KNOPF
American book publisher

1897
IRÈNE JOLIOT-CURIE
French nuclear physicist, joint winner of the 1935 Nobel Prize in chemistry, daughter of Nobel Prize winners Pierre and Marie Curie

1910
ALEXANDER D. LANGMUIR
American epidemiologist who created and led the U.S. Epidemic Intelligence Service

1913
JESSE OWENS
American track-and-field athlete who won four medals at the Berlin Olympics in 1936

1931
KRISTIN HUNTER
American author (*The Survivors; God Bless the Child*)

1931
GEORGE JONES
American country singer ("Why Baby Why"; "White Lightning")

---

secret courtship. Barrett's father disliked Browning. To escape him, the couple fled to Italy, where they lived happily for 15 years until Elizabeth's death.

1873 In the United States, the Remington Company manufactures the first successful commercial typewriter.

1877 The Chase National Bank is organized in New York.

1890 Pioneers of the British South Africa Company arrive at what will be the capital of Rhodesia and begin to take up prospecting claims without permission of native Ndebele residents.

1908 Future British prime minister Winston Churchill, age 33, marries Clementine Hozier.

1912 Plans are announced for America's first transcontinental highway, to be called the Lincoln Highway—eventually known as Route 66.

1918 American motorcycle endurance rider Erwin "Cannonball" Baker completes a 17,000-mile, 78-day trip to all 48 state capitals—a significant trek in a time of limited roads and little pavement.

1923 Great Britain annexes Southern Rhodesia as a self-governing colony. In 1922,

> *"Conscience is the inner voice that warns us that someone may be looking."*
> —H. L. Mencken

Howard Hughes

the colony's European residents voted for self-government rather than joining South Africa.

🏆 **1935** American aviation pioneer and future recluse Howard Hughes sets an air-speed record in a plane of his own design: 352.46 miles per hour.

🎭 **1940** Near Montignac, France, four teenagers following their dog into a cave tunnel discover the Lascaux cave paintings. The 15,000- to 17,000-year-old paintings, consisting mostly of animal representations, are among the finest examples of art from the Upper Paleolithic period.

💥 **1942** A German U-boat sinks the British troop ship *Laconia*, killing more than 1,400 men during World War II.

1943 German forces rescue deposed Italian dictator Benito Mussolini from prison during World War II, expecting to set him up as a puppet ruler of Italy.

⚖️ **1947** In the United States, the Screen Actors Guild adopts a voluntary "loyalty oath," in which members must swear they are not members of the Communist Party.

1953 Massachusetts senator John F. Kennedy weds Jacqueline Lee Bouvier in Rhode Island.

1953 Six months after the death of Soviet leader Joseph Stalin, Nikita Khrushchev succeeds him as first secretary of the Communist Party of the Soviet Union.

🏆 **1956** American boxer Carmen Basilio, the "Canastota Clouter," wins the world welterweight championship. A year later he would beat Sugar Ray Robinson for the middleweight title.

1974 Ethiopian ruler Haile Selassie is deposed by army officers wishing to establish a socialist state.

1990 The United States, Great Britain, France, and the Soviet Union relinquish occupation rights in Germany. The largely symbolic action cleared the way for East and West Germany to reunite a month later.

M I L E S T O N E

Violence in Boston Over Racial Busing

In Boston, Massachusetts, opposition to court-ordered school busing turns violent on the opening day of classes in 1974. Schoolbuses carrying African-American children were pelted with eggs, bricks, and bottles. Police in combat gear fought to control angry white protestors besieging the schools. U.S. district judge Arthur Garrity had ordered the busing of black students to predominantly white schools and vice versa in an effort to integrate Boston's geographically segregated public schools. Protests continued for months, and many parents, white and black, kept their children at home. In October, the National Guard was mobilized to enforce the federal desegregation order.

Police escort school buses from the Gavin School in South Boston (milestone)

81 Roman emperor Flavius Vespasianus Titus, who brutally sacked Jerusalem in 70 and destroyed its Jewish temple, dies in Rome.

1321 Italian poet Dante Alighieri, author of *The Divine Comedy*, dies in Ravenna.

1515 In Italy, the Battle of Marignano opens with French and Venetian forces fighting Swiss mercenaries for control of Milan.

1577 Italian Jesuit missionary Matteo Ricci arrives on the west coast of India during his voyage to China, where he would introduce Christianity and live for nearly 30 years.

1645 In a decisive battle of the English Civil War, Scottish antiroyalists rout supporters of King Charles I at Philiphaugh.

1759 During the French and Indian War, British forces win supremacy in Canada by scaling the heights above Quebec and defeating a French army on the Plains of Abraham.

1791 Revolutionary France, espousing the radical doctrine of a people's right to self-determination, reunites with the papal territory of Avignon.

1812 With the French army on the outskirts of Moscow, Russian general Mikhail Kutuzov tells his subordinates, "Napoleon is a torrent which as yet we are unable to

"What we play is life."
—Louis Armstrong

BORN ON THIS DAY

1761
CASPAR WISTAR
American anatomist after whom the plant genus wisteria is named

1819
CLARA SCHUMANN
German pianist and composer, wife of composer Robert Schumann

1847
MILTON HERSHEY
American founder of the Hershey candy company

1851
WALTER REED
U.S. Army doctor who discovered a cure for yellow fever

1860
JOHN J. PERSHING
American general who led the campaign against Pancho Villa in Mexico and commanded the American Expeditionary Force in France during World War I

1863
FRANZ VON HIPPE
German naval commander at the Battle of Jutland in World War I

1874
ARNOLD SCHOENBERG
Austrian composer

1886
ALAIN LOCKE
Author and first African-American Rhodes scholar

1894
J. B. PRIESTLEY
English novelist (*The Image Men; The Good Companions*) and playwright (*An Inspector Calls; Bright Shadow*)

1911
BILL MONROE
American musician, considered the father of bluegrass music

1916
ROALD DAHL
Welsh-born British author (*James and the Giant Peach; Charlie and the Chocolate Factory; Tales of the Unexpected*)

1957
HANS ZIMMER
Academy Award-winning German composer for films (*Rain Man; The Lion King*)

"The Star Spangled Banner" poster

stem. Moscow will be the sponge that will suck him dry."

1814 During the War of 1812, a British fleet bombards Fort McHenry in Baltimore harbor, Maryland, inspiring witness Francis Scott Key to write "The Star-Spangled Banner." It later became the U.S. national anthem.

1826 A rhinoceros is exhibited for the first time in the United States, in New York.

1847 In the last battle of the Mexican-American War, U.S. forces storm the ancient Chapultepec fortress at the edge of Mexico City and eliminate the last significant Mexican resistance.

1862 In events leading up to the major American Civil War Battle at Antietam, Union soldiers resting in a meadow find a copy of Confederate general Robert E. Lee's battle plan. Union general George McClellan failed to exploit the serendipitous intelligence coup.

1882 British troops rout an Egyptian army at the Battle

of Tel-el-Kebir and begin a 72-year occupation of the country.

1899 In the first recorded auto fatality in the United States, a New York City motorist runs over a pedestrian at the corner of Central Park West and 74th Street.

1900 While conducting experiments in Cuba to determine how yellow fever is transmitted, physician Jesse Lazear, 34, is bitten by a mosquito carrying the disease. His death two weeks later confirmed the transmission process.

1922 The world's highest shade temperature, 136.4 degrees Fahrenheit, is recorded at a Libyan village south of Tripoli.

1940 Italian dictator Benito Mussolini launches Italy's ill-advised invasion of Egypt during World War II.

1945 British troops arrive in Vietnam to disarm defeated Japanese units during World War II.

1956 Large-scale production of taconite, a low-grade iron ore, begins in the United States, at Silver Bay, Minnesota, on Lake Superior.

1959 The Soviet Union launches *Lunik II*, the first man-made object to land on the moon.

1965 In the midst of rock and roll's ascendancy, American jazz great Louis Armstrong wins a Grammy for best male vocalist for "Hello Dolly!"

1968 In the Vietnam War, U.S. and South Vietnamese infantry and armor move into the Demilitarized Zone to attack two North Vietnamese divisions preparing an offensive.

1971 Chinese leader Lin Biao, an opponent of Mao Zedong during the Cultural Revolution, dies after a failed coup attempt, allegedly in a plane crash in Outer Mongolia.

1979 An underwater earthquake in Indonesia causes tidal waves that destroy an entire village and kill more than 100 people.

President Clinton, center, with Israeli prime minister Yitzhak Rabin, left, and PLO chairman Yāsir Arafāt, right (milestone)

407 Saint John Chrysostom, an early Church Father renowned for his preaching, dies in Helenopontus.

1224 While at prayer, Saint Francis of Assisi experiences a vision of a crucified figure and receives the marks of the stigmata.

1368 In China, forces of the Ming dynasty drive the Mongols out of Ta-tu (modern-day Beijing) and occupy the capital city.

1523 Pope Adrian VI, the only Dutch pope and the last non-Italian until John Paul II, dies in Rome.

1716 The first lighthouse in America, Boston Light, glows for the first time on Little Brewster Island at the entrance to Boston Harbor.

1752 British subjects turn their clocks 11 days ahead as Great Britain switches from the old Julian calendar to the Gregorian one, so what would have been September 3, 1752 is now September 14, 1752.

1781 During the American Revolutionary War, General George Washington and his army arrive in Williamsburg, Virginia, and prepare to besiege the British Army trapped on Yorktown peninsula.

Boston Light, Boston, Massachusetts

MILESTONE

American Canonized as Saint

Elizabeth Ann Seton is canonized on this day in 1975 by Pope John III at the Vatican in Rome, becoming the first American-born Catholic saint. She devoted much of her time to charity work with the poor and in 1797 founded the Society for the Relief of Poor Widows with Small Children in New York. After she herself was widowed and left with five children, Seton went to Baltimore, Maryland, to establish a Catholic school for girls. She founded the United States' first religious order, the Sisters of Mercy of St. Joseph. She continued to teach until her death in 1821.

Elizabeth Ann Seton

"Where there is hatred, let me sow love. Where there is injury, pardon. Where there is doubt, faith."

—*Saint Francis of Assisi*

1812 French general Napoleon Bonaparte's *Grande Armée* enters Moscow and finds the capital city deserted and its larders bare. Later that night, fires break out and in three days destroy most of the city.

1829 The Russian-Ottoman War officially ends with the signing of the Treaty of Adrianople.

1847 Fighting ends in the Mexican-American War as U.S. forces under General Winfield Scott enter Mexico City and raise the American flag over the Hall of Montezuma.

1848 The Second Sikh War escalates as the Sikh army joins in a national revolt against the British.

1854 During the Crimean War, a French and British amphibious force lands near Sevastopol and prepares to capture the important Russian naval base.

1862 During the American Civil War, Union and Confederate forces battle for three strategic passes on South Mountain, a 50-mile ridge in western Maryland. By nightfall, Union general George McClellan had taken the passes and was in position to destroy General Robert E. Lee's scattered army.

1886 The first typewriter ribbon is patented by George Anderson of Tennessee.

1901 U.S. president William McKinley, mortally wounded by an assassin, dies from gangrene and 42-year-old vice president Theodore Roosevelt becomes the nation's 26th president.

1905 Great Britain's Royal Automobile Club holds its first race on the Isle of Man.

1911 Russian prime minister Pyotr Stolypin is assassinated at the theatre in Kiev, in the presence of the Czar and Czarina.

1916 The Italian Army launches the Seventh Battle of the Isonzo, one in a series of failed attempts to cross the Isonzo River in present-day Slovenia.

1923 After being knocked out of the ring in the first round of a heavyweight bout, American boxer Jack Dempsey ferociously pounds Salvadoran Luis Angel Firpo to defeat in the second.

1927 American dancer Isadora Duncan dies in France when her trademark long scarf catches in the rear wheel of a speeding Bugatti motorcar.

1930 German voters elect 107 Nazis to the Reichstag, elevating the Nazis to major-party status.

1942 In Russia, German troops penetrate Stalingrad during World War II. In the Pacific, American Marines on Guadalcanal stop a Japanese offensive in the "Battle of Bloody Ridge" and force a general Japanese retreat across the island.

1956 American surgeons perform the first U.S. prefrontal lobotomy, at George Washington University Hospital in Washington, D.C.

1960 In an attempt to stabilize oil prices and unify oil policies, five oil-rich nations met in Baghdad, Iraq, to form the Organization of the Petroleum Exporting Countries. OPEC developed into one of the world's most influential organizations.

1982 Princess Grace of Monaco, an American actress who had abandoned a successful Hollywood film career to marry Prince Rainier, dies of injuries sustained in a car crash.

53 According to tradition, future Roman emperor Trajan is born. He was the first of Rome's emperors born outside of Italy.

1347 Moroccan sultan Abu al-Hasan captures Tunis as part of his short-lived North African Empire.

1590 Urban VII is elected pope. He died 12 days later of malaria.

1644 Innocent X succeeds Urban VIII as pope.

1752 In the first production by a professional acting troupe in the American colonies, Lewis Hallam and his company present William Shakespeare's *Merchant of Venice* in Williamsburg, Virginia.

1776 During the American Revolutionary War, British forces occupy New York.

1789 The U.S. Congress creates the Department of State from the previous Department of Foreign Affairs.

BORN ON THIS DAY

1789
JAMES FENIMORE COOPER
American author (*The Pioneers; The Last of the Mohicans*)

1857
WILLIAM HOWARD TAFT
26th president of the United States (1909–13)

1889
ROBERT BENCHLEY
American humorist, critic, actor, and author (*From Bed to Worse; My Ten Years in a Quandry*)

1890
DAME AGATHA CHRISTIE
English mystery author (*Murder in Mesopotamia; Death on the Nile; Appointment With Death*)

1890
CLAUDE MCKAY
American poet and novelist (*Home to Harlem; Banjo; Banana Bottom*)

1894
JEAN RENOIR
French film director (*Grand Illusion; The Rules of the Game*)

1901
SIR HOWARD BAILEY
English engineer who gave his name to a prefabricated bridge used extensively during World War II

1903
ROY ACUFF
American Country Music Hall of Fame musician

1794 Future U.S. president James Madison marries Dolley Payne Todd.

1810 In Mexico, revolutionary priest Miguel Hidalgo y Costilla delivers a speech called the Cry of Dolores, repeated now each year in Mexico to celebrate national independence.

1821 In his Central American Declaration of Independence, Guatemalan patriot José Cecilio del Valle proclaims freedom from Spain.

1830 English railroad pioneer George Stephenson opens the 36-mile Liverpool-Manchester line, marking the birth of the railroad age.

1830 In the first recorded railway accident involving a moving locomotive, English statesman William Huskisson is killed on the opening day of the Liverpool & Manchester Railway after being hit by Stephenson's *Rocket*.

1857 Timothy Alden obtains a U.S. patent for the first practical typesetting machine.

1857 After President James Buchanan's appointment of a non-Mormon as governor of Utah territory, Mormon leader Brigham Young issues an order forbidding the entry of U.S. troops into Utah.

1858 The Overland Mail Company inaugurates America's first transcontinental mail service, operating horse-drawn stagecoaches between St. Louis, Missouri, and San Francisco, California.

Trajan, emperor of Rome

"If one sticks too rigidly to one's principles, one would hardly ever see anybody."

—*Agatha Christie*

1862 Confederate forces capture Harper's Ferry, Virginia, along with 73 artillery pieces, 13,000 rifles, and 12,500 men. It was the largest single Union surrender of the American Civil War.

1864 Napoleon III agrees to withdraw French troops from Rome within two years. Italy, in turn, agrees not to invade Rome.

1910 In a scientific journal, Jesuit priest and physicist Theodor Wulf reports that cosmic radiation is more intense at the top of the Eiffel Tower than at ground level, supporting the idea that the radiation originates from space.

1916 During the Battle of the Somme in World War I, the British employ battle tanks for the first time in history.

1921 The U.S. government issues the first regular broadcasting license to radio station WBZ in Springfield, Massachusetts.

1924 A military junta ejects Chile's elected president, Arturo Palma.

1934 Bruno Hauptmann, kidnapper of American aviation hero Charles Lindbergh's baby, passes a marked ransom bill at a filling station in the Bronx, New York, more than two years after the crime. He was arrested, convicted, and executed.

1938 British prime minister Neville Chamberlain meets with Nazi German dictator Adolf Hitler at Berchtesgaden, as prelude to the Munich Conference two weeks later.

1940 In the Battle of Britain during World War II, the Royal Air Force beats off 1,300 invading German aircraft, downing 56 in two dogfights lasting less than an hour.

Services for Carol Robertson, one of four girls killed in the bombing of 16th Street Baptist Church

World War I tank

1253 French Franciscan William of Rubrouck leaves the camp of Mongol leader Batu Khan on a great journey to Karakorum, the Mongol capital. His account of the trip became a classic of history and travel.

1394 Clement VII, first antipope of the Great Schism, dies in Avignon, France, still convinced he was the true pope.

1398 In events later celebrated by William Shakespeare's play *Richard II*, England's King Richard banishes the dukes of Norfolk and Hereford, though he failed to save his throne.

1498 One of history's great villains dies in Avila, Spain. Tomás de Torquemada, head of the Spanish Inquisition, was said to be responsible for the torturing of innumerable heretics, Jews, apostates, and other nonconformers, some 2,000 of whom were burned at the stake.

1776 During the American Revolutionary War, George Washington's retreating army fights a delaying action—

MILESTONE

Mayflower Departs England

The *Mayflower* sails from Plymouth, England, on this day in 1620, bound for the New World with 102 passengers. The ship was headed for Virginia, where the colonists had been authorized to settle by the British crown. However, stormy weather and navigational errors forced it off course, and on November 21 the Pilgrims reached Massachusetts, where they founded the first permanent European settlement in New England in late December. Thirty-five of the Pilgrims were members of the radical English Separatist Church, who had traveled to America to escape the jurisdiction of the Church of England, which they found corrupt.

---

the Battle of Harlem Heights—in what would later be 103rd to 120th streets in New York City.

1798 Would-be Irish revolutionary James Napper Tandy lands in Ireland hoping to raise an army to fight the British. Despite having been made a general in France, he abandons the effort on the day of his arrival.

1810 Miguel Hidalgo y Costilla, a Catholic priest, launches the Mexican War of Independence.

1835 HMS *Beagle*, the British ship bearing naturalist Charles Darwin, arrives at the Galápagos Islands. Darwin's observations of Galápagos finches contributed greatly to his developing theory of natural selection and the evolution of species.

1839 The first daguerreotypes in America are made, less than a month after French inventor Louis Daguerre published the method and declared it "free to the world."

1845 Phineas Wilcox is stabbed to death by fellow Mormons in Nauvoo, Illinois, because he is believed to be a Christian spy. It was an act of "blood atonement," a doctrine stating that murder was sometimes necessary to save a sinful soul.

> *"A man who dares to waste one hour of time has not discovered the value of life."*
>
> —*Charles Darwin*

The defeat of Tandy's invasion of Ireland

A Palestinian woman brandishes helmets worn by those who massacred Palestinians at the Sabra refugee camp in Lebanon

1893 The largest land run in American history begins with more than 100,000 people pouring into the Cherokee Strip of Oklahoma to claim valuable land that had once belonged to Native Americans.

1903 English automaker Frederick Henry Royce, of Rolls-Royce Ltd., successfully tests his first gasoline engine, a two-cylinder, 10-horsepower device.

1911 English mountaineer Edward Whymper, first to climb the Matterhorn and survivor of a famous accident that killed four of his companions, dies peacefully in Chamonix, France, at age 71.

1920 In New York City's financial district, a horse-drawn wagon filled with explosives detonates near the subtreasury. Thirty-three people were killed and about 400 were wounded. The bombers were never identified.

1941 Mohammad Reza Shah Pahlavi, the shah of Iran, replaces his father on the throne.

1963 Malaysia is established from a federation of former British colonies.

1964 Canada ratifies the Columbia River Treaty, which regulates the use of the river's hydroelectric power by the United States and Canada.

1975 Papua New Guinea achieves full independence from Australia, triggering an unsuccessful secession effort by Bougainville.

1977 Celebrated American soprano Maria Callas dies in Paris, France, at the age of 53.

1978 Zia ul-Haq, former chief of staff of the Pakistani army and administrator of martial law, is proclaimed president.

1982 Hours after Israeli forces enter West Beirut, Christian Phalangist militiamen begin a massacre of Palestinians at the Sabra and Shatila refugee camps. Within two days, 1,000 men, women, and children were dead.

14 The Roman Senate makes a deity of the late emperor Caesar Augustus, officially enrolling him among the Roman pantheon of gods.

1019 Afghan astronomer Biruni makes a detailed observation of a lunar eclipse above Ghazni.

1635 French trader Pierre Belain claims Martinique for Louis XIII.

1683 Dutch scientist Anton van Leeuwenhoek reports the discovery of live bacteria, which he had seen in plaque picked from his own teeth.

1745 Scottish noble Charles Edward, the last Stuart to make an attempt on the English throne, enters Edinburgh with 2,400 men.

1787 The newly drafted Constitution of the United States

MILESTONE

Antietam: The Bloodiest Day in American History
On this day in 1862, Confederate general Robert E. Lee's Army of Northern Virginia and Union general George B. McClellan's Army of the Potomac fight to a standstill along a Maryland creek on the bloodiest day in American history. Although the battle was a tactical draw, it forced Lee to end his invasion of the North and retreat to Virginia. After Lee's decisive victory at the Second Battle of Bull Run, the Confederate general had steered his army north into Maryland. Lee and Confederate president Jefferson Davis believed that another Rebel victory might bring recognition and aid from Great Britain and France.

"Time is a storm in which we are all lost."

—*William Carlos Williams*

of America is signed by 38 of 41 delegates to the constitutional convention in Philadelphia, Pennsylvania. The document then required ratification by nine of 13 states to become law.

1820 English poet John Keats, age 24, sets off for Italy in the hope that the Mediterranean climate will improve his tuberculosis.

1844 Inventor Thomas Adams of Philadelphia, Pennsylvania, patents the first U.S. color printing press.

1871 The eight-mile Mont-Cenis Tunnel opens in the Alps, linking Savoy with the rest of Italy via a 20-minute train ride.

The Battle of Antietam (milestone)

From left, Egyptian president Anwar el-Sādāt, U.S. president Jimmy Carter, and Israeli prime minister Menachem Begin

1884 A judge in Oakland, California, sets a new speed record for verdicts, disposing of 13 criminal cases in just six minutes.

1915 Great Britain announces the loss of a submarine with its crew in the Dardanelles Strait during World War I.

1932 English auto racer Sir Malcolm Campbell sets a land-speed record of 76.27 miles per hour over a half mile.

1935 Scottish physicist Robert Alexander Watson-Watt, working for the National Physical Laboratory in Great Britain, files a patent for what he calls radio detection and ranging, later known as radar.

1939 Soviet troops sweep into eastern Poland during World War II, taking advantage of a pact with Germany to carve up the vulnerable Slavic nation.

1939 During World War II, the British aircraft carrier *Courageous* is torpedoed by a German submarine and sinks

with the loss of 518 men southwest of Ireland.

1944 In Europe, three divisions of Allied airborne troops parachute into the Netherlands and launch Operation Market-Garden, an attempt to outflank the German West Wall in France during World War II.

1954 In New York, heavyweight boxing champion Rocky Marciano knocks out Ezzard Charles for his 47th consecutive win. Marciano retired in 1956 as undefeated world champion with a professional record of 49 wins from 49 bouts.

1978 In New Orleans, Muhammad Ali beats Leon Spinks to regain his world heavyweight title and become the first boxer to win the heavyweight title three times.

1978 In ceremonies at the U.S. White House, Egyptian president Anwar el-Sādāt and Israeli prime minister Menachem Begin sign the Camp David Accords, which laid the foundation for a peace agreement between the two nations.

324 Constantine I defeats his rival emperor Licinius at Chrysopolis and takes control of the entire Roman Empire, east and west.

1634 English Puritan Anne Hutchinson, who would become the first notable female religious leader in the American colonies, arrives in Massachusetts.

1759 French forces surrender Quebec, Canada, to the British.

1793 U.S. president George Washington lays the silver cornerstone of the Capitol Building in Washington, D.C.

1830 The first American-built locomotive, *Tom Thumb*, loses a nine-mile race against a horse, thanks to a boiler leak.

1850 The U.S. Congress passes the Fugitive Slave Act, which mandates the return of runaway slaves regardless of where in the Union they are captured.

1851 The *New York Daily Times* (now the *New York Times*) publishes its first issue. In it, publishers Henry J. Raymond and George Jones state, "we intend to issue it every morning (Sundays excepted) for an indefinite number of years."

1860 In the Italian War of Independence, some 40,000 Sardinian troops defeat a papal army of 4,000 at the Battle of Castelfidardo.

1862 In the American Civil War, Union general George McClellan misses a chance to defeat Confederate

---

BORN ON THIS DAY

1709
SAMUEL JOHNSON
English lexicographer, essayist, poet, and moralist (*The Idler and the Adventurer; The Rambler*)

1819
LEON FOUCAULT
French physicist who invented the pendulum and the gyroscope

1827
JOHN TOWSEND TROWBRIDGE
English author of books for boys (*The Jack Hazzard and Toby Trafford series*)

1893
ARTHUR BENJAMIN
Australian composer

1895
JOHN G. DIEFENBAKER
Prime minister of Canada (1957–63)

1905
GRETA GARBO
Swedish-born American actress (*Flesh and the Devil; Anna Karenina; Two-Faced Woman*)

Greta Garbo

1932
NIKOLAI N. RUKAVISHNIKOV
Russian cosmonaut

1939
FRANKIE AVALON
American pop singer ("Venus"; "Bobby Sox to Stockings"; "Why")

1951
DR. BENJAMIN SOLOMON CARSON SR.
American neurosurgeon and author (*Gifted Hands; THINK BIG; The Big Picture*)

1971
LANCE ARMSTRONG
American cyclist and five-time winner of the Tour de France

Jane Addams, right

general Robert E. Lee after the Battle of Antietam. Vulnerable, exhausted, and outnumbered three-to-one, Lee's army is allowed to withdraw.

1889 American social reformer Jane Addams establishes Hull House, in Chicago, Illinois, to provide educational and cultural opportunities for working-class immigrants.

1895 Daniel David Palmer gives the first chiropractic adjustment to one Harvey Lillard, of Davenport, Iowa.

1896 French physicist Armand Fizeau, the first to directly measure the speed of light, dies in France.

1904 Mr. and Mrs. Charles Glidden complete the first automobile crossing of the Canadian Rockies,

> *"Life would be so wonderful if we only knew what to do with it."*
>
> —*Greta Garbo*

arriving in Vancouver, British Columbia, after a harrowing 3,536-mile drive from Boston, Massachusetts, in a 24-horse-power Napier.

1915 During World War I, Germany temporarily suspends its submarine campaign in the English Channel and west of the British Isles in response to American protests over the sinking of the *Lusitania* and other civilian passenger liners.

1917 English author Aldous Huxley, 23, takes a day job as a schoolmaster at Eton.

1926 A devastating hurricane strikes downtown Miami, killing 193 and taking the wind out of a south Florida real-estate boom.

1932 Imprisoned Indian nationalist leader Mahatma Gandhi begins a hunger strike in order to unite the Hindu community in its opposition to British rule.

1941 U.S. president Franklin D. Roosevelt asks Congress for $5.9 billion for Lend-Lease, his program to provide war materiel to nations fighting the Axis powers in World War II. On the same day, U.S. Navy ships for the first time begin escorting an eastbound transatlantic convoy.

1943 The Battle of Salerno ends in Italy as German forces, hammered by Allied air attacks during World War II, withdraw.

1945 American general Douglas MacArthur moves his World War II command headquarters to Tokyo and prepares to oversee Japan's conversion to democracy.

1961 U.N. secretary general Dag Hammarskjöld dies in a mysterious plane crash in Africa while trying to broker an end to the Congo crisis.

Miami River Bridge in Miami Beach, after the hurricane of 1926

"Time flies like an arrow. Fruit flies like a banana."

—*Groucho Marx*

1356 At the Battle of Poitiers, during the Hundred Years' War, French king John II suffers a disastrous defeat against the English archers of Edward, the Black Prince.

1468 By the Accord of Toros, Castilian king Henry IV recognizes his half-sister Isabella I as his heir.

1586 Anthony Babington, convicted in a plot to assassinate Queen Elizabeth I of England, writes to the queen offering £1,000 pounds for his freedom, to no avail. He was executed the next day.

1657 By the Treaty of Wehlau, Polish king John Casimir gives up suzerainty over Prussia in return for military aid against Sweden.

1777 Continental forces withstand an attack by British troops under General John Burgoyne at the First Battle of Saratoga, in New York. A month later, Burgoyne surrendered—an event that marked a turning point in the American Revolutionary War.

1778 During the American Revolutionary War, the Committee on Finance of the Continental Congress presents the nation's first budget.

1783 The Montgolfier brothers, French ballooning pioneers, launch a hot-air balloon over Versailles. The

---

M I L E S T O N E

New Zealand First in Women's Vote

With the signing of the Electoral Bill by Governor Lord Glasgow on this day in 1893, New Zealand becomes the first country in the world to grant national voting rights to women. The bill was the outcome of years of suffragette meetings in towns and cities across the country, with women often traveling considerable distances to hear lectures and speeches, pass resolutions, and sign petitions. They first went to the polls in the national elections of November 1893. The United States granted women the right to vote in 1912, and Great Britain guaranteed full voting rights for women in 1928.

---

passengers were a sheep, a rooster, and a duck. The first manned untethered flight was made in November.

1796 U.S. president George Washington publishes his Farewell Address and retires to Mount Vernon.

1827 After a duel turns into an all-out brawl, American frontiersman Jim Bowie disembowels a banker in Alexandria, Louisiana, with an early version of his famous Bowie knife, a foot-long instrument probably invented by his equally belligerent brother, Rezin Bowie.

1863 In the American Civil War, forces under Union general William Rosecrans and Confederate general Braxton Bragg begin one of the bloodiest battles of the War at Chickamauga, Georgia.

1865 American cabinetmaker turned railway contractor George Pullman is granted U.S. patent number 4992 for his railway sleeping carriage, and Pullman soon became a byword for luxury railway travel.

The Battle of Chickamauga

1900 Robert Parker and Harry Longbaugh, better known as Butch Cassidy and the Sundance Kid, rob the First National Bank in Winnemucca, Nevada, marking the first time the duo worked as a team.

1902 American aviation pioneers Orville and Wilbur Wright begin a series of nearly 1,000 glider flights south of Kitty Hawk in North Carolina. The flights helped them refine the design of the powered craft that they would first fly a year later.

1918 During World War I, British forces supported by Jewish Brigades begin the last major offensive against the Turks in what would become the state of Israel.

1918 British forces under Lord Edmund Allenby win a decisive victory against the Ottoman Turks at Megiddo. Subsequent victories at Damascus and Aleppo ended Ottoman rule in Syria.

1932 At the Bonneville Salt Flats in Utah, Ab Jenkins completes the first 24-hour solo run, driving 2,710 miles non-stop in a single day. His stock Pierce Arrow V-12 averaged 112.94 miles per hour.

1941 In a particularly brutal World War II attack, German bombers blast through Leningrad's antiaircraft defenses and kill more than 1,000 Russians.

1944 Finland and the Soviet Union sign an armistice in which Finland is forced to accept the 1940 Treaty of Moscow.

Earthquake destruction in Mexico City

1955 Argentine president Juan Domingo Perón is deposed in a military coup.

1956 American comedian Groucho Marx's radio game show *You Bet Your Life* airs its last episode.

1959 In one of the more surreal moments in the history of the Cold War, Soviet leader Nikita Khrushchev explodes with anger when he learns that he cannot visit Disneyland.

1985 A large earthquake devastates Mexico City, killing more than 10,000.

1991 A German hiker in the Tyrolean Alps discovers the Ice Man, a mummified corpse frozen in a glacier.

1994 Twenty thousand U.S. troops land unopposed in Haiti to oversee the country's transition to elected government under Roman Catholic priest Jean-Bertrand Aristide, who had been deposed in a bloody military coup.

Pedro Menéndez de Avilés

☪ **693** Nicephorus II marries Theophano, the beautiful young empress of Byzantium. A popular military leader, Nicephorus had been crowned by public demand a month earlier.

▮▮ **1378** Dissident French cardinals elect Robert of Geneva as antipope Clement VII, launching a schism that would last 40 years.

1405 In feuding between his guardians, Faraj, the young 26th Mamluk ruler of Syria and Egypt, is deposed. He was later reinstated. The disagreement was a portent of the Mamluk kingdom's demise.

1519 Portuguese navigator Ferdinand Magellan sets sail from Spain with five ships and 270 men in search of a western sea route to the Spice Islands of Indonesia.

🔫 **1565** Spanish forces under Pedro Menéndez de Avilés

> *"Mistakes are part of the dues one pays for a full life."*
> —*Sophia Loren*

capture the French Huguenot settlement of Fort Caroline, near present-day Jacksonville, Florida. It was the first instance of colonial warfare between European powers in America.

🔫 **1643** In the English Civil War, 6,000 men die as Parliamentary forces defeat the Royalists at Newbury.

▬ **1697** The first Treaty of Rijswijk is signed in Holland. Along with the second treaty, signed in October, it ended the War of the Grand Alliance.

⚖ **1761** Jesuit Gabriel Malagrida is burned to death in Portugal, having been convicted of conspiring to assassinate the king (he was later vindicated) in what was called the Conspiracy of the Távoras.

🔫 **1792** French forces under Charles Dumoriez beat back invading Prussians at the Battle of Valmy.

🔬 **1851** A railroad first employs a telegraph when

Charles Minot, the superintendent of the Erie Railroad, sends a telegram 14 miles to Goshen, New York, to delay a train.

1853 American inventor Elisha Otis sells his first elevator. Called a "safety hoist," it was the first to employ a device to keep it from falling if the hoisting cable broke.

1854 In the Crimean War, British and French forces defeat the Russians at the Battle of Alma.

1863 In the American Civil War, Rebel forces win the Battle of Chickamauga Creek in northern Georgia. Although one of the bloodiest battles of the war, it had little impact on the military situation in the region.

1870 Italian troops enter Rome, completing the unification of Italy. Days later, a proclamation freed Jews from the city's 315-year-old ghetto.

1945 A month after the surrender of Japan in World War II, Packard joins American auto manufacturers in stopping military production, turning out its last wartime Rolls-Royce Merlin engine.

U.S. Embassy bombing in Beirut, Lebanon

1984 Twelve people are killed when a suicide car bomber attacks the U.S. embassy complex in Beirut, Lebanon.

1984 Marvin Gaye Sr. agrees to a plea bargain that will keep him out of jail for fatally shooting his son, singer Marvin Gaye, after an investigation revealed that he had received massive bruises from their violent argument.

1995 The cross-Channel ferry *Stena Challenger*, en route from England to France, runs aground near Calais, trapping 245 passengers before the ship is refloated.

480 B.C. Persian king Xerxes I pillages Athens.

454 Roman emperor Valentinian III murders with his own hands Flavius Aetius, the able patrician who had run the Roman government for nearly 20 years, while the emperor spent his life in the pursuit of pleasure.

1327 Edward II is murdered in Berkeley Castle, Gloucestershire on the orders of his wife, Isabella, who was known as the "she-wolf of France."

1348 Riots against Jews spread to the Swiss cities of Bern, Chillon, and Zurich. Jews were blamed for the plague after Jews under torture in Switzerland said they had been given poison to place in wells in Venice.

1526 During the wars of the Italian Renaissance, Rome is attacked by Spanish and German mercenaries.

1629 Jan Pieterszoon Coen, founder of the Dutch commercial empire in the East Indies, dies in Jakarta.

MILESTONE

Monarchy Abolished in France

In Revolutionary France, the Legislative Assembly votes to abolish the monarchy and establish the First Republic on this day in 1792. The measure came one year after King Louis XVI reluctantly approved a new constitution that stripped him of much of his power. In 1789, food shortages and economic crises led to the outbreak of the French Revolution. The king and his queen, Marie Antoinette, were imprisoned in August 1792. After the monarchy was abolished, evidence of Louis's counter-revolutionary intrigues with foreign nations was discovered, and he was tried for treason. In January 1793, Louis was convicted and condemned to death by guillotine.

> *"Remember if people talk behind your back, it only means you're two steps ahead!"*
> —Fannie Flagg

1745 At the outset of the final Jacobite rebellion in Scotland, forces under Stuart prince Charles Edward win the Battle of Prestonpans.

1776 Delaware proclaims its existence as an independent state.

1779 Spain takes advantage of the American Revolution and captures Baton Rouge, Louisiana, from the British.

1780 American traitor Benedict Arnold meets with a British major in Stony Point, New York, to arrange the betrayal of West Point.

1809 Great Britain's foreign secretary, George Canning, fights a duel with the war secretary, Viscount Castlereagh, and is wounded in the thigh.

Henry Ford, left, wife Clara Bryant, center, and Henry Ford II, right

Car bombing of former Chilean ambassador and his aides in Washington, D.C.

1860 French forces defeat the Chinese Army near Beijing and prepare to enter the capital city.

1898 In China, the Hundred Days of Reform comes to an abrupt end when the reform-minded emperor is overthrown and replaced by the ultra-conservative empress dowager.

1904 Chief Joseph, the Nez Perce leader who conducted a brilliant fighting retreat across the American West in 1877, dies at age 64 on the Colville reservation in northern Washington.

1914 German colonial forces in New Guinea surrender to the Australians.

1915 Bulgaria mobilizes its army and enters World War I as an ally of Germany and the Central Powers.

1931 Great Britain abandons the gold standard; the pound sterling plunges from $4.86 to $3.49, and worried U.S. depositers make a run on American banks that would soon force 827 banks to close their doors.

1938 The Great New England Hurricane, with winds up to 120 miles per hour, smashes without warning into Long Island, New York, and southern New England, killing nearly 600 people, devastating coastal communities, and sinking some 3,000 ships.

1942 Soviet Red Army troops counterattack near the vital oil distribution point of Stalingrad, Russia, during World War II.

1945 Henry Ford II, grandson of American automaker Henry Ford, takes over as president of Ford Motor Company.

1949 After winning the Chinese Civil War, a triumphant Mao Zedong announces that the Communist Party will lead the nation's new government.

1976 A car bomb in Washington, D.C., kills Orlando Letelier, a former official under Chile's first socialist president, Salvador Allende, who had been deposed and killed three years before.

1981 Belize gains its independence from Great Britain.

1429 After being rebuffed at the walls of Paris, Joan of Arc and King Charles VII return to Gien, where they disband their army.

1499 After fighting an unsuccessful war in Switzerland, Holy Roman Emperor Maximilian I signs the Peace of Basel, which recognizes the virtual independence of the Swiss Confederation.

1554 Spanish conquistador Francisco Vásquez de Coronado, whose chimeric quest for treasure-laden cities in the North American Southwest ended in failure, dies in disgrace in Mexico.

1598 English playwright, actor, and verbal pugilist Ben Jonson is indicted for manslaughter after killing a fellow actor in a duel.

1692 Seven alleged witches, six women and one man, are hanged in Salem, Massachusetts.

1711 Tuscarora Indians massacre settlers on the Chowan and Roanoke rivers in the Carolinas.

1776 During the American Revolutionary War, American patriot Nathan Hale is summarily hanged in New York City by the British for spying. On the same day, U.S. naval hero John Paul Jones

> *"Every time I look at my pocketbook, I see Jackie Robinson."*
>
> —*Willie Mays*

attacks a British fishing fleet in Nova Scotia.

1780 In Virginia, followers of Captain William Lynch sign an execution pact, thus becoming the first "lynch mob."

1792 France's National Convention declares the country a republic.

1828 Shaka, founder of the Zulu Kingdom of southern Africa, is murdered by his two half-brothers after his mental illness threatens to destroy the Zulu tribe.

1851 Telegraphed dispatching of trains begins in the United States.

1862 U.S. president Abraham Lincoln issues his Emancipation Proclamation, which would free slaves in Confederate-controlled territory as of January 1, 1863, and lift the tenor of the American Civil War to a higher plain.

1893 America's first automobile, built by bicycle makers Charles and Frank Duryea, debuts on the streets of Springfield, Massachusetts.

The first reading of the Emancipation Proclamation

Raoul Wallenberg

1893 The *Fram*, a ship specifically designed by Norwegian explorer Fridtjof Nansen to be frozen into the arctic's pack ice, accomplishes its purpose at 78 degrees 50 minutes North, 133 degrees 37 minutes East.

1914 During World War I, a single German U-boat sinks three British cruisers in the North Sea within an hour, killing 1,400 British sailors and alerting the Admiralty to the hitherto underestimated submarine threat.

1918 On World War I's Mideast front, Turkish forces east of the Jordan River begin to retreat in the face of advancing British army units.

1921 Lithuania joins the League of Nations as a recognized member, though its borders have yet to be defined.

1927 American boxer Jack Dempsey loses his bid to regain the heavyweight title when he fails to return to a neutral corner after knocking down champ Gene Tunney in a title match in Chicago, Illinois.

1938 Prior to World War II, Nazi dictator Adolf Hitler ups the ante in the crisis over Czechoslovakia by demanding that German troops occupy the Sudetenland and that all Czechs be evacuated from the area.

1943 British midget submarines succeed in badly damaging the German battleship *Tirpitz*, which is in a supposedly safe anchorage in a Norwegian fjord.

1945 U.S. general George S. Patton proves himself a political novice by publicly questioning the need to rid Germany of Nazis and by comparing the controversy over Nazism to a "Democratic and Republican election fight."

1949 The Soviet Union tests its first nuclear bomb, thus exponentially raising the stakes of the Cold War.

1953 The world's first four-level freeway interchange opens in Los Angeles, California.

1969 American baseball great Willie Mays hits his 601st homer, the first since Babe Ruth to top 600.

1981 The U.S. Congress confers honorary citizenship upon Raoul Wallenberg, the missing Swedish businessman and diplomat who rescued Hungarian Jews during World War II. The honor had been granted just once before, to Winston Churchill.

1989 American songwriter Irving Berlin, who composed 1,500 songs including "Puttin' on the Ritz" and "God Bless America," dies in New York at age 101.

Young Iranian soldiers

867 Byzantine emperor Michael III ("The Drunkard") is assassinated in Constantinople.

1408 Rebellious citizens of Liège (in present-day Belgium) are defeated by John, Duke of Burgundy, on the field of Othée.

1777 German composer Christoph Gluck's opera *Armide* premieres in Paris.

1779 During the American Revolutionary War, the U.S. ship *Bonhomme Richard*, commanded by John Paul Jones ("I have not yet begun to fight!"), wins a hard-fought engagement against the British warships *Serapis* and *Countess of Scarborough* off the east coast of England.

1803 Arthur Wellesley, later the Duke of Wellington, wins his first major engagement as a commander at the Battle of Assaye, India.

1806 American explorers Meriwether Lewis and William

"Great art picks up where nature ends."

—*Marc Chagall*

Clark receive a boisterous greeting on their return to St. Louis, Missouri, having made the first recorded overland journey from the Mississippi River to the Pacific coast and back.

1810 Residents of Baton Rouge, in what was then the Spanish territory of West Florida, launch a rebellion. They proclaimed the West Florida Republic, which the United States annexed three months later.

1821 French religious educator André Coindre founds the Brothers of the Sacred Heart.

1846 German astronomer Johann Gottfried Galle discovers the planet Neptune at the Berlin Observatory. The blue gas giant, which has a diameter four times that of Earth, was named for the Roman god of the sea.

Revolutionary War battle between John Paul Jones of the Bonhomme Richard and Captain Pearson of the British ship Serapis

Jack Henry Abbott

🔫 **1853** Great Britain sends its fleet to Constantinople, an act that led to the Crimean War.

🎭 **1862** Russian author Count Leo Tolstoy, 34, marries 17-year-old Sophie Andreyevna Behrs. The couple proceeded to have 13 children over the next 17 years.

🔫 **1863** In the wake of the Union's defeat at Chickamauga, U.S. president Abraham Lincoln meets with military planners to discuss the desperate situation at Chattanooga, Tennessee. Their decision to send General Joseph Hooker's army as reinforcement resulted in the most impressive logistical accomplishment of the American Civil War.

⚖️ **1875** Fifteen-year-old William Bonney ("Billy the Kid") is arrested for the first time in his criminal career. The offense: helping to steal a bag of clothes from a Chinese laundry.

🏴󠁧󠁢󠁥󠁮󠁧󠁿 **1897** In Great Britain, Nine-year-old Stephen Kempton becomes the world's first recorded automobile fatality on a public road. Trying to steal a ride from a taxi by hanging on to a spring, he lost his grip and died under a wheel. The first motoring fatality of all occurred the previous year on a private road at the Crystal Palace in London.

🔫 **1917** Legendary German fighter ace Werner Voss, flying alone, is shot down by Captain J. B. McCudden after a dogfight with five airplanes of No. 56 Squadron, Royal Flying Corps.

🏆 **1926** American boxer Gene Tunney wins the world heavyweight championship by decision over heavily favored Jack Dempsey.

🇮🇹 **1943** Deposed Italian dictator Benito Mussolini, having been rescued from prison by his German masters, fashions the new fascist Republic of Salo, an imaginary country ruled by a powerless puppet.

🎭 **1964** France's Paris Opéra unveils a stunning new ceiling painted as a gift by Belorussian-born artist Marc Chagall.

⚖️ **1981** Jack Henry Abbott is captured in the oil fields of Louisiana two months after killing Richard Adan in New York City. Abbott, author of *In the Belly of the Beast,* was out on parole with the support of author Norman Mailer, who had convinced officials that he had a great writing talent.

🏴 **1989** Azerbaijan declares sovereignty from the Soviet Union.

🏳️ **1991** Following the collapse of the Soviet Union, Armenia becomes an independent nation.

BORN ON THIS DAY

484 B.C.
EURIPIDES
Greek playwright (*Trojan Women; Hippolytus; Medea*)

63 B.C.
OCTAVIAN (AUGUSTUS CAESAR)
First Roman emperor

1838
VICTORIA CHAFLIN WOODHULL
American feminist reformer and presidential candidate

1865
BARONESS ORCZY
Hungarian-born British novelist and playwright (*The Scarlet Pimpernel*)

1889
WALTER LIPPMANN
American journalist and political commentator

Walter Lippmann

1920
MICKEY ROONEY
American actor (*Boys' Town; The Bridges at Toko-Ri; Andy Hardy Comes Home*)

1926
JOHN COLTRANE
American composer and jazz musician ("Soultrane"; "My Favorite Things"; "Crescent")

1930
RAY CHARLES
American singer and songwriter ("Born to Lose"; "Georgia On My Mind"; "Money")

1943
JULIO IGLESIAS
Spanish singer/songwriter ("To All the Girls I've Loved Before"; "All of You"; "Fragile")

1949
BRUCE SPRINGSTEEN
American rock singer ("Born in the U.S.A."; "Born to Run"; "The Rising"; "Streets of Philadelphia")

366 In an early papal power dispute, two Roman deacons are elected pope and Ursinus is swiftly consecrated. Violence followed, and Ursinus was exiled to Gaul.

622 The Prophet Muhammad, fleeing from Mecca, arrives at Medina. The higira, his flight to the desert oasis, marked the start of the Muslim calendar.

813 In Iraq, al-Amin, the sixth Abbasid caliph, is captured and executed in Baghdad by the forces of his elder half-brother.

911 The 18-year-old East Frankish king Louis IV dies in Frankfurt.

1180 Upon the death of his father Manuel I Comnenus, Alexius II Comnenus becomes the emperor of Byzantium at age 11.

1332 Edward de Balliol is crowned king of Scotland at Scone. An ally of Edward III of England, he opposed supporters of Scotland's independence.

1398 Central Asian conqueror Timur, also called Tamerlane, crosses the Indus on his way to the bloody destruction of Delhi.

1706 During the Second Northern War, Sweden and Poland sign the first Treaty of Atranstädt, by which Augustus II, king of Poland, gives up the throne. Three years later he reclaimed it.

1812 In Argentina, revolutionary forces under General Belgrano defeat royalist troops north of Tucumán.

MILESTONE

The First Supreme Court
The Judiciary Act of 1789 is passed by Congress and signed by President George Washington on this day, establishing the Supreme Court of the United States as a tribunal made up of six justices who were to serve on the court until death or retirement. On September 26, the U.S. Senate confirmed all six appointments. The Constitution granted the Supreme Court ultimate jurisdiction over all laws, especially those in which their constitutionality was at issue. The high court was also designated to oversee cases concerning treaties of the United States, foreign diplomats, admiralty practice, and maritime jurisdiction.

James Doolittle

1826 Scottish explorer Alexander Laing, the first European to see Tombouctou in western Africa, leaves that ancient fabled city only to be murdered two days later.

1827 In Dublin, Ireland, Catherine McAuley, founder of the Religious Sisters of Mercy, opens the House of Mercy to serve orphans and the poor.

1834 In Portugal, the War of Two Brothers ends with the death of King Pedro four months after the exile of his brother Miguel.

1849 Johann Strauss the elder, the hugely popular Austrian composer of waltzes, dies in Vienna at age 45.

1852 French inventor Henri Giffard makes the first-ever powered, controlled flight in his new invention, the dirigible. It flew 17 miles from Paris to Trappe in three hours.

1869 Gold prices plummet on "Black Friday," the result of a swindle by American financier Jay Gould and his robber-baron partner, James Fisk, who conspired to inflate and then corner the gold market.

1877 Saigo Takamori, Japanese samurai leader and

"The measure of success is not whether you have a tough problem to deal with, but whether it is the same problem you had last year."

—*John Foster Dulles*

rebel against the Meiji government he helped restore, kills himself as an act of honor.

1889 British inventor Alexander Dey patents the late employee's bane, a time clock that records when each worker "punches in" to work.

1890 Under pressure by the U.S. government, Mormon leaders issue the "Mormon Manifesto," abandoning polygamy as a tenet of the Church of Jesus Christ of Latter-day Saints.

1908 Ford rolls out its factory-built Model T. The "Tin Lizzy" revolutionized the American automotive industry by providing an affordable, reliable car for the average person.

1918 U.S. Navy flier Lieutenant David Ingalls downs his fifth enemy plane, becoming the Navy's first ace.

1924 At Mitchel Field, New York, Lieutenant James Doolittle takes off and lands in a windowless airplane. It was the first all-instrument blind flight.

1941 Japan instructs its consul in Hawaii to divide Pearl Harbor into five zones, calculate the number of warships in each zone, and report the findings back to Japan. American intelligence intercepted the message, but dismissed it as unimportant.

1947 Chinese Communist forces under Chen Yi rout the garrison at Chi-nan. The victory opened the road to the vital railroad center of Suchow.

1953 In a speech, U.S. secretary of state John Foster Dulles declares that the United States will not "cringe or become panicky" in the face of Soviet nuclear weapons.

1960 The USS *Enterprise,* the first nuclear-powered aircraft carrier is launched in Newport, Virginia. Its range, without refueling, is 470,000 miles.

1964 The Warren Commission finishes its investigation, concluding that Lee Harvey Oswald acted alone in the assassination of U.S. president John F. Kennedy.

The Warren Commission, from left, Allen W. Dulles, Hale Boggs, John Sherman Cooper, Chief Justice Earl Warren, Richard Russell, John J. McCloy, and Gerald Ford

1066 At the Battle of Stamford Bridge, English king Harold II defeats a Norwegian invasion force and kills the Norwegian king, Harald III Hardraade, who had laid claim to the English throne.

1396 Turkish forces consolidate control over the Balkans as they defeat a large European army near Nicopolis on the Danube River.

1493 Italian explorer Christopher Columbus ships out from Cadiz, Spain, on his second voyage to the Americas, this time in command of at least 17 ships.

1513 Spanish explorer Vasco Núñez de Balboa walks across the Isthmus of Panama and becomes the first European to see the Pacific Ocean.

1555 The Peace of Augsburg, which established a legal basis for both Lutheranism and Catholicism in Germany, is issued by the Diet of the Holy Roman Empire.

1643 During the English Civil Wars, Scotland agrees in the Solemn League and Covenant to support English parliamentary disputes with the royalists, and both parties agree to work toward the civil and religious union of the British Isles.

1697 England's Banishment Act requires all

> *"I not only use all the brains that I have, but all that I can borrow."*
> —*Woodrow Wilson*

Catholic clergy to leave the realm by May 1, 1698.

1776 British Army troops capture the American capital of Philadelphia, Pennsylvania, during the Revolutionary War.

1789 The American Bill of Rights, 10 amendments to the U.S. Constitution that guarantee basic freedoms, passes Congress and goes to the states for ratification.

1799 The French defeat a large Russian army in the Second Battle of Zurich, which helped to prevent an invasion of France.

1805 During the Napoleonic Wars, the pivotal Battle of Ulm opens as the French Grand Army crosses the Rhine River and heads south to meet the Austrian Army. The month-long series of maneuvers and battles ended in a major strategic victory for Napoleon Bonaparte's forces, which captured more than 50,000 of the 72,000 Austrians.

1818 James Blundell performs the world's first transfusion of human blood at Guy's Hospital in London, England.

Simón Bolívar

Charlie Chaplin movie poster

1828 South American revolutionary Simón Bolívar, who had liberated northern South America from Spain, survives an assassination attempt by liberal conspirators in the presidential palace in Bogotà.

1908 In Casablanca, Morocco, three German deserters from the French foreign legion are seized from a German consular official, thus touching off an international incident known as the Casablanca Affair.

1913 English actor Charlie Chaplin, 24, signs his first movie contract with Keystone for $175 a week and starts his meteoric rise to fame. Within three years, he would be raking in $10,000 a week from Mutual Studios.

1915 As part of a major Allied offensive on World War II's Western Front, British forces launch the Third Battle of Artois, during which they would use poison gas for the first time.

1919 U.S. president Woodrow Wilson, touring the United States to promote the League of Nations, collapses. A week later, he suffered a massive stroke.

1941 The German *Wehrmacht* isolates the Crimean Peninsula from the rest of Russia during World War II.

1943 The Soviet Red Army recaptures Smolensk during World War II.

1956 The first call is placed from New York City to London, England, over the recently installed transatlantic telephone cable, which could handle 36 simultaneous calls.

1957 Racial integration finally begins in Little Rock, Arkansas, as U.S. Army paratroopers escort nine black students through the doors of all-white Central High School.

1970 The brief, bloody war called "Black September," which pitted Palestinian guerrillas and Syrian armored units against the Jordanian Army, ends in stalemate with Palestinians still controlling portions of northern Jordan.

1974 Scientists first report that freon gas from spray cans is destroying Earth's ozone layer.

Sandra Day O'Connor is sworn in by Chief Justice Warren Burger as husband John J. O'Connor holds two family bibles (milestone)

1519 Portuguese navigator Ferdinand Magellan, sailing on behalf of Spain, reaches Tenerife, off the northwest coast of Africa, during the early weeks of the first circumnavigation of the planet.

1580 English sailor Francis Drake completes the first British circumnavigation of Earth as he returns to Plymouth in the *Golden Hind*.

1687 The Parthenon, occupied by Turks and used as a powder magazine, explodes when Venetian artillery score a direct hit on the ancient building.

1772 The first U.S. law to license medical practitioners is passed in New Jersey.

1781 As the American Revolutionary War draws to a close, the French fleet defeats the British at Yorktown, Virginia.

1820 Daniel Boone, the great American frontiersman who blazed a path through the Cumberland Gap into Kentucky, dies in Missouri at age 86.

1864 In the American Civil War, the Confederate Army under General Sterling

The Parthenon

BORN ON THIS DAY

1774
JOHNNY APPLESEED (CHAPMAN)
American pioneer and orchardist

1887
SIR BARNES WALLIS
English aeronautical engineer

1888
T. S. ELIOT
American-born British poet ("The Wasteland"; "The Love Song of J. Alfred Prufrock"; "Four Quartets")

1897
PAUL VI
262nd Roman Catholic pope (1963–78)

1898
GEORGE GERSHWIN
American composer ("Rhapsody in Blue"; "An American in Paris"; *Porgy and Bess*)

1915
JACK LALANNE
American fitness guru

1925
MARTY ROBBINS
American Country Music Hall of Fame singer ("El Paso"; "Devil Woman"; "Streets of Laredo")

1948
OLIVIA NEWTON-JOHN
English-born Australian and American pop singer ("Please Mr. Please"; "If Not For You"; "Downtown")

1949
JANE SMILEY
Pulitzer Prize-winning American author (*The Age of Grief; Ordinary Love; A Thousand Acres*)

Levi Strauss

Price invades Missouri and captures a Union fort at Pilot Knob. The battle and subsequent raids alienated Missouri voters, who soon elected a slate of staunch Union supporters.

1871 Portland cement, patented in Great Britain by English bricklayer Joseph Aspdin in 1824, is patented in the United States by David Oliver Saylor of Allentown, Pennsylvania. Aspdin named his invention after the Isle of Portland in Dorset, England, where Portland stone is quarried.

1888 Norwegian arctic explorer Fridtjof Nansen reaches the west coast of Greenland after a six-week ski trek across Greenland's colossal ice cap.

1892 Fame comes to Russian composer Sergei Rachmaninoff with the premiere of his *Piano Concerto No. 2 in C Minor*, in Moscow.

1902 American entrepreneur Levi Strauss, inventor of blue jeans, dies.

1918 The final Allied offensive of World War I begins as American and French forces push off along the Meuse River through the Argonne Forest. On the same day, 115 American sailors die when the Coast Guard cutter *Tampa*, apparently torpedoed by a German submarine, explodes and sinks off Wales.

1934 Cunard's largest ocean liner to date, RMS *Queen Mary*, is launched at Clydebank, Scotland, by Queen Mary herself. *Queen Mary* set sail on her maiden transatlantic voyage on May 27, 1936, and in 1967 was sold to an American company and berthed off Long Beach, California, as a tourist museum and hotel.

1940 Vichy French forces bomb the British at Gibraltar during World War II.

1942 Germany's SS begins cashing in possessions taken from murdered Jews at the concentration camps in Auschwitz and Majdanek, Poland, sending foreign currency, gold, jewels, and other valuables to SS headquarters, distributing clothing to German families, and sending watches, clocks, and pens to frontline troops during World War II.

1944 Thousands of Allied soldiers are killed, wounded, or taken prisoner around the Dutch city of Arnhem as Operation Market-Garden, an ill-fated World War II bid to seize Rhine River bridges, fails. Of the 10,000 British and Polish troops engaged, only 2,900 escaped.

> *"I would've made a good pope."*
> —Richard Nixon

1945 The first American soldier is killed in Vietnam while searching for missing World War II pilots.

1957 American composer Leonard Bernstein's classic musical about star-crossed lovers, *West Side Story*, premieres in New York City to mixed reviews.

1960 John F. Kennedy and Richard M. Nixon face off in the first televised debate between major-party U.S. presidential candidates.

1996 Astronaut Shannon Lucid returns to Earth after setting a new space endurance record for an American: 188 days aboard the Russian space station *Mir*.

1997 In Indonesia's worst aviation disaster, a jetliner flying low through smoke from forest fires hits a tree and explodes, killing 234.

1997 Two earthquakes in central Italy kill 10 people and severely damage the Basilica of St. Francis of Assisi.

Shannon Lucid

Emperor William I and his generals

1066 Norman duke William, soon to be conqueror of England, assembles his army of cavalry and infantry and sets sail from France for Sussex.

1331 Polish king Wladyslaw I defeats the Germanic Knights of the Teutonic Order at the Battle of Plowce.

1540 Pope Paul III charters the Society of Jesus (the Jesuit order), which had been founded six years earlier by Ignatius de Loyola, a Spanish soldier turned priest.

1590 Pope Urban VII dies of malaria just 12 days after his election to the papacy.

1815 In the aftermath of the Napoleonic Wars, William I ascends the throne of the Kingdom of the Netherlands, a country assembled for the convenience of Europe from Dutch and Belgian territories.

1825 In England, the world's first freight and passenger steam railway, the Stockton & Darlington Railway, makes its inaugural eight-mile run with 450 passengers aboard.

1864 During the American Civil War, a band of

BORN ON THIS DAY

1722
SAMUEL ADAMS
American Revolutionary War leader who became governor of Massachusetts

1792
GEORGE CRUIKSHANK
English caricaturist, illustrator, and reformer

1817
HIRAM R. REVELS
First African-American U.S. senator

1840
THOMAS NAST
American political cartoonist

1862
LOUIS BOTHA
First prime minister of South Africa

1918
SIR MARTIN RYLE
English radio astronomer

1922
ARTHUR PENN
American movie director (*Bonnie and Clyde*; *The Missouri Breaks*; *Alice's Restaurant*)

Arthur Penn

1941
DON CORNELIUS
American television host (*Soul Train*)

1947
MEATLOAF (MARVIN LEE ADAY)
American rock singer ("Bat Out of Hell"; "Two Out of Three Ain't Bad")

1958
SHAUN CASSIDY
American actor (*The Hardy Boys*) and singer ("Da Doo Ron Ron")

Confederate guerrillas sack the town of Centralia, Missouri, murder 22 unarmed Union soldiers who had just stepped off a train, and then annihilate a pursuing force of 120 Yankees.

1869 "Wild Bill" Hickok, in his first job as a sheriff, stops a bar fight in Hays City, Kansas, by shooting one of the participants in the head.

1892 Book matches are patented by Ohio's Diamond Match Company.

1916 Ethiopia's emperor Iyasu is deposed by the country's aristocrats after he courts the Central Powers during World War I.

1918 During the final Allied offensive of World War I, British troops attack the Germans' Hindenburg Line between Cambrai and Saint-Quentin, France.

1935 American child actress Judy Garland, who would later star as Dorothy in *The Wizard of Oz,* signs her first contract with MGM.

1938 Queen Elizabeth, consort of George VI, launches the Cunard ocean liner *Queen Elizabeth* at Clydebank, in Scotland.

1939 Warsaw surrenders to the German army, 140,000

> *"There is no security on this earth; there is only opportunity."*
>
> —Douglas MacArthur

Polish troops are taken prisoner, and the Nazis prepare for a campaign of terror against the country's Jews, Roman Catholics, and its upper and middle classes during World War II.

1940 World War II belligerents Germany, Italy, and Japan join forces by signing the Tripartite Pact, which calls for mutual assistance in case any of the Axis powers is attacked by a formerly neutral country, i.e., the United States.

1941 The United States launches the first Liberty ship, the SS *Patrick Henry,* in Baltimore, Maryland. Liberty ships were built by the hundreds to carry cargo to the war zones during World War II.

1950 American boxer Charles Ezzard outpoints Joe Louis to win the world heavyweight title in New York City.

1950 During the Korean War, American

Marines recapture Seoul. On the same day, the U.S. Joint Chiefs of Staff order General Douglas MacArthur to destroy the North Korean armed forces.

1959 Soviet leader Nikita Khrushchev heads home after a two-week visit to the United States that included a summit conference with President Dwight D. Eisenhower and a tantrum at Disneyland.

1960 English social activist Sylvia Pankhurst dies in Ethiopia. She had championed women's suffrage, had vociferously opposed racism and the rise of fascism in Europe, and had helped settle Jewish refugees from Germany.

1998 The Taliban capture Kabul and hang Mohammad Najibulla, the last communist president of Afghanistan.

Judy Garland, left, in The Wizard of Oz

545

Chinese characters engraved by Confucius

551 B.C. Tradition claims this date for the birth of Confucius, the great Chinese philosopher.

48 B.C. Roman general Pompey, recently defeated in Greece by Julius Caesar, is murdered as he tries to come ashore in Egypt, where he had sought refuge.

235 Pope Pontian, exiled to the mines of Sardinia by Roman emperor Maximinus, abdicates the papacy.

1066 William, duke of Normandy, lands unopposed in England and begins preparing his army for battle against King Harold II of Britain.

1105 Roger II, age nine, succeeds his older brother as grand count of Sicily but still has to obey his mother, who becomes his regent.

1106 English king Henry I defeats and captures his rebellious older brother Robert at the Battle of Tinchebrai, in Normandy.

BORN ON THIS DAY

1573
MICHELANGELO MERISI DA CARAVAGGIO
Italian Baroque painter (*Adoration of the Shepherds; St. Francis in Ecstasy*)

1769
JOHN "GENTLEMAN" JACKSON
English champion boxer, mentioned in the poetry of Lord Byron, who he taught to box

1803
PROSPER MÉRIMÉE
French writer whose novel *Carmen* was adapted for Bizet's opera

1856
EDWARD THOMPSON
American archaeologist who explored the Mayan ruins

1902
ED SULLIVAN
American newspaper columnist and television show host (*The Ed Sullivan Show*)

1925
SEYMOUR CRAY
American inventor of the Cray I computer

1934
BRIGITTE BARDOT
French actress (*And God Created Woman; The Truth; Ms. Don Juan*)

1938
BEN E. KING
American singer/songwriter ("Stand by Me"; "Save the Last Dance for Me"; "There Goes My Baby")

1948
PHIL HARTMAN
American comedian and actor (*Saturday Night Live*)

> *"One must be frank to be relevant."*
> —*Corazón Aquino*

1238 James I, king of Aragon, conquers the kingdom of Valencia in Spain.

1542 In the first known European encounter with California, Portuguese navigator João Rodrigues Cabrilho sails into San Diego Bay on behalf of Spain.

1634 John Milton, age 25, debuts his masque *Comus* for the Earl of Bridgewater. It was the young English poet's first attempt to deal with the themes of good struggling with evil, a subject he would explore in his masterpiece, *Paradise Lost.*

1810 In Mexico, independence fighters under parish priest Miguel Hidalgo y Costilla sack the city of Guanajuato and massacre upper-class Spaniards and Creoles.

1850 Congress outlaws flogging as a means of discipline on U.S. Navy ships.

1858 English photographer William Usherwood snaps the first photo of a comet, Donati's.

1863 During the American Civil War, Union generals Alexander McCook and Thomas Crittenden take the fall for losing the Battle of Chickamauga, in Tennessee. Both were relieved of their command but subsequently exonerated.

1865 Elizabeth Garrett Anderson becomes the first woman to obtain a license to practice as a physician and surgeon in Great Britain. She later became England's first female mayor, when she was elected Mayor of Aldeburgh in 1908.

1868 During the Spanish Revolution of 1868, rebels seize a strategic bridge at Alcolea, opening the way to Madrid and forcing Queen Isabella II to flee into exile.

1914 German artillery begins bombarding the besieged Belgian city of Antwerp during World War I.

1915 An Anglo-Indian force routs the Turks at Kut-al-Amara in eastern Iraq during World War I.

1917 During World War I, British troops supported by armored cars attack and encircle the strategic Iraqi city of Ramadi, whose Turkish defenders surrendered the following morning.

Estonia memorial in Stockholm, Sweden

1918 Belgian troops begin an attack aimed at capturing Ghent during the final Allied offensive of World War I.

1942 The U.S. Army Air Force begins developing two long-range bombers for transatlantic use in case Great Britain is overrun by the Nazis. Neither plane was deployed during the war, but the tailless B-35 later became the prototype for the B-2 Stealth bomber built in 1989.

1989 Corrupt Filipino tyrant Ferdinand Marcos dies in exile in Hawaii, three years after being driven from power by a popular uprising led by Corazón Aquino.

1994 More than 900 people die in one of the worst maritime disasters of the century when Sweden's *Estonia*, a large car-and-passenger ferry, sinks in the Baltic Sea during a storm.

48 B.C. A Greek fleet of some 370 triremes savages and scatters a much larger Persian fleet in the Battle of Salamis, the first major naval battle of recorded history. The victory turned the tide against Persian king Xerxes's invasion of Greece.

1349 Albert II of Austria forcibly suppresses anti-Jewish riots, thus making his country one of the few relatively safe havens for Jews as a plague sweeps Europe.

1399 In a series of meetings in the Tower of London, English king Richard II agrees to abdicate the throne. Henry Bolingbroke, who had deposed Richard, soon became King Henry IV.

1651 In the English Civil War, Royalist commander James Stanley is court-martialed and condemned to death by Parliamentarians.

1793 Wage and price controls come to revolutionary France as a means for rationing goods and provisioning the nation's armies.

1862 During the American Civil War, a Union general quarrels with his commanding officer, then chases him through a Louisville, Kentucky, hotel and shoots him. General Jefferson C. Davis was never court-martialed for killing General William Nelson.

> *"If you obey all the rules, you miss all the fun."*
> —*Katharine Hepburn*

BORN ON THIS DAY

1547
MIGUEL DE CERVANTES
Spanish author (*Don Quixote*)

1755
ROBERT LORD CLIVE
Founder of the British empire in India

1758
HORATIO NELSON
British admiral who won the Battle of Trafalgar

1810
MRS. ELIZABETH CLEGHORN GASKELL
English novelist (*Mary Barton; Wives and Daughters*)

1907
GENE AUTRY
American singer and actor, "The Singing Cowboy"

1908
GREER GARSON
British-born American actress (*Goodbye, Mr. Chips; Pride and Prejudice; The Miniver Story*)

1916
TREVOR HOWARD
English actor (*Brief Encounter; The Third Man; Sons and Lovers*)

1916
CARL GILES
English cartoonist

1930
COLIN DEXTER
English crime writer, creator of Inspector Morse

1930
RICHARD BONYNG
Conductor of the Australian Orchestra

1935
JERRY LEE LEWIS
American Rock and Roll Hall of Fame singer ("Great Balls of Fire"; "You Win Again"; "Breathless")

1943
LECH WALESA
Polish political reformer and Nobel Peace Prize winner

General Jefferson C. Davis

1864 The inconclusive Battle of New Market Heights opens during the American Civil War with a Union attack against Confederate fortifications around Richmond and Petersburg, Virginia.

1898 French forces in West Africa capture and deport Muslim reformer and military leader Samory Toure, who for nine years had resisted French colonial expansion.

1907 French aviation pioneers Louis and Jacques Breguet make a short, tethered flight in their primitive helicopter, the Gyroplane No. 1, which attained an altitude of about two feet.

1911 Italy declares war on the Ottoman Empire as its invasion of Libya continues.

1913 Rudolf Diesel, the German inventor of the engine that bears his name, leaps to his death from a ship in the English Channel. He was 55.

1915 The first transcontinental radio telephone call is made, from New York City to Honolulu, Hawaii.

1918 A bad day for the German effort in World War I: Its ally Bulgaria drops out of the war, its Turkish allies sue for peace, and British troops break through the Hindenburg Line and take 22,000 prisoners. General Erich von Ludendorff urges his superiors to negotiate an armistice.

1930 Filming begins for the classic American-made horror film *Dracula*, starring Bela Lugosi, who had played the title role on stage beginning in 1927.

1932 American actress Katharine Hepburn, age 24, makes her film debut in *A Bill of Divorcement*.

1938 As the crisis over Czechoslovakia reaches its climax, the prime ministers of Great Britain and France, Neville Chamberlain and Edouard Daladier, meet in Munich, Germany, with the dictators of Germany and Italy, Adolf Hitler and Benito Mussolini.

1938 The British Home Office issues plans for the evacuation of London in the event of war, proposing the evacuation of two million adults and children to the country from the most heavily populated areas of the capital.

1939 Nazi Germany and the Soviet Union officially carve up occupied Poland during World War II, with the fascists taking everything, and everyone, west of the Bug River and the communists taking the east.

1941 During World War II, German soldiers machine-gun thousands of unarmed Jewish men, women, and children as the infamous Babi Yar massacre begins north of Kiev. After two days of slaughter, nearly 34,000 lay dead in a ravine.

1941 In a classic example of Nazi Party double-speak, SS fanatic Reinhart Heydrich is appointed protector of Bohemia and Moravia, in Czechoslovakia.

Two granite slabs honor the victims of Babi Yar in Babi Park in Aurora, Colorado

"Failure is the condiment that gives success its flavor."

—*Truman Capote*

circa 420 According to tradition, St. Jerome, who translated the Bible into Latin, dies on this day in Bethlehem.

1189 Richard the Lion-Heart becomes king of England after driving his own father from power with the help of French king Philip II.

1399 Henry Bolingbroke, duke of Lancaster, is proclaimed King Henry IV of England upon the abdication of Richard II.

1626 Nurachi, one of the founders of China's Manchu dynasty, dies of battle wounds after attempting to invade China from Manchuria.

1777 The American Continental Congress, driven from Philadelphia by the British during the American Revolutionary War, sets up shop in York, turning the southeastern Pennsylvania city into the nation's temporary capital.

1791 Austrian composer Wolfgang Amadeus Mozart's opera *The Magic Flute* debuts in Vienna.

1864 During the American Civil War, Union general Ulysses S. Grant launches the Battle of Poplar Springs Church in an attempt to cut an important rail line and force Confederate troops from their trenches around Petersburg, Virginia. The attack failed.

BORN ON THIS DAY

1788
LORD RAGLAN
English field marshal, commander in chief of British forces during the Crimean War

1832
LORD ROBERTS
English field marshal, commander in chief of British forces during the Boer War

1861
WILLIAM WRIGLEY JR.
American chewing-gum tycoon

1882
HANS GEIGER
German physicist after whom the Geiger counter is named

1917
BUDDY RICH
American jazz musician

1921
DEBORAH KERR
Scottish-born American actress (*The King and I*; *The Night of the Iguana*; *An Affair to Remember*)

1924
TRUMAN CAPOTE
American author (*In Cold Blood*; *A Tree of Night*; *Breakfast at Tiffany's*)

Truman Capote

1934
FREDDIE KING
American blues singer ("Hide Away"; "Stumble"; "I'm Tore Down")

1935
JOHNNY MATHIS
American singer ("The Twelfth of Never"; "Chances Are"; "Wonderful! Wonderful!")

1981
MARTINA HINGIS
Slovakian professional tennis player

Women at the polls in Cheyenne, Wyoming

1868 American author Louisa May Alcott publishes the first volume of her beloved children's novel *Little Women*.

1882 The world's first hydroelectric power plant opens on the Fox River in Appleton, Wisconsin.

1889 Wyoming becomes the first state to grant women the right to vote.

1901 France requires registration for all motor vehicles driving over 18 miles per hour.

1918 Belgian troops drive back the Germans and capture the high ground around Ypres.

1938 Nazi Germany is allowed to have its way with Czechoslovakia as British and French prime ministers Neville Chamberlain and Edouard Daladier sign the Munich Pact with Adolf Hitler. The pact ceded the Sudetenland to Germany and forced the evacuation of Czechs from the region. Chamberlain thought he had averted a major war.

1939 During World War II, Polish leaders ousted

by the German-Soviet invasion of Poland form a government-in-exile in Paris, France. On the same day, the German pocket battleship *Admiral Graf Spee* sinks the British ship SS *Clement*.

1940 Germany begins night bombing raids over England during World War II.

1949 The Berlin Airlift ends after 15 months and more than 250,000 flights that delivered food, clothing, and medical supplies to West Berlin, which lay in the Soviet zone of occupation.

1953 Swiss physicist Auguste Piccard dives to a then-record 10,330 feet in a bathyscaphe off the Italian coast.

1954 The world's first nuclear-powered submarine, the USS *Nautilus*, is commissioned by the U.S. Navy. Representing an enormous technological leap, the sub was much larger than its diesel electric predecessors, boasted a submerged speed of more than 20 knots, and could remain submerged almost indefinitely.

1962 Race riots break out in Oxford, Mississippi, as James H. Meredith, escorted by federal marshals, attempts to enroll as the first African-American student at the University of Mississippi.

1975 In the so-called "Thrillah in Manila," boxer Muhammad Ali beats Joe Frazier to retain his world heavyweight title.

1991 Haitian president Jean-Bertrand Aristide, whose reforms for the nation's poor angered the military and Haiti's elite, is ousted in a coup.

1993 A 6.4-magnitude earthquake strikes the Maharashtra state in India, killing more than 9,700 and flattening a dozen villages.

1994 In Geneva, the World Health Organization announces that polio has been completely eradicated from the western hemisphere.

James Dean on the set of the film Giant (milestone)

366 Damasus I is elected pope in the midst of a bloody struggle for the papacy after the death of Pope Liberius.

959 Edgar, king of the Mercians and Northumbrians, becomes king of all England.

965 John XIII becomes pope but is soon kidnapped by Roman nobles who opposed him.

1536 The Pilgrimage of Grace, an uprising against the Reformation legislation of Henry VIII, begins with riots in the north of England.

1569 English playwright William Shakespeare's father, John, is elected mayor of Stratford-upon-Avon.

1795 Revolutionary France annexes the southern Netherlands and the principality of Liège.

1811 The first steamboat to sail down the Mississippi, the *New Orleans,* arrives in its namesake city after a month-long cruise from Pittsburgh, Pennsylvania.

1814 Spanish royalists in South America defeat Chilean independence fighters in the Battle of Rancagua.

1846 English biologist Charles Darwin begins a four-volume study of barnacles.

1847 Maria Mitchell, America's first woman astronomer, discovers a comet in the vicinity of the North Star.

1856 The first installment of French author Gustave

BORN ON THIS DAY

1207
HENRY III
King of England (1216–72)

1685
CHARLES VI
Holy Roman emperor (1711–40) and patron of learning and the arts

1735
AUGUSTUS HENRY FITZROY, 3RD DUKE OF GRAFTON
British prime minister (1768–70)

1791
SERGEI AKSAKOV
Russian novelist (*Chronicle of a Russian Family*)

1903
VLADIMIR HOROWITZ
Ukrainian-born American virtuoso concert pianist

Vladimir Horowitz

1920
WALTER MATTHAU
American actor (*A Shot in the Dark; The Odd Couple; Grumpy Old Men*)

1924
JIMMY CARTER
39th U.S. president (1977–81), winner of the Nobel Peace Prize (2001)

1924
WILLIAM REHNQUIST
U.S. Supreme Court chief justice

1935
JULIE ANDREWS
English singer and actress (*Mary Poppins; The Sound of Music; Victor/Victoria*)

1945
ROD CAREW
American Hall of Fame baseball player

1963
MARK MCGWIRE
American professional baseball player who set a single-season home run record of 70 in 1998

Flaubert's *Madame Bovary* appears in the *Revue de Paris.* The novel, about a country doctor's wife and her adulterous liaisons, was a popular success but led to an obscenity trial for Flaubert (who was acquitted).

1864 During the American Civil War Confederate spy Rose Greenhow drowns off North Carolina when the British ship she was traveling in is run aground by a Union warship. She passed information that helped the South win the First Battle of Bull Run.

1880 Prolific American martial composer John Philip Sousa is named director of the U.S. Marine Corps Band.

1880 American inventor Thomas Edison opens his first light-bulb factory, in Menlo Park, New Jersey.

1890 Yosemite National Park is established in California, setting aside 1,500 square miles of spectacular alpine terrain in the Sierra Nevada mountains.

1898 Czar Nicholas II bars Jews from living in major Russian cities.

1914 The First Battle of Arras opens during World War I, as French forces try to outflank the Germans in the famous "race for the sea."

> *"We must adjust to changing times and still hold to unchanging principles."*
>
> —*Jimmy Carter*

Joseph Stalin

✈ **1916** German zeppelins raid the east coast of England during World War I, but the British down one airship.

✈ **1917** World War I Allied troops repulse five major German attacks on the Western Front.

✈ **1918** During World War I, a combined British and Arab force captures Damascus from the Turks, thus completing the liberation of Arabia. Among the commanders is T. E. Lawrence, the legendary British soldier known as Lawrence of Arabia.

▬ **1928** Soviet dictator Joseph Stalin announces the First Five Year Plan, a catastrophe for peasants that would collectivize agriculture and industrialize the Soviet economy.

1936 During the Spanish Civil War, fascist Francisco Franco is named head of state and establishes a Nationalist government in Burgos.

1940 America's first toll superhighway, the Pennsylvania Turnpike, opens to traffic, cutting travel time between Pittsburgh and Harrisburg by three hours.

1944 Nazi German "scientists" begin castrating homosexuals at the Buchenwald concentration camp as part of a medical experiment during World War II.

⚖ **1946** A dozen high-ranking Nazis are sentenced to death in Nuremberg by the International War Crimes Tribunal after World War II. They include Joachim von Ribbentrop, minister of foreign affairs; Hermann Goering, founder of the Gestapo and chief of the German Air Force; and Wilhelm Frick, minister of the interior.

1949 A half million American steelworkers go on strike for improved retirement benefits.

1995 A magnitude-6.0 earthquake rocks western Turkey, killing at least 84. Meanwhile, in the Philippines, a devastating tropical storm kills more than 100 in floods, landslides, and volcanic mudflows.

1998 Europol, Europe's cross-border police force, officially begins operations.

Earthquake wreckage in Dinar, Turkey

OCTOBER 2

☙ **479 B.C.** A total eclipse of the sun encourages Persian king Xerxes to invade Greece when it is interpreted as a sign of Athens's impending doom.

🏴 **1066** English king Harold II learns of the landing in Sussex of William, duke of Normandy, and hurries south from the Battle of Stamford Bridge with his already-exhausted army.

☙ **1187** Saladin, the great Muslim leader, recaptures Jerusalem, allows wealthy Christians to buy their freedom, and sells many of the rest into slavery.

🔬 **1608** Dutch spectacle-maker Hans Lippershey offers to sell his new invention to the military: the world's first telescope.

▬ **1656** In Holland, Amsterdam authorities raid a Yom Kippur service in the mistaken belief that the gathering is a secret meeting of Catholic papists. When they learned that the community was Jewish, they released the leaders and allowed them to worship in peace.

⚖ **1780** American revolutionaries hang British major

BORN ON THIS DAY

1452
RICHARD III
King of England (1483–85)

1800
NAT TURNER
African-American slave who led a major slave rebellion

1851
FERDINAND FOCH
French marshal who became Allied commander in chief toward the end of World War I

1852
SIR WILLIAM RAMSAY
Scottish chemist, first British winner of the Nobel Prize in chemistry

1869
MAHATMA (MOHANDAS K.) GANDHI
Indian political and spiritual leader whose nonviolent efforts led to Great Britain's granting independence to India

1890
GROUCHO MARX
American comedian and actor, one of the Marx Brothers (*Duck Soup; A Night at the Opera; Room Service*)

1891
H. V. PORTER
American basketball pioneer who created the fan-shaped backboard

1904
GRAHAM GREENE
English novelist (*Stamboul Train; Brighton Rock; The Third Man; Our Man in Havana*)

"Truth never damages a cause that is just."
—*Mahatma (Mohandas K.) Gandhi*

John Andre as a spy in Tappan, New York. Andre had been carrying papers showing that U.S. general Benedict Arnold had offered to surrender West Point for a bribe of 20,000 pounds.

☙ **1835** The Texas Revolution against Mexico begins as Texans in Gonzales drive off a Mexican army unit that had attempted to disarm the town's citizens.

🔬 **1836** English naturalist Charles Darwin returns to England after his five-year scientific voyage aboard the *Beagle* in the south Atlantic and Pacific oceans.

☙ **1864** As the American Civil War enters its final phase, a large Union cavalry column tries to seize the Confederacy's main supply of salt, used as a preservative for army rations. Though vastly outnumbered, the Confederates beat off the Union attack to win the Battle of Saltville. They also massacred wounded African-American Union soldiers.

▮◆ **1865** Mexican emperor Maximilian, a French puppet, orders that any captured republican guerrilla be court-martialed and shot within 24 hours.

🔬 **1866** Inventor J. Osterhoudt of New York City patents the first tin can with a key opener.

☙ **1914** During the early months of World War I, Belgian

The capture of John Andre

Nazi German troops on their drive to Moscow

forces retreat across the Nethe River from Antwerp as German artillery pounds the city.

1915 Bulgaria agrees to enter World War I on the side of Germany and the Central Powers.

1917 The British armored cruiser HMS *Drake* is torpedoed off the north Irish coast, but her captain manages to beach her and save all but 19 of her crew.

1918 German troops withdraw along a wide front as the Allies continue their last offensive of World War I.

1919 U.S. president Woodrow Wilson suffers a massive stroke, which would incapacitate him for the remainder of his term.

1923 Turkish nationalists occupy Istanbul.

1935 As Italian troops pour across the Ethiopian border, Emperor Haile Selassie abandons hope in the collective security allegedly offered through the League of Nations and orders his army to mobilize.

1941 On the verge of the Russian winter during World War II, Nazi Germany launches an intense attack, Operation Typhoon, with Moscow as the goal. Though the invading German armies advanced quickly over a broad front, the Russians employed a scorched-earth policy, leaving behind nothing of value to support Adolf Hitler's troops.

1944 During World War II, the Warsaw Uprising ends as surviving Poles surrender to the Germans after 63 days of intense street fighting. The Poles, who supported the Polish government-in-exile in London, England, had hoped to free Warsaw before the Soviet army occupied it.

1958 In Africa, Guinea declares independence from France and establishes a left-leaning government that would play both sides of the fence during the Cold War.

1995 In the second of five controversial weapons tests, France detonates a nuclear device at Mururoa atoll in the South Pacific. The test prompted 16 South Pacific nations to suspend official links with Paris.

Thurgood Marshall

701 John VI is consecrated pope. He ruled for less than four years.

1210 John of Brienne, a penniless count who managed to wed Mary, queen of the crusader state of Jerusalem, is crowned king of Jerusalem.

1247 William of Holland becomes king of Germany with papal support in opposition to rival King Conrad IV.

1519 Portuguese explorer Ferdinand Magellan sets sail from Tenerife for Brazil.

1605 Officials of the decaying Ming dynasty could not have known that a child born on this day in Shensi Province, Li Zicheng, would overthrow the last Ming emperor in 1644.

1691 The Treaty of Limerick is signed, marking the completion of England's conquest of Ireland.

MILESTONE

Britain Tests A-Bomb

Great Britain successfully tests its first atomic bomb at the Monte Bello Islands off the coast of Australia on this day in 1952. During World War II, 50 British scientists and engineers worked on the successful U.S. atomic bomb program in New Mexico. After the war, many of these scientists were enlisted into the secret effort to build an atomic bomb for Great Britain. In February 1952, Prime Minister Winston Churchill publicly announced plans to test a British nuclear weapon. A 25-kiloton device was successfully detonated in the hull of the frigate HMS *Plym* anchored off the Monte Bello Islands. The test made Great Britain the world's third atomic power.

> *"Life has got a habit of not standing hitched. You got to ride it like you find it."*
> —*Woody Guthrie*

1776 Needing money to fuel the American Revolution, the U.S. Congress approves the nation's first loan, borrowing $5 million at 4 percent interest and giving colonial officials in Paris, France, authority to borrow an additional two million pounds.

1799 Near London, England, live-in housekeeper Sarah Lloyd lets her boyfriend burglarize her employer's home. For this, the 22-year-old was sentenced to death and executed.

1862 In the American Civil War, Confederate forces suffer a major defeat at Corinth, a vital rail center in northern Mississippi. The devastating loss allowed the Union to focus on

The Battle of Corinth

capturing Vicksburg, the last Rebel stronghold on the Mississippi River.

1866 After the Seven Weeks' War between Prussia and Austria, the Peace of Vienna treaty forces Austria to cede Venetia to Italy.

1873 The U.S. military hangs four Modoc Indians found guilty of murdering a Civil War hero, General Edward Canby, during the Modoc War in Oregon. Canby was the highest-ranking military official—and the only general—ever killed by Native Americans.

1899 American inventor John Thurman patents a gasoline-powered vacuum cleaner, a large machine mounted on a horse-drawn wagon. One housecleaning cost four dollars.

1922 The first facsimile photo transmission by phone line is made in Washington, D.C. The image came out not on curly thermal paper, but on a photographic plate.

1932 With Iraq's entry into the League of Nations, Great Britain ends its mandate over the Arab nation, making Iraq independent after 17 years of British rule and centuries of Ottoman rule.

1932 In London, England, *The Times* adopts a new typeface designed by typographer Stanley Morrison, called Times New Roman.

1941 *The Maltese Falcon* premieres, starring Humphrey Bogart as hard-boiled detective

O. J. Simpson reacts to not-guilty verdict

Sam Spade. It was the first time an American actor's name appeared above the title of a movie on a film credit.

1967 America loses a great champion of the downtrodden with the death of folk singer and songwriter Woody Guthrie.

1968 A military junta headed by Juan Velasco Alvarado takes control of Peru.

1981 A hunger strike by Irish nationalists at the Maze Prison in Belfast, Northern Ireland, is called off after seven months and 10 deaths. The first to die was Irish Republican Army leader Bobby Sands.

1990 Less than one year after the destruction of the Berlin Wall, East and West Germany come together as one nation on what became known as Unity Day.

1995 At the end of a sensational trial, former American football star O. J. Simpson is acquitted of the brutal 1994 double murder of his estranged wife, Nicole Brown Simpson, and her friend Ronald Goldman.

OCTOBER 4

> *"An intellectual is a man who takes more words than necessary to tell more than he knows."*
>
> —*Dwight D. Eisenhower*

23 Peasant rebels burst through the gates of the Chinese Hsin imperial capital, Chang-an. Two days later, the emperor Wang Mang was killed in his palace.

578 Tiberius II Constantinus becomes sole ruler of Byzantium upon the death of his adoptive father and sponsor, the former emperor Justin II.

1190 English king Richard the Lion-Heart, on his way to join the Third Crusade, stops in Sicily, storms Messina, and frees his sister Joan.

1535 The first printed English Bible, an inexpert translation by bishop of Exeter Miles Coverdale, is published.

1582 Pope Gregory XIII proclaims the New Style or Gregorian calendar, which goes into effect with a 10-day adjustment. The day after October 4 was reckoned October 15, but it took centuries for most of the world to recognize the change.

1636 At the Battle of Wittstock during a critical time in the Thirty Years' War, Swedish general Johán Banér makes a brilliant flanking move and defeats the imperial Saxon army.

1777 In the American Revolutionary War, Patriot troops attempt unsuccessfully to

BORN ON THIS DAY

1289
LOUIS X (THE STUBBORN)
King of France (1314–16) who sold the serfs their liberty

1626
RICHARD CROMWELL
Lord protector of England (1658–59), son of Oliver Cromwell

1814
JEAN FRANCOIS MILLET
French painter

1822
RUTHERFORD B. HAYES
19th U.S. president (1877–81)

1860
SIDNEY PAGET
English artist who illustrated the original Sherlock Holmes stories

1861
FREDERIC REMINGTON
American artist (*The Snow Trail; The Last March; The Apaches Are Coming*)

1880
DAMON RUNYON
American author (*Guys and Dolls; Blue Plate Special; Money from Home*)

1895
BUSTER KEATON
American actor (*The Navigator; The General; Sunset Boulevard*)

Buster Keaton

1924
CHARLTON HESTON
American actor (*Ben-Hur; The Ten Commandments; Planet of the Apes*)

1928
ALVIN TOFFLER
American futurist and author (*Future Shock; War and Anti-War; Powershift*)

1931
DICK TRACY
American comic-strip police detective

break through the defenses around British-occupied Philadelphia, Pennsylvania. Both sides suffered heavy losses, but the battle demonstrated General George Washington's ability as a leader and helped convince France to support the revolution.

1830 American inventor Isaac Adams wins a patent for the first motorized book-printing press.

1853 At the outset of the Crimean War, the Turks declare war on Russia.

1859 Voters in what would become the state of Kansas approve the Wyandotte Constitution, leading to Kansas's admission to the Union in 1861 as a free state.

1876 Swiss missionary and African explorer Johannes Rebmann—the first European to see Mount Kilimanjaro, and much ridiculed by ignorant geographers for his claim that snow lay on its summit—dies in Germany.

1897 Boxer George Dixon, the first African American to hold a world championship, loses his featherweight title to Solly Smith after 20 rounds. He regained it a year later.

1910 In Portugal, rebels under Antonio Machado Santos launch a republican revolution. The 20-year-old king Manuel II escaped aboard his yacht to exile in England.

1918 Ferdinand I, king of Bulgaria, abdicates in favor of his son, Boris III.

Boris III

1943 Heinrich Himmler, head of the Nazi German SS, praises his troops for having murdered more than one million Russian Jews during World War II. To have piled up thousands of corpses, he said, "and at the same time . . . to have remained decent fellows, that is what has made us hard. This is a page of glory in our history."

1944 U.S. general Dwight D. Eisenhower warns his World War II commanders to guard their men against "shell shock," the debilitating psychological toll of battle.

1957 The Soviet Union launches *Sputnik*, the world's first artificial satellite. With a diameter of 22 inches and weighing 183 pounds, it was visible at night with binoculars. Americans reacted with dismay that the Soviets accomplished this before the supposedly superior United States space program.

1958 The British Overseas Airways Corporation (BOAC) inaugurates the first scheduled transatlantic passenger-jet service.

1958 France adopts a new constitution.

1959 The Soviet Union launches *Luna 3*. The first space probe to circle the moon, it sent back pictures of its previously unseen far side.

1966 Addressing 150,000 people in St. Peter's Square, Pope Paul VI calls for a negotiated end to the war in Vietnam. His comments were symbolic of growing sentiment against the war.

1970 American singer Janis Joplin dies from a heroin overdose at the Landmark Hotel in Hollywood, California.

1983 Scottish driver Richard Noble sets a new land-speed record in his jet-powered *Thrust 2*, a 17,000-pound vehicle that reached 633.468 miles per hour in Nevada's Black Rock Desert.

1988 American televangelist Jim Bakker is indicted on federal charges of mail and wire fraud and of conspiring to defraud the public. The case exploded in the press when it was revealed that moralist Bakker had sex with a former church secretary and paid her $350,000 to keep silent.

1992 A Boeing 747 jumbo jet operated by El Al as a cargo plane crashes into two nine-story blocks of apartment buildings in Amsterdam shortly after taking off from Schipol Airport bound for New York.

Pope Paul VI (milestone)

OCTOBER 5

23 In China, peasant armies rebelling against Emperor Wang Mang overrun the imperial palace in Beijing and set it on fire.

1789 In the early months of the French Revolution, Parisians march on the palace at Versailles to force Louis XVI to accept the Declaration of the Rights of Man.

1793 Revolutionary France abandons the Gregorian calendar in favor of one free of any ecclesiastical connections.

1795 During the White Terror in revolutionary France, royalists attempting to seize power in Paris are crushed by the young Napoleon Bonaparte.

1813 In the War of 1812, American troops decisively defeat a combined British and Indian force at the Battle of Thames, in Ontario, Canada, to win the old Northwest. Among the dead is Shawnee chief Tecumseh, who had fought against the Americans during the revolution and had organized intertribal resistance to white settlement.

Death of Tecumseh at the Battle of Thames

"If you want others to be happy, practice compassion. If you want to be happy, practice compassion."

—the Dalai Lama

1831 An unsuccessful Polish revolt against Russian rule, known as the November Insurrection, ends with the Polish Army's surrender in Prussia.

1864 After Atlanta falls to the Union during the American Civil War, Confederate general John Bell Hood attacks Union general William T. Sherman's supply lines at Allatoona Pass, in Georgia. The attack is repulsed, with the loss of 897 Rebels and 706 Yankees.

1871 American Fenian leader John O'Neill launches an armed raid on Manitoba from the United States. It was his third such bid to capture Canada for the secretive Irish nationalist faction, which intended to hold Canada until Great Britain freed Ireland.

1877 Nez Perce tribal leader Chief Joseph and his people surrender to U.S. general Nelson Miles in the Bear Paw mountains of Montana after their epic, fighting retreat across the American West.

1892 Most of the notorious Dalton Gang are shot to death by townspeople when the outlaw band of brothers attempts to rob two banks in their old hometown of Coffeyville, Kansas.

Laura Ingalls

🔫 **1915** Allied troops land in Salonika, Macedonia, during World War I, to oppose the Bulgarians.

🔫 **1918** During World War I, British troops break through on the Western Front and pursue swiftly withdrawing German forces.

🏆 **1919** Enzo Ferrari, 21, makes his auto-racing debut in an Italian hill climb. Twenty-one years later, he would found his own car-making company.

🔬 **1919** The first radio conversation between a ship and a submerged submarine takes place between American vessels in the Hudson River.

🔬 **1923** The first Cepheid variable star is identified by American astronomer Edwin Hubble.

🇺🇸 **1930** American pilot Laura Ingalls becomes the first woman to fly across North America, from New York to Glendale, California, in 30 hours, 27 minutes.

▐ ▐ **1930** R101, at the time the world's largest dirigible, crashes in France. The dead included Lord Thompson,

British secretary of state for air, and Major-General Sir Sefton Brancker, British director of civil aviation.

🔫 **1942** Soviet premier Joseph Stalin orders Red Army forces to liberate and hold all of Stalingrad, a vital rail and water hub on the Volga River during World War II.

🎭 **1950** American comedian Groucho Marx's game show *You Bet Your Life* makes its television debut.

🎭 **1961** The film version of American author Truman Capote's novel *Breakfast at Tiffany's* opens in New York, starring Audrey Hepburn as Holly Golightly, an elusive, whimsical city girl with a dark secret.

🇺🇸 **1969** In an embarrassing breach of U.S. air-defense capability, a Cuban defector flies undetected into U.S. airspace and lands his MiG-17 at Homestead Air Force Base near Miami, Florida. President Richard M. Nixon's jet, *Air Force One*, was parked nearby.

Norwegian diplomat Kjeld Vibe, left, and the Dalai Lama at Nobel Peace Prize ceremony (milestone)

105 B.C. At the Battle of Arausio in what is now southern France, Teutoni and Cimbri invaders hand the Roman army a crushing defeat.

69 B.C. Armenian king Tigranes II the Great, who built a considerable empire in some 20 years, is beaten by invading Roman armies under Lucullus. Though his empire was quickly swallowed by Rome, he stayed on as a client ruler.

23 Wang Mang, the only emperor of China's short-lived Hsin dynasty, is killed by peasant rebels.

891 Formosus is elected pope. He is best remembered for his posthumous trial, conducted by his successor, in which his exhumed body was set upon a throne and it was decided that he was not a pope after all.

1683 Encouraged by William Penn's offer of 5,000 acres of land in the colony of Pennsylvania and the freedom to practice their religion, the first Mennonites arrive from Germany aboard the *Concord*.

1781 During the American Revolutionary War, French and Continental troops dig trenches to begin the siege of Yorktown, Virginia—essentially the last battle of the revolution. On October 19, British general Cornwallis surrendered.

1783 Benjamin Hanks patents the self-winding clock.

1789 Marquis de Lafayette, who helped Americans in their revolutionary war and

---

1809
ALFRED, LORD TENNYSON
English poet ("Ulysses"; "In Memoriam"; "The Charge of the Light Brigade")

1820
JENNY LIND
Swedish soprano

1824
HENRY CHADWICK
English-born American baseball pioneer

1846
GEORGE WESTINGHOUSE
American inventor who founded Westinghouse Electric Company

George Westinghouse

1882
KAROL SZYMANOWSKI
Ukrainian-born Polish opera and orchestral composer (*Lottery for Men; Mandragora; Love Songs for Hafiz*)

1887
CHARLES ÉDUOARD JEANNERET
Swiss-born French architect known as Le Corbusier

1888
LI TA-CHAO
Co-founder of the Chinese Communist Party

1908
CAROLE LOMBARD
American actress (*Man of the World; My Man Godfrey; The White Ball*)

1914
THOR HEYERDAHL
Norwegian ethnologist, explorer, and author (*Kon Tiki*)

1930
HAFEZ AL ASSAD
President of Syria

"A ruffled mind makes a restless pillow."
—*Charlotte Brontë*

now serves as commander of the revolutionary national guard in Paris, rescues Louis XVI and Marie Antoinette from an angry mob storming the palace at Versailles. Lafayette took them to Paris as prisoners of the French Revolution.

1790 German Jacob Schweppe demonstrates how to make artificial mineral water.

1847 *Jane Eyre* is published under the pseudonym Currer Bell, who was actually English author Charlotte Brontë.

1848 Revolution erupts in Vienna, Austria, together with a rash of revolts breaking out across Italy.

1863 Confederate guerrilla leader William Clarke Quantrill, on a bloody rampage through Kansas during the American Civil War, fails to capture the stronghold of Baxter Springs, but massacres a Union detachment that happened to be traveling nearby.

1895 Sir Henry Wood begins the "Proms," an immensely popular annual concert series at Queens Hall in London, England. The promenade concerts continue to this day and are now held at the Royal Albert Hall.

1911 The first transpacific radio conversation takes place between Japan and California.

Tokyo Rose

1942 American inventor Chester Floyd Carlson obtains a patent on the xerography process for making electrostatic copies.

1945 Former French premier and Vichy collaborator Pierre Laval attempts suicide on the day he is to be executed for treason.

1945 Higashikuni Naruhiko, imperial prince of Japan, ends his brief stint as the first post-World War II prime minister, a job he took for its symbolic, healing value.

1945 French general Jacques Leclerc lands in Saigon to retake Vietnam for France. A month earlier, having defeated Japanese occupying forces with help from the United States, Ho Chi Minh had triumphantly—and prematurely—declared Vietnamese independence.

1949 Iva Toguri D'Aquino, a.k.a. Tokyo Rose, is sentenced to 10 years in prison for treason. Her broadcasts from Japan during World War II were intended to demoralize Allied troops. Later, mitigating evidence led to a pardon by U.S. president Gerald R. Ford.

1973 Hoping to win back territory lost during the third Arab-Israeli war, Egypt and Syria launch a coordinated attack against Israel on Yom Kippur, the holiest day in the Jewish calendar.

1978 Iraqi president Saddam Hussein orders exiled Iranian cleric Ruhollah Khomeini to leave Iraq. Khomeini moved to France until the Iranian revolution forced the shah of Iran into exile, and then made a triumphant return to Iran in February 1979.

1981 On the eighth anniversary of the Yom Kippur War, Islamic extremists assassinate Egyptian president Anwar el-Sādāt as he reviews troops. Ten others also died in the attack.

2000 In the face of massive public anger, Serbian president Slobodan Milosevic, having lost an election he tried not to recognize, reluctantly capitulates.

Egyptian gunman attacking Anwar el-Sādāt's reviewing stand

"It is well that war is so terrible, or we should grow too fond of it."

—*Robert E. Lee*

✡ **3761 B.C.** According to Jewish tradition, God created the world on this date, day one of *anno mundi*, or "year of the world."

1072 Having attacked and beaten his two brothers, who held León and Galicia, Sancho II dies in his attempt to take the fortress of Zamora from his sister.

1492 At the suggestion of Martín Pinzón, commander of the *Pinta*, Italian-born explorer Christopher Columbus changes his course. Five days later, he made landfall in the Bahamas.

1571 Christian and Ottoman naval forces clash at the Battle of Lepanto, and in four hours of fighting the Turkish fleet is defeated. At issue was Venetian control of Cyprus.

● **1684** Japanese statesman Hotta Masatoshi, chief councilor to the shogun Tsunayoshi, is assassinated by a jealous cousin.

1708 Gobind Singh, last of the Sikh gurus and creator of the Sikh military brotherhood, is assassinated by a Pashtun tribesman in Maharashtra, India.

1727 Jeanne-Agnes Berthelot de Pleneuf, Marquise de Prie, commits suicide rather than live on in exile. As mistress of the duke of Bourbon, she had been a de facto ruler of France.

BORN ON THIS DAY

1573
WILLIAM LAUD
English prelate, archbishop of Canterbury (1633–45)

1849
JAMES WHITCOMB RILEY
American poet (*Little Orphan Annie; The Runaway Boy*)

1885
NIELS BOHR
Danish Nobel Prize-winning physicist

1888
HENRY WALLACE
33rd vice president of the United States (1941–45)

1900
HEINRICH HIMMLER
German Gestapo chief

1927
R. D. LAING
Scottish psychiatrist (*The Divided Self*)

1931
DESMOND TUTU
South African clergyman and civil rights leader who won the Nobel Peace Prize

1935
THOMAS KENEALLY
American author (*Schindler's Ark*)

1943
OLIVER NORTH
American Marine Corps lieutenant colonel who was at the center of the Iran-Contra Affair

1951
JOHN COUGAR MELLENCAMP
American singer/songwriter ("Hurts So Good"; "Lonely Ol' Night"; "Small Town")

1952
JACQUES RICHARD
Canadian professional hockey player

1952
VLADIMIR PUTIN
Former Soviet spy and Russian prime minister

1955
YO-YO MA
French-born American cello virtuoso ("Hush"; "Appalachia Waltz"; "The Silk Road Journeys: When Strangers Meet")

MISS CAVELL
FUSILLÉE PAR LES ALLEMANDS À BRUXELLES le 12 OCTOBRE 1915

K. B. Cº PARIS   DÉPOSÉ

French poster mourning Edith Cavell

1735 As the Ching dynasty emperor lies dying, Hung-li (later known as Qian-long) is proclaimed heir apparent. One of China's most powerful emperors, he reigned for 61 years.

1780 During the American Revolutionary War, Patrick Ferguson, leader of Tory forces in the Battle of Kings Mountain, dies while leading a suicide charge against what he called a "band of banditti."

1816 The first double-decked river steamboat, the *Washington*, arrives in New Orleans, Louisiana. It offered passenger and cargo service between New Orleans and Louisville, Kentucky, steaming upstream at the then dizzying speed of 16 miles per hour and downstream at as much as 25 miles per hour.

1864 During the American Civil War, Union troops repulse General Robert E. Lee's assault along Darbytown Road in Virginia.

Lee was trying to roll back Union gains around the besieged Confederate capital, Richmond.

1864 During the American Civil War, the Union warship *Wachusett* captures the famed Confederate raider *Florida* while the Rebel ship is in port at Bahia, Brazil, and sails it out to sea. When Brazil protested the violation of its neutrality, the Union gave the ship back, but it sank soon after.

1879 During the Afghan War of 1879, invading British forces under General Frederick Sleigh Roberts advance on Kabul, having defeated Afghan defenders at Charasia.

1905 During the Russian Revolution of 1905, a railroad strike begins. It grew into a general strike in cities across the country.

1908 Austria annexes Bosnia and Herzegovina, setting off a Balkan crisis.

1913 Henry Ford's American automobile factory begins to run on a moving assembly line, with subassemblies such as magnetos, engines, and transmissions. A system for assembling the entire car was soon to follow.

1915 English nurse Edith Cavell goes on trial in Brussels, Belgium, for secretly helping some 200 Allied soldiers escape German-occupied Belgium. She confessed, was convicted, and was shot three days later.

1919 The Dutch airline KLM is founded.

1922 The first program to be broadcast by a network of radio stations airs the 1922 World Series to the region around New York City.

1940 Nazi German dictator Adolf Hitler occupies Romania as part of his World War II strategy to build an unbroken eastern front against the Soviet Union.

1943 During World War II, American forces capture New Georgia in the Solomon Islands.

1944 In Washington, D.C., representatives from Great Britain, China, the Soviet Union, and the United States wrap up the Dumbarton Oaks Conference, during which they laid plans for the United Nations.

1985 Four Palestinian terrorists from the Popular Front for the Liberation of Palestine board and hijack the Italian cruise ship *Achille Lauro* in the Mediterranean. Their killing of a 69-year-old wheelchair-bound American, Leon Klinghoffer, triggered worldwide outrage.

MILESTONE

East Germany Created
On this day in 1949, less than five months after Great Britain, the United States, and France established the Federal Republic of Germany in West Germany, the Democratic Republic of Germany (East Germany) is proclaimed within the Soviet occupation zone. Wilhelm Pieck was named East Germany's first president, with Otto Grotewohl as prime minister. Approximately half the size of West Germany, East Germany consisted of five German states. Berlin, the former German capital, remained divided between West and East German authorities. The West was critical of this division and of East Germany's lack of autonomy, and the two nations were reunited in 1990.

Youssef Magied al-Molqi, the Palestinian terrorist convicted of killing American Leon Klinghoffer

1515 Spanish explorer Juan Diaz de Solis sails for South America in three ships from Sanlucar de Barrameda.

1741 Russian explorer Aleksei Ilich Chirikov returns to Kamchatka with the tattered remnants of his crew after a voyage to southern Alaska. He was second in command to Vitus Bering, who died on the trip.

1777 In a pivotal moment of the American Revolutionary War, 20,000 American troops under General Horatio Gates surround British general John Burgoyne's army of 5,000 at Saratoga, New York.

1823 About 40,000 people attend ceremonies in Albany, New York, to open the Erie Canal to boat traffic.

1862 During the American Civil War, the Confederate invasion of Kentucky is turned back with heavy losses for both sides at the Battle of Perryville.

1871 The Great Chicago Fire begins as a cow reportedly kicks over a lantern in a barn. Wind-driven flames killed 250 people during the next two days, destroyed the homes of 90,000, and ravaged the city's thriving downtown.

1879 Chilean naval forces sink the Peruvian warship *Huascar*, thus permitting the Chilean Army to land on the Peruvian coast and sack Lima.

1895 American recording pioneer Emil Berliner founds the Berliner Gramophone Company to produce gramophones and

1869
J. FRANK DURYEA
American inventor of the first automobile built and operated in the United States

1873
EJNAR HERTZSPRUNG
Danish astronomer

1890
EDDIE RICKENBACKER
American aviator in World War I

1895
JUAN PERÓN
President of Argentina (1946–55 and 1973–74)

1929
DAME BETTY BOOTHROYD
English politician, first female Speaker of the House of Commons

1941
REVEREND JESSE JACKSON
American civil rights leader

1943
CHEVY CHASE
American comedian and actor (*Saturday Night Live; Fletch; National Lampoon's Vacation*)

1948
JOHNNY RAMONE
American rock musician (The Ramones)

1949
SIGOURNEY WEAVER
American actress (*Alien; Gorillas in the Mist; The Ice Storm*)

The Great Chicago Fire

"If one is forever cautious, can one remain a human being?"
—Aleksandr Solzhenitsyn

flat gramophone records of his own invention.

1904 Frenchman George Heath wins the first major international auto-racing event in the United States, the Vanderbilt Cup, held in Hicksville, New York. Heath's average speed: 52.2 miles per hour.

1906 The first permanent wave, or "perm," is demonstrated by German hairdresser Karl Ludwig Nessler (later known as Charles Nestlé), in his salon at 245 Oxford Street, London, England. The procedure took five hours and required the supplicant to wear a dozen brass curlers, each weighing nearly two pounds.

1912 Montenegro touches off the First Balkan War by declaring war on Turkey.

1918 During the final Allied offensive of World War I, U.S. Army corporal Alvin C.

Hurricane Pauline damage in Acapulco, Mexico

Che Guevara Captured
A Bolivian guerrilla force led by Marxist revolutionary Che Guevara is defeated in a skirmish with a special detachment of the Bolivian army on this day in 1967. Guevara was wounded, captured, and executed the next day. He played a pivotal role in the Cuban Revolution of 1956–59 and encouraged Fidel Castro to pursue his communist, anti-American agenda. After holding several positions in Castro's government, he disappeared from Cuba in 1965 and resurfaced the next year in Bolivia as leader of another guerrilla group. Since his death, Guevara has been idolized as a hero of leftist Third World revolutions.

Ernesto "Che" Guevara

York kills 25 Germans in France's Argonne Forest, captures 132, and saves his small unit from annihilation by a German machine-gun nest.

1918 In reply to German peace overtures, the United States demands total German withdrawal from all Allied territory.

1919 The first round-trip transcontinental air race across North America begins with 63 competitors taking to the sky from airfields in New York and California.

1970 Russian author Aleksandr Solzhenitsyn, a leading critic of Soviet domestic oppression, wins the Nobel Prize in literature.

1972 Rumors arise of a breakthrough at the secret Paris peace talks between the United States and North Vietnam as the Vietnamese offer a plan calling for a cease-fire.

1990 Israeli police kill 17 Palestinians and wound more than 100 on Jerusalem's Temple Mount, a sacred site for both Jews and Muslims.

1993 The United Nations lifts economic sanctions against post-apartheid South Africa, paving the way for its normalizing of relations with the rest of the world.

1997 Hurricane Pauline rips through Acapulco, Mexico, and devastates communities throughout Oaxaca and Guerrero with winds up to 185 miles per hour and 30-foot waves. More than 200 were killed and 20,000 rendered homeless.

1998 The U.S. House of Representatives votes 258–176 to conduct impeachment hearings against President Bill Clinton for perjury, obstruction of justice, witness tampering, and abuse of power in connection with an extramarital affair.

2000 A month-long world chess championship match opens in London, England, between Vladimir Kramnik and Gary Kasparov. Kramnik eventually won with two victories, 13 draws, and no losses.

> *"Power is when we have every justification to kill, and we don't."*
> —Oskar Schindler

1308 Italian painter Duccio di Buoninsegna begins painting the second version of his masterwork, the *Maestà*, a double-sided altarpiece for the cathedral of Siena.

1514 At the insistence of her brother, Henry VIII of England, 20-year-old Mary Tudor weds the dying 52-year-old king Louis XII of France.

1562 During the Wars of Religion in France, Catholic leader Seigneur de Monluc defeats the Huguenots at Vergt.

1601 Christian forces battle the Turks under Sultan Mehmed III at Stuhlweissenburg, Hungary. The battle lasted five days and ended in Turkish defeat.

1635 Religious dissident Roger Williams is banished from the Massachusetts Bay Colony by the General Court of Massachusetts. Williams had spoken out against the right of civil authorities to punish religious dissension and to confiscate Indian land.

1772 Christian Jacobsen Drakenberg dies in Scandinavia at the reported age of 145 years and 325 days. If true, he had the longest recorded life span.

1779 During the American Revolutionary War, Polish volunteer General Casimir Pulaski is wounded in fighting at Savannah, Georgia. He died two

days later, and is remembered as a revolutionary hero.

1818 Great Britain, Austria, Russia, Prussia, and France sign a treaty at Aix-la-Chapelle intended to tackle the mess left in the wake of the Napoleonic Wars.

1831 Count I. A. Kapodístrias, president of Greece, is assassinated.

1864 George "Little Bighorn" Custer participates in the humiliating defeat of Confederate cavalry by Union cavalry at Tom's Brook, Virginia. It was the most complete Union cavalry victory in the eastern theater of the American Civil War.

1871 The Great Chicago Fire, which burned four square miles of the city including the business district and left 90,000 out of a population of 500,000 homeless, is brought under control with the help of a rainstorm.

1876 Scottish-born American inventor Alexander Graham Bell calls his assistant Thomas Watson, who was about two miles away, in the first

General Casimir Pulaski

BORN ON THIS DAY

1757
CHARLES X
Reactionary king of France (1824–30) who was ultimately deposed

1835
CAMILLE SAINT-SAËNS
French composer

1859
ALFRED DREYFUS
French artillery officer falsely accused of treason

1890
AIMEE SEMPLE MCPHERSON
American pentecostal evangelist and radio preacher

1899
BRUCE CATTON
American historian and author (*A Stillness at Appomattox; Mr. Lincoln's Army; The Army of the Potomac*)

1900
ALASTAIR SIM
Scottish actor (*The Belles of St. Trinian's; School for Scoundrels; A Christmas Carol*)

1903
WALTER O'MALLEY
American baseball team owner (Brooklyn/Los Angeles Dodgers)

1908
JACQUES TATI
French film director and comedic actor

1909
LORD COGGAN
English prelate, 101st Archbishop of Canterbury (1974–80)

1940
JOHN LENNON
English singer/songwriter who was a member of The Beatles

1944
PETER TOSH
Jamaican reggae musician ("Where You Gonna Run"; "Fools Die"; "Burial")

1975
SEAN ONO LENNON
American musician ("Into the Sun"; "Spaceship"), son of John Lennon and Yoko Ono

phone call using outdoor wires. As proof to skeptics that the conversation had taken place, the *Boston Advertiser* published Bell's and Graham's separate accounts of the conversation.

1890 French aviation pioneer Clément Ader takes off in a steam-powered airplane and flies approximately 160 feet, in the world's first powered "hop" from level ground in a heavier-than-air machine, but he is unable to achieve sustained controlled flight.

1894 The first magic lantern feature presentation, a precursor to cinema using slides and imitated motion, is shown in New York City. The show, *Miss Jerry*, featured a plot, characters, and titles.

1899 Boer leader Paul Kruger ignites war in South Africa by demanding that British troops withdraw from the border of the Transvaal.

1934 Alexander I, king of Yugoslavia, is assassinated by Croatian terrorists during a visit to France.

1936 Hoover Dam, tallest in the world at the time, begins sending electricity over transmission lines spanning 266 miles of mountains and deserts to run the lights, radios, and stoves of Los Angeles, California.

1962 Uganda gains independence, with Milton Obote as its first president.

1967 Ernesto Guevara de la Serna, better known as "Che" Guevara, is executed by Bolivian armed forces. The

Oskar Schindler

Argentine-born Guevara rose to fame as a comrade of Fidel Castro during the Cuban revolution, and was trying to carry the revolution to Bolivia.

1974 German businessman Oskar Schindler, credited with saving 1,200 Jews from the Holocaust and subject of the film *Schindler's List*, dies at the age of 66. He was buried at a Catholic cemetery in Israel.

1992 A 30-pound meteorite slams into a Chevy Malibu in Peekskill, New York. Thousands of people saw it streak across the sky on its way across the United States.

Hoover Dam near Boulder City, Nevada

MILESTONE

African-American Radio Show Debuts

The radio variety show *Jubilee* airs for the first time on this day in 1942, broadcast through the U.S. War Department for service personnel. The program, starring prominent African-American performers, was intended to boost the morale of black troops serving overseas. Network radio had largely ignored African-American talent until *Jubilee's* launch. The show featured some of the most important jazz bands, singers, and entertainers of the early 20th century, including Duke Ellington, Count Basie, Lena Horne, and Ella Fitzgerald.

OCTOBER 10

680 Husayn Ibn Ali, grandson of the prophet Muhammad, dies in battle in what is now Iraq. Modern Shiite Muslims revere him as the third imam, and commemorate his death with the holy day of Ashura.

732 At the Battle of Tours near Poitiers, France, Frankish leader Charles Martel, a Christian, defeats a large army of Spanish Moors, halting the Muslim advance into Western Europe. Martel's grandson was the emperor Charlemagne.

1733 In the War of Polish Succession, France declares war on Austria.

1774 Upon the death of her husband in the settlers-versus-Indians battle of Point Pleasant, Ohio frontierswoman Ann Bailey dons men's clothing and starts her career as a scout and Indian fighter, the legendary "Mad Ann."

1795 The U.S. Mint hires its first two female employees.

1845 The U.S. Naval Academy opens in Annapolis, Maryland, with 50 midshipmen students and seven professors.

1846 English astronomer William Lassell discovers Neptune's moon Triton.

1868 Cuban revolutionary Carlos Manuel de Céspedes issues the "Cry of Yara," proclaiming Cuban independence. His revolution did not succeed.

1874 The South Pacific island group of Fiji becomes a British crown colony.

1877 The U.S. Army holds a West Point funeral with full military honors for Lieutenant Colonel George Armstrong Custer, who had graduated from the academy in 1861 at the bottom of his class.

1879 Sentimental poet Ethel Beers, author of *The Picket Guard*, which was popular during the American Civil War, publishes a collection of her poems. She died the next day, having predicted that publication of her collected work would mark her death.

1881 A year before his death, Charles Darwin publishes *The Formation of Vegetable Mold Through the Action of Worms*, a work he viewed as more important than his great achievement, *The Origin of Species*.

1899 American outlaw Butch Cassidy's pal and Wild Bunch gang member Elzy Lay is sentenced to life in prison for a train robbery. Pardoned in 1906, he ended up in Los Angeles, California, where he died in 1934.

1901 American automaker Henry Ford enters his first and last automobile race, and wins. He found the experience so terrifying that he retired as a competitive driver, reportedly explaining that "once is enough."

> *"Man still bears in his bodily frame the indelible stamp of his lowly origin."*
>
> —*Charles Darwin*

Yuan Shi Kai

1911 Violence erupts in Wuhan, China, over nationalization of railway lines. The revolt led to the fall of China's last imperial dynasty, the Ching.

1913 Would-be Chinese emperor Yuan Shi Kai is inaugurated president.

1928 Chinese nationalists establish a reorganized Republic of China with Nanking as its capital.

1929 Habibollah II, deposed emir of Afghanistan, is executed with 17 of his followers by Mohammad Nader Khan, who himself was assassinated in 1933.

1935 The American jazz opera *Porgy and Bess*, by George Gershwin, opens. The show included the classic song "Summertime."

1944 At the concentration camp in Auschwitz, Poland, during World War II, Germans use poison gas to murder 800 Gypsy children.

1957 An embarrassed President Dwight D. Eisenhower apologizes to Ghana's finance minister, Komla Agbeli Gbdemah, who had been refused service at a restaurant in Dover, Delaware, for being black.

1961 The entire population of the island of Tristan, part of a group of islands in the South Atlantic known collectively as Tristan da Cunha, is evacuated to Great Britain following the eruption of the volcano that forms the island. Most of those evacuated chose to return to the island in 1963.

1962 In the first public demonstration of a relay satellite in stationary orbit, the opening ceremonies of the Tokyo Olympics are shown live on U.S. television.

1967 The Outer Space Treaty takes effect. Ratified by the United States, the Soviet Union, and other countries, it prohibits nuclear weapons in space.

1970 In Canada, the Quebec Liberation Front, a militant separatist group, kidnaps Quebec labor minister Pierre Laporte in Montreal.

1985 The hijacking of the Italian cruise ship *Achille Lauro* reaches a dramatic climax when U.S. Navy F-14 fighters force an Egyptian airliner carrying the Palestinian hijackers to land at a NATO base in Sicily.

1995 University of Chicago professor Robert E. Lucas Jr. wins the Nobel Prize in economic science, becoming the school's sixth professor to win a Nobel in as many years.

Spiro T. Agnew

1503 Portuguese navigator Vasco da Gama returns from his second voyage to India, during which he burned to death several hundred Muslims and massacred dozens of Hindu fisherman.

1643 During the first phase of the English Civil Wars, Parliamentarians defeat Royalists at Winceby.

1649 English Parliamentary general Oliver Cromwell crushes Royalist forces in Wexford, Ireland, massacring both soldiers and townspeople.

1698 The First Partition Treaty, which carved up the Spanish Empire and determined who would succeed to the Spanish throne, is signed by England, Holland, and France. It angered the Spanish king, Charles II, whom the other powers had not bothered to consult.

1776 In the naval Battle of Valcour Island during the

MILESTONE

Color TV License Issued
The U.S. Federal Communications Commission issues the world's first license to broadcast color television on this day in 1950 to CBS. However, RCA charged that CBS's color technology was inadequate and contested the license. The challenge worked, and a restraining order was issued on November 15. Despite this setback, CBS did broadcast the first commercial color TV program in June 1951. Color television technology continued to evolve during the 1950s. In 1956, a Chicago, Illinois, station became the first to broadcast entirely in color. Color television sets, however, remained less popular than black-and-white sets until the late 1960s.

"Politics is supposed to be the second-oldest profession. I have come to realize that it bears a very close resemblance to the first."
—Ronald W. Reagan

American Revolution, future American traitor Benedict Arnold valiantly delays a British fleet for two crucial days while Patriot ground forces prepare the defense of New York.

1797 Admiral Duncan leads the British fleet to victory against the Dutch in the Battle of Camperdown off the north coast of Holland.

1809 American western explorer Meriwether Lewis, who led the famous Lewis and Clark Expedition across western North America, kills himself in Tennessee at age 35.

The Crystal Palace at the Great Exhibition

Israeli tank in the Golan Heights

1851 The Crystal Palace, a vast glass-and-iron structure enclosing nearly one million square feet of Hyde Park in London, England, closes its doors after serving as the site of the Great Exhibition of 1851. It was later rebuilt at a different site, where it survived until it was destroyed by fire in 1936.

1862 In the American Civil War, a Confederate cavalry unit under General J. E. B. Stuart raids the vital Union supply center of Chambersburg, Pennsylvania, and cuts telegraph lines, seizes horses and supplies, and destroys everything else.

1890 The Daughters of the American Revolution is founded as a patriotic society limited to those of direct lineal descent from Revolutionary soldiers or others who aided the cause of American independence.

1899 The South African Boer War begins between the British Empire and the Boers of the Transvaal and Orange Free State.

1914 German forces capture Ghent, in Belgium, during the early months of World War I before the fighting stalemated into trench warfare.

1915 On World War I's Balkan front, Bulgaria attacks eastern Serbia in concert with Germany and the other Central Powers.

1942 In the Pacific Battle of Cape Esperance during World War II, U.S. Navy ships intercept a Japanese troop convoy bringing reinforcements to Guadalcanal and sink one cruiser and three destroyers.

1954 The Vietminh occupy Hanoi and take control of North Vietnam after a nine-year guerrilla war against French colonial forces.

1961 At a meeting of the U.S. National Security Council, President John F. Kennedy is told that 40,000 U.S. troops could defeat the Vietcong in South Vietnam and that another 120,000 could deflect intervention by the North Vietnamese or Chinese.

1973 During the Yom Kippur War, Israeli forces beat back the Syrian invasion in the Golan Heights.

1986 U.S. president Ronald W. Reagan and Soviet leader Mikhail Gorbachev meet in Reykjavik, Iceland, to discuss limiting intermediate nuclear missile arsenals in Europe.

1995 A report to the U.N. Security Council estimates that Saddam Hussein has enough chemical and biological weapons to destroy the population of the world several times over.

539 B.C. Persian general Gobyras captures Babylon, in line with the prediction of the Hebrew prophet Daniel. Babylon's co-regent Belshazzar died soon after.

322 B.C. Athenian statesman and orator Demosthenes commits suicide by poison rather than surrender to Macedonian soldiers.

1428 The earl of Salisbury, an English commander in the Hundred Years' War, launches the siege of Orléans, which would lead to his death on November 3.

1549 In the Wars of the Roses in England, Yorkist forces defeat Lancastrians at the Battle of Blore Heath but themselves are routed later in the day at Ludford Bridge.

1565 In Florida, French Huguenot naval officer Jean Ribaut is executed for being a

---

MILESTONE

Columbus Reaches the New World

After sailing across the Atlantic Ocean, Italian explorer Christopher Columbus sights a Bahamian island, believing he has reached East Asia, on this day in 1492. His expedition went ashore the same day and claimed the land for Isabella and Ferdinand of Spain. Although educated Europeans of Columbus's day did believe that the world was round, Columbus underestimated its size, calculating that East Asia must lie approximately where North America sits on the globe. He returned to Spain with gold, spices, and Native American captives whom he named Indians because of his error. He was the first European to explore the Americas since the Vikings in the 10th century.

"Small opportunities are often the beginning of great enterprises."

—*Demosthenes*

Protestant heretic by Spanish forces that had earlier massacred the Huguenot colony of Fort Caroline.

1730 Upon the death of his father, Frederick IV, Christian VI becomes king of Denmark and Norway.

1810 The wedding of Bavarian crown prince Louis to Princess Therese von Sachsen-Hildburghausen gives rise to the annual beer-lover's celebration, Oktoberfest, first celebrated on October 17, 1810.

1860 Anglo-French troops capture Beijing, China, during the second Opium War, a victory that gave Great Britain perpetual control of the Kowloon Peninsula.

1870 General Robert E. Lee, commander of the Confederate Army of Northern Virginia, dies peacefully at his home in Lexington, Virginia. He was 63 years old.

1898 Ten people are killed in a miner's riot near Virden, Illinois—a milestone in the campaign for an eight-hour workday.

1899 Boers begin the siege of Mafeking (now Mafikeng), a British military outpost in northwestern South Africa. The British held out for six dramatic months until relieved in May, touching off big celebrations in London.

Columbus in the New World (milestone)

1938 Production begins on *The Wizard of Oz*, the movie that would boost American actress Judy Garland to international fame. Garland was the lowest-paid member of the principal cast, earning only $500 a week.

1938 Japanese forces capture the Chinese city of Canton, and would soon control most of eastern China.

1940 Tom Mix, the highest-paid actor in silent films during the 1920s and best-known cowboy star of the era, dies in a car accident in Arizona, still wearing his cowboy costume from a performance the previous day.

1945 Desmond T. Ross of Lynchburg, Virginia, wins the Congressional Medal of Honor for outstanding bravery as a medical corpsman. He was the first conscientious objector in American history to receive the nation's highest military award.

1946 American general Joseph Stilwell, who commanded U.S. and Chinese Nationalist resistance in China and Burma during World War II, dies at age 63. He made no secret of his dislike for corrupt Nationalist leader Chiang Kai-shek, whom he nicknamed "the Peanut."

1948 The Soviet Union recognizes the North Korean government under Kim Il Sung as Korea's only legal government.

1960 Soviet leader Nikita Khrushchev removes his shoe and pounds a table with it in protest against a speech critical of Soviet policy in Eastern Europe.

USS Cole after terrorist bomb exploded

1964 The Soviet Union launches *Voskhod 1* into Earth orbit with three cosmonauts aboard. It was the first spacecraft to carry a multiperson crew.

1968 Spain's former West African colony gains independence and becomes the Republic of Equatorial Guinea.

1975 Saint Plunket, an Irish bishop who was hanged, disemboweled, and quartered in London in 1681, is canonized. He was the last Catholic martyr to die in England.

1999 Pakistan's prime minister Nawaz Sharif fires armed forces chief Pervez Musharraf, who was on a foreign visit, and tries to keep his plane from landing at Karachi. Instead, the armed forces seized the airport and deposed Sharif.

2000 Seventeen American sailors are killed and 38 wounded when a motorized rubber dinghy loaded with explosives and piloted by two suicide terrorists connected with the al Qaeda network blows a 40-by-40-foot hole in the side of the USS *Cole*, a Navy destroyer refueling at Aden, Yemen.

54 Tiberius Claudius, the emperor of Rome, dies at age 63.

1066 On the eve of the Battle of Hastings, English king Harold II and his ill-trained army, lacking cavalry and archers, occupy a ridge top and await the approach of William, duke of Normandy.

1307 Philip IV, king of France, orders the arrest of all Knights Templar in his campaign to exterminate the religious military order.

1534 Italian cardinal Allesandro Farnese is elected pope, and takes the name Paul III. Rumors had it that his support resulted largely from the romantic affair between his sister and the previous pope, Alexander VI.

1660 English diarist Samuel Pepys notes in his journal: "I went out to Charing Cross to see Major-general Harrison hanged, drawn and

---

MILESTONE

White House Cornerstone Laid

The cornerstone is laid for a presidential residence in the newly designated capital city of Washington on this day in 1792. In 1800, John Adams became the first U.S. president to reside in the executive mansion, which was soon named the White House because its white-gray Virginia freestone contrasted with the red brick of nearby buildings. Washington was created to replace Philadelphia, Pennsylvania, as the nation's capital because of its geographical position in the center of the existing new republic. Work was completed on the White House in the 1820s. It is the capitol's oldest federal building.

"Judge a man by his questions rather than by his answers."

—*Voltaire*

quartered; which was done there, he looking as cheerful as any man could do in that condition." Harrison had been one of those who condemned Charles I to death in 1649.

1761 The son of French Huguenot cloth merchant Jean Calas is found hanged. Catholic mobs accused Calas of murdering his son to prevent his conversion to the true faith. Convicted, he was brutally executed, an act that prompted the philosher Voltaire to mount his famous campaign for religious tolerance.

1775 The Continental Congress authorizes the first American naval force. Esek Hopkins commanded the seven ships of the Continental navy.

1812 During the War of 1812, British and Indian forces under Sir Isaac Brock defeat Americans at the Battle of Queenstown Heights, on the Canadian frontier, effectively ending U.S. plans to conquer Canada. Brock died in the battle.

1843 B'nai B'rith, the world's oldest Jewish service organization, is founded in New York City.

1845 Voters of the independent Republic of Texas approve a proposed constitution that, when accepted by the U.S. Congress, will make Texas the 28th American state.

Battle of Queenstown Heights

1860 Balloonist and photographer James W. Black makes the first aerial photograph in America, from an altitude of 1,200 feet. His subject: Boston.

1884 In Washington, D.C., delegates from 25 nations agree to adopt the Greenwich meridian—the line of longitude passing through Greenwich, England—as the prime meridian.

1905 English suffrage campaigners Christabel Pankhurst and Annie Kenney are arrested and sent to prison for "assaulting" police. Their action won nationwide publicity for their movement.

1917 Some 70,000 pilgrims gather at Fátima, Portugal, hoping to see a miracle during the sixth appearance of the Virgin Mary to three shepherd children. On the same day in 1967, Pope Paul VI visits the shrine with the last surviving shepherd child, Lucia dos Santos, and about one million pilgrims.

1923 Ankara is chosen to be the capital of the new Republic of Turkey.

1940 In the first telecommunication between deaf people, two deaf women communicate in sign language via two-way television sets installed at the New York World's Fair and at a television station eight miles away.

1943 During World War II, the government of post-Mussolini Italy declares war on its former Axis partner Germany and joins the battle on the side of the Allies. On the same day, the U.S. Fifth Army crosses the

Hijacked Lufthansa airliner

Volturno River, breaking an important German defense line.

1957 American movie audiences gasp and chuckle to the science-fiction thriller *The Amazing Colossal Man*. The film revolves around a character who strayed too close to the test of an atomic device in the Nevada desert. Bombarded with "plutonium rays," he experiences the world's greatest growth spurt.

1977 Four Palestinians hijack a Lufthansa airliner and demand the release of 11 imprisoned members of Germany's Baader-Meinhof terrorist group, also known as the Red Army Faction.

1998 At least 16 people die in a huge explosion at a secret, illegal fireworks factory in Tultepec on the outskirts of Mexico City.

2000 South Korean president Kim Dae Jung is awarded the Nobel Peace Prize, in part for his efforts to smooth relations with North Korea.

William the Conqueror

222 Pope Calixtus I is beaten to death in Rome and his remains thrown into a well.

530 A brief schism within the Roman Catholic Church ends when Dioscorus, one of two rival popes, dies just 23 days after his consecration. His demise left the field clear for Boniface II.

1066 William the Conqueror defeats English king Harold II at the Battle of Hastings. Harold himself was killed at the end of the battle, by an arrow in the eye, according to legend.

1758 Austria defeats Prussia in the Battle of Hochkirk.

1806 French general Napoleon Bonaparte crushes the Prussian Army at the Battle of Jena-Auerstadt, in modern Germany. The victory helped Napoleon conquer Prussia before Russian forces could intervene.

1822 French writer Victor Hugo *(Les Misèrables)* marries his childhood sweetheart, Adèle Foucher.

BORN ON THIS DAY

1618
SIR PETER LELY
Dutch-born British portrait painter

1633
JAMES VII OF SCOTLAND AND II OF ENGLAND
King of what he called Great Britain (1685–88), though the Act of Union with Scotland was not passed by Parliament until 1707

1644
WILLIAM PENN
English colonist who founded Pennsylvania as a haven for Quakers

1712
GEORGE GRENVILLE
English politician, British prime minister (1763–65)

1882
ÉAMON DE VALERA
American-born Irish statesman, president of the Irish Republic (1959–73)

1888
KATHERINE MANSFIELD
New Zealand writer (*The Garden Party and Other Stories*)

1890
DWIGHT D. EISENHOWER
Five-star U.S. Army general who became the 34th U.S. president (1953–61)

1893
LILLIAN GISH
American actress (*Madonna of the Storm; The Birth of a Nation; La Bohème*)

1894
E. E. CUMMINGS
American poet, playwright, and author (*The Enormous Room;* "anyone lived in a pretty how town"; "Buffalo Bill's")

1905
EUGENE FODOR
English travel author

1916
C. EVERETT KOOP
U.S. surgeon general (1981–89)

1927
ROGER MOORE
English actor who succeeded Sean Connery in James Bond films

1834 Henry Blair of Glenross, Maryland, becomes the first African American to receive a patent, for a corn planter.

1863 In the Battle of Bristol Station during the American Civil War, Union Army troops stop Confederate general Robert E. Lee's advance in Virginia.

1863 Swedish arms manufacturer Alfred Nobel patents the explosive nitroglycerin.

1899 The American magazine *Literary Digest* predicts that automobiles will never be as popular as bicycles.

1912 Former U.S. president Theodore Roosevelt is shot at close range by a saloonkeeper in Milwaukee, Wisconsin, but suffers only a flesh wound and goes on to make a one-hour speech with the bullet still in his chest.

1914 German forces capture the Belgian city of Bruges during World War I.

1915 Bulgaria and Serbia declare war on one another.

1922 The first automated telephone exchange begins operating in New York City.

1933 Nazi Germany withdraws from the League of Nations.

"Our lives begin to end the day we become silent about things that matter."

—*Dr. Martin Luther King, Jr.*

1936 As tensions rise in Europe, Belgium renounces its interwar alliance with France and declares itself neutral. On the same day, the first members of the International Brigades arrive in Spain to help fight Francisco Franco's fascists.

1939 The British battleship *Royal Oak* is torpedoed and sunk off the Orkney Islands by a German U-boat during World War II, killing 833 men.

1942 During World War II, Germans and their Ukrainian collaborators machine-gun 1,700 Jewish men, women, and children from the Mizocz ghetto.

1943 Jewish slave laborers revolt at the Nazis' Sobibor extermination camp in Poland during World War II, killing several SS supervisors and guards. All inmates were executed the following day.

1944 German general Erwin Rommel, the "Desert Fox," kills himself with cyanide rather than face a public treason trial for conspiring in the failed assassination attempt on Adolf Hitler.

1947 U.S. Air Force test pilot Chuck Yeager becomes the first person to fly faster than the speed of sound, reaching a velocity of more than 662 miles per hour at 40,000 feet in the *X-1* rocket plane.

1958 Madagascar proclaims itself the Malagasy Republic, an autonomous unit within the French Community.

1962 The Cuban Missile Crisis begins, as spy plane photos offer incontrovertible evidence that Soviet-made missiles had been stationed just 90 miles off the American coast. The crisis would bring the world to the brink of nuclear war.

1993 Haiti's justice minister is murdered in his office by opponents of exiled president Jean Bertrand Aristide.

1998 More than 45 people die when a bus in central India plunges off a bridge into the Karam River.

Chuck Yeager and the X-1

879 Boso is proclaimed the king of Provence, France.

1384 Breaking an early sex-role barrier, Polish queen Jadwiga is crowned king.

1417 Pope Gregory XII resigns, one of the few times in history that a pope has left office before his death.

1795 Chian-long picks his fifth son to succeed him as emperor of China, and announces he will abdicate on the new year. He continued to rule behind the scenes, exercising power for longer than any other Chinese emperor.

1821 Lord Byron notes in his diary: "Whenever an American requests to see me (which is not infrequently) I comply—1stly because I respect a people who acquired their freedom without excess—and 2ndly because these transatlantic visits . . . make me feel as if talking with posterity from the other side of the Styx."

1863 During the American Civil War, the CSS *Hunley,* the first combat submarine, sinks during a test run, killing its inventor and seven crew members. Recovered and fitted with a new crew, it stuck a torpedo in a Union ship and sank it, but also sank in the attempt.

1878 American inventor Thomas Edison opens the Edison Electric Company, with funding help from J. P. Morgan and other investors.

1880 The warrior Victorio, one of the greatest

Mata Hari

"The higher we soar, the smaller we appear to those who cannot fly."
—Friedrich Nietzsche

Apache military strategists, dies in the Tres Castillos Mountains south of El Paso, Texas. Victorio had led his people from the bleak San Carlos reservation in Arizona in search of freedom on better land, an act that made him an outlaw.

1914 During World War I, Otto Weddigen, the German U-boat commander who sank three British cruisers in an hour on September 22 at a cost of 1,400 lives, sinks another off Scotland. The *Hawke* went down with some 500 British sailors.

1918 Leading film studios in the United States announce that due to the great influenza epidemic, and the chance of contracting flu in theaters, they will temporarily stop releasing films.

1939 La Guardia Airport (originally named New York Municipal Airports) is dedicated.

1940 Charlie Chaplin's satiric social commentary *The Great Dictator* opens. The American actor directed the film and starred as both a Jewish barber and dictator Adenoid Hynkel in the fictional country of Tomania.

1945 Pierre Laval, the puppet leader of Nazi-occupied Vichy France, is executed by firing squad for treason against France. He attempted suicide by

New York Municipal Airports poster

poison but was nursed back to health in time for his execution.

1946 Hermann Goering, commander of the German *Luftwaffe* and Adolf Hitler's designated successor, commits suicide at the end of World War II. Convicted of war crimes at Nuremburg and sentenced to be hanged, he swallowed a cyanide tablet he had hidden from his guards.

1950 The first radio paging service begins business. The first page went to a doctor on a golf course 25 miles from New York City.

1964 At Bonneville Salt Flats, Utah, Craig Breedlove breaks the 500-miles-per-hour land-speed barrier to set a new record of 526.277 miles per hour in his jet-powered vehicle, the *Spirit of America*.

1965 In New York, David Miller, a young Catholic pacifist, becomes the first U.S. war protestor to burn his draft card in direct violation of a recently passed law. For his gesture, he was sentenced to two years in prison.

1966 A 75-year-old Texan qualifies as the worst driver in American history. He received 10 traffic tickets, drove on the wrong side of the road four times, committed four hit-and-run offenses, and caused six accidents, all within 20 minutes.

1970 Thirty-three people die in Melbourne when the West Gate Bridge, the largest bridge in Australia, collapses.

1989 Playing against his old team, the Edmonton Oilers, Canadian ice-hockey legend Wayne Gretzky breaks Gordie Howe's scoring record of 1,850 points. Gretzky retired in 1999 with 2,857 career points.

1990 Soviet leader Mikhail Gorbachev wins the Nobel Peace Prize, in recognition of his work in ending Cold War tensions.

1997 British race-car driver Andy Green, in his Thrust SSC jet-powered car, sets another new land-speed record of 763.035 miles per hour in Nevada.

Andy Green

1495 Pope Alexander VI issues an order trying to silence Florentine leader Girolamo Savonarola, who ignored the order and continued to preach against tyrants and corrupt clergy.

1555 English Protestant martyrs Bishop Hugh Latimer and Bishop Nicholas Ridley are burned at the stake for heresy opposite Balliol College in Oxford.

1710 The British capture Port Royal, in the French colony of Acadia. It became Annapolis Royal, Nova Scotia, and several thousand of its inhabitants became the Cajuns of Louisiana.

1756 Robert Clive (a.k.a. Clive of India) departs Madras, India, with a force of Europeans and Indians to retake the East India Company's trading center of Calcutta, which had been seized by the Mughal viceroy, Siraj-ud-Dawlah. Clive's victory there established British control of Bengal.

1777 During the American Revolutionary War, British forces burn Kingston, the seat of New York's revolutionary government.

1793 Marie Antoinette is beheaded by guillotine nine months after her husband, the

> *"In this world there are only two tragedies. One is not getting what one wants, and the other is getting it."*
>
> —*Oscar Wilde*

Marie Antoinette

former king Louis XVI of France, lost his head to the same device. Showing imperious disregard for starving peasants who could not afford bread, she allegedly said, "Let them eat cake."

1813 185,000 French troops under Napoleon Bonaparte face 320,000 allied troops at the Battle of Leipzig. The battle lasted three days, ending in a decisive defeat for the French.

1854 In response to a speech by his Illinois presidential rival, U.S. senator Stephen A. Douglas, Abraham Lincoln denounces slavery.

1859 Abolitionist John Brown leads a raid against an arsenal in Harpers Ferry, Virginia, in an attempt to incite an insurrection and bring an end to slavery in America. Later convicted of treason, he was hanged for the crime.

1891 A Chilean mob attacks a group of U.S. Navy sailors on shore leave in Valparaiso, killing two and seriously wounding several others. The event nearly led to war between the United States and Chile.

1893 In St. Petersburg, Russia, Peter Ilyich Tchaikovsky premieres his masterpiece sixth symphony, the *Pathétique,* which he knew, despite unenthusiastic reviews, was among his best works.

1899 Italian physicist and inventor Guglielmo Marconi demonstrates his wireless telegraph in a broadcast of yacht racing results off the coast of Long Island, New York.

1901 Swedish explorer Otto Nordenskjöld embarks aboard the ship *Antarctic* to spend a winter in Antarctica. He spent two winters there, owing to the destruction of his ship in pack ice.

1905 The British government of India partitions Bengal in the face of enormous opposition by Indian residents. The move politicized millions to oppose British rule.

1918 Austrian prime minister Max Hussarek, in a last-ditch effort to save the Hapsburg empire, declares the federalization of Austria. The plan did not succeed.

1925 Great Britain, France, Germany, Belgium, and Italy initial the Locarno Pact, a series of treaties meant to guarantee peace in Western Europe.

1946 U.S. President Harry S. Truman lifts wartime price controls on meat.

1946 At Nuremberg, Germany, 10 high-ranking Nazi officials are executed by hanging for crimes against humanity, crimes against peace, and war crimes during World War II. Among them were Joachim von Ribbentrop, minister of foreign affairs; Wilhelm Frick, minister of the interior; and Alfred Rosenberg, primary formulator of Nazi ideology.

1949 Greek communist radio announces the end of the country's second communist rebellion, a conflict that cost Greece some 50,000 lives.

1964 The People's Republic of China detonates an atom bomb and becomes the fifth nuclear nation, joining the United States, the Soviet Union, Great Britain, and France.

1973 U.S. secretary of state Henry Kissinger and North Vietnamese diplomat Le Duc Tho are awarded the Nobel Peace Prize for negotiating the Paris peace accords. Kissinger accepted, but Tho declined the award until such time as "peace is truly established."

MILESTONE

The Long March

The embattled Chinese Communists break through Nationalist enemy lines on this day in 1934 and begin an epic flight from their encircled headquarters in southwest China. Known as the Long March, the retreat lasted 368 days and covered 6,000 miles. Civil war in China between the Nationalists and the Communists broke out in 1927. In 1931, Communist leader Mao Zedong was elected chairman of the newly established Soviet Republic of China. Secrecy and rearguard actions confused the Nationalists, and it was several weeks before they realized that the main body of the Red Army had fled.

Chinese Communists, from right, Mao Zedong, Chu Teh, Chou En-Lai, and Qin Bangxia, during the Long March (milestone)

"Without alienation, there can be no politics."

—Arthur Miller

456 Flavius Ricimer, an influential general in the Western Roman Empire, deposes the Western emperor Avitus.

1346 The English decisively defeat an invading Scottish army at the Battle of Neville's Cross, near Durham.

1404 Innocent VII is elected to the papacy. His election was opposed in both Rome and Avignon, France, where the antipope Benedict XIII ruled.

1438 The Spanish Inquisition broadens its scope as the powers of its first grand inquisitor, Tomás de Torquemada, are extended from Castile and León to Aragon, Catalonia, Valencia, and Majorca.

1448 The Battle of Kosovo opens between the Ottomans and a combined force of Hungarian, Albanian, and papal soldiers. During the following three days, the Ottomans crushed the western army.

1651 Having been defeated by Cromwell's forces at the Battle of Worcester, the fugitive king Charles II escapes to France, thus effectively ending the English Civil Wars.

1707 The great German composer Johann Sebastian Bach marries his cousin Maria Barbara Bach.

1761 German composer Christoph Willibald Gluck

BORN ON THIS DAY

1711
JUPITER HAMMON
First published African-American poet ("A Poem for Children With Thoughts on Death"; "Master"; "Legacy")

1813
GEORG BÜCHNER
German dramatist (*Danton's Death*; *Woyzeck*)

1817
SAMUEL RINGGOLD WARD
American minister, abolitionist, and author (*Autobiography of a Fugitive Negro*)

1880
CHARLES KRAFT
American processed-cheese mogul who co-founded the Kraft Food Company

1912
ALBINO LUCIANI
Pope John Paul I, 263rd pope of the Roman Catholic Church

1915
ARTHUR MILLER
Pulitzer Prize-winning American playwright (*Death of a Salesman*; *All My Sons*; *After the Fall*)

1918
RITA HAYWORTH
American actress (*The Strawberry Blonde*; *Blood and Sand*; *Gilda*)

1920
MONTGOMERY CLIFT
American actor (*Suddenly Last Summer*; *From Here to Eternity*; *Raintree County*)

premieres his dramatic ballet *Don Juan*, in Vienna, Austria.

1777 In a major turning point of the American Revolutionary War, besieged British general John Burgoyne surrenders 5,000 troops at Saratoga, New York. The American victory led to French recognition of U.S. independence.

1781 During the American Revolutionary War, a British fleet with 7,000 troops sails too late to relieve the British Army trapped on the Yorktown Peninsula.

1793 In the Battle of Cholet, French republican forces win a major victory against royalist Roman Catholic rebels in the country's Vendée region.

1813 During the War of 1812, American forces launch a campaign against Montreal, Canada.

1835 The Texas Rangers, a corps of armed and mounted lawmen, is created to range and guard the Lone Star republic's frontier from Mexican and Indian raiders.

Surrender of General John Burgoyne to General George Washington

Workers check earthquake damage to Interstate 880 in Oakland, California (milestone)

MILESTONE

Earthquake Rocks San Francisco

The deadliest earthquake to hit the San Francisco area in California since 1906 occurs on this day in 1989. The quake measured 7.1 on the Richter scale, and its aftermath was witnessed on live television by millions of people watching the third game of baseball's World Series between the San Francisco Giants and the Oakland Athletics. The tremor hit moments before the start of the game, and sportscasters were soon performing the duties of news anchors as they reported on the pandemonium in the stadium. The earthquake killed 63 people, injured more than 3,000 others, and damaged more than 100,000 buildings.

1850 In northern Syria, anti-Christian rioters pillage Christian neighborhoods in Aleppo, killing several residents and injuring others.

1864 In the American Civil War, Confederate general James Longstreet returns to command after recovering from wounds inadvertently inflicted upon him by his own troops during the Battle of the Wilderness.

1885 English metallurgist Sir Harry Bessemer patents his blast-furnace method for mass-producing inexpensive steel.

1907 The first regular transatlantic radio messaging service opens as a coded dispatch is sent from Ireland to the *New York Times* in New York City.

1931 American gangster Al Capone, kingpin of Chicago's Prohibition-era underworld, is sentenced to 11 years in prison for tax evasion and is fined $80,000.

1941 During World War II, antifascist Japanese prime minister Fumimaro Konoye resigns, leaving control of the country's foreign and domestic policies in the hands of Hideki Tōjō.

1947 During China's civil war, Communist forces capture Chin-chou, a Nationalist supply and transport hub.

1961 Paris police kill 200 as they fire on a crowd of 30,000 Algerians marching in the city in support of peace talks to end their country's war of independence against France.

1973 The Arab oil embargo begins as the Organization of Petroleum Exporting Countries decides to cut exports to the United States and other nations that aided Israel during the Yom Kippur War.

1974 U.S. president Gerald R. Ford voluntarily appears before a House subcommittee to explain why he pardoned former president Richard M. Nixon.

1995 Algerian terrorists bomb a subway train in Paris, France, injuring 29.

1998 More than 700 people die in southern Nigeria when a gasoline pipeline explodes.

33 Agrippina the Elder starves to death on the Mediterranean island of Pandeteria. The daughter of Roman emperor Augustus, wife of Germanicus, and mother of Caligula, she was exiled to the island for political reasons.

456 Avitus, who repulsed the Huns under Attila during their invasion of Gaul, abdicates from his brief stint as Western Roman emperor when defeated at Placentia by Ricimer.

816 Pope Stephen IV crowns Louis I, the son and successor of Charlemagne, Holy Roman emperor, thereby solidifying the ties between the papacy and secular power in Europe.

1016 English king Edmund II is defeated at Ashington, Essex, by Danish king Canute. The two kings agreed to divide England, but Canute became sole ruler when Edmund died in November.

1216 John, the English king who was forced to sign the Magna Carta, dies in Nottinghamshire at age 48.

1377 Andronicus IV Palaeologus is crowned Byzantine emperor after deposing and imprisoning his father, John VI Cantacuzenus, who escaped and deposed him in return.

1469 Ferdinand of Aragon marries Isabella of Castile in Valladolid, Spain, thus beginning a cooperative reign that would unite the nation and make it a dominant world power.

1672 By the Treaty of Buczacz, the Ottomans acquire

MILESTONE

End of a Monarchy

On this day in 1955 Vietnam's last emperor, Bao Dai, tries to dismiss prime minister Ngo Dinh Diem, telling the Vietnamese people that he could no longer support "a man who will drag you into ruin, famine, and war." Diem suppressed the message and the people never heard it. Five days later Diem won a dubiously conducted referendum set up with the help of American intelligence agents. This effectively abolished the monarchy in Vietnam and established Diem, an ardent anticommunist and puppet of American interests, in political control of the southern half of the country. On October 26, Diem proclaimed a republic and declared himself as South Vietnam's first president.

Tom Sayers

---

a large chunk of Poland, including the Polish Ukraine.

1685 Louis XIV rescinds the Edict of Nantes, depriving French Protestants of all civil rights.

1735 Hung-li becomes the fourth Ching dynasty emperor of China. Taking the name Chian-long, he ruled more than 60 years.

1748 The Treaty of Aix-la-Chapelle ends the eight-year War of Austrian Succession.

1842 The first telegraph cable is laid by Samuel Morse in New York harbor.

1853 English boxer Tom Sayers loses the only match of his life, to Nat Langham after 61 rounds.

1854 In the Ostend Manifesto, three U.S. diplomats urge Secretary of State William Marcy to seize Cuba from Spain. The motive: to expand American slave territory and prevent a slave uprising like the one in Haiti.

1858 In a letter, future U.S. president Abraham Lincoln writes, "I believe the declaration that 'all men are created equal' is the great fundamental principle upon which our free institutions rest."

1860 French and British troops occupying Beijing, China, loot and then burn the Yuanmingyuan, the fabulous summer residence built by the Manchu emperors in the 18th century.

Hungarian border guards cut a down barbed wire fence on the Austrian border

1867 The United States formally takes possession of Alaska, having purchased the vast territory from Russia for less than two cents an acre.

1898 One year after Spain granted Puerto Rico self-rule, American troops take control of the Caribbean nation. U.S. forces invaded Puerto Rico near the end of the Spanish-American War, and took it with almost no resistance.

1912 The First Balkan War erupts. It lasted only a few months and ended with Ottoman concessions.

1913 English suffragette Emmeline Pankhurst arrives in New York but is ordered to be deported from the United States on grounds of moral turpitude. In her autobiography, *My Own Story,* published the following year, Pankhurst wrote: "Women had always fought for men, and for their children. Now they were ready to fight for their own human rights."

1922 *Robin Hood*, starring American actor Douglas Fairbanks, opens at Grauman's Egyptian Theater in Hollywood. Fairbanks was not much of an archer. As a publicity stunt, he loosed arrows from a New York hotel and accidentally shot a man through an open window.

1989 Having disbanded the Communist Party and torn down the barbed wire separating Hungary from Austria, the Hungarian government amends its constitution to allow a multiparty political system and free elections.

1989 NASA launches the U.S. space probe *Galileo* on its successful journey to Jupiter.

> *"It takes a clever man to turn cynic and a wise man to be clever enough not to."*
>
> —Fannie Hurst

"It is not the size of a man but the size of his heart that matters."

—Evander Holyfield

439 Gaiseric, king of the Vandals, captures Carthage. He built an empire from parts of Roman Africa, and sacked Rome itself in 455.

1774 Patriot ruffians of Annapolis, Maryland, hold their own version of the Boston Tea Party, attacking a ship. The ship's owner burned the vessel and the tea.

1781 Hopelessly trapped at Yorktown, Virginia, British general Lord Cornwallis surrenders 8,000 British soldiers and seamen to a larger Franco-American force, effectively bringing an end to the American Revolutionary War.

Sheridan's Ride

MILESTONE

Gulf and Western Goes to the Movies

Gulf and Western Industries Inc., an umbrella company for a wide array of business enterprises, shifts gears and places its focus squarely on media on this day in 1966 with its purchase of Paramount Pictures Corporation, the legendary film company that boasted top talent like Rudolph Valentino and Cecil B. DeMille. The newly formed company produced a number of hits, including the *Godfather* and *Indiana Jones* trilogies, before Gulf and Western, since renamed Paramount Communications, was snapped up by fellow media giant Viacom Inc.

1781 Holy Roman emperor Joseph II issues the Edict of Toleration, which allows limited religious rights to non-Catholic Christians.

1812 One month after Napoleon Bonaparte's massive invading force entered a burning and deserted Moscow, the starving French army, the largest European military force ever assembled to that date, begins a disastrous retreat from Russia. Napoleon lost more than 400,000 of his troops.

1813 French general Napoleon Bonaparte loses the Battle of Leipzig, along with some 68,000 men killed or captured and his imperial holdings east of the Rhine River.

1864 At the Battle of Cedar Creek, Virginia, during the American Civil War, Union general Philip Sheridan averts a near disaster when he rallies his

troops after a surprise Rebel attack that threatened to destroy the Union force. His fierce rallying gallop became known as "Sheridan's Ride."

1864 In the American Civil War, Confederate raiders cross the Canadian border to attack St. Albans, Vermont.

1869 Prussian-born mining engineer Adolph Sutro begins one of the most ambitious western engineering projects of the day: a four-mile water-drainage tunnel through solid rock in the Comstock mining district at Virginia City, Nevada. It took nine years to complete and earned Sutro a fortune.

1899 According to his diary, American rocket pioneer Robert Goddard gets inspiration for his life's work when he climbs a cherry tree and imagines building a machine that could go beyond the tree all the way to Mars.

1900 American painter Henry O. Tanner wins the Medal of Honor at the Paris Exposition.

1911 Norwegian explorer Roald Amundsen departs his base in the Bay of Whales on the Antarctic coast with a party of four companions, four sledges, and 52 dogs. He became the first man to reach the pole on December 14.

1915 During World War I, Russia and Italy declare war on Bulgaria, joining Great Britain, France, and Serbia, who declared a few days earlier.

1935 In response to Italy's invasion of Ethiopia, the League

Mike Hawthorn

of Nations imposes deliberately ineffectual economic sanctions, fearing that effective action would ignite hostilities in Europe.

1936 In a race around the world by commercial airlines, H. R. Ekins of the *New York World-Telegram* beats two other journalists. His time: 18.5 days.

1939 The American film *Mr. Smith Goes to Washington* debuts, starring James Stewart as an earnest young senator persevering against corruption.

1943 In North Borneo, local Chinese and native Suluks rise up against the Japanese occupation and kill 40 Japanese soldiers. The Japanese reprisal was far more violent.

1954 The Himalayan peak Cho Oyu (8,201 meters), one of the world's 14 peaks higher than 8,000 meters, is climbed for the first time.

1958 By finishing second to his countryman Stirling Moss in the Moroccan Grand Prix near Casablanca, English driver Mike Hawthorn becomes the first British Formula One world champion, just one point ahead of Moss after a season's racing.

1097 During the First Crusade, Christian forces begin the long and difficult siege of Antioch, in Syria.

1314 German electors choose their second king in two days, Louis of Bavaria, thus setting up a rivalry with Frederick that would lead to eight years of warfare.

1517 Portuguese navigator Ferdinand Magellan arrives in Seville in order to offer his services to the king of Spain.

1600 The Battle of Sekigahara establishes the Tokugawa shogunate, a military dictatorship that would rule Japan for 265 years.

1629 In England, the Massachusetts Bay Company elects Puritan John Winthrop governor of the colony it intends to establish in the New World.

1794 Navigator George Vancouver returns to England after his meticulous survey of North America's northwest coast.

1805 French admiral Pierre Villeneuve sails his fleet out of Cádiz, Spain, to confront the British the following day in the fateful Battle of Trafalgar.

1807 After bombarding Copenhagen, a British fleet seizes the entire Danish fleet and sails away.

BORN ON THIS DAY

1632
SIR CHRISTOPHER WREN
English architect, astronomer, and mathematician who designed St. Paul's Cathedral and other great buildings after London's fire in 1666

1822
THOMAS HUGHES
English writer and reformer (*Tom Brown's Schooldays*)

1854
ARTHUR RIMBAUD
French symbolist poet

1856
JAMES MANN
American lawyer and U.S. congressman who authored the Mann Act

1859
JOHN DEWEY
American psychologist and philosopher (*How We Think; Democracy and Education; A Common Faith*)

1874
CHARLES IVES
Pulitzer Prize-winning American composer (*Concord Sonata; Symphony No. 3*)

1882
BELA LUGOSI
Hungarian-born American actor (*Casanova; The Thirteenth Chair; Dracula*)

1905
FREDERIC DANNAY
American author who co-created the mystery-novel character Ellery Queen

1931
MICKEY MANTLE
American Hall of Fame baseball player

"Education is not preparation for life. Education is life itself."
—John Dewey

1824 The U.S. Navy schooner *Porpoise* seizes four pirate ships in the waters off Cuba.

1827 During the Greek War for Independence from Turkey, a European armada annihilates the Turkish and Egyptian fleets in the Battle of Navarino.

1842 German opera great Richard Wagner, 29, premieres his *Rienzi* in Dresden to wide acclaim.

1905 The Russian Revolution of 1905 reaches its climax as a railroad strike develops into a general strike in most of the nation's large cities.

1910 In the United States, a baseball with a cork center is used for the first time during a World Series game.

1914 Germany reports that it has captured some 300,000 French, Russian, Belgian, and British soldiers during the opening months of World War I.

1917 Disguised Bolshevik leader Vladimir Lenin sneaks into Petrograd to organize an armed takeover of the Russian government.

Game two of the 1910 World Series

Sherlock Holmes poster

1930 English fictional sleuth Sherlock Holmes makes his radio debut, played by William Gillette. The series would run, with some interruptions, for the next 26 years.

1935 Mao Zedong's Long March ends as he and 4,000 Chinese communist survivors arrive in Shensi Province in northwest China. The communists had covered 6,000 miles in 368 days as they fled from Chiang Kai-shek's Nationalist forces.

1941 Nazi Germany's siege of Moscow begins during World War II.

1944 American Army troops capture Aachen, the first German city to fall to the Allies during World War II, and Belgrade, Yugoslavia, falls to the Soviets.

1944 In the Pacific, more than 100,000 American soldiers, including General Douglas MacArthur, land on Leyte Island and take on a Japanese garrison of 80,000. The ensuing two-month battle for the island was among the bloodiest of the war, especially for the Japanese, who lost virtually all of Leyte's defenders.

1956 German physician Hannes Lindemann begins a transatlantic voyage in a 17-foot, foldable, wood-and-fabric kayak. His successful crossing took 76 days.

1960 The world's first fully automated post office, capable of sorting and canceling mail at 18,000 pieces per hour, goes into service in Providence, Rhode Island.

1968 Jacqueline Kennedy, widow of assassinated President John F. Kennedy, marries Greek shipping magnate Aristotle Onassis.

1973 As the Watergate scandal blossoms, U.S. president Richard M. Nixon's attorney general and deputy attorney general both resign after refusing to fire Watergate special prosecutor Archibald Cox. Nixon finally got his solicitor general, Robert Bork, to do the deed. The incident became known as the Saturday Night Massacre.

OCTOBER 21

■ ■ **63** Roman consul Cicero convinces a skeptical Senate to declare a state of martial law in the face of rebel aristocrat Cataline's attempt to overthrow the republic.

💥 **1096** During the First Crusade, Turkish forces destroy the ragged army of Peter the Hermit, a passionate monk but a poor military leader.

■ ■ **1422** Not yet one year old and king of England for the past seven weeks, Henry VI is declared king of France as well.

💥 **1508** Safavid leader Shah Ismail I captures Baghdad and within eight years had established Shiite control over all of Persia.

▨ **1520** Portuguese explorer Ferdinand Magellan begins the first passage of the stormy and dangerous sea channel at the tip of South America that would eventually bear his name. It took him six weeks to cross from the Atlantic Ocean to the Pacific.

▨ **1559** Protestant nobles depose Mary of Guise (mother of Mary, Queen of Scots, and pro-French Catholic regent of Scotland during the queen's minority) after she initiates a policy of religious intolerance.

▬ **1797** The USS *Constitution*, a 44-gun U.S. Navy frigate, is launched in Boston harbor. During the War of 1812, the ship won its nickname "Old Ironsides" after defeating a British warship off the coast of Nova Scotia.

🔬 **1803** English chemist John Dalton, father of the atomic

Battle of Ball's Bluff

theory, presents his first account of the Table of Atomic Weights to the Manchester Literary and Philosophical Society.

💥 **1805** In one of the most decisive naval battles ever fought, a British fleet under Admiral Lord Nelson defeats a combined French and Spanish fleet at the Battle of Trafalgar. Victory ensured that Napoleon Bonaparte would never invade Great Britain, but Nelson died from a sniper's bullet.

💥 **1861** Union troops suffer a humiliating defeat in the second major engagement of the American Civil War. After the Battle of Ball's Bluff, the Union commanding general was arrested for treason and jailed for six months.

▬ **1867** More than 7,000 Southern Plains Indians gather in Kansas as their leaders sign the Medicine Lodge Treaty, by which the Indians—who may not have understood what they were signing—gave up their traditional nomadic way of life and agreed to move to a reservation in Oklahoma.

🏆 **1891** A one-mile dirt track opens for harness races at the site of the present-day Nashville Speedway in Tennessee. The

BORN ON THIS DAY

1772
SAMUEL TAYLOR COLERIDGE
English poet ("The Rime of the Ancient Mariner"; "Kubla Kahn"; "Desire")

Samuel Taylor Coleridge

1833
ALFRED BERNHARD NOBEL
Swedish chemist who invented dynamite and willed his fortune to create the Nobel Prizes, awarded annually for achievements in physics, chemistry, medicine, literature, and peace

1912
SIR GEORG SOLTI
Hungarian-born American conductor

1917
DIZZY GILLESPIE
American musician called by many the creator of modern jazz ("Salt Peanuts"; "I Can't Get Started"; "Hot House")

1921
SIR MALCOLM ARNOLD
English composer

1928
WHITEY (EDWARD) FORD
American Hall of Fame baseball player

1940
FRANCES FITZGERALD
Pulitzer Prize-winning American journalist (*Fire in the Lake: The Vietnamese and the Americans in Vietnam*)

1949
BENJAMIN NETANYAHU
Israel's ninth prime minister

1950
RONALD E. MCNAIR
American physicist, astronaut, and mission specialist aboard the *Challenger* space shuttle

track eventually became a top NASCAR course.

1904 Russia's newly refitted Baltic fleet, on its way to a disastrous defeat by the Japanese, fires by mistake upon British fishing trawlers in the North Sea, nearly inciting war with Great Britain.

1910 A massive explosion destroys the *Los Angeles Times* building in the California city's downtown area, killing 20 and injuring many more. The villains were two brothers, one a labor union official, reacting to the anti-union stance of the newspaper's publisher.

1915 The first transatlantic message to be transmitted over radiotelephone is placed from Arlington, Virginia, to the Eiffel Tower in Paris, France.

1925 The first demonstration of a photoelectric cell takes place at the Electrical Show in New York City. The light-sensitive cell was used to count objects as they interrupted a light beam.

1941 To crush resistance in the country they were dismembering during World War II, German soldiers go on a rampage, killing thousands of Yugoslavian civilians, including whole classes of schoolboys.

> *"I intend to leave after my death a large fund for the promotion of the peace idea, but I am skeptical as to its results."*
>
> —*Alfred Nobel*

1944 American forces under General Douglas MacArthur take Tacloban, in the Philippines, during World War II. The city served as an interim capital until Manila was recaptured.

1945 Upon the post–World War II proclamation of independent Indonesia, the Indonesian communists reestablish their party, the PKI.

1948 The first high-speed radio fax is sent from a radio station to the U.S. Library of Congress. All 1,047 pages of the novel *Gone with the Wind* were sent in two minutes and 21 seconds.

1969 After the assassination of Somalia's president, the military stages a coup, bringing Muhammed Siad Barre to power.

American peace demonstrators (milestone)

Since 1200 B.C. The morning sun penetrates the innermost sanctuary of the temple of the sun god Amon-Re. The sun's position on October 22 and again on February 22 each year determined the design of the temple, built by Egyptian King Ramses II at Abu Simbel.

1641 Sir Phelim O'Neill, an Irish Catholic rebel, touches off a bloody but unsuccessful 11-year revolt by capturing Charlemont Castle in Ireland.

1764 In India, troops of the British East India Company defeat Mughal forces at the Battle of Baksar. After the victory, company officials took charge of ruling Bengal themselves rather than through an Indian puppet governor.

1797 The first parachute jump of note is made by French daredevil André-Jacques Garnerin from a hydrogen balloon 3,200 feet above Paris. Riding in a basket below a cloth canopy 23 feet in diameter, he landed shaken but unhurt.

1812 French general Claude François de Malet, who opposed Napoleon Bonaparte, escapes from prison and nearly succeeds in an attempted coup d'état. He was executed several days later.

1844 The second coming of Christ would occur on this day, according to followers of William Miller, an American farmer and leader of the Millerite movement. They were wrong.

1883 New York City's Metropolitan Opera opens its

MILESTONE

Gay Sergeant Challenges the Air Force
On this day in 1975, U.S. Air Force sergeant Leonard Matlovich is given a general discharge after publicly declaring his homosexuality. Matlovich, who appeared on the cover of *Time* magazine, was challenging the ban against homosexuals in the U.S. military. In 1979, after winning a much-publicized case against the Air Force, his discharge was upgraded to honorable. In 1988, Matlovich died of AIDS at 44. He was buried with full military honors in Washington, D.C. His tombstone reads: "A gay Vietnam Veteran. When I was in the military they gave me a medal for killing two men and a discharge for loving one."

distinguished career with a performance of Charles Gounod's *Faust*.

1884 The Royal University of Ireland grants degrees to female graduates for the first time in Irish history.

1903 The infamous hired killer Tom Horn is hanged for the murder of Willie Nickell, the 14-year-old son of a southern Wyoming sheep rancher. Horn worked for the Wyoming Cattlemen's Association, who opposed sheep ranchers to the point of having them killed.

1914 The U.S. Congress passes the Revenue Act, mandating the country's first income tax. It applied to annual incomes over $3,000.

1925 Greece invades Bulgaria over frontier tensions.

1934 Depression-era outlaw Charles "Pretty Boy" Floyd meets his end in an Ohio cornfield, shot by FBI agents who had pursued him for years.

Ferdinand Porsche with Volkswagen gift for Nazi German official Herman Goering

Soviet ship Volgoles, about 40 miles from Cuba, with shrouded missiles

1936 German automaker Ferdinand Porsche submits a proposal to Adolf Hitler's government to build a small, reliable car for the average German—to be called the Volkswagen, or people's car.

1938 American inventor Chester Carlson demonstrates for the first time his copying technique called xerography, which would lead to the modern photocopier.

1958 China announces the departure of the last Chinese troops from North Korea.

1962 In a televised speech, President John F. Kennedy reveals that U.S. spy planes have discovered Soviet missile bases under construction in Cuba and announces a naval blockade to prevent Soviet ships from bringing more weapons to the communist island.

> *"Life begets life. Energy creates energy. It is by spending oneself that one becomes rich."*
>
> —*Sarah Bernhardt*

1962 Soviet military intelligence officer and double agent Oleg Penkovsky is arrested in the Soviet Union and charged with spying for the United States and Great Britain. He was convicted and executed.

1963 Great Britain's newly formed National Theatre (later the Royal National Theatre) opens in its temporary home, London's Old Vic Theatre, with a performance of *Hamlet*.

1964 French novelist and philosopher Jean-Paul Sartre is awarded the Nobel Prize in literature. He turned it down.

1965 During the Vietnam War, 18-year-old Private First Class Milton Lee Olive, of Chicago, Illinois, throws himself on an enemy grenade, saving the lives of four fellow soldiers. His selfless act won him a posthumous Medal of Honor.

1968 In the lead-up to America's landing on the moon, *Apollo 7* returns to Earth after an 11-day mission involving the first manned flights of the Command and Service modules.

42 B.C. During the Roman civil wars that followed Julius Caesar's assassination, imperial forces crush the republican army of Marcus Junius Brutus at Philippi, and Brutus kills himself.

1086 In Spain, a Muslim army from North Africa defeats the forces of King Alfonso I near Badajoz. Alfonso's oppression of his Muslim vassals had prompted the invasion.

1526 Ferdinand is elected king of Bohemia.

1642 The first major battle of the English Civil Wars, the Battle of Edgehill, is fought to a draw in Warwickshire. There, Oliver Cromwell, future ruler of the commonwealth of England, Scotland, and Ireland, made his first appearance at the head of the troops, as a captain.

1812 In an attempt to seize power in France, a Parisian general announces that Napoleon Bonaparte has died in Russia. The news prompted Napoleon to rush back to France ahead of his retreating army.

1813 During the War of 1812, Americans operating the Pacific Fur Company trading post in Astoria, Oregon, sell the post to their rivals in the British North West Company rather than risk an armed takeover.

1855 As tensions rise in Kansas over slavery, Kansas Free

"For three days after death, hair and fingernails continue to grow but phone calls taper off."
—Johnny Carson

State forces establish a rival governor and legislature to oppose the fraudulently elected pro-slavery legislature.

1864 In the largest Civil War engagement west of the Mississippi River, Union forces drive Confederate general Sterling Price's raiders out of Missouri at the Battle of Westport, near Kansas City.

1911 An Italian pilot makes the world's first use of an airplane in warfare as he makes a one-hour reconnaissance flight over Turkish positions during the Italo-Turkish War in Libya.

1917 In Petrograd, Bolshevik leader Vladimir Lenin prevails during a secret 10-hour debate, and the Bolshevik Central Committee decides to prepare for the armed overthrow of the Russian government.

1918 During World War I, U.S. president Woodrow Wilson replies to German overtures for peace by saying that armistice

The Blue Flame, driven by Gary Gabelich at the Bonneville Salt Flats in Utah

Wounded U.S. Marine after truck bombing in Beirut, Lebanon (milestone)

terms must prevent Germany from renewing hostilities.

1934 Swiss-born American balloonist Jean-Felix Piccard and his wife make the first successful flight into the stratosphere, rising to a height of 11 miles.

1935 New York gangster Dutch Schultz and three of his bodyguards are gunned down in a restaurant in Newark, New Jersey.

1941 Soviet official Georgi K. Zhukov assumes command of Red Army operations to stop the German advance into the heart of Russia. He would retain command throughout World War II, planning and executing virtually all major Soviet engagements.

1942 During World War II, the Battle of el-Alamein opens in North Africa as British infantry forces under General Bernard Montgomery launch a massive attack against weakened German and Italian positions.

1944 The decisive Battle of Leyte Gulf opens in the Pacific as American submarines sink two Japanese heavy cruisers.

1945 Jackie Robinson, the first African-American baseball player in the major leagues, signs with a Brooklyn Dodger farm team.

1950 Al Jolson, the most famous American singer of his day and star of the first feature-length film with sound, *The Jazz Singer,* dies.

1956 Street fighting breaks out in Hungary between Hungarian security forces, fighting alongside pro-democracy protesters, and Soviet soldiers. In the next few days, hundreds of protesters were killed.

1970 American driver Gary Gabelich sets a new average land-speed record of 631.367 miles per hour average speed in *The Blue Flame,* a rocket-powered vehicle, on the Bonneville Salt Flats in Utah.

> *"If you're going to make rubbish, be the best rubbish in it."*
>
> —*Richard Burton*

1071 Michael VII Ducas becomes sole Byzantine emperor at age 12. His policies weakened the empire to the benefit of its Turkish rivals. Michael quit and became a monk just before his death at age 19.

1273 King Rudolf I, first of the Hapsburg dynasty, is crowned at Aachen, Germany.

1307 Jacques de Molay, the last grand master of the Knights Templar, confesses under torture to charges brought against the knights by their enemy, French king Philip IV, who eventually burned Molay alive.

1537 Jane Seymour, the third wife of English king Henry VIII, dies 12 days after giving birth to the future Edward VI.

1648 The Treaty of Westphalia is signed, ending the Thirty Years' War and resulting in dissolution of the Holy Roman Empire. The war devastated Europe, particularly Germany, which was plundered and ravaged by unpaid armies of mercenaries.

1658 French comedic writer and actor Molière gets

MILESTONE

First Barrel Ride Down Niagara Falls

Daredevil Annie Edson Taylor initiates a famous stunt tradition when she goes over Niagara Falls in a wooden barrel on this day in 1901. She went over Horseshoe Falls on the Canadian side of Niagara inside a barrel five feet high and three feet in diameter, emerging shaken but unhurt in the river below. Taylor hoped that after the stunt she could make a fortune touring the world, displaying the famous barrel and relating the adventure. Although the stunt did receive international attention, she reaped few financial rewards and died in poverty after 20 years as a street vendor.

his big break when he performs *The Amorous Doctor* before King Louis XIV.

1795 In the Third Partition of Poland, Russia and Prussia carve up the remains of the nation between them after intervening in an uprising led by Polish nationalist Tadeusz Kosciuszko. Poland no longer existed as a sovereign state.

1836 American inventor Alonzo Phillips wins a U.S. patent for safety matches. Their friction-ignited heads were made of sulphur, phosphorous, chalk, and glue.

1851 English astronomer William Lassell discovers the Uranian moons Umbriel and Ariel.

1861 In Utah, the Western Union Telegraph Company links wires from the east and west coasts, completing the first transcontinental telegraph line and allowing instantaneous communication between Washington, D.C., and San Francisco, California.

1882 German physician Robert Koch discovers the cause of tuberculosis, the tubercle bacillus.

1908 The Locomobile company's Old 16 becomes the first American-made car to beat European competition, winning at the fourth annual Vanderbilt

Robert Koch

Niagara Falls, right (milestone)

Major Vidkun Quisling

Cup in New York. Driver George Robertson covered the 297-mile course at an average speed of 64.38 miles per hour.

1917 During World War I, Italy suffers a major military disaster at the Battle of Caporetto when an Austro-German offensive breaks a two-year stalemate. Italy lost more than 600,000 soldiers captured or deserted, and nearly lost the war.

1929 Wall Street suffers through "Black Thursday." In the gathering storm of the 1929 stock market crash, investors on the New York Stock Exchange traded a record 12,894,650 shares as financial panic mounted.

1930 With Brazil in economic collapse, opposition forces stage a successful coup to oust President Washington Luis.

1939 The first nylon stockings, a product of DuPont intended to replace silk, go on sale in the United States.

1945 Less than two months after the end of World War II, the United Nations is formally established by ratification of its enabling charter. The first U.N. General Assembly, with 51 nations represented, opened in London, England, on January 10, 1946.

1945 Vidkun Quisling, Norwegian army officer and would-be Nazi ruler of Norway, is executed for treason in Oslo. His surname has become a synonym for traitor.

1958 American mystery writer Raymond Chandler *(The Big Sleep; Farewell My Lovely)* starts working on his last novel, *The Poodle Springs Story*. He died the following March before completing it.

1964 Zambia gains independence from Britain.

1969 English movie star Richard Burton dazzles wife Elizabeth Taylor—and their legions of fans—when he buys her a 69-carat Cartier diamond ring costing $1.5 million.

1970 Salvador Allende, an avowed Marxist, is elected president of Chile against determined American opposition. U.S. efforts to destabilize his government bore fruit with a 1973 coup by the Chilean military, who overthrew Allende and assassinated him.

🎯 **1147** During the Second Crusade, Turks destroy the army of German emperor Conrad III at Dorylaeum, in Asia Minor.

🎭 **1400** Geoffrey Chaucer, English poet and author of *The Canterbury Tales*, dies in London.

🎯 **1415** During the Hundred Years' War between England and France, Henry V, the young king of England, leads his forces to victory at the Battle of Agincourt in northern France. The pivotal weapon for the beleaguered English was the six-foot-long bow.

🏳️ **1553** Spanish theologian Michael Servetus is convicted of heresy by the Inquisition. Two days later he was burned alive for the good of his soul.

⚖️ **1586** Mary, Queen of Scots is convicted of plotting to assassinate Queen Elizabeth I of England.

🇺🇸 **1764** Abigail Smith marries future U.S. president John Adams. Her minister father disapproved at first, believing Adams's prospects too limited for his daughter.

🎯 **1854** In the Battle of Balaclava, English general James Thomas Brudenell, seventh earl of Cardigan, leads a charge of the Light Brigade cavalry against well-defended Russian artillery during the Crimean War. His brigade suffered 40 percent casualties, and inspired Alfred, Lord Tennyson's famous poem *Charge of the Light Brigade*.

🇨🇳 **1860** After invading Beijing, China, and making off with priceless loot, France negotiates increased indemnities and land cessions with the Ching government.

🇺🇸 **1896** Adolph Simon Ochs, new owner of the *New York Times*, first uses the paper's famous slogan, "All the News That's Fit to Print."

🏆 **1902** American race-car driver Barney Oldfield launches his legendary auto-racing career, and long association with the Ford Motor Company, at the Manufacturer's Challenge Cup in Grosse Point, Michigan.

1922 Japanese troops who had entered Vladivostok in 1917 during the Russian Civil War evacuate the city, leaving it to the temporary Soviet buffer state called the Far Eastern Republic.

1936 Germany and Italy announce an axis, which binds their mutual fates. The term was later applied to the Axis Powers in World War II.

🇺🇸 **1940** Benjamin Davis becomes the first African-

Brigadier General Benjamin Davis conducting close rifle inspection

American general in the U.S. Army.

🛩 **1944** During the Battle of Leyte Gulf in World War II, the Japanese launch kamikaze ("divine wind") suicide bombers for the first time. Japan employed both conventional aircraft and specially designed rocket-powered planes dropped at high altitude from bombers.

🏳 **1948** Communist Czechoslovakia establishes forced labor camps to deal with dissenters.

🏳 **1951** India begins its first general election, which would last four months.

🏳 **1956** The German Federal Republic (West Germany) declares Adolf Hitler dead.

➕ **1960** The world's first electronic watch, the Accutron, goes on sale. Produced by Bulova Watch Company in Bienne, Switzerland, it used transistorized electronic circuits and a miniature power cell instead of springs and gears.

🎸 **1964** The English rock group the Rolling Stones make their first U.S. appearance on Ed Sullivan's television variety show.

🇺🇳 **1971** Reversing its policy of not recognizing the communist People's Republic of China, the

> *"I am always doing things I can't, that's how I get to do them."*
>
> —*Pablo Picasso*

Japanese kamikaze attack

U.S. votes to seat the PRC as a permanent member of the United Nations. Over American objections, Taiwan was expelled.

🛩 **1972** During the Vietnam War, U.S. president Richard M. Nixon orders a suspension in the bombing of Vietnam north of the 20th parallel to signal approval of recent North Vietnamese concessions at the secret peace talks in Paris.

🎨 **1981** Spanish artist Pablo Picasso's masterwork *Guernica* is shown in Madrid. It had been in New York since 1939.

🔫 **1983** Citing the threat posed to American nationals on the Caribbean nation of Grenada by that nation's Marxist regime, President Ronald W. Reagan orders a military invasion.

🏆 **1990** American boxer Evander Holyfield knocks out Buster Douglas in three rounds to win the undisputed world heavyweight title.

M I L E S T O N E

Pablo Picasso Born

Pablo Picasso, one of the greatest and most influential artists of the 20th century, is born on this day in 1881 in Málaga, Spain. Picasso's father was a professor of drawing who bred his son for a career in academic art. Picasso's work comprises more than 50,000 paintings, drawings, engravings, sculptures, and ceramics produced over 80 years and is described in a series of overlapping periods. Known for his penetrating gaze and domineering personality, he had a series of intense and overlapping love affairs throughout his life that are reflected in his work. Picasso continued to produce art with undiminished force until his death in 1973.

Pablo Picasso

366 Rival papal factions fight a bloody battle at Rome's Basilica Liberia over who should lead the Catholic Church.

ca. 900 English monarch Alfred the Great, renowned for his unstinting efforts to encourage education during the Dark Ages, dies.

1440 French nobleman Gilles de Rais is hanged for heresy and the abduction, torture, and murder of more than 140 children.

1640 During a war between France and Spain, the young Jules Mazarin (later Cardinal Mazarin) prevents a battle by galloping a horse between the two opposing armies shouting, "Peace, peace!" as if an armistice had been negotiated.

1709 An Anglo-Dutch-Austrian army captures Mons, France, during the War of the Spanish Succession.

1788 The British discovery ship *Bounty*, under the notorious Captain William Bligh, arrives in Tahiti to collect breadfruit.

1813 During the War of 1812, British forces head off an American attack on Montreal, Canada, in the Battle of Chateauguay.

1840 Bare-knuckle boxer Benjamin Caunt becomes the English champion after beating John Leechman in 101 rounds.

1858 Inventor Hamilton Smith of Philadelphia,

BORN ON THIS DAY

1685
DOMENICO SCARLATTI
Italian composer and harpsichordist

1754
GEORGES JACQUES DANTON
French revolutionary leader

1854
C. W. POST
American founder of Post Cereals

C. W. Post

1874
ABBY ROCKEFELLER
American philanthropist, co-founder of the New York Museum of Modern Art

1879
LEON TROTSKY
Russian revolutionary, president of the first Soviet

1894
JOHN S. KNIGHT
Pulitzer Prize-winning American reporter and editor

1911
MAHALIA JACKSON
American gospel singer ("Move On Up a Little Higher"; "Amazing Grace")

1916
FRANÇOIS MITTERAND
President of France (1981–95)

1919
MOHAMMED REZA PAHLAVI
Last shah of Persia

1930
JOHN ARDEN
English playwright

1947
HILLARY RODHAM CLINTON
U.S. senator from New York; first lady of 42nd U.S. president Bill Clinton

Pennsylvania, patents the rotary washing machine.

1864 During the American Civil War, Union forces ambush and kill notorious Confederate guerrilla leader William "Bloody Bill" Anderson, who had killed Union troops at Centralia, Missouri, and massacred civilians at Lawrence, Kansas.

1881 Three men die in the famous shootout at the OK Corral in Tombstone, Arizona, between the Earp brothers and the Clanton-McLaury gang.

1900 American writers Henry James and Edith Wharton begin corresponding with one another and would soon become great friends.

1915 During World War I, the British troop transport *Marquette* is torpedoed in the Aegean Sea.

1918 As Allied troops advance across Europe during World War I, German general Erich Ludendorff resigns.

1939 During World War II, Nazi Germany makes slaves of all Polish Jews ages 14 to 60.

1942 During the three-day Battle of Santa Cruz,

> *"It's easy to be independent when you've got money. But to be independent when you haven't got a thing—that's the Lord's test."*
>
> —*Mahalia Jackson*

General Erich Ludendorff

American naval forces once again stop a Japanese fleet from its repeated attempt to reinforce Guadalcanal. Japanese planes so damaged the U.S. aircraft carrier *Hornet* that it had to be abandoned.

1944 The largest air-naval battle in history, the World War II Battle of Leyte Gulf, ends after four days of intense combat with a decisive American victory that destroyed the Japanese fleet and gave the Allies control of the Pacific.

1948 A fluoride-laced smog descends on the working-class town of Donora, Pennsylvania, killing 20 and leading to the hospitalization of 7,000 (half the town's population) over the next few days. It was the nation's worst air pollution disaster.

1951 American former heavyweight boxing champion Joe Louis is knocked out in eight rounds by future champ Rocky Marciano.

1955 South Vietnamese prime minister Ngo Dinh Diem proclaims himself president of the new Republic of Vietnam.

 1955 American teen idol James Dean appears in the film *Rebel Without a Cause*, one of only three movies he made in a brief career cut short by a fatal car crash.

1963 The U.S. Navy successfully test-launches a Polaris A-3 missile from a submerged submarine, the USS *Andrew Jackson*, off Cape Canaveral, Florida.

1966 A fire aboard the U.S. aircraft carrier *Oriskany* off Vietnam kills 35 sailors and threatens to detonate a cache of some three hundred 500-pound, 1,000-pound, and 2,000-pound bombs.

1972 After negotiations with the North Vietnamese in Paris, U.S. national security advisor Henry Kissinger announces that "peace is at hand" in Vietnam. The Vietnam War continued for another three years.

1995 In Iceland, an early-morning avalanche strikes the fishing village of Flateyri and kills 20 people.

Joe Louis, left, and Rocky Marciano

312 At the Battle of Milvian Bridge a few miles north of Rome, Constantine slays Roman emperor Maxentius. Legend tells that Constantine saw a vision of a cross in the heavens, and the words "Conquer by This."

1428 Thomas Montagu, fourth earl of Salisbury, suffers a fatal wound while surveying the siege of Orleans from a castle window.

1449 Timurid ruler Ulugh Beg is assassinated on orders of his son, in Samarkand. The grandson of conqueror Tamerlane, his interests were cultural and scientific, not military, which left him open to militant rivals.

1539 Spanish explorer Hernando de Soto arrives on the site of modern Tallahassee, Florida.

1553 Spanish theologian Michael Servetus is burned alive in Switzerland for heresy.

1561 Lope de Aguirre, disreputable explorer and murderer famed for a disastrous expedition in search of legendary El Dorado, is executed by Spanish forces in what is now Venezuela.

1659 William Robinson and Marmaduke Stevenson, two Quakers who came to America from England in 1656 to escape religious persecution,

> *"He who laughs most, learns best."*
> —John Cleese

BORN ON THIS DAY

1728
JAMES COOK
English explorer who discovered the Sandwich Islands

1782
NICCOLÒ PAGANINI
Italian composer, violin virtuoso ("Sonata a Movement Perpetual")

1858
THEODORE ROOSEVELT
26th U.S. president (1901–09)

1872
EMILY POST
American authority on social behavior and author (*Etiquette*)

1914
DYLAN THOMAS
Welsh poet and author (*Portrait of the Artist as a Young Dog; Under Milk Wood; A Child's Christmas in Wales*)

1917
OLIVER TAMBO
President of South Africa's African National Congress

1923
ROY LICHTENSTEIN
American pop artist (*Grrrrrrrrr!!; Stepping Out; Vicki*)

1932
SYLVIA PLATH
American poet and author (*The Colossus; The Bell Jar*)

1939
JOHN CLEESE
English comedian and actor (*Monty Python's Flying Circus; The Life of Brian; A Fish Called Wanda*)

---

are executed in the Massachusetts Bay Colony for their religious beliefs. A year earlier, a law had been passed banning Quakers from the colony under penalty of death.

1795 Spain and the United States agree to the Treaty of San Lorenzo, which set the southern U.S. boundary at 31 degrees north latitude (roughly the current northern boundary of Florida).

1806 French general Napoleon Bonaparte occupies Berlin, Germany.

1864 At the Battle of Hatcher's Run, during the American Civil War, Union troops fail in a disastrous attempt to cut the last rail line supplying Confederate forces in Petersburg, Virginia. Also on this day, the CSS *Albemarle* sinks. It was the only Confederate ironclad destroyed by the Union during the war.

1870 During the Franco-German War, French marshal Achille Bazaine surrenders Metz and 140,000 men, an act for which he was sentenced to death.

Armstrong's mill and Confederate positions at the Battle of Hatcher's Run

The sentence was commuted, but Bazaine was ruined.

1873 Illinois farmer Joseph Glidden applies for a patent on his clever new design for barbed wire, an invention that would forever change the face of the American West.

1901 Russian composer and pianist Sergei Rachmaninoff scores his first important success with the debut performance, in Moscow, of his *Piano Concerto No. 2 in C Minor*.

1936 In England, Wallis Warfield Simpson is granted a preliminary decree of divorce. King Edward VIII would abdicate the British throne on December 10 in order to marry her.

1940 French general Charles de Gaulle forms a government-in-exile during World War II. Speaking for the Free French Forces from his temporary headquarters in equatorial Africa, he called on all French men and women "to attack the enemy wherever it is possible, to mobilize all our military, economic, and moral resources . . . to make justice reign."

1945 German automaker Ferdinand Porsche, builder of the Volkswagen, is arrested by U.S. military officials for his pro-Nazi activities. Sent to France, he was held for two years and then went back to designing cars.

1946 The American travel show *Geographically Speaking* debuts. It was the first television program with a commercial sponsor.

1954 American actress Marilyn Monroe and baseball star Joe DiMaggio divorce after DiMaggio allegedly struck Monroe following the filming of her famous "skirt scene" in *The Seven-Year Itch*. The scene, showing Monroe laughing as a blast of air from a subway grating lifts her skirt, infuriated DiMaggio, who felt it was exhibitionistic.

1954 Walt Disney's first television series, *Disneyland*, premieres on ABC. The show, which ran for 34 years under various names, was the longest-running prime-time series on American network television.

1962 Tense negotiations between the United States and the Soviet Union finally result in a plan to end the two-week-old Cuban Missile Crisis.

1991 Turkmenistan declares itself an independent republic.

1991 Israeli authorities give scholars open access to the Dead Sea Scrolls.

Marilyn Monroe

306 Angry citizens revolt in Rome against tax increases ordered by Flavius Severus, augustus of the West. In the spring, Severus marched toward Rome to set things right, but his army deserted him and before long he was executed by his rival, Maximilian.

1225 Jien, an aristocratic Buddhist monk and early historian of Japan, dies in Omi province. His masterwork was titled *Jottings of a Fool*.

1359 During the Hundred Years' War, Edward the Black Prince lands in Calais, France, to enforce the Treaty of London, which he had forced upon French king John II. He had captured John at the Battle of Poitiers in 1356 and held him captive in England.

1492 Italian explorer Christopher Columbus lands on the coast of Cuba and thinks he has found Cipangu (Japan). A few days later he decided he was wrong and that Cuba was in fact mainland China.

1577 In the Spanish-controlled Netherlands, Calvinist troops and townsfolk attack neighboring Catholics. Pillaging and destroying and burning monks alive, they took over the government of Ghent.

1636 The "Great and General Court of Massachusetts"

> *"The reward for work well done is the opportunity to do more."*
>
> —*Dr. Jonas Salk*

George Bernard Shaw

designates 400 pounds to establish a "schoale or college." The first classes were held two years later, and the college was named Harvard.

1746 A monster earthquake hits Peru, destroying the cities of Lima and Callao. Thirty minutes after the quake, a tsunami devastated the coast. One wave was estimated to be 80 feet high.

1776 In the early days of the American Revolutionary War, British forces defeat George Washington's army at the Battle of Chatterton Hill, in New York.

1790 Spain and Great Britain sign the Nootka Sound Convention, by which Spain gives up its claim to absolute sovereignty over fishing, sailing, trading, and living on the northwest coast of North America—a claim based on the pope having given it to Spain in 1493.

1859 In Kentucky, a pro-slavery mob destroys the office and press of the state's only antislavery newspaper, *The Free South*. The editor fled to Ohio.

1864 In the American Civil War, Union forces withdraw from Fair Oaks, Virginia, after failing to breach the Confederate defenses around Richmond. The assault was actually a diversion to draw attention from the larger, also unsuccessful, Union offensive at Hatcher's Run near Petersburg.

1905 Irish writer George Bernard Shaw's play *Mrs. Warren's Profession*, which deals frankly with prostitution, is performed at the Garrick Theater in New York. Already banned in Great Britain, it was closed by New York censors, who arrested the performers on obscenity charges.

1914 Gavrilo Princip, the Serbian assassin who shot Archduke Francis Ferdinand and his consort Sophie in Sarajevo (the event that triggered World War I), is sentenced to 20 years in prison.

1919 The U.S. Congress passes the Volstead Act, which enforced the 18th Amendment to the U.S. Constitution, also known as the Prohibition Amendment, which banned the consumption and sale of alcohol.

1922 Italian Blackshirt fascists launch an insurrection called the March on Rome.

King Victor Emmanuel III refused to order the army to oppose them, and the fascists carried Benito Mussolini to power.

1929 Mrs. T. W. Evans becomes the first woman to give birth in the air, to a girl aboard a passenger flight in Florida.

1930 Burmese monk, astrologer, and anti-British rebel leader Saya San has himself declared king of Burma. His revolt, and his army of dispossessed peasants, was crushed by British forces.

1940 In a self-destructive act of hubris, Italian dictator Benito Mussolini invades Greece in what will prove to be a short and disastrous military campaign for Il Duce's forces during World War II.

Statue of Liberty (milestone)

53 B.C. Babylon, the greatest city of the ancient world, falls to Cyrus the Great of Persia.

1618 Sir Walter Raleigh, founder of the first English settlement in America, is beheaded in London for conspiring against King James I.

1787 Austrian composer Wolfgang Mozart premieres his opera *Don Giovanni* in Prague, Czechoslovakia, to great acclaim.

1811 The first steamboat on the Ohio River cruises downriver from Pittsburgh, Pennsylvania, on its way to New Orleans, Louisiana.

1814 The U.S. Navy launches its first steam-powered warship, the *Fulton I*, in New York Harbor.

1858 The first store opens in the frontier town of Denver, Colorado, to serve miners working the placer gold deposits along Cheery Creek and the South Platte River.

1872 An all-metal windmill is patented by one J. S. Risdon of Genoa, Illinois.

1901 U.S. president William McKinley's assassin, the anarchist Leon Czolgosz, is executed by electrocution.

BORN ON THIS DAY

1740
JAMES BOSWELL
Scottish author who was Samuel Johnson's biographer (*The Life of Johnson; Journal of a Tour of the Hebrides*)

1815
DANIEL DECATUR EMMETT
American composer ("Dixie")

1882
JEAN GIRAUDOUX
French dramatist (*The Madwoman of Chaillot; Judith; Tiger at the Gates*)

1891
FANNY BRICE
American comedienne

1897
JOSEPH GOEBBELS
German minister of propaganda under Adolf Hitler

1921
BILL MAULDIN
American war correspondent and Pulitzer Prize-winning editorial cartoonist

1926
JON VICKERS
Canadian opera singer

1938
RALPH BAKSHI
American writer, director, and animator (*Fritz the Cat; American Pop; Wizards; Spicy City*)

1947
RICHARD DREYFUSS
American actor (*Close Encounters of the Third Kind; American Graffiti; What About Bob?*)

1971
WINONA RYDER
American actress (*Girl, Interrupted; Little Women; Beetlejuice*)

"One of the privileges of the great is to witness catastrophes from a terrace."

—*Jean Giraudoux*

1914 The Turkish fleet attacks the Ukrainian port city of Odessa during World War I.

1917 During World War I, German planes bomb the French cities of Dunkirk, Calais, and Belfort.

1918 The World War I battle of Sharqat, the final engagement on the Mesopotamian Front, opens in what is now Iraq with British forces seeking to control the Mosul oil fields north of Baghdad. On the same day, Italian and British troops advance five full miles along a 30-mile line on the war's southern front. Meanwhile, the German High Seas Fleet is ordered to leave port for a last-ditch battle, but mutinies instead.

1922 The Italian king Victor Emmanuel III invites fascist Benito Mussolini to form a government.

1923 The Turkish Republic is proclaimed.

Nineteenth century American river steamboat

1940 During World War II, British forces occupy Crete. On the same day, the United States begins drafting 1.2 million troops and 800,000 reserves.

1942 At a public meeting in Great Britain during World War II, leading clergymen and politicians register their outrage over the Nazi persecution of Europe's Jews. "The systematic cruelties," Prime Minister Winston Churchill wrote in a message to the gathering, "place an indelible stain upon all who perpetrate and instigate them."

1942 During World War II, Japanese infantry land in the Aleutian Islands.

1945 The first American ballpoint pen (an unauthorized knock-off of an invention by the Hungarian Laszlo Biró) goes on sale for $12.95 and rakes in $100,000 for its manufacturer.

1947 American weather scientists douse a New Hampshire forest fire by seeding cumulus clouds with dry ice to produce rain.

1954 The last of the line of true Hudson automobiles, renowned during the early 1950s for their style and handling, is produced in Detroit, Michigan.

1956 Israeli Army forces invade Egypt in response to the Egyptian nationalization of the Suez Canal. French and British troops would soon join them, precipitating the Suez Crisis.

1958 The first coronary angiogram is performed at the Cleveland Clinic by American pediatric cardiologist F. Mason Sones Jr.

1960 American boxing great Muhammad Ali (then named Cassius Clay) wins his first professional bout in six rounds in his hometown of Louisville, Kentucky.

1999 A devastating cyclone hits eastern India, destroying villages, touching off terrible floods, and killing at least 9,463 people.

Black Tuesday on Wall Street (milestone)

Antinoöpolis

130 Roman emperor Hadrian establishes Antinoöpolis on the Nile River. The city was the western terminus of the Via Hadriana, a road between the Red Sea and the Nile.

1340 At the Battle of Rio Salado in southern Spain, allied Christian forces defeat an enormous invading army of Muslim Marinids from North Africa.

1411 After decades of fighting with each other, Portugal and Spain reach a final peace.

1697 The second of two treaties of Rijswijk, in western Netherlands, marks the end of the War of the Grand Alliance between France on one side and much of Europe on the other. The treaties restored conditions to their pre-war status.

1811 English author Jane Austen's *Sense and Sensibility* is published anonymously. Most of the British public knew only that the popular novel had been written "by a Lady."

1862 During the American Civil War, Union general Ormsby Mitchell dies at Beaufort, South Carolina. A college professor and liberal

thinker, he protected slaves who escaped to his lines well before the practice was mandated by federal policy.

1864 Helena, Montana, is founded by four gold miners who struck it rich at the appropriately named "Last Chance Gulch." Their find produced some $19 million worth of gold in just four years. Helena became the state capital.

1888 American inventor John Loud is granted the first patent for a ballpoint pen. Loud could not devise a suitable ink feed, so the pen was never made.

1890 Oakland, California, enacts one of America's first antinarcotic laws, limiting opium, morphine, and cocaine to doctors' prescriptions.

1905 Czar Nicholas II, under pressure from the Russian Revolution of 1905, issues the October Manifesto, ending autocratic rule in favor of a constitutional monarchy and granting a range of civil liberties.

1918 The Armistice of Mudros, signed on the island of Lemnos in the Aegean Sea, marks the surrender and dissolution of the Ottoman Empire after World War I.

1922 Fascist leader Benito Mussolini becomes premier of Italy.

> *"The best impromptu speeches are the ones written well in advance."*
> —*Ruth Gordon*

1925 Scottish television pioneer John Logie Baird makes the world's first television transmission of a moving image: 15-year-old office boy William Taynton, who thereby became the first person to appear on television. Baird's transmitter was built from items including a tea chest, darning needles, and piano wire.

1941 President Franklin D. Roosevelt, determined to keep the United States out of World War II while helping the Allies already mired in it, approves $1 billion in Lend-Lease loans to the Soviet Union.

1943 Italian film director Federico Fellini marries his favorite actress, Giulietta Masina.

1953 U.S. president Dwight D. Eisenhower formally approves National Security Council Paper No. 162/2, a secret document advising expansion of the nation's nuclear arsenal as a cost-efficient way to fight the Cold War.

1959 In the United States, Piedmont Airlines flight 349 crashes, killing 26. One man, E. Phil Bradley, survived—the only sole survivor of a commercial air crash on record.

1974 American boxer Muhammad Ali scores an upset victory over George Foreman in eight rounds. The match, called the "Rumble in the Jungle," was held in Zaire.

1975 Prince Juan Carlos becomes Spain's acting head of state after Generalissimo Francisco Franco, the dictator of Spain since 1938, concedes that he is too ill too govern. On November 22, Juan Carlos would be crowned king.

1983 In Turkey, a 7.1-magnitude earthquake kills 1,000.

1995 By a bare majority of 50.6 percent to 49.4 percent, voters in the province of Quebec decide not to secede from the federation of Canada.

George Foreman takes a right from challenger Muhammad Ali

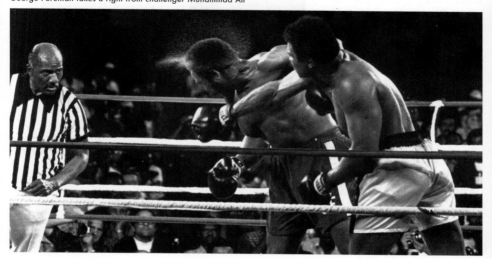

475 Orestes, master of soldiers for the Western Roman Empire, puts his young son on the throne after deposing the rightful Western emperor, Julius Nepos. He and his hopes died when his army switched allegiance to the German war leader Odoacer, Italy's first barbarian king.

1756 The notorious Italian libertine Giovanni Casanova, imprisoned in Venice for being a magician, makes a dramatic escape and flees to Paris, France.

1815 English chemist Humphrey Davy patents a safety lamp that warns coal miners of the presence of explosive methane gas.

1822 Mexican emperor Agustín I, only five months on the throne, dismisses the civilian congress and sets up a junta government. Disgruntled rivals would soon overthrow him under the banner of Santa Anna.

1828 William Burke and William Hare murder their last victim. Keepers of a lodge in Edinburgh, Scotland, they took to murdering the occasional traveler and selling the corpses to a local school of anatomy. Killing a local woman got them caught.

1861 During the American Civil War, General

> *"Many have original minds who do not think it—they are led away by custom."*
>
> —John Keats

Martin Luther Posts 95 Theses

Martin Luther, a professor of biblical interpretation at the University of Wittenberg in Germany, nails his 95 revolutionary theses on the door of the Castle Church on this day in 1517, marking the beginning of the Protestant Reformation in Germany. Luther's theses condemned the excesses and corruption of the Roman Catholic Church, especially the papal practice of asking payment, called indulgences, for the forgiveness of sins. In 1521, Pope Leo X excommunicated him. Three months later, Luther was called to defend his beliefs before Holy Roman emperor Charles V at the Diet of Worms, where he was famously defiant.

Martin Luther

Miners with safety lamps

Winfield Scott, commander of the Union forces, retires, citing bad health. He was criticized for early losses, but his general strategy prevailed in the end.

1863 George I, a Danish prince selected to become the constitutional monarch of Greece, ascends to the throne. He would reign successfully for 50 years.

1864 The U.S. Congress, anxious to have support of the Republican-dominated Nevada Territory for President Abraham Lincoln's reelection, quickly admits Nevada as the 36th state in the Union.

1870 The Blanquists, followers of French socialist revolutionary Auguste Blanqui, stage an unsuccessful uprising against the provisional government of the Third Republic. Napoleon III had surrendered to the Germans, who were marching on a disorganized Paris.

1873 During a Cuban rebellion, Spanish authorities seize the *Virginius*, a Cuban ship carrying false U.S. registration, and execute 53 of its crew and passengers, including Britons and Americans. The incident nearly led to war with the United States.

1876 Months after their spectacular victory over General George Custer at the Battle of the Little Bighorn, some 3,000 Sioux surrender to the U.S. Army in Montana.

1888 Scottish veterinary surgeon, bicyclist, and inventor John Dunlop patents the pneumatic bike tire, but his patent is later revoked when it is discovered that the idea had previously been patented in 1845 by fellow Scotsman Robert William Thompson. Thompson's invention had been used only for horse-drawn carriages and had since been forgotten.

1918 In the final battles of World War I, American and French troops drive German forces from the Argonne Forest.

1956 During the Suez Crisis, British and French troops arrive in the canal zone to join Israeli troops already on the scene. Their goal was to foil Egypt's plans to nationalize the Suez canal.

1961 Five years after Soviet leader Nikita Khrushchev

Communist supporters commemorate Stalin's death

denounced Stalinism and the "personality cult" of Soviet rulers, Joseph Stalin's embalmed body is removed from public display at Lenin's tomb in Moscow's Red Square.

1961 Hurricane Hattie and its accompanying storm surge destroy much of Belize City, the main port and then the capital of Belize. The capital was later moved to a safer inland location.

1970 South Vietnamese president Nguyen Van Thieu claims that 99.1 percent of the country has been "pacified," and that military victory in the Vietnam War is close at hand.

1984 Indira Gandhi, the prime minister of India, is assassinated in New Delhi by two of her own bodyguards. Both men were Sikhs, apparently reacting to Gandhi's having ordered an army raid on a Sikh temple in Punjab to flush out armed Sikh extremists.

1992 In Rome, Italy, the Vatican finally admits that Galileo was right: Earth does revolve around the sun.

1254 Hayton, king of a region in what is now Turkey, leaves the Mongol capital of Karakorum after a six-week visit. His account of the trip is one of the first and most detailed chronicles of the powerful Mongol Empire.

1492 Italian explorer Christopher Columbus, realizing he is not in Japan, decides that Cuba is the Chinese mainland.

1501 Italian navigator Amerigo Vespucci discovers Bahia de Todos Santos (All Saints Bay) on the coast of Brazil.

1700 The last Spanish Hapsburg monarch, Charles the Mad, dies in Madrid at age 38, leaving no offspring. His death touched off the War of the Spanish Succession.

1755 A great earthquake wrecks the Portuguese capital of Lisbon, destroying about 12,000 homes. About 60,000 people died, including many in church for All Saints' Day mass and others killed in the subsequent tsunami.

1765 The Stamp Act, a tax on the American colonies to pay for British military operations in America officially goes into effect. It caused an uproar. "Taxation without representation" became an incentive for revolution.

1803 In Great Britain's campaign against the Maratha

> *"The harder you work, the luckier you get."*
> —*Gary Player*

Michelangelo's Sistine Chapel Ceiling Goes on View

The ceiling of the Sistine Chapel, one of Italian artist Michelangelo Buonarroti's finest works, is exhibited to the public for the first time on this day in 1512. Central in a complex system of decoration featuring numerous figures are nine panels devoted to biblical history. The most famous of these is *The Creation of Adam*, a painting in which the arms of God and Adam are stretching toward each other. After 15 years as an architect in Florence, Michelangelo returned to Rome in 1534, where he worked and lived for the rest of his life.

Michelangelo Buonarroti

Stamp Act protestors

Confederacy in India, General Gerard Lake defeats Daulat Rao Sindhia's army at Laswari, after earlier capturing Delhi.

1858 Shaken by the recent Indian Mutiny, Great Britain announces a new policy that leaves the princely states intact, rather than annexing them into a unified India.

1893 Supporters of basing the U.S. dollar on gold win a key victory, as Congress votes to repeal the three-year-old Sherman Silver Purchase Act.

1894 Nicholas II succeeds his father as czar of Russia. He was the last of the czars.

1895 The first automobile club in the United States, the American Motor League, holds its preliminary meeting in Chicago, Illinois, with 60 members.

1899 During the Boer War, Boer forces begin the siege of Ladysmith, South Africa.

1913 In an American football game between Notre

Dame and Navy, the forward pass is used for the first time.

1914 The German Far Eastern Squadron under Admiral Graf von Spee defeats the British 4th Cruiser Squadron off the coast of Chile during World War I.

1914 Russia declares war on the Ottoman Empire after the Ottoman fleet attacks the Black Sea port of Odessa, sinking two Russian ships.

1922 Two years after the first commercial radio station began broadcasting in the United States (KDKA in Pittsburgh, Pennsylvania), 524 stations have received licenses.

1927 For the first time since the Model T was introduced in 1908, the Ford Motor Company begins production on a significantly redesigned automobile—the Model A.

Hungarian rebels atop a Soviet tank in Budapest, Hungary

1950 Puerto Rican nationalist radicals Griselio Torresola and Oscar Collazo attempt to assassinate U.S. president Harry S. Truman in Washington, D.C. A few years earlier, Truman had escaped a similar attempt by the right-wing Israeli Stern Gang. "A president has to expect these things," he remarked.

1952 The United States detonates the world's first thermonuclear weapon, the hydrogen bomb, on Eniwetok atoll in the Pacific. The Soviet Union would explode its own H-bomb the following year.

1954 Independent India takes de facto control of the last French possessions on the subcontinent.

1956 During the Hungarian Revolution against communist rule, rebel premier Imre Nagy declares Hungary a neutral country and appeals, in vain, for support from the United Nations.

"It is easy to be popular. It is not easy to be just."

—Rose Elizabeth Bird

1164 Archbishop of Canterbury Thomas à Becket begins a six-year exile in France.

1388 At age 19, Charles the Mad dismisses his uncles, who have served as advisors, and declares that he will rule France by himself. He was alternately sane and mad for most of his 42-year reign.

1637 John Harvard arrives in Charlestown, Massachusetts Bay Colony. His donation to a newly established college set the school on a firm foundation. In 1639 it was named Harvard College.

1721 The Russian Senate elevates Peter the Great from czar to emperor.

1781 Up-and-coming actor John Kemble makes his first big-city appearance, as Hamlet, in Dublin, Ireland. As manager of the Covent Garden and Drury Lane theaters in London, England, he became a popular favorite.

1783 After the American Revolutionary War, Congress disbands the Continental Army.

John Brown

1802 French general Charles Leclerc dies of yellow fever in Haiti while trying to put down a rebellion. The French were beaten, and Haiti became independent in 1804.

1840 At Parwan, Afghan partisans under Dost Mohammad have one day of success in their campaign to drive the British from their country. The next day they surrendered.

1859 Abolitionist John Brown, whose raid on Harper's Ferry, Virginia, inflamed tensions leading to the American Civil War, is found guilty of treason and murder. He was hanged a month later.

1861 During the American Civil War, President

Abraham Lincoln removes controversial Union general John C. Fremont from command in the Western Department. Fremont had endangered a delicate political balance by declaring martial law and the emancipation of slaves in Missouri.

1878 Edward Scripps publishes his first newspaper, the *Cleveland Penny Press.* He went on to found the first large syndicate of papers in the United States, the Scripps-McRae League of Newspapers.

1917 Great Britain issues the Balfour Declaration, stating the British intent to establish a Jewish homeland in Palestine. The declaration was included in the British mandate over Palestine, approved by the League of Nations in 1922 over the objection of Arabs.

1920 Pittsburgh, Pennsylvania, radio station KDKA broadcasts the results of the 1920 presidential race between Warren G. Harding and James M. Cox. This was the first significant public radio news broadcast in the United States.

1930 The new emperor of Ethiopia assumes a new name, Haile Selassi, which

means "Might of the Trinity." Previously Ras Tafari Makonnen, he claimed descent from the Queen of Sheba and King Solomon.

1939 Nazi German dictator Adolf Hitler's minister of propaganda, Joseph Goebbels, visits Lodz, Poland. Of the city's 200,000 Jews, he reported, "They were no longer people, but beasts. . . . Here one must make a radical incision. Otherwise Europe will be ruined by the Jewish sickness."

1948 In the greatest upset in U.S. presidential election history, Democratic incumbent Harry S. Truman defeats his Republican challenger, Governor Thomas E. Dewey of New York, by just over two million votes. Long before all the votes were counted, the *Chicago Tribune* published an early edition with the banner headline "DEWEY DEFEATS TRUMAN."

Harry S. Truman

361 Roman emperor Constantius II, who spent years shuttling from one end of the empire to the other to confront a series of invaders and usurpers, dies in Turkey on his way back to Gaul.

1295 During the Mongol occupation of Iran, Mahmud Ghazan takes the throne of Il-Khan (subordinate to the Great Khan) and launches a ruthless career of conquest.

1428 During the Hundred Years' War between England and France, Thomas de Montacute, earl of Salisbury, dies of wounds received in the decisive siege of Orléans.

1440 After 25 years as a prisoner in England, Charles, duc d'Orleans, arrives home in France. He was captured at the Battle of Agincourt during the Hundred Years' War.

1493 Italian explorer Christopher Columbus sights the Caribbean island of Dominica. It was a Sunday; *dies dominica* is Latin for "the Lord's day."

1529 British lord chancellor Sir Thomas More opens the Parliament that will later sentence him to death for not supporting Henry VIII's marriage plans.

1839 Ottoman sultan Abdulmecid I issues the "Noble

> *"Man is not what he thinks he is, he is what he hides."*
> —André Malraux

BORN ON THIS DAY

1611
HENRY IRETON
Parliamentarian commander in the English Civil War, son-in-law of Oliver Cromwell

1718
JOHN MONTAGU, FOURTH EARL OF SANDWICH
English politician and inventor of the sandwich, for whom the Sandwich Islands were named

1749
DANIEL RUTHERFORD
Scottish discoverer of nitrogen

1794
WILLIAM CULLEN BRYANT
American poet ("Thanatopsis")

1801
KARL BAEDEKER
German publisher who created a series of guide books

1801
VICENZO BELLINI
Italian composer (*La Sonnambula; Norma*)

1901
ANDRÉ MALRAUX
French Resistance fighter in World War II and novelist (*The Voices of Silence*)

1908
BRONKO NAGURSKI
American professional football player

1912
ALFREDO STROESSER
President and dictator of Paraguay (1954–89)

1921
CHARLES BRONSON
American actor (*Death Wish; The Stone Killer; Battle of the Bulge*)

1933
MICHAEL DUKAKIS
Massachusetts governor and 1988 Democratic presidential candidate

1933
KEN BERRY
American actor (*F-Troop; Mayberry, RFD*)

Edict of the Rose Chamber," a decree granting equality to all his subjects, regardless of race or creed.

1844 English author William Makepeace Thackeray completes *The Luck of Barry Lyndon: A Romance of the Last Century*. It was first published in serialized form in Fraser's Magazine.

1863 J. T. Alden wins a U.S. patent for a method to preserve yeast in a dried, granular form.

1864 Antonio Dias, Brazil's national poet, dies in a shipwreck while sailing home from a visit to Europe.

1883 California bandit and infamous stagecoach robber Black Bart makes his last robbery. He got away, but was caught later and sent to prison.

1883 In the central Sudan region of Kordofan, Mahdist rebels annihilate Egyptian troops sent to suppress their revolt.

1892 The first telephone exchange in the world to use automatic switching devices

William Makepeace Thackeray

Ku Klux Klan violence in Greensboro

opens for public use in LaPorte, Indiana.

1900 America's first car show opens in New York City.

1903 With the support of the U.S. government, Panama issues a declaration of independence from Colombia. The revolution opened the way for construction of the Panama Canal.

1914 Mary Jacob of New York City wins a patent for the first soft brassiere. Her prototype was made from two silk handkerchiefs and pink ribbon: no whalebone, no metal rods.

1918 At the end of World War I, Austria-Hungary signs an armistice with the victorious Allies. The war finally ended eight days later when Germany signed the Armistice.

1919 Fueled by a post-Armistice "inflation boom" in the United States, the Dow posts a high of 119.62. In August 1920, it bottomed out at 63.90.

1939 As World War II erupts in Europe, and at the urging of President Franklin D. Roosevelt, the U.S. Congress revises the Neutrality Act to allow the sale of weaponry to France and England.

1946 In Japan, the first post-World War II Diet passes a new constitution prepared by the American occupation forces. It placed sovereignty with the people and renounced war.

1952 American frozen-food pioneer Clarence Birdseye introduces the first frozen peas.

1961 Burmese diplomat U Thant is unanimously elected secretary general of the United Nations. His predecessor, Dag Hammarskjöld, had died in a plane crash in Northern Rhodesia while on a diplomatic mission.

1964 In one of the biggest U.S. presidential election landslides, incumbent president Lyndon B. Johnson defeats Republican challenger Barry M. Goldwater.

1969 President Richard M. Nixon coins two new terms, appealing to the "great silent majority" of Americans for their support as he worked for "peace with honor" in Vietnam.

1970 Socialist president Salvador Allende is inaugurated in Chile.

1979 Five members of the Communist Workers Party, participating in a "Death to the Klan" rally in Greensboro, North Carolina, are shot to death by a group of Klansmen and neo-Nazis. Seven others were wounded.

Laika, the Soviet space dog

> *"Everything is funny as long as it is happening to somebody else."*
>
> —*Will Rogers*

1493 Italian explorer Christopher Columbus pays a short visit to the Caribbean island of Guadeloupe.

1520 The king of Denmark and Norway, Christian II, is crowned king of Sweden. His first act would be the Stockholm Bloodbath, which resulted in a rebellion that ended in Swedish independence.

1530 English cardinal Thomas Wolsey, who failed to acquire a papal annulment of Henry VIII's marriage to Catherine of Aragon, is arrested for treason. He died before facing charges.

1791 U.S. general Arthur St. Clair, sent with an undisciplined army of 3,000 men and camp followers to punish Indian raiders in present-day Ohio, is surprised at dawn and disastrously defeated. More than 600 militiamen died.

1796 The United States and Tripoli sign a treaty giving American ships some relief from pirate attacks.

1839 Extreme members of the Chartist parliamentary reform movement stage an armed uprising in Newport, Wales. The revolt was suppressed, and its leader, John Frost, was convicted of treason.

MILESTONE

Entrance to King Tut's Tomb Discovered

English archaeologist Howard Carter and his workmen discover a step leading to the tomb of King Tutankhamen in the Valley of the Kings in Egypt on this day in 1922. After World War I, Carter had begun an intensive search for King Tut's tomb. On November 26, 1922, Carter and Lord Carnarvon entered the interior chambers of the tomb, finding them miraculously intact. Inside the coffin was the mummy of the boy-king Tutankhamen, preserved for more than 3,000 years. Most of the tomb's treasures are now housed in the Cairo Museum.

Golden mask of King Tutankhamen (milestone)

1842 After a stormy three-year courtship marked by a broken engagement, future U.S. president Abraham Lincoln marries Kentucky-born Mary Todd.

1846 In the United States, Benjamin Palmer wins a patent for his advanced design of a jointed artifical leg.

1879 California dentist John Beers patents artificial gold tooth crowns that can be glued rather than hammered in place.

1880 James and John Ritty of Dayton, Ohio, invent the first cash register. It had a round face like a clock, whose hands indicated the amount of purchase.

1890 In London, England, the world's first electric-powered underground railway opens. Precursor to London's famous Underground, or Tube, this first line ran three miles. The fare: tuppence.

1911 In the Second Moroccan Crisis, France and Germany settle a dispute over their African interests. France got protectorate rights over Morocco, and Germany got land in the French Congo.

1913 Chinese Republic president Yuan Shikai purges the national assembly of Guomindang (Nationalist Party) members.

Yuan Shikai

1917 In Germany, the mutiny of sailors refusing to leave the harbor of Kiel and engage the British spreads to other seaports. On November 9, the emperor would abdicate.

1918 Just one week before the Armistice ended World War I, English soldier and poet Wilfred Owen is killed in action on the Western Front.

1942 After losing the final and most famous battle at El Alamein, Egypt, German field marshal Erwin Rommel disobeys Hitler's order to fight to the death and begins his five-month retreat.

1943 The world's first self-sustaining nuclear fission reaction is achieved at Oak Ridge National Laboratory.

1952 Russia's far eastern Kamchatka Peninsula is rocked by the fourth largest earthquake of the century, measuring 9.0 on the Richter scale.

1952 On Election Day in the United States, UNIVAC, the world's first commercially available electronic computer, predicts a landslide victory for Dwight D. Eisenhower over Adlai Stevenson. The computer's

prediction was more accurate than conventional polls.

1956 Soviet tanks roll into Budapest to stop Hungary's political reform movement, and to prevent the country from leaving the communist bloc. Thousands were killed and wounded, and nearly a quarter-million Hungarians fled the country. Reformist premier Imre Nagy was captured and executed.

1965 Lee Ann Roberts Breedlove, wife of land-speed record-holder Craig Breedlove, becomes the first female driver to exceed 300 miles per hour, hitting 308.50 miles per hour at the Bonneville Salt Flats in Utah.

1979 In Iran, student followers of the Ayatollah Khomeini storm the U.S. embassy in Tehran, taking 90 hostages. The ayatollah released all non-U.S. captives and all female and minority Americans but kept 52 men for 444 days.

1995 Israeli prime minister Yitzhak Rabin is fatally shot after attending a peace rally held in Tel Aviv. He later died in surgery. The assassin was a 27-year-old Jewish law student who opposed Rabin's efforts to make peace.

Adlai Stevenson, left, and President Dwight D. Eisenhower

BORN ON THIS DAY

1577
FRANCOIS LE CLERC DU TREMBLAY
French advisor to Cardinal Richelieu, known as "l'Éminence Grise"

1650
WILLIAM III (WILLIAM OF ORANGE)
Netherlands-born king of Britain and Ireland, ruling jointly with his wife Mary II

1740
AUGUSTUS MONTAGUE TOPLADY
English clergyman and hymn writer ("Rock of Ages")

1879
WILL ROGERS
American humorist and entertainer

1916
WALTER CRONKITE
American journalist (*CBS Evening News*)

1918
MARTIN BALSAM
Academy Award-winning American actor (*A Thousand Clowns; Mission: Impossible*)

1919
ART CARNEY
American comedian and Academy Award-winning actor (*The Honeymooners; Harry and Tonto*)

1937
LORETTA SWIT
American actress (*M.A.S.H.*)

1940
DELBERT MCCLINTON
American country singer ("Sending Me Angels"; "Giving It Up For Your Love")

1946
LAURA W. BUSH
U.S. first lady, wife of President George W. Bush

1962
RALPH MACCHIO
American actor (*The Karate Kid; Crossroads*)

1969
MATTHEW MCCONAUGHEY
American actor (*Amistad; U-571; The Wedding Planner*)

"Our knowledge is a receding mirage in an expanding desert of ignorance."

—Will Durant

1556 North of Delhi, India, a Mughal army defeats the forces of Hemu, a Hindu general trying to usurp the Mughal throne from the recently proclaimed emperor, 14-year-old Akbar. With able regents and his own brilliant leadership, Akbar brought the Mughal Empire to unprecedented glory.

1688 William of Orange and his army land at Brixham, England, having been asked by English malcontents to rescue them from the pro-French, Catholic policies of James II. James fled, and in what was known as the Glorious Revolution, William and his wife Mary, James's daughter, came to the throne.

1735 The Jewish community of Mantua, Italy, agrees to send gifts to a local school. In return, the students agree not to exercise their right to throw things at passing Jews.

1781 John Hanson, sometimes called the first American president, is elected "President of the United States in Congress Assembled" by the Continental Congress. He was a presiding officer, not a chief executive.

1824 America's first engineering college, the Rensselaer School, is established in Troy, New York. Its name was later changed to Rensselaer Polytechnic Institute.

MILESTONE

Gunpowder Plot

James I of England and VI of Scotland escapes death in the Gunpowder Plot on this day in 1605. A group of Catholic conspirators led by Robert Catesby had conceived the plot, angered by laws restricting religious practice and banning many priests, especially Jesuits, from the country. The Catholic Lord Monteagle received an anonymous letter warning him not to attend the State Opening of Parliament. He showed the letter to Robert Cecil, James I's chief minister, and a search was undertaken of the cellars on November 4th. Guy Fawkes was found with 36 barrels of gunpowder and arrested. Under torture, Fawkes revealed the names of his co-conspirators, who were arrested and executed. In the aftermath, far harsher anti-Catholic laws were passed.

1854 During the Crimean War, Florence Nightingale and her cadre of nurses arrive at the Barracks Hospital in Turkey to tend wounded British soldiers. On the same day, British infantry defeat Russian forces at the bloody battle of Inkerman, despite being outnumbered four to one. Nineteen Victoria Crosses were awarded to British soldiers.

1862 More than 300 Santee Sioux are found guilty of raping and murdering Anglo settlers during the Minnesota Uprising, and are sentenced to hang. President Abraham Lincoln, citing the long history of Anglo injustice and abuse against the Santee, commuted all but 39 of the death sentences.

1862 U.S. president Abraham Lincoln removes General George B. McClellan from command of the Army of the Potomac. McClellan ably built the army in the early stages of the war but proved a

Florence Nightingale

sluggish and paranoid field commander.

1889 Citizens of Wyoming Territory approve their state constitution, the world's first constitution to grant women full voting rights.

1891 Future Nobel Prize winner and physicist Marie Curie enrolls for classes at the Sorbonne, in France. On the same day in 1906, she begins lecturing as the university's first female physics instructor.

1893 Columns by the 20-year-old Willa Cather begin appearing in the *Nebraska State Journal.* She won a Pulitzer Prize in 1922 for *One of Ours,* and her 1927 novel *Death Comes for the Archbishop* is a classic.

1895 American inventor George B. Selden wins a patent for his gasoline-powered automobile. His impractical design was far behind those of other innovators, but he collected royalties on the idea of combining a motor with a carriage until 1911, when a court declared his concept outdated.

1912 Woodrow Wilson is elected the 28th president of the United States. Running against one former and one incumbent president, Wilson won 435 electoral votes. Incumbent William Howard Taft drew eight and Theodore Roosevelt won 88.

1913 Water diverted from the Owens Valley on the east slope of the Sierra Mountains begins flowing into water-starved Los Angeles, California, the result of a controversial,

Sinclair Lewis and his wife

corrupt, and visionary development scheme.

1930 Sinclair Lewis, author of *Babbitt, Arrowsmith,* and *Elmer Gantry,* wins the Nobel Prize in literature. The Minnesota native was the first American to win the distinguished award.

1963 Archaeologists working in Newfoundland discover the ruins of a Viking settlement that predated Christopher Columbus in the New World by 500 years.

1990 Meir Kahane is shot dead in New York City. An American-born rabbi and founder of the far-right Kach movement, Kahane advocated expulsion of all Arabs from Israel. El Sayyid Nosair, an Egyptian, was later convicted.

1991 English publishing magnate Robert Maxwell disappears from his yacht off the Canary Islands. After his body was discovered, his death was ruled a suicide, perhaps driven by legal and financial trouble.

355 Julian, at age 23, is made Caesar (and successor-in-waiting) by his cousin Emperor Constantius II. As an enemy of Christianity, he publicly converted to paganism when he became emperor in 361.

963 In the merry-go-round of papal politics, Holy Roman Emperor Otto I calls a council that replaces the 25-year-old pope John XII with Leo VIII. John later deposed Leo, and three months later died in bed with his mistress.

1398 Central Asian conqueror Tamerlane sweeps across the Indus River in his bloody invasion of India.

1455 Johannes Gutenberg, German inventor of movable type and printer of the first typeset Bible, loses his print shop in a lawsuit with a creditor.

1528 Spanish conquistador Álvar Núñez Cabeza de Vaca is shipwrecked on a low, sandy island off the coast of Texas. Starving, dehydrated, and desperate, he was the first European to visit the future Lone Star state.

1600 Japanese warrior Ishida Mitsunari is executed after losing the Battle of Sekigahara. His loss assured the acendancy of the Tokugawa family, which held the position of shogun until 1868.

> *"The ignorant man always adores what he cannot understand."*
>
> —*Cesare Lombroso*

BORN ON THIS DAY

1558
THOMAS KYD
English playwright (*The Spanish Tragedie*)

1671
COLLEY CIBBER
English actor, playwright (*Love's Last Shift; Xerxes*) and poet ("The Blind Boy")

1814
ADOLPHE SAX
Belgian inventor of the saxophone

1851
CHARLES H. DOW
American journalist who was the first editor of the *Wall Street Journal* and who co-founded the Dow Jones company

1854
JOHN PHILIP SOUSA
American composer and bandleader ("Stars and Stripes Forever")

1861
JAMES NAISMITH
American inventor of basketball

1887
WALTER PERRY JOHNSON
American Baseball Hall of Fame pitcher who threw 110 shutouts, still the all-time record

1892
SIR JOHN ALCOCK
British pilot of the first nonstop transatlantic flight

1900
HEINRICH HIMMLER
Nazi German SS leader

1921
JAMES JONES
American author (*From Here to Eternity*)

1931
MIKE NICHOLS
German-born American director, winner of Tony (*The Odd Couple; The Prisoner of Second Avenue; The Real Thing*) and Academy awards (*The Graduate*)

1836
CESARE LOMBROSO
Italian criminologist and author (*L'umo Delinquente*)

1813 Mexican revolutionaries behind José Morelos declare independence from Spain, but the revolution would be suppressed.

1860 Abraham Lincoln is elected the 16th president of the United States, the first Republican to win the office. Southern states had been threatening secession if he was elected. On the day of his inauguration the following March, seven rebel states will have already formed the Confederate States of America.

1861 Jefferson Davis is elected president of the Confederate States of America. He ran without opposition, and the election simply confirmed the decision made by the Confederate Congress earlier in the year.

1869 Rutgers and Princeton universities play the first intercollegiate football game at Rutgers in New Brunswick, New Jersey. Rutgers won, 6–4.

1893 Russian composer Pyotr Ilich Tchaikovsky dies at the age of 53. The official

Jefferson Davis

1899 Packard Model A

explanation for his death was that he had drunk water contaminated with cholera, but many believe he had been forced to commit suicide as details of a homosexual affair with the czar's nephew were about to be revealed.

🔬 **1899** The first Packard automobile is completed and test-driven through the streets of Warren, Ohio. The Model A featured a one-cylinder engine, a single seat, and a chain drive. Cost: $1,250.

🎭 **1909** American theatrical producer Winthrop Ames opens a distinguished New York career with a production of *Antony and Cleopatra* at the New Theatre, the city's largest.

🏴 **1911** Revolutionary leader Francisco Madero is elected president of Mexico, having ousted dictator Porfirio Díaz with the support of Pancho Villa.

💥 **1914** During World War I, after six weeks of terrible fighting, the French offensive called the Second Battle of Champagne ends with no appreciable gain.

🏴 **1917** Behind Bolshevik Party leader Vladimir Lenin, leftist revolutionaries launch a nearly bloodless coup d'état against Russia's ineffectual Provisional Government in the Russian capital, Petrograd. Bolshevik Russia, later renamed the Union of Soviet Socialist Republics, was the world's first Marxist state.

💥 **1917** After three months of horrific fighting during World War I, the Third Battle of Ypres ends when Canadian forces take the village of Passchendaele in Belgium. Nearly 250,000 casualties were suffered by both sides, and the Allies advanced five miles.

🎭 **1921** *The Sheik*, starring American silent-film actor Rudolph Valentino, opens to negative reviews. But Valentino caught the attention of women across the country, who were soon literally swooning in the aisles at his movies.

🔬 **1928** The first electric flashing sign signals election results from all four sides of the New York Times building in New York City. It took more than 14,000 lamps and one million feet of wire.

Segregated bus in apartheid South Africa

305 B.C. Ptolemy, Macedonian general and follower of Alexander the Great, assumes the kingship of Egypt. Cleopatra VII, who died in 30 B.C., was the last of the Ptolemaic dynasty.

1497 Searching for a sea route to India, Portuguese explorer Vasco de Gama arrives at Santa Helena Bay near the Cape of Good Hope on the southern tip of Africa. He reached India the following May.

1504 Italian-born Spanish explorer Christopher Columbus arrives in Spain after his disappointing fourth voyage, still believing he had reached the fringes of Asia.

1659 Spain and France sign the Treaty of the Pyrenees, ending the war that stretched back to 1622 and was an extension of the Thirty Years' War.

1811 Shawnee Indians under Tecumseh's brother Laulewasikau, "The Prophet," are defeated by future U.S. president General William Harrison at the Battle of Tippecanoe.

1859 Immigrants to the Rocky Mountains form the illegal Territory of Jefferson and set up a provisional government. It lasted until the U.S. Congress created the Territory of Colorado in 1861.

1869 English bicyclist James Moore wins the first city-to-city bicycle race, from Paris to Rouen, France. He pedaled 84 miles in 10 hours, 25 minutes.

1875 British explorer Verney Lovett Cameron reaches the coast of Angola, becoming

BORN ON THIS DAY

1867
MARIE CURIE
Nobel Prize-winning Polish-born French physicist and chemist who co-discovered the radioactive elements polonium and radium and coined the term "radioactivity"

1879
LEON TROTSKY
Soviet communist politician

1903
DEAN JAGGER
American actor (*Game of Death; King Creole*)

1905
WILLIAM ALWYN
English composer, best known for his film scores (*A Night to Remember; The Swiss Family Robinson*)

1913
ALBERT CAMUS
Nobel Prize-winning French philosopher and author (*The Stranger*)

1918
BILLY GRAHAM
American Christian evangelist and author (*Revival in Our Times; America's Hour of Decision*)

1922
AL HIRT
American jazz trumpeter

1926
DAME JOAN SUTHERLAND
Australian opera singer

1943
JONI MITCHELL
American musician, poet, and artist ("The Circle Game;" "California;" "Big Yellow Taxi")

1959
KEITH LOCKHART
American conductor of the Boston Pops Orchestra

1964
DANA PLATO
American actress (*Diff'rent Strokes*)

1970
NEIL HANNON
Northern Irish singer/songwriter with The Divine Comedy ("Something for the Weekend"; "The Frog Princess")

General William H. Harrison

the first person on record to cross equatorial Africa from the Indian Ocean to the Atlantic. His expedition was meant to carry aid to missionary David Livingstone, but he arrived after Livingstone's death.

1885 At a remote spot called Craigellachie in the mountains of British Columbia, the last spike is driven into Canada's first transcontinental railway.

1912 Russia and Outer Mongolia sign a treaty securing Mongolia's autonomy.

1914 Having declared war on Germany, and having violated China's neutrality, Japan captures the German concession area of Qingdao in Shandong Province, China.

1916 Montana suffragist Jeannette Rankin is elected to the U.S. House of Representatives. She was the first woman to win a seat in the U.S. Congress.

> *"I don't want to be a genius—I have enough problems just trying to be a man."*
>
> —*Albert Camus*

1917 On this date in the West, Premier Aleksandr Kerensky flees Russia and the Bolsheviks take over. The event was known as the October Revolution, as Russia was still using the Julian calendar, under which the date was October 25th.

1917 After Italy's catastrophic defeat in the Battle of Caporetto during World War I, retreating Italian units finally hold their positions at the Piave River.

1917 Revolution erupts in Bavaria behind socialist leader Kurt Eisner. The result was the end of the Bavarian monarchy.

1918 British forces occupy Mosul, in northern Iraq, during World War I.

1918 On rumors of an armistice in Europe, the New York Stock Exchange closes early to celebrate. The Armistice was signed four days later.

1921 In Italy, the national congress picks Benito Mussolini as its leader.

1938 Herschel Grynszpan, a Polish-Jewish student, shoots German diplomat Ernst vom Rath in Paris, France. Adolf Hitler used vom Rath's death two days later as a pretext for the Nazi attacks on Jews called *Kristallnacht*.

1940 Four months after its completion, the Tacoma Narrows Bridge in Washington state suffers a spectacular collapse. Having earned the nickname "Galloping Gertie" for its bending and twisting on windy days, the bridge was destroyed by harmonic vibrations induced by a 42-mile per hour wind.

1940 Democrat Franklin D. Roosevelt is reelected president of the United States for a record third time, handily defeating his Republican challenger, Thomas E. Dewey, the governor of New York.

1944 Soviet master spy Richard Sorge is hanged in Japan after spending two years in prison. Under the cover of being a German journalist, he passed valuable information to Joseph Stalin, which gained him a posthumous award as Hero of the Soviet Union.

The Tacoma Narrows Bridge crashes into the Puget Sound in Tacoma, Washington

392 The Roman Empire outlaws paganism.

1047 Theofilatto, the licentious pope Benedict IX, claims the papacy for a third time. He sold it once, was deposed once, and the third time was driven from Rome.

1519 Spanish conquistador Hernán Cortés enters the Aztec capital, Tenochtitlán, now Mexico City. Montezuma, regarding him as the god Quetzalcoatl, received him with honor.

1520 A few days after becoming king of Sweden, Danish king Christian II begins the Stockholm Bloodbath, murdering more than 80 Swedish nobles in two days. Outraged Swedes joined forces to drive the Danes from their country.

1605 Robert Catesby, chief conspirator in the Gunpowder Plot to blow up the English Parliament, is caught and killed by government troops.

1620 At the beginning of the Thirty Years' War, forces of the Catholic League rout the Protestant Bohemian army at the Battle of the White Mountain near Prague, Czechoslovakia.

1861 During the American Civil War, a Union frigate seizes the *Trent*, a neutral British ship carrying two Confederate emissaries. A U.S. apology narrowly averted war with Great Britain.

MILESTONE

Louvre Museum Opens

After more than two centuries as a royal palace, the French revolutionary government opens the Louvre in Paris as a public museum on this day in 1793. Today, the Louvre's collection is one of the richest in the world. The Louvre palace was begun by King Francis I in 1546 on the site of a 12th-century fortress built by King Philip II. In the spirit of the Enlightenment, many in France began calling for the public display of the royal collection. Not until the outbreak of the French Revolution was real progress made in establishing a permanent museum.

Sarah Bernhardt

> *"The time to repair the roof is when the sun is shining."*
>
> —John F. Kennedy

1864 Despite military defeats and a sense that the American Civil War would never end, northern voters overwhelmingly reelect President Abraham Lincoln to a second term. With his reelection, the fate of the Confederacy was sealed and recent talk of a negotiated settlement vanished.

1867 Scottish missionary and explorer David Livingstone, searching for the source of the Nile and already reported dead, discovers Lake Mweru, part of the Congo River drainage.

1876 The *New York Times*, voicing a view contrary to that of other newspapers, asserts that neither Samuel Tilden nor Rutherford B. Hayes has won the U.S. presidential election. Hayes was selected months later by an electoral commission and Congress.

1880 French actress Sarah Bernhardt makes her first appearance on the New York stage, in *La Dame aux Camelias*, by Alexandre Dumas.

1887 Doc Holliday—gunslinger, gambler, and occasional dentist—dies from tuberculosis at a sanitarium in Glenwood Springs, Colorado, at age 36.

Captured Marxist city councilman, left, during Beer Hall Putsch in Munich, Germany

1895 German physicist Wilhelm Roentgen becomes the first person to observe x-rays.

1923 Adolf Hitler launches the Beer Hall Putsch, his first attempt at seizing control of Germany. Crashing a meeting of Bavarian officials at a Munich beer hall with a group of Nazi storm troopers, Hitler fired his pistol into the air and declared, "the national revolution has begun." Hitler was imprisoned as a result, dictating *Mein Kampf (My Struggle)* to Rudolf Hess while in jail.

1933 President Franklin D. Roosevelt unveils the Civil Works Administration, a program to provide temporary work for Americans who would otherwise have to endure a winter of unemployment during the Great Depression.

1933 Afghan ruler Muhammad Nadir Shah is assassinated, and his son Sahir Shah takes the throne.

1935 United Mine Workers chief John L. Lewis and other American labor leaders announce the Committee for Industrial Organization, which is charged with pushing the cause for industrial unionism.

1939 A bomb explodes in a beer hall in Munich, Germany, minutes after Adolf Hitler leaves the scene. He made the appearance to celebrate the 16th anniversary of his Beer Hall Putsch and took his narrow escape as a sign of God's support for his work. So did the archbishop of Munich, who held a mass to celebrate the miracle.

1942 During World War II, British and American forces land in French North Africa. At the time it was the biggest amphibious landing ever attempted, involving 850 ships.

1945 In the wake of World War II, the U.S. Revenue Act of 1945 rolls back heavy temporary wartime taxes by some $6 billion.

1949 Israel begins Operation Magic Carpet, a program to bring 40,000 Yemeni Jews to Israel.

1960 John F. Kennedy becomes the youngest man—and the first Catholic—to be elected president of the United States, narrowly beating Republican vice president Richard M. Nixon.

1729 British prime minister Sir Robert Walpole's intervention during a fast-rising crisis leads to the signing by Great Britain and Spain of the Treaty of Seville.

1799 In France, one revolutionary government (the Consulate) overthrows the incumbent revolutionary government (the Directory), opening the way for the dictatorship of Napoleon Bonaparte.

1813 After victory at the Battle of Leipzig, the Allies (Sweden, Russia, Austria, and Prussia) offer French emperor Napoleon Bonaparte a peace settlement, which he spurns. Six months later, he was exiled to the island of Elba.

1862 General Ambrose Burnside reluctantly takes command of the Union Army during the American Civil War, following the removal of controversial George B. McClellan. Within months, Burnside was also replaced.

1869 American author Mark Twain writes a review of East-Coast attitudes in a letter:

General Ambrose Burnside

1801
GAIL BORDEN
American publisher, surveyor, and inventor of evaporated milk and juice concentrate, founder of the Borden Company

1818
IVAN TURGENEV
Russian author (*Fathers and Sons; First Love*) and playwright (*A Month in the Country*)

1841
EDWARD VII
British king, son of Queen Victoria

Edward VII

1880
SIR GILES GILBERT SCOTT
English architect of Liverpool Anglican cathedral and Bankside power station (now the Tate modern art gallery) and designer of the classic red telephone box

1913
HEDY LAMARR
American actress (*Ecstasy; White Cargo*)

1918
SPIRO AGNEW
39th vice president of the United States (1969–73)

1934
CARL SAGAN
American pioneer of space exploration, lecturer, and author (*Cosmos*)

1934
RONALD HARWOOD
South African-born British playwright and screenwriter (*The Dresser; Cry, the Beloved Country; The Pianist*)

1936
MARY TRAVERS
American folk singer (Peter, Paul, and Mary)

"Tonight I appear for the first time before a Boston audience—4,000 critics."

1872 A year after the Chicago Fire in Illinois, another great fire engulfs Boston, Massachusetts, destroying 775 buildings.

1875 The U.S. government orders free-roaming Sioux and Cheyenne Indians to reservations, despite impossible winter travel conditions. As expected, the Sioux missed the deadline, and punitive forces were sent out, including a cavalry unit led by George Armstrong Custer.

1903 In the United States, the Panic of 1903, also known as the "Rich Man's Panic," reaches its nadir, with the Dow dropping to a paltry 42.15.

1906 On the first foreign trip by a U.S. president, Theodore Roosevelt departs for Panama aboard the battleship *Louisiana*. He went to inspect the construction site of the Panama Canal.

1914 In the South Pacific, the Australian naval ship *Sydney* sinks the German cruiser *Emden*.

1918 A day after the abdication of Bavarian king Ludwig III, and with rebellion in the seaports, German socialists proclaim the Weimar Republic.

> *"If you want to make an apple pie from scratch, you must first create the universe."*
>
> —Carl Sagan

1923 In Munich, armed policemen and troops loyal to Germany's democratic government crush Adolf Hitler's Beer Hall Putsch, the first attempt by the Nazi Party at seizing control of the German government.

1936 An American hunting party captures a live baby panda in China. Su-Lin was the first panda exhibited in the United States and survived for about one year.

1938 German Nazis launch the *Kristallnacht* ("Night of Broken Glass") pogrom, attacking Jews and their property. Some 30,000 Jewish men were transported to prison camps; more than 1,000 synagogues and 7,500 Jewish-owned businesses were damaged or burned; and the Jewish community had to pay for the damage.

1961 U.S. Air Force pilot Robert White sets a world speed record of 4,093 miles per hour when he takes an X-15 rocket plane to an altitude of 101,607 feet.

1961 Liverpool, England, record store manager Brian Epstein goes to the Cavern nightclub to hear a local band called The Beatles.

1965 Declaring, "I'm against wars, all wars. I did this as a religious act," Roger Allen LaPorte, a 22-year-old member of the Catholic Worker movement, immolates himself in front of the United Nations headquarters in New York.

1970 The U.S. Supreme Court rejects a Massachusetts state law allowing residents to refuse military service in an undeclared war.

1989 East Germany opens the Berlin Wall, allowing free travel from East Berlin to West Berlin. The following day, exuberant Germans began to tear down the wall.

1990 In the face of mounting public pressure, King Birendra of Nepal approves a new constitution allowing a multiparty democracy.

1991 In a two-second reaction, scientists in Culham, England, produce 1.7 megawatts of power from the first controlled nuclear fusion reaction.

1993 Croatian artillery destroys the beautiful 16th-century Ottoman bridge across the Neretva River in the Bosnian town of Mostar.

M I L E S T O N E

The Great Northeast Blackout

At dusk, the biggest power failure in U.S. history occurs as all of New York state, portions of seven neighboring states, and parts of eastern Canada are plunged into darkness on this day in 1965. The Great Northeast Blackout began at the height of rush hour, delaying millions of commuters, trapping 800,000 people in New York's subways, and stranding thousands more in office buildings, elevators, and trains. Ten thousand National Guardsmen and 5,000 off-duty policemen were called into service to prevent looting. The blackout was caused by the tripping of a 230-kilovolt transmission line near Ontario, Canada.

Blackout traffic on New York's 42nd Street (milestone)

Osage Indian chief

1202 At the start of the Fourth Crusade, French crusaders lay siege to the former Venetian city of Zara, Croatia. By conquering Zara—a Christian city—the crusaders paid for transport on Venetian ships.

1241 Pope Celestine IV dies two weeks after becoming the first pope elected by a conclave of cardinals.

1444 By defeating Hungarian forces in the Battle of Varna, the Ottoman Empire confirms its control over the Balkan region.

1808 Osage Indians agree to abandon their lands in Missouri and Arkansas in exchange for a reservation in Oklahoma. Treaty-makers had no idea that oil and gas deposits on the new reservation would someday make the Osage rich.

1820 The British House of Lords abandons an attempt to retract the title of queen from Caroline of Brunswick-Lüneburg, and to dissolve her marriage to her cousin King George IV. She had been accused of adulterous relationships.

Marine recruiting poster

1861 French naturalist Henri Mouhot, best known for bringing Cambodia's vast temple complex at Angkor Wat to Western attention, dies of malaria near Luang Prabang, Laos.

1865 Henry Wirz, a Swiss immigrant and the commander of Andersonville Prison in Georgia, is hanged for war crimes. Nearly a third of the prison's 46,000 inmates had died from inhumane conditions. Walt Whitman wrote, "There are deeds, crimes that may be forgiven, but this is not among them."

1871 At Ujiji, on the shore of Lake Tanganyika, Welsh-born American journalist Henry Stanley catches up with the ailing Scottish missionary and explorer David Livingstone and utters his famous words, "Dr. Livingstone, I presume?" Stanley had been commissioned by the *New York Herald* to locate Livingstone, who had been reported dead.

1885 German automaker Gottlieb Daimler unveils a new transportation concept, the motorcycle. It was meant only as a testing device for his single-cylinder engine.

1888 Jack the Ripper commits the last known murder in a series of seven in the East End of London, England. He was never caught or identified.

1918 During World War I, Allied forces cut the rail line

> *"The fewer the words, the better the prayer."*
> —*Martin Luther*

at Sedan in the Meuse-Argonne sector. The next day, the Armistice was declared.

1921 Anatole France, the French writer whose novels often championed social justice, wins the Nobel Prize in literature.

1924 Chicago gang leader and bootlegger Dion O'Bannion is murdered by gunmen working for his rival and fellow gangster Al Capone.

1928 Michinomiya Hirohito is enthroned as the 124th Japanese monarch in an imperial line dating back to 660 B.C. Emperor Hirohito presided over Japan's rapid military expansion from 1931 to its crushing defeat in 1945.

1931 American actor Lionel Barrymore wins the Best Actor Oscar for his performance in *Free Soul*. Between 1911 and 1953, he appeared in more than 250 movies.

1937 Brazilian president and Fascist admirer Getúlio Vargas, who took control of the country through a coup in 1930, cancels elections and proclaims himself dictator.

1942 During World War II, Germany invades its puppet-run conquest, Vichy France, in reaction to Vichy admiral Jean François Darlan's announcement of an armistice with the Allies following the Allied landing in North Africa.

1950 During the Chinese invasion of Tibet, the isolated Himalayan country appeals to the United Nations for help.

1960 America's first commercial nuclear power plant goes on line at Rowe, Massachusetts.

1975 The American SS *Edmund Fitzgerald,* a 729-foot-long freighter carrying a load of iron ore, sinks during an early winter storm on Lake Superior, taking all 29 crew members with her.

1995 After a hasty trial, Ken Saro-Wiwa, a Nigerian playwright, environmental activist, and Nobel Peace Prize nominee, is hanged in Nigeria despite worldwide objections.

Protest in London, England, against the execution of Ken Saro-Wiwa in Nigeria

887 The Welsh monk Asser begins teaching Latin to Alfred the Great, beginning a relationship that led to his writing *Life of King Alfred*, an important addition to another book of the time, the invaluable *Anglo-Saxon Chronicle*.

1493 Italian explorer Christopher Columbus sights an island on St. Martin's Day and names it St. Martin. It is now one of the five Netherlands Antilles.

1572 Danish astronomer Tycho Brahe notices "a new and unusual star, surpassing the other stars in brilliancy." So brilliant it could be seen in daylight for about two weeks, it was a supernova, an exploding star.

1778 During the American Revolutionary War, Iroquois Indians destroy the fortified settlement of Cherry Valley, New York, in reprisal for the earlier American destruction of two Indian towns.

1813 At the Battle of Crysler's Farm during the War of 1812, British troops turn back American forces trying to capture Montreal, Canada.

1831 Nat Turner, the leader of a bloody slave revolt in Southampton County, Virginia, is hanged in Jerusalem, the county seat. Turner's rebellion was the largest slave revolt in U.S. history and led to a

---

MILESTONE

World War I Ends

At the 11th hour of the 11th day of the 11th month of 1918, the Great War ends. Germany, bereft of manpower and supplies and faced with imminent invasion, signs an armistice agreement with the Allies outside Compiègne, France. Nine million soldiers died, 21 million were wounded, and at least five million civilians were killed. World War I was known as "the war to end all wars" because of the slaughter and destruction it caused, but the punitive terms imposed on Germany as a result led to deep resentment that allowed Hitler's fanatical policies to flourish.

Armistice celebration in New York City (milestone)

> *"You know you are getting old when the candles cost more than the cake."*
>
> —Bob Hope

new wave of oppressive legislation prohibiting the movement, assembly, and education of slaves.

1838 Four hundred Canadian rebels, members of the secret Hunters' Lodges, invade Ontario in an unsuccessful attempt at sparking a revolution against British rule.

1852 The *Saturday Evening Gazette* publishes *The Rival Painters: A Story of Rome*, by American author Louisa May Alcott, who would later write the beloved children's book *Little Women*.

1853 Scottish explorer and missionary David Livingstone departs Linyanti in southern Africa. He headed northwest, saying, "I shall

---

open up a path into the interior, or perish."

⚖️ **1880** Outlaw and bushranger Ned Kelly, who had become a popular hero, is hanged in Melbourne, Australia.

🇬🇧 **1885** Nathan Adler, chief rabbi of the British Empire, founds Jews' College, a teachers' college, in London, England.

⚖️ **1886** August Spies and three co-defendants are hanged for their alleged (but never proven) part in the Haymarket Riot in Chicago, Illinois—a labor protest in which a bomb killed seven policemen.

🇺🇸 **1921** Exactly three years after the end of World War I, the Tomb of the Unknowns is dedicated at Arlington Cemetery in Virginia by President Warren G. Harding.

🇺🇸 **1933** A massive dust storm rips through South Dakota, one of a series of disastrous windstorms that devastated the West during the droughts of the 1930s—a region that would become known as the Dust Bowl.

🔬 **1935** American balloonists Albert W. Stevens and Orvil Anderson set a manned-balloon altitude record, rising to 72,395 feet, a record that would stand for 21 years.

🔬 **1938** Typhoid Mary, blamed as the prime carrier of infection during the 1904 typhoid epidemic, dies in New York following a paralytic stroke.

💥 **1940** The British Royal Navy launches the first major aircraft-carrier strike in history.

Ho Chi Minh Trail

Planes from the new carrier *Illustrious* sank two battleships at Taranto, Italy, during World War II. Their success inspired Japanese admiral Gombei Yamamoto to plan his attack by aircraft carriers on Pearl Harbor in Hawaii in 1941.

👡 **1942** The American comedy *The Road to Morocco* opens. It was the third in the series of road pictures that brought fame and fortune to its stars: Bob Hope, Bing Crosby, and Dorothy Lamour.

🏴 **1965** Colonial prime minister Ian Smith declares Rhodesian independence as a way of resisting British pressure to adopt a constitution that would lead to black-majority rule.

💥 **1968** During the Vietnam War, the United States launches Operation Commando Hunt, a bombing campaign to block communist traffic on the Ho Chi Minh Trail through Laos to South Vietnam. By 1973, nearly two million tons of bombs had fallen on Laos, but traffic on the trail continued.

1660 English Puritan preacher John Bunyan is arrested and sentenced to jail for unauthorized nonconformist preaching. While in prison, he wrote the Puritan classic *Pilgrim's Progress*.

1794 Four months after Maximilien Robespierre's execution, the Reign of Terror, in which more than 17,000 opponents of the French Revolution were executed, officially comes to an end.

1798 Wolfe Tone, an Irish rebel who organized French-sponsored raids on British-occupied Ireland, takes a knife to his throat on the day he was supposed to be hanged. He died a week later.

1864 During the American Civil War, Union general William T. Sherman orders the business district of Atlanta, Georgia, destroyed. He captured the city in September and did not want to leave it intact when he continued his march to the sea.

1867 After more than a decade of ineffective military campaigns and infamous atrocities, talks begin at Fort Laramie in present-day Wyoming. The

Maximilien Robespierre

German soldiers outside Moscow

hope was to find peaceful solutions to the "Indian problem."

1874 A year after Scottish missionary David Livingstone's death in Africa, American journalist Henry Morton Stanley leaves Zanzibar with an expedition to further clarify the question of the Nile River sources, and to survey the lakes of central Africa.

1905 Voters overwhelmingly approve the first king of newly independent Norway. Christian Frederick Carl Georg Valdemar Axel (Prince Carl) took the name Haakon VII.

1912 Members of the shore party of British explorer Robert Scott's Antarctic expedition arrive at the lonely tent in which Scott and two companions died more than seven months earlier on their return from the South Pole.

1919 The Macpherson brothers take off on the first flight from England to Australia. The Australian aviators flew a Vickers Vimy twin-engine biplane and made the journey in just under a month, winning a cash award and knighthoods: Sir Keith and Sir Ross.

1938 The day after *Kristallnacht*, Nazi field marshal Hermann Goering presides at a meeting of government officials regarding the status of Jews. His concluding comment: "I would not like to be a Jew in Germany."

1941 During World War II, winter arrives on the Moscow front, and for the first time Soviet ski troops are deployed. For German soldiers, frostbite emerged as an unexpected, crippling foe.

1944 British warplanes sink the last major German battleship, the *Tirpitz,* off the coast of Norway during World War II.

1948 An international war crimes tribunal in Tokyo pronounces death sentences on seven Japanese military and government officials, including General Hideki Tōjō, who served as premier of Japan from 1941 to 1944.

> *"Nothing is a waste of time if you use the experience wisely."*
>
> —Auguste Rodin

1970 In the century's worst natural disaster, a monster cyclone strikes Bangladesh, killing hundreds of thousands.

1980 More than three years after its launch, the U.S. planetary probe *Voyager 1* flies to within 77,000 miles of Saturn. Photos beamed 950 million miles back to California showed that Saturn has not six, but hundreds of rings.

1990 English computer scientist Tim Berners-Lee circulates a draft proposal for a hypertext system, which he calls the World Wide Web.

1990 Crown Prince Akihito, the 125th Japanese monarch along an imperial line dating back to 660 B.C., is enthroned as emperor of Japan two years after the death of his father.

Infrared image of Saturn

938 Vietnam turns back Chinese Han invaders at the Bach Dang River. So ended a thousand-year domination of Vietnam by China.

1002 Ethelred II—English king of poor judgment, assassin of his brother, and one whose rule was marked by constant invasions from Denmark—launches the St. Brice's Day massacre of Danish settlers, which provoked new invasions.

1715 The Battle of Sheriffmuir in Scotland ends in a draw, bringing to an end the hopes of Jacobite supporters of the Fifteen Rebellion, an attempt to restore the Catholic Stuart monarchy.

1775 American revolutionary troops capture and occupy Montreal, Canada. The occupation lasted only a few weeks, until the unsuccessful attempt to capture Quebec resulted in a retreat to New York.

1789 The new American president George Washington completes his first presidential tour. For four weeks, Washington traveled by stagecoach on a visit to all the northern states that had ratified the U.S. Constitution.

1789 American statesman Benjamin Franklin lamented in a letter to a friend, "In this world nothing can be said to be certain, except death and taxes."

> *"Keep your fears to yourself, but share your courage with others."*
>
> —*Robert Louis Stevenson*

BORN ON THIS DAY

354
SAINT AUGUSTINE OF HIPPO
Christian philosopher

1312
EDWARD III
King of England (1327–77)

1817
BAHÁ'U'LLÁH (MIRZA HUSAYN ALI)
Persian-born patrician who founded the Bahá'í faith

1831
JAMES CLERK MAXWELL
Scottish physicist whose work advanced understanding of electromagnetism

1850
ROBERT LOUIS STEVENSON
Scottish author (*Treasure Island; Dr. Jekyll and Mr. Hyde*)

1856
LOUIS BRANDEIS
U.S. Supreme Court justice

1866
SUN YAT-SEN
Revolutionary reformer known as the father of modern China

1881
LUDWIG KOCH
German naturalist famous for making the first outdoor recordings of birdsong

1935
GEORGE CAREY
Archbishop of Canterbury (1991–2002)

1938
JEAN SEBERG
American actress (*St. Joan; Bonjour Tristesse; A Bout de Souffle*)

1943
JOHN PAUL HAMMOND
American blues singer (*So Many Roads*)

1947
JOE MANTEGNA
American actor (*House of Games; Weeds; Liberty Heights*)

1949
WHOOPI GOLDBERG
Academy Award-winning American comedienne and actress (*The Color Purple; Ghost*)

1790 German-born English astronomer William Herschel observes an unusual nebula, which appeared to be a star at the center of a luminous cloud. It led him to devise a new theory of nebulae as stars condensing, under the force of gravity, from surrounding gases.

1805 Following his October 20 victory over Austria at the Battle of Ulm, French general Napoleon Bonaparte enters Vienna.

1861 U.S. president Abraham Lincoln pays a late-night visit to General George McClellan, whom Lincoln had recently named general in chief of the Union Army. The general, who had called his boss "nothing more than a well-meaning baboon," refused to see him.

1879 The New York Stock Exchange goes modern, installing its first telegraph and phone lines.

1913 Indian poet Rabindranath Tagore wins the Nobel Prize in literature.

General George McClellan

Mickey Mouse in Fantasia

1916 During World War I, the First Battle of the Somme ends after more than four months of terrible fighting, with more than one million casualties on both sides and nothing won by either.

1917 Aleksandr Kerensky, leader of the revolutionary government of Russia, goes into hiding after the Battle of Pulkovo ends his effort to oppose Vladimir Lenin's Bolsheviks.

1940 Walt Disney's *Fantasia* opens in New York City. An ambitious animated film with no plot, it was an artistic attempt to marry music and animation.

1942 During World War I, the naval battle of Guadalcanal begins in the Solomon Islands when a Japanese fleet attacks a smaller American task force.

1942 British forces, victorious at el-Alamein, recapture the Libyan port of Tobruk.

1946 In Massachusetts, cloud seeding with pellets of dry ice creates the first artificially induced snowstorm—a limited success, considering that the snow evaporated before reaching the ground.

1950 Venezuelan junta leader Colonel Carlos Chalbaud is assassinated one year after his overthrow of popular elected president Rómulo Gallegos.

1953 Mrs. Thomas J. White of the Indiana Textbook Commission calls for removal of Robin Hood's name from state school books "because he robbed the rich and gave it to the poor. That's the Communist line." She also attacked Quakers for their pacifist beliefs.

1970 In a military coup, Syrian defense minister Hafez Al-Asad takes control of Syria. He became president in 1971.

1985 Nevado del Ruiz, the highest active volcano in the Colombian Andes, erupts with catastrophic results. Fast-moving torrents of water, ice, mud, and rock, swelled by heavy rain, killed some 26,000 people and buried the town of Armero.

Vietnam Veterans Memorial in Washington, D.C. (milestone)

⚖️ **1553** Lady Jane Grey, a political pawn at age 16 who had held the title of English queen for nine days, is hauled to court for high treason and later beheaded on orders of Mary Tudor.

🎭 **1587** English navigator Thomas Cavendish, while leading the third circumnavigation of the globe, captures the Spanish treasure ship *Santa Ana* off the coast of California.

1770 British explorer James Bruce reaches Lake Tana, source of the Blue Nile in Ethiopia. His book about the journey, *Travels to Discover the Source of the Nile,* is a classic.

1799 In revolutionary France, following the fall of the Directory and creation of the Consulate, Napoleon Bonaparte becomes first consul, a step on his road to despotism.

🎭 **1851** Harper & Brothers in New York publishes *Moby-Dick,* by Herman Melville. The book flopped, and it was many years before it was recognized as an American classic.

💥 **1862** During the American Civil War, President

Lady Jane Grey

BORN ON THIS DAY

1765
ROBERT FULTON
American inventor and artist who put the steamboat design into practice

1776
HENRI DUTROCHET
French botanist who discovered the process of osmosis

1816
JOHN CURWEN
English Christian minister who invented the tonic sol-fa scale for music teaching

1840
CLAUDE MONET
French Impressionist painter (*Water Lilies*)

1863
LEO BAEKELAND
Belgian chemist who invented Bakelite, the world's first fully synthetic plastic

1889
PANDIT JAWAHARLAL NEHRU
First prime minister of independent India (1947–64)

1900
AARON COPLAND
American composer (*Billy the Kid; Appalachian Spring*)

1909
JOSEPH R. MCCARTHY
Senator from Wisconsin who led a fanatical anticommunist campaign in the early 1950s

1919
VERONICA LAKE
American actress (*This Gun For Hire; I Married a Witch; The Blue Dahlia*)

1922
BOUTROS BOUTROS-GHALI
Egyptian secretary general of the United Nations (1992–96)

1929
MCLEAN STEVENSON
American actor (*M.A.S.H.*)

1935
HUSSEIN IBN TALAL I
King of Jordan

1948
PRINCE CHARLES
Prince of Wales, heir to the British throne

Abraham Lincoln approves of General Ambrose Burnside's plan to capture the Confederate capital at Richmond, Virginia. It proved a bad move: the disastrous Battle of Fredericksburg turned into one of the worst Union defeats in the war.

🏴 **1882** In Tombstone, Arizona, notorious gunslinger Buckskin Leslie shoots Billy the Kid Claiborne dead in the street.

💥 **1885** Great Britain invades Upper Burma to settle a trade dispute. This was accomplished by capturing Mandalay and deposing the last Burmese king, Thibaw.

💥 **1885** Serbia declares war on Bulgaria over possession of Eastern Rumelia. Five days later, underdog Bulgarian forces trounced the invading Serbs at Slivnitza.

🏴 **1889** *New York World* reporter Nellie Bly sails from New York on her celebrated attempt to circle the globe in less than the 80 days of Jules Verne's fictional hero Phineas Fogg. She made it in just over 72 days.

🏴 **1908** Guangxu, the nominal Ching emperor, dies under suspicious circumstances. Nephew and puppet of the Empress Dowager, he was completely dominated by his aunt, who replaced him with his three-year-old nephew P'u-yi, China's "last emperor," on the throne.

"All the time I feel I must justify my existence."
—*Prince Charles*

The Empress Dowager of China

🏆 **1945** Tony Hulman buys the dilapidated, disused Indianapolis Motor Speedway from Edward Rickenbacher. Renovations allowed the post-war resumption of the famous 500-mile races.

1965 In Vietnam's Ia Drang Valley, regular U.S. and North Vietnamese forces clash in their first major engagement of the Vietnam War. Despite serious American losses (one company suffered 93 percent casualties), U.S. commanders were encouraged and declared a significant victory.

1977 Hare Krishna movement founder A. C. Bhaktivedanta dies in India.

1982 Lech Walesa, leader of communist Poland's outlawed Solidarity movement, returns to Gdansk after public pressure effected his release from 11 months in jail.

1914 U.S. Marines withdraw from Veracruz, Mexico, after a seven-month occupation triggered by a shipment of weapons from Germany to Mexico's revolutionary government. U.S. forces left after a new Mexican government was in place.

Coventry Cathedral in 1940 (milestone)

"If I had my choice I would kill every reporter in the world, but I am sure we would be getting reports from Hell before breakfast."

—General William T. Sherman

1315 At the Battle of Morgarten, peasant soldiers of the Swiss Confederation ambush and rout a Hapsburg army—the first important victory in a long struggle leading to establishment of an independent nation.

1492 Italian explorer Christopher Columbus, in his journal, describes an interesting custom among the Indians of the New World—the use of tobacco.

1532 Spanish conquistador Francisco Pizarro springs a trap on the Inca emperor Atahualpa. The Spanish invitation to a feast became a massacre. Atahualpa, captured, ordered up a vast treasure as ransom. Once the Spanish had the gold, they killed Atahualpa after forcing his conversion to their religion.

1805 The Corps of Discovery, under American captains Lewis and Clark, arrives at the stormy mouth of the Columbia River and prepares to settle down for the winter.

1806 Approaching the Colorado foothills of the Rocky

MILESTONE

Articles of Confederation Adopted

After 16 months of debate, the Continental Congress, sitting in its temporary capital of York, Pennsylvania, agrees to adopt the Articles of Confederation and Perpetual Union on this day in 1777. On March 4, 1781, following final ratification by the 13th state, the Articles of Confederation became the law of the land. By 1786 defects in the Articles were apparent, such as the lack of central authority over foreign and domestic commerce. The United States was in danger of breaking apart. On March 4, 1789, the modern United States was established when the U.S. Constitution formally replaced the Articles of Confederation.

Mountains during his second exploratory expedition, U.S. lieutenant Zebulon Pike spots a distant mountain peak that looks "like a small blue cloud." The mountain was later named Pike's Peak in his honor.

1818 In the wake of the Napoleonic Wars, Russia, Prussia, Great Britain, and France conclude the Congress of Aix-la-Chapelle. Among decisions they made, France agreed to pay an indemnity for war damage, and the allies agreed to end their occupation of France.

1859 English author Charles Dickens publishes the final installment of his serialized novel *A Tale of Two Cities*, in his weekly circular of fiction, poetry, and essays called *All the Year Round*.

1864 During the American Civil War, Union general William T. Sherman leaves Atlanta, Georgia, in smoking ruins and begins his six-week scorched-earth march to the sea.

1867 The stock ticker is unveiled in New York City. Its main use was to give stock traders a stream of data on ribbons of paper; it also gave rise to that festive public event, the ticker-tape parade.

1884 European representatives begin a conference in Berlin, Germany, to settle colo-

Atlanta, before being burnt by order of General Sherman

Heinrich Himmler

nial divisions in the Congo River basin.

1889 After a 49-year reign, Pedro II, the second and last emperor of Brazil, is deposed in a military coup.

1923 Apparently framed by the Ku Klux Klan, James Montgomery, a black man, is sentenced after a 20-minute trial to life in prison for the rape of a mentally disabled white woman. He studied law in prison and was released after 25 years, when the conviction was overturned.

1926 The National Broadcasting Company is launched on 24 stations across the United States. The first program, broadcast from New York City's Waldorf-Astoria Hotel, included remote pickups from Chicago, Illinois, and Kansas.

1938 The first live on-the-scene television news broadcast covers a fire on Ward's Island, New York. NBC station W2XBT was able to film and broadcast the fire live.

1943 During World War II, Heinrich Himmler, leader of the German SS, orders that Gypsies and "part-Gypsies" are to be put "on the same level as Jews and placed in concentration camps." In cases of doubt, local SS commanders were to determine for themselves who were Gypsies.

1957 Soviet leader Nikita Khrushchev boasts of Soviet missile superiority and challenges the United States to a shooting match. He said in an interview, "Let's have a peaceful rocket contest just like a rifle-shooting match" to prove the point.

1988 In Algiers, Algeria, Palestine Liberation Organization leader Yāsir Arāfat proclaims the independent state of Palestine but specifies no borders for the prospective country.

1996 The Stone of Destiny, the ancient Scottish coronation stone, is returned to Scotland 700 years after it was stolen by English king Edward I. The reputed pillow on which Jacob had his vision of angels ascending a ladder to heaven, it is also known as the Stone of Scone after Scone Palace, coronation place of Scottish kings.

1632 During the Thirty Years' War, king Gustavus Adolphus of Sweden, the "Lion of the North," is slain during his nation's victory over the Austrians at the Battle of Lützen.

1722 Jack Sheppard, a burglar from London, England, is hanged at Tyburn in front of a crowd believed to number 200,000. Sheppard, who was only 22, had become a popular hero, immortalized in songs and stories, for his exploits and four escapes from prison.

1776 During the American Revolutionary War, a force of 3,000 Hessian mercenaries overwhelm Patriot riflemen protecting Fort Washington on Long Island, New York. The Hessian victory was made possible by the desertion of American William Demont who gave the British information on Fort Washington's defenses. Demont was the first traitor to the Patriot cause.

1798 Kentucky becomes the first state to nullify an act of the U.S. Congress, specifically the Alien and Sedition Acts, through the Kentucky Resolutions, written by Thomas Jefferson. The Resolutions were a severe attack on a broad interpretation of the Constitution that would have extended the powers of the federal government over the states.

> *"An adult is a child who has more ethics and morals. That's all."*
> —*Shigeru Miyamoto*

BORN ON THIS DAY

42 B.C.
TIBERIUS
Second emperor of Rome

1811
JOHN BRIGHT
English Liberal politician and social reformer

1839
WILLIAM FREND DE MORGAN
English ceramics designer

1895
PAUL HINDEMITH
German composer ("The Four Temperaments")

1896
SIR OSWALD MOSLEY
English fascist politician

Sir Oswald Mosley

1908
BURGESS MEREDITH
American actor (*Of Mice and Men; Rocky; Batman*)

1916
DAWS BUTLER
American actor who was the voice of many Hanna-Barbera cartoon characters, including Yogi Bear, Huckleberry Hound, and Snagglepuss

1952
SHIGERU MIYAMOTO
Japanese creator of Nintendo games

1958
MARG HELGENBERGER
American actress (*C.S.I.: Crime Scene Investigation; Species II*)

1961
FRANK BRUNO
English heavyweight boxing champion

1964
DWIGHT GOODEN
American professional baseball player

Thomas Jefferson

1798 British seamen impress U.S. crewmen as alleged deserters as they board the U.S. frigate *Baltimore*, a practice that contributed to the War of 1812.

1821 Missouri Indian trader William Becknell arrives in Santa Fe, New Mexico, sells his goods at an enormous profit, and makes plans to return the next year over a short-cut route of his own that would become known as the Santa Fe Trail.

1824 Australian explorer Hamilton Hume discovers the Murray River, the longest in Australia at 1,609 miles.

1901 A. C. Bostwick becomes the first American racer to exceed the speed of a mile a minute (63.83 miles per hour) on the Ocean Parkway racetrack in Brooklyn, New York.

1913 The first volume of French author Marcel Proust's classic autobiographical novel, *Remembrance of Things Past,* is published in Paris.

1914 The U.S. Federal Reserve Bank opens. A continuous cycle of bank panics prompted the formation of the National Monetary Commission, which issued a report that the nation's banks had essentially engaged in life-and-death contests with each other. The report triggered the passage of the Federal Reserve Act of 1913, which paved the way for the formation of the Federal Reserve Bank.

1918 Hungary declares independence from the Austro-Hungarian Empire and is proclaimed a republic.

1920 The Russian Civil War ends with victory for the Bolsheviks.

1933 Diplomatic relations are established between the United States and the Soviet Union.

1938 During a soccer match between England and Ireland at Old Trafford, Englishman Willie Hall scores three goals in 3.5 minutes, a record for an international soccer event.

1945 The United States imports 88 German scientists to assist in developing rocket technology. Most of these men had served under the Nazi regime, and critics questioned the morality of the move. But fearful that the Russians were also utilizing captured German scientists for the same end, the government welcomed the men with open arms.

1955 *Bluebird II*, the British jet hydroplane owned and driven by Donald Campbell, becomes the first speedboat to exceed 200 miles per hour.

1957 Infamous killer Edward Gein murders his last

victim, Bernice Worden of Plainfield, Wisconsin. His grave robbing, necrophilia, and cannibalism provided the inspiration for the movie characters Norman Bates in *Psycho* and serial killer Buffalo Bill in *The Silence of the Lambs*.

1959 The Rodgers and Hammerstein musical *The Sound of Music* opens on Broadway in New York City.

1988 Pakistanis, voting in their first open election in more than a decade, choose Benazir Bhutto as prime minister. She was the first woman leader of a Muslim country in modern history.

1993 Russian leader Vladimir Lenin's mausoleum in Moscow is shut down by the Russian authorities.

Pro-communist Muskovites lined up to view Lenin's mausoleum

John Adams

1695 Mustafa II becomes the Ottoman sultan in Istanbul. His reign marked the first time the Ottoman Empire began to lose territory.

1800 John Adams becomes the first U.S. president to live in the White House. Also on this same day, Congress convenes for the first time in Washington, D.C.

1825 The U.S. Congress formally adopts an Indian removal policy east of the Mississippi River, which was carried out extensively in the 1830s by presidents Andrew Jackson and Martin Van Buren.

1837 Italian composer Giuseppe Verdi's first opera, *Oberto, Conte di San Bonifacio*, debuts at La Scala in Milan. The next day, Bartolomeo Merelli, the impresario at La Scala, commissioned Verdi to write three more operas.

1863 U.S. president Abraham Lincoln begins to write the first draft of his Gettysburg Address.

1869 The Suez Canal in Egypt is formally inaugurated.

MILESTONE

The Elizabethan Age Begins

The Elizabethan Age begins on this day in 1558 when Queen Mary I, the monarch of England and Ireland since 1553, dies and is succeeded by her 25-year-old half sister, Elizabeth. The long reign of Elizabeth, who became known as the Virgin Queen for her reluctance to endanger her authority through marriage, coincided with the flowering of the English Renaissance, associated with such renowned authors as William Shakespeare and Christopher Marlowe. By her death in 1603, England had become a major world power in every respect, and Queen Elizabeth I passed into history as one of the nation's greatest monarchs.

Elizabeth I

The canal took 10 years to build and was the brainchild of Ferdinand de Lesseps, who oversaw its construction.

1900 Foreign diplomats in Beijing, China, demand that the Imperial Government discipline the Boxer Rebels, a movement against Westerners and Western influence.

1913 The first ship sails through the Panama Canal, which was built by the United States on the Isthmus of Panama.

1924 Russian revolutionary leader Vladimir Ilyich Lenin's body is laid to rest in a marble tomb in Red Square near the Kremlin.

1930 The first Irish Sweepstakes is held. It was an Irish government effort to raise money to build hospitals. Because of a general prohibition against gambling in the United States and Canada, the tickets were sold internationally on the black market to great success. The Sweepstakes was held four times a year, and was based on the results of four well-known horse races. It was discontinued in 1987.

1931 American aviator Charles Lindbergh inaugurates air service from Cuba to South America in the Pan American flying boat *American Clipper*.

> *"We have to be able to grow up. Our wrinkles are our medals of the passage of life."*
>
> —*Lauren Hutton*

1941 German World War I flying ace Ernst Udet commits suicide. A celebrity in the interwar years, Udet had been promoted to a senior position in the Luftwaffe, but was uneasy with the Nazi regime and had tried to resign. The Nazi authorities claimed he had died testing a new aircraft.

1941 Joseph C. Grew, ambassador to Japan, cables the U.S. State Department that he heard that Japan had "planned, in the event of trouble with the United States, to attempt a surprise mass attack at Pearl Harbor." The Office of Naval Intelligence ignored his warning.

1944 Following the murder of Lord Moyne, a British official in the Middle East, Prime Minister Winston Churchill warns Zionist terrorists that continued actions will damage their cause and calls on the Jewish community to police itself.

1970 The Soviet *Luna 17*, soft-lands on the moon. Hours later, *Lunokhod 1*, a self-propelled vehicle controlled by Soviet mission control, rolled out and became the first wheeled vehicle to travel on the surface of the moon.

1974 The first general election in Greece in more than 10 years gives a decisive victory for the New Democracy Party of Constantine Karamanlis.

1977 Egyptian president Anwar el-Sādāt formally accepts an invitation to visit Israel. Sādāt's visit marked the beginning of a process that finally ended the 30-year war between Israel and Egypt.

1979 Iran's Ayatollah Khomeini orders the release of 13 female and African-American hostages being held at the U.S. Embassy in Tehran.

1993 The U.S. House of Representatives passes the North American Free Trade Agreement (NAFTA), a controversial regional trade agreement among Canada, Mexico, and the United States.

NAFTA protestors

1210 Pope Innocent III excommunicates Roman Catholic emperor Otto IV after Otto begins seizing church property.

1307 According to legend, the story of Swiss patriot William Tell shooting an apple off his son's head is first told on this day.

1421 A seawall at the Zuider Zee dike in the Netherlands breaks, flooding 72 villages and killing an estimated 10,000 people.

1477 The first dated book printed in England is published by William Caxton, a translation from the French of *The Dictes and Sayings of the Philosophers*, by Earl Rivers.

1497 Vasco da Gama reaches the Cape of Good Hope at the southern tip of Africa.

1626 Pope Urban VIII dedicates St. Peter's Basilica in Rome, Italy.

1820 U.S. Navy captain Nathaniel B. Palmer is the first person to reach Antarctica.

1865 "The Celebrated Jumping Frog of Calaveras County," American author Mark Twain's first story, is published in the *New York Saturday Press*.

1869 Lucy Stone and Henry Blackwell form the American Woman Suffrage

> *"An epic is the easiest kind of picture to make badly."*
> —Charlton Heston

1789
LOUIS DAGUERRE
French painter who created the first usable photographic process, the Daguerreotype

1836
SIR W. S. GILBERT
English playwright and lyricist who collaborated with Sir Arthur Sullivan on the Savoy Operas (*The Pirates of Penzance; The Mikado; HMS Pinafore; Iolanthe*)

1899
EUGENE ORMANDY
Hungarian-born American conductor and musical director of the Philadelphia Orchestra

1901
GEORGE GALLUP
American journalist and statistician who created the opinion poll

1908
IMOGENE COCA
American actress (*Your Show of Shows; National Lampoon's Vacation*)

1909
JOHNNY MERCER
American songwriter ("Lazybones"; "One for My Baby (and One More for the Road)")

1923
ALAN SHEPARD JR.
Chief of the U.S. Astronaut Office, the first American to travel into space in 1961

1939
BRENDA VACCARO
American actress (*Midnight Cowboy; The Mirror Has Two Faces*)

1942
LINDA EVANS
American actress (*Beach Blanket Bingo; Dynasty*)

1960
ELIZABETH PERKINS
American actress (*Big; He Said, She Said; The Flintstones*)

1962
KIRK LEE HAMMET
American rock guitarist (Metallica)

Dr. V. K. Zworykin, seated

Association in their quest to win women the right to vote.

1883 At noon, American and Canadian railroads begin using four continental time zones to end the confusion of dealing with thousands of local times.

1902 Morris Michton, a Brooklyn, New York, toymaker, names the teddy bear after U.S. president Theodore Roosevelt.

1905 Prince Charles of Denmark is elected the first king of Norway after independence is restored.

1916 Douglas Haig, commander of the British Expeditionary Force in World War I, calls off the Battle of the Somme in France after nearly five months of mass slaughter that resulted in tens of thousands of British dead and wounded. Although Haig was severely criticized for the costly battle, his willingness to commit massive amounts of men and resources along the Western Front eventually contributed to the defeat of Germany in 1918.

1929 Russian inventor Vladimir K. Zworykin demonstrates the "kinescope," an early version of television.

1959 *Ben-Hur,* the American biblical-era spectacle directed by William Wyler and starring Charlton Heston, has its world premiere at Loew's Theater in New York City. It won 11 Academy Awards.

1976 Spain's parliament votes to establish a democracy after 37 years of dictatorship.

1987 A special-edition 1963 Ferrari 250 GTO hardtop is sold for $1,600,000 at an automobile auction in Italy, setting a new public auction record.

1987 The joint U.S. congressional investigating committee looking into the Iran-Contra scandal concludes that the Reagan administration exhibited "secrecy, deception, and disdain for the law." The scandal involved a plan to send funds from secret weapons sales to Iran to finance a war against the Sandinista government in Nicaragua. A number of government officials were convicted of various crimes as a result.

1993 South Africa approves a new democratic constitution that gives blacks the vote and ends white minority rule.

1995 The Vatican proclaims that the Roman Catholic ban on women as priests is a definitive, infallible, and unquestionable part of the Church's doctrine.

1998 In a move that provokes international condemnation, the Zimbabwean government of president Robert Mugabe begins seizing 841 white-owned farms, with the aim of distributing them to landless black peasant farmers. Taking the land out of the hands of experienced farmers may have contributed to famine in Zimbabwe in subsequent years.

MILESTONE

Mass Suicide in Jonestown

People's Temple leader Jim Jones leads hundreds of his followers in a mass murder-suicide at their agricultural commune in remote northwestern Guyana on this day in 1978. Jones was becoming distressed at the defection of his members. The few cult members who refused to take a cyanide-laced fruit-flavored drink were either forced to do so at gunpoint or shot as they fled. With Jones exhorting the beauty of dying over a loudspeaker, hundreds drank the lethal concoction. Most of the 913 dead were lying side by side in the clearing where Jones had preached to them for the last time.

People's Temple suicide victims in Jonestown, Guyana (milestone)

1493 Italian explorer Christopher Columbus discovers Puerto Rico on his second voyage.

1530 Augsburg emperor Karel I enables the "Edict of Worms," which bans the ideas of Martin Luther from the empire. Luther's main point was that the Bible is the word of God and people did not need the Church to worship God.

1620 The Pilgrims, who left England on the *Mayflower* in search of a new life free of restrictions on religious worship, reach Cape Cod, Massachusetts. They would land at Plymouth on December 26.

1703 During the reign of Louis XIV of France, a masked prisoner in the Bastille in Paris dies. His true identity was never revealed but caused much intrigue. The incident became the basis of literary works by François Voltaire and Alexandre Dumas.

1794 The United States and Great Britain sign the Jay Treaty to resolve postrevolution issues pertaining to compensation for certain losses and damages, the regulation of commerce and navigation, and to provide for extradition.

1850 The first U.S. patent for magic lantern slides made of glass plate is issued to their

> *"People tend to forget their duties but remember their rights."*
>
> —*Indira Gandhi*

BORN ON THIS DAY

1600
CHARLES I
King of England, Scotland, and Ireland, beheaded after his defeat in the English Civil War

1805
VISCOMTE FERDINAND DE LESSEPS
French engineer who constructed the Suez Canal and planned the Panama Canal

1831
JAMES GARFIELD
20th president of the United States

1905
TOMMY DORSEY
American jazz trombonist and trumpet player, brother of jazz clarinetist Jimmy Dorsey

1917
INDIRA GANDHI
Prime minister of India (1966–67 and 1980–84)

1933
LARRY KING
American broadcast journalist who created the first nationwide phone-in television program

1936
DICK CAVETT
American television talk-show host (*The Dick Cavett Show*)

1938
TED TURNER
American television network executive, owner of MGM/UA Entertainment Company and vice chairman of AOL Time Warner

1942
CALVIN KLEIN
American fashion designer

1961
MEG RYAN
American actress (*When Harry Met Sally; French Kiss; Kate and Leopold*)

1962
JODIE FOSTER
Academy Award-winning American actress (*Taxi Driver; The Accused; The Silence of the Lambs*)

1997
MCCAUGHEY SEPTUPLETS
American septuplets Kenneth, Alexis, Natalie, Kelsey, Brandon, Nathan, and Joel

---

Julia Ward Howe

inventor, Frederick Langenheim of Philadelphia, Pennsylvania.

1850 The first life insurance policy issued to a woman in the United States is purchased by 26-year-old Carolyn Ingraham of Madison, New Jersey.

1850 Alfred, Lord Tennyson becomes British poet laureate.

1861 While visiting Union troops near Washington, D.C., during the American Civil War, Julia Ward Howe writes "The Battle Hymn of the Republic."

1869 The Hudson Bay Company sells the Northwest Territories to Canada.

1916 In the United States, Samuel Goldfish and Edgar Selwyn establish the Goldwyn Company. Goldfish, who changed his name to Goldwyn, became one of the world's most successful independent filmmakers and launched the careers of Danny Kaye, Gary Cooper, Will Rogers, and Lucille Ball. Among the writers he employed were Robert Sherwood, Sinclair Lewis, and Ben Hecht.

1919 The U.S. Senate rejects the Treaty of Versailles,

which attempted to create the League of Nations, the forerunner to the United Nations.

1926 Communist revolutionary Leon Trotsky is expelled from the Politburo in the Soviet Union.

1933 Women are allowed to vote in Spain for the first time.

1940 During World War II, Belgian king Leopold III visits German dictator Adolf Hitler. His visit achieved the release of 50,000 Belgian prisoners of war and secured an improved food supply for occupied Belgium.

1942 Soviet general Georgi Zhukov launches Operation Uranus, the great World War II counteroffensive that turned the tide against the Germans and thousands of Romanian, Hungarian, and Italian troops in the Battle of Stalingrad.

1949 Rainier III is officially crowned as the 30th ruling prince of Monaco. He married American movie star Grace Kelly, who became known as Princess Grace.

1969 Brazilian soccer great Pelé scores his 1,000th professional goal in a game against Vasco da Gama in Rio de Janeiro's Maracana stadium.

1969 U.S. astronauts Charles Conrad and Alan L. Bean of *Apollo 12* make the second landing on the moon.

1977 In an unprecedented move for an Arab leader, Egyptian president Anwar el-Sādāt travels to Jerusalem to seek a permanent peace settlement with Israel after decades of conflict.

Alan L. Bean departs the Lunar Module

269 Diocletian is proclaimed emperor of Rome. He was the first emperor to formally divide the empire and set up a genuine autocracy.

1272 Edward I is proclaimed king of England. Although his reign was characterized by warfare, he is better known for his legal and constitutional reforms and his insistence that church courts be confined to ecclesiastical cases.

1616 Bishop (later Cardinal) Armand Richelieu becomes French secretary of state. While encouraging commercial capitalism overseas, Richelieu is known for policies aimed at consolidating and centralizing royal authority, resulting in the destruction of the power of the Huguenots.

1759 A French invasion of England is prevented as Admiral Hawke leads the British fleet to victory at the Battle of Quiberon Bay.

1789 New Jersey becomes the first state to ratify the U.S. Bill of Rights.

1818 Simón Bolívar formally declares Venezuelan independence from Spain.

1820 The American whaler *Essex* is attacked and sunk by an 80-ton sperm whale 2,000 miles from the western coast of South America. Herman Melville's classic novel

> *"Curiosity is free-wheeling intelligence."*
> —*Alistair Cooke*

Queen Elizabeth II and Prince Philip

Moby-Dick was inspired in part by this event.

1866 The first U.S. patent on a rotary-crank bicycle is issued to Pierre Lallemont of Paris, France. Using pedals applied directly to the front wheel, it was a major advance on the so-called hobby-horse bicycle, which had to be pushed with the feet.

1866 James L. Haven and Charles Hittrick of Cincinnati, Ohio, receive the first U.S. patent for a yo-yo.

1875 American-born British writer Henry James publishes his first novel, *Roderick Hudson*. His other novels include *The American, Daisy Miller*, and *The Portrait of a Lady*.

1888 William Bundy is issued the first U.S. patent for a timecard clock.

1889 Austrian composer Gustav Mahler's First Symphony is first performed in Budapest, Hungary.

1902 George Lefevre and Henri Desgrange create the Tour de France bicycle race.

1906 English automaker Charles Stewart Rolls and Frederick Henry Royce form Rolls-Royce.

1917 The first tank battle takes place at Cambrai, France, as 350 British tanks roll over German positions during World War I.

1923 American inventor Garrett Morgan patents the automatic traffic signal. Distress after seeing an automobile crash into a horse-drawn carriage prompted his invention.

1931 In the United States, the first commercial teletype service is inaugurated by AT&T.

1931 Japan, having invaded Manchuria, rejects the terms for peace offered by the League of Nations. The League's inability to stop Japan assisted in the rise of militaristic nationalism in that country.

1943 One of the bloodiest battles in the history of the U.S. Marine Corps begins on Tarawa Atoll in the Gilbert Islands during World War II. Approximately 1,000 American soldiers were killed in just 70 hours. The battle was still considered an undisputed victory, as 4,690 Japanese had been killed.

1947 In a lavish wedding ceremony at Westminster Abbey in London, heir to the British throne Princess Elizabeth marries her distant cousin Philip Mountbatten, a dashing former prince of Greece and Denmark who renounced his titles in order to marry her.

1953 Flying a Douglas Skyrocket, American aviator Scott Crossfield becomes the first to travel faster than Mach 2 (1,300 miles per hour).

MILESTONE

Nuremberg Trials Begin
High-ranking Nazis go on trial in Nuremberg, Germany, on this day in 1945 for atrocities committed during World War II. The Nuremberg Trials were conducted by an international tribunal made up of representatives from the United States, the Soviet Union, France, and Great Britain. They were the first trials of their kind in history, and the defendants faced charges ranging from crimes against peace and humanity to crimes of war. The proceedings lasted 10 months. Twelve architects of Nazi policy were sentenced to death. Seven others were sentenced to prison terms ranging from 10 years to life, and three were acquitted.

U.S. Marines on Tarawa

1620 Leaders of the British *Mayflower* expedition frame the Mayflower Compact, a social contract providing for the temporary government of the Plymouth Colony in America.

1695 Henry Purcell, possibly the greatest English composer of all time, dies at age 36.

1783 French physician Jean-François Pilâtre de Rozier and François Laurent, the marquis d'Arlandes, make the first untethered hot-air balloon flight, flying 5.5 miles over Paris in about 25 minutes. Their cloth balloon was crafted by French papermaking brothers Jacques-Étienne and Joseph-Michel Montgolfier, inventors of the world's first successful hot-air balloons.

1806 French emperor Napoleon I begins a blockade of Great Britain. The object was to strike a blow at Great Britain's supremacy by cutting off all intercourse with the continent of Europe.

1831 English physicist Michael Faraday reads the first in a series of papers on

MILESTONE
Edison's First Great Invention

On this day in 1877, Thomas Edison announces his invention of the phonograph, a way to record and play back sound. He stumbled on his great invention while working on a way to record telephone communication at his laboratory in Menlo Park, New Jersey. Edison's work led him to experiment with a stylus on a tinfoil cylinder, which played back the short song he had recorded. Public demonstrations of the phonograph made the American inventor world famous, and he was dubbed the "Wizard of Menlo Park."

Thomas Edison with phonograph

The Pilgrims signing the Mayflower Compact

"Experimental Research into Electricity" at the Royal Society in London.

1843 Thomas Hancock of England patents vulcanized rubber. He produced the first toy balloons in Great Britain, utilizing a bottle of rubber solution and a condensing syringe.

1846 American physician Oliver Wendell Holmes coins the word "anesthesia" in a letter to William Thomas Green Morton, the surgeon who gave the first public demonstration of ether.

1871 The first human cannonball, Emilio Onra, posing as a woman, is shot from a catapult-like device in London, England.

1904 Horse-drawn carriages are replaced by motorized "omnibuses" in Paris, France.

1906 The emperor of China issues an edict declaring an end to all opium traffic within 10 years. By some estimates, as much as half of China's population had either become opium addicts or were otherwise involved in the opium trade.

1907 The Cunard liner *Mauritania* travels 624 nautical miles in one day, a new speed record for steamship travel.

1911 The British Parliament in London is stormed by suffragettes. All were arrested, and all chose prison terms.

1917 During World War I, German ace Rudolf von Eschwege attacks a booby-

> *"Love is a canvas furnished by nature and embroidered by imagination."*
>
> —*Jean François Voltaire*

trapped observation balloon packed with explosives over Macedonia and is killed.

⚓ **1938** During World War II, Nazi forces occupy western Czechoslovakia and declare its people to be German citizens.

🏴 **1974** Despite President Gerald R. Ford's veto, the U.S. Congress passes the Freedom of Information Act.

🏴 **1974** In England, terrorist bombs planted by the Irish Republican Army in two pubs in Birmingham kill 17 people and wound 120.

🔬 **1977** The supersonic Concorde airliner, developed by Great Britain and France, takes off on its first flight from London to New York City.

⚖️ **1985** Jonathan Pollard, a civilian U.S. Navy intelligence analyst and Jewish-American, is arrested on charges of illegally passing classified U.S. security information about Arab nations to Israel. He was eventually convicted and sentenced to life in prison.

🏴 **1985** Thirteen black South Africans are shot dead by police in Mamelodi township.

⚖️ **1990** The career of American stockbroker Michael Milken, Wall Street's "junk-bond king," comes to a halt as he is

Michael Milken

sentenced to a 10-year prison term for various securities law infractions including insider trading and "stock manipulation." The sentence topped off an intensive four-year probe into the actions of one of the financial world's wealthiest and most powerful figures.

🏆 **1992** Three world swimming records are broken. Jan Karlsson of Sweden swims the men's 50-meter butterfly in 23.80 seconds; Jani Sievinen of Finland swims the men's 100-meter medley in 53.78 seconds; and Sweden's Louise Karlsson swims the women's 50-meter freestyle in 31.19 seconds.

🏴 **1995** The Dayton peace plan is accepted, with reservations, by the leaders of Serbia, Croatia, and Bosnia, paving the way for an end to the Bosnian conflict. The agreement created a new state of Bosnia-Herzegovina, divided into self-governing Muslim-Croat and Bosnian Serb areas.

"How can anyone govern a nation that has two hundred and forty-six kinds of cheese?"

—*Charles de Gaulle*

1220 Frederick II is crowned emperor of the Holy Roman Empire after promising Pope Honorius III to participate in the Fifth Crusade.

1497 Portuguese explorer Vasco de Gama, in his search for a sea route to India, is the first to successfully sail around the Cape of Good Hope.

1542 Laws are passed in Spain giving Indians in America protection against enslavement.

1699 Denmark, Saxony-Poland, and Russia create an alliance to break Swedish dominance in northern Europe. The resulting Great Northern War began in 1700, and while Swedish king Charles XII was initially successful in defeating the alliance, the Russians got the upper hand in the Battle of Poltava in 1709. It was the beginning of the end of Sweden as a great power.

1718 Edward Teach, also known as the pirate Blackbeard, is killed off North Carolina's Outer Banks during a bloody battle with a British Navy force sent from Virginia.

1809 Peregrine Williamson of Baltimore, Maryland, is issued the first U.S. patent for a steel pen.

1906 Delegates of the International Radio Telegraphic

BORN ON THIS DAY

1808
THOMAS COOK
English package tour pioneer

1819
GEORGE ELIOT (MARY ANN EVANS)
English novelist (*Middlemarch; The Mill on the Floss; Daniel Deronda*)

1890
CHARLES DE GAULLE
French general, president of France (1959–69)

1899
HOAGY CARMICHAEL
American composer ("Stardust")

1901
JOAQUÍN RODRIGO
Spanish composer ("Concierto de Aranjuez")

1913
BENJAMIN BRITTEN
English composer (*Easter 1916; Peter Grimes; The Turn of the Screw*) and co-founder of the Aldeburgh Festival with his life partner, tenor Peter Pears

1914
LEW HAYS
American who founded the PONY League baseball program for children

1921
RODNEY DANGERFIELD
American comedian and actor (*Caddyshack*)

1930
SIR PETER HALL
English director, former artistic director of the Royal National Theatre

1932
ROBERT VAUGHN
American actor (*The Man From U.N.C.L.E.*)

1940
TERRY GILLIAM
American actor (*Monty Python's Flying Circus*), animator, and director (*Twelve Monkeys; The Fisher King*)

1943
BILLIE JEAN KING
American tennis player who won 20 Wimbledon championships

Mike Tyson, right, and Trevor Berbick

Convention meeting in Berlin, Germany, vote to use SOS as the new international signal calling for help.

1910 The first U.S. patent for a tubular steel shaft for a golf club is issued to A. F. Knight of Schenectady, New York. The first recorded steel-shafted club was made by Scottish blacksmith Thomas Horsburgh in 1893, but his solid shaft was heavy and did not prove popular.

1918 Following his heroic resistance to the German invasion of Belgium during World War I and his leadership in an Allied offensive that recovered the Belgian coast, King Albert I heads a triumphant procession through Brussels.

1919 An eight-hour workday and a 48-hour workweek is urged at a labor conference committee in the United States.

1927 Carl Eliason of Sayner, Wisconsin, is granted the first patent for a snowmobile design. His first snowmobile

used everything from bicycle parts to a radiator from a Model T Ford.

1928 French composer Maurice Ravel's "Bolero" is publicly performed in Paris for the first time.

1935 Pan American Airlines inaugurates the first transpacific airmail service, flying 100,000 pieces of mail from Alemeda, California, to Manila, the Philippines.

1943 U.S. president Franklin D. Roosevelt, British prime minister Winston Churchill, and Generalissimo Chiang Kai-Shek of China gather in Cairo, Egypt, for a discussion on the future of Japan following World War II. The most important implication of the conference, however, was that China would be conferred "Great Power" status in the postwar world.

1967 The U.N. Security Council approves Resolution 242, calling for Israel to withdraw from territories it captured in 1967 and for adversaries to recognize Israel's right to exist.

1972 A 22-year-old ban on American travel to China is lifted by U.S. president Richard M. Nixon.

1975 Juan Carlos is sworn in as king of Spain two days after the death of Generalissimo Francisco Franco. He returned the country to democracy after Franco's long dictatorship.

1986 American prizefighter Mike Tyson becomes the youngest boxer to wear the world heavyweight crown as he knocks out Trevor Berbick in Las Vegas, Nevada. He was only 20 years old.

1165 Pope Alexander III returns to Rome from exile in France. He was forced into exile by Holy Roman Emperor Frederick I after his election to the papacy was opposed by several cardinals. Considered one of the great medieval popes, Alexander III established the procedure for canonizing saints and inaugurating the two-thirds rule for papal elections.

1803 Arthur Wellesley, who will later become the duke of Wellington, secures victory in the Battle of Assaye in India, his first major battle as commander.

1835 The first machine for manufacturing horseshoes is created by Henry Burden of Troy, New York. Burden went on to make almost all the horseshoes used by the Union Army during the American Civil War.

1863 The Battle of Chattanooga, one of the most decisive battles of the American Civil War, begins as Ulysses S. Grant and William T. Sherman drive the Confederate Army

MILESTONE

Billy the Kid Born

Infamous outlaw Billy the Kid (William Bonney) is born today in New York in 1859. Billy found work as a rancher and bodyguard for John Tunstall, a New Mexico rancher. When a rival cattle gang killed Tunstall, Billy got involved in the Lincoln County War and became leader of a vigilante posse of regulators sent to arrest the killers. After more than two years on the run, he was arrested by Sheriff Pat Garrett, but he escaped before his scheduled execution. In 1881, Garrett tracked him down and shot him dead at the age of 21. Billy the Kid had reportedly killed 27 people in the American West.

"The monster was the best friend I ever had."

—Boris Karloff

under Braxton Bragg out of Tennessee and back to Georgia.

1874 English author Thomas Hardy's novel *Far from the Madding Crowd* is published. In the novel, three suitors court farm owner Bathsheba Everdene, each showing a different face of love and human nature. Although the book ends happily, it contains many of the tragic elements, a grim view of human nature, and a pessimistic outlook, that characterize Hardy's later masterworks.

1876 William Marcy "Boss" Tweed, leader of New York City's corrupt Tammany Hall political organization during the 1860s and early 1870s, is delivered to municipal authorities after his capture in Spain. Tweed became a powerful figure in New York City's Democratic political machine, which openly bought votes, encouraged judicial corruption, and extracted millions from city contracts.

The Battle of Chattanooga

Warren G. Harding

🔬 **1889** Louis Glass and William S. Arnold install the first jukebox at the Palais Royale Saloon in San Francisco, California. The device was a coin-operated Edison cylinder phonograph. For a nickel, a patron could listen to one of four songs.

🔬 **1897** American Andrew J. Beard invents the "jenny coupler," a device to automatically hook railroad cars together by simply allowing them to bump into each other. It remains in use today.

🎭 **1903** Italian tenor Enrico Caruso makes his American debut in a production of Giuseppe Verdi's *Rigoletto* at New York City's Metropolitan Opera House.

⚖️ **1906** Joseph Smith, leader of the Church of Jesus Christ of Latter-day Saints (the Mormons), is convicted of polygamy. According to the *Deseret Evening News,* he entered a plea of guilty, was fined three hundred dollars, and was dismissed.

⚖️ **1910** American-born dentist Dr. Hawley Crippen is hanged at Pentonville prison in London for murdering his wife. Crippen had attempted to escape to Canada after the murder, but was arrested on board ship after a radio message revealed his identity.

🇺🇸 **1921** U.S. president Warren G. Harding signs the Willis Campell Act, forbidding doctors from prescribing beer or liquor for medical purposes.

🇺🇸 **1936** In the United States, the first issue of the pictorial magazine *Life* is published. The cover featured a photo of the Fort Peck Dam by Margaret Bourke-White.

🔬 **1948** Dr. Frank G. Back of New York City patents the first zoom lens, which eliminated the need for multiple focal-length lenses mounted on a turret.

✠ **1964** The Vatican abolishes Latin as the official language of Roman Catholic liturgy.

🇺🇳 **1971** The People's Republic of China becomes a member of the United Nations Security Council.

⚖️ **1979** Thomas McMahon, a member of the Irish Republican Army, is sentenced to life imprisonment for preparing and planting the bomb that killed Lord Louis Mountbatten three months before. The assassination was the first blow struck against the British royal family by the IRA during its long campaign to drive the British out of Northern Ireland.

🇮🇹 **1980** A series of earthquakes devastates southern Italy and kills 4,800 people.

1105 Rabbi Nathan ben Yehiel of Rome completes his classic Talmudic dictionary, a book tracing the root of each word and citing the text in which it appears. The Talmud is a vast compilation of the Oral Law of the Jews, as opposed to what is written in Scripture.

1642 Dutch navigator Abel Tasman discovers an island that he names Van Diemen's Land, after his captain. It was later renamed Tasmania.

1655 After conflicts over laws in Parliament aimed at limiting the power of the Anglican Church, English lord protector Oliver Cromwell bans Anglican services in favor of Puritan forms.

1835 The Texas Provincial Government authorizes a horse-mounted police force called the Texas Rangers.

1874 Joseph Glidden receives a U.S. patent for barbed wire, a product that transformed the American West. Before this, settlers on the plains had no easy way to fence livestock and prevent herds from roaming away.

Texas Ranger

BORN ON THIS DAY

1632
BENEDICT SPINOZA
Dutch philosopher and author (*Ethics Demonstrated with Geometrical Order*)

1713
LAURENCE STERNE
Irish-born British author (*The Life and Opinions of Tristram Shandy*)

1784
ZACHARY TAYLOR
12th U.S. president (1849–50)

1815
GRACE DARLING
Scottish lighthouse-keeper's daughter who rescued storm-wrecked sailors in 1838

1821
WILLIAM HENRY VANDERBILT
American businessman, president of the New York Central Railroad, and son of Cornelius Vanderbilt

1849
FRANCES HODGSON BURNETT
English author (*Little Lord Fauntleroy; The Secret Garden*)

1853
BAT MASTERSON
American buffalo hunter, gun-fighter, and lawman

1868
SCOTT JOPLIN
Oft-cited date for African-American musician and composer of ragtime music ("Maple Leaf Rag"; "The Entertainer")

1888
DALE CARNEGIE
American lecturer and author (*How to Win Friends and Influence People*)

1894
CORINNE GRIFFITH
American actress (*The Girl Problem; The Bramble Bush*)

1921
JOHN V. LINDSAY
American politician, mayor of New York City (1966–73)

1925
WILLIAM F. BUCKLEY JR.
American author and commentator, editor of the *National Review*

1938
OSCAR ROBERTSON
American Hall of Fame basketball player

King George II of Greece

1903 Clyde J. Coleman of New York City receives a patent for an automobile electric self-starter. It was eventually modified and was first installed on Cadillacs in 1912.

1935 King George II of Greece returns to his homeland after 12 years in exile in London, England. He left in 1923 before Greece was declared a republic, and returned after a national plebiscite called for the restoration of the monarchy following a decade of political instability.

1941 The United States grants Lend-Lease aid to the Free French government. Lend-Lease was a program initially instituted to send aid to Great Britain during World War II while the United States was still theoretically neutral. By the end of the war, 44 countries had received Lend-Lease aid,

> *"If you want to be different from the past, study the past."*
>
> —*Benedict Spinoza*

totaling more than $50 billion in war supplies.

1944 During World War II, U.S. bombers based on Saipan attack Tokyo in the first raid against the Japanese capital by land-based planes.

1947 The U.S. House of Representatives votes to approve citations of contempt against 10 Hollywood writers, directors, and producers who had refused to cooperate at hearings dealing with communism in the movie industry. As a result, Hollywood quickly established its "blacklist," a collection of names of Hollywood personalities suspected of having communist ties.

1948 Ireland votes for independence from the United Kingdom, a move recognized by England the following year.

1960 American basketball star Wilt Chamberlain establishes an NBA record with 55 rebounds in a single game.

1962 Dawn Fraser, an Australian swimmer, sets the 11th of her 12 world records and the eighth of nine in a row in the 100-meter freestyle with a time of 59.5 seconds.

1962 The English satirical television program *That Was the Week That Was* is first broadcast. Breaking new ground in TV production, it introduced personalities David Frost and John Cleese.

1969 During the Vietnam War, U.S. Army officials announce that First Lieutenant William Calley will be court-martialed for the premeditated murder of 109 Vietnamese civilians at My Lai. Calley was found guilty of murdering 22 civilians and sentenced to life imprisonment, but his sentence was reduced twice, and President Richard M. Nixon paroled him in 1974.

1969 The nuclear nonproliferation treaty is signed by the United States and the Soviet Union. Fifty-nine other nations eventually signed the treaty.

1971 A hijacker calling himself D. B. Cooper parachutes from a Northwest Orient Airlines 727 into a raging thunderstorm over Washington state with $200,000 in ransom money. His fate remains a mystery.

1977 The tomb of King Philip II, father of Alexander the Great, is found in Greece.

1985 Fifty-eight people die as Egyptian commandos storm a hijacked EgyptAir jetliner parked on the ground in Malta.

EgyptAir flight 648 in flames after troops stormed the jet

1120 The heir to the English throne, William, son of Henry I, is drowned when the royal yacht the *White Ship* sinks en route from Normandy to England. His death led to a struggle for the crown between Henry's daughter Matilda and nephew Stephen.

1500 Governor Francisco de Bobadilla of Santo Domingo, sent by Spain's Isabella and Ferdinand to investigate wretched conditions in the colony of Hispaniola, sends Italian explorer Christopher Columbus back in chains. Columbus was released, but his favor began to wane.

1715 American Sybilla Masters is granted the first English patent for processing corn.

1758 The British capture Fort Duquesne in present-day Pittsburgh, Pennsylvania, during the French and Indian War.

1783 Nearly three months after the Treaty of Paris ends the American Revolutionary War, the last British soldiers withdraw from New York City, their last military position in the United States. After they departed, General George Washington entered the city in triumph to the cheers of New Yorkers.

1792 The first *Farmer's Almanac* is published in the United States.

1834 Delmonico's, one of New York's most famous restaurants, provides a meal of soup, steak, coffee, and pie for 12 cents.

Alfred Nobel

1837 William Crompton of Taunton, Massachusetts, receives a patent for the silk power loom.

1867 Dynamite is patented in the U. S. by Swedish chemist Alfred Nobel. Extremely concerned about the potential harmful uses of his invention, he eventually created the Nobel Prize to promote advances toward peace.

1884 The U.S. patent for evaporated milk is granted to John B. Meyenberg of St. Louis, Missouri.

1914 During World War I, German field marshal Friedrich von Hindenburg calls off the two-week Lodz offensive in Poland. The Russians lost 90,000 to the Germans' 35,000 soldiers.

1921 Hirohito becomes regent of Japan. Although he held little real military power, as emperor he became the figurehead around which Japan engaged the United States during World War II.

1922 English archaeologist Howard Carter opens the

> *"As I grow older I pay less attention to what men say. I just watch what they do."*
>
> —Andrew Carnegie

first of two doorways to the tomb of King Tutankhamen.

1923 Transatlantic radio broadcasting begins for the first time from England to America.

1936 Japan and Germany sign the Anti-Comintern Pact to collaborate against the spread of communism.

1940 The American cartoon character Woody Woodpecker debuts in Walter Lantz's *Knock Knock*.

1947 The New Zealand Parliament finally confirms the 1931 Statute of Westminster, granting independence from Great Britain.

1947 Meeting in what a newspaper report called "an atmosphere of utter gloom," representatives from the United States, France, Great Britain, and the Soviet Union convene to discuss the fate of postwar Europe, particularly that of Germany, which had been divided into sections occupied by the four nations since the end of the war.

1948 Ed Parsons, who ran a radio station in Astoria, Oregon, invents cable television. He detected a usable signal from a TV station 150 miles away and ran a cable from an antenna on the hotel where he lived to his living room. Then he put a TV set in a store window and brought the signal to it with coaxial cable, the first recorded use of coaxial to carry TV.

1965 In a struggle for power, Republic of the Congo Army chief of staff Seko Sese Mobutu leads a military coup deposing President Joseph Kasavubu. Mobutu had previously helped Kasavubu oust Patrice Lumumba, the Congo's first premier and secretary of defense. Mobutu changed the name of Congo to Zaire.

1990 Poland holds its first popular presidential election following Communist rule. Solidarity founder Lech Walesa received a plurality of votes and won a runoff on December 9.

1998 The English Law Lords rule that the former Chilean dictator General Augusto Pinochet, currently staying in England, is not immune from prosecution. The ruling paved the way for his eventual extradition on charges of torture and genocide.

MILESTONE

International Day to Eliminate Violence Against Women

The United Nations General Assembly passes a resolution designating November 25 the International Day to Eliminate Violence Against Women. The resolution marked the anniversary of the death of three sisters who were brutally murdered in the Dominican Republic in 1961. Not all U.N. members formally recognized this day until 1999. Many organizations worldwide have successfully pulled together for increased awareness and support of their cause. Although this is a sign of positive change, statistics show there is still much work left. It is estimated that one in every four women worldwide has been, or will be, raped.

Women's demonstration in Dhaka, Bangladesh (milestone)

1716 Captain Arthur Savage exhibits the first lion to be seen in America, at his house in Boston, Massachusetts.

1778 English captain John Cook discovers the island of Maui in the Sandwich Islands. It was later renamed Hawaii.

1789 George Washington proclaims this a National Thanksgiving Day to honor the signing of the U.S. Constitution.

1812 Stalked by hunger after suffering terrible defeats in Russia, the remnants of French general Napoleon Bonaparte's army begin crossing two hastily constructed bridges over the Beresina River toward Poland, in a desperate attempt to escape to safety. After crossing, his retreat became a rout.

1832 The first horse-drawn streetcar in the United States begins operation in New York City.

1861 Westerners in the state of Virginia, having earlier nullified the state's ordinance of secession from the Union, meet to draft a constitution that will eventually lead to the creation of West Virginia.

MILESTONE

FDR Establishes Modern Thanksgiving Holiday

On this day in 1941, President Franklin D. Roosevelt signs a bill officially establishing the fourth Thursday in November as Thanksgiving Day in the United States. The tradition of celebrating the holiday on Thursday dates back to the early history of the Plymouth and Massachusetts Bay colonies. In 1939, Roosevelt departed from tradition by declaring November 23, the next-to-last Thursday that year, as Thanksgiving Day. Considerable controversy surrounded this deviation and some Americans refused to honor his declaration. After two years, he admitted his mistake and signed the bill officially making the last Thursday in November the national holiday of Thanksgiving.

"A work of art is above all an adventure of the mind."

—Eugene Ionesco

1862 Oxford mathematician Charles Lutwidge Dodgson sends a handwritten manuscript called "Alice's Adventures Under Ground" to 10-year-old Alice Liddell. Better known as Lewis Carroll, the English author made up the story one day on a picnic with young Alice and her two sisters. It became one of the earliest children's books written simply to amuse children, not to teach them.

1867 J. B. Sutherland of Detroit, Michigan, patents the refrigerated railroad car. The car was little more than a huge, rolling icebox, insulated by large ice bunkers on each end. Air was circulated through the bunkers by the movement of the train. This invention enabled railroads to transport perishables great distances.

1885 A meteor trail is first photographed, in Prague, Czechoslovakia.

1913 Jesse Lasky forms the Jesse L. Lasky Feature Play Company in partnership with

Horse-drawn streetcar

his brother-in-law, Samuel Goldfish (later Goldwyn), and his friend Cecil B. DeMille. The American company's first production, *The Squaw Man*, directed by DeMille, was an instant hit and the first silent feature film to be shot in Hollywood, California.

1927 The Ford Motor Company announces the introduction of the Model A, the first new Ford to enter the market since the Model T was introduced in 1908. With prices starting at $460, nearly five million Model As, in several body styles and a variety of colors, rolled onto America's highways until production ended in 1931.

1940 During World War II, Nazi soldiers begin to wall in the ghetto of Warsaw, Poland, where a half-million Jews live.

1941 A Japanese fleet of six aircraft carriers, commanded by Vice Admiral Chuichi Nagumo, leaves Hitokapu Bay for Pearl Harbor, Hawaii, during World War II.

1942 The American movie *Casablanca* has its world premiere at the Hollywood Theatre in New York City.

1944 To hide Nazi German war crimes during World War II, Heinrich Himmler gives the order to dismantle the Auschwitz and Birkenau concentration camps in Poland and to destroy the gas chambers and crematories.

1949 India becomes a sovereign republic under a constitution.

Vice Admiral Chuichi Nagumo

1960 The Minneapolis-St. Paul major-league baseball club officially adopts the name of the Minnesota Twins.

1965 France successfully launches the *Asterix-1* satellite into space, becoming the world's third space power after the Soviet Union and the United States.

1966 French president Charles de Gaulle opens the world's first (and still most powerful) tidal power station at the Rance estuary, in Brittany.

1983 Great Britain's (and possibly the world's) greatest robbery takes place as some 25 million pounds' worth of gold (approximately $38.7 million at the time) in the form of 6,800 bars is stolen from the Brinks-Mat security warehouse at London's Heathrow Airport.

2000 In one of the most contested presidential races in U.S. history, Florida secretary of state Katherine Harris certifies Governor George W. Bush as the winner in the state's presidential election by a 537-vote margin.

43 B.C. To secure Rome following the death of Julius Caesar, Octavian, Antony, and Lepidus form the Second Triumvirate. Now allied, they move to attack and defeat Brutus and Pompeius.

1095 In Clermont, France, Pope Urban II, responding to false rumors of atrocities in the Holy Land, makes an appeal for the faithful to wrest Jerusalem from the Muslims, giving rise to the Crusades.

1495 After failing in an attempt to invade England, 21-year-old Perkin Warbeck, a pretender to the English throne, is warmly received by Scottish king James IV, who gives him Lady Catherine Gordon in marriage. Warbeck's later attempts to invade England also failed, and he was eventually hanged.

1798 Rabbi Shneur Zalman, author of the *Tanya,* a sacred religious text for followers of the orthodox Hasidic movement, is released from a prison in St. Petersburg, Russia. He had been arrested on charges of high treason for allegedly sending money to the sultan of Turkey (the money was meant for the poor of the Holy Land, which was under Turkish rule at the time).

1826 English pharmacist John Walker invents the first practical, strike-anywhere friction

"Creativity can be described as letting go of certainties."

—*Gail Sheehy*

match. He refused to patent his creation.

1834 Thomas Davenport of the United States invents the first commercially successful electric motor, which operated on direct current.

1868 U.S. general George Armstrong Custer leads an attack on peaceful Cheyenne living along the Washita River in Texas, destroying the village and killing 103 Indians. The attack helped restore Custer's reputation and succeeded in persuading many Cheyenne to move to the reservation.

1870 The *New York Times* dubs American baseball "the national game."

1895 Swedish engineer Alfred Nobel, inventor of dynamite, draws up his will in Paris, France. In it, he provides for most of his fortune to be put in trust to establish the Nobel Prizes.

1910 The world's largest railway terminal, New York City's Pennsylvania Station, is officially opened.

General George Armstrong Custer

C.A.R.E. package in Japan

1924 Macy's department store in New York City holds its first Thanksgiving Day parade down a two-mile stretch of Broadway. The event was created to boost holiday sales. With an audience of more than a quarter-million people, it was subsequently declared an annual event.

1940 Two months after General Ion Antonescu seized power in Romania and forced King Carol II to abdicate, his "Iron Guard" arrests and executes more than 60 of the king's aides. The Iron Guard was an extreme right-wing movement imitating Germany's Nazi Party.

1942 During World War II, the French fleet in Toulon is scuttled to keep it from being used by the advancing Germans.

1945 The nonprofit organization Cooperative for American Relief Everywhere is founded to help war-ravaged Europe. C.A.R.E. was soon expanded to include underdeveloped nations worldwide.

1954 After 44 months in prison, former U.S. government official Alger Hiss is released. One of the most famous figures of the Cold War period, he was convicted in 1950 of perjury over his complicity in passing secret government documents to Whittaker Chambers, who passed them along to Soviet agents. Hiss never stopped proclaiming his innocence.

1957 Indian prime minister Jawaharlal Nehru makes an impassioned speech in New Delhi for the United States and the Soviet Union to end nuclear tests and begin disarmament, which, he said, would "save humanity from the ultimate disaster."

1971 The Soviet Union's *Mars 2* becomes the first spacecraft to land (crash) on Mars.

1983 Stores across the United States report being flooded by sometimes-violent shoppers trying to buy "Cabbage Patch Kids" dolls.

Cabbage Patch Kids commemorative stamp

NOVEMBER 28

1340 The Portuguese, in alliance with Castile's Alfonso XI, defeat Muslims from Granada and North Africa at the Battle of Salado in Spain. It was the Muslims' last real attempt to establish or expand their domain in the peninsula.

1520 After sailing through the dangerous straits below South America, Portuguese navigator Ferdinand Magellan enters the Pacific Ocean with three ships, becoming the first European explorer to reach the Pacific from the Atlantic.

1569 The duke of Alva, a fierce military commander under Philip II of Spain, forces Bishop Nicolaas van Nieuwland of Haarlem (the capital of the Province of North Holland) to resign after the area suffered a religious war that led to the devastation of 150 towns and villages.

1582 William Shakespeare, 18, and Anne Hathaway, 26, pay a 40-pound bond for their marriage license in Stratford-upon-Avon, England.

1660 The Royal Society of London is founded. It is the oldest scientific organization in Great Britain and one of the oldest in Europe.

1678 King Charles II of England accuses his wife, Catherine of Braganza, of treason for not bearing him children.

1775 The U.S. Navy is formally established by the Second Continental Congress.

MILESTONE

Lady Astor Becomes MP
American-born Nancy Astor, the first woman ever to sit in the British House of Commons, is elected to Parliament with a substantial majority on this day in 1919. Lady Astor succeeded her husband, Waldorf Astor, who was moving up to an inherited seat in the House of Lords, as a Coalition Unionist candidate. Her flamboyant campaign attracted international attention. Her impassioned speeches on women's and children's rights, her modest black attire, and her occasional irreverence won her a significant following. Repeatedly reelected by her constituency in Plymouth, she sat in the House of Commons until her retirement in 1945.

Lady Astor

"It takes most men five years to recover from a college education, and to learn that poetry is as vital to thinking as knowledge."
—Brooks Atkinson

1871 Ku Klux Klan trials begin in South Carolina as part of a federal effort to halt growing violence against African Americans in the former Confederate states.

1893 Female New Zealanders become the world's first women to vote in a general election in an independent country.

1905 Sinn Fein, a political party dedicated to independence for all of Ireland, is founded in Dublin by Irish nationalist Arthur Griffith. At its inception, the party became the unofficial political wing of militant Irish groups in their struggle to throw off British rule.

1907 Scrap-metal dealer Louis B. Mayer opens a small movie theater in Massachusetts.

668 B-24 Liberator

Emiliano Zapata

Although Fairbanks was already an established star, this was the first time he played a swash-buckling adventurer.

1922 Captain Cyril Turner of Great Britain's Royal Air Force gives the first public skywriting exhibition in the United States, over New York City's Times Square.

1925 The American country-variety show *The Grand Ole Opry* debuts. It remains the longest-running live music show, and celebrates its 79th anniversary in 2004.

Ten years later he started his own production company, which, through a series of mergers, became part of Metro-Goldwyn-Mayer.

1911 Mexican revolutionary Emiliano Zapata issues his "Plan of Ayala," calling for the return of stolen Indian lands.

1918 Emperor Wilhelm of Germany formally abdicates after U.S. president Woodrow Wilson makes it a prerequisite for peace negotiations following World War I.

1920 The American movie *The Mask of Zorro* opens, starring Douglas Fairbanks.

1942 The first production B-24 Liberator rolls off the assembly line at Ford's massive Willow Run plant in Ypsilanti, Michigan. By July of 1944, using the type of assembly-line production that had made Ford an industrial giant, the plant was producing one B-24 every hour.

1948 The Polaroid Land camera first goes on sale, at a department store in Boston, Massachusetts. It was the first commercially successful self-developing camera system.

1516 The Treaty of Freiburg, promising eternal peace, is signed between the Swiss and the French.

1787 Civil status is granted to Protestants in France as Louis XVI issues an edict of tolerance.

1825 In New York City, *The Barber of Seville* is the first Italian opera to premiere in the United States. Also on this day in 1948, *Othello* becomes the first opera to be televised.

1864 Colonel John Chivington and his Colorado volunteers massacre a peaceful village of Cheyenne near Sand Creek in Colorado Territory, setting off a long series of bloody retaliatory attacks by Indians. Because of the depraved manner of slaughter, many Americans strongly condemned Chivington, who spent the rest of his life trying to escape the stigma of the attack.

1887 The United States first gains rights at Pearl Harbor when the Hawaiian monarchy grants permission for the maintenance of a coaling and repair station.

1890 In the United States, the first Army-Navy American football game is played. Navy beat Army, 24–0.

1890 The Imperial Diet, forerunner of Japan's national legislature, opens its first session. It consisted of a House of Peers and a House of Representatives.

1897 The first motorcycle race takes place in Surrey, England. Charles Jarrot won

BORN ON THIS DAY

1797
GAETANO DONIZETTI
Italian operatic composer (*Lucrezia Borgia; Lucia di Lammermoor*)

1832
LOUISA MAY ALCOTT
American author (*Little Women*)

1843
GERTRUDE JEKYLL
English garden designer who worked with architect Sir Edwin Lutyens

1849
SIR JOHN AMBROSE FLEMING
English physicist and engineer, inventor of the thermionic valve

1898
C. S. LEWIS
Irish-born English author (*The Lion, the Witch, and the Wardrobe; The Silver Chair; Miracles*)

1908
ADAM CLAYTON POWELL JR.
American politician, civil rights activist, and congressman from New York City (1944–66, 1969–72)

Adam Clayton Powell Jr.

1918
MADELEINE L'ENGLE
American Newberry and American Book Award-winning author (*A Wrinkle in Time; A Swiftly Tilting Planet*)

1927
VIN SCULLY
Los Angeles Dodgers baseball announcer

1933
JOHN MAYALL
American singer/songwriter (The Bluesbreakers)

Richard E. Byrd

the one-mile race in a time of two minutes, 8 seconds.

1929 American explorer Richard E. Byrd and three companions make the first flight over the South Pole, flying from their base on the Ross Ice Shelf to the pole and back in 18 hours, 41 minutes.

1934 The marriage of the Duke of Kent and Princess Marina is the first English royal wedding to be televised.

1944 The first open-heart surgery, a fix for the fetal heart defect tetralogy of Fallot, or "blue baby syndrome," is performed at Johns Hopkins University in Baltimore, Maryland, by surgeon Alfred Blalock and assistant Vivien Thomas.

1947 Despite strong Arab opposition, the United Nations votes for the partition of Palestine and the creation of an independent Jewish state.

1948 Australian prime minister Ben Chifley and 1,200 other people attend the unveiling of the first car to be manu-

> *"Aim at heaven and you get Earth thrown in, aim at Earth and you get neither."*
>
> —*C. S. Lewis*

factured entirely in Australia—an ivory-colored, six-cylinder motorcar officially designated the 48-215, but fondly known as the Holden FX. It was an instant success, and 100,000 were sold in the first five years of production.

1950 Three weeks after U.S. general Douglas MacArthur first reported Chinese communist troops in action in North Korea, U.S.-led United Nations troops begin a desperate retreat out of North Korea under heavy fire from the Chinese. By May 1951 the communists were pushed back to the 38th parallel, where the battle line remained for the rest of the Korean War.

1961 Freedom Riders, volunteers from across the country who traveled to the South to challenge segregation in U.S. interstate bus travel, are attacked by a mob at a bus station in McComb, Mississippi.

1961 In a prelude to John Glenn's orbital space flight, the first U.S. satellite carrying an animal, a five-year-old chimpanzee named Enos, is launched from Cape Canaveral, Florida.

1963 U.S. president Lyndon B. Johnson establishes a special commission, headed by Supreme Court chief justice Earl Warren, to investigate the assassination of John F. Kennedy. After 10 months of gathering

evidence and questioning witnesses, the Warren Commission concluded that there was no conspiracy in the assassination and that Lee Harvey Oswald, the alleged assassin, acted alone.

1974 Prompted by recent terrorist atrocities, Great Britain passes the Prevention of Terrorism Act, which outlawed the Irish Republican Army.

1990 The U.N. Security Council votes to authorize military action if Iraq does not withdraw from Kuwait and release all foreign hostages by January 15, 1991.

1993 The British government reveals it has had secret talks with the Irish Republican Army. The news provoked an angry response from some MPs, but the contact led to an IRA cease-fire the following year.

1999 Fifty thousand protestors gather in Seattle, Washington, to oppose the World Trade Organization's "corporate globalization."

World Trade Organization protester in Seattle, Washington

1215 Pope Innocent III closes the Fourth Lateran Council, which first officially used the term "transubstantiation" in referring to the Eucharist (Lord's Supper).

1609 The true face of the moon is first seen as Galileo Galilei in Padua, Italy, turns his telescope toward it for the first time and makes a drawing to record his discovery. Galileo's revolutionary treatise *Starry Messenger,* which appeared the following March, showed an astonished public that the moon was a cratered world, a new land to be explored.

1774 The left-wing political activist and writer Thomas Paine arrives in Philadelphia, Pennsylvania. An advocate and fighter for the American revolutionary cause, Paine wrote several ground-breaking political works including *The Rights of Man.*

1782 The British sign a preliminary agreement in Paris recognizing American independence.

1803 France officially takes control of the Louisiana Territory from Spain. Spain ceded it to France to avoid continued deficits and the growing possibility that it might have to fight the Americans to retain control.

1864 During the American Civil War, the Confederate Army of Tennessee suffers a devastating defeat when its commander, General John Bell Hood, orders a frontal assault on strong Union positions around Franklin, Tennessee. The loss cost Hood

BORN ON THIS DAY

1554
SIR PHILIP SIDNEY
English soldier, politician, and poet (*Astrophel and Stella; Arcadia*)

1667
JONATHAN SWIFT
English author, poet, and satirist (*Gulliver's Travels; A Modest Proposal*)

1835
MARK TWAIN (SAMUEL CLEMENS)
American author (*Tom Sawyer; Huckleberry Finn; Roughing It; Life on the Mississippi*)

1874
LUCY M. MONTGOMERY
Canadian author (*Anne of Green Gables; Anne of Avonlea*)

1874
SIR WINSTON CHURCHILL
British statesman, historian (*A History of the English-speaking Peoples*), and biographer

1912
GORDON PARKS
American photographer, director (*Flavio; Shaft*), and author (*The Learning Tree; Born Black*)

1914
CHARLES HAWTREY
English comedy actor in the *Carry On…* films

1929
DICK CLARK
American disk jockey, television producer, and TV host (*American Bandstand; New Year's Rockin' Eve*)

1936
ABBIE HOFFMAN
American author (*Steal This Book*), antiwar activist, and 1960s cultural revolutionary

1937
SIR RIDLEY SCOTT
English movie director (*Alien; Blade Runner; Gladiator*)

1947
DAVID MAMET
American playwright (*Speed-the-Plow; American Buffalo*) and screenwriter (*Glengarry Glen Ross; Wag the Dog*)

Folies Bergère poster

six of his finest generals and nearly a third of his force.

1872 The world's first international soccer match is played at Hamilton Crescent in Glasgow between Scotland and England. The match was a goalless draw.

1886 The Folies Bergère stages its first revue-style music hall show, featuring scantily clad chorus girls. Among the performers who got their start at the French theater were Yvette Guilbert, Maurice Chevalier, and Mistinguett. The African-American dancer and singer Josephine Baker made her Folies debut in 1926.

1887 The first softball game is held indoors at the Farragut Boat Club in Chicago, Illinois.

1900 The French government denounces British actions involving annexations in South Africa and declares sympathy for the Boers (inhabitants of Dutch or French Huguenot descent, also known as Afrikaners).

1902 American outlaw Harvey "Kid Curry" Logan, the second-in-command in Butch Cassidy's Wild Bunch crew, is sentenced to 20 years' hard labor in a Tennessee prison. Though the Hollywood movie *Butch Cassidy and the Sundance Kid* portrayed Harry Longabaugh as Cassidy's main partner, Logan was his true sidekick and right-hand man.

1906 U.S. president Theodore Roosevelt publicly denounces the segregation of schoolchildren of Japanese descent in San Francisco, California.

1919 Women are allowed to cast votes for the first time in French elections.

1939 The Russo-Finnish War begins as Soviet premier Joseph Stalin attacks Finland. The Finnish used forest combat to inflict heavy damage on the Russian invaders, and the British and French came to their defense in mid-December. But the following March, the "Peace of Moscow" was signed and Finland ceded 16,000 square miles to the Soviet Union.

1956 In the United States, *Douglas Edwards and the News* makes the first use of videotape on television.

1956 American prizefighter Floyd Patterson, age 21, becomes the youngest boxer to

John Paul II

win the world heavyweight title as he defeats Archie Moore in Chicago, Illinois.

1979 John Paul II attends an Eastern Orthodox mass, the first pope to do so in 1,000 years. He and Patriarch Dimitros I of Constantinople agreed to set up a joint commission to explore the prospects of ecumenical unity.

1993 U.S. president Bill Clinton signs the Brady handgun-control bill into law. The law requires a prospective handgun buyer to wait five business days while the authorities perform a background check.

President Clinton signs Brady Bill; back row left to right, Vice President Al Gore, Attorney General Janet Reno; Mrs. Brady; front left, James Brady

> *"Invention is the talent of youth, as judgment is of age."*
>
> —Jonathan Swift

1167 Northern Italian towns form an alliance called the Lombard League to resist the authority claimed by Holy Roman Emperor Frederick I.

1626 The pasha Muhammad ibn Farukh is deposed for his tyrannical governorship of Jerusalem.

1640 Portugal reclaims its independence after 60 years of Spanish rule.

1824 Congress announces that no candidate received a majority of electoral votes in the U.S. presidential election. The House of Representatives, as dictated by the 12th Amendment, made a decision from among Andrew Jackson; John Quincy Adams, the son of the second president John Adams; Secretary of State William H. Crawford; and Representative Henry Clay. Adams was selected.

1835 Danish author Hans Christian Andersen's first book of fairy tales is published.

1838 Mexico declares war on France and orders the expulsion of all French citizens. France had established a naval blockade and begun bombarding the port of Veracruz after delivering an ultimatum demanding reparations for criminal damages suffered by French citizens residing in Mexico.

1862 U.S. president Abraham Lincoln addresses conservative concerns over emancipation in his State of the Union address and speaks of gradual, compensated emancipation of slaves, which many

---

BORN ON THIS DAY

1761
MADAME TUSSAUD
Swiss-born creator of waxwork mannequins who founded the famous London exhibition

1844
QUEEN ALEXANDRA
Queen consort of British king Edward VII, mother of Edward VIII and George VI

1886
REX STOUT
American author of more than 70 detective novels, most of which feature a sleuth named Nero Wolf (*Triple Jeopardy; The Golden Spiders; Gambit*)

1910
DAME ALICIA MARKOVA
English ballerina

1911
WALTER ALSTON
American manager of major-league baseball teams

1911
CALVIN GRIFFITH
American owner of major-league baseball teams

1925
CALVIN COOLIDGE JULIUS CAESAR TUSKAHOMA MCLISH
American professional baseball pitcher

1935
WOODY ALLEN
Academy Award-winning American writer, director, and actor (*Annie Hall; Manhattan; Bullets over Broadway*)

1939
LEE TREVINO
American golf champion

1940
RICHARD PRYOR
American comedian and actor (*Stir Crazy; Blue Collar*)

---

moderates and conservatives desire. But he also asserted that slaves liberated thus far would remain forever free.

1878 U.S. president Rutherford B. Hayes has the first telephone installed in the White House. Its inventor, Alexander Graham Bell, personally installed it.

1879 English librettist Arthur Gilbert's and composer William Sullivan's operetta *HMS Pinafore* has its first performance, at the Opéra Comique in London. Sullivan conducted the orchestra, while Gilbert was a sailor in the chorus.

1881 Virgil, Wyatt, and Morgan Earp are acquitted of any crime for their actions in Tombstone, Arizona, during the gunfight at the O.K. Corral.

1887 Scottish author Sir Arthur Conan Doyle's character Sherlock Holmes first appears in print in *Study in Scarlet*.

1891 Canadian doctor James B. Naismith invents the game of basketball at the YMCA in Springfield, Massachusetts.

1903 The world's first western movie, *The Great Train Robbery*, is released in the United

The Great Train Robbery poster

Cuban airlift to Miami, Florida

States by Thomas Edison's production company. It revived flagging interest in motion pictures with a 12-minute story that first introduced editing and the chase scene.

1906 The world's first movie theater, the Cinema Omnia Pathé, opens in Paris, France.

1918 The Kingdom of Serbs, Croats, and Slovenes is formed from two independent kingdoms and parts of seven other areas. In 1929, King Alexander I renamed it Yugoslavia.

1933 Nazi storm troopers become an organ of Germany's Third Reich.

1934 American jazz clarinet pioneer Benny Goodman, the "King of Swing," debuts as a regular on the radio variety show *Let's Dance*.

1959 Twelve nations, including the United States and the Soviet Union, sign the Antarctica Treaty, banning military activity and weapons testing on that continent. It was the first

> *"If you want to make God laugh, tell Him your future plans."*
>
> —Woody Allen

arms control agreement signed in the Cold War period.

1959 A camera mounted on the nose of a Thor missile takes the first color photo of Earth from space.

1965 An airlift of refugees from Cuba to the United States begins as thousands of Cubans, dissatisfied with Fidel Castro's revolution, are allowed to leave.

1990 Great Britain is connected with the European mainland for the first time since the Ice Age when workers from England and France break through to connect the two ends of a tunnel 132 feet beneath the English Channel. The Channel Tunnel, sometimes referred to as the "Chunnel," was officially opened in May 1994.

Rosa Parks riding the bus (milestone)

MILESTONE

Rosa Parks Ignites Bus Boycott

In Montgomery, Alabama, Rosa Parks is jailed on this day in 1955 for refusing to give up her seat on a public bus to a white man, a violation of the city's racial segregation laws. The successful Montgomery Bus Boycott, organized by Martin Luther King, Jr., followed Parks's historic act of civil disobedience. The boycott stretched on for more than a year, and participants carpooled or walked miles to work and school. On December 20, 1956, Montgomery's buses were finally desegregated.

St. Paul's Cathedral

1682 The first earl of Shaftesbury flees to Amsterdam, Holland, from England following charges of treason. He fought to keep the Roman Catholic duke of York (later King James II) from the throne on suspicion of royal efforts to elevate the position of Roman Catholics.

1697 St. Paul's Cathedral in London, England, designed by Sir Christopher Wren following the destruction of the former cathedral in the Great Fire of London, is opened.

1793 Fleeing his debtors, 21-year-old Samuel Taylor Coleridge enlists in the Light Dragoons, an English cavalry unit. He is probably best known for his poem "The Rime of the Ancient Mariner."

1804 In Notre Dame Cathedral, in Paris, France, Napoleon Bonaparte is crowned Emperor Napoleon I. Pope Pius VII handed Napoleon the crown that he then placed on his own head.

1805 On the first anniversary of his coronation, Napoleon defeats the Russian and Austrian armies at the

---

BORN ON THIS DAY

1837
DOCTOR JOSEPH BELL
Scottish physician held to be the model on which Sir Arthur Conan Doyle based Sherlock Holmes

1859
GEORGES SEURAT
French painter (*Sunday Afternoon on the Island of Grand Jatte; The Bathers at Asnières*)

1896
GENERAL GEORGY ZHUKOV
Russian military commander who led the attack on Berlin toward the end of World War II

1899
SIR JOHN BARBIROLLI
English conductor who led the Hallé and New York Philharmonic orchestras

1915
ADOLPH GREEN
American screenwriter and collaborator with Betty Comden on Broadway musicals (*Singin' in the Rain; On the Town; Bells Are Ringing; On a Clear Day You Can See Forever*)

1924
ALEXANDER HAIG
American general and NATO commander, chief of staff to presidents Nixon and Ford and secretary of state under President Reagan

1925
JULIE HARRIS
Tony Award-winning American actress (*I Am a Camera; Member of the Wedding*)

1949
CATHY LEE CROSBY
American actress (*Wonder Woman*) and television show host (*That's Incredible*)

1960
RICK SAVAGE
English rock musician (Def Leppard)

1962
TRACY AUSTIN
American professional tennis player who became the youngest U.S. Open champion

---

"As of now, I am in control here in the White House."
—Alexander Haig

Battle of Austerlitz, sometimes called the "Battle of the Three Emperors."

1823 President James Monroe proclaims a new U.S. foreign policy initiative that would become known as the Monroe Doctrine. It forbade European interference in the American hemisphere but also asserted U.S. neutrality with regard to future European conflicts.

1848 Franz Josef I becomes emperor of Austria. His reign represented a slow and steady decline of Austria as a world power.

1859 Antislavery activist John Brown is hanged for treason in Virginia.

1867 English writer Charles Dickens gives his first public reading in the United States, in a New York City theater. The line of people anxious to see him stretched for more than a mile.

1877 Louis-Paul Cailletet of France becomes the first to liquefy oxygen.

1901 American inventor King Camp Gillette patents the disposable safety razor.

1908 Zxuan Tong, at age 2, becomes China's last emperor.

1930 Desperately seeking ways to halt the nation's financial free fall, President Herbert C. Hoover goes before the U.S. Congress to make a plea for a $150 million public works program. A few weeks later, Congress appropriated $116 million in hopes of putting Americans back to work.

1942 Italian-born Nobel Prize-winning physicist Enrico Fermi directs and controls the first nuclear chain reaction beneath the bleachers of Stagg Field at the University of Chicago in Illinois, ushering in the nuclear age.

1969 The Boeing 747 jumbo jet is publicly demonstrated for the first time.

1971 The Soviet *Mars 3* enters orbit around Mars. Its lander became the first to soft land on the planet.

Laid-off Enron employees

1979 Iranian electors vote overwhelmingly in favor of a new constitution giving the Ayatollah Khomeini absolute power.

1990 The first free parliamentary elections are held in newly reunified Germany.

2001 In a response to terrorist attacks on September 11, U.S. bombers hit Taliban defenses around Kandahar in Afghanistan.

2001 The Enron Corporation, under CEO Kenneth Lay, files for bankruptcy. It was the largest bankruptcy in U.S. history and one of the most controversial. Just days before filing, the company paid $55 million in bonuses to some 500 high-level employees.

Boeing model 747 accompanied by a Sabre V chase plane to observe the test flight

Lorenzo Piero de' Medici

1347 Pope Clement VI declares Roman leader Cola di Rienzi a heretic. Rienzi dreamed of a popular Italian empire with Rome as its capital and had set about to crush the power of the ruling barons. Clement VI became concerned over his motives.

1468 Lorenzo the Magnificent succeeds his father, Piero de' Medici, as ruler of Florence, Italy. The Medicis, particularly Lorenzo, fueled Italy's growing passion for classical literature and created new centers of learning as part of the Italian Renaissance.

1557 The "First Covenant" of Scottish protestant nobles is formed to oppose Mary marrying the Roman Catholic dauphin of France.

1586 Potatoes are introduced to England by Sir Thomas Herriot by way of Colombia.

1762 France cedes all lands west of the Mississippi, known as Upper Louisiana, to Spain.

1800 The Battle of Hohenlinden, between France and Austria, takes place during the Napoleonic Wars. French general Jean Moreau advanced toward Munich, Germany, with 100,000 troops, while Austria's Archduke John planned to use 130,000 men to cut off his supply lines. Austria lost and was forced to sign an armistice three weeks later.

1868 The treason trial of Jefferson Davis, president of the Confederacy, begins in Richmond, Virginia. President Andrew Johnson issued amnesty on February 15, 1869, and the charges were dropped.

1879 American inventor Thomas Edison gives the first demonstration of his light bulb. This private demonstration was done for financial backers J. P. Morgan and the Vanderbilt family only. English inventor Joseph Swan had given the first public demonstration of an incandescent light bulb in January of the same year, but Edison was the first to bring the product to market.

1896 American inventor Hermann Hollerith incorporates his Tabulating Machine Company. His machine counted punched cards, inspired by a card system developed by Joseph Jacquard of France to program patterns into textile looms. Through a series of mergers and reorganizations, the company eventually became IBM.

BORN ON THIS DAY

1753
SAMUEL CROMPTON
English inventor of Crompton's Mule, a cotton spinning machine

1755
GILBERT STUART
American artist (*Portrait of Mr. Webb; George Washington*)

1795
SIR ROWLAND HILL
English creator of the postal system where the sender pays, and inventor of adhesive postage stamps

1820
THOMAS BEECHAM
English inventor of Beecham's pills; grandfather of conductor Sir Thomas Beecham

1857
JOSEPH CONRAD
Polish-born English author (*Heart of Darkness; The Secret Sharer; The Secret Agent*)

1907
CONNIE BOSWELL
American singer (The Boswell Sisters)

1923
MARIA CALLAS
American opera singer

1925
FERLIN HUSKY
American country singer ("Gone"; "Wings of a Dove")

1930
JEAN-LUC GODARD
French New Wave film director (*Alphaville; À Bout de Souffle* (*Breathless*); *Hélas pour Moi* (*Unfortunately for Me*))

1930
ANDY WILLIAMS
American singer ("Canadian Sunset"; "Moon River")

1931
JAYE P. MORGAN
American singer ("That's All I Want From You"; "The Longest Walk")

1948
OZZY OSBOURNE
English rock singer (Rare Breed, Black Sabbath)

"The truth is that there is no terror untempered by some great moral idea."

—Jean-Luc Godard

Anti-Union Carbide protest in Bhopal, India

1907 Future movie star Mary Pickford and future director Cecil B. DeMille appear in the Broadway play *The Warrens of Virginia* in New York City.

1910 Neon lighting, developed by French physicist Georges Claude, has its first public demonstration at the Paris Motor Show.

1925 The League of Nations orders Greece to pay for its October invasion of Bulgaria. Greece had invaded Bulgaria in an attempt to annex it. Bulgaria appealed to the League and Greece withdrew, but mostly as a result of the League's collective security rather than "moral force."

1931 The British Parliament adopts the Statute of Westminster, the founding charter for the British Commonwealth of Nations.

1944 Civil war breaks out in Athens as communist guerrillas battle democratic forces for control of a liberated Greece. By February 1945 they were forced to surrender and disband.

1947 American playwright Tennessee Williams's *A*

Streetcar Named Desire opens on Broadway with Jessica Tandy as Blanche Dubois and Marlon Brando as Stanley Kowalski.

1968 American major-league baseball reduces the height of the pitcher's mound from 15 inches to 10 inches in an attempt to increase scoring.

1971 The third Indo-Pakistani War begins as India intervenes in a Pakistani civil war. The war ended with independence for East Pakistan, now Bangladesh.

1984 In one of the worst industrial disasters in history, a Union-Carbide pesticide plant located in Bhopal, India, leaks a highly toxic cloud of methyl isocyanate into the air. Two thousand people were killed immediately, at least 600,000 were injured, and at least 6,000 have died since.

1997 Responding to growing concerns over B.S.E., known as "mad cow disease," the British government announces plans to ban the sale of beef on the bone, which is believed to carry a higher theoretical risk of transmitting the disease to humans.

2001 American inventor Dean Kamen unveils his battery-powered, 12-miles-per-hour Segway Human Transporter. Kamen spent $100 million to develop the two-wheeled vehicle.

Dean Kamen on the Segway

771 Charlemagne becomes sole ruler of the Frankish Empire.

963 Pope John XII is deposed by Holy Roman emperor Otto for plotting an armed conspiracy.

1110 The Syrian harbor city of Saida surrenders to Crusaders. Along with Tripoli and Beirut, it was one of three major cities to fall within 18 months.

1154 Adrian IV (born Nicholas Breakspear) becomes the only English pope.

1259 The Treaty of Paris is signed between English king Henry III and French king Louis IX. Louis wanted the political unification of France and yielded Limoges, Cahors, and Perigeux to Henry in exchange for Henry's abandonment of claims to Normandy, Anjou, Maine, Touraine, and Poitou.

1674 Father Jacques Marquette of France builds the first dwelling at what will be Chicago, Illinois, near the mouth of the Chicago River at the present intersection with Damen Avenue. He and Louis Joliet were the first European explorers to pass through the area.

1732 John Gay, English author best known for *The Beggar's Opera*, dies at age 47. He was buried in Westminster Abbey in London, England.

"Not what I have, but what I do is my kingdom."

—*Thomas Carlyle*

MILESTONE

Senate Approves U.S. Participation in United Nations

In an overwhelming vote of 65 to 7, the U.S. Senate approves full U.S. participation in the United Nations on this day in 1945. The United Nations officially came into existence on October 24, 1945, when its charter was ratified by China, France, the Soviet Union, the United Kingdom, the United States, and a majority of other signatories. Senate approval allowed the United States to join most of the world's nations in the international organization, which aims to arbitrate differences between countries and stem military aggression.

1783 General George Washington bids farewell to his officers at Fraunces Tavern in New York City at the end of the American Revolutionary War.

1791 The oldest Sunday newspaper in world, Great Britain's *Observer*, is first published.

1808 The Inquisition in Spain is abolished by French emperor Napoleon Bonaparte.

1829 Great Britain bans "suttee" in India, the practice of a widow throwing herself on her husband's funeral pyre.

1843 Manila paper is patented in Massachusetts.

1867 Former Minnesota farmer Oliver Hudson Kelley founds the Order of the Patrons

Promotional print for the Grange

Dan Jansen

of Husbandry, better known as the Grange. Begun primarily as a social organization for farmers, it evolved into a major political force for state and federal controls over pivotal economic issues, including the federal regulation of railroads.

1872 The *Dei Gratia,* a small British brig under Captain David Morehouse, spots the *Mary Celeste,* an American vessel, sailing erratically but at full sail near the Azores in the Atlantic Ocean. The ship was seaworthy, its stores and supplies were untouched, but not a soul was onboard. The crew was never found and the reason for the ship's abandonment has never been determined.

1918 Woodrow Wilson departs Washington, D.C., for France on the first European trip by a U.S. president. He headed the American delegation to the Versailles Peace Conference, seeking an official end to World War I.

1933 *Tobacco Road,* based on American author Erskine Caldwell's book, has its first performance at the Masque Theatre in New York City. The play ran for eight years.

1942 During World War II, a group of Polish Christians led by two women, Zofia Kossak and Wanda Filipowicz, put their own lives at risk when they set up the Council for the Assistance of the Jews. The fates of Kossak and Filipowicz are unclear.

1977 Jean-Bedel Bokassa, ruler of the Central African Republic (which he would later rename the Central African Empire), crowns himself emperor in a $100 million ceremony. He was deposed in 1979.

1993 American speed skater Dan Jansen skates the 500-meter race in a world-record 35.92 seconds. On the same day, Johann Koss of Norway skates the 5K in a world-record six minutes, 35.53 seconds.

Catherine de' Medici

1301 Trying to stop illegal French levies on the clergy, Pope Boniface VIII issues the bull *Ausculta fili,* which summons a synod of French to Rome to discuss the reformation of French affairs.

1349 Five hundred Jews in Nuremberg, Germany, believed to be a cause of the Black Death (the Plague), are tortured, burned at the stake, or simply murdered.

1484 Pope Innocent VIII issues a statement deploring witchcraft in Germany. He also ordered that all cats belonging to witches who were scheduled to be burned also be burned.

1492 Italian explorer Christopher Columbus reaches Hispaniola (Haiti), the last discovery on his first voyage to the New World before returning to Spain and a hero's welcome.

1560 Charles IX becomes king of France. Under the influence of his mother, Catherine de' Medici, he approved the massacre of St. Bartholomew's Day (August 24), in which thousands of Huguenots were murdered in 1572.

BORN ON THIS DAY

1782
MARTIN VAN BUREN
Eighth U.S. President (1837–41)

1830
CHRISTINA ROSSETTI
English poet ("Remember"; "De Profundis"; "In an Artist's Studio")

1839
GEORGE ARMSTRONG CUSTER
American military officer who led the Seventh U.S. Cavalry to its annihilation at the Battle of Little Bighorn in 1876

1859
JOHN, LORD JELLICOE
Admiral of the British Grand Fleet during World War I

1894
PHILLIP K. WRIGLEY
American corporate executive (Wrigley's Gum)

1901
WALT DISNEY
American cartoonist, producer, and creator of Mickey Mouse, Disneyland, Walt Disney World, and many animated feature films

1902
STROM THURMOND
Governor of South Carolina (1947–51) and U.S. senator (1956–2003)

1906
OTTO PREMINGER
Austrian-born American movie director (*Porgy and Bess; Laura; Anatomy of a Murder*)

1932
"LITTLE" RICHARD
American singer ("Good Golly Miss Molly"; "Tutti Frutti")

1934
JOAN DIDION
American author (*Run River; A Book of Common Prayer; Salvador*)

1946
JOSÉ CARRERAS
Spanish operatic tenor

1953
CHRISTOPHER GUARD
English actor (*Great Expectations; I, Claudius; The Lord of the Rings*)

"Fancy being remembered around the world for the invention of a mouse!"
—*Walt Disney*

1766 James Christie, founder of the famous London, England, auction house, holds his first sale. Christie's was eventually sold to François Pinault, a French businessman and art collector, in 1998.

1776 The first American college Greek-letter fraternity, Phi Beta Kappa, is organized at William and Mary College in Williamsburg, Virginia.

1791 Austrian composer Wolfgang Amadeus Mozart dies at age 35 in Vienna. He was buried in a pauper's grave.

1792 The trial of King Louis XVI of France, husband of Marie Antoinette, begins. He was tried (and later beheaded) on charges of treason in dealing with foreign powers after being forced to accept a constitution and becoming a mere figurehead.

1797 French general Napoleon Bonaparte arrives in Paris to lead troops on an invasion of England.

1848 A statement by U.S president James Knox Polk confirming the existence of gold in California encourages the great Gold Rush of 1849.

1861 Dr. Richard Gatling of Indianapolis, Indiana, patents his Gatling Gun, a six-barreled hand-cranked weapon capable of firing 200 rounds per minute.

It was the forerunner of all modern machine guns.

🔬 **1879** Daniel and Thomas Connolly and Thomas McTighe receive a U.S. patent for the first automatic telephone system.

🔬 **1893** The Toronto Railway Company of Canada builds the first electric streetcar. It could go 15 miles between charges and was in service until 1915.

🎭 **1926** *Battleship Potemkin*, Russian director Sergei Eisenstein's film based on a real mutiny aboard a Russian ship in 1905, premieres in New York. The depiction of the czar's troops firing at people as they flee down the steps of Odessa is one of the most famous scenes in movie history.

🇺🇸 **1945** Five U.S. Navy torpedo planes take off from Florida on a routine mission over an area of the Atlantic known as the Bermuda Triangle. After reporting instrument failures and radio difficulties, the planes vanished. The story cemented the legend of the Bermuda Triangle as an area where ships and aircraft disappear without a trace.

🇪🇬 **1977** Egypt breaks off diplomatic relations with five Arab states that expressed hostility toward President Anwar el-Sādāt's peace overtures to Israel.

🇪🇬🇷🇺 **1978** In an effort to prop up an unpopular pro-Soviet regime in Afghanistan, the Soviet Union signs a "friendship treaty" with the Afghan government, agreeing to provide economic and military assistance. The treaty moved the Russians closer to their disastrous involvement in the Afghan Civil War, which officially began in 1979.

Kegs of beer being unloaded after prohibition ended (milestone)

683

1240 Mongols under Batu Khan, grandson of Genghis Khan, conquer Kiev. Assigned to the conquest of Europe, Batu also conquered Moscow and, in the following two years, defeated Hungary and Poland and invaded Germany.

1534 Quito, Ecuador, is captured from the Inca for Spain by Sebastian de Benal Cazar, a subordinate of Francisco Pizarro.

1631 German astronomer Johann Kepler successfully predicts the transit of Venus across the face of the sun. He not only predicted this particular transit but also worked out that such transits of Venus occur in a cycle of approximately 120 years.

1648 During the English Civil War, Thomas Pride, a parliamentary soldier, expels 143 members of Parliament on the grounds they are royalist sympathizers. This event, called Pride's Purge, led to the trial of King Charles I for treason.

1768 The first *Encyclopaedia Britannica* is published, in Scotland.

1774 The world's first state education system starts when Johann von Felbiger's Educational Statute goes into effect in Austria.

1790 The U.S. Congress moves from New York City to Philadelphia, Pennsylvania.

> *"The sooner you get behind, the more time you have to catch up."*
> —Steven Wright

BORN ON THIS DAY

1421
HENRY VI
The youngest king of England (1422–61, 1470–71)

1778
JOSEPH GAY-LUSSAC
French scientist who investigated the physical properties of gases

1806
GEORGE MONCK, DUKE OF ALBEMARLE
English Civil War soldier who switched from the Royalist to the Parliamentary side and later negotiated the restoration of Charles II

1816
SIR JOHN BROWN
English engineer who created the first steel rails and armor plating for warships

1872
WILLIAM S. HART
American actor, director, and silent screen star (*The Silent Man; Tumbleweeds*)

1886
JOYCE KILMER
American poet ("Trees")

1892
OSBERT SITWELL
English poet and author (*Scarlet Tree; Winters of Content; Laughter in the Next Room*)

1896
IRA GERSHWIN
American musician and lyricist ("Lady Be Good"; "The Man I Love"; "The Man That Got Away")

1900
AGNES MOOREHEAD
American actress (*Citizen Kane; Jane Eyre; Bewitched*)

1913
ELEANOR HOLM
American Olympic gold medalist swimmer and actress (*Tarzan's Revenge*)

1920
DAVE BRUBECK
American jazz musician ("Take Five")

1955
STEVEN WRIGHT
American comedian

Washington Monument

1842 The world's first propeller-driven ship, the *Napoleon*, is launched by the French navy.

1847 Abraham Lincoln becomes a member of the U.S. House of Representatives.

1865 The 13th Amendment to the U.S. Constitution is ratified, officially ending the institution of slavery.

1884 The 555-foot-tall Washington Monument is completed 101 years after George Washington approved its location. Construction did not begin until July 4, 1848, and it was stopped in 1854 for lack of funds. President Ulysses S. Grant authorized its completion in 1876. When the capstone was set in place, it was the tallest structure in the world.

1907 In West Virginia's Marion County, an explosion in a network of mines owned by the Fairmont Coal Company in Monongah kills 361 coal miners.

It was the worst mining disaster in American history.

1917 Czar Nicholas II and his family are imprisoned by the Bolsheviks in Tobolsk.

1917 During World War I, the most devastating man-made explosion in the pre-atomic age occurs when the *Mont Blanc*, a French munitions ship packed with more than 2,500 tons of munitions, explodes after colliding with another vessel. The explosion killed more than 1,800 people, injured another 9,000, and destroyed almost the entire north end of the city of Halifax, Nova Scotia.

1921 The Irish Free State is declared, ending a five-year Irish struggle for independence from Great Britain. Ireland was to remain part of the British Commonwealth, but it later severed ties with Great Britain, was renamed Éire, and is now called the Republic of Ireland.

Everglades National Park in southern Florida

1922 General Electric launches its service in Utica, New York, with the opening of its Utica Gas and Electric Company plant. The lines could carry both power and voice signals, and one line could carry numerous frequencies simultaneously.

1945 British scientist and Raytheon engineer Percy Spencer invents the microwave oven after observing that a candy bar in his pocket melted as he stood in front of a magnetron tube that had been switched on.

1947 Florida's Everglades National Park, the third-largest national park in the United States, is established.

1956 In South Africa, Nelson Mandela and 156 others are jailed on political charges. After spending years in jail, Mandela was set free and became the nation's president.

1957 America's first attempt at putting a satellite into orbit fails when a Vanguard rocket blows up on its launching pad at Cape Canaveral, Florida.

1978 Spanish voters go to the polls in a referendum on a new constitution that will limit the powers of the monarchy and restore full democracy after decades of dictatorship under the late Generalissimo Franco. The proposal was overwhelmingly supported.

1984 After winning 74 matches over 11 months, Czech-born American tennis champion Martina Navratilova loses to Helena Sukova, ending the longest winning streak in women's singles tennis.

DECEMBER 7

"If we don't believe in freedom of expression for people we despise, we don't believe in it at all."

—*Noam Chomsky*

185 The appearance of a "guest star" (supernova) is noted in the Houhanshu of the Later Han dynasty in China. This is generally regarded as the first of only some 50 supernovas to have been recorded historically.

983 At age three, Otto III becomes German king after his father's death. He was crowned Holy Roman emperor in 996 and sought to create an empire that included German, Italian, and Slavic lands, with Rome as the seat of power. Otto was forced to flee the city when riots erupted over his establishment of a permanent imperial administration.

1354 Empress Margaretha van Bavarian signs a peace treaty with her own son, Willem V, over control of Holland.

1783 At age 24, William Pitt, the Younger, becomes the

MILESTONE

Pearl Harbor Bombed
At 7:55 A.M. Hawaii time on this day in 1941, a Japanese dive bomber bearing the red symbol of the Rising Sun of Japan on its wing appears out of the clouds above the island of Oahu. A swarm of 360 Japanese warplanes followed, descending on the American naval base at Pearl Harbor, Hawaii, in a ferocious aerial assault. The surprise attack struck a critical blow against the U.S. Pacific fleet and drew the United States immediately into World War II. A total of 2,400 Americans were killed and 1,200 were wounded, while Japan's losses were fewer than 100 men. Although most of the American battleship fleet was sunk or damaged, no aircraft carriers, a principal Japanese target in the raid, were present in the harbor that day. American aircraft carriers proved decisive in the Pacific war.

youngest British prime minister on record. He is remembered for his policies against corruption, fiscal reform, the shifting of power to the House of Commons, and union with Ireland.

1842 The New York Philharmonic Orchestra gives its first performance, with works by Ludwig van Beethoven and Karl Maria von Weber.

1872 The HMS *Challenger,* the first vessel specifically equipped for general oceanographic research, sets sail on a three-year world cruise. The British ship opened the era of descriptive oceanography.

1907 At the National Sporting Club in London, England, Eugene Corri becomes the first referee to officiate inside a boxing ring.

1909 Belgian-born American inventor Leo Baekeland creates the modern plastics industry when he introduces the process for making Bakelite.

1917 The United States enters World War I when it declares war on Austria-Hungary.

🏆 **1925** Future Tarzan actor Johnny Weissmuller sets the world record for the 150-yard freestyle swim.

🔬 **1926** In the United States, the Electrolux Servel Corporation (now noted for vacuum cleaners) patents a gas-operated household refrigerator.

🇺🇸 **1931** The last Ford Model A is produced in the United States.

🔬 **1934** Famed American aviator Wiley Post flies over Bartlesville, Oklahoma, and discovers the jet stream, a narrow, swift current of air found seven to eight miles above Earth.

🇺🇸 **1942** The U.S. Navy launches the largest battleship ever built, the USS *New Jersey*.

🇨🇳 **1949** Following an unsuccessful campaign against communists for control of China after World War II, Chiang Kai-shek and his nationalist government flee to Taiwan.

🏆 **1963** In the United States, instant replay is shown for the first time during an Army-Navy football game in Philadelphia, Pennsylvania.

1970 West Germany and Poland sign an agreement renouncing the use of force to settle disputes and transferring 40,000 square miles of German territory to Poland while recognizing the Oder-Neisse River as Poland's western border.

1975 Indonesian forces launch an invasion of the former Portuguese half of the island of Timor, which lies near Australia, nine days after the democratically elected government of East Timor declared independence.

1988 In the Soviet Union, an earthquake of magnitude 6.9 on the Richter scale hits northwestern Armenia, affecting an area 50 miles in diameter. More than 25,000 people were killed, at least 15,000 were injured, and some 500,000 Armenians were left homeless.

DECEMBER 8

● **1326** Zen master Daito Kokushi establishes the Daitoku-ji temple in Kyoto, Japan. Now the site of one of Japan's most famous Zen gardens, it was particularly significant in the development of the tea ceremony and Zenga painting.

1660 Margaret Hughes is the first actress in England to appear in public on stage. She starred as Desdemona in Shakespeare's *Othello* at a theater in Clare Market, London. Before this, only men were allowed to perform in public.

1813 Ludwig von Beethoven's Seventh Symphony in A debuts.

1854 Pope Pius IX proclaims the doctrine of the Immaculate Conception, in which Mary, mother of Jesus, was free of Original Sin from the moment she was conceived.

1863 Tom King of England claims the world's first heavyweight boxing title when he beats American John Heenan in the southern English county of Kent.

1886 The American Federation of Labor is founded by the leaders of some 25 labor organizations representing 150,000 workers, in Columbus, Ohio, during four days of meetings beginning on this date.

1914 Four German cruisers are sunk by a British force in the Battle of the Falkland Islands. More than 2,500 lives were lost in a single day.

1920 Even though he was a chief figure in its establish-

BORN ON THIS DAY

65 B.C.
QUINTUS HORATIUS FLACCUS (HORACE)
Roman lyric poet (*Odes; Epistles; Ars Poetica*)

1765
ELI WHITNEY
American inventor of the cotton gin and the uniformity method of musket manufacturing

1865
JEAN SIBELIUS
Finnish composer ("En Saga"; "Finlandia")

Jean Sibelius

1894
JAMES THURBER
American author (*The Secret Life of Walter Mitty; My World and Welcome to It; The Last Flower*)

1903
ADELE SIMPSON
American fashion designer

1922
LUCIAN FREUD
English artist (*Francis Bacon; Girl with a White Dog*), grandson of Sigmund Freud

1925
JIMMY SMITH
American modern jazz organist ("Walk on the Wild Side")

1925
SAMMY DAVIS JR.
American entertainer, dancer, and singer ("The Candy Man"; "What Kind of Fool Am I?")

1930
MAXIMILIAN SCHELL
Academy Award-winning Austrian actor (*Judgment at Nuremberg; The Odessa File*)

1943
JIM MORRISON
American singer/songwriter (The Doors)

Pope Pius IX

ment, U.S. president Woodrow Wilson decides not to send a representative to the League of Nations in Geneva, Switzerland, when the Senate refuses to ratify the Treaty of Versailles.

1931 A U.S. patent is issued to American inventors Lloyd Espenschied and Herman A. Affel for coaxial cable that, with its ability to carry a wide range of transmission frequencies simultaneously, is widely used today for television and high-speed internet connections.

1941 One day after the surprise Japanese attack on Pearl Harbor, Hawaii, the United States formally enters World War II when President Franklin D. Roosevelt addresses the congress, describing the previous day as "a date which will live in infamy." Great Britain also declared war on Japan the same day.

1942 U.S. president Franklin D. Roosevelt and British prime minister Winston Churchill issue a declaration, signed by representatives of 26 countries, called the "United Nations."

*"I am fond of pigs.
Dogs look up to us.
Cats look down.
Pigs treat us as equals."*

—*Sir Winston Churchill*

1945 Following World War II, the Toyota Motor Company receives permission from the Allied occupation government to start production of buses and trucks to keep Japan running. It was the first rumble of the postwar auto industry in Japan. By 2000, Toyota was selling 1.7 million new cars annually in the U.S.

1946 The first test of a snow-melting device embedded in a sidewalk is made in New York City.

1951 The Zenith Radio Corporation of Chicago, Illinois, demonstrates the first pay television system, called Phonevision. The company sent movies over the telephone line via scrambled signals, and the 300 families who participated in the test could decode the movies for $1 each.

1952 The first acknowledgment of pregnancy on American television occurs during the *I Love Lucy* episode "Lucy Is Enceinte" (the word "pregnant" was not allowed).

1953 At the United Nations, U.S. president Dwight D. Eisenhower calls on the major powers to contribute to the peaceful development of atomic energy and proposes the creation of an international atomic energy agency.

1983 Great Britain's House of Lords votes to allow its proceedings to be televised for an experimental period.

1991 The Soviet national government is declared dead by Russia, Byelorussia, and Ukraine. They would forge a new alliance known as the Commonwealth of Independent States.

1993 Daisy Adams, the oldest person in Great Britain, dies at the age of 113.

1995 China attempts to force Tibetans to accept its choice of a new six-year-old Panchen Lama for Buddhism's second-ranking monk, instead of one named by the god-king, the 14th Dalai Lama, who had been driven into exile.

1997 Swiss Bank and Union Bank of Switzerland announce plans to form a single bank, United Bank of Switzerland, with assets of more than a half trillion dollars. The new bank would be the world's largest money manager.

Gyaltsen Norbu, the 6-year-old boy China installed as the 11th Panchen Lama

🪈 **536** Belisarius, a Byzantine general for Justinian I, captures Rome under orders to recover Italy from the Ostrogoths (Germans).

🦁 **1165** William I the Lion becomes king of Scotland. He fought to recover Northumbria (lost to England in 1157) but was forced to abandon the quest in 1209.

1425 Pope Martin V founds the Catholic University of Leuven in the Netherlands. It is the oldest Catholic university still in existence.

🇬🇧 **1688** King James II flees England for France after his efforts to fill positions of authority and influence with Roman Catholics (instead of Protestants) fails.

🇺🇸 **1792** Henry Laurens is the first person in the United States to be formally cremated, near Charleston, South Carolina.

🪈 **1824** Spaniards are defeated by Peruvian patriots at the Battle of Ayacucho, resulting in Peru's independence.

🪈 **1835** The newly created Texan Army takes possession of the city of San Antonio, an important victory for the Republic of Texas in its war for independence from Mexico.

> *"If you want to know about a man you can find out an awful lot by looking at who he married."*
>
> —*Kirk Douglas*

BORN ON THIS DAY

1608
JOHN MILTON
English poet (*Paradise Lost*)

1837
ÉMILE WALDTEUFEL
French composer ("The Skaters' Waltz")

1847
GEORGE GROSSMITH
English actor and author (*Diary of a Nobody*)

1898
EMMETT KELLY
American clown for Ringling Bros. Circus

Emmett Kelly

1906
FREDDY MARTIN
English musician and bandleader ("I've Got a Lovely Bunch of Coconuts"; "April in Portugal")

1911
LEE J. COBB
American actor (*On the Waterfront; Twelve Angry Men; Exodus; The Virginian*)

1912
TIP O'NEILL
Speaker of the U.S. House of Representatives

1915
DAME ELIZABETH SCHWARZKOPF
German operatic soprano

1916
KIRK DOUGLAS
American actor (*Young Man with a Horn; Spartacus*)

1922
REDD FOXX
American comedian and actor (*Sanford & Son*)

Girl selling Christmas Seals

🇬🇧 **1843** In England, the first Christmas cards are created, by Henry Cole with artist John Horsley. Involved in many ventures, Cole had little time to inscribe personal greetings and so decided to create a lithographed image on rigid folded paper that would just require his signature.

🎭 **1854** Alfred, Lord Tennyson's poem "The Charge of the Light Brigade" is published. It commemorates the courage of 600 British soldiers charging a heavily defended position during the Battle of Balaklava, in the Crimean War.

🇺🇸 **1878** Greenbacks, paper money issued during the American Civil War to support the Union, pull even with gold for the first time since 1862. The victory was short lived, however, as greenback supporters eventually shifted their allegiance to silver.

🔬 **1884** Levant M. Richardson of Chicago, Illinois, receives the first U.S. patent for ball-bearing roller skates.

🇺🇸 **1907** The first American Christmas Seals, created to raise money to fight tuberculosis, go on sale in Wilmington, Delaware.

1940 Two British divisions, half of them composed of Indian troops, attack seven Italian divisions in Egypt during World War II. Overwhelmed, the Italian position in Egypt collapsed and the end of the Italian occupation of North Africa had begun.

1950 Harry Gold, who had confessed to serving as a courier for a British scientist who stole top-secret information on the atomic bomb for the Soviets, is sentenced to 30 years in jail. Gold's confession eventually led to the implication of Americans Julius and Ethel Rosenberg, who were later convicted and executed for espionage.

1985 Former Argentine president Jorge Videla is sentenced to life imprisonment for his part in the war against communist guerrillas in which as many as 9,000 people disappeared.

1987 In the Israeli-occupied Gaza Strip, the first riots of the Palestinian *intifada* ("shaking off") begin, one day after an Israeli truck crashed into a station wagon killing four Palestinian workers and wounding 10. Palestinians saw this as an act of retaliation for the killing of a Jew several days before, and they took to the streets throwing rocks and Molotov cocktails.

1992 U.S. Marines storm into Mogadishu, Somalia, to spearhead an international effort to stop one of the worst famines of the 20th century.

MILESTONE

Joint Committee on the Conduct of the War Created

To monitor both military progress and the Lincoln administration, the U.S. Congress creates the Joint Committee on the Conduct of War on this day in 1861. Created in the aftermath of the disastrous Battle of Ball's Bluff, the War Committee was designed to provide a check over the executive branch's management of the war. It was often at odds with the Lincoln administration's handling of the war effort and had problems with their military decisions. Although the committee did help uncover fraud in war contracts, its members' lack of military expertise complicated the northern war effort.

U.S. troops delivering food in Somalia

1508 Holy Roman emperor Maximilian I, Pope Julius II, Louis XII of France, and Ferdinand II of Aragon form the League of Cambrai, an alliance against the republic of Venice to check its territorial expansion.

1520 Martin Luther publicly burns the papal edict demanding that he recant his attack on the papacy as a mediator between God and man and its authority over secular life or face excommunication.

1768 King George III of Great Britain founds the Royal Academy of Arts in London.

1810 In England, Tom Cribb of Great Britain defeats African American Tom Molineaux in the first interracial boxing championship. The fight lasted for 40 rounds.

1831 In the United States, William Trotter Porter publishes the first issue of *Spirit of the Times*. The weekly publi-

---

MILESTONE

First Nobel Prizes Awarded

On this day in 1901, the first Nobel Prizes are awarded in the fields of physics, chemistry, medicine, literature, and peace. The ceremony came on the fifth anniversary of the death of Swiss engineer Alfred Nobel, inventor of dynamite. In his will, Nobel directed that his fortune be placed in a fund where the interest would be "annually distributed in the form of prizes to those who, during the preceding year, shall have conferred the greatest benefit on mankind." It is widely believed he created the prizes out of moral regret over the increasingly lethal uses of his inventions in war.

---

cation was created to raise the reputation of horse racing, prize fighting, and even cricket. It was, for a while, the country's leading sports journal.

1845 Robert Thompson, a Scottish civil engineer, patents the first pneumatic tire in London, England.

1864 During the American Civil War, Union general William T. Sherman completes his "March to the Sea" when he arrives at Savannah, Georgia. Since mid-November, Sherman's army had been sweeping from Atlanta toward Savannah, destroying farms and railroads, burning storehouses, and feeding off the land.

1869 Motivated by interest in free publicity and the possibility of attracting more marriageable women to the region, Wyoming territorial legislators grant women the right to vote. Wyoming thus became the first U.S. territory or state to grant women this fundamental right of citizenship.

Signing of the Spanish-American Treaty of Paris

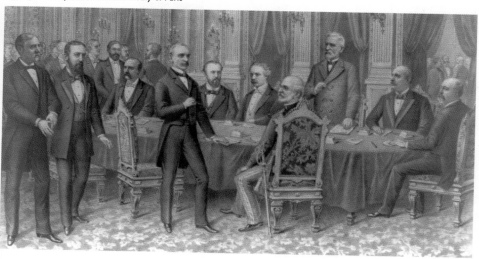

1898 In France, the Treaty of Paris is signed, formally ending the Spanish-American War and granting the United States its first overseas empire.

1915 In the United States, the 1,000,000th Model T Ford is produced.

1930 American jazz musician Duke Ellington and his orchestra record what would become one of his most famous standards, "Mood Indigo," for Victor Records.

1932 King Rama VII presents a permanent constitution to Thailand, creating a constitutional monarchy.

1938 Filming finally begins on the epic American movie *Gone with the Wind.* Producer David O. Selznick had not yet cast an actress to play the leading role of Scarlett O'Hara, so the first day's shooting was of the burning of Atlanta, which didn't require close footage of Scarlett.

1941 During World War II, 4,000 Japanese troops land on the Philippine Islands, while Japanese aircraft sink the British warships *Prince of Wales* and *Repulse.* Guam, an American-controlled territory, was also seized. British prime minister Winston Churchill finally exclaimed, "We have lost control of the sea."

> *"Success is counted sweetest by those who ne'er succeed."*
>
> —*Emily Dickinson*

Imelda and Ferdinand Marcos

1948 The Universal Declaration on Human Rights is adopted by the U.N. General Assembly.

1953 American publisher Hugh Hefner publishes the first *Playboy* magazine with an investment of $7,600. There is no date printed on the issue, as Hefner doubted that a second one would ever be printed.

1962 English director David Lean's epic film *Lawrence of Arabia,* starring Peter O'Toole as British officer T. E. Lawrence, has its premiere in London.

1984 The discovery of the first planet outside our solar system, orbiting a star 21 million light years from Earth, is reported by the U.S. National Science Foundation.

1997 The Swiss high court rules that the $100 million former dictator Ferdinand Marcos has in banks will be returned to the Philippine government.

1998 Researchers report the first complete genetic blueprint of an animal upon mapping all 97 million genetic "letters" of the worm *Caenorhabditis elegans.*

🏴 **1205** In England, John Grey, bishop of Norwich, becomes King John's appointee for archbishop of Canterbury. This placed the king in opposition to Pope Innocent III, who had appointed Stephen Langton. By custom it was the ruler of England who had the authority, as the archbishop was also a baron, holding immense territory.

🇺🇸 **1620** The *Mayflower* pilgrims land at Plymouth Rock in Massachusetts. The date is sometimes given as either December 21 or 22, as both the Julian and Gregorian calendars were in use at the time and England didn't officially recognize the Gregorian calendar until 1752.

🔬 **1769** Edward Bevan of London, England, patents venetian blinds.

🔬 **1844** Nitrous oxide ("laughing gas") becomes the first dental anesthetic when Dr. John M. Riggs uses it for a tooth extraction on Dr. Horace Wells, in Hartford, Connecticut.

🏆 **1866** The first transatlantic yacht race takes place, sponsored by the New York Yacht Club and England's Royal Yacht Squadron.

🎭 **1872** Already appearing as a well-known figure of the Wild West in popular dime novels, Buffalo Bill Cody makes his first stage appearance in a production of *The Scouts of the Prairie* in Chicago, Illinois.

🔬 **1882** The Bijou Theatre in Boston, Massachusetts, becomes the first theater lit by electricity. Some 650 lamps were

---

"It is easier to be wise for others than for ourselves."

—*Aleksandr Solzhenitsyn*

used for a performance of Gilbert and Sullivan's *Iolanthe*.

🔬 **1894** The world's first auto show, the Exposition Internationale de Velocipidie et de Locomotion Automobile, opens in Paris, France. Four makes of automobile were on display.

▬ **1917** German-occupied Lithuania proclaims its independence from Russia.

🏴 **1938** Noted English architect Sir Edwin Lutyens, famous for designing the Cenotaph and the Viceroy's House in New Delhi, India, is elected president of the Royal Academy.

🎭 **1939** German actress Marlene Dietrich records her hit song "Falling in Love Again."

⚔ **1941** Nazi German dictator Adolf Hitler declares war on the United States, bringing America, which had been neutral, into the European conflict during World War II.

🔬 **1945** A Boeing B-29 Superfortress crosses the United States in five hours and 27 minutes, setting a new speed record.

🏳 **1946** In the aftermath of World War II, the General Assembly of the United Nations

---

votes to establish the United Nations International Children's Emergency Fund (UNICEF), an organization to help provide relief and support to children living in countries devastated by the war.

1946 John D. Rockefeller Jr. offers a six-block area of Manhattan in New York City for the world headquarters of the United Nations. The offer was accepted the next day.

1956 The American movie industry's tight restriction of language and subject matter, known as the Hays Code or the Production Code, is eased slightly for the first time since its adoption in 1930. The easing of the code meant that actors could now mention abortion, drugs, kidnapping, and prostitution.

1961 The first U.S. helicopters arrive in South Vietnam aboard the ferry carrier USNS *Core*. Their assignment was to airlift South Vietnamese Army troops into combat.

Concorde 001

1967 The world's first supersonic airliner, the Concorde, is unveiled in Toulouse, France. The plane had been jointly developed by France and Great Britain.

1969 The Moscow writers' union declares that nudity as displayed in the popular play *Oh! Calcutta!* is a sign of decadence in Western culture.

1972 U.S. *Apollo 17* lands on the moon's surface for a three-day exploration. It was the final Apollo mission to the moon.

1978 Massive riots and demonstrations take place in Tehran against the Shah of Iran.

1994 In the largest Russian military offensive since the 1979 invasion of Afghanistan, thousands of troops and hundreds of tanks pour into the breakaway Russian republic of Chechnya. Encountering only light resistance, Russian forces had by evening pushed to the outskirts of the Chechen capital of Grozny, where several thousand Chechen volunteers vowed a bitter fight against the Russians.

1997 One hundred sixty nations meeting in Kyoto, Japan, endorse a treaty to cut greenhouse gases.

Edward VIII

695

1098 During the First Crusade, the Saracens are defeated and the city of Mara, in Syria, is captured and plundered.

1474 In Spain, Isabella contests the succession to the throne of Castile after the death of her half-brother, Henry IV. A civil war ensued, which Isabella won in 1479. Isabella is probably best known for her support of explorer Christopher Columbus.

1524 In an ecumenical gesture of protection, Pope Clement VII approves the Organization of Jewish Community of Rome.

1770 Seven British soldiers are acquitted but two are found guilty of manslaughter during the "Boston Massacre" in Massachusetts, when soldiers fired into a rioting crowd, killing five men. The two were punished and discharged from the army.

1792 In Vienna, Austria, Franz Joseph Haydn gives 22-year-old German student Ludwig van Beethoven one of his first lessons in music composition.

1800 The capital of the United States is moved from Philadelphia, Pennsylvania, to Washington, D.C.

1822 The United States formally recognizes the Republic of Mexico as an independent nation.

> *"Anything becomes interesting if you look at it long enough."*
> —Gustave Flaubert

BORN ON THIS DAY

1731
ERASMUS DARWIN
English naturalist and poet (*The Botanic Garden; Zoonomia*), grandfather of Charles Darwin

1745
JOHN JAY
American statesman, first chief justice of the U.S. Supreme Court (1789–95)

1821
GUSTAVE FLAUBERT
French author (*Madame Bovary; The Temptation of St. Anthony*)

1863
EDVARD MUNCH
Norwegian expressionist painter (*The Scream; Puberty; The Dance of Life*)

1893
EDWARD G. ROBINSON
American actor (*Little Caesar; Key Largo; Double Indemnity; Scarlet Street*)

1915
FRANK SINATRA
American singer ("The Lady Is a Tramp;" "New York, New York"; "My Way") and actor (*On the Town; From Here to Eternity*)

1918
JOE WILLIAMS
Emmy Award-winning American jazz singer ("I Just Want to Sing") and actor (*The Bill Cosby Show*)

1929
JOHN OSBORNE
English playwright (*Look Back in Anger; The Entertainer*)

1899 The wooden golf tee is patented by George F. Bryant of Boston, Massachusetts.

1900 Charles Schwab, J. Pierpont Morgan, and Andrew Carnegie announce the formation of a giant steel conglomeration called U.S. Steel.

1913 Two years after it was stolen from the Louvre Museum in Paris, France, Leonardo da Vinci's masterpiece *The Mona Lisa* is recovered inside Italian waiter Vincenzo Peruggia's hotel room in Florence. Peruggia had previously worked at the Louvre and had participated in the heist with a group of accomplices dressed as janitors.

1915 The German Junkers J1, the first all-metal plane, flies for the first time.

1925 The first motel, the Motel Inn, is opened by Arthur Heinman, in San Luis Obispo, California.

1941 Following the fall of France to German forces during World War II, the U.S. Navy takes control of the largest and most luxurious

East view of the first Washington, D.C., Capitol building

ocean liner at that time, France's *Normandie*, while it is docked at New York City. Shortly thereafter, its conversion for U.S. wartime use began.

1955 In the United States, the Ford Foundation makes the biggest donation to charity the world had ever seen: $500 million to hospitals, medical schools, and colleges.

1955 English engineer Christopher Cockerell files for a patent on the first hovercraft.

1959 In Sebring, Florida, Bruce McLaren becomes the youngest driver to win a Grand Prix race. He was 22 years, 104 days old.

1963 *John Fitzgerald Kennedy: A Memorial Album* becomes the fastest-selling record of all time when four million copies are sold in six days between December 7 and 12.

1963 Kenya becomes an independent state within the British Commonwealth with Jomo Kenyatta as prime minister. On the same day in 1964 it becomes a republic, with Kenyatta as president.

1968 Arthur Ashe becomes the first African American to be ranked number one in tennis.

1975 A six-day siege in which four members of the Irish Republican Army had held two civilians hostage at a house in London, England, ends peacefully with the surrender of the terrorists. The gang, who were responsible for a wave of attacks on the British mainland, were jailed for 10 murders and 20 bombings.

1980 Computer programs are protected under U.S. copyright law for the first time.

1980 American oil tycoon Armand Hammer pays $5.28 million for a 36-page notebook of writings by Leonardo da Vinci, in London, England.

1988 In London, England, the first satellite pictures are beamed to some 2,200 betting shops to allow gamblers to watch several races from different locations live.

1988 During the morning rush hour in London, England, 35 people are killed and more than 100 injured in a crash involving three trains near Clapham Junction, Europe's busiest railroad station.

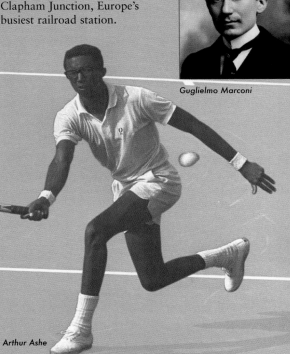
Arthur Ashe

1545 The Council of Trent begins. Summoned by Pope Paul III, it was convoked to deal with the Protestant Reformation.

1577 Francis Drake sets out from Plymouth in England with five ships and 164 men on a mission to raid Spanish holdings on the Pacific coast of the New World and explore the Pacific Ocean. Three years later, Drake's return marked the first circumnavigation of Earth by a British explorer.

1621 The first American furs to be exported from the continent leave for England aboard the *Fortune*. One month before, the ship had arrived with colonists at Plymouth Colony in present-day Massachusetts with the idea of making a living through cod fishing. Within a few years, however, they began concentrating almost entirely on the fur trade.

1642 Dutch navigator Abel Tasman becomes the first European explorer to sight the South Pacific island group now known as New Zealand. On November 24, Tasman had discovered Tasmania, off the coast of Australia.

1812 After its failed Russian campaign, the last remnants of Napoleon Bonaparte's *Grand Arméé* reaches the safety of Kovno, Poland.

1816 In Boston, Massachusetts, the Provident Institution for Savings becomes the first chartered savings bank in the United States.

1847 Ellis Bell's novel *Wuthering Heights* is published.

MILESTONE

The Rape of Nanking
On this day in 1937 during the Sino-Japanese War, the Chinese capital of Nanking falls to Japanese forces and the Chinese government flees to Hankow. To break the spirit of Chinese resistance, Japanese general Matsui Iwane ordered that Nanking be destroyed. In what became known as the Rape of Nanking, the Japanese butchered an estimated 150,000 male war prisoners, massacred an additional 50,000 male civilians, and raped at least 20,000 women and girls, many of whom were mutilated or killed in the process. Shortly after World War II, Matsui was found guilty of war crimes by the International Military Tribunal for the Far East and was executed.

Japanese bugler in Nanking, China

Bell was the pseudonym used by English author Emily Brontë.

1862 During the American Civil War, Confederate general Robert E. Lee's Army of Northern Virginia repulses a series of attacks by General Ambrose Burnside's Army of the Potomac at Fredericksburg, Virginia. The defeat was one of the most decisive losses for the Union Army, and it dealt a serious blow to Northern morale.

1893 The first tuberculosis diagnostic laboratory in the United States is opened by the New York City Department of Health.

1903 In the United States, Italo Marchiony is granted a patent on the mold for edible waffle cups, better known today as ice-cream cones.

1910 American radio pioneer Lee De Forest arranges the first opera broadcast. Although few people had radio receivers, De Forest arranged for a broadcast from the stage of New York City's Metropolitan Opera, featuring Enrico Caruso.

1914 The British submarine B-11 dives under a heavily mined area of the Dardanelles to successfully torpedo the Turkish battleship *Messudieh*. The action won Commander Norman Douglas Holbrook the first Victoria Cross to be awarded to a submariner.

"Now is then's only tomorrow."
—Kenneth Patchen

1918 Woodrow Wilson arrives in France, becoming the first U.S. president to visit Europe while in office.

1920 The International Court of Justice in The Hague, Netherlands, is established by the League of Nations.

1928 The New York Philharmonic, playing at Carnegie Hall in New York City, debuts George Gershwin's *An American in Paris*.

1939 The first production Lincoln Continental rolls off the assembly line in the United States. The Lincoln Continentals of the 1940s are commonly considered some of the most beautiful production cars ever made.

1957 The last original two-seater Thunderbird is produced. The 1958 version of the American classic was a four-passenger car, 18 inches longer and half a ton heavier. It packed a 300-horsepower V-8 engine, making it one of the most muscular cars on the road, and one of the most popular. Thunderbird sold more cars in 1958 than 1957, despite a nationwide slump in auto sales.

First Lincoln Continental

1962 The United States launches the first active communications satellite, *Relay*. It handled 12 simultaneous two-way telephone conversations or one television channel, and provided the first satellite communications link between North and South America and Europe.

1967 King Constantine of Greece flees the country after his attempt to overthrow a military junta failed.

1968 Mexican president Gustavo Diaz Ordaz and U.S. president Lyndon B. Johnson meet on a border bridge at El Paso, Texas, for ceremonies marking the return of the long-disputed El Chamizal area to Mexico.

1991 North and South Korea sign a non-aggression pact aimed at improving ties with the goal of eventual reconciliation.

1994 The first meeting of the World Wide Web Consortium takes place at the Massachusetts Institute of Technology. The group was established as an international association to promote common protocols on the World Wide Web.

1287 Fifty thousand lives are lost when the Netherlands' Zuider Zee seawall collapses.

1640 Aphra Behn is baptized at Harbledown, near Canterbury in England. She has been called the first Englishwoman to make her living as a writer and was the first woman to be buried in Westminster Abbey in recognition of her own achievements.

1656 The basic modern technique of making imitation pearls is developed in Paris, France, by a rosary-bead maker named Jacquin. He made them by coating the inside surface of hollow glass beads with a fish-scale mixture.

1774 During the first organized fight of the American Revolutionary War, Massachusetts militiamen successfully attack Fort William and Mary to keep gunpowder and shot from royal troops. Paul Revere had warned them, during the first of his famous rides, that the British planned to station troops nearby.

1790 Secretary of the Treasury Alexander Hamilton floats a proposal to create the Bank of the United States. Under Hamilton's plan, the bank would assume responsibility for easing the nation's Revolutionary War debt as well as establishing a healthy line of credit.

1798 American mechanical engineer David Wilkinson receives a patent for the slide-rest lathe for cutting screw threads, a device of immense significance to the machine tool industry.

BORN ON THIS DAY

1503
NOSTRADAMUS
French physician, writer, astrologer, and prophet whose verses are believed by many to have predicted numerous events in the centuries since his death

1546
TYCHO BRAHE
Danish astronomer who established that comets orbit the sun in the same way as planets

1866
ROGER FRY
English artist and critic who coined the term "Post-Impressionism"

1895
KING GEORGE VI
King of Great Britain (1936–1952), father of Queen Elizabeth II

1896
JAMES H. DOOLITTLE
American aviator who was awarded the Congressional Medal of Honor for leading the first U.S. bombing raid against Japan in World War II

James H. Doolittle

1897
MARGARET CHASE SMITH
American politician, first woman elected to both houses of Congress

1911
SPIKE JONES
American musician and bandleader ("Cocktails for Two"; "Der Fuhrer's Face")

1935
LEE REMICK
American actress (*The Long, Hot Summer; Days of Wine and Roses; Anatomy of a Murder*)

1822 During the Congress of Verona, Great Britain protests the decision to suppress a Spanish revolution against Ferdinand VII. It led to a growing rift between Great Britain and the other powers. The Congress was the last European conference under the provisions of the Quadruple Alliance of 1814.

1885 The steamship *Umbria* sails from San Francisco, California, to London, England, in 14 days, a new record.

1900 German physicist Max Planck publishes his groundbreaking quantum theory. The theory helped to resolve previously unexplained natural phenomena such as the behavior of heat in solids and the nature of light absorption on an atomic level. Today, the combination of quantum theory with Einstein's theory of relativity is the basis of modern physics.

1901 The London Royal Aquarium in England holds the world's first table tennis tournament.

1902 A ship begins to lay out the first transpacific telegraph cable, connecting San Francisco, California, with Honolulu, Hawaii, some 2,620 miles away.

1906 The first German U-boat (the U-1) is brought into service.

> *"When people keep telling you that you can't do a thing, you kind of like to try it."*
>
> —*Margaret Chase Smith*

Josef Kramer

committed at Nazi concentration camps during World War II.

🏆 **1947** The National Association for Stock Car Auto Racing (NASCAR) is founded at the Streamline Hotel in Daytona Beach, Florida.

🔬 **1962** The U.S. *Mariner 2* space probe approaches to within 21,600 miles of Venus. It discovered the planet lacks radiation belts and a strong magnetic field.

🇮🇱 **1981** Israel annexes the Golan Heights, which it had seized from Syria in the War of 1967.

🔬 **1986** The experimental aircraft *Voyager* takes off on the first nonrefueled, nonstop flight around the globe. At an average speed of 115.8 miles per hour, the trip took nine days and almost doubled the previous distance record set in 1962 by an Air Force B-52H.

🇬🇷 **1913** Greece formally incorporates the island of Crete.

🇬🇧 **1918** Women vote in a British general election for the first time. The first woman MP was elected as a result, Constance, Countess Markievicz, a Sinn Fein member in Dublin. However, she was unable to take her seat as, being a republican, she refused to swear an oath of allegiance to the King.

🇬🇧 **1920** The first aircraft disaster involving a scheduled airline occurs when a plane carrying six passengers and two crew members takes off on a flight from London, England, to Paris, France. The plane crashed into a house just after takeoff, killing the crew and two passengers.

1927 Great Britain formally recognizes Iraq as an independent nation.

👣 **1944** The American movie *National Velvet* premieres at Radio City Music Hall in New York City. It boosted 12-year-old English actress Elizabeth Taylor to stardom.

⚖️ **1945** The "Beast of Belsen," Josef Kramer, is hanged in Hamelin, Germany, for crimes

MILESTONE

Amundsen Reaches South Pole

Roald Amundsen of Norway becomes the first explorer to reach the South Pole on this day in 1911, beating his British rival, Robert Falcon Scott. Amundsen's expedition returned safely to base camp late in January. After his historic Antarctic journey, Amundsen established a successful shipping business. He later made attempts to become the first explorer to fly over the North Pole.

Mariner 2

1025 Byzantine emperor Basil II is succeeded by his brother and former co-ruler, Constantine VIII. During Basil's reign, the schism between the Roman and Eastern churches widened.

1488 Bartholomeu Dias returns to Portugal after becoming the first European to sail around the Cape of Good Hope at the southern tip of Africa. His voyage opened the trade route to India.

1593 Holland grants a patent for a windmill crankshaft.

1815 Italian composer Gioacchino Antonio Rossini begins work on his masterpiece, *Il Barbiere di Siviglia (The Barber of Seville)*.

1854 The first practical street cleaning machine goes into operation, in Philadelphia, Pennsylvania.

1864 During the American Civil War, the once powerful Confederate Army of Tennessee is nearly destroyed when the Union Army swarms over the Rebel trenches around Nashville. More than 6,000 Rebels were killed or wounded and 3,000 Union troops lost their lives. The Army of Tennessee retreated to Mississippi, no longer a viable offensive fighting force.

1899 The British are defeated in South Africa by the Boers at the Battle of Colenso.

1903 A 15-year ban on whale fishing in Norway is enacted by Great Britain.

BORN ON THIS DAY

37
NERO
Roman emperor (54–68) who committed suicide following condemnation by the Senate

1734
GEORGE ROMNEY
English portrait painter

1832
GUSTAVE EIFFEL
French structural engineer who built the Eiffel Tower and created the frame for the Statue of Liberty

1852
ANTOINE BECQUEREL
French physicist who discovered radioactivity

1879
RUDOLF VON LABAN
German choreographer who created a system of notation for dance movements

1892
J. PAUL GETTY
American oil magnate who founded Getty Oil and was once the richest man in the world

1911
STAN KENTON
American bandleader and jazz innovator

1918
JEFF CHANDLER
American actor (*Broken Arrow; Away All Boats; Merrill's Marauders*)

1928
ERNEST ASHWORTH
American singer ("Talk Back Trembling Lips")

1933
TIM CONWAY
American actor and comedian (*McHale's Navy; The Tim Conway Show; The Carol Burnett Show*)

1936
EDNA O'BRIEN
Irish novelist (*In the Forest; Wild Decembers; Irish Revel*)

1938
JERRY WALLACE
American singer ("Primrose Lane"; "Shutters and Boards")

Lena Horne

1922 The British Broadcasting Company Limited is formally registered in London, England.

1939 The American film *Gone with the Wind* premieres, in Atlanta, Georgia. The movie, based on Margaret Mitchell's Pulitzer Prize-winning novel, became an instant hit, breaking all previous box-office records and winning nine Oscars.

1939 The first commercial use of nylon, to make women's stockings, takes place.

1941 American singer Lena Horne first croons her classic "Stormy Weather" for Victor Records.

1944 The battle for Luzon, the largest of the Philippine Islands, begins as U.S. general Douglas MacArthur orders troops ashore on the nearby island of Mindoro during World War II.

1945 Following World War II, U.S. general Douglas MacArthur, in his capacity as supreme commander of Allied powers in the Pacific severs all ties between the Japanese state and the Shinto religion.

> *"If you can count your money, you don't have a billion dollars."*
>
> —J. Paul Getty

1950 American golfer Babe Didrikson Zaharias sets a women's single-season money-winning record of $14,800 by winning her sixth tournament. She helped found the Ladies Professional Golf Association.

1954 An audience of 40 million watches as Walt Disney's American television series *Davy Crockett, Indian Fighter* premieres. The Davy Crockett craze swept the United States, resulting in a number-one pop song ("Davy, Davy Crockett, King of the Wild Frontier") and the popularity of coonskin hats.

1961 In Tel Aviv, Israel, Adolf Eichmann, the Nazi SS officer who organized Adolf Hitler's "final solution of the Jewish question," is condemned to death by an Israeli war-crimes tribunal.

1964 Canada's House of Commons approves a new design for its national flag, featuring a big red maple leaf.

1965 The U.S. spacecraft *Gemini* 6 and *Gemini* 7 achieve the first space rendezvous, flying within 10 feet of each other.

1980 American baseball outfielder Dave Winfield becomes the wealthiest player in the history of American team sports as he signs a 10-year contract with the New York Yankees said to be worth more than $22 million.

1989 A popular uprising results in the downfall of Romania's Nicolae Ceauçescu.

1997 In the United States, the last *Minuteman II* missile silo is destroyed, in Dederick, Missouri. The missiles and silos, aimed at the Soviet Union, were destroyed as a result of the 1995 Strategic Arms Reduction Treaty.

2000 The Chernobyl nuclear power plant is permanently shut down in the Ukraine, more than 14 years after a meltdown of one of its reactors resulted in one of the world's worst nuclear disasters.

2001 After 10 years, Italy's Leaning Tower of Pisa is reopened to the public following completion of a $27 million effort to keep it from falling.

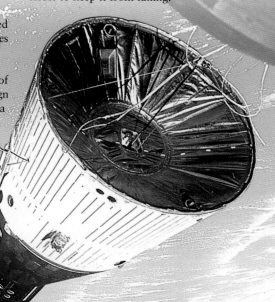

A photograph of Gemini 6 taken by Gemini 7

1431 The English proclaim King Henry VI as king of France when his grandfather, Charles VI of France, dies. The French, who recognized the son of Charles as the rightful heir, disputed this.

1617 On his recommendation, Spanish colonial governor Hernando Arias de Saavedra receives a royal order for the separation of Guaira (Paraguay) from the province of Río de la Plata (Argentina).

1653 Granted the title of lord protector of the commonwealth, Oliver Cromwell assumes dictatorial powers over England, Scotland, and Ireland.

1689 The English Parliament adopts a bill of rights setting forth conditions for ascending the throne and proclaiming that all English citizens have certain inviolable civil and political rights.

Boston Tea Party (milestone)

MILESTONE

The Boston Tea Party

A group of Massachusetts colonists disguised as Mohawk Indians board three British tea ships and dump 342 chests of tea into Boston harbor on this day in 1773. The Boston Tea Party protested the British Parliament's Tea Act of 1773, a bill designed to save the faltering East India Company by greatly lowering its tea tax and granting it a virtual monopoly on the American tea trade. The low tax allowed the East India Company to undercut tea smuggled into America by Dutch traders, and many colonists viewed the act as another example of taxation tyranny.

"Those who cannot remember the past are condemned to repeat it."

—*George Santayana*

1838 A few hundred Boers (Afrikaners), looking to escape British rule, encounter and then defeat 10,000 Zulu warriors in the Battle of Blood River.

1884 William H. Fruen of Minneapolis, Minnesota, receives the first U.S. patent for an automatic liquid vending machine.

1892 The first Sheffield Shield cricket competition is held in Australia. It is named after Lord Sheffield, who used the sport to promote intercolonial competition by bringing an English team to Australia for the 1891–92 season.

1901 Unable to find a publisher, English children's-book author Beatrix Potter publishes *The Tale of Peter Rabbit*

independently. It was picked by a mainstream publisher in 1902.

1905 The U.S. entertainment trade weekly *Variety* is first published. The first issue had 16 pages and cost five cents.

1908 The first U.S. credit union is created in Manchester, New Hampshire.

1913 Young English actor Charles Chaplin reports to work at Keystone Studios for the first time. In his first film, *Making a Living,* he played a mustachioed villain with a monocle. With his third film, *The Tramp,* Chaplin won the hearts of American moviegoers and became one of the best-loved actors of the silent-film era.

1915 German physicist Albert Einstein's *General Theory of Relativity* is first published.

1920 One of the deadliest earthquakes in history hits the Gansu province of China, causing massive landslides and the deaths of an estimated 200,000 people.

1944 The Battle of the Bulge begins during World War II as the Germans launch their last major offensive to push the Allied front line west from northern France to northwestern Belgium. The battle was so-named because the Germans created a "bulge" around the Ardennes forest in pushing through the American defensive line. It was the largest battle fought on the Western Front.

1949 The Swedish company Svenska Aeroplan

German soldier in the Ardennes

Aktiebolaget produces its first motorcar, engineered with the precision of fighter planes, the company's other main product. By the late 1960s, the concern had shortened its name to Saab.

1971 Two weeks after the Indian invasion of East Pakistan in support of the independence movement there, 90,000 Pakistani troops surrender to the Indian forces. East Pakistan was subsequently declared the independent nation of Bangladesh.

1997 The U.S. spacecraft *Galileo* flies to within 124 miles of the surface of the Jovian moon Europa. Its recordings of volcanic ice floes suggested a vast ocean below the surface.

1997 Approximately 700 television viewers in Japan suffer epilepsy-like spasms and nausea after watching a cartoon show featuring bright, flashing colors.

2000 The source of the Amazon River is discovered at the Carhuasanta Creek on the peak of Nevado Mismi in southern Peru.

1399 During the Mongol invasion, Tamerlane's Mongols destroy the army of Mahmud Tughluk, sultan of Delhi (India).

1526 Ferdinand I, younger brother of Charles V, is chosen king of Bohemia. He was crowned Holy Roman emperor in 1558.

1538 Pope Paul III excommunicates England's King Henry VIII after he declares himself supreme head of the Church of England.

1788 The Russian Army of Grigorij Potemkin, in a campaign against the Turks, occupies the fortress of Ochárov. Potemkin was a favorite of Russian empress Catherine the Great.

1790 Mexico's greatest Aztec relic, the 24-ton "Sun Stone," is discovered in Mexico City. Made in 1479, it was used to predict the seasons and natural events as well as to regulate economic and social activities.

1843 English author Charles Dickens's classic story "A Christmas Carol" is published.

1892 Russian composer Peter Tchaikovsky's *The*

MILESTONE

First Airplane Flies

Near Kitty Hawk, North Carolina, American inventors Orville and Wilbur Wright make the first successful flight of a self-propelled, heavier-than-air aircraft in history on this day in 1903. The aircraft ran down a monorail track and into the air, staying aloft for 12 seconds and flying 120 feet. Orville piloted the gasoline-powered, propeller-driven biplane on its inaugural flight. The Wright brothers both possessed extraordinary technical ability and a sophisticated approach to solving mechanical design problems. In 1908, they traveled to France and made their first public flights, arousing widespread public excitement.

Charlie McCarthy, left, and Edgar Bergen

Nutcracker premieres at St. Petersburg (now Leningrad).

1936 American ventriloquist Edgar Bergen and his wisecracking dummy Charlie McCarthy debut on Rudy Vallee's popular radio show. Despite the incongruity of a ventriloquist act on radio, Bergen became a hit radio star and had his own show for more than 20 years.

1939 Believing resistance against the British is futile, German captain Hans Langsdorf sinks his own battleship, the *Graf Spee*, following the Battle of the River Plate near Montevideo, Uruguay, during World War II.

1944 During World War II, the United States approves the end of the internment of Japanese Americans when Major General Henry C. Pratt issues Public Proclamation No. 21, declaring that, effective January 2,

Orville Wright at the controls and Wilbur running alongside of the first flight (milestone)

> *"I think we have a need to know what we do not need to know."*
>
> —William Safire

1945, Japanese-American "evacuees" from the West Coast can return to their homes.

1957 The United States successfully test-fires the *Atlas*, its first intercontinental ballistic missile, for the first time.

1963 The U.S. Congress passes the Clean Air Act, a sweeping set of laws designed to protect the environment from air pollution. It was the first legislation to place pollution controls on the automobile industry.

1965 Ferdinand Marcos is declared president of the Philippines after a bitter and violent election campaign.

1965 The *New York Times* produces the largest newspaper ever, a 946-page Sunday edition.

1969 Finding no evidence that UFO sightings have any extraterrestrial origin, the U.S. Air Force closes its "Project Blue Book."

1990 Jean-Bertrand Aristide, a radical Roman Catholic priest and opponent of the dictatorship of Jean-Claude Duvalier, is elected president of Haiti in a landslide victory. It was the first free election in Haiti's history.

1991 A long meeting between Soviet president Mikhail Gorbachev and president of the Russian Federation Boris Yeltsin, resolves details for the dissolution of the Soviet Union on or before New Year's Eve.

1996 In Lima, Peru, members of the Tupac Amaru leftist rebel movement, disguised as waiters and caterers, slip into the home of Japanese ambassador Morihisa Aoki during a celebration and take 490 people hostage. A commando raid on April 22, 1997, ended the ordeal with the deaths of all the rebels, two commandos, and one hostage.

1996 Intel Corporation and the U.S. Energy Department announce the development of a high-speed computer capable of performing more than one trillion calculations per second.

1118 Alfonso the Battler, king of Aragon, captures Zaragossa, Spain. He fought energetically against the Moors and encouraged Christians in Muslim lands to settle in his domain. The capture of Zaragossa was a major blow to Muslim Spain.

1378 Charles V of France denounces the treacherous designs of John IV of Brittany and confiscates his domain. Charles led France in a phenomenal recovery from the first phase of the Hundred Years' War.

1603 Dutch admiral Steven van der Haghen's fleet departs to the East Indies, one of the first voyages in support of the Dutch East India Company (a response to the English enterprise). He is noted as the founder of Dutch navigation to the East Indies.

1621 The English House of Commons makes a written protestation that they have a full right to deal with matters concerning King and State without punishment. King James I promptly tore up the protestation and disbanded parliament.

1719 The U.S. claim to "Mother Goose" begins with the publication in Boston, Massachusetts, of *Mother Goose's Melodies for Children*, by Thomas Fleet. Fleet said the tales originated with his mother-

> *"In baiting a mousetrap with cheese, always leave room for the mouse."*
>
> —Saki

John William Draper

in-law, Elizabeth Vergoose. Others trace Mother Goose's nursery rhymes to both England and France.

1796 The *Baltimore Monitor* publishes the first U.S. Sunday edition of a newspaper.

1813 During the War of 1812, the British take Fort Niagara, strategically located on Lake Ontario.

1839 English photographer John William Draper takes the first celestial photograph, a Daguerreotype of the moon.

1865 Following its ratification by the requisite three-quarters of the states earlier in the month, the 13th Amendment is formally adopted into the U.S. Constitution, ensuring an end to slavery.

1878 John Kehoe, the last of the Molly Maguires, is executed in Pennsylvania. The Molly Maguires were an Irish secret society that had allegedly been responsible for incidents of vigilante justice in the coal fields of eastern Pennsylvania. They are often regarded as one of the first organized labor groups.

🏆 **1898** Count Gaston de Chasseloup-Laubat of France sets the world's first official land-speed record in Acheres Park near Paris: 39.245 miles per hour.

💥 **1915** Twenty thousand Australian and New Zealand troops withdraw from Gallipoli, Turkey, during the night, completely undetected by Turks defending the peninsula.

💥 **1916** During World War I, the Battle of Verdun ends after 10 months with a French victory. On February 21, German forces had launched an offensive against Verdun, a city 137 miles east of Paris. When it was over, 23 million shells had been fired and 650,000 lives lost.

🇺🇸 **1936** Su-Lin, the first giant panda to come to the United States from China, arrives in San Francisco, California.

💥 **1940** German dictator Adolf Hitler reveals "Operation Barbarossa," his plan for invading the Soviet Union, to his generals.

💥 **1941** During World War II, the island of Guam, defended by just 610 Americans, falls to more than 5,000 Japanese in a three-hour battle.

🇬🇧 **1946** The British House of Commons votes in favor of the Labour government's plan to nationalize the railroads, ports, and road haulage industry.

1956 Japan is admitted to the United Nations.

⚗️ **1957** The Shippingport Atomic Power Station in

Pennsylvania becomes the first U.S. nuclear facility to generate electricity.

🏆 **1961** The U.S. Associated Press names Olympic gold medalist Wilma Rudolph as Female Athlete of the Year for the second year in a row.

🇬🇷 **1974** Just 10 days following a referendum that abolished the Greek monarchy, legal scholar Michalis Stasinopoulos is elected president.

⚖️ **1987** American financier Ivan Boesky, one of the wealthiest and most powerful players on Wall Street, is sentenced to a three-year prison term for insider trading and other sizable but shady transactions. He ended up serving two years and paid over $100 million in fines.

The Telstar *satellite (milestone)*

1154 Henry II is crowned king of England. Among his achievements were strengthening the administration of the country and the establishment of the Exchequer (a separate organization responsible for revenue collection). It was also during his reign that the conquest of Ireland began.

1562 The battle of Dreux marks the beginning of the French Wars of Religion between Huguenots and Catholics.

1732 Benjamin Franklin first publishes *Poor Richard's Almanack*. The book, filled with proverbs preaching industry and prudence, became one of the most popular publications in colonial America, selling an average of 10,000 copies a year for 25 years.

1776 English and American political activist Thomas Paine's first "American Crisis" essay is published. In it, he writes, "These are the times that try men's souls."

1777 With the onset of the bitter winter cold, the Continental Army under General George Washington enters its winter camp at Valley Forge, 22 miles from British-occupied Philadelphia, Pennsylvania, during the American Revolutionary War.

1793 During the French Revolutionary War, forces under Napoleon Bonaparte and General Dugommier recapture the city of Toulon from the English.

1863 Frederick Walton of London, England, applies for a patent on linoleum.

1871 Albert Jones of New York City receives a patent for corrugated paper.

1887 Jake Kilrain of the United States and Jem Smith of England participate in France in a bare-knuckles fight that lasts 106 rounds. The 2-hour fight was ruled a draw.

1891 Charles Uncles of Baltimore, Maryland, becomes the first African American ordained priest.

1900 The French Parliament agrees to grant amnesty for those involved in the Dreyfus Affair.

1905 The first motorized ambulance service for traffic victims is created in London, England.

1910 Rayon is first commercially produced, in Marcus Hook, Pennsylvania. It was

Washington's prayer at Valley Forge

"I'd hate this to get out but I really like opera."

—Ford Frick

known as artificial silk, the term "rayon" was not adopted until 1924.

🏆 **1917** The first National Hockey League ice hockey game is played, in Montreal, Canada.

🇬🇧 **1924** The last Rolls-Royce Silver Ghost manufactured in England is sold in London. The Silver Ghost, a custom touring car, was introduced in 1906 and was called by some the best car in the world.

🔬 **1930** American aviator Amelia Earhart becomes the first autogyro pilot to carry a passenger, at Pitcairn Field in Willow Grove, Pennsylvania. The autogyro was the predecessor to the helicopter.

💥 **1941** Dissatisfied with the German offensive against Moscow, Russia, Adolf Hitler assumes the position of commander in chief of the German Army.

🎭 **1961** *Judgment at Nuremberg,* a multiple Academy Award-winning film about the post-World War II trial of Nazis, opens in New York City.

🇺🇸 **1972** The U.S. Apollo lunar-landing program ends as *Apollo 17* splashes down safely in the Pacific Ocean.

🔬 **1974** The personal computer revolution is launched when the Altair 8800, a do-it-yourself computer kit, goes on sale for $397. The computer used switches for input and flashing lights as a display.

⚖️ **1979** George Nichopoulos, Elvis Presley's personal physician, is charged with illegally prescribing drugs for the American rock-and-roll star during the months preceding his death.

▬ **1986** Soviet leader Mikhail Gorbachev releases Andrei Sakharov and his wife, Elena Bonner, from their internal exile in Gorky, a closed city on the Volga River.

🏆 **1987** Gary Kasparov of the Soviet Union defeats Anatoly Karpov in Seville, Spain, retaining his title as world chess champion.

🇬🇧 **1994** Great Britain's prestigious Rolls-Royce announces that its future cars will feature 12-cylinder motors manufactured by Germany's BMW. It was an ironic change; in earlier years, Rolls-Royce made a name for itself in automobile and aircraft engines.

British prime minister Margaret Thatcher and Chinese premier Zhao Ziyang (milestone)

> *"If you choose the lesser of two evils, always remember that it is still an evil."*
>
> —*Max Lerner*

69 Vespasian (Titus Flavius Vespasianus), a former general under Nero, enters Rome to claim the title of emperor. His reign was noted for its order and the beginning of a century of peace.

1192 On his way home after having concluded a treaty with Saladin to end the Third Crusade, England's Richard the Lion-Heart is captured and imprisoned by Leopold V of Austria over an argument they had during the crusade.

1606 Virginia Company settlers board three ships and set sail from London to establish Jamestown, Virginia, the first permanent English settlement in the New World.

1688 The Netherlands' William III marches into London with 15,000 troops, resulting in the overthrow of James II (who was allowed to escape to France on December 23) and William's ascension to the throne of England, reigning jointly with his wife, Queen Mary II.

1699 Russian czar Peter the Great orders the New Year changed from September 1 to January 1.

1790 Samuel Slater opens the first successful spinning mill in the United States, at Pawtucket, Rhode Island.

MILESTONE

United States Invades Panama

The United States invades Panama on this day in 1989 in an attempt to overthrow military dictator Manuel Noriega, who had been indicted in the United States on drug trafficking charges and accused of suppressing democracy in Panama and endangering U.S. nationals. Noriega's Panamanian Defense Forces were crushed, forcing him to seek asylum with the Vatican nuncio in Panama City, where he surrendered on January 3, 1990. In 1992, Noriega was found guilty on eight counts of drug trafficking, racketeering, and money laundering, marking the first time in history that a U.S. jury had convicted a foreign leader of criminal charges.

Peter the Great

1803 The U.S. and French governments put the finishing touches on the Louisiana Purchase. For the relatively small price tag of $15 million, the United States acquired an area that would become Arkansas, Missouri, Iowa, and the Dakotas, as well as chunks of Minnesota, Montana, Wyoming, Colorado, and, of course, Louisiana.

1860 In a prelude to the American Civil War, South Carolina becomes the first state to secede when it officially ratifies an article of secession. It was followed within a few weeks by six other states, who collectively formed the Confederate States of America.

1880 Electricity is used for the first time to light New York City's Broadway, and the street becomes known as the "Great White Way."

1907 Physicist Albert Michelson becomes the first American scientist to receive the Nobel Prize. His work contributed to the development of Einstein's theory of relativity.

1917 Felix Dzerzhinsky creates the Russian secret police in Czechoslovakia. He was instrumental in the Bolshevik revolution and eventually set up the "Cheka," which later became the KGB.

1920 English-born comedian Leslie Downes becomes an American citizen. He eventually became known as Bob Hope.

1938 Russian-born American inventor Vladimir Kosma Zworykin patents two revolutionary devices that lead to modern television. One, the kinescope (also known as the cathode-ray receiver), is still used today in TV and computer monitors. The other was for the iconoscope, a cathode-ray trans-mitter, which was used in all TV cameras for the next 50 years.

1941 The Flying Tigers, American pilots fighting against the Japanese in China during World War II, take to the air for the first time in their P-40 fighters, inflicting heavy losses on Japanese bombers attacking Kunming.

1951 The first electricity ever generated by atomic power begins flowing from the Experimental Breeder Reactor-1 turbine generator at the Argonne National Laboratory in the United States.

1962 The Dominican Republic, in its first free election in 38 years, chooses Juan Bosch Gavino for president. However, the army toppled him shortly afterward, as his plans for land reform would have broken up sugar plantations that were owned by generals.

1971 Pakistani president Mohammad Yahya Khan resigns and hands power over to Zulfikar Ali Bhutto.

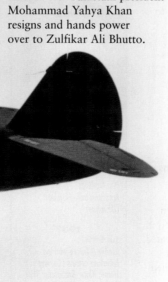

1708 French and Native American forces capture the English settlement at St. John's in Newfoundland, Canada, giving the French control of the eastern shoreline.

1784 John Jay becomes the first U.S. secretary of state for foreign affairs.

1846 The first surgical operation under anesthesia in Great Britain is performed at University College Hospital in London, England, for a leg amputation.

1861 In the most serious diplomatic crisis between England and the United States during the American Civil War, Lord Lyons, the British minister to the United States, meets with U.S. secretary of state William Seward concerning James Mason and John Slidell, Confederate envoys arrested by the U.S. Navy aboard the British mail steamer *Trent*. The United States was eventually forced to release the Confederates.

1898 French scientists Pierre and Marie Curie discover radium. They formally announced the discovery on December 26.

1910 The An-Hul province of China reports more than 2.5 million victims of the plague.

1913 The first modern crossword puzzle is published in *New York's World*. It was created by Liverpool-born journalist Arthur Wynne, who redesigned a Victorian-era game called "The Magic Square."

BORN ON THIS DAY

1639
JEAN BAPTISTE RACINE
French dramatist (*Alexandre; Britannicus; Mithridate*)

1804
BENJAMIN DISRAELI
English author (*The Life and Reign of Charles I*) and Conservative statesman, twice prime minister

Benjamin Disraeli

1879
JOSEPH STALIN
Russian Soviet dictator (1928–53) infamous for the numerous mass exterminations of his own people

1892
DAME REBECCA WEST
English novelist and journalist (*The Fountain Overflows; The Meaning of Treason*)

1892
WALTER HAGEN
American golf champion

1905
ANTHONY POWELL
English novelist (*A Dance to the Music of Time*)

1908
PAT WEAVER
American president of NBC-TV who is credited with the idea for the *Today* and *Tonight* shows

1935
PHIL DONAHUE
American talk-show host (*Donahue*)

1937
JANE FONDA
Academy Award-winning American actress (*Coming Home; Klute; Barbarella; They Shoot Horses Don't They?*)

SEE ONE OF THE ALL TIME GREATS!

WALT DISNEY'S
Snow White
and the Seven Dwarfs
Color by TECHNICOLOR

Snow White and the Seven Dwarfs poster

1921 Labor injunctions and picketing are ruled unconstitutional by the U.S. Supreme Court.

1923 Nepal becomes an independent nation after having been a British protectorate.

1933 Dried human blood serum is prepared for the first time at the University of Pennsylvania's School of Medicine in Philadelphia. It was used for the prevention of childhood diseases.

1937 *Snow White and the Seven Dwarfs* debuts. The American film, created by Walt Disney's animation company, was the first feature-length animated movie. It became a classic, and box-office receipts recouped the film's cost of $1.5 million by the end of its first year in circulation.

1958 Three months after a new French constitution was approved, Charles de Gaulle is elected the first president of the Fifth Republic by a sweeping majority of French voters. The previous June, France's World War II hero was called out of

> *"No government can be long secure without a formidable opposition."*
>
> —*Benjamin Disraeli*

retirement to lead the country when a military and civilian revolt in Algeria threatened France's stability.

1963 The Turkish minority in Cyprus riots to protest anti-Turkish revisions to the constitution.

1966 The Soviet Union launches *Luna 13*, which successfully soft-lands on the moon.

1968 *Apollo 8*, the first manned mission to the moon, is successfully launched from Cape Canaveral, Florida, with astronauts Frank Borman, James Lovell Jr., and William Anders aboard. On Christmas Eve it entered into orbit around the moon, the first manned spacecraft ever to do so.

1973 The first peace conference between Israel and her Arab neighbors opens in Geneva, Switzerland.

1975 Terrorists, led by the infamous Venezuelan "Carlos the Jackal," raid OPEC headquarters in Vienna, Austria, and hold 11 oil ministers and their staff hostage.

1986 In Shanghai's People's Square, a half-million Chinese students call for democratic reforms.

1989 Hard-line communist Romanian president Nicolae Ceauçescu is visibly stunned as listeners begin booing his speech. The next day, the army defected to the demonstrators and Ceauçescu and his wife fled the capital in a helicopter, only to be captured by the armed forces.

1993 Russian president Boris Yeltsin abolishes the KGB, proclaiming the security police force was incapable of being reformed.

MILESTONE

Pan Am Flight 103 Explodes Over Lockerbie
On this day in 1988, Pan Am Flight 103 from London, England, to New York City explodes in midair over Lockerbie, Scotland. A bomb hidden inside an audio-cassette player detonated inside the cargo area when the plane was at 31,000 feet. All 259 passengers were killed, as were 11 people on the ground. Authorities accused Islamic terrorists of having placed the bomb on the plane while it was at a low-security airport in Germany. In the early 1990s, investigators identified Libyan intelligence agents Abdel Basset Ali al-Megrahi and Lamen Khalifa Fhimah as suspects, but Libya refused to turn them over to be tried in the United States. The men were eventually tried under Scottish law in the Netherlands. In 2001, al-Megrahi was convicted of murder and sentenced to life in prison; Fhimah was acquitted.

Pan Am Flight 103 investigation (milestone)

640 The Saracens, under Amrou Ibn el-Ass, conquer Alexandria and destroy its famous library.

1135 Stephen of Blois is crowned king of England. A courageous soldier and a generous king, his abilities were inadequate to the requirements of his position and his reign was a continuous struggle to retain the crown.

1216 Pope Honorius III approves the Order of Preachers (Dominicans). A large number of Dominicans became missionaries with the Portuguese and Spanish as they explored the New World.

1772 Moravian missionaries begin construction of the first school west of the Allegheny Mountains, in Schoenbrunn, Pennsylvania.

1775 With $100,000, Ezek Hopkins begins to organize seven ships into a Continental Navy fleet for the American colonies.

1807 Hoping to stay out of the Napoleonic Wars, the U.S. House of Representatives passes President Thomas Jefferson's Embargo Act, barring trading between the United States and European nations. Unfortunately, it took a severe toll on U.S. agricultural and mercantile interests and, by 1809, was repealed with the exception of Great Britain and France.

1849 Russian writer Fyodor Dostoyevsky is led before a firing squad. He had been convicted and sentenced to death on November 16 for

MILESTONE

Comedian Convicted in Obscenity Case
On this day in 1964, American comedian Lenny Bruce is sentenced to four months in a New York jail for violating obscenity laws during his nightclub act. He performed his typical, inflammatory routine at a Greenwich Village theater, where his audience included New York City police officers. A few days later, Bruce and the owner of the theater were arrested. After the longest and costliest obscenity trial in history, Bruce was convicted for his "anthology of filth," as the prosecutor termed it. Bruce never served time because he died of a drug overdose in August 1966 while the case was on appeal.

Lenny Bruce at the police station

allegedly taking part in antigovernment activities. However, at the last moment he was reprieved and sent into exile. Dostoyevsky is known for such works as *Crime and Punishment* and *The Brothers Karamazov*.

1879 Swiss chemist and physicist Raoul Pierre Pictet announces the liquefaction of oxygen.

1882 American inventor Thomas Edison's associate, Edward H. Johnson, creates the first string of Christmas tree lights. Prior to this, trees were traditionally decorated with wax candles.

1885 La Marcus Thompson of Coney Island in Brooklyn, New York, receives the first U.S. patent for a 600-foot-long switchback gravity-powered railway, which would become known as the roller coaster.

1894 In a highly irregular trial smacking of anti-Semitism, French officer Alfred Dreyfus is convicted of treason by a court-martial and sentenced to life in prison for his alleged crime of passing military secrets to the Germans. After evidence of a cover-up was made public, Dreyfus was pardoned in 1899.

1894 The United States Golf Association is founded.

"The first lady is, and always has been, an unpaid public servant elected by one person, her husband."

—*Lady Bird Johnson*

1900 In Germany, a new 35-horsepower car built by Daimler from a design by Emil Jellinek is completed. The car was named for Jellinek's daughter, Mercedes.

1929 Soviet troops leave Manchuria after the Japanese and Chinese accept the Soviet position over claims to a lease to operate a railway running from Port Arthur to the Chinese Eastern Railway. The original lease was up, and Japanese and Chinese forces had sought to end Soviet control.

1938 A coelacanth, a five-foot-long prehistoric fish thought to be extinct, is discovered by Marjorie Courtenay-Latimer of Cape Town, South Africa, from among a trawler's catch. It was hailed as one of the greatest scientific discoveries of the century.

1939 Seventeen-year-old Gloria Jacobs of the United States establishes a new world pistol record, scoring 299 out of a possible 300. The previous record, 298, had been held by Walter Walsh, an FBI agent.

1943 In the United States, synthetic rubber is approved for the core of baseballs, which makes them "livelier" and allows them to be hit farther.

1956 The Columbus Zoo in Ohio becomes the site of the first gorilla born in captivity.

1964 The U.S. Lockheed SR-71 spy plane achieves a world record speed of 2,118 miles per hour.

1972 An earthquake in Managua, Nicaragua, kills more than 12,000 people. Later, President Anastasio Somoza was accused of diverting millions of dollars in foreign aid, which led to a revolution in 1979.

1973 Because of an Arab oil embargo, a federal speed limit of 55 miles per hour is imposed across the United States to increase fuel economy and safety.

1990 Lech Walesa, well-known Polish labor leader and winner of the Nobel Peace Prize, is sworn in as the first noncommunist president of Poland since the end of World War II.

2001 Richard Reid is subdued on American Airlines Flight 63 from Paris, France, to Miami, Florida, as he tries to ignite a fuse on his shoes. The FBI later confirmed that his shoes were packed with explosives. Reid, from south London in England, who became known as the "shoe bomber," later pleaded guilty to the charges against him and was jailed for life.

Richard Reid

1588 King Henry III of France orders the assassination of Henri, third duc de Guise, and his brother Louis, to put down a rebellion that forced him from Paris. While the assassination was successful, it only made matters worse and Henry was eventually forced to leave France.

1620 Persecuted French Huguenots rebel against the rule of King Louis XIII.

1690 English astronomer John Flamsteed observes Uranus but doesn't realize its significance as an undiscovered planet. Credit for discovering Uranus went to Sir William Herschel in 1781, who originally thought it was a comet.

1788 Maryland votes to give 100 square miles to the U.S. federal government, two-thirds of which are now the District of Columbia.

1823 "A Visit from St. Nicholas," a poem once attributed to American author Clement C. Moore, is first published. The poem is popularly known as "The Night Before Christmas."

1834 In England, Joseph Aloysius Hansom, a well-known architect, patents his Patent Safety Cab, a two-wheeled, horse-driven vehicle that would become better known as the hansom cab.

1861 The principalities of Wallachia and Moldavia become Romania.

1888 Dutch painter Vincent van Gogh, suffering from severe depression, mutilates the

BORN ON THIS DAY

1722
BARON AXEL CRONSTEDT
Swedish scientist who discovered the element nickel

1732
SIR RICHARD ARKWRIGHT
English inventor and pioneer of manufacturing techniques who created the spinning frame

1812
SAMUEL SMILES
Scottish writer (*Self Help*)

1885
VINCENT SARDI
American restaurateur who founded Sardi's Bar & Grill in New York City

1907
DON MCNEILL
American radio host (*The Breakfast Club*)

1911
JAMES GREGORY
American actor (*The Manchurian Candidate; Barney Miller; PT 109; Beneath the Planet of the Apes*)

1918
JOSÉ GRECO
Spanish flamenco dancer and actor (*Ship of Fools*)

1924
DAN DEVINE
American football coach

1925
HARRY GUARDINO
American actor (*Hell Is for Heroes; Dirty Harry; The Enforcer*)

1926
ROBERT BLY
American poet, translator, and author (*The Light Around the Body; The Kabir Book; Iron John*)

1929
DICK WEBER
American professional bowler

1929
CHET BAKER
American jazz trumpeter and singer

1933
AKIHITO (HEISEI TENNO)
Emperor of Japan since 1989

John Bardeen, left, and Walter H. Brattain

lower portion his left ear with a razor while staying in Arles, France. The event is documented in his *Self-Portrait with Bandaged Ear.*

1912 In the United States, Keystone Pictures releases its first "Keystone Kop" movie, *Hoffmeyer's Release.* Directed by Mack Sennett, the silent, black-and-white Keystone Kop films starred comedians playing a crew of bumbling policemen who bumped into and fell over each other in a frenetic sequence of slapstick gags.

1913 The U.S. Congress passes the Federal Reserve Act, which paved the way for the Federal Banking System, a network of 12 regional banks designed to provide resources to aid and stabilize the nation's other banks.

"I know a lot of men who are healthier at age fifty than they have ever been before, because a lot of their fear is gone."
—Robert Bly

1919 The United States' first hospital ship, the USS *Relief,* is launched.

1928 The first permanent U.S. coast-to-coast radio network is established by the National Broadcasting Company.

1930 American actress Bette Davis signs with Universal Studios after years of struggling to succeed. She made her film debut the next year in *Bad Sister,* but played unremarkable roles until the mid-1930s.

1933 Pope Pius XI condemns the Nazi racial sterilization program directed at the Jews.

1944 Private Eddie Slovik's death sentence is confirmed by General Dwight D. Eisenhower. Slovik was the only American shot for desertion since the Civil War.

1947 American inventors Walter H. Brattain and John Bardeen first demonstrate the transistor at a meeting at Bell Laboratories. The original device was later improved by William Schockley, and all three shared the 1956 Nobel Prize in physics.

1948 In Tokyo, Hideki Tōjō, former Japanese premier and chief of the Kwantung Army, is executed along with six other top Japanese leaders for war crimes during World War II. Seven of the defendants were also found guilty of committing crimes against humanity, especially in regard to their systematic genocide of the Chinese people.

1950 Pope Pius XII announces that St. Peter's tomb has been discovered in Rome, Italy, beneath St. Peter's Basilica.

1951 The first U.S. coast-to-coast televised football game is broadcast on the Dumont Network. The event was an NFL championship game in which the Los Angeles Rams beat the Cleveland Browns, 24–17.

MILESTONE

Voyager Completes Global Flight
After nine days and four minutes in the sky, the experimental aircraft *Voyager* lands at Edwards Air Force Base in California on this day in 1986, completing the first nonstop flight around the globe on one load of fuel. Piloted by Americans Dick Rutan and Jeana Yeager, *Voyager* was made mostly of plastic and stiffened paper and carried more than three times its weight in fuel when it took off from Edwards on December 14. *Voyager* is on permanent display at the National Air and Space Museum in Washington, D.C.

Voyager (milestone)

1476 Some 400 soldiers of Burgundy's Charles the Bold freeze to death during the siege of Nancy, France, by Swiss troops under René II of Lorraine.

1568 The bloody Rebellion of Morisco takes place in Granada in southern Spain as all the city's Moors are forced to convert to Christianity from Islam.

1638 The Ottomans under the ruthless Sultan Murad IV recapture Baghdad from Shah Abbas I of Persia. Murad was the last of the warrior sultans of the Ottoman Empire.

1773 England is petitioned by the Massachusetts Assembly to remove Governor Thomas Hutchinson. Hutchinson's harsh methods against colonial discontent were partly responsible for the Boston Tea Party on December 16, 1773.

1784 In Baltimore, Maryland, legal status is conferred upon Methodism in the United States.

1801 Richard Trevithick drives a three-wheeled steam-powered vehicle carrying seven passengers in Camborne,

Sultan Murad IV

BORN ON THIS DAY

1167
KING JOHN
King of England, son of Henry II

1491
ST. IGNATIUS LOYOLA
Spanish founder of the Jesuit order

1754
GEORGE CRABBE
English clergyman and poet whose work depicted the lives of the poor (*The Village*; *The Borough*)

1809
KIT CARSON
American frontiersman, fur trapper, guide, and Indian agent

Kit Carson

1818
JAMES JOULE
English physicist who gave his name to the S.I. unit of energy

1822
MATTHEW ARNOLD
English poet and critic (*Thyrsis*; *Dover Beach*)

1893
HARRY WARREN
American composer ("Lullaby of Broadway"; "You'll Never Know"; "On the Atcheson, Topeka and Santa Fe"; "You Must Have Been a Beautiful Baby")

1905
HOWARD HUGHES
American industrialist and eccentric billionaire who founded Hughes Aircraft and designed and built the "Spruce Goose," a plywood seaplane that is still the largest aircraft ever to fly

1905
I. F. STONE
American journalist

Cornwall, England. It was one of the first automobiles in history. Sometimes called the "Father of the Steam Locomotive," Trevithick adapted his engine to hoist loads in mines, drive locomotives and ships, and run rolling mills.

1814 The War of 1812 ends as the Treaty of Peace and Amity between Great Britain and the United States is signed at Ghent, Belgium. By terms of the treaty, all conquered territory was to be returned, and commissions were planned to settle the boundary of the United States and Canada.

1818 "Silent Night" is sung for the first time, during midnight mass at the Church of St. Nicholas at Oberndorf, Austria. Franz Gruber of Oberndorf, Germany, composed the music, with words written by Josef Mohr.

1851 A devastating fire at the Library of Congress in Washington, D.C., destroys about two-thirds of its 55,000 volumes, including most of Thomas Jefferson's personal library.

1865 In Pulaski, Tennessee, a group of

> *"When you are younger you get blamed for crimes you never committed and when you're older you begin to get credit for virtues you never possessed. It evens itself out."*
>
> —I. F. Stone

Confederate veterans convenes to form a secret society that they name the Ku Klux Klan. The KKK rapidly grew into a paramilitary force bent on reversing the federal government's Reconstruction Era activities in the South.

1871 The world premiere of Italian composer Giuseppe Verdi's *Aida* takes place in Cairo, Egypt.

1893 American automotive pioneer Henry Ford completes his first successful gasoline engine and tests it in his kitchen.

1906 The world's first radio entertainment program is broadcast. Canadian scientist Reginald Fessenden of Brant Rock, Massachusetts, broadcast a poetry reading, a violin solo, and a speech.

1914 The first air raid on Great Britain is launched when a German airplane drops a bomb on Dover. There were no casualties. The first deaths from aerial bombardment occurred in the county of Norfolk the next month.

1942 The first surface-to-surface missile, the V-1 Flying Bomb, also known as the buzz bomb or doodlebug, is successfully tested at Peenemunde in Germany. The weapons caused terror and devastation when they were unleashed on southern England eighteen months later.

1947 Led by General Markos Vafthiades, approximately 20,000 communists declare a free Greek government in northern Greece and issue a revolutionary edict to establish the government throughout the nation.

1951 Libya gains its independence from Italy.

1997 Venezuelan revolutionary Ilich Ramirez Sanchez ("Carlos the Jackal") is sentenced in France to life in prison for the murders of two French investigators and a Lebanese national in 1975.

Carlos the Jackal, standing between two gendarmes, and judge Yves Corneloup at right

274 Lucius Domitius Aurelianus (also known as Aurelian), one of Rome's greatest emperors, tries to achieve more unity in the Empire by establishing Sol invictus (a sun god) as supreme god. He inaugurated a new temple to celebrate the god's birth on this day and made it a national holiday.

336 The earliest historical mention of Christmas being celebrated in Rome on this day is found in a book written by Furius Dionysius Philocalus in A.D. 354.

800 The Holy Roman Empire begins as Charlemagne is proclaimed emperor by Pope Leo III.

875 Charles the Bald becomes emperor of Rome. His reign was marked by a rise in the

---

MILESTONE

Washington Crosses the Delaware

During the American Revolutionary War, General George Washington crosses the Delaware River with 2,400 troops on this day in 1776, hoping to surprise a British Hessian mercenary force celebrating Christmas at their winter quarters in Trenton, New Jersey. The unconventional attack came after several months of substantial defeats for Washington's army that had resulted in the loss of New York City and other strategic points in the region. The army commenced its crossing of the half-frozen river at three locations. The 2,400 soldiers led by Washington reached the New Jersey side of the Delaware just before dawn.

---

power of nobles that ultimately resulted in the local beginnings of feudalism.

967 Otto II is crowned Holy Roman emperor. He considered Italy and Germany to be a united realm and fought many battles to maintain that belief, although he never recovered from a disastrous defeat at the hands of Arabs in southern Italy.

969 Byzantine John Tzmisces, with the aid of Emperor Nicephorus II's wife, has his uncle Nicephorus murdered and proclaims himself emperor. He extended Byzantine power in Syria at the expense of Muslims.

1066 Norman invader William the Conqueror becomes king of England. The construction of Windsor Castle began under his reign.

Washington crossing the Delaware (milestone)

1223 St. Francis of Assisi creates what may be the first "Christmas crib" (the forerunner of the nativity scene) in the town of Greccio, Italy, to allow the community to better picture the miracle of Christ's birth in Bethlehem.

1241 The Mongols, under Batu Khan, overrun Budapest and leave it in ashes.

1651 The General Court of Boston, Massachusetts, makes it a crime to observe Christmas and levies a five-shilling fine on anyone caught doing so.

1741 Swedish astronomer Anders Celsius creates the Centigrade (or Celsius) temperature scale, in which the freezing point of water is set at zero and the boiling point at 100.

1799 French emperor Napoleon Bonaparte's new constitution goes into effect, giving him powers to create laws, nominate officials, control finances, and conduct foreign affairs.

1809 Dr. Ephraim McDowell of Danville, Kentucky, performs the first successful ovarian tumor operation.

1830 French composer Louis-Hector Berlioz's *Symphony Fantastique* premieres in Paris.

1896 American composer John Philip Sousa completes "Stars & Stripes Forever."

> *"Peace is more precious than a piece of land."*
>
> —*Anwar el-Sādāt*

Restoration of the Giza Sphinx

1914 German troops in World War I cease firing and commence to sing Christmas carols. At points along the Eastern and Western fronts, the soldiers of Russia, France, and Great Britain joined in. The "Christmas Truce of 1914" was one of the last examples of the notion of chivalry between enemies in warfare.

1923 The U.S. White House has its first Christmas tree lit exclusively by electric lights.

1941 The British garrison in Hong Kong surrenders to the Japanese during World War II.

1950 Scottish nationalists steal the Coronation Stone (known as the "Stone of Scone") from Westminster Abbey. Edward I in 1296 originally took the 485-pound stone from Scone in Scotland. The stone was returned to Westminster Abbey in April 1951.

1979 Egypt begins major restoration work on the Sphinx.

DECEMBER 26

1492 Italian explorer Christopher Columbus founds the first Spanish settlement in the New World, La Navidad, on Haiti. The native Indians eventually destroyed it.

1606 William Shakespeare's play *King Lear* is performed at the court of King James I of England.

1610 Count Gyorgy Thurzo visits Csejthe Castle in Hungary on orders from King Matthias and discovers Countess Elizabeth Bathory directing a torture session of girls. Bathory was already infamous for her activities, but her title and high-ranking relatives made her untouchable. Her bloodthirsty activities have led many to cite her as one of history's first vampires.

1786 Daniel Shay, an American Revolutionary War veteran, leads a rebellion in Massachusetts to protest a tax increase to pay off war debts. Those who couldn't pay were evicted from their property or sent to prison.

1825 The Erie Canal opens to great fanfare as American statesman De Witt Clinton pours a barrel of Lake Erie water into the Atlantic Ocean.

1854 The first useful process for making paper from wood fiber is patented in the United States by Hugh Burgess and Charles Watt. Most paper was made primarily of rag pulp, which had become increasingly expensive.

1862 Thirty-eight Sioux Indians are executed in

Minnesota for an uprising that claimed the lives of 800 settlers and soldiers.

1865 The first U.S. patent for a coffee percolator is issued to James H. Mason of Franklin, Massachusetts.

1906 What may be the world's first feature film, *The Story of the Kelly Gang*, premieres at the Athenaeum Hall in Melbourne, Australia. At an hour long, it is considered the first continuous film of any significant length.

1908 Jack Johnson becomes the first African American to win the world heavyweight title when he knocks out Tommy Burns of Canada in a fight near Sydney, Australia.

1917 During World War I, U.S. president Woodrow Wilson places the nation's railroads under government control.

Jack Johnson

1926 The first overland journey across Africa from south to north is completed as Major C. Court Treatt arrives in Cairo, Egypt. Treatt had set out from Capetown, South Africa, some 27 months earlier in two military-style Crossley automobiles.

1928 Johnny Weissmuller retires from amateur swimming, having never lost a freestyle race.

1931 *Of Thee I Sing*, a George Gershwin musical, opens in New York City. It became the first American musical to receive a Pulitzer Prize.

1933 The Nissan Motor Company is organized in Tokyo, Japan, under the name Dat Jidosha Seizo Company.

1941 Winston Churchill becomes the first British prime minister to address the U.S. Congress. He urged the legislative body to back President Franklin D. Roosevelt's proposal that America become the "great arsenal of democracy."

1943 During World War II, the German battle cruiser *Scharnhorst* is sunk by British warships in the Arctic after decoded naval signals reveal that it is on a mission to attack an Anglo-American convoy to Russia.

> *"One of the nice things about problems is that a good many of them do not exist except in our imaginations."*
>
> —Steve Allen

General George S. Patton

1944 Literally wheeling his Third Army a sharp 90 degrees in a counterthrust movement, U.S. general George S. Patton breaks through the German lines and enters Bastogne, Belgium, during the Battle of the Bulge in World War II. The action relieved the defenders and ultimately pushed the Germans east across the Rhine.

1955 In one of the most publicized cultural exchanges of the Cold War, *Porgy and Bess,* an opera featuring an African-American cast, opens in Leningrad, the Soviet Union, and receives a 10-minute standing ovation.

1962 Eight people from East Berlin, Germany, escape to West Berlin by crashing an armor-plated bus through a gate in the Berlin Wall.

1978 Indira Gandhi, India's prime minister from 1966 to 1977, is released after serving 10 days in jail on corruption charges. She served again as prime minister from 1980 until her assassination in 1984.

MILESTONE

The First Kwanzaa
The first day of the first Kwanzaa is celebrated in Los Angeles, California, under the direction of Maulana Karenga on this day in 1966. The seven-day holiday, which has strong African roots, was designed by Dr. Karenga as a celebration of African-American family, community, and culture. The name Kwanzaa is derived from the phrase *matunda ya kwanza,* which means "first fruits" in Swahili. Today, Kwanzaa is celebrated by millions of people of African descent all across the United States and Canada.

The first candle of Kwanzaa

1512 Spain's Laws of Burgos become the first systematic code to govern the conduct of settlers in the Americas, providing provisions for the protection of Native Americans.

1703 England and Portugal sign the Methuen Treaty, whereby the Portuguese agree to admit previously prohibited English textiles while the English agree to import wine at a lower duty rate than that imposed on France.

1831 English naturalist Charles Darwin sets out from Plymouth, England, aboard the HMS *Beagle* on a five-year surveying expedition of the southern Atlantic and Pacific oceans. The voyage to such diverse places as the Galápagos Islands and New Zealand led to the development of his groundbreaking scientific work of 1859, *On the Origin of Species by Means of Natural Selection.*

1845 Ether is first used as an anesthetic in childbirth, given by Dr. Crawford W. Long of Jefferson, Georgia, to his wife. She successfully gave birth to a baby girl.

1846 The ragtag army of 500 volunteers known as Doniphan's Thousand, led by U.S. colonel Alexander W. Doniphan, wins a major victory against 1,200 Mexican soldiers in the war with Mexico, leading to the occupation of El Paso.

1871 The Crystal Palace in London, England, is the site of the world's first cat show.

1900 American prohibitionist Carry Nation begins the

1571
JOHANNES KEPLER
German astronomer who devised laws describing the motion of the planets

1773
SIR GEORGE CAYLEY
English engineer and aviation pioneer who built the first successful piloted glider and developed the first vehicle with caterpillar tracks

1822
LOUIS PASTEUR
French scientist who discovered that most diseases are caused by germs and who developed the pasteurization process

1879
SYDNEY GREENSTREET
English actor (*The Maltese Falcon; Casablanca*)

1901
MARLENE DIETRICH
German-born American actress (*Shanghai Express; A Foreign Affair*)

1906
OSCAR LEVANT
American composer, concert pianist, humorist, and author (*A Smattering of Ignorance; The Unimportance of Being Oscar*)

1931
WALTER NORRIS
American pianist and composer ("Drifting")

1939
JOHN AMOS
American actor (*The West Wing; The Fresh Prince of Bel Air; Roots*)

1941
LESLIE MAGUIRE
English rock pianist (Gerry and The Pacemakers)

1943
COKIE ROBERTS
Emmy-winning American journalist and author (*We Are Our Mothers' Daughters*)

1948
GERARD DEPARDIEU
French actor (*Cyrano de Bergerac; The Man in the Iron Mask*)

Sir James M. Barrie

first of her infamous bar smashings, at the Carey Hotel in Wichita, Kansas.

1903 The barbershop quartet favorite "Sweet Adeline" is sung for the first time, in New York City. Henry Armstrong composed the music, with words by Richard Gerard.

1904 The play *Peter Pan*, by English author James M. Barrie, opens at the Duke of York's Theatre in London.

1927 The musical *Show Boat* opens on Broadway. The show, with music by Jerome Kern and lyrics by Oscar Hammerstein, helped set the future direction of American musical theater.

1927 Leon Trotsky is expelled from the Communist Party when Joseph Stalin's faction comes out on top at the All-Union Congress in the Soviet Union.

1942 The German military begins enlisting Soviet prisoners of war in their World War II battle against Russia, eventu-

> *"Happiness isn't something you experience; it's something you remember."*
>
> —*Oscar Levant*

ally creating a 50,000-man army known as the Russian Liberation division. Tens of thousands eventually ended up turning back against the Germans, then finally surrendering to the Americans rather than to the advancing Soviets when the German cause was lost.

1945 Following World War II, the Allied Powers divide Korea into two occupation zones, with Soviet forces occupying the North and American forces the South. War broke out in June 1950, but while a truce halted the fighting in 1953, the Korean War was never officially ended.

1945 Twenty-eight nations sign an agreement in Washington, D.C., creating the International Monetary Fund and the World Bank.

1946 The Davis Cup international tennis championship is won by the American team for the first time since 1938.

1949 After more than three centuries of Dutch rule, Queen Juliana of the Netherlands grants sovereignty to Indonesia.

1950 Concern over the Korean War prompts the United States to reconcile relations with Spain for the first time since the Spanish Civil War of the 1930s.

1968 U.S. *Apollo 8*, the first manned mission to the moon, returns safely to Earth after a historic six-day journey.

1972 Belgium becomes the first NATO nation to launch diplomatic relations with East Germany.

1978 Following its approval in a national referendum, King Juan Carlos ratifies Spain's first democratic constitution in nearly five decades.

1989 Egypt and Syria resume diplomatic relations after 12 years.

Hafizullah Amin

Soviet army officer and Nazi collaborator Andrei Vlasov, center

1784 The first American ship to visit China, the *Empress of China*, begins its return voyage from Guangzhou.

1793 Thomas Paine, who had moved to France to become involved in the French Revolution, is arrested for treason by Robespierre and thrown into prison. Paine became a French citizen and member of the National Assembly and was arrested because he had voted against the execution of Louis XVI. An instrumental figure in the American Revolution, his imprisonment caused an uproar in the United States. President James Monroe got Paine released in November 1794.

1832 Citing political differences with President Andrew Jackson and a desire to fill a vacant Senate seat in South Carolina, John C. Calhoun becomes the first vice president in U.S. history to resign the office.

1869 The Knights of Labor, a union of tailors in Philadelphia, Pennsylvania, hold the first Labor Day ceremonies in American history. Established as a secret society, it grew into a national body that played an important role in the labor movement of the late 19th century.

1869 William Finley Semple of Mount Vernon, Ohio, first patents chewing gum, though he would never commercially produce it. Chewing gum as we know it was invented by Thomas Adams of Staten Island, New York, who unsuccessfully experimented with vulcanized chicle as a rubber substitute and instead gave us all something to chew on in 1871.

1856
WOODROW WILSON
28th U.S. president (1913–21)

Woodrow Wilson

1860
PHILIP WILSON STEER
English artist (*The Beach at Walberswick*)

1882
SIR ARTHUR EDDINGTON
English astrophysicist and author (*The Expanding Universe*)

1905
CLIFF ARQUETTE
American comedian (*The Jack Paar Show*), pianist, and composer ("It's Xmas in Mount Idy")

1905
EARL HINES
American jazz pianist and big band leader

1908
LEW AYRES
American actor (*All Quiet on the Western Front; Young Dr. Kildare; Johnny Belinda*)

1911
SAM LEVENSON
American humorist and television personality (*The Price Is Right; Two for the Money*)

1934
DAME MAGGIE SMITH
Academy Award-winning English actress (*The Prime of Miss Jean Brodie; California Suite; Hook; Gosford Park*)

1954
DENZEL WASHINGTON
Academy Award-winning American actor (*Glory; Malcolm X; Training Day*)

1874 Alfonso XII is proclaimed king of Spain. He had been in exile with his parents since childhood following a revolt in 1868, but returned to Madrid with great popular support.

1877 A U.S. patent for a flour-rolling mill is applied for by John Stevens, of Neenah, Wisconsin. The mill boosted flour production by 70 percent.

1879 The Tay Bridge crossing the estuary near Dundee in eastern Scotland collapses in a gale while a train is passing over it. More than seventy people were killed, and plans for the same engineer, Sir Thomas Bouch, to build the Forth bridge were scrapped.

1902 The first indoor professional American football game (now called arena football) is played in New York City's Madison Square Garden. Syracuse won over the Philadelphia Nationals, 6–0.

1904 Wireless telegraphy is used for the first time to relay weather reports, in London, England.

1908 The most destructive earthquake in recorded European history strikes the Straits of Messina in southern Italy, leveling the cities of Messina in Sicily and Reggio di Calabria on the Italian mainland. The earthquake and tsunami it

> *"Insanity is hereditary— you get it from your children."*
>
> —*Sam Levenson*

Seabees recruiting poster

caused killed an estimated 100,000 people.

1911 Sun Yat-sen is elected provisional president of China. He resigned two months later.

1941 U.S. rear Admiral Ben Moreell requests authority to create a contingent of construction units able to build everything from airfields to roads under battlefield conditions. These units would be known as the "Seabees," for the first letters of Construction Battalion.

1941 American heavyweight boxing champion Joe Louis is named fighter of the year for the fourth time.

1945 The U.S. Pledge of Allegiance is officially recognized by Congress.

1946 With full-scale war all but inevitable, France declares martial law in Vietnam.

1947 American blues singer Wynonie Harris records the hit song "Good Rockin'

Tonight." The hard-driving number popularized the word "rock" and associated it with the fast, exciting blues-based music that would dominate in the 1950s.

1950 During the Korean War, Chinese troops intervene on behalf of communist North Korea and cross the Yalu River to help fight American-led United Nations forces.

1964 Principal filming of the English classic *Dr. Zhivago*, directed by David Lean and based on the novel by Russian author Boris Pasternak, begins near Madrid, Spain. The film won five Academy Awards, including Best Original Score.

1973 Aleksandr Solzhenitsyn's "literary investigation" of the police-state system in the Soviet Union, *The Gulag Archipelago, 1918–1956*, is published in the original Russian in Paris, France.

1989 Playwright Vaclav Havel is sworn in as president of Czechoslovakia.

1989 Alexander Dubcek, former Czech leader and architect of the "Prague Spring," a series of far-reaching political and economic reforms, including increased freedom of speech and an end to state censorship, is elected chairman of the new multiparty Czech parliament.

1993 The Vatican and Israel sign a formal document recognizing each other.

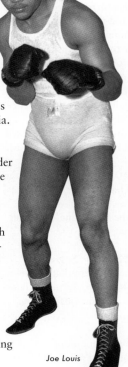

Joe Louis

Pocahontas

BORN ON THIS DAY

1721
MADAME DE POMPADOUR
Mistress of French king Louis XV

1766
CHARLES MACINTOSH
Scottish chemist who invented rubberized waterproof fabric and hence gave his name to a kind of raincoat

1800
CHARLES GOODYEAR
American inventor who created vulcanized rubber

1808
ANDREW JOHNSON
17th U.S. president (1865–69) who succeeded to the presidency upon the death of Abraham Lincoln

1809
WILLIAM EWART GLADSTONE
English Liberal statesman and philanthropist, four-time prime minister

1813
ALEXANDER PARKES
English chemist who invented celluloid

1876
PABLO CASALS
Spanish cellist

1893
VERA BRITTAIN
English pacifist and writer (*Testament of Youth*)

1938
JOHN VOIGHT
American actor (*Midnight Cowboy; Deliverance; The Tin Soldier; Mission: Impossible*)

1946
MARIANNE FAITHFULL
English singer ("As Tears Go By"; "Summer Nights")

1947
TED DANSON
Emmy Award-winning American actor (*Cheers; Three Men and a Baby; The Onion Field; Gulliver's Travels*)

1953
YVONNE ELLIMAN
American actress (*Jesus Christ Superstar*) and singer ("If I Can't Have You")

> *"It's a damn poor mind that can only think of one way to spell a word."*
> —Andrew Johnson

1170 Thomas Becket, the archbishop of Canterbury, is murdered in Canterbury Cathedral by four Norman knights. Their actions are widely held to have been prompted by an overheard outburst from King Henry II: "Who will rid me of this turbulent priest?" Becket and the king had had a long-running dispute as to whether the king was subject to the church or in charge of it.

1223 Pope Honorius III formally approves the Order of the Friars Minor (the Franciscans), originally founded in 1209 by St. Francis of Assisi.

1607 After listening to the pleas of his daughter, Pocahontas, Chief Powhatan of Virginia spares the life of English settler John Smith.

1675 The English Parliament orders that coffeehouses be closed, citing them as hotbeds of malicious rumors and revolution.

1845 Six months after the congress of the Republic of Texas accepted U.S. annexation of the territory, Texas is admitted into the United States as the 28th state.

1848 During the administration of U.S. president James Knox Polk, gaslights are first installed at the White House.

1849 In the United States, the Christmas hymn "It Came Upon a Midnight Clear," by Edmund Sears, is first published, in *The Christian Register*.

1851 The first Young Men's Christian Association in America is organized, in Boston, Massachusetts.

1852 In violation of the law in Boston, Massachusetts, Emma Snodgrass is arrested for wearing pants in public.

1862 The bowling ball is invented in the United States.

1867 Groesbeck & Company of New York becomes the first brokerage house to use a telegraph ticker to provide up-to-the-minute stock prices.

1890 In the tragic final chapter of America's long war against the Plains Indians, the U.S. Cavalry kills 146 Sioux Indians at Wounded Knee, South Dakota, after Colonel James W. Forsyth of the Seventh Cavalry tries to disarm Chief Big Foot and his followers.

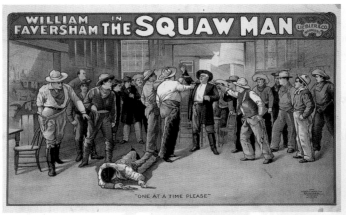

WILLIAM FAVERSHAM IN THE SQUAW MAN

LIEBLER & CO.

"ONE AT A TIME PLEASE"

The Squaw Man poster

1891 American inventor Thomas Edison is granted a patent for wireless radio. His patent indicated that signals could be transmitted between two points without a wire.

1895 In the South African Republic, Leander Jameson leads a raid into the Transvaal in an attempt to trigger an uprising by foreigners (mainly British settlers) against President Paul Kruger.

1913 Shooting begins on *The Squaw Man*, the first feature-length film made in Hollywood, California. The movie, produced by the Jesse L. Lasky Company, helped establish the careers of Cecil B. DeMille and Samuel Goldfish (later Goldwyn). It tells the story of an English aristo-crat who comes to America and marries a Native American.

1914 Belgian newspapers cease production to protest German censorship.

1916 Irish author James Joyce's book *Portrait of the Artist as a Young Man* is pub-lished in New York.

1940 London, England, suffers its most devastating air raid when Germans firebomb the city during World War II. Hundreds of fires caused by the exploding bombs engulfed areas of the city, but firefighters showed a valiant indifference to the bombs falling around them and saved much of London from destruction.

1950 Trusts and would-be monopolies are put on notice as the Celler-Kefauver Antimerger Act, a potent piece of antitrust legislation, makes its way into the law books. The legislation was designed to help stanch monopolistic mergers and acquisitions, as well as reign in super-sized corporations that threatened competition.

United States Prepares New Strategic Plan for Middle East

On this day in 1956, President Dwight D. Eisenhower asks Congress for the resolutions supporting greater U.S. eco-nomic and military presence in the Middle East. Days before an official announce-ment was to be issued by the Eisenhower administration, the *New York Times* leaked the news that the United States was preparing a major policy statement on the Middle East. Secretary of State John Foster Dulles was set to ask for congressional support of a declaration by the administration that the nation would oppose Soviet military intervention in the Middle East and would establish a major economic assistance plan there.

London firefighters after German air raid

1460 During England's Wars of the Roses, Richard, duke of York, is defeated by Queen Margaret and the Lancastrians at the Battle of Wakefield.

1622 In the American colonies, Robert Gorges is appointed the first lieutenant general of the New England Territory.

1731 The first musical concert in America is held, in Boston, Massachusetts.

1853 James Gadsden, the U.S. minister to Mexico, and General Antonio López de Santa Anna, the Mexican president, sign the Gadsden Purchase in Mexico City. The treaty settled the dispute over the location of the Mexican border west of El Paso, Texas, and established the final boundaries of the southern United States.

1861 American banks suspend the redemption of paper money for metal currency.

1862 The USS *Monitor* sinks in a storm off Cape Hatteras, North Carolina. Just nine months earlier, the ship

Collective farming in eastern Europe under communist control

M I L E S T O N E

Soviet Union Established
In postrevolutionary Russia, the Union of Soviet Socialist Republics is established on this day in 1922, comprising a confederation of Russia, Belarus, the Ukraine, and the Transcaucasian Federation. Also known as the Soviet Union, the new communist state was the successor to the Russian Empire and the first country in the world to be based on Marxist socialism. All levels of government were controlled by the Communist Party; and the party's politburo, with its increasingly powerful general secretary, effectively ruled the country. In 1991, the Soviet Union was dissolved following the collapse of its communist government.

had been part of a revolution in naval warfare when the ironclad dueled to a standstill with the CSS *Virginia* (formerly the captured Union ship USS *Merrimac*) off Hampton Roads, Virginia, during the American Civil War, in one of the most famous naval battles in U.S. history.

1873 The American Metrological Society is created to improve upon the U.S. system of weights, measures, and money.

1879 Gilbert and Sullivan's comic opera *The Pirates of Penzance* premieres in the town of Paignton in Devon, England.

1880 In South Africa, the Transvaal declares itself a republic.

1905 French driver Victor Hemery, in a gasoline-powered Darracq automobile, sets a new land-speed record in Arles-Salon, France. He reached a speed of 109.589 miles per hour.

1906 Iran becomes a constitutional monarchy.

1916 Rasputin, the "mad monk," is assassinated by two relatives of Czar Nicholas II. Rasputin, who had exercised considerable influence over the Czarina, was shot and beaten after poison failed to kill him.

"Take everything you like seriously, except yourselves."

—*Rudyard Kipling*

1924 American astronomer Edwin Hubble announces the existence of another galaxy in addition to the Milky Way. Until then, astronomers were not certain whether the Milky Way was the only galaxy.

1927 Tokyo, Japan, opens the first subway in Asia. Following several extensions, it is now 135 miles long, the sixth longest in the world, after those in London, New York, Paris, Moscow, and Washington, D.C.

1932 The Soviet Union eliminates free food for housewives less than 36 years old.

1942 American singer Frank Sinatra opens at New York's Paramount Theatre and an estimated 400 policemen are called in to curb screaming teenage girls.

1944 Trying to stop the spread of a civil war with communists in Athens following Allied liberation of Greece in World War II, British prime minister Winston Churchill convinces King George II not to return immediately to Greece. The king had been in exile in London.

1947 Soviet-backed communists force the abdication of Romania's King Michael, placing all of Eastern Europe under communist control.

1951 The American television western *The Roy Rogers Show* debuts.

1959 The first U.S. ballistic missile submarine, the USS

George Washington, is commissioned.

1965 Philippines Senate president Ferdinand Marcos is inaugurated president of the nation. Marcos's regime would span 20 years and become increasingly authoritarian and corrupt. He was eventually indicted by the United States on charges of embezzling billions of dollars from the Philippine economy.

1985 Pakistani president Mohammad Zia-ul-Haq lifts martial law. He had seized power in 1977 and ruled with an iron fist in the belief that the country's law and culture should be guided by strict Islamic principles.

1989 Dmitri Volkov of the Soviet Union swims the 50-meter freestyle in a world-record 27.15 seconds.

1992 Afghanistan's interim president Burhanuddin Rabbani is elected to lead the country for two years. He was the sole candidate on the ballot.

Burhanuddin Rabbani

1600 Queen Elizabeth I of England grants a formal charter to London merchants trading to the East Indies, hoping to break the Dutch monopoly of the spice trade in what is now Indonesia. But the East India Company had better results in India itself and, by the 1630s, began concentrating almost entirely on Indian textiles and Chinese tea.

1762 Austrian composer Wolfgang Mozart moves his family to Salzburg from Vienna.

1775 During the American Revolutionary War, forces under generals Benedict Arnold and Richard Montgomery are defeated by British defenders of the city of Quebec in Canada. On the same day, recruiting officers are ordered by General George Washington to accept free blacks into the army.

1851 The Austrian constitution of 1849 is abolished, increasing royal power.

1852 The best year of the California Gold Rush comes to an end. An estimated $81.3 million in gold had been produced.

1857 Ottawa is made the capital of Canada by Queen Victoria of Great Britain.

1862 In the American Civil War, Confederate general Nathan Bedford Forrest narrowly escapes capture during a raid in western Tennessee. Despite the close call, the raid was instrumental in forcing Union general Ulysses S. Grant to abandon his first attempt to capture Vicksburg, Mississippi.

MILESTONE

Edison Demonstrates Incandescent Light

In the first public demonstration of his incandescent light bulb, American inventor Thomas Edison lights up a street in Menlo Park, New Jersey, on this day in 1879. Although the first incandescent lamp had been produced 40 years earlier, Edison was the first to bring the product to the commercial market, a few months before his English rival, Joseph Swan. After countless tests, he developed both a high-resistance carbon-thread filament that burned steadily for hours and an electric generator sophisticated enough to power a large lighting system. Swan had given the world's first public demonstration of a practical incandescent lightbulb in January of the same year. Having both filed patents, the two men launched law suits against each other, eventually settling out of court and joining forces in the Edison & Swan United Electric Company.

Incandescent light bulb

Marie Curie

1879 The cornerstone is laid for the only royal palace in the United States, Iolani Palace in Honolulu, Hawaii.

1904 For the first time, a light descends from a pole in New York City's Times Square to mark the beginning of the New Year.

1911 French physicist Marie Curie becomes the first person to be awarded a second Nobel Prize, for her isolation of metallic radium. Eight years earlier, she had become the first woman to ever win the honor.

1929 Guy Lombardo and his Royal Canadians play *Auld Lang Syne* as a New Year's Eve song for the first time, at the Hotel Roosevelt Grill in New York City.

1938 The first successful blood-alcohol breath test for car drivers, the "drunkometer," is introduced in Indianapolis, Indiana. Dr. Rolla N. Harger, of the Indiana University School of Medicine, invented it.

1942 Japanese emperor Hirohito allows his commanders at Guadalcanal to retreat after five months of battle during World War II.

> *"Nothing is too good to be true, nothing is too wonderful to happen, and nothing is too wonderful to ask."*
>
> —*Sir Anthony Hopkins*

1944 Liberated from German rule by Soviet troops, the provisional government of Hungary officially declares war on Germany, bringing an end to its World War II cooperation—sometimes free, sometimes coerced—with the Axis power.

1950 Willie Shoemaker and Joe Culmone are the first jockeys to ride 388 winners in a single year. On this same day in 1953, Shoemaker set a new record when he won his 485th race of the year.

1955 General Motors becomes the first American company to earn more than a billion dollars in one year.

1960 The last compulsory recruits in Great Britain's National Service system receive their call-up papers. On the same day, the farthing, a coin worth a quarter of a penny in Great Britain's pre-decimal system, ceases to be legal tender. The farthing had been in use since the 13th century.

1965 California becomes the largest state in the United States in terms of population.

1968 The Soviet Union's TU-144 supersonic airliner makes its first flight, several months ahead of the Anglo-French Concorde. The TU-144 so closely resembled the Concorde that the Western press dubbed it the "Konkordski."

1973 Great Britain introduces a three-day workweek as an energy conservation measure during a miners' strike.

1974 For the first time in more than four decades, U.S. citizens are allowed to own gold.

1978 The United States ends official relations with Nationalist China, officially recognizing the government of the People's Republic of China in Beijing the next day.

1981 President Hilla Limann's civilian government in Ghana is overthrown in a military coup.

1987 Robert Mugabe is sworn in as Zimbabwe's first president.

1993 Scientists, looking to continue research, stop the destruction of the last samples of the smallpox virus, the world's most dreaded disease until it was declared eradicated in 1977.

Hilla Limann

American Honda Motor Co., Inc. Used by permission: 125b

AP/Wide World Photos: 7a, 7b, 9a, 9b, 11, 13b, 15c, 16-17, 19, 21, 24-25, 27a, 28a, 29b, 31a, 33a, 33b, 34-35, 35, 36-37, 38, 39, 41b, 43a, 45, 46b, 47, 49, 51b, 55b, 56-57, 59, 61a, 65, 67, 69, 71b, 73b, 75, 81a, 83b, 85a, 85b, 87b, 89a, 89b, 91, 93a, 93b, 95, 97a, 97b, 99b, 101a, 101c, 107c, 109, 111, 113b, 115, 117a, 117b, 119a, 119b, 121b, 122b, 123b, 125a, 127, 128, 129, 132b, 133b, 135a, 137a, 139a, 140, 143, 145a, 145b, 149, 151a, 151a, 153, 157, 159b, 163a, 163b, 165b, 166b, 167, 169, 171, 175a, 175b, 177, 178, 179, 182, 183, 185b, 187, 191b, 193a, 193b, 194b, 195a, 197a, 197b, 199a, 199b, 201a, 201b, 203a, 203b, 205b, 207a, 209a, 210b, 219a, 219b, 223a, 223b, 224-225, 226b, 227, 229a, 229b, 231a, 231b, 232, 233a, 233b, 235a, 235b, 237a, 237b, 238-239, 239, 240, 241, 242-243, 243b, 245b, 247b, 248b, 249, 251a, 251b, 253a, 253b, 255a, 255b, 257, 259, 260b, 261, 263a, 263b, 265a, 265b, 267, 269a, 269b, 271a, 271b, 273b, 274, 275b, 277b, 278, 278-279, 280-281, 283a, 283b, 285, 287a, 289b, 291a, 292-293, 294-295, 295, 297, 301b, 303a, 303b, 305, 306, 307a, 307b, 309, 311a, 311b, 313a, 315a, 315b, 317, 319a, 321b, 323a, 323b, 325a, 327, 329b, 331b, 333a, 333b, 335b, 337b, 339a, 339b, 341a, 343, 345a, 346b, 347, 348-349, 349, 351a, 351b, 353b, 355, 357, 361a, 361b, 362, 363a, 363b, 365a, 365b, 366b, 367, 369b, 371a, 371b, 373a, 373b, 375a, 377, 379b, 380-381, 385a, 385b, 386-387, 389b, 393a, 393b, 395b, 397a, 397b, 398, 399a, 399b, 400-401, 401a, 401b, 403, 405b, 407c, 409a, 409b, 411, 412a, 413, 415b, 416, 417, 420, 421b, 422, 423, 425b, 427, 429, 431, 433, 435, 436-437, 437, 439a, 439b, 440, 440-441, 442, 445a, 445b, 446, 447b, 449b, 450-451, 452b, 453, 455, 457a, 459, 461a, 461b, 463b, 465a, 465b, 467b, 469a, 469b, 471b, 473, 474, 475, 477a, 477b, 478, 479b, 480b, 481, 483, 484, 485, 487b, 491a, 491b, 496-467, 497a, 498a, 499, 501, 503a, 505, 507, 508, 509, 511a, 512-513, 513, 515a, 515b, 517, 523a, 525, 526a, 527, 529, 531, 532, 533, 535a, 535b, 537a, 539, 541b, 542a, 545, 546, 546-547, 547, 549, 551, 553b, 555a, 557, 559b, 561b, 563b, 565, 567a, 569a, 569b, 571b, 573a, 575a, 577a, 579b, 581c, 583, 585, 587, 589a, 593, 595a, 596-597, 597, 599, 601a, 603b, 609, 611, 613, 615, 616-617, 619a, 619b, 620, 621b, 625a, 625b, 627, 631, 633, 634, 635, 636a, 639b, 641b, 643, 645, 647, 649, 655, 656-657, 656-657, 661, 662, 663, 665, 667a, 667b, 671, 673b, 675a, 676-677, 677, 679a, 679b, 681, 683, 685b, 689, 691, 693, 694-695, 697b, 698, 699, 701a, 701b, 703, 705, 709, 711, 715, 717b, 718, 719, 721, 723, 725b, 727a, 729b, 731b, 733b, 734b, 735

Dammen Photography: 99a (Drisine replica located in the Deke Slayton Memorial Space & Bicycle Museum in Sparta, WI.)

© Dorling Kindersley, Ltd.: 359, 452a

Duke University, Durham, North Carolina: 60b (Image of Edgar Allen Poe from a set of "Poor Boys Images" in the W. Duke Sons & Co. Records located in the Rare Book, Manuscript, and Special Collections Library), 156a (Sheet music cover of "How are you greenbacks!" located in the sheet music collection Duke University,)

Florida State Archives: 104

Henry Ford Museum & Greenfield Village & Ford Motor Company Collections: 30-31

Jimmy LaRocca. Used by permission: 63 (Current performing band and general history can be seen at www.odjb.com)

Library of Congress, Prints and Photographs Division: 1a (LC-USZC4-3277), 1b (LC-USZC4-6894), 1c (LC-USZC4-4242), 1d (LC-USZC62-105453), 1e (LC-USZC2-724), 1f (LC-DIG-ppmsca-808), 1g (LC-USZ62-52000), 1h (LC-USZ62-79125), 1i (LC-USZC2-1855), 1j (LC-USZ62-116060), 1k (LC-USZC4-2995), 1m (LC-USZ62-111438), 1n (LC-USZ62-78301), 1o (LC-USZ62-127237), 1p (LC-USZ6-1823), 1q (LC-USZ62-127777), 1r (LC-USZ62-112535), 1s (LC-USZ62-84988), 1t (LC-USZC4-4642), 1u (LC-USZC4-10733), 1v (LC-USZ62-2070), 1w (LC-USZ62-117755), 1x (LC-USZC4-4856), 1y (LC-USZ62-78555), 3 (LC-W861-35), 5a (LC-USZ62-123070), 6 (LC-USZ62-115121), 12 (LC-USZ62-60976), 14 (LC-USZC4-630), 17 (LC-USZ62-118841), 18 (LC-USZC4-6878), 22 (LC-USZC4-2542), 24a (LC-USZ62-45002), 25b (LC-USZ62-119710), 26b (LC-USZ62-92268), 27b (LC-USZ62-119955), 28b (LC-USZC2-2802), 29a (LC-USZ62-122694), 30 (LC-USZ62-116520), 32 (LC-USZC4-1731), 34a (LC-USZ62-107503), 34b (LC-USZ62-123257), 36b (LC-USZ62-97430), 40a (LC-USZ62-94018), 40b (LC-USZ62-103899), 41a (LC-USZ62-124392), 42 (LC-USZ62-97748), 43b (LC-USZ62-128470), 44b (LC-USZ62-124552), 48 (LC-USZ62-29717), 50a (LC-USZC2-4903), 50b (LC-USZ62-106325), 51a (LC-USZ62-121182), 52 (LC-USZ62-111438), 52-53 (LC-USZ62-125093), 54a (LC-USZ62-25791), 55a (LC-USZ62-128346), 56b (LC-USZ62-99747), 61b (LC-USZ62-126187), 62 (LC-USZ62-125925), 64a (LC-USZ62-115014), 64b (LC-L9-54-3566-O), 66a (LC-USZ62-121998), 68a (LC-USZ62-105453), 68b (HABS, CAL, 49-FORO,1-5), 70b (LC-USZ62-104244), 71a (LC-USZ62-74515), 72b (LC-USZ62-117116), 73a (LC-USZ62-93263), 74a (LC-USZ62-107848), 76 (LC-USZC2-1985), 77a (LC-USZ62-93193), 77b (LC-USZ6-557), 78a (LC-USZ61-694), 78b (LC-USZC4-3040), 80 (LC-USZC2-2038), 81b (LC-USZ62-97180), 82b (LC-USZC4-5800), 83a (LC-USZ62-114995), 84 (LC-USZ62-120704), 88b (LC-USZ62-83450), 92 (LC-USZ62-84711), 94-95 (6a22671), 96 (LC-USZC4-1764), 101b (LC-USZ62-125119), 102a (LC-USZ62-116193), 102b (LC-USZ62-79125), 103a (LC-USZ62-114802), 103b (LC-USZ62-108760), 105a (LC-USZ62-110154), 106 (LC-USZC4-5802), 107b (LC-USZC4-4113), 108 (LC-USZC4-2957), 113a (LC-USZC2-2370), 114a (LC-USZ62-98798), 114b (5a52510), 118a (LC-B8171-7753), 120 (LC-D416-128), 121a (LC-USZ62-120867), 122a (LC-USZ62-51767), 123a (LC-USE6-D-9178), 126 (LC-USZ62-15392), 130b (LC-USZC4-7157), 131a (LC-USZ62-116347), 134 (LC-USZCN4-23), 136 (LC-USZ62-15278), 137b (LC-USZ6-180), 138 (LC-USZC2-3005), 139b (LC-USZ62-58677), 140-141 (LC-USZC2-3066), 144b (LC-USZ62-104073), 146a (LC-USZ62-87523), 146b (LC-USZ62-116769), 148 (LC-USZ62-75616), 150a (LC-USZ62-120800), 154 (LC-USZ62-13004), 154-155 (6a35561), 155 (LC-USZ62-127237), 156b (LC-USZC2-2758), 158 (LC-USZ62-1505), 159a (LC-USZ62-125079), 160-161 (6a01791), 164a (LC-USZ62-126846), 164b (LC-USZC4-3432), 166a, 168a (LC-D416-9855), 170a (LC-USZ62-79673), 170b (LC-USZ62-120880), 172-173 (6a23792), 173a (LC-USZ62-83570), 173b (LC-USW361-474), 174 (LC-USZ62-94149), 176a (LC-USZ62-95948), 176b (LC-USZ62-107179), 180a (LC-USZC2-2715), 180b (LC-USZ62-78311), 181a (LC-USZC4-6198), 181b (LC-USZ62-112559), 185a (LC-USZC4-10733), 186a (LC-USZ62-103112), 186b (LC-USZC4-1759), 190b (LC-USZC4-2458), 192 (LC-USZ62-118276), 194a (LC-USZC4-3368), 196 (LC-USZ62-14654), 198 (LC-USZC4-1910), 200a (LC-USZ62-111688), 200b (LC-USZ61-1814), 204b (LC-USZ62-93370), 205a (LC-USZ62-92227), 206 (LC-USZC2-1989), 208 (LC-USZC2-2663), 209b (LC-USZ62-113267), 212a (5a52024), 212b (LC-USZ62-78299), 213 (LC-USZ62-121014), 214 (LC-USZ62-12421), 215a (LC-USZC4-6144), 215b (LC-USZ62-116256), 217a (LC-USZ62-15070), 218 (LC-USZC4-6208), 220 (LC-USZ62-78551), 220-221 (LC-USZ62-123408), 221 (LC-G412-T-5023-3), 222 (LC-D418-7746), 225a (LC-USZC4-1297), 228 (LC-USZ62-77823), 234 (LC-USZC2-2963), 236 (LC-USZ62-2073), 238b (LC-USZ62-77201), 242a (LC-USZC4-5658), 242b (LC-USZ62-125934), 245a (LC-USZC4-4856), 246 (LC-USZC2-3394), 247a (LC-USZC4-7177), 248a (LC-D4-18531), 250 (LC-USZ62-118858), 252b (LC-USZC4-1033), 254 (LC-USZ62-97857), 256a (LC-USZ62-77370), 258-259 (LC-USZC2-64956 & LC-USZ62-64957), 262 (LC-USZ62-79466), 266a (LC-USZ62-126070), 266b (LC-USZC4-2462), 268 (LC-USZC2-2454), 270 (LC-D4-13038), 272 (LC-USZ62-47071), 273a (LC-USZC4-95255), 275a (LC-USZ62-103206), 276 (LC-USZC4-1291), 279 (LC-USZ62-124428), 280a (LC-USZC4-2569), 280b (LC-USZ62-105425), 284a (LC-USZC4-2069), 284b (LC-USZ62-90389), 286 (LC-USZ62-104325), 287b (LC-USZC4-1281), 290 (LC-USW3-9849), 291b (LC-USZC4-2459), 292 (LC-USZC2-3252), 296a (LC-USZC4-6894), 296b (LC-USZ62-105941), 298-299 (HAER,

CAL,38-SANFRA,140-43), 299 (LC-USZ62-104537), 300 (LC-USZ62-94750), 301a (LC-USZ62-109602), 302 (LC-USZ62-115562), 304-305 (6a22919), 304b (LC-USZC2-5591), 308 (LC-USZ62-119343), 310 (bbc 1743), 312 (LC-USZ61-776), 313b (LC-USZ62-111578), 314 (LC-USZ62-52000), 316 (LC-USZC4-9018), 318 (LC-USZ62-107077), 320 (LC-USZ6-119), 322 (LC-USZC4-3934), 324 (LC-USZ62-91062), 325b (LC-USZ62-122087), 326a (LC-USZ62-99147), 326b (LC-USZ62-128723), 328 (LC-USZ62-96168), 329a (LC-USZ62-105582), 330 (LC-D419-53), 331a (LC-USZ62-114909), 332 (LC-USZC4-4526), 334a (LC-USZC4-2997), 334b (LC-USZ62-101797), 335a (LC-USZ6-1818), 336 (LC-USZ62-78555), 337a (LC-USZ61-380), 338 (LC-USZ61-823), 340 (LC-USZC4-4970), 341c (LC-USZC2-724), 342a (LC-USZC4-9736), 344 (LC-USZC2-3749), 345b (LC-USZ62-113398), 346a (LC-USZC4-2108), 350a (LC-USZC4-3157), 350b (LC-USZC4-3158), 352 (LC-USZ62-2583), 354 (LC-USZ62-3029), 354-355 (6a16301), 356b (LC-USZC2-2161), 358a (LC-USZ62-100824), 358b (LC-G412-T-6033-5-A), 360 (LC-USZ62-71036), 364 (2a03712), 366a (LC-USZC4-741), 368 (LC-USZC4-1316), 370 (LC-USZ62-7622), 372 (LC-USZC4-2737), 376a (LC-USZC4-10026), 379a (LC-USZ62-116060), 381 (LC-USZ62-103183), 383 (LC-USZ62-84002), 386 (LC-USZ62-117301), 388 (LC-USZ62-75928), 390a (LC-USZC2-2734), 392a (LC-USZ62-103880), 392b (LC-USZC2-2598), 394 (LC-USZC2-2371), 395a (LC-USZ62-113276), 396 (LC-USZ62-120683), 402a (LC-USZ62-79597), 402b (LC-USZ62-111582), 404 (LC-USZ62-5535), 405a (LC-USZ62-87206), 406 (LC-USZC4-7960), 407a (LC-USZC4-1653), 407b (LC-USZ62-122951), 408 (LC-USZC4-1796), 410a (LC-G412-T-5154-5), 410b (LC-USZ62-53145), 412b (LC-USZ62-114740), 416-417 (LC-USZ62-107357), 418 (LC-USZC4-3576), 421a (bbc 0745), 424 (LC-USZ62-91133), 426a (LC-USZ62-87210), 428a (LC-USZC4-6877), 428b (LC-USZ62-120437), 430 (LC-USZ62-104753), 432 (LC-USZ62-96711), 434a (LC-USZ62-99981), 434b (LC-USZ62-78301), 438 (LC-USZC4-8136), 441 (LC-USZC4-3277), 442-443 (6a22748), 443 (LC-USZ62-77328), 444 (LC-USZ62-105894), 447a (LC-USZC2-5641), 448a (LC-USZ62-15887), 449a (LC-USZ62-131567), 450 (LC-USZ62-113641), 454b (LC-USZ62-100477), 456 (LC-DIG-ppmsca-808), 457b (yan 1a37978), 458 (LC-USZC4-7110), 458-459 (LC-USZ62-109321, LC-USZ62-109322, LC-USZ62-109323), 460 (LC-USZ62-70643), 462 (LC-USZC4-2995), 464 (LC-USZ62-100317), 466 (LC-USZC4-2960), 467a (LC-DIG-ppmsc-6102), 470 (LC-USZC2-5233), 471a (LC-D416-29478), 472 (LC-USZ62-2455), 476 (LC-USZ62-114629), 479a (LC-USZ62-117576), 480a (LC-USZ62-103896), 482-483 (LC-USZ62-111722), 487a (LC-USZ62-114755), 488b (LC-USZ62-98186), 490 (LC-USZ62-121591), 492-493 (LC-USZ62-39698), 493b (LC-USZ62-99252), 494 (LC-USZ62-96518), 497b (LC-USZ62-121305), 500 (LC-USZ62-100825), 502 (LC-USZC2-5377), 504 (LC-USZC2-3756), 506a (LC-USZC4-4169), 510 (LC-USZC4-6893), 511b (LC-USZC2-5845), 514 (LC-USZ62-126805), 516, 518-519 (LC-D4-18915), 520 (LC-USZ62-127029), 520-521 (LC-USZ62-115011), 521 (LC-USZ62-121453), 523b (LC-USZ62-115527), 524 (LC-USZC4-1179), 526b (LC-USZC4-2395), 528 (LC-USZC4-1762), 530 (LC-USZ62-102263), 530-531 (LC-USZC4-9299), 534 (LC-USZ62-2070), 536 (LC-USZC2-1855), 537b (LC-USZ62-115610), 538 (LC-USZ62-90021), 540 (LC-USZ62-80182), 541a (LC-USZC4-4714), 542b (LC-USZC2-108932), 544a (LC-USZ62-101364), 544b (LC-USZ61-278), 548 (LC-USZ62-112548), 550a (LC-USZ62-106109), 550b (LC-USZ62-119327), 552 (LC-USZ62-86916), 553a (LC-USW33-19081-C), 554 (LC-USZC4-2395), 555b (LC-USZ62-84486), 556 (LC-USZC4-1765), 558 (LC-USZC2-126201), 559a (LC-USZ62-80736), 560 (LC-USZC4-1581), 561a (LC-USZ62-128699), 562 (LC-USZ62-93492), 563a (LC-USZ62-117755), 564 (LC-USZC2-4004), 566 (LC-USZC2-3788), 567b (LC-USZC4-4446), 571a (LC-USZ62-102508), 572 (LC-USZ62-93899), 573b (LC-USZ62-25812), 574 (LC-USZC2-1687), 575b (LC-USZ62-77384), 576 (LC-USZ62-70450), 580 (LC-USZ62-111086), 581a (LC-USZC4-4242), 581b (LC-USZ62-116779), 584 (LC-D434-T01-50234), 586 (LC-USZ62-841), 588 (LC-USZC4-1964), 589b (LC-USZ62-118273), 590-591 (6a28646), 591, 592a (LC-USZC2-2229), 592b (LC-USZ62-104646), 594 (LC-USZ6-1479), 598 (LC-USZ62-5912), 598-599

(6a15249), 600 (LC-USW33-373-ZC), 602 (LC-USZ62-105445), 603a (LC-USZC4-6419), 604 (LC-USZ62-111189), 605b (LC-D4-17287), 605b (LC-USZ62-118272), 606 (LC-USZ62-87186), 607 (LC-USZC2-3397), 608-609 (ppmsc 02241), 610b (LC-USZ62-117754), 612a (LC-USZ62-97319), 612b (LC-USZ62-106323), 616 (LC-USZ62-89569), 617 (LC-USZ62-115068), 618 (LC-USZ62-128495), 622 (LC-USZC4-4239), 623 (LC-USZ62-108427), 626 (LC-USZC2-2416), 628 (LC-D4-90053), 628-629 (LC-USZ62-120707), 629 (LC-USZ62-76614), 632a (LC-USZ62-126407), 632b (LC-USZC4-10224), 639a (LC-USZ62-22017), 641a (LC-USZ62-25833), 642-643 (LC-USZ62-115232), 644a (LC-USZC4-3254), 644b (LC-USZ62-105822), 646a (LC-USZ62-119056), 648 (LC-USZ62-103252), 652a (LC-USZ62-127777), 654a (LC-USZ62-98128), 654b (LC-USZ61-206), 658 (LC-USZC4-1763), 659 (LC-USZ62-91485), 660a (LC-USW33-19082-C), 660b (LC-USZ62-124160), 664 (LC-D420-2719), 668 (LC-USZ62-46647), 668-669 (LC-USW33-20786-C), 669 (LC-USZ62-97787), 670a, 670b (LC-USZ62-124573), 672 (LC-USZC4-5163), 674 (LC-USZ62-13506), 675b (LC-USZ62-111235), 678 (LC-USZ62-112535), 680 (LC-USZC4-4642), 684 (LC-USZC4-3763), 685a (LC-USZ62-115887), 688a (LC-USZC2-2924), 688b (LC-USZ62-122946), 690a (LC-USZ62-94273), 690b (LC-USZ62-105923), 692 (LC-USZ62-28012), 695 (LC-USZ62-111576), 696, 697a (LC-USZ62-77563), 700 (LC-USZ62-103905), 702 (LC-USZ62-116372), 706 (LC-USZ62-119954), 706-707 (LC-USZ62-6166A), 712-713 (LC-USE6-D-9488), 714a (LC-USZC4-9480), 716 (LC-USZ62-118200), 717a (LC-USZ62-92303), 720a (LC-BH8301-1371), 720b (LC-USZ62-98779), 722 (LC-USZC2-3156), 724 (LC-USZ6-1823), 725a (LC-USZ62-84988), 726 (LC-USZ62-89798), 727b (LC-USZ61-35), 728 (LC-USZ62-13028), 729a (LC-USZC2-5428), 731a (LC-USZC4-7516), 732 (LC-USW33-24196-C)

Mount St. Vincent-on-Hudson. Courtesy of: 518

NASA: 10 (MSFC-9248168), 13a (KSC-81PC-136), 16b (GPN-2000-451), 58b (MSFC-8910708), 64-65 (GPN-2000-1120), 79 (S84-27017), 105b (MSFC-9702743), 181c (KSC-73P-539), 211 (MSFC-7008011), 216 (AS16-113-18339), 244 (S81-25295), 389a (MSFC-102088), 391 (GPN-2000-1421), 419 (MSFC-7022567), 425a, 489 (GNP-2000-1078), 543 (GPN-2000-1034), 637 (STScI-PRC98-18), 651 (GPN-2000-1317)

NASA/NSSDC: 23

National Archives: 5b (90-G-22D-42), 8 (148-GW-331), 15a (179-WP- 1563), 87a (111-SC-260486), 131b (NLK-EHEMC-AFRICA-8HH), 189 (NWDNA-353-EAPC-6-M713a), 288 (NWDNS-69-N-13606C), 319b (26-G-2343), 374 (148-GW-662), 378a (19-N12445), 653 (127-N-63458), 704 (148-GW-439), 710 (148-GW-2OI)

National Motor Museum, Beaulieu: 147

Naval Historical Center: 495 (USA C-2719), 686-687 (KN-32031)

Peter A. Juley & Son. Used by permission: 112a

Private Collection: 15b, 16a, 20, 24b, 26a, 31b, 36a, 44a, 46a, 53, 54b, 56a, 58a, 60a, 66b, 70a, 72a, 74b, 82a, 86, 88a, 90, 94, 98, 100, 107a, 110, 112b, 116, 118b, 124, 130a, 132a, 133a, 135b, 142a, 142b, 144a, 150b, 151b, 152a, 152b, 160, 162, 165a, 168b, 184, 188a, 188b, 190a, 191a, 195b, 202, 204a, 207b, 210a, 217b, 225b, 226a, 230, 238a, 252a, 256b, 260a, 264, 277a, 282, 289a, 294, 304a, 321a, 341b, 342b, 348, 353a, 356a, 369a, 375b, 376b, 378b, 382a, 382b, 382c, 384, 390b, 414, 415a, 426b, 448b, 454a, 463a, 468, 486a, 486b, 488a, 493a, 498b, 503b, 506b, 522, 568, 570, 577b, 578, 579a, 582, 595b, 601b, 610a, 614a, 614b, 621a, 624, 630a, 630b, 636b, 638, 640, 646b, 650, 652b, 666, 673a, 676, 682, 694, 708, 712, 714b, 730, 733a, 734a

William Randolph Hearst, Jr. Courtesy of: 243a

JULIAN TO GREGORIAN CALENDAR SWITCHOVER

The official switch from the Julian to the Gregorian calendar was decreed by Pope Gregory XIII for October 4, 1582. Unfortunately, not every country made the change at that time. According to our research, the dates for the changeover are as follows:

Albania: Dec. 1912

Austria:
Brixen, Salzburg: Oct. 5, 1583 was followed by Oct. 16, 1583
Carinthia, Styria: Dec. 14, 1583 was followed by Dec. 25, 1583
Other areas: Jan. 6, 1584 was followed by Jan. 17, 1584

Belgium:
Brahant, Flanders, Hainant: Dec. 21, 1582 was followed by Jan. 1, 1583
Liege: Feb.10, 1583 was followed by Feb. 21, 1583

Bulgaria: Oct. 31, 1915 was followed by Nov. 14, 1915

China: Lunisolar calendar to Jan. 1, 1912

Czechoslovakia (i.e. Bohemia and Moravia):
Jan. 6, 1584 was followed by Jan. 17, 1584

Denmark (including Norway):
Feb. 18, 1700 was followed by Mar. 1, 1700

Egypt: Sometime in 1875

Estonia: Jan. 31, 1918 was followed by Feb. 14, 1918

Finland: Then part of Sweden, Feb. 17, 1753 was followed by Mar. 3, 1753 (However, Finland became part of Russia in 1809, which then still used the Julian calendar. The Gregorian calendar remained official in Finland, but some use of the Julian calendar was made.)

France and Lorraine: Dec. 9, 1582 was followed by Dec. 20, 1582 in most areas
Alsace: Oct. 13, 1583 was followed by Oct. 24, 1583
Strasburg: Feb. 5, 1682 was followed by Feb. 16, 1682

Germany: Catholic states on various dates in 1583–1585
Prussia: Aug. 22, 1610 was followed by Sep. 2, 1610
Protestant states: Feb. 18, 1700 was followed by Mar. 1, 1700

Great Britain and Dominions (including what is now the USA): Sep. 2, 1752 was followed by Sep. 14, 1752

Greece:
Greek Orthodox Church: Feb. 15, 1923 was followed by Mar. 1, 1923 or Mar. 9, 1924 was followed by Mar. 23, 1924

Hungary: Oct. 21, 1587 was followed by Nov. 1, 1587

Italy: Oct. 4, 1582 was followed by Oct. 15, 1582

Japan: Lunisolar calendar to Jan. 1, 1873

Latvia: Sometime in 1617

Lithuania: Nov. 15, 1915

Luxembourg: Dec. 14, 1582 was followed by Dec. 25, 1582

Netherlands:
Brabant, Flanders, Holland, Artois, Hennegau: Dec. 14, 1582 was followed by Dec. 25, 1582 or, some say Dec. 21, 1582 was followed by Jan. 1, 1583
Geldern, Friesland, Groningen: Dec. 31, 1700 was followed by Jan. 12, 1701
Zeuthen, Utrecht, Overysel: Nov. 30, 1700 was followed by Dec. 12, 1700

Norway: See Denmark

Poland (in Catholic areas): Oct. 4, 1582 was followed by Oct. 15, 1582

Portugal: Oct. 4, 1582 was followed by Oct. 15, 1582

Romania: Mar. 31, 1919 was followed by Apr. 14, 1919

Russia: Jan. 31, 1918 was followed by Feb. 14, 1918
Silesia: Jan. 12, 1584 was followed by Jan. 23, 1584

Spain: Oct. 4, 1582 was followed by Oct. 15, 1582

Sweden: Feb. 17, 1753 was followed by Mar. 1, 1753

Switzerland:
Catholic cantons: Jan. 11, 1584 was followed by Jan. 22, 1584
Zurich, Bern, Basel, Schafhausen, Neuchatel, Geneva: Dec. 31, 1700 was followed by Jan. 12, 1701
St. Gallen: 1724

Transylvania: Dec. 14, 1590 was followed by Dec. 25, 1590

Turkey: Islamic calendar to Jan. 1, 1926

Tyrol: Oct. 5, 1583 was followed by Oct. 16, 1583

USA: See Great Britain, of which it was then a colony.

Yugoslavia: Jan. 14, 1919 was followed by Jan. 28, 1919, but some regions changed over earlier